P9-APD-081

GEORGE WHITEFIELD

REVD GEORGE WHITEFIELD, B.A.

AGED 24

The earliest portrait, engraved by J. Cochran, 1739

GEORGE WHITEFIELD

The Life and Times of the Great Evangelist of the Eighteenth-Century Revival

VOLUME I

*

Arnold A. Dallimore

THE BANNER OF TRUTH TRUST

THE BANNER OF TRUTH TRUST
3 Murrayfield Road, Edinburgh EH12 6EL
PO Box 621 Carlisle, Pennsylvania 17013, USA

First published 1970
Reprinted 1971
Reprinted 1975
Reprinted 1979
Reprinted 1989
Reprinted 1995
Reprinted 2001

ISBN 0 85151 026 4

*

Printed and bound in Great Britain by
The Bath Press, Bath

Giving no offence in anything, that the ministry be not blamed: but in all things approving ourselves as the ministers of God, in much patience, in afflictions, in necessities, in distresses, in stripes, in imprisonments, in tumults, in labours, in watchings, in fastings;

By pureness, by knowledge, by longsuffering, by kindness, by the Holy Ghost, by love unfeigned, by the word of truth, by the power of God, by the armour of righteousness on the right hand and on the left, by honour and dishonour, by evil report and good report:

As deceivers, and yet true; as unknown, and yet well known; as dying, and, behold we live; as chastened, and not killed; as sorrowful, yet alway rejoicing; as poor, yet making many rich; as having nothing, and yet possessing all things.

THE APOSTLE PAUL

Acknowledgements

Several persons have rendered assistance in the preparation of this work and with deep gratitude I make mention of the following:

Mr Geoffrey Williams of the Evangelical Library, London, has provided several rare books and, at his own initiative, has located certain documents that otherwise would not have been available. His interest and encouragement have been constant over the years.

The late the Rev Tom Beynon of Aberystwyth and the Rev Gomer M. Roberts, of Llanydbie, Wales, officials of the *Welsh Calvinistic Methodist Historical Society*, have freely drawn upon their stores of knowledge in response to my many queries. The same is true of the officials of the *Wesley Historical Society*, particularly the late the Rev Wesley F. Swift, Dr C. J. Bowmer and Dr Frank Baker, now of Duke University, S.C., U.S.A. Authorities in both England and America on the subject of the Moravian movement have likewise rendered valuable assistance. Librarians of several libraries – civic, university and ecclesiastical – on both sides of the Atlantic, have granted their fullest co-operation. Mr Brian Frith, an archivist of Gloucester, England, has located certain source materials regarding Whitefield's boyhood. The Rev Richard Owen Roberts of California, who has compiled an immense *Bibliography on Revival* (a work that deserves to be published) has provided me with his extensive section on Whitefield.

My thanks are due also to Mrs Schulkins of Toronto and Mrs Lawson of Leamington, Ontario, for their work in typing the manuscript, and to Mrs Catherwood of London, England, for her labours in reading through the first draft of the work. Mr Ernest C. Reisinger of Carlisle, Pennsylvania, has provided material assistance at points of particular need.

I am especially grateful to the Banner of Truth Trust for many valuable suggestions, and to Dr D. M. Lloyd-Jones, who has encouraged my endeavour and has written the accompanying *Foreword*.

To these and several others who have assisted in various ways, I acknowledge my indebtedness and gratitude.

ARNOLD A. DALLIMORE

Cottam Baptist Church
Cottam, Ontario, Canada
1969

Foreword

THIS volume is something for which I have been waiting for over forty years. It was then that I first read Luke Tyerman's *Life of George Whitefield.* Ever since, I have read everything that I could discover on Whitefield, and by him, and never have I failed to be thrilled as I have done so, and stimulated to become a better Christian and a better preacher. But I waited for something more, and felt that in some respects justice had still to be done.

It is, therefore, with the greatest possible pleasure that I write a Foreword to this new Life of Whitefield, appearing on the bi-centenary of his death. Arnold Dallimore's Volume One is a moving account, and it achieves excellence in those areas of Whitefield's thought where more thorough work was needed. That Mr Dallimore has succeeded in doing this while in the pastoral charge of a Canadian village is a testimony both to his love of his subject and to the persistence which has carried him through his twenty years of thorough research. His zeal was such that he has twice crossed the Atlantic and in the course of his travels he has discovered information on Whitefield from many hitherto little used, or even unknown, sources. Justice has at last been done to Whitefield and without a trace of special pleading or injustice to his contemporaries.

Of all the men of that century Whitefield was the most lovable. He radiated warmth and joy, and wherever he went he moved others to greater zeal and activity. Above all he was the greatest preacher – indeed one can say that he was the greatest preacher that England has ever produced. He had in abundant measure all the qualities of a great preacher. His appearance was pleasing in spite of his squint, and his whole personality conveyed the impression of a man who 'knew his God' and at the same time had a loving concern for the souls of men. As an orator there has scarcely ever been his equal. His voice was not only powerful but beautifully modulated and under perfect control. From all contemporary accounts one gathers that it had a most moving and melting quality that none could resist and which was the envy of the famous actor David Garrick. He gesticulated freely, and, as I once heard it said by an orator of the earlier part of this century, he could 'pull out all the stops of the entire gamut of the human emotions'.

More important than these things was the certainty with which Whitefield knew his message and how it should be applied to the human mind and heart of all classes. He was as much the favourite preacher of the aristocracy that gathered to listen to him in the home of Lady Huntingdon as of the common rabble that listened to him in Moorfields or Kennington. His converts were numbered in thousands and competent historians are agreed that both in America and in Great Britain he was, as one of his biographers has described him, 'The Awakener'. He was the pioneer in open-air preaching as in other matters; and though not to be compared with his contemporary and friend John Wesley as an organiser, he easily eclipsed him as an innovator and promoter. His mind was more original and fertile and he was less bound by tradition and logic.

But above all he was a great saint, and Wesley and others bore noble tribute to this during his life and after his death. This was the ultimate secret of his preaching power. He was 'filled with the Spirit' and endued with exceptional unction while preaching. He could say with the Apostle Paul 'I am what I am by the grace of God'.

To read the wonderful story of his life is to be reminded again of what is possible to a truly consecrated Christian, and how even in the darkest and most sinful ages God in His sovereign power is able to revive His work and shower blessings upon His people.

I not only commend this first volume of this new biography of this great man of God, I urge all who bemoan the evil of these days and long for 'days of heaven on earth' to read it and to learn its lessons. These present days in many ways are not dissimilar to the days prior to 1735. God is still the same and is able to do again what He did in the eighteenth century through George Whitefield and others.

May the reading of this book produce in us the same spirit of utter submission, ready obedience, and unshakeable reliance upon the power of the Holy Spirit that characterised his life and ministry. Whitefield never drew attention to himself but always pointed people to his God and exalted his Lord and Saviour. May he, though now dead for nearly 200 years, do the same for countless thousands through the reading of this book!

London, February 1970 D. M. LLOYD-JONES

Contents

PART III
The Period of Transition

Illustrations

INTRODUCTORY

And now is it not time that the world should deal righteously with itself as to its ancient quarrel with one like Whitefield? The world has a long score to settle in this behalf, for it pursued him, from first to last, with a fixed and furious malignity; and even now, where Wesley is spoken of with fairness, and perhaps with commendation, a line of reluctant praise, coupled with some ungracious insinuation, is the best treatment Whitefield can obtain . . . No one can dare to say that his life was not blameless; and that his intentions were benevolent is manifest. His temper was not arrogant; for meekly he received rebuke and patiently he endured so many revilings. It was with the courage of a noble nature that he confronted violence; and with the simplicity of a child that he forgave injuries.

Yet among those who by their flagitious vices and outrageous crimes have the most deeply sinned against society, it would be difficult to find a wretch upon whose guilty pate has been showered so much rancorous abuse as, year after year, was heaped upon the head of the love-fraught, self-denying and gentle-natured Whitefield.

There is a mystery here which 'philosophy' should do its best to clear up . . .

ISAAC TAYLOR

Wesley and Methodism, 1860

On Knowing Whitefield

GEORGE WHITEFIELD as the eighteenth century knew him, and George Whitefield as he is thought of today, are two widely different persons.

Whitefield lived from 1714 to 1770, and throughout much of his adult life was as famous as any man in the English-speaking world. From the age of twenty-two till his death he was the foremost figure of the immense religious movement that held the attention of multitudes on both sides of the Atlantic. Although his evangelistic labours provoked bitter opposition they also won profound praise, and several of the great among his contemporaries in both Britain and America counted him their familiar friend. Certain highly knowledgeable appraisals of his career have estimated it in the superlative. 'The history of preaching since the apostles does not contain a greater or worthier name than that of George Whitefield',[1] asserts an authority on the subject, and another – an author noted for the precision of his statements – declares:

> . . . if a list could be made from the experience of all nations and ages, of the twenty men that have produced the greatest effects, by means of their single personal influence, it is highly probable that the name of Whitefield must there hold a place.[2]

One would suppose that such a life would be treasured by the Christian world. It would be expected that this career would receive thorough research, that its documents would be carefully preserved and its story told and retold for all to read.

[1] E. C. Dargan, *A History of Preaching* (second ed, Baker, Grand Rapids, USA, 1954), Vol 2, *p* 307.

[2] John Foster, *Critical Essays* (Bohn ed, 1856), Vol 2, *p* 63.

Such would be the expectancy, but the treatment that Whitefield has received has been very much the opposite. During the years that followed his death mankind's attitude towards him became characterized by a strange carelessness. Precise investigation was largely lacking, the accusations made by his enemies were given wide circulation, the great accomplishments of his life were gradually forgotten and his memory was allowed to sink into neglect. When nearly a century had passed, Bishop Ryle, reflecting on this curious turn of events, stated 'There are few men whose characters have suffered so much from misrepresentation and ignorance as George Whitefield!'

This practice has continued to constitute the method by which the general opinion of Whitefield has been formed. Granted, there are people to-day who recognize and deplore this oversight and regard it as a grievous loss to all Christendom; others there are who consider him worthy of commemoration for his oratory, and still others who view him as a sort of secondary helper to John Wesley. But apart from such persons, among those who remember Whitefield at all, it is usually assumed that he may be of interest as a peculiar religious phenomenon, but that otherwise he hardly merits attention.

*

The causes of this long deterioration are many. In fact, almost as if they had been formed according to some preternatural design, adverse circumstances, one after another have occurred, and these, singly and in combination, have served to prevent the true Whitefield from being known.

As a preparation for our study of Whitefield, we must familiarize ourselves with the more important of these causes.

The blame for this situation must be laid first at the door of Whitefield himself. Though he wrote *Journals* of his ministry during its first three years, he thereafter refused to take any steps towards making a correct knowledge of his life available. With his eye fixed on his accounting in heaven, he sought no justification of himself on earth. When urged by friends to reply to certain false accusations, lest he be lastingly stigmatized, he replied, 'I am content tc wait till the judgment day for the clearing up of my character. When I am dead I desire no epitaph but this: "Here lies G. W. What kind of man he was the great day will discover." ' To his followers' frequent demands that he perpetuate his memory by forming a denomination with himself at its head, he invariably answered, 'Let the name of Whitefield perish, but Christ be glorified!' So noble an attitude renders his life all the more worthy of attention, but in adopting it Whitefield set events moving in the wrong direction – the direction they have followed ever since.

A further cause of misunderstanding lay in Whitefield's *Journals*,[1] for the *Journals* lent themselves to a distorted view of his life. These accounts told Whitefield's story only to a point shortly after he had turned twenty-six, and though they reported a most amazing ministry, they were marked by the exaggerative tendencies which usually attend youth. However, since the information in the *Journals* was readily at hand and that of his later years much more difficult to come by, the path of least resistance led several authors into the error of portraying Whitefield's youthful characteristics as features of his whole life. The youth in his early twenties is depicted and his mistakes displayed, but the man of later years, humbly apologetic for his earlier errors and marked by a true maturity, is largely overlooked.

Whitefield's memory also suffered from the lack of editorial help in the publishing of his *Works*.[2] Following his death, Dr John Gillies of Glasgow gathered his literary remains and published them in six volumes. Productions of this nature customarily receive editorial attention in the form of introductions and explanatory notes, but Gillies provided almost nothing of this kind. These volumes went forth to the public augmented by but a brief phrase here and there, and one has but to compare them with Wesley's *Journal*, replete as it is with Dr Curnock's extensive introductions and copious footnotes, to see how the memory of Whitefield has suffered from the absence of such aids.

Three volumes of the *Works* contain Whitefield's correspondence, but a deletion that occurs throughout them all has proved particularly injurious. Nearly fifteen hundred letters are published, but because many of the persons addressed were still living, Dr

[1] *George Whitefield's Journals*. References herein made are to the Banner of Truth edition (London, 1960).

[2] *The Works of the Reverend George Whitefield, M.A.* (London, 1771).

Gillies removed their names, leaving merely the initials. This was a prudent step at the time, but it has robbed the letters of much of their value since. A lack of knowledge as to who the recipient was, usually makes it impossible to know the context of a letter and to understand the matters to which it refers. As a result, the whole body of correspondence takes on a vagueness and an emptiness. Only the religious sentiments remain easily intelligible – a condition which has led to the charge that Whitefield's letters contain nothing else.

By this deletion a prime source of information on Whitefield was all but destroyed. During the last twenty-five years of his life he purposely published little of any kind. But he wrote letters and they came from his pen with unfailing frequency. Were we able in each case to identify the recipient, our knowledge of that period would be richly increased, and we should see that Whitefield's letters, instead of being limited to religious sentiments, reveal a man alive to the many realms associated with the lives of his correspondents. A study of the internal evidence in a given letter will sometimes enable one to ascertain the recipient's identity and to grasp the significance of the contents, but despite the information thus retrievable, much other remains forever sealed.

The question arises, however, 'Why not republish the letters, this time supplying the names from the originals?' The answer is that in this matter Whitefield's memory has suffered tragedy. His original papers are lost!

From Dr Gillies Whitefield's literary remains passed into the hands of an Aaron Seymour, a nephew of the Countess of Huntingdon. Along with these, Seymour gathered also the mass of papers left by the Countess and by a great Welsh preacher named Daniel Rowland. Whitefield's papers undoubtedly contained, besides his letters, diaries covering the entire period of his ministry, several unpublished sermons and many miscellaneous manuscripts. Rowland's records, we may be sure, would have revealed much concerning his life, which in the absence of them is but little known. Lady Huntingdon's papers consisted chiefly of her correspondence, much of which manifested the remarkable Christian witness that she maintained among Britain's nobility. Thus Seymour had in his possession a virtual treasury of documents, for which he ought to have provided the most careful guardianship, and one can but wonder that he did not place them in the safe-keeping of Lady Huntingdon's College.

But all of this wealth of manuscripts disappeared. Little is known as to what happened, but it is believed that one of Seymour's descendants took them to Ireland, where they were either lost or destroyed.

There can be no doubt that the disappearance of this mass of documents has robbed us of extensive and invaluable information on Whitefield, and that it has placed severe limitations on the measure of the knowledge of the revival that it is possible for any one to gain. Moreover, since these were the records of the Calvinistic section of the movement, the loss has given exaggerated prominence to the Wesleyan, the documents of which have been well preserved. It is possible, however, that these papers did not suffer destruction, and though extensive searches among family records inherited by several of Lady Huntingdon's descendants have thus far proved fruitless, hope is entertained that somewhere, perhaps in England or possibly in Ireland, they may yet be found.

The first biography of Whitefield was written by Dr Gillies[1] in 1772, and this also left much to be desired. Gillies wrote from a position of advantage, for besides possessing Whitefield's papers, he had known Whitefield personally for nearly thirty years. Moreover, hundreds of persons of similar acquaintance with the evangelist were then living from whom he could have obtained copious information. A thorough work at that early date could have been highly effective towards setting the true Whitefield before posterity, but Gillies did not meet the demands of his task. His research was small, and though his book contains much that is valuable, it amounts to but 357 pages and leaves certain highly important areas of Whitefield's life untouched. Gillies did well, but it is to be regretted that he did not do better.

In 1820 England's Poet Laureate, Robert Southey, produced a *Life of Wesley*.[2] This book became a strong factor in the 'mis-

[1] John Gillies, *Memoirs of the Life of the Reverend George Whitefield, M.A.* (London, 1772).

[2] Robert Southey, *The Life of Wesley*. References herein are to the Bohn ed, 2 volumes (London, 1858).

representation and ignorance' of Whitefield, of which Bishop Ryle spoke.

Southey's *Wesley* is an evidence that no man, however gifted, can easily acquire a thorough understanding in several realms. Turning from his many interests to this subject, Southey wrote with literary skill, but with too hurried a preparation and little insight. As a result, on both Wesley and Whitefield he manifests a curious combination of knowledge and superficiality. One edition of this work contains extensive footnotes by S. T. Coleridge, and these often evince a discernment far superior to that of the text. Nevertheless, though stoutly denounced by the Methodists when it first appeared, in its final effect Southey's book did much to enhance the prestige of Wesley. Whitefield, however, by reason of certain of Southey's false statements and unfounded judgments, is made to appear cheap and inconsistent.[1] Coming from so eminent an author these insinuations were readily received, and there can be no doubt that this book marks the point at which the public concept of Wesley experienced a sharp change for the better and that of Whitefield its major change for the worse.

In the aftermath of Southey's work Robert Philip produced a life of Whitefield.[2] He wrote as a doughty champion of his subject and asserted that as a result of his volume, 'Whitefield will be known to the public; which he was not until now'. The book drew stinging criticism from the eminent reviewer, Sir James Stephen. 'This chronicle', said Stephen, 'illuminated by no eloquence or philosophy, arranged on no intelligible method, is a sore exercise for the memory and patience of the reader. . . . Whitefield's life still remains to be written by someone who shall bring to the task other qualifications than an honest zeal for his fame and a cordial adoption of his opinions.'[3]

[1] The author of *The Life and Times of the Countess of Huntingdon* (London, 1840), Vol 1, *p* 475, in reference to Southey's *Life of Wesley*, speaks of 'the numerous blunders, false statements and wilful misrepresentations with which his work everywhere abounds'.

[2] Robert Philip, *The Life and Times of the Reverend George Whitefield, M.A.* (London, 1837).

[3] Sir James Stephen, *Essays in Ecclesiastical Biography* (London, 1883), *p* 385. Stephen's review of Philip first appeared in the *Edinburgh Review* in 1838.

Thus, for more than a century after his death[1] it was chiefly by these works – Gillies, Southey and Philip, and his own *Journals* and sermons – that Whitefield was known. But limited by Gillies, suffering the vagueness of the letters, the misrepresentations in Southey and the confusion in Philip, the life of Whitefield proved of steadily declining interest, and the image received by the public was a distorted rather than a true one.

In 1876, however, a much more suitable life of Whitefield appeared. This was the work of the Reverend Luke Tyerman,[2] two large volumes that he wrote as by-product of his three-volume life of Wesley. It was a major accomplishment which published numerous documents for the first time and dealt with aspects of Whitefield's life which others had left virtually untouched. But since Tyerman was a devoted disciple of John Wesley,[3] he displayed strong bias in Wesley's favour – bias which led him, in narrating the controversy between the two men and assessing their respective places in the movement, into certain serious omissions and foolish statements. But despite these weaknesses, Tyerman's work is a storehouse of information; from it later biographers have drawn and to it the present author expresses his frequent indebtedness.

Tyerman's *Whitefield* has never exercised the influence that it deserves. It has long been out of print and is now seldom encountered on the American continent, and common opinion regarding Whitefield has remained oblivious to important information that it presents.

Even in the realm of the artist events have militated against Whitefield. His life, in the high drama of his open-air preaching, presented a rare challenge to creative art, and his personal characteristics – the radiant countenance and grace of body described in the eye-witness accounts – rendered him an exceptional subject for portraiture. One or two masterly paintings would have

[1] During this period there were produced also further and enlarged editions of Gillies and eight other biographies. The most complete of the latter was the one by J. P. Gledstone, which appeared in 1871.

[2] Luke Tyerman, *The Life of the Rev George Whitefield* (London, 1876, 2 volumes).

[3] J. H. Rigg, a Methodist writer, in his *The Living Wesley* (London, 1891), says, 'Mr Tyerman had passed his life among those who almost worship the memory of John Wesley; some of whom thought him absolute perfection, and cherished toward him a blind and unintelligent admiration' (*pp* 16, 17).

done much towards offsetting the lack of adequate biography, but though something like ten artists of merit made him their subject, the majority of these works contain some prominent distortion. There is no satisfactory portrait of Whitefield during his early ministry and probably only Flaxman's medallion can be considered a first-rate likeness of him in his later years. Engravings of several paintings are common, but most are of such poor workmanship as to do his memory more harm than good. Both John and Charles Wesley have received some excellent portraiture, but that accorded Whitefield has seldom risen above the mediocre.

*

While by this strange combination of adverse circumstances Whitefield was being increasingly neglected, John Wesley was coming into a steadily enlarging fame. As contemporary documents show, during the eighteenth century Whitefield was the foremost figure and Wesley the secondary one, but such has been the neglect of Whitefield and the emphasis on Wesley that these positions are now entirely reversed.

The John Wesley known to-day is, to a great extent, a semi-legendary figure. Few men have been the object of such militant loyalty among their followers as was he during the last years of his life. After his death this admiration became even more intense and amidst the next two generations of his people he was regarded with such unthinking veneration that certain later Methodist scholars term the attitude an apotheosis.

It was, however, while these conditions prevailed that the first biographies of Wesley were written. Holding him in such affection, the authors of these works[1] proved incapable of viewing his career without bias. In keeping with his teaching of *Christian Perfection* they passed over those aspects of his personality and those areas of his life which reveal him as other than faultless. They portrayed him as always the master of himself and as invariably correct in his judgments. Though much of their

[1] These were particularly the biographies by Coke and Moore, by Whitehead and by Watson. Though Hampson had left the Methodist body at the time he wrote, and was somewhat more objective, his work was much after the same non-critical order.

picture is contradicted by Wesley's own *Journal* and *Diary*, the image they created was tenaciously defended by the Methodist rank and file and, with the passing of the years, became fixed in the public mind.

In recent years much scholarship of the finest order has been devoted to the study of John Wesley. It has produced a wealth of information, yet appears to have approached the semi-legendary image with the assumption that its basic features are true. The areas that were untouched by the early biographers have been largely left untouched; they have not been subjected to impartial historical enquiry, or, if they have, the results have not been applied, for the image created by the early writers remains almost entirely unchanged.

Out of deference to so great and good a man as John Wesley this situation might well be overlooked, were it not for its wider effect. The early authors made little, if any, mention of his fellow-evangelists and gave him credit, not only for his own magnificent labours, but, by their omissions, made him appear responsible for a considerable amount of the accomplishment of Whitefield too. Charles Wesley, Lady Huntingdon, Howell Harris, John Cennick, Daniel Rowland – these and several others have not been correctly recognized for their contributions to early Methodism, and the bias in John Wesley's favour has coloured much that has been written about them. But above all, this magnifying of John Wesley has been effected by the minifying of George Whitefield.

Thus have these several factors arisen during the past two centuries to rob us of a true understanding of Whitefield. Inadequate biography, poorly edited *Works*, lost documents, ineffective portraiture and the undue aggrandizement of his associate – these have joined with his own unconcern about human opinion to prevent him from being properly known.

*

This neglect of Whitefield – loss enough in itself – has occasioned a further loss: the failure to recognize the true nature of the spiritual movement of which he was part.

It is common knowledge that there were religious revivals throughout several lands during the eighteenth century, but these have usually been looked upon as separate activities.[1] A large literature exists on the work that took place in England, terming it *The Evangelical Revival* or *The Wesleyan Revival*. Several books depict the powerful spiritual movement that occurred in America, which was known as *The Great Awakening*, and still others chronicle the Revivals which were experienced in Scotland and Wales.

The truth is, however, that these activities were not unconnected. Viewed in their entirety they are seen to be one in spirit and one in effect. Though intentionally not an organized unity, they actually comprised a single movement of vast extent, a movement which spanned the Atlantic, reached much of the English-speaking world of that time and continued in force for more than half a century.

This movement, in its unified nature, must not be overlooked. It requires a designation which recognizes its oneness and expresses its historic position, and for this purpose I have chosen the term *The Eighteenth-Century Revival*. In the sense of a spiritual movement this mighty work of God deserves a place in Christian thought alongside the Reformation, and as an evangelical revival it must be considered the greatest since the Apostles.

This is the movement which, in overlooking Whitefield, mankind has also largely overlooked. Whitefield's ministry was the one human factor which bound this work together in all the lands it reached. He alone carried the Gospel throughout England, Wales and Scotland and to parts of Ireland, even to Bermuda and, again and again to all the American Colonies, and the story of his life is also the story of this unparalleled revival.

*

It is in an attempt to meet the need for a more adequate knowledge of Whitefield and the Revival that this book has been written. A few personal words about the effort may be in order.

I have tried to discover and present the George Whitefield who was known to the eighteenth century. Accordingly, I have laboured to obtain documents from those times, and while such a

[1] The following works, exceptions to this rule, recognize the unity of the Revival: A. W. Harrison, *The Evangelical Revival and Christian Reunion* (Epworth, 1942); A. Skevington Wood, *The Inextinguishable Blaze* (Paternoster, London, 1960); C. H. Maxson, *The Great Awakening in the Middle Colonies* (Peter Smith, Gloucester, Mass., 1920, reprinted 1958).

search always has its disappointments, I have had a measure of success, and have located several source materials not heretofore used. Moreover, I have put some of the well-known materials to new use, extracting from them information usually overlooked. I have also endeavoured to look thoroughly into certain aspects of the subject which have commonly been given but a cursory treatment, and these various efforts have enabled me to shed light on several areas of Whitefield's life which were otherwise either shadowed or dark.

In the use of the materials, I have sought to be objective. I make no attempt to hide my personal adherence to the great doctrines of evangelical Christianity which were the basis of the Revival and which were held in common by Whitefield, the Wesleys, Edwards and all others who had part in that work. Nevertheless, I have made it my purpose to approach the documents with an open mind, there to discover precisely what took place and how it took place and to present my findings without exaggeration or diminution. I trust that in a suitable measure I have succeeded.

I have endeavoured to give my portrait of Whitefield both reality and depth. I make known, not only his accomplishments and abilities, but also his foibles and his mistakes. I must confess, however, that I have almost wished his faults had been more pronounced, lest by reason of their fewness and feebleness, I should be charged with favouritism. It has been my constant attempt to penetrate below the surface of the man, to understand him in such elements of personality as motives and desires, and to grasp the basic principles that underlay his life.

But despite some degree of accomplishment in these aims, I am conscious of much failure. Though I have lived with the study of Whitefield for twenty years, I have constantly felt that his greatness defied my understanding as I sought to know him, and my powers of expression as I endeavoured to portray his life.

Nevertheless, this book goes forth with a mission. It is written with the profound conviction that the paramount need of the twentieth century is a mighty evangelical revival such as that which was experienced two hundred years ago. Thus, I have sought to show what were the doctrines used of God in the eighteenth-century Revival, and to display the extraordinary fervour which characterized the men whom God raised up in that blessed work. Yea, this book is written in the desire—perhaps in a measure of inner certainty—that we shall see the great Head of the Church once more bring into being His special instruments of revival, that He will again raise up unto Himself certain young men whom He may use in this glorious employ. And what manner of men will they be? Men mighty in the Scriptures, their lives dominated by a sense of the greatness, the majesty and holiness of God, and their minds and hearts aglow with the great truths of the doctrines of grace. They will be men who have learned what it is to die to self, to human aims and personal ambitions; men who are willing to be 'fools for Christ's sake', who will bear reproach and falsehood, who will labour and suffer, and whose supreme desire will be, not to gain earth's accolades, but to win the Master's approbation when they appear before His awesome judgment seat. They will be men who will preach with broken hearts and tear-filled eyes, and upon whose ministries God will grant an extraordinary effusion of the Holy Spirit, and who will witness 'signs and wonders following' in the transformation of multitudes of human lives.

Indeed, this book goes forth with the earnest prayer that, amidst the rampant iniquity and glaring apostasy of the twentieth century God will use it toward the raising up of such men and toward the granting of a mighty revival such as was witnessed two hundred years ago.

Righteousness exalteth a nation; but
sin is a reproach to any people.

Proverbs 14:34

I love those that thunder out the word! The Christian world is in a deep sleep. Nothing but a loud voice can waken them out of it!

WHITEFIELD, 1739

Spiritual and Moral Conditions in England before the Revival

FOR the past thirty years numerous evangelical people have been saying, 'There can never be another revival! The times are too evil. Sin is now too rampant. We are in the midst of apostasy and the days of revival are gone for ever!'

The history of the eighteenth-century Revival entirely contradicts that view. It demonstrates that true revival is the work of God – not man – of God who is not limited by such circumstances as the extent of human sin or the degree of mankind's unbelief. In the decade between 1730 and 1740 the life of England was foul with moral corruption and crippled by spiritual decay, yet it was amidst such conditions – conditions remarkably similar to those of the English-speaking world to-day – that God arose in the mighty exercise of His power which became the eighteenth-century Revival.

In an over-all view of a century of British history we are able to observe these conditions, not only in themselves, but as to their cause, their effect and their cure.

*

Our glance goes back to 1660. In the violent rejection of Puritanism that then accompanied the Restoration of the monarchy, Englishmen were given to believe that the life of unfettered licentiousness might be indulged in with impunity. In this assurance much of the nation threw off restraint and plunged itself heedlessly into a course of godlessness, drunkenness, immorality and gambling. Legislation was enacted which distressed the Puritan conscience, and in 1662, on one of the darkest days in all British history, nearly two thousand ministers – all those who would not submit to the *Act of Uniformity* – were ejected from their livings. Hundreds of these men suffered throughout the rest of their lives, and a number died in prison. Yet these terrible conditions became the occasion of a great volume of prayer; forbidden to preach under threat of severe penalties – as John Bunyan's Bedford imprisonment bore witness – they yet could pray, and only eternity will reveal the relationship between this burden of supplication and the revival that followed.

During these years a teaching known as Deism was introduced into England. Deism was not an organized cult, but was a form of religious rationalism advocated by a number of authors.[1] It taught that whatever God there may be is nothing more than the First Cause, a force that made the world the way a clock-maker makes a clock, and having set its mechanism to operate according to certain laws, simply winds it up and lets it run. This Deity, they said, had revealed himself only in creation and that man's sole responsibility towards Him was that of recognizing His being. This vague contemplation they termed *Natural Religion*, and, strangely enough, they claimed that it, and it alone, was true Christianity.

The Deists carried on a vigorous warfare against *supernatural religion* – Biblical Christianity – and in doing so made loud boast about the reasonableness and logic of their views. They claimed that the Bible could not be a revelation of the Deity, for, had He chosen to reveal Himself, He would not have done so through one small, ancient nation and in a book rendered unreliable by divergent readings. They sought to explain away the argument from fulfilled prophecy by stating that the prophecies were either written after their supposed fulfilment or were so ambiguous as to admit of many fulfilments. They argued that the miracles were unproved and that such dogmas as the Virgin birth and literal resurrection were no more than pious imagination. Jesus, they said, was merely a man, earnest but deluded,

[1] The following are some of the principal Deistic writers:
Matthew Tindal (1653–1733) *Christianity as Old as the Creation.*
John Toland (1670–1722) *Christianity Not Mysterious.*
Thomas Woolston (1670–1733) *The Miracles of Our Saviour.*
Bernard de Mandeville (1670–1733) *The Fable of the Bees.*
Lord Shaftesbury (1671–1713) *Characteristics of Men, Manners, Opinions and Times.*
Anthony Collins (1671–1729) *Discourse of Free Thinking.*
Lord Bolingbroke (1678–1751) *Essays.*

and raised to an imagined Saviourhood by the fancies of His disciples.

To Englishmen who had already rejected the idea of moral restraint Deism proved especially welcome. It removed from their thoughts the God of the Bible, the God of holiness and justice whom the Puritans had preached, and substituted this vague Deity found, as they believed, in nature. In its assertion that man was not held responsible for his actions and that there was no judgment day, it rationalized the *sin with impunity* concept and, as a result, was widely received.

Deism gradually made its way into the thought of the nation. Its influence began to be felt between 1660 and 1670, and the successive appearance of each of its books increased its popularity. Tindal's *Christianity as Old as the Creation*, published in 1730, brought it to the peak of its fame.

*

Confronted by the challenge of Deism the Church displayed both its strength and its weakness.

Its strength was manifested in the intellectual force of its reply. From the ranks of the Church of England such men as Berkeley, Conybeare, Warburton and Butler, and, from the Dissenters Watts, Doddridge, Lardner and Leland – these and many others – took up their pens and replied to the Deists with consummate skill.[1] It deserves to be noticed that these men very largely adhered to the supernatural in Christianity and the works they produced still stand as the greatest body of apologetics in the English language.

But the Church's weakness was also revealed in these efforts. The works against Deism ought to have radiated the beauty

[1] The following are the more important of the works against Deism:
Bishop Berkeley, *Alciphron.*
Bishop Conybeare, *A Defence of Revealed Religion.*
Bishop Sherlock, *The Tryal of the Witnesses of the Resurrection of Jesus.*
Bishop Warburton, *The Divine Legation of Moses.*
Bishop Newton, *A Dissertation on the Prophecies.*
Bishop Butler, *The Analogy of Revealed Religion.*
William Law, *An Appeal to all that Doubt the Truths of Revelation.*
Isaac Watts, *A Treatise on the Trinity.*
Nathaniel Lardner, *The Credibility of the Gospel History.*
John Leland, *A View of the Deistical Writers.*

and warmth of Christianity, but actually contained little besides logic, and most were as cold as they were correct. Their appeal was almost solely to the intellect, and few persons apart from those of sufficient mental strength to pore through such treatises as Conybeare's *Defence* or Butler's *Analogy* could be influenced by them. They were also merely defensive, for, whereas the Christian forces ought to have mounted a mighty offensive against sin and unbelief, Deism alone took the initiative and the Church politely replied. English Christianity proved itself to be little more than a religious ethic, sedate and timid – a disposition admirably exemplified in Dr John Tillotson, Archbishop from 1691 to 1694 – and this remained the vogue until challenged by the militant evangelism of the revival.

Moreover, much of the Church was in no way strong enough to withstand the onslaught of Deism. After the ejection of the two thousand pastors in 1662, the Church of England accepted as their substitutes whatever men were available, and many whom it received were sadly lacking in both learning and Christian principles. In turn, the ministerial standards suffered a long and steady decline, insomuch that, nearly a century later, a member of the clerical ranks, Archdeacon Blackburne, saw fit to state:

> The collective body of the clergy, excepting a very inconsiderable number, consists of men whose lives and occupations are most foreign to their profession – courtiers, politicians, lawyers, merchants, usurers, civil magistrates, sportsmen, musicians, stewards of country squires, tools of men in power, and even companions of rakes and infidels, not to mention the ignorant herd of poor curates to whom the instruction of common people is committed, who are, accordingly, in religious matters, the most ignorant common people who are in any Protestant, not to say in any Christian society upon the face of the earth.[1]

Among clergy of this kind Deism easily gained acceptance, and it was not uncommon for them to drone its tenets from their pulpits. And even among better men, doctrines that had once been considered essential to Christianity were regarded as open to

[1] Alfred Plummer, *The Church of England in the Eighteenth Century* (Methuen, London, 1910), *p* 114.

dispute, and for more than half a century a great debate over the Deity of Christ – the Trinitarian Controversy – was waged within the Church.

Large numbers of the people, both high and low, believing Christianity to be false, dropped all pretence of religious profession. The majority of the populace, however, in keeping with the belief that the Church of England was a necessary support of the monarchy and a key factor in maintaining the peace of the realm, asserted that, despite its outworn dogmas, it ought to be retained. To such persons its rituals were but empty formality; an incident revealing this attitude among the highest circles comes from the record of the death of Queen Caroline:

She had been out of health for a long time, and in November, 1737 was on her death-bed . . . And now we have a painful but very characteristic scene. People wondered that the Queen did not have anyone to pray with her. To stop these remarks, Robert Walpole [the Prime Minister] asked the Princess Emily to suggest to the Queen that Archbishop Potter should be sent for. The Princess hesitated. Then, although about a dozen persons were present, Walpole added: 'Pray, Madam, let this farce be played; the Archbishop will act it very well. You may bid him be as short as you will. It will do the Queen no hurt, no more than any good; and it will satisfy all the good and wise fools, who will call us atheists if we don't profess to be as great fools as they are.[1]

The attitude revealed in this very characteristic scene could doubtless have been found in many a home and many a pulpit throughout the nation.

There was, however, one aspect of the religious question on which the people of England were in general unity. This was the fear of what they called 'enthusiasm'. The term meant as much as or more than the word 'fanatic' to-day, and they applied it to anyone whose practice of Christianity manifested any true fervour. In the belief that the wars of the mid-seventeenth century had been caused by over-zealous religion, it was commonly assumed that prayer and preaching which displayed a vital earnestness would prove a threat to the peace of the realm, and in fear of such an outcome public opinion decreed that everything to do with religion must be quietly dispassionate. Thus, empty

[1] *Ibid*, *p* 109.

formality was the order of the day, and an unwritten law demanded that it remain so.

*

Among the Nonconformists (Presbyterians, Independents and Baptists) conditions were undoubtedly better, but very little so, than in the Church of England. Though persecuted from the time of The Great Ejection of 1662 onward, they came into liberty with the Act of Toleration of 1689. In the joy of this new freedom they immediately began to conduct themselves with great vitality; yet their fervour lasted but a short time, and before many years had passed the spiritual lethargy of the times had descended on them too.

The strength of the Nonconformist bodies became sapped, as had that of the Church, by scepticism. Certain men who held to the fundamental principles of Christianity endeavoured to contend for them, but amidst the majority of the ministers Arianism was common, and some preached nothing more than the vagaries of Deism. With but a few notable exceptions, the pulpits were cold, and discord and stagnancy were the chief features of denominational life. By the year 1700 such divisions had taken place that in London there were three separate groups of Presbyterians, four of Independents and six of Baptists. The growth was so small that a report covering the work of these three denominations for the period from 1695 to 1730 stated:

> One church only had been erected, but by enlargements, increased accommodation had been made for four thousand persons. Twelve of the old congregations had been dissolved and ten new congregations organized; fourteen had increased, fifteen had declined and twenty remained in about the same state.[1]

The plain truth is that the churches of England had failed. Much is made in some quarters to-day of the fact that the ecclesiastical machinery was all functioning the same as ever. Nevertheless, in their lack of spiritual authority, their lack of earnestness and lack of power, the churches had failed.

Furthermore, they had failed at a time when they were most sorely needed. Subjected to the effects of Restoration licentious-

[1] Herbert S. Skeats, *A History of the Free Churches of England,* (Jas. Clarke, London, 1868), *p* 334.

ness, and robbed of a sense of the reality of God by Deism, the people of England stood more in need of the Gospel of Jesus Christ than at any time since the Reformation. But they were denied the message of its transforming power and, as a result, found themselves in the bondage of sinful habit.

Nowhere was the nation's weakness more evident than in the *Gin Craze*. With the prohibition, in 1689, of the importation of liquor, Englishmen began to brew their own, and so large was the demand that, within a generation, every sixth house in London had become a gin shop and the nation was in an uncontrollable orgy of gin drinking. 'What must become', asked Magistrate Fielding, 'of the infant who is conceived in gin, with the poisonous distillations of which it is nourished both in the womb and at the breast.'[1] 'Those cursed liquors', asserted Bishop Benson, 'will, if continued to be drunk, destroy the very race of the people themselves.' The nation which had been taught to scoff at self-restraint learned that it had not the strength to withstand the slavery of alcohol. We shall need to remember that it was among a people broken by gin that Whitefield and the Wesleys went about in the nobility of their ministries and that there was triumphant meaning to Charles Wesley's lines on the deliverance effected by the Gospel:

> Hear Him, ye deaf! His praise ye dumb,
>   Your loosened tongues employ;
> Ye blind, behold your Saviour come,
>   And leap ye lame for joy!
>
> He breaks the power of cancelled sin,
>   He sets the prisoner free!
> His blood can make the foulest clean,
>   His blood availed for me!

Perhaps the worst effect of the Gin Craze was that indicated by Bishop Benson, when, towards the close of his life he stated, 'Gin has made the English people what they never were before – cruel and inhuman'. From almost every aspect of British life there arises evidence that an unwonted heartlessness had come over the nation. The Puritans had prohibited sports which indulged in cruelty to animals, but in the age of gin a traffic in games which

[1] Henry Fielding, *An Enquiry into the Late Increase in Robbers* (London, 1751), *p* 19.

found their pleasure in torturing beasts was carried on throughout the land, and people had become so callous that they could look on suffering and delight in it.

The generality of England's upper class manifested a deep-seated inhumanity. Their lives were marked by pride and ostentation; they created homes of boastful magnificence and lived in luxury, but although they gave lip service to the Church, Deism was the creed of many hearts and polite thievery went hand-in-hand with their intrigues for political power.

Far below them there existed the vast numbers of the poor. Of course, every country has its poor in every age, but, as England became more and more enfeebled by its long rejection of moral restraint and its indulgence in gin, larger and larger numbers of them became unable or unwilling to work. The indigent increased in such a fashion that by 1740–50 the arrangements throughout the country for collecting and expending the Poor Rate proved inadequate and the increase in the local Poor Rate alarmingly high. Conditions in the slums of London have been described in the words:

> Behind the streets there was hidden, in a squalid confusion of buildings, fever-laden haunts of vice and wretchedness, . . . a maze of alleys and lanes fading into the unwholesome vapour that always overhung them, of dirty tumble-down houses, with windows patched with rags and blackened paper, and airless courts crowded with quarreling women and half-naked children, wallowing in pools and kennels.[1]

The men of the Restoration had pictured the licentious life as one of unalloyed pleasure, but England learned to its sorrow that it also brought lawlessness and violence. Crime became rampant and the authorities resorted to the only hope they had of checking it: the increase of punishment. They made as many as 160 offences punishable by death, but lawlessness still mounted. London erected a permanent scaffold at Kennington and another at Tyburn, and a hanging became a gala event with a boisterous crowd making merry around the gallows. Jail sentences were meted out with great freedom, and many persons spent the major

[1] Cited by J. V. McAree, *Centuries Compared* (The Globe and Mail, Toronto, August 1955). Original source not given.

portion of their lives in the prisons amidst conditions of unspeakable wretchedness.

The prisoners were huddled together [says the *Encyclopedia Americana*], utterly regardless of their influence on each other, the young and the old, the first offender and the hardened criminal, and the treatment of women was almost worse than that of men. Hundreds of women were crowded together in London prisons, some of them women of the streets, and others accused of little thefts to keep their children alive; and with many of the prisoners, children were allowed to be there because there was no one but their mother to care for them. Poor women were often hanged for passing a counterfeit pound note which sometimes they did not know was counterfeit, and the fact that they had children at the breast or were in pregnancy, was no mitigation of their offence.[1]

John Howard said of the Knaresborough jail, 'Only one room ... earth floor; no fireplace; very offensive; a common sewer from the town running through it uncovered ... An officer confined here took with him a dog to defend him from vermin; but the dog was soon destroyed ... by them.'[2] We shall need to bear these conditions in mind when we witness the ministrations of the men of the revival among the prisoners, and see, for instance, Charles Wesley as he shewed mercy to a 'poor sick negro in the condemned hole', and saying as he told him and his companions the Gospel, 'I found myself overcome with the love of Christ to sinners.'

Much more might be said in description of the evils of the times: the treatment of the insane, cruelties to children, the London mob – Sir Mob it called itself – the incredible extent of gambling, the obscenity of the stage – 'that sink of all corruption' as John Wesley termed it – these and similar aspects of English conditions might be depicted at length. We notice, however, a contemporary note on the corruption of the printed page. Dr Stanhope, Dean of Canterbury and Chaplain to the King, in a sermon preached in 1723, described certain productions of the press as,

... those monsters of irreligion and profaneness, of heresy and

[1] *Encyclopedia Americana* (1949 ed), Vol 10, *p* 31.

[2] Cited by J. W. Bready, *England: Before and After Wesley* (Hodder and Stoughton, London, 1939), *p* 133.

schism, of sedition and scandal, of malice and detraction, of obscenity and ribaldry, which mercenary wretches, void of shame, published for the sake of a paltry present gain, thereby not only debauching the principles of the age, but, if such detestable compositions can survive so long, propagating the poison to posterity . . .[1]

Some will assert, however, that such a statement may be discounted since it comes from a clergyman, and that ministers invariably describe conditions that surround them as especially corrupt. But evidence that during the first half of the eighteenth century England was suffering moral and religious decay to an extraordinary degree comes also from such writers as Richard Steele and Joseph Addison, Samuel Johnson and Henry Fielding. Lady Mary Wortley Montagu, a learned and witty member of high society, made such statements as, 'To be styled a rake is now as genteel in a woman as in a man', and 'There are now more atheists among genteel women than men'. She made the claim, 'Honour and virtue, which we used to hear of in our nursery, are as much laid aside as crumpled ribbons', and joked that Parliament was 'preparing a bill to have "not" taken out of the *Commandments* and inserted in the *Creed*',[2] in order to render these documents more in harmony with the times. Lord Chesterfield, the elegant worldling who instructed his son in the arts of seduction as part of a polite education, came to the place where he too deplored the evils of the age. Addressing Parliament in 1737 on the obscenity of the theatre he carried the matter to its basic cause. 'When we complain of the licentiousness of the stage', he asserted, 'I fear we have more reason to complain of the general decay of virtue and morality among the people.'[3]

In 1732 *The Weekly Miscellany*, London's foremost religious paper, published an article deploring the prevailing conditions – an article later summarized as follows:

It broadly asserts that the people were engulfed in voluptuousness and business, and that a zeal for godliness looked as odd upon a man as would the antiquated dress of his great grand-father. It states that freethinkers were formed into clubs, to propagate their tenets,

[1] Cited from Tyerman's *Life of Whitefield*, Vol 1, *p* 71.
[2] A letter to the Countess of Mar, cited by Julia Wedgwood in her *John Wesley* (London, 1870), *p* 117.
[3] *Ibid.*

and to make the nation a race of profligates; and that atheism was scattered broadcast throughout the kingdom. It affirms that it was publicly avowed that vice was profitable to the state; that the country would be benefited by the establishment of public stews; and that polygamy, concubinage, and even sodomy were not sinful.[1]

*

Such conditions as these, however, did not exist without there being several efforts made to correct them. The love of righteousness – a legacy from the Reformation and more particularly from the Puritan age – still existed in many a heart throughout the nation, and England was not wanting in hundreds – probably thousands – who refused to bow the knee to Baal.

Important among the attempts which such persons made towards the betterment of conditions was the Religious Societies movement. In 1673 Dr Anthony Horneck, a Church of England minister in London, preached a number of what he called 'awakening sermons'. As a result several young men began to meet together weekly in order to build up one another in the Christian faith. They gathered in small groups at certain fixed locations and their places of meeting became known as Society Rooms. In these gatherings they read the Bible, studied religious books and prayed; they also went out among the poor to relieve want at their own expense and to show kindness to all. This activity was recognized by the Church of England, rules were laid out to govern it, and the work so grew that by 1730 nearly one hundred of these Societies existed in London, and others – perhaps another hundred – were to be found in cities and towns throughout England. The Societies movement became, in many senses, the cradle of the Revival, and a knowledge of it is essential to an understanding of Whitefield's early ministry and of John Wesley's organization.

But there were also several other steps taken in the attempt to improve conditions, and the principal ones may be listed as:

1. *The establishment of hospitals.* The years 1720–40 saw unprecedented activity in this field. These institutions not only did much to relieve suffering, but also aided considerably in the increase then being made in medical knowledge.

[1] Tyerman, *The Life and Times of John Wesley* (London, 1880), Vol 1, *p* 217.

2. *The publicizing of the conditions of the prisons.* In 1728 a Parliamentary Committee headed by James Oglethorpe, made a study of England's prisons and presented a report, severely condemning the conditions they found and calling for vigorous reforms. Nothing, however, came of the attempt at the time, for Englishmen in general had little heart for such things.

3. *Legislation against the sale of gin.* Queen Caroline became so deeply concerned about the effects of the Gin Craze that, under her influence, *The Gin Act* – a law prohibiting much of the liquor traffic – was passed in 1736. But it was supported by so few and defied by so many that it proved impossible to enforce. Further legislation of a similar nature was passed in 1743, but this met the same fate.

4. *The Charity Schools movement.* In the early years of the eighteenth century Queen Anne led in the establishment of a number of free schools. William Lecky, the historian, says 'Ninety-six grammar schools were founded in England between 1684 and 1727', and others set the number much higher. But this noble effort was hindered by the vicious circle of the times in which competent teachers were difficult to obtain and dissolute parents were often more desirous that their children earn a few pence than that they learn to read and write.[1]

5. *The Society for the Reformation of Manners.* Failing by persuasion to influence evil-doers to desist from their practices, certain good men formed this organization in order to force them to behave. They scouted out cases of blasphemy and immorality and, in a report issued in 1735, stated that, during the previous forty years, they had effected '99,380 prosecutions for debauchery and profaneness in London and Westminster alone'.[2]

6. *The Society for Promoting Christian Knowledge.* Coming into existence in 1699, this movement provided Christian literature for distribution among the common people. Its efforts were highly beneficial and contributed much toward the work of the Revival.

But despite these many commendable endeavours, there was no

[1] No mention is made here of the Welsh Circulating Schools, for they were a fruit of the Revival, not antecedent to it.

[2] William Lecky, *A History of England in the Eighteenth Century* (New York, 1887), Vol 2, *p* 595.

noticeable improvement in the moral and religious state of the nation. In fact, conditions became not better, but worse, until responsible men began to grow alarmed and to warn of dire consequences. Henry Fielding, speaking as a London magistrate, said concerning the Gin Craze, 'Should the drinking of this poison be continued at its present height during the next twenty years, there will, by that time, be very few of the common people left to drink it'.[1] Bishop Butler declared that scepticism was so rampant that Christianity was treated as though 'it was now discovered to be fictitious . . . and nothing remained but to set it up as the subject of mirth and ridicule'.[2] Archbishop Secker, writing in 1738, asserted:

> In this we cannot be mistaken, that an open and professed disregard to religion is become, through a variety of unhappy causes, the distinguishing character of the present age. This evil has already brought in such dissoluteness and contempt of principle in the higher part of the world, and such profligate intemperance and fearlessness of committing crimes in the lower, as must, if this torrent of impiety stop not, become absolutely fatal.[3]

But how was 'this torrent of impiety' to be stopped? It was evident that the writing of scholarly books in defence of Christianity would not suffice, for it had been tried, but with little avail. Nor would the threat of punishment, for the informing on wrongdoers and the increase of hangings had but hardened the criminal mind. The successive failures of the several attempts to better conditions simply proved that the nation's trouble lay basically with the individual human heart and that the 'torrent of impiety' would flow until some power was found that could stanch it at its source.

During the very months in which Bishop Secker wrote his foreboding words, England was startled by the sound of a voice. It was the voice of a preacher, George Whitefield, a clergyman but twenty-two years old, who was declaring the Gospel in the pulpits of London with such fervour and power, that no church would hold the multitudes that flocked to hear.

[1] Fielding, *op cit*, *p* 19.

[2] Joseph Butler, *Works* (New York, 1842) Advertisement prefixed to the first edition of *The Analogy of Religion.*

[3] Thomas Secker, *Works* (Porteus and Stinton ed), Vol 5, *p* 306.

His voice continued to be heard, and then was joined by the voices of John and Charles Wesley and of many others, in a tremendous chorus of praise and preaching that rang throughout the land and was sustained in strength for more than half a century.

The effect has been described in the words:

> . . . a religious revival burst forth . . . which changed in a few years the whole temper of English society. The Church was restored to life and activity. Religion carried to the hearts of the people a fresh spirit of moral zeal, while it purified our literature and our manners. A new philanthropy reformed our prisons, infused clemency and wisdom into our penal laws, abolished the slave trade, and gave the first impulse to popular education.[1]

It is the story of this, the eighteenth-century Revival, rich with its lessons for our own needy age, which is before us now.

[1] J. R. Green, *A Short History of the English People* (Harper ed, 1899), *pp* 736–7.

PART I
The Years of Preparation

Many Whitefield biographers present his life as an enigma which cannot be explained. This is largely due to a failure to recognize the character of his ancestry and the nature of his boyhood environment . . . Whitefield came from a clerical, educated and cultured ancestry.

EDWIN NOAH HARDY

George Whitefield, the Matchless Soul Winner

I

Whitefield's Ancestry

On the last evening of his life George Whitefield started to mount the stairs of the Presbyterian manse at Newburyport, Massachusetts. Though but fifty-five, he was tired and weak, utterly worn out from his lifetime of evangelistic labours, and for days he had been so infirm that he ought not to have left his bed.

But as he ascended the stairs people came pressing in at the door, begging to hear the Gospel from his lips once more. In response he paused on the landing and began to preach. There he stood, candle in hand, and such was his zeal that he spoke on, heedless of the passing of time, till the candle finally flickered, burned itself out in its socket and died away.

That candle was strikingly representative of Whitefield's life – a life that in its holy burning had long given forth brilliant light and constant heat, but burned its last that night.

Though such is the story before us, its episodes of flaming zeal must be left waiting for the moment. If we are to gain a true understanding of this life we have no choice but to approach it by so cold a consideration as the nature of the ancestry and so uneventful an account as that of the boyhood.

*

From what kind of people did George Whitefield come?

For many years little was known on the subject. Whitefield himself provided the minimal information that his parents were inn-keepers, and his first biographer, Dr Gillies, went a little further and stated that there were two ministers and a retired gentleman among his forbears.[1] But apart from these fragments the lineage remained largely unknown.

[1] Gillies, *op cit*, *p* 1 fn.

This has long proved a misleading situation, for in the absence of a fuller understanding several false assumptions have been made. The background has frequently been pictured as marked by ignorance and poverty, and this error has in turn been a foundation on which further errors have been built.

In more recent years, however, a much larger knowledge of Whitefield's ancestry has been available. A work of extensive research by C. Roy Hudleston[1] traces the lineage, both paternal and maternal, over the course of the four preceding generations. Hudleston brings to light numerous points of information that otherwise were unknown, and, though many details still remain hidden, the evidence that he presents forms a fairly comprehensive picture of the evangelist's background.

Hudleston's findings, amplified by information from the *Alumni Oxoniensis*, show that the Whitefield family had long sustained a relationship with Oxford University and with the priesthood of the Church of England. As is demonstrated on the accompanying *Paternal Pedigree Chart*, seven of the Whitefield men attended Oxford and two of the Whitefield women married Oxford men. These nine obtained their Bachelor of Arts degree, six proceeded to the degree of Master and one held the office of chaplain of Magdalen College for five years. All of these men devoted their lives to the service of the Church and their combined ministries amounted to approximately three hundred years.

This ancestry could hardly have failed to bestow hereditary qualities upon George Whitefield. Though he was descended directly from only two of these men, five of the others were related to this direct line by birth. The extent of the association with Oxford shows most plainly in Thomas (the great-grandfather of George), for not only was he one of its graduates, but so also were his father, two of his brothers, a son, two sons-in-law, a nephew and a grandson. This lengthy relationship indicates that attendance at England's great seat of learning and a life in the ministry were something of a tradition in the family and suggests that in some measure, Oxonian culture and ecclesiastical acumen had undoubtedly found their way into the Whitefield blood.

[1] C. Roy Hudleston, 'George Whitefield's Ancestry', published in *The Transactions of the Bristol and Gloucestershire Archaeological Society for* 1937, *pp* 221–42. Also published by the Society in monograph form.

PATERNAL PEDIGREE CHART OF GEORGE WHITEFIELD

Showing particularly the relationship of the family to Oxford University and the ministry of the Church of England

(1) WILLIAM WHITEFIELD. d 1610
B.A. Magdalen, 1576. M.A. 1580
Chaplain, Magdalen 1580–85
Incorporated at Cambridge, 1584
Rector, Emmington, Oxford, 1584
Vicar, Mayfield, Sussex, 1605

OBERT WHITEFIELD
86
. St Alban's, 1607
. St Alban's, 1611
:or Liddiard Millicent,
ts., 1614

(3) SAMUEL WHITEFIELD
b 1598
B.A. Magdalen, 1621
M.A. Magdalen, 1624
Rector, Dorchester, 1628

(4) THOMAS WHITEFIELD
b 1607 d 1667
B.A. Magdalen 1628
M.A. (?) Magdalen 1631
Rector, Halstead, Kent,
Rockhampton, Glos., 1665

)HN WHITEFIELD
15
. Lincoln, 1636
. Lincoln, 1639
ar, Pembury, Kent

AMUEL WHITEFIELD
51 d 1728
. Hart Hall, 1671
tor, Rockhampton,
s. 1683–1727

(7) ANDREW WHITEFIELD
b 1654 d 1711
Lived retired as gentleman on estate near Thornbury, Glos.

(8) MARY WHITEFIELD
b 1640 d 1724
Married Jonathan Luffingham, who was
B.A. Magdalen, 1671
M.A. Magdalen, 1674
Rector, Fretherne, Glos.

(9) SUSAN WHITEFIELD
b 1644 d 1720
Married George Perkins, who was
B.A. Magdalen, 1667
M.A. Magdalen, 1672
Rector, Rockhampton, Glos.

MUEL WHITEFIELD
95 d 1741
. St Mary Hall, 1716
tor, Rockhampton,
s., 1728–1741

(11) THOMAS WHITEFIELD m. ELIZABETH EDWARDS
b 1681 d 1716 b 1681 (?) d 1751
Proprietor, Bell Inn, Gloucester.

(12) GEORGE WHITEFIELD m. ELIZABETH JAMES
b 1714 d 1770
B.A. Pembroke, 1736

Andrew b 1703 d 1730
Thomas b 1706
Richard b 1708
James b 1710
Joseph b 1712
Elizabeth b 1713

JOHN
b 4 Oct. 1743
Buried St. Mary de Crypt 8 Feb. 1744

This chart is composed on the basis of information provided in C. Roy Hudleston's *George Whitefield's Ancestry* and Foster's *Alumni Oxoniensis*.

During the sixteenth and seventeenth centuries the name was spelled in many forms: Whytfield, Whitfield, Whitfeld, Whitefeld and Whitfeild. The evangelist himself generally used the form 'Whitefield', although there were occasions when he signed 'Whitfield'. Since Howell Harris frequently refers to him in his *Diary* as 'Brother Whit', we may be sure the pronunciation was 'Witfeeld'.

But the life of trade and the holding of civic office also marked George Whitefield's background. His paternal grandfather, Andrew Whitefield, is said by Gillies to have been 'a private gentleman and lived retired upon his estate'.[1] It would appear, however, that Andrew had previously engaged in business in Bristol, and it is probable that it was his success in that realm which made possible his apparently early retirement. His place of residence was a country estate near Thornbury,[2] and we may well assume that it was there that his children (among them, Thomas, the father of George) grew up, enjoying those comforts which a country gentleman's home provided.

The faculty of youthful enterprise which is thus suggested in Andrew is still more evident in his son Thomas. After having been 'bred to the employment of a wine merchant in Bristol',[3] Thomas appears to have been too ambitious to remain in the service of another, for he soon made plans to enter into business for himself. First he took unto himself a wife and, although but about nineteen years old, launched out into a weighty commercial undertaking – the proprietorship of the Bell Inn at Gloucester.

Thomas's bride, Elizabeth Edwards, was a Bristol girl of approximately the same age as her husband. She also came from a background of goodly quality. A Bristol historian says she 'was related to (two) reputable civic families',[4] and Hudleston shows that three of her uncles and four other relatives were burgesses and that another held the offices of alderman and mayor.[5] Elizabeth's father, Richard Edwards, was also a burgess and was in the trade of manufacturing cutlery. From such documents as wills, tax records and covenants covering the sale of property, it is evident that Elizabeth's parents and relations were solid

[1] Gillies, *op cit*, *p* 1.

[2] Andrew is spoken of by contemporary writers as being 'a Bristolian' and as 'of Rockhampton'. Rockhampton, a village in the lower Severn River valley, not far north of Bristol, was the home of his father Thomas. Other documents link Andrew with Thornbury, and it may be assumed that his estate was somewhere between Thornbury and Rockhampton.

[3] Gillies, *p* 2.

[4] Latimer, *Annals of Bristol in the 18th Century*, *p* 201.

[5] This man, John Blackwell, was a vintner and therefore may have been the wine merchant to whom Thomas Whitefield was apprenticed. If so, Thomas was employed by the mayor of the city, and it was doubtless through Mr Blackwell and his wife that he made the acquaintance of their niece, Elizabeth Edwards.

middle-class citizens, and that one branch of the family must be considered as comparatively wealthy.[1]

Such then was George Whitefield's ancestry. With these generations of Oxford graduates and priests of the Church, and these successful business people and civic servants, the background was obviously above the commonplace. A knowledge of this lineage will prove important, for when we come to the study of Whitefield's ministry, and witness his extraordinary array of natural gifts, we shall not need to regard them as a mystery, but may have some understanding as to their source. It was manifestly by means of this ancestry that God prepared the man whom He was raising up as a prime instrument in the eighteenth-century Revival.

[1] This branch of the family was descended from John Dymer, the brother of Elizabeth's maternal grandfather. To each of his three sons Dymer bequeathed a country property, one of which was described as '. . . all that capital messuage or tennement, with the coach house, stable, gardens, outhouses and appurtenances in Ridland, together with all the lands, feedings and commons belonging thereto' (Hudleston, *pp* 236, 239). This was manifestly a property of some value, and those bequeathed to the other sons, one at Putney and the other at Chippenham, appear to have been of a similar nature and worth.

John Dymer's wife, who died three years after her husband, made bequest of a city house, a country estate, many household goods, silverware, pewter, brass, jewellery, 'my biggest diamond' and several sums of money which amounted to £1,294. (*Ibid*, 236, 238.)

How much is £1,294 worth to-day? Since the wage paid to a labouring man is a basic element of the economy of any nation in any age, it will serve as a basis of comparison. In the early eighteenth century an English labourer earned approximately 8 or 9 shillings a week (see M. Dorothy George, 'Wages and Living Standards circa 1700 to 1756', in her *Social Life in the Eighteenth Century*, Sheldon, London, 1923). Thus the £1,294 bequeathed by Mrs Dymer would equal the wages paid to a labouring man for more than 3,000 weeks of work. The reader may make his own calculations in present-day currencies on this basis.

All the man can be traced in the boy – delight in the emotional and exciting, a ready power of appropriating and applying to himself and to his enemies the words of Scripture, fondness for using his elocution, and aptness of imitation. And a strange contrast, as well as resemblance, is there between the man and the boy, when they are placed side by side in St Mary de Crypt, Gloucester. In the church where the infant was baptized and the boy of ten mocked, the deacon of twenty-one preached his first sermon.

J. P. GLEDSTONE

The Life and Travels of George Whitefield, M.A.

2

George, the Boy of the Bell

THE goodly conditions to which Thomas and Elizabeth Whitefield had been accustomed in childhood were in no way lost when they became proprietors of the Bell Inn.

The Bell, strategically located at the heart of Gloucester, was the city's largest and finest hostelry. A building of three storeys, it had a breadth of nearly a hundred feet and a depth which, with its carriage-yard and stables, extended all the way through to the street behind. It was a centre of social activity and its main hall was one of the two auditoriums in the city in which plays were staged for public entertainment.

Two contemporary notes afford us a glimpse of the quality and function of the Bell. Henry Fielding says of a pair of travellers in his *Tom Jones*, 'Being arrived at Gloucester, they chose for their house of entertainment the sign of the Bell, an excellent house indeed, and which I do most seriously recommend to every reader who shall visit this ancient city'.[1] A private letter carried the news, 'To-morrow the city of Gloucester is to be entertained at Mr Whitefield's great room with "The Miser", performed by the celebrated Cheltenham Strollers, with an assembly and ball, the whole to conclude with a supper'.[2] The writer of this letter was a cultured Gloucestershire lady, and the recipient, her sister, was a famous and elegant woman who moved in London's brightest circles, and whom Edmund Burke described as 'the woman of fashion of all ages'. The letter suggests that such

[1] Henry Fielding, *The History of Tom Jones*, Book VIII, chapter 8.

[2] *The Autobiography and Letters of Mrs Delany*. At the time of this correspondence the recipient was yet Mrs Pendarves. The writer was Miss Ann Granville, and these women were respectively the Aspasia and Selima of John Wesley's early correspondence. Since the letter was written in 1740 the 'Mr Whitefield' to whom it refers was not Thomas, but his son Richard.

persons as these were interested in the Bell and the social life that it provided.

It was this place, with its responsibilities for the comfort of the travelling public, the management of its dining-room, the care of its tavern and the overseeing of its servants that Thomas and Elizabeth took on themselves at so early an age. There can be no doubt that the proprietors of such an establishment would be classed among the more prominent and prosperous of Gloucester's citizens.

This estimate finds corroboration from another contemporary source. In those days each parish assisted its poor by a tax which it levied against its members. The Whitefields attended the Church of St Mary de Crypt and its Registers show that the Poor Rate paid by Thomas Whitefield year after year was among the two or three highest in the parish. It was twice as much as most and four times as much as many, and his fellow parishioner, Robert Raikes – then a printer, but soon to become the founder of the *Gloucester Journal* – paid but half as much as he.

The Poor Rate figures also give us grounds to believe that the Bell prospered under Thomas's management. During his first two years his weekly payment of Poor Rate was 4 pence, but the following year it was raised to 4½d. and later to 5 pence, and there can be little doubt that the increased assessment reflected a corresponding increase in the volume of his business.[1] Moreover, in writing his will in 1716 Thomas listed 'all that stable I recently bought and purchased', and this acquisition would also indicate growth. It suggests, either that the stable attached to the Inn was no longer adequate, or that he had undertaken the operating of a livery stable as an additional business.

During their years together at the Bell, Thomas and Elizabeth saw not only their business prosper, but their family also. Seven children were born to them: first, five boys, then a girl, and finally

[1] Though the system of assessment for the Poor Rate differed from parish to parish and was fraught with many inequalities, the amount of assessment indicated, in a general way, the financial standing of the assessed. During the years in which Thomas's Rate was raised that of others either remained level or was lowered – a circumstance which could have resulted only from an increase in either his property holdings, his stock in trade or the volume of his business. This is true also of the increased Rate charged to Elizabeth in the years of her management of the Bell.

the boy whom they named George. There can be little doubt that the home into which these children came was representative of England's upper middle class, and that the father and mother – he as the son of a country gentleman and she as the daughter of successful business people – would plan to see their family raised amidst conditions similar to those of their own background.

Such prospects, however, were suddenly changed: Thomas's promising career was cut short by death. The immediate cause is unknown, but it would appear that he was sick but a short while, for on December 23, 1716, he wrote his will and on the 26th he passed away. He was thirty-five years old.

As to Thomas's religious associations, we know only that he was a member of the Church of St Mary de Crypt (Church of England) and that he served as one of its wardens in 1712.[1] Perhaps the most that can be said of him is that he was an enterprising and successful young tradesman, and there is no reason to doubt that had he lived, his family would have continued to enjoy their accustomed measure of prosperity.

With Thomas laid within the grave the responsibilities of managing the Inn and bringing up the family were borne by Elizabeth. She appears to have succeeded with the business, for during the years of her widowhood the Poor Rate levied against her not only remained as high as when Thomas was alive, but even increased at times. The little that is recorded of her indicates a woman of forthright decision and upright principles. If it be, however, that the mind of a man is received from his mother, we can but wonder whether Elizabeth possessed some of the qualities which later shone in her youngest son, yet we must assume that if such were the case, she found no opportunity to express them amidst the burdens of her widowed life.

*

Only one item regarding George's infancy has come down to us. Due to neglect on the part of his nurse at a time when he had the measles, he contracted a permanent misfocus of his eyes. This does

[1] There is an entry in the records of St Mary de Crypt for 1703: 'Spent at the Receiving Mr Whitefield's gift, 00.02.06.' It is possible that Thomas donated a certain fixture or item of furniture which cost this amount to install.

not seem to have been serious enough to be termed cross-eyes.[1] But during the days of his ministry it afforded his detractors a point of ridicule, and he was long referred to among the riff-raff of London as 'Doctor Squintum'.

Similarly, we know of only one of Whitefield's boyhood companions. This was Gabriel Harris, whose father (also a Gabriel Harris) was proprietor of Gloucester's foremost book store.[2] The father was long active in civic affairs and filled successively the offices of elder sheriff, alderman and mayor, and the son grew up to follow in his father's footsteps, both in the book business and the mayoralty. It is probably a further indication of the status of the Whitefield family, that the one of George's childhood friends of whom we have record was the son of the mayor of the city.

*

The principal source of information on Whitefield's boyhood is an autobiographical *Account*[3] which he wrote in 1739. At that time he was twenty-four and had been preaching for two years. Its opening paragraphs are as follow:

I was born in Gloucester, in the month of December, 1714. My father and mother kept the Bell Inn. The former died when I was two years old; the latter is now alive, and has often told me how she endured fourteen weeks' sickness after she brought me into the world; but was used to say, even when I was an infant, that she expected more comfort from me than any other of her children. This, with the circumstance of my being born in an inn, has often been of service to me in exciting my endeavours to make good my mother's expectations, . . .

I can truly say, I was froward from my mother's womb. I was so brutish as to hate instruction and used purposely to shun all opportunities of receiving it. I can date some very early acts of uncleanness. I soon gave pregnant proofs of an impudent temper. Lying, filthy

[1] J. P. Gledstone, *The Life and Travels of George Whitefield, M.A.* (London, 1871), *pp* 2–3, speaks of Whitefield's condition as 'a squint, which is said not to have marred the extreme sweetness of his countenance, nor diminished the charm of his glance'. For an eyewitness description of Whitefield's appearance, see *pp* 364–5.

[2] The first book ever published in Gloucester, *The History of Britain from the Tower of Babel,* bore the inscription, 'Printed by R. Raikes and W. Dicey for the author, and sold by Gabriel Harris in Gloucester, &c., 1722.'

[3] *A Short Account of God's Dealings with the Reverend George Whitefield, A.B., from His Infancy to the Time of His entering into Holy Orders*, published in Whitefield's *Journals*, *pp* 33–72.

talking, and foolish jesting I was much addicted to, even when very young. Sometimes I used to curse, if not swear. Stealing from my mother I thought no theft at all, and used to make no scruple of taking money out of her pocket before she was up. I have frequently betrayed my trust, and have more than once spent money I took in the house, in buying fruits, tarts, etc., to satisfy my sensual appetite. Numbers of Sabbaths have I broken, and used generally to behave myself very irreverently in God's sanctuary. Much money have I spent in plays and the common entertainments of the age. Cards and reading romances were my heart's delight. Often have I joined with others in playing roguish tricks . . .

I had some early convictions of sin; and once, I remember when some persons (as they frequently did) made it their business to tease me, I immediately retired to my room, and kneeling down, with many tears, prayed over that Psalm wherein David so often repeats these words – *'But in the Name of the Lord will I destroy them.'* I was always fond of being a clergyman, and used frequently to imitate the ministers reading prayers, etc. Part of the money I used to steal from my parent I gave to the poor, and some books I privately took from others, for which I have since restored fourfold, I remember were books of devotion.

My mother was very careful of my education, and always kept me, in my tender years, for which I can never sufficiently thank her, from intermeddling in the least with the public business.

About the tenth year of my age, it pleased God to permit my mother to marry a second time . . .

When I was about twelve, I was placed at a school called St Mary de Crypt, in Gloucester – the last grammar school I ever went to. Having a good elocution and memory, I was remarked for making speeches before the corporation at their annual visitation. . . .

During the time of my being at school, I was very fond of reading plays, and have kept from school for days together to prepare myself for acting them. My master seeing how mine and my schoolfellows' vein ran, composed something of this kind for us himself, and caused me to dress myself in girls' clothes, which I had often done, to act a part before the corporation. The remembrance of this has often covered me with confusion of face, and I hope will do so, even to the end of my life.

And I cannot but here observe, with much concern of mind, how this way of training up youth has a natural tendency to debauch the mind, to raise ill passions and to stuff the memory with things as contrary to the Gospel of Jesus Christ, as light to darkness, Heaven to

Hell. However, though the first thing I had to repent of was my education in general, yet I must always acknowledge my particular thanks are due to my master, for the great pains he took with me and his other scholars, in teaching us to speak and write correctly.[1]

In order to understand Whitefield's *Account* we must notice the unusual circumstances under which it was produced. At the time of writing he had, for two years, experienced a most phenomenal popularity, and he sought to take away attention from himself by directing it to the grace of God in his life. Moreover, as we shall see, he was then undergoing a tremendous conviction of the holiness of God and of the sinfulness of sin; this, in turn, made him consider faults that most Christians would entirely overlook, as grievous iniquities. He made much of abasing himself and magnifying the Lord.

The *Account* does not prove that in comparison with others around him Whitefield was a particularly evil boy. In all probability he was much like his brothers and playmates, and was simply what one might expect of a lad growing up in an inn during an exceptionally dissolute age.

A public house is seldom a savoury place in which to bring up a child, but in the early years of the eighteenth century it could hardly have failed to abound with evil. Though the Whitefields sought to attract the better class of trade, all manner of humanity must have made 'ye signe of ye Bell' their stopping-place and the tavern must often have witnessed the sights and sounds of drunken degradation. Highway robbers frequented the inns, there to pick their victims and plan their attacks, and many of the lowest of mankind made a hostelry a place of debauchery. It was in this environment with its unavoidable familiarity with the ways of sin that George Whitefield spent the first sixteen years of his life.

The *Account* reveals, however, something of Whitefield's boyhood personality. It shows a high-spirited, merry lad who plays 'roguish tricks', yet it also portrays a deeply sensitive boy who, when teased by his playmates, runs home to weep and pray. This combination of vigorous animal spirits and extraordinary sensitivity – the chief components of many of the world's

[1] Gledstone, *op cit, pp* 37–9.

greatest personalities – will be seen again and again throughout Whitefield's career.

Moreover, the *Account* depicts a constant conflict between natural inclinations to wrong and what Whitefield calls 'the movings of the blessed Spirit upon my heart'. He read romances, but turned from them to read the Bible; he misbehaved in church, yet played a game of church with himself as the minister; he stole from his mother and gave to the poor; he purloined books, but they were books of religion.

This conflict is further seen in an item which comes from his own pen. Not far from the Bell there was an Independent Meeting House where a Thomas Cole was the pastor, and Whitefield tells us:

I must acquaint you with the following anecdote of old Mr Cole, a most venerable Dissenting minister; whom I was always taught to ridicule, and (with shame I write it) used, when a boy, to run into his meeting house and cry, 'Old Cole! Old Cole! Old Cole!' Being asked once by one of his congregation what business I would be of? I said, 'a minister, but I would take care never to tell stories in the pulpit, like old Cole.'[1]

Here again is the rollicksome lad who chooses as the object of his merriment a man of God, yet who stays listening at the chapel door, and is there at least long enough to know that the preaching is interspersed with stories.

*

The most important information in the *Account*, however, is that which pertains to Whitefield's early education. Because he says, 'When I was about twelve, I was placed at a school called St Mary de Crypt', certain writers assume that he was not in school before that time. They suggest a virtually idle childhood and on that basis suppose that he went to Oxford with little education and remained an unlearned man throughout life.

Thus the question arises, 'When did Whitefield first attend school?' In reply we notice that during his days at St Mary de Crypt he was not a mere beginner, learning his *A, B, C* s. Rather, he was a fairly mature lad who had both the eloquence and

[1] *Works*, Vol 2, *p* 27. When Whitefield began to preach Mr Cole displayed much delight in his ministry. He heard him as often as possible and once remarked jovially, 'I find that young Whitefield can now tell stories, as well as Old Cole'.

understanding to make speeches before the city fathers and who was able to learn and perform dramatic roles with ease. He read plays for his own delight and used Bishop Ken's *Manual for Winchester Scholars* with 'great benefit to [his] soul'. By the time he was sixteen he was reading the *Greek New Testament* for his spiritual edification and had laid the foundation for the proficiency in Latin that we shall notice later.

In describing St Mary's as 'the last grammar school I ever attended', Whitefield implies that he had previously attended other schools. We know of one of these: the school conducted by the Gloucester Cathedral, popularly known as The College. Its enrolment records for 1726 contain the following entry:

> Georgius Whitefield, ann: 11, Jan. 10.
> Dom. Elizabethae Whitefield, vid: Glous; filius.[1]

Nothing has been recorded of George's days here except that his Master was the Reverend William Alexander, M.A.[2] He remained, however, for but one year, after which he went directly to St Mary's. The reason for the change may have been that the latter was but a stone's throw or so from the Bell.

Whitefield must, however, have attended a school before entering The College, for the *Account* makes it evident that he could read at a fairly early age. It is in his narration of what he calls 'my younger days' that he speaks of himself as reading romances, praying over a Psalm and imitating ministers reading prayers. Moreover, the degree of learning that he possessed while at St Mary's was not something that he could have acquired in his one year at The College, and these factors together require the belief that he had previously attended some other school.

This belief is but part of a larger picture which emerges regarding Whitefield's boyhood. In his report of certain events which took place when he was fifteen (we shall notice his words later)[3] he twice implies that he and his mother had long taken it for granted that he was to attend the University. Moreover, his statement in the *Account*, 'My mother . . . was used to say, even

[1] Cited by Roland Austin, *George Whitefield's Schooldays*, in *Gloucestershire Notes and Queries* (1913), Vol 8, *pp* 384–5.

[2] Fosbrooke's *History of Gloucester* mentions Alexander's work as a schoolmaster and says, 'Among Alexander's pupils was George Whitefield'.

[3] See *pp* 56–7.

when I was an infant, that she expected more comfort from me than any other of her children', suggests that she saw special promise in him. It may well have been the case that both she and Thomas had planned that the family tradition of an Oxford education and a life in the ministry was to be maintained in one of their sons, and decided that George should be the child thus privileged. It would appear that after Thomas' death, Elizabeth continued – apparently with increased tenacity – to hold to this purpose; for Dr Gillies tells us, 'He was regarded by his mother with peculiar tenderness and educated with more than ordinary care'.[1] The same thought arises from Whitefield's statement, 'My mother was very careful of my education and always kept me in my tender years . . . from intermeddling in the least with the public business.' The other children might work in the Inn, but not Elizabeth's favoured George. He was being prepared for better things: he was to attend the University!

Thus we may be sure that Whitefield did not spend an idle childhood and did not arrive at the age of eleven in ignorance. Though there is no recorded statement on the matter, the above evidence would require us to conclude that his mother put him under instruction at an early age – probably as soon as he was old enough to receive it – and that throughout his boyhood she looked on him as being prepared to enter Oxford.

*

The *Account* possibly sheds light on George's appearance. It speaks of him as playing feminine roles. There are no descriptions of him during his boyhood, but those during his early ministry depict him as having a very fair countenance, and it is probable that this was the reason he was chosen for these parts.

Whitefield's sentence about staying home from school in order to practise plays reveals something further about his personality. His words conjure up a picture of him. There he is in his room at the Bell. Though but a lad of thirteen or fourteen he becomes so excited, so engrossed as he prepares to act his role that he cannot leave it to go to school. He reads and re-reads the play, acting and re-acting his part (and perhaps the other parts too), entering into the whole performance with such intensity that he

[1] Gillies, *op cit*, *p* 2.

cannot tear himself away. He has become enraptured in a world of his own making and this goes on 'for days together'. These gifts of vivid imagination and intense emotion, along with those of 'a good elocution and memory', are the prerequisites of the true actor and true orator, and reveal the qualities which we shall see in him in rare abundance in the days of his ministry.

Though the master of St Mary's School, the Reverend Daniel Bond, M.A., nurtured young Whitefield's natural inclinations towards the stage, he also assisted in his preparation toward the ministry. Without realizing the effects of his actions, in training his pupils 'to speak and write correctly' Mr Bond was educating young Whitefield for the work he was to perform so soon and with such extraordinary skill.

*

At this point, however, we must retrace somewhat in our narrative. When George was almost eight years old[1] his mother remarried and brought her new husband to live at the Bell. This man was a long-time neighbour by the name of Capel Longden. He came of worthy stock, for his father had been a prosperous tradesman and mayor of the city.[2] On his mother's side, one ancestor had thrice been mayor, and another Richard Capel, after some years as Dean of Magdalen College, Oxford, moved to Gloucester where he became famous as a medical doctor, a theologian and a preacher.

Elizabeth had reason to believe that the marriage gave promise of happiness, for she and Capel Longden had much in common. His wife's death had occurred but ten months before that of Thomas and therefore each had been in the widowed state for six years. He was the owner of an ironmonger (hardware) business, not far from the Bell, and his assessment for the Poor Rate was sometimes as high as that of the Whitefields. And he too was a

[1] The marriage took place on December 8, 1722, at which time George was not quite eight years old. His *Journals* state that the marriage took place 'about the tenth year of my age', showing that his chronology is not to be trusted in these early parts of his record. Wherever possible the chronology must be tested by other sources.

[2] The *Apprenticeship Lists for the City of Gloucester* record: '25 Nov., 1695, Capel Longden, son of Thomas Longden of the city of Gloucester, Ironmonger, now Mayor, hath putt himself apprentice to his Father (and Anne his wife) for seven years from 25th March last.'

member of the Church of St Mary de Crypt, and had repeatedly been chosen as a sidesman and one of its 'examiners of accounts'.

But though this marriage began with hopes of success, before long it showed signs of failure. Looking back upon it years later, George wrote:

> It proved [to be] what the world would call an unhappy match as for temporals, but God overruled it for good. It set my brethren upon thinking more than otherwise they would have done and made an uncommon impression on my own heart in particular.[1]

George was wise enough to say no more about this family affair, and it is evident that as a minister he was ashamed of it. Nevertheless, there is much more behind his words than appears on the surface and we must piece together the shreds of information that are available.

It would appear that upon marrying Elizabeth, Longden seized control of the Bell. Thomas had bequeathed one half of his estate to his wife; the other half was to be divided equally among the children, each of whom was to come into possession of his share at the age of fourteen. Longden, however, was able to take over both the management and the proprietorship, and the Bell was referred to in the *Gloucester Journal* as 'in the possession of Capel Longden'. Beginning with the year following the marriage, the Poor Rate assessment was made out in his name and the church's annual payment for sacramental wine is shown in its books as paid to him. Richard Whitefield, the third son in the family, though he had grown up in the Inn and was virtually a part owner, was required to enter into an apprenticeship contract with this step-father who had never learned the business.[2] All of this points to a severe struggle within the Whitefield home.

George's statement that this was 'an unhappy match as for temporals' is amplified by his further words, 'my mother's circumstances being much on the decline . . .' These assertions indicate that the Bell did not prosper under Longden's hand. Something in his person or behaviour may have repulsed

[1] *Journals*, p 39.

[2] The *Apprenticeship Lists for the City of Gloucester* record: '1 Jan. 1723/4, Richard Whitfield, son of Thomas Whitfield, late of the city of Gloucester, Innholder, deceased, has putt himself apprentice to Capel Longden of the city aforesaid, Ironmonger, and Elizabeth his wife for 7 years.'

customers, but whatever the cause, Elizabeth apparently saw the endowment that Thomas had left being steadily reduced, till the comforts she and her children had known were diminished and they faced critical conditions.[1] And as the business declined, so there declined also Elizabeth's hope of sending George to Oxford, insomuch that, by the time he was fifteen the idea was temporarily dropped.

When Elizabeth had endured this marriage for six years, matters came to the breaking-point. Perhaps some bitter crisis provoked her final decision, but George simply says, '. . . my mother was obliged to leave the Inn. My brother, who had been bred up for the business, married; whereupon all was made over to him.'[2] Therewith Elizabeth not only left the Bell, but left Longden too. She obtained a little cottage of her own,[3] where henceforth she and her daughter lived alone.

The brother, Richard, apparently sought to remove the Longden association from the Bell and restore the good name of Whitefield, for he advertised in the *Gloucester Journal*:

The Bell Inn and Tavern in Southgate Street, Gloucester, which hath been lately in the Possession of Capell Longden, and formerly kept by Elizabeth his Wife, Relict of Thomas Whitefield, is now held, By Richard Whitefield, his Son; who hath always been in the Business, and will continue the same, fit for accommodating Gentlemen and Others. NOTE. He sells all sorts of Wines, Wholesale or Retale, at very reasonable Rates.[4]

As to what became of Longden, little is recorded. It is possible that he tried to retain his hold on the Bell – or else had reduced it to such a condition that others had claims upon it – for Richard had difficulty in securing a satisfactory lease.[5] From the time when

[1] In 1728 the Poor Rate charged against Longden dropped from £1 to 12 shillings.
[2] *Journals, p* 40.
[3] About this time Elizabeth sold a stable. This was not the one mentioned by Thomas in his will, and therefore must indicate a further business venture on Elizabeth's part. The proceeds of this sale may have assisted her in the purchase of her cottage. The document covering the sale of the stable is in the possession of the *Gloucester Public Library*.
[4] The *Gloucester Journal*, Tuesday, March 11, 1728/9.
[5] *Ibid*, February 9, 1730/1: 'To be lett at Lady Day, the Bell Inn and Tavern, in the City of Gloucester, now in the possession of Richard Whitefield. Enquiries of William Jones, Attorney at Law, in Gloucester, or of Mr Richard Gastrell, of

Elizabeth separated from him, Longden is but once alluded to in any record that has come down to us and that is a brief sentence in George's *Diary*.[1] The church *Registers*, where he had been listed among the sidesmen and examiners of accounts for several years show that he had been dropped entirely from office. Only once do they so much as mention his name and that in a cryptic entry in the *Register of Deaths*; '13 February, 1737/8. Breaking ground for Capel Longden: 2 shillings.'

As we look back upon the presence of Longden in the Whitefield home we ask what effect it may have had on George. The circumstance of growing up in a fatherless condition, along with the self-consciousness occasioned by his eye affliction, may well have caused feelings of insecurity in so sensitive a child. Without doubt, Longden afforded him none of the strength and confidence which a child should derive from a father's presence. On the contrary, during the highly formative years from eight to fifteen, George lived in a home which was marred by this unpleasant personality, by increasing financial difficulty, by a sorrowing mother and finally a broken marriage. He could not but have been affected by such things and we may be sure that the shyness we shall see in him later arose primarily from these boyhood conditions.

*

A further result of the trouble in the home was that it caused George to discontinue his schooling for a time. He wrote:

> Before I was fifteen, having, as I thought, made a sufficient progress in the classics, and, at the bottom, longing to be set at liberty from the confinement of a school, I one day told my mother, 'Since her circumstances would not permit her to give me a University education, more learning I thought would spoil me for a tradesman; and therefore, I judged it best not to learn Latin any longer.' She at first refused to consent, but my corruptions soon got the better of her good nature.
>
> Hereupon, for some time I went to learn to write only. But my mother's circumstances being much on the decline, and being tractable

Cirencester.' Whatever the difficulties, Richard was able to overcome them and advertised the following week, 'The Bell Inn and Tavern is still kept by Richard Whitefield, who has taken a long lease of the same'.

[1] See *p* 93.

that way, I from time to time began to assist her occasionally in the public-house, till at length I put on my blue apron and my snuffers,[1] washed mops, cleaned rooms, and in one word, became professed and common drawer for nigh a year and a half.[2]

Such employment could hardly be considered a preparation for the ministry. Nevertheless, in Whitefield's case, it proved of real value. It provided an insight into the world of business and taught him to bear responsibility, for he 'sometimes had the care of the whole house upon [his] hands'. It enabled him to know people and life, for there are few occupations which afford as good an opportunity to assess mankind as that of an inn-keeper. The knowledgeable rapport which Whitefield so easily established in later life with all ranks of humanity, arose in some measure from this experience in the Inn.

Nor were his better ambitions lost. He soon yearned to continue his education and confessed, '. . . seeing the boys go by to school has often cut me to the heart'. Though he served liquor during the day, he read the Bible and composed sermons at night. Furthermore, he still entertained the hope of attending the University: '. . . a dear youth would often come', he wrote, 'entreating me to go to Oxford. My general answer was, "I wish I could!" '[3]

Before George was seventeen this long-cherished goal again became a possibility. Because of disagreement with Richard's wife who was then mistress of the Inn, he left the place and determined never to have anything more to do with it. He went to live with his mother, but her cottage was so small that it was necessary for him to sleep on the floor. It was a difficult period for him, yet he told his sister, 'God intends something for me which we know not of', and before long the something appeared. A youth who had spent a term at Oxford happened to mention to him and his mother that he had been able to defray his University costs by working as a servitor.

To Elizabeth, who apparently had never heard of a servitorship,

[1] Snuffers were wristlets the shape of the metal snuffers used on candles. These were made of the same material as the 'blue apron' and were worn as a protection to the lower portion of the sleeve. The 'blue apron and snuffers' were regarded as the badge of the trade of the domestic employee in the eighteenth-century inn.

[2] *Journals*, *pp* 39, 40.

[3] *Ibid*, *p* 40.

this news was cause for rejoicing. 'This will do for my son!' she cried out. 'George, will you go to Oxford?' And George, who appears to have been equally overjoyed, replied, 'With all my heart,'[1] And so it was settled, George was to attend Oxford as a servitor, and there can be little doubt that, in keeping with the family tradition he intended to enter the ministry and viewed the University as the principal step towards it.

With this prospect before him George immediately returned to St Mary's School. He said of his first day there:

My Master addressed me thus, 'I see, George, you are advanced in stature, but your better part must needs have gone backwards.' This made me blush. He set me something to translate into Latin, and though I had made no application to my classics for so long a time, yet I had but one inconsiderable fault in my exercises.[2]

Whitefield entered upon his renewed school career with diligence. 'I spared no pains', he wrote, 'to go forward in my book.' Before long, however, his higher aspirations were forgotten, for he 'got acquainted with a set of debauched, abandoned, atheistical youths', and soon 'was in a fair way of being as infamous as the worst of them'. But his *Account* goes on to report:

Oh, stupendous love! God even here stopped me, when running on in a full career to hell! For, just as I was upon the brink of ruin, He gave me a distaste of their principles and practices . . .

Being thus delivered out of the snare of the Devil, I began to be more and more serious, and felt God, at different times, working powerfully and convincingly upon my soul . . .

Being now near the seventeenth year of my age, I was resolved to prepare myself for the holy sacrament, which I received on Christmas Day. I began now to be more and more watchful over my thoughts, words and actions. I kept the following Lent, fasting Wednesday and Friday, thirty-six hours together. My evenings, when I had done

[1] *Ibid, p* 42. Elizabeth's immediate response, 'This will do for my son', upon hearing of the practice of servitorship shows that the desire that George might attend the University was already in her mind. This is also to be seen in George's words, cited earlier, 'I one day told my mother, "Since her circumstances would not permit her to give me a University education . . ." ' Similarly George's reply, 'I wish I could', to the youth who mentioned his going to Oxford while he was serving in the Inn, indicates that Oxford was not an afterthought. These three references are a strong confirmation of the view that Elizabeth had long planned that this favoured son should maintain the family tradition of Oxford.

[2] *Ibid.*

waiting upon my mother, were generally spent in acts of devotion, reading *Drelincourt on Death*, and other practical books, and I constantly went to public worship twice a day. Being now upper-boy, by God's help I made some reformation amongst my schoolfellows. I was very diligent in reading and learning the classics, and in studying my *Greek Testament*...[1]

In this disciplined and religious manner of life Whitefield continued 'for a twelvemonth'. This period of his schooling has often been overlooked, but because he applied himself with such earnestness, it was probably of greater value than any previous portion of his education. Though as yet he knew nothing of the redemption by grace that God was to teach him at Oxford, he was given strength to leave his evil companions entirely and to pursue his programme of study and religious duty with unremitting diligence. Sir James Stephen, reflecting on this time of reformation declared, 'From his seventeenth year to his dying day, Whitefield lived amongst embittered enemies and jealous friends, without a stain on his reputation'.[2]

Shortly before he 'was eighteen years of age, it was judged proper for (him) to go to the University'.[3] We see the scene as he prepares to mount the stage-coach and relatives and friends have gathered to bid him farewell. His mother is deeply affected by the event; she tearfully recalls the years of her widowhood, his fatherless boyhood and the tragedy of Longden, but in the realization that her long-standing desire is at last coming to fulfilment, her tears of sorrow become tears of joy. She sees him as he stands before her, fairly tall and slim and marked by an easy, gracious bearing, and, knowing his extraordinary vitality of spirit, she is certain that some outstanding future awaits him.

And for George too, the occasion is a poignant one. Into his mind there crowd memories of his childhood, of his days of drudgery in the Inn and his struggles to overcome evil. Yet now he may well forget all such things, for before him there lie new surroundings, new companions – yea, a new life, the life of books and study amidst the storied halls and ancient colleges of Oxford University.

[1] *Journals*, *pp* 43, 44. [2] Stephen, *op cit*, *p* 382. [3] *Journals*, *p* 44.

I began to fast twice a week for thirty-six hours together, prayed many times a day and received the sacrament every Lord's Day. I fasted myself almost to death all the forty days of Lent, during which I made it a point of duty never to go less than three times a day to public worship, besides seven times a day to my private prayers. Yet I knew no more that I was to be born a new creature in Christ Jesus than if I had never been born at all.

WHITEFIELD, 1769

3

Oxford, the Holy Club and Conversion

WHITEFIELD matriculated at Pembroke College, Oxford, on November 7, 1732.[1] The day was not clouded for him, as it might have been for many a man, by the fact that he entered in the lowest of its categories: as a servitor.

The servitor, in exchange for free tuition, served as lackey to three or four more highly placed students. He might be required to waken them in the morning, black their shoes, run their errands and tidy their rooms, and might even be asked to do their college exercises for them. He received what money and discarded clothing and books they chose to give. His inferior position was marked by a special garb that he wore and custom forbade students of a higher rank to talk to him.[2] The Statutes ordered that the servitors were not to take part with other students in the weekly Disputations in Philosophy, but were to dispute by themselves on a different day,[3] and even when a whole college attended the Holy Sacrament the servitors were still separated and partook at another time.[4] It was not uncommon for men who

[1] As he was probably at Oxford, preparing for the matriculation, for some days before this, it may be assumed that his schooling at Gloucester lasted until sometime after the middle of October. The poet Shenstone entered Pembroke at the same time; Samuel Johnson had left it twelve months earlier.

[2] A. D. Godley, *Oxford in the Eighteenth Century* (Methuen, London, 1908), *p* 119, quotes a biographer of Shenstone: 'Mr Shenstone had one ingenious and much valued friend in Oxford, whom he could only visit in private, as he wore a servitor's gown; it being then deemed a great disparagement for a commoner to appear in public with one in that situation; which would make one wish with Dr Johnson there were no young people admitted in that servile state.'

[3] Douglas Macleane, *A History of Pembroke College, Oxford* (Oxford Historical Society, 1897), *p* 189.

[4] V. H. H. Green, *The Young Mr Wesley* (Edward Arnold, London, 1961), *p* 162, quotes Charles Wesley, who reported, 'On Whitsunday the whole College received

began in a servitorship to leave the University rather than endure its humiliations.

This was a most unsuitable environment for one like Whitefield. Having already suffered an insecure boyhood, he needed surroundings which would minister to the development of self-assurance. But he was subjected instead to this self-abasement and the more than three years of enforced servility left lasting scars on his personality.

*

The question arises as to what value there was in a course at Oxford at that time.

It cannot be doubted that the general deterioration which then existed throughout the nation had affected the University also. The Statutes had established academic standards which fully justified the claim, 'Oxonians are required to take all knowledge for their province'. 'There is a course of study', says an Oxford historian, 'intended to cover the seven years from matriculation to the M.A. degree, . . . which, had it been duly followed, was catholic enough to satisfy the demands of that or any age.'[1] But by the third and fourth decades of the eighteenth century these standards had fallen into grave neglect.

This condition was manifest, for instance, in the practice of relegating the work of teaching into the hands of the tutors. Adam Smith who attended Balliol in 1740, stated, 'The greater part of the public professors have, for these many years, given up altogether, even the pretence of teaching', and several other graduates made similar criticisms.

Though some tutors were men of industry and learning, the majority were characterized by slothfulness. Most were holders of a Fellowship – a system by which a graduate was granted an income in order that he might pursue further studies – but so many remained at the University in idleness for the rest of their days that a Fellowship became known as 'a pension in indolence'

the Sacrament, except the servitors (for we are too well bred to communicate with them, though in the body and blood of Christ) to whom it was administered the next day'.

[1] Godley, *op cit*, *p* 56.

and the holders were made the sport of the 'college wits'.[1]

The descriptions of the University's decadence at the time, however, have doubtless been carried too far. Though sloth and indifference plainly marked certain areas of its life, it must be recognized that among the heads of its colleges there were several men of the highest erudition and sincerity. Advancements of historic importance were then being made in the fields of astronomy, medicine and law, and, despite its publicized failings, the University was still a rich repository of scholarship.

Under these conditions an Oxford degree might represent little or it might represent much. The University merely made an opportunity for thorough learning available, and the possibility of a student's acquiring it depended on two things – his own diligence and the competence and interest of his tutor.

The religious and moral character of the University was also in a state of decline. In earlier years several of Oxford's best intellects had been active in the defence of the basic principles of the Christian faith, but by 1730 departures from both Christian belief and practice were generally regarded with an easy *laissez-faire*. Since most Fellowships required the holder to remain unmarried, the practice brought its inevitable toll of scandal. Admittedly, immorality and drunkenness are found in university life in any age, but during this period of Oxford's history they were particularly prevalent. Thomas Sheridan stated that Oxford taught 'a continuation of the classics learned at school, the rudiments of logic, natural philosophy, astronomy, metaphysics and heathen morality thrown in'.

Charles Wesley speaks of Oxford as the place,

[1] The following parody appeared in *The Oxford Sausage*:

> Within those walls, where thro' the glimmering shade,
> Appear the pamphlets in a mould'ring heap,
> Each in his narrow bed till morning laid,
> The peaceful Fellows of the College sleep.
>
> The tinkling bell proclaiming early prayers,
> The noisy servants rattling o'er their head,
> The calls of business and domestic cares,
> Ne'er rouse these sleepers from their downy bed.
>
> Oft have they bask'd along the sunny walls,
> Oft have the benches bow'd beneath their weight;
> How jocund are their looks when dinner calls!
> How smoke the cutlets on their crowded plate!

Where learning keeps its loftiest seat,
And hell its firmest throne.

And he goes on to state that, while there,

Satan and sloth had smoothed my way,
To pleasure's paradise,
Yet still I paused, afraid, to stray,
Or plunge the gulf of vice.[1]

*

Into life amidst these conditions Whitefield entered with resolute purpose. He not only bore the servitorship without complaint, but so desirous was he of succeeding at Oxford that he did double duty. Though one of his brothers had told him that when he got to the University he would forsake the strong habits of religion and study that he had developed during his last year at Gloucester, this was not the case:

I was quickly solicited [he writes], to join in the excess of riot with several who lay in the same room. God . . . gave me grace to withstand them; and once in particular, it being cold, my limbs were so benumbed by sitting alone in my study, because I would not go out amongst them, that I could scarce sleep all night. But I soon found the benefit of not yielding, for, when they perceived they could not prevail, they let me alone as a singular odd fellow.[2]

Instead of lessening, Whitefield increased his religious duties, recording, 'I now began to pray and sing Psalms thrice every day, and to fast every Friday and to receive the Sacrament at a parish Church near our College, and at the Castle . . . once a month.'[3]

The one feature which most stands out in Whitefield's reports of these days is his seriousness. To him any form of time-wasting was unthinkable, and the importance he attached to academic effort is seen in his attitude towards indolence in others. 'It has often grieved my soul', he declared, 'to see so many young students spending their substance in extravagant living, and thereby entirely unfitting themselves for the prosecution of their studies.'[4] Though we know little about his academic progress, except that it was sufficient to earn his degree, it is clear that as a student he was extremely diligent.

[1] Charles Wesley's *Journal* (Epworth, nd), Vol 2, *p* 434.
[2] Whitefield's *Journals*, *p* 45. [3] *Ibid*, *p* 46. [4] *Ibid*, *p* 45.

This earnestness was providentially combined with the assistance of a good tutor. Whitefield spoke of him as 'my kind tutor' and stated, 'He lent me books, gave me money, visited me and furnished me with a physician when I was sick. In short, he behaved in all respects like a father.'[1] This man possessed a doctor's degree[2] (in those days a doctorate was much more rare than to-day) and he appears to have required thorough effort on the part of his students. Perhaps he saw particular promise in this youth, but, be that as it may, at a time when the value of an Oxford course depended so much on the tutor, Whitefield had reason to be thankful for so conscientious a man.

*

But because of his refusal to join in the levity of other students, Whitefield was lonely. 'My soul', he confessed, 'was athirst for some spiritual friends to lift up my hands when they hung down', and he went on to speak of 'the despised Methodists', saying,

> The young men so called were then much talked of at Oxford. I had heard of, and loved them before I came to the University, and so strenuously defended them when I heard them reviled by the students, that they began to think that I also in time should be one of them.
>
> For above a twelvemonth my soul longed to be acquainted with some of them, and I was strongly pressed to follow their good example, when I saw them go through a ridiculing crowd to receive the Holy Eucharist.[3]

Although he yearned to know these men, as a servitor he was not allowed to introduce himself to them. But his serious demeanour had already caught the attention of one of their number, Charles Wesley, and, heedless of Oxford's rules, Charles invited him to breakfast. 'I thankfully embraced the opportunity', Whitefield stated, 'and blessed be God, it was one of the most profitable visits I ever made in my life.'[4] To Charles also the occasion became a noteworthy one and many years later, as he looked back upon it, he wrote:

[1] *Ibid*, *p* 51.

[2] In 1748 Whitefield attended a service at Bristol Cathedral and reported: 'My old Tutor, Dr R—, one of the Prebendaries, was very cordial when I waited on him.' *Works*, Vol 2, *p* 210. Dr R— was probably George Henry Rooke.

[3] *Journals*, *p* 46.

[4] *Ibid.*

Can I the memorable day forget,
When first we by Divine appointment met?
Where undisturbed the thoughtful student roves
In search of truth, through academic groves;
A modest, pensive youth, who mused alone,
Industrious the frequented path to shun,
An Israelite without disguise or art,
I saw, I loved, and clasped him to my heart,
A stranger as my bosom-friend caress'd,
And unawares received an angel-guest.[1]

Though allowance must be made for a measure of poetic licence, these lines contain a description of Whitefield by one who knew him well. Since other descriptions also spoke of his exceptionally fair countenance we may be sure it was this quality which caused Charles to refer to him as 'an angel-guest'. The words, 'a modest, pensive youth', and 'without disguise or art', also deserve notice, and in the mental image which we form of Whitefield at this stage of his life we must see him as reticent, meditative and transparently sincere.

Much that Whitefield thirsted for awaited him in this new friendship, for Charles soon introduced him to the other Methodist men – a group to whom we may best refer as The Holy Club. This work had been begun in 1728 by three men: Robert Kirkham, William Morgan and Charles Wesley. The following year, John Wesley, who had been absent from Oxford for some time, returned to the University, and the leadership of their activities fell to him. Several names besides the Holy Club were applied to them: Bible Moths, Bible Bigots, the Godly Club, Sacramentarians and Methodists, but John Wesley simply used the term 'our Company'. At the time when Whitefield was introduced – the summer of 1733[2] – this group consisted of ten or eleven true devotees and an equal number of more casual associates.

[1] Charles Wesley, *An Elegy on the Death of the Late Rev. George Whitefield, M.A.*, lines 50–59. Here cited from Charles Wesley's *Journal*, *op cit*, Vol 2, *p* 419. Referred to as *Elegy*. In a sermon, *God, the Believer's Glory*, which he preached late in his life, Whitefield said, 'When I was performing my first exercises at Oxford, I used to take delight to walk and read the *Epistle of St Ignatius*, and could not help noting, and putting down, from time to time, several important passages.'

[2] The first date showing an acquaintance between Whitefield and the Wesleys comes from John's *Oxford Diary*, where he records that he and Whitefield were

In making the acquaintance of Charles and John Wesley, Whitefield was entering upon the most important friendships of his life. From this point onward his career became so closely associated with theirs that it is impossible to seek a true understanding of the one without seeking also a true understanding of the other.

As is well known, the Wesleys were extraordinary men. They were marked by wide learning and personal attractiveness, and such was their academic skill that they could have remained at Oxford, engaged in scholarly undertakings throughout their lives. Though small of stature, they possessed an innate dignity and a force of character that set them apart. They were men of culture, manifesting a rich appreciation of music and the emotions of the true poet.

But though usually benign in their manner, the Wesleys were also men of unbending self-assertion. They delighted in exercising their powers of logic and indulging in disputation. They were highly opinionated and strongly disliked being contradicted; and[1] John, in particular, found it instinctive to dominate the sphere of his associations.

These varied traits and abilities made John the unquestioned leader of the Holy Club. They enabled him to bear with calmness and even disdain, the storm of ridicule which the Club's activities attracted.

The Holy Club was not a new idea. In both spirit and aim it was akin to the Religious Societies of England and the *Collegia Pietatis* of Germany. Its members practised early rising and lengthy devotions, and strove for a self-discipline which left no moment wasted throughout the day. At nightfall they wrote a diary which enabled them to scrutinize their actions and condemn themselves for any fault. They partook of the Eucharist every Sunday, fasted each Wednesday and Friday, and hallowed

together at *The King's Head* in Oxford on September 6, 1733 (Green, *op cit*, *p* 190). The first meeting between Whitefield and Charles must have taken place a few days earlier.

[1] During his Oxford days John confessed that he had 'disputed warmly on a trifle' (*Journal*, Vol 1, *p* 59) and displayed 'devilish anger' (Green, *op cit*, *p* 82). Southey said, 'At the commencement of his career, Wesley was of a pugnacious spirit, the effect of his sincerity, his ardour and his confidence', and Tyerman stated that this remark was made 'with great truthfulness' (Tyerman, *Life of Wesley*, Vol 1, *p* 312).

Saturday as the Sabbath of Preparation for the Lord's Day. They revered the Church of England with unthinking devotion, believed in the Apostolic succession of its priesthood and obeyed many of its unused canons. They sought to persuade others to refrain from evil and attend church. They regularly visited Oxford's prisons (the Castle and the Bocardo) and the Poor House, and each member contributed to a fund with which they relieved the needs of the inmates and maintained a school for the prisoners' children. This programme of endeavour, aided by these works of charity, they believed, somehow ministered towards the salvation of their souls.

The practices of the Holy Club held a deep fascination for Whitefield.

Never did persons [he wrote,] strive more earnestly to enter in at the strait gate. They kept their bodies under, even to an extreme. They were dead to the world, and willing to be accounted as the dung and offscouring of all things, so that they might win Christ. Their hearts glowed with the love of God and they never prospered so much in the inner man as when they had all manner of evil spoken against them falsely without.[1]

He quickly entered into their activities:

I now began, like them, to live by rule, and to pick up the very fragments of my time, that not a moment of it might be lost. Whether I ate or drank, or whatsoever I did, I endeavoured to do all to the glory of God. Like them, having no weekly Sacrament at our own College, though the rubric required it, I received every Sunday at Christ Church. I joined with them in keeping the stations by fasting Wednesdays and Fridays and left no means unused which I thought would lead me nearer to Jesus Christ.[2]

For Whitefield, in his lack of self-confidence, this identification of himself with the Holy Club was a distinct victory. He admits that he found some difficulty at first and experienced a twinge of shame in being seen in public with Charles Wesley, but before long such fears were overcome. These men made much of Professor Francke's treatise *Against the Fear of Man* and frequently referred to the Pauline declarations, 'a fool for Christ's sake', and 'It is a little thing with me if I be judged of you or of man's judgment'.

[1] *Journals*, *p* 48. [2] *Ibid*, *p* 47.

Under such influence Whitefield could soon say, 'I walked openly with them and chose rather to bear contempt with those people of God, than to enjoy the applause of almost-Christians for a season'. He faced many acts of opposition, but spoke of them as 'useful trials' and stated, 'They inured me to contempt, lessened self-love and taught me to die daily'.

Charles Wesley describes Whitefield among the Holy Club:

> Associating with the derided few, . . .
> Outcasts of men, and fools for Jesus' sake;
> He long'd their glorious scandal to partake,
> Courageously took up the shameful cross,
> And, suffering all things in the Saviour's cause,
> Vow'd to renounce the world, himself deny,
> And following on with them, with them to live and die.[1]

*

Although the religious values of the Holy Club are widely known, its academic benefits have been largely overlooked. As these men met – usually in John Wesley's rooms at Lincoln College – the atmosphere in which they gathered was one of thorough scholarship. This is seen particularly in the scholastic attainments of its leading personnel. We notice:

John Wesley was a Master of Arts, a lecturer in Greek, a Fellow of Lincoln and an ordained priest. At this point in our narrative he was thirty years old.

Charles Wesley was twenty-six, a Master of Arts and a tutor at Christ Church.

John Clayton was an M.A. from Brasenose, where he had been Hulme's Exhibitioner in 1729 and after that time a Tutor. He possessed a measure of learning similar to that of the Wesleys, and held a position of influence in the Club, second only to that of John Wesley.

John Gambold held the Master's degree from Christ Church, and in later life became an outstanding Moravian Bishop.

Thomas Broughton, who in after life spent forty years as the Secretary of the S.P.C.K., was at this time a Master of Arts and a Fellow of Exeter.

Charles Kinchin was an M.A. and a Fellow of Corpus Christi, where, in four years' time, he was appointed Dean.

James Hervey was an undergraduate; he manifested extraordinary

[1] *Elegy, op cit,* lines 41–49.

ability as a Hebraist and later earned a lasting place in English literature as a writer of religious prose.[1]

Among the undergraduate members of the Holy Club there must also be mentioned Benjamin Ingham who became a famous Moravian evangelist, and John Hutchings (not Dr Richard Hutchins, as has often been assumed) who remained a close friend of Whitefield for some years.

These were the truly zealous of the Holy Club members and any gathering of such men could not fail to be marked by their learning. At their meetings the Greek New Testament was used as the basis of the Bible study and the writings of learned men from various ages were read and discussed.

Moreover, to inculcate thoroughness in study as much as in religion was part of their function. Dr Curnock says of John Wesley, 'In one of the Rules for "our Company", he regards scholarship as a Christian virtue, emphasizing "the necessity of method and industry, in order to either learning or virtue" ',[2] and John Gambold, reporting his experiences as a Holy Club member, says that the Wesleys and Clayton, 'took great pains with the younger members of the University, to rescue them from bad company, and encourage them in a sober, studious life . . . They would help them in those parts of learning which they stuck at, . . . and watch over them with great tenderness.'[3]

During the whole of his time at Oxford, with the exception of its first eleven months, Whitefield was under this strong influence. While many a student wasted his days in frivolity, he practised the Club's rigid discipline, planning the duty of each hour and forcing himself to do as he planned, 'that not a moment be lost'. His personality became cast in this mould of self-mastery and in our study of his life a recognition of these habits will enable us to understand the otherwise inexplicable immensity of

[1] Dr Ryland, a biographer of Hervey, tells of his desire to learn Hebrew, and says 'a Fellow of Lincoln College' (doubtless Dr Richard Hutchins), 'conducted him to the first chapter of Genesis, and analysed every word; he taught him to reduce every noun to its proper pattern; he instructed him to trace every verb to its proper root, and to work every verb through the active and passive conjugations . . . After Mr Hervey had learnt to analyse the first chapter of Genesis, he went on like a giant, and to my certain knowledge, became one of the first scholars in Europe for a familiar knowledge of the Hebrew Bible.' Luke Tyerman, *The Oxford Methodists* (London, 1873), *p* 212.

[2] John Wesley's *Journal*, Vol 1, *p* 39. [3] *Ibid*, Vol 8, *p* 266.

his accomplishments. If education be, as William James defined it, 'the training of the whole man so that he will do what ought to be done, when it ought to be done, whether he likes it or not', then the Holy Club was a notable educational force.

Because, however, of certain misconceptions which have grown up around the Holy Club, we must look more carefully at it. We notice:

1. *It was not famous.* For its first three or four years, news of its existence spread but little beyond the University. In 1733, however, a letter which harshly attacked the Holy Club's practices appeared in *Fogg's Weekly Journal*, and was answered by the publication of an anonymous 30-page pamphlet entitled *The Oxford Methodists*. The pamphlet had but one edition at that time.[1]

2. *It was not evangelical.* Its members knew nothing of the inward miracle of the new birth, and in their search for spiritual satisfaction, turned increasingly to outward ritual. John Clayton was the chief advocate of this trend, and under his influence the Wesleys and the others went so far in the Anglo-Catholic direction that they began to regard the opinions of the Fathers as all but equal in authority to the statements of Scripture, they considered setting themselves up as auricular confessors,[2] and adopted a view of the Holy Eucharist which was very near to transubstantiation.[3] The Oxford Methodists were walking the same path as that taken a century later by Keble and Pusey and it might even have become that on which Newman and Faber were to find themselves.

3. *It was not the beginning of the revival.* The Holy Club men were not only without the Gospel which they were later to preach to the multitudes, but were also without the least anticipation of such preaching or such multitudes. Some quiet English parish where they might enforce their discipline on self and hearer, or

[1] A second edition appeared in 1738, but this was occasioned by the extraordinary attention then being given to Whitefield's preaching. Its title page announced that it contained 'A Short Ep'stle to the Rev Mr Whitefield'. A third edition was printed by a certain publisher under the same cover as several of Whitefield's sermons, and these attempts to associate his name with it were doubtless planned in order to give it sale.

[2] See a letter from Emilia Wesley to her brother John in Stevenson's *Memorials of the Wesley Family* (London, 1876), *p* 271.

[3] See Tyerman, *The Oxford Methodists*, *op cit*, *pp* vi and 39.

some missionary enterprise where privation would further mortify their natures – these were the prospects they entertained. The Methodism of Oxford was destined to die away with the dispersal of its members in 1735; the Methodism of the revival was to be born in 1737 and 1739 under Whitefield's flaming ministry, and thereafter to be assisted by the ministry of the Wesleys. The Methodism of the Holy Club could never have created the Methodism of the revival; the two were vastly different and the distinction between them must be clearly understood.

4. *It did not bring its members the satisfaction that they sought.* The failure arose primarily from the lack of a thorough doctrinal foundation. Strange as it may seem to-day, such subjects as systematic theology and Biblical exegesis were not taught to undergraduates at Oxford, and the Wesleys and their friends failed to make up for the lack in their private study. They read widely, but their choice ran largely to books on devotion, mysticism, self-discipline and good works, and they appear to have given little attention to those store-houses of Biblical scholarship and doctrinal teaching: the works of the Reformers and Puritans.

In fine, the Holy Club men knew little or nothing of grace as taught in the Scriptures. Their iron-clad régime was one of human effort, that provided no assurance and left the all-important salvation of the soul a distant uncertainty. Its practices brought little joy and, as Dr Curnock, the learned editor of Wesley's *Journal* points out, had Wesley's *Hymn Book* been in existence then, its section *Hymns for Believers Rejoicing* would have been a mystery to him. These ardent men strove on and on, yet saw no point of arrival.

*

The spiritual dissatisfaction experienced in the Holy Club, though later to be expressed by almost all its members, was first evident in Whitefield. The immediate human cause was a book, *The Life of God in the Soul of Man*,[1] written in the previous century by a young Scotsman, Henry Scougal.

This little work so directly contradicted all that he and his

[1] Henry Scougal, *The Life of God in the Soul of Man* (republished Westminster, Philadelphia, 1958).

fellows believed about salvation that it alarmed him. He says that by it:

God showed me that I must be born again, or be damned! I learned that a man may go to church, say his prayers, receive the sacrament, and yet not be a Christian. How did my heart rise and shudder, like a poor man that is afraid to look into his account-books, lest he should find himself a bankrupt.

'Shall I burn this book? Shall I throw it down? Or shall I search it?' I did search it; and, holding the book in my hand, thus addressed the God of heaven and earth: 'Lord, if I am not a Christian, or if I am not a real one, for Jesus Christ's sake, show me what Christianity is that I may not be damned at last!'

God soon showed me, for in reading a few lines further, that, 'true religion is a union of the soul with God, and Christ formed within us', a ray of Divine light was instantaneously darted in upon my soul, and from that moment, but not till then, did I know that I must become a new creature.[1]

Aroused by Scougal's book Whitefield began to search for the life of which it spake. He knew not where to seek it, but stumbled along in the darkness of his own efforts, yet after months of striving he found that the light of grace shone on his path and that God was leading him to Himself.

His first endeavour was the increase of his bodily austerities, and his actions were immediately met by new opposition. His relatives at Gloucester 'were alarmed and conceived strong prejudices against [him]', the Master of the College threatened to expel him, students threw dirt at him and 'others took away their pay' for his servitor's duties. Even some of the Holy Club thought that he went too far and grew ashamed of him; yet he was unmoved and spoke of his willingness to suffer and even to die for Christ.

Amidst his fear of being lost and his frustration in being unable to find salvation, he became subject to strange and terrible emotions.

My comforts were soon withdrawn [he wrote], and a horrible fearfulness and dread permitted to overwhelm my soul. One morning in

[1] Sermon, 'All Men's Place', published in *Sermons on Important Subjects* by the Reverend G. Whitefield (Baynes, London, 1825), *p* 702.

particular, rising from my bed, I felt an unusual impression and weight upon my breast, attended with inward darkness . . .

In a short time I perceived this load gradually increase, till it almost weighed me down, and fully convinced me that Satan had as real possession of, and power given over, my body, as he had once over Job's. All power of meditating, or even thinking, was taken from me . . . My whole soul was barren and dry, and I could fancy myself to be like nothing so much as a man locked up in iron armour.

Whenever I kneeled down, I felt great heavings in my body, and have often prayed under the weight of them till the sweat came through me . . .

God only knows how many nights I have lain upon my bed groaning under the weight I felt, and bidding Satan depart from me in the name of Jesus. Whole days and weeks have I spent in lying prostrate on the ground, and begging for freedom from those proud hellish thoughts that used to crowd in upon and distract my soul.[1]

Whitefield's story goes on in this vein at some length, and when these attempts failed to bring 'the life of God' within his soul, he devised means to increase his asceticism, saying,

By degrees I began to leave off eating fruits and such like, and gave the money I usually spent in that way to the poor. Afterward, I always chose the worst sort of food, . . . I wore woollen gloves, a patched gown and dirty shoes.[2]

These efforts still failing, his next attempt was the practice of Quietism, which developed from reading an author named Castaniza:

When the Holy Spirit put into my heart good thoughts or convictions, he (Satan) always drove them to extremes . . . When Castaniza advised to talk but little, Satan said I must not talk at all, so that I, who used to be the most forward in exhorting my companions, have sat whole nights almost without speaking at all. Again, when Castaniza advised to endeavour after a silent recollection and waiting upon God, Satan told me I must leave off all forms, and not use my voice in prayer at all.[3]

As was to be expected, his scholastic work began to suffer from this fearful preoccupation of his mind. Twice he failed to have his composition ready, and although his tutor fined him a half crown the first time, on the second, after imposing a fine again,

[1] *Journals*, *p* 52. [2] *Ibid*, *p* 53. [3] *Ibid*, *p* 53.

Imagining that I would not willingly neglect my exercise, he afterwards called me into the Common Room, and kindly enquired whether any misfortune had befallen me, or what was the reason I could not make a theme. I burst into tears and assured him it was not out of contempt of authority, but that I could not act otherwise. Then, at length, he said, he believed I could not, and when he left me, told a friend, as he very well might, that he took me to be really mad.[1]

But if this seemed mad behaviour, Whitefield's next step appeared even more so. Again we have his own words,

It was now suggested to me that Jesus Christ was among the wild beasts when He was tempted, and that I ought to follow His example; and being willing, as I thought, to imitate Jesus Christ, after supper I went into Christ Church Walk, and continued in silent prayer under one of the trees for near two hours, sometimes lying flat on my face, sometimes kneeling upon my knees . . . The night being stormy, it gave me awful thoughts of the day of judgment. I continued, I think, till the great bell rung for retirement to the College, not without finding some reluctance in the natural man against staying so long in the cold . . . The next night I repeated the same exercise.[2]

Still finding only failure in all these attempts, he cast around for something further that he might do, something else that he could give up, in hope that in so doing he might find the longed-for 'life of God' within his soul. The precious object on which he fixed was his friendship with the other members of the Holy Club, thinking that to turn away from them was the supreme sacrifice which might prove the necessary act. No wonder he says,

This was a sore trial; but rather than not be, as I fancied, Christ's disciple, I resolved to renounce them, though as dear to me as my own soul.[3]

Thus he parted from his friends, but was never, even in his loneliest hours, without a sense that God was with him and would finally bring him to salvation.

My soul was inwardly supported [is his testimony], with great courage

[1] *Ibid, p* 54. The period of Whitefield's intense anxiety, during which he was unable to do his academic work, probably lasted from late autumn or early winter of 1734 until shortly after Easter of 1735. Some have assumed that it characterized most or all of his time at Oxford, but his tutor recognized that '[he] would not willingly neglect [his] exercise'.

[2] *Ibid, p* 55.

[3] *Ibid.*

and resolution from above. Every day God made me willing to renew the combat, . . . Thomas à Kempis, Castaniza's *Combat*, and the Greek Testament, every reading of which I endeavoured to turn into a prayer, were of great help and furtherance to me.[1]

Whitefield had been undergoing these strivings, probably since the autumn of 1734, and with the approach of Lent in the spring of 1735, matters became even worse. He now determined that throughout the six weeks of the holy season, he would allow himself little food except coarse bread and sage tea without sugar. Though burdened and perplexed in mind, dangerously weakened in body, unable to do his studies, praying 'with strong cryings and tears' during much of the day and night, he nevertheless pressed into his Lenten mortifications with renewed zeal;

I constantly walked out in the cold mornings [he wrote], till part of one of my hands was quite black. This, with my continued abstinence and inward conflicts, at length so emaciated my body, that at Passion-week, finding I could scarce creep upstairs, I was obliged to inform my kind tutor of my condition, who immediately sent for a physician to me.[2]

His plight was now serious. Just two years earlier, William Morgan, one of the ablest of the Holy Club men, had continued such practices until he had lost, first his mind, and finally his life, and now it looked as though Whitefield, who had said 'I was resolved to die or conquer', might do the same. His physician confined him to bed, where he lay for seven weeks, but he knew no relenting in his search, and recorded of these days,

The blessed Spirit was all this time purifying my soul. All my former gross and notorious, and even my heart sins also, were now set home upon me, of which I wrote down some remembrance immediately,

[1] *Ibid, p* 56.
[2] *Ibid, p* 57. On April 1, 1735, Whitefield wrote to John Wesley who was then at Epworth, asking for his advice regarding his physical condition. Whitefield had been trying to diagnose and cure his ailments by using a medical book written by the celebrated physician, Dr Cheyne, and asks Wesley to give his interpretation of Dr Cheyne regarding his case. He describes his symptoms, suggests they indicate the possibility of diabetes and speaks of suffering from what he calls 'general distemper'. Whitefield writes as one who knew Wesley somewhat from a distance – certainly not on terms of familiarity – and the relation is that of the young and poor undergraduate and servitor to the older and experienced Fellow and Master of Arts. This letter is not published, but the original is in the Methodist Archives, City Road, London.

and confessed them before God morning and evening. Though weak, I often spent two hours in my evening retirements, and prayed over my Greek Testament, and Bishop Hall's most excellent *Contemplations*, every hour that my health would permit.[1]

But now, when he had come to an end of all human resources, when there was nothing else that he could do to seek salvation, God revealed Himself in grace, and granted him that which he had found could never be earned. Somehow, we know not exactly how: somewhere, perhaps in his room, or more likely, in one of the secluded Oxford walks, in a sense of utter desperation, in rejection of all self-trust, he cast his soul on the mercy of God through Jesus Christ, and a ray of faith, granted him from above, assured him he would not be cast out. He testified of this experience,

God was pleased to remove the heavy load, to enable me to lay hold of His dear Son by a living faith, and by giving me the Spirit of adoption, to seal me even to the day of everlasting redemption.

O! with what joy – joy unspeakable – even joy that was full of and big with glory, was my soul filled, when the weight of sin went off, and an abiding sense of the pardoning love of God, and a full assurance of faith, broke in upon my disconsolate soul! Surely it was the day of mine espousals – a day to be had in everlasting remembrance! At first my joys were like a spring tide, and overflowed the banks![2]

Late in life, as he looked back on this momentous occasion, Whitefield declared:

I know the place! It may be superstitious, perhaps, but whenever I go to Oxford I cannot help running to that place where Jesus Christ first revealed himself to me and gave me the new birth.[3]

[1] *Ibid, p* 57. [2] *Ibid, p* 58, fn. [3] Sermon, 'All Men's Place', *op cit, p* 702.

Every man who is rightly in the ministry must have been moved thereto of the Holy Ghost. He must feel an irresistible desire to spend his whole life in his Master's cause. No college, no bishop, no human ordination, can make a man a minister; but he who can feel, as did Bunyan, Whitefield, Berridge or Rowland Hill, the strugglings of an impassioned longing to win the souls of men, may hear in the air the voice of God saying, 'Son of man, I have made thee *a watchman'.*

C. H. SPURGEON, 1854

When it pleased God who separated me from my mother's womb, and called me by his grace, to reveal his Son in me, that I might preach him among the heathen; immediately I conferred not with flesh and blood.

THE APOSTLE PAUL

4

Ordination – Divine and Human

WHITEFIELD'S conversion was the supreme turning-point of his life. His joy was such that he could not contain it. 'I fell a writing', he says, 'to all my brethren and to my sister and talked to the students as they came in my room.' But the months of strain had so undermined his health that it became necessary for him to return to Gloucester to recuperate.

He arrived at the city penniless and unwell, but the Harrises, the book-seller people, opened their home to him. They were a prominent family, for Gabriel Harris, the father, had recently finished his second term as mayor, and Gabriel his son,[1] who was yet unmarried and lived with his parents, was now Younger Sheriff and was anticipating his rise to the mayoralty. They and Mrs Harris showed Whitefield much kindness during the nine months he was in the city, and other friends came to his help in various ways.

In returning among the people of Gloucester, Whitefield gave evidence that he had truly become 'a new creature in Christ'. When some of his former associates sought to dissuade him from his 'weekly abstinence and receiving the blessed sacrament', he proved adamant against their suggestions. Learning that the Strollers were coming to town (we may well suppose to the

[1] Shortly after Whitefield had first gone to Oxford the younger Gabriel Harris had written, asking him to use his influence to get him a position in Oxford and suggested he would prefer some form of civic employment. Apparently, nothing came of the request.

Whitefield's will, written in 1770 contained the following clause, 'To my dear old friend, Gabriel Harris, who received and boarded me in his house when I was helpless and destitute, above thirty-five years ago, I give and bequeath the sum of fifty pounds.' Gillies, *op cit*, *p* 351.

Great Room at the Bell), he wrote an abridgement of William Law's *The Absolute Unlawfulness of the Stage Entertainment* and had Robert Raikes publish it serially (it ran for six weeks) in the *Gloucester Journal*. Remembering the little thefts of which he had been guilty as a boy, as soon as he was financially able he made restitution and sent a letter of confession along with the goods that he returned.

Our knowledge of this period of Whitefield's life comes from two sources. The first is his *Journals,* which are well known, and the second is a *Diary* that he wrote during these months, which has never been published and has long remained unknown.

The *Diary* begins with a list of criteria which he used each night as a basis of judging himself on his actions during the day. The list is,

Have I,

1. Been fervent in private prayer?
2. Used stated hours of prayer?
3. Used ejaculation every hour?
4. After or before every deliberate conversation or action, considered how it might tend to God's glory?
5. After any pleasure, immediately given thanks?
6. Planned business for the day?
7. Been simple and recollected in everything?
8. Been zealous in undertaking and active in doing what good I could?
9. Been meek, cheerful, affable in everything I said or did?
10. Been proud, vain, unchaste, or enviable of others?
11. Recollected in eating and drinking? Thankful? Temperate in sleep?
12. Taken time for giving thanks according to Law's rules?[1]
13. Been diligent in studies?
14. Thought or spoken unkindly of anyone?
15. Confessed all sins?

Each day's entry in the *Diary* is in two parts, a page to a part. On one page he lists the specific activities of each hour of the day and makes a self-examination, on the basis of the criteria, of the merits or demerits of each hour. On the second page he records any unusual activity throughout the day, but above all,

[1] That is, William Law.

gives expression to his inner self. The longings of his soul, a searching of his motives, severe self-reproach for the slightest wrong and bursts of praise to God, are all recorded without inhibition.

The Whitefield revealed in the *Journal* and *Diary* of these months is a new man indeed. Gone entirely are the gloom and fear of his pre-conversion days and, notwithstanding his but partially recovered health, he is full of vigour in the things of God. He continues to govern his time according to the system he practised at Oxford, but now the rigid schedule is one of joy, and, perhaps without fully admitting it, he is fervently preparing himself for the ministry.

He tells us of his delight in the law of the Lord:

> My mind being now more open and enlarged, I began to read the Holy Scriptures upon my knees, laying aside all other books and praying over, if possible, every line and word. This proved meat indeed and drink indeed to my soul. I daily received fresh life, light and power from above. I got more true knowledge from reading the Book of God in one month than I could *ever* have acquired from *all* the writings of men.[1]

He experienced a similar joy in prayer:

> Oh, what sweet communion had I daily vouchsafed with God in prayer, after my coming again to Gloucester! How often have I been carried out beyond myself when sweetly meditating in the fields! How assuredly have I felt that Christ dwelt in me and I in Him! And how did I daily walk in the comforts of the Holy Ghost and was edified and refreshed in the multitude of peace![2]

His *Diary* shows his unyielding adherence to his 'stated hours of prayer', first thing in the morning, again at noon and finally at night. It reveals also one occasion on which he was lax in his evening season of prayer and severely reproached himself for his omission the following day. But it is evident from his words above that prayer was something more than merely the 'stated hours'; it was an attitude of heart all the day long.

Along with his English Bible Whitefield read his Greek New Testament. This had become his custom during his last months at school and he had continued it during his years at Oxford.

[1] *Journals, p* 60. [2] *Ibid, p* 61.

In this regard we do well to notice that a two-volume *Greek Testament* which he used at some period of his life is now among the Methodist archives at London. It is an edition which is interleaved with blank pages for notes and the late Mr George Stampe of the *Wesley Historical Society* says that the notes he made reveal 'a wide, if not deep, knowledge of the Greek language'.[1]

Among other books which he read he mentions 'Burkitt's and Henry's *Expositions*', and 'Alleine's *Alarm*, Baxter's *Call to the Unconverted* and Janeway's *Life*'. Books were then much less common and, in comparison, much more expensive than to-day, and, though the set of Matthew Henry's *Commentary* cost £7 (equal to the wages received by a labouring man for fifteen or sixteen weeks of work) he obtained it from Harris and paid him for it a year later.[2]

This set became his inseparable companion. 'For many months', he wrote, 'I have been almost always upon my knees, to study and pray over these books' (Burkitt and Henry). His *Diary* shows his use of Henry every morning from five till six or even seven, sometimes again later in the morning and the afternoon and, invariably, for an hour or two in the evening. The *Diary* reveals that when he was dejected he used the Scripture as expounded by Henry as a means of comfort and, when he sought guidance in a decision, Henry helped him to know the Divine leading through some Scripture passage. 'What a means has Henry's Comment been of building me up!' he stated. 'I hope I shall never forsake that candle of the Lord', he recorded at another time; and at still another, 'O how sweetly did my hours in private glide away in reading and praying over Mr Henry's Comment on the Scripture'.

Again his words conjure up a picture in the mind. There he is at five in the morning, in the room above the Harris book-store. He is on his knees with his English Bible, his *Greek New Testament* and Henry's *Commentary* spread out before him. He reads a portion in the English, gains a fuller insight into it as he studies words and tenses in the Greek and then considers Matthew

[1] 'George Whitefield's Greek Testament', in the *Proceedings of the Wesley Historical Society*, Vol 10, part 2, June 1915.

[2] Nov. 5, 1736, Whitefield wrote to Harris to say, 'Herewith I have sent you seven pounds to pay for Mr Henry's *Commentary*'. *Works*, Vol 1, *p* 23.

Henry's explanation of it all. Finally, there comes the unique practice that he has developed: that of 'praying over every line and word' of both the English and the Greek till the passage, in its essential message, has veritably become part of his own soul.

Such was Whitefield's study of the Bible in the months following his conversion. There were branches of learning to which he gave little or no attention, but he concentrated on the all-important, the Word of God. When, in later chapters, we see him preaching forty and more hours a week, with little or no time for preparation, we may well look back on these days in Gloucester and recognize that he was then laying up a store of Biblical knowledge on which he was able to draw amidst the haste and tumult of such a ministry.

But the blessings of this new life could not be kept to himself. He must tell them to others and thus we find him writing:

> After importunate prayer one day, I resolved to go to the house of Mrs W—, to whom I had formerly read plays, *Spectators,* Pope's *Homer* and such-like trifling books, hoping the alteration she might now find in my sentiments, might, under God, influence her soul. She wanted to be taught the way of God more perfectly and soon became a fool for Christ's sake. Not long after God made me instrumental to awaken several young persons, who soon formed themselves into a little Society, and had quickly the honour of being despised at Gloucester, as we had been before them at Oxford.[1]

This Society appears to have met each evening in the week. Whitefield conducted it after the fashion of the Religious Societies, with the singing of Psalms, the reading of the Bible and prayer. He also read and enlarged upon certain books of doctrine and devotion and finally gave an exhortation to holy living. He records that, at times, his exhortation lasted an hour and even two hours.

The founding of this little Society was an historic event. This was the first Methodist Society in the permanent sense of the word, and it remained a unit of Whitefield's work throughout his lifetime.

Nor was this all, for he also began a separate Society for women. He speaks of it as 'a Society of 6 or 7 female disciples',[2] and '7 or 8 females who are all in the narrow road to Heaven'.

[1] *Journals, pp* 59, 60. [2] *Diary*, March 6, 1736.

Along with this activity he carried on a programme of good works. He says:

I always observed, as my inward strength increased, so my outward sphere of action increased proportionately. In a short time, therefore, I began to read to some poor people twice or thrice a week . . . I generally visited one or two sick persons every day, and though silver and gold I had little of my own, yet in imitation of my Lord's disciples . . . I used to pray unto Him, and He . . . inclined several that were rich in this world to give me money, so that I generally had a little stock for the poor in my hand. One of the poor whom I visited in this manner was called effectually by God as at the eleventh hour. She was a woman above three score years old, and I really believe died in the true faith of Jesus Christ.[1]

Of his visitation of the prisoners he reported:

I constantly read to and prayed with them . . . I also begged money for them, whereby I was enabled to release some of them and cause provision to be distributed weekly amongst them, as also to put such books into their hands as I judged most proper. I cannot say any one of the prisoners was effectually wrought upon; however, much evil was prevented, many were convinced and my own soul was much edified and strengthened in the love of God and man.[2]

*

These were manifestly happy days for Whitefield. His programme of Bible study, reading, prayer and good works filled him with delight, and at the same time he was gradually gaining in physical health. Furthermore, his intellectual apprehension of Christian truth was also increasing and he tells us:

About this time God was pleased to enlighten my soul, and bring me into the knowledge of His free grace and the necessity of being justified in His sight by *faith only*. This was more extraordinary, because my friends at Oxford had rather inclined to the mystic divinity . . .[3]

What did Whitefield mean by these words? Several statements that he made during the following year or two reveal that he was not yet fully clear on the matter of grace and that some remnant of the Holy Club's ideas of works lingered with him. Certainly

[1] *Journals*, *p* 61. [2] *Ibid*, *p* 63. [3] *Ibid*, *p* 62.

the terms 'free grace' and 'justified by *faith only*' did not, at this early time, have the immense meaning for him which, as we shall see, he enunciated with clarity and conviction in 1739. Nevertheless, it is evident that he had grasped certain fundamental truths: he knew that salvation was a Divine work – the placing of 'the life of God in the soul of man' – and that it was an eternal work. These truths were already a foundation upon which, he was, from this time forth, to build a steadily increasing understanding and finally a system of theology. This was the beginning of his lifelong adherence to what he called 'the doctrines of grace' – the system commonly known as 'Calvinism'.

*

The feature which most noticeably marked Whitefield during these days was the extent to which he was given over to the Lord. Most Christians seem to need an experience subsequent to conversion in which grace effects a new and deeper consecration, but with him, this full measure of devotion characterized his life from the time of conversion itself. Almost every day's entry in his *Diary* has some such exclamation as, 'I have thrown myself blindfold into His Almighty hands', or, 'I am Thine, Thine alone!' He was subject, at times, to a fluctuation of spirits as the weakness of the body weighed upon the soul, but beneath it all there was an unfailing peace and joy. Even the ordinary pursuits of young men in sports or the seeking of feminine company, had no part in his life and his devotion to the Lord filled all his waking hours.

His activity became fervent in its zeal. His *Diary* makes such a report as 'Met a new poor sinner; God sanctify my advice to him'.[1] Charles Wesley describes him during these months in the words:

> He now begins, from every weight set free,
> To make full trial of his ministry;
> Breaks forth on every side and runs and flies,
> Like kindling flames that from the stubble rise;
> Where'er the ministerial Spirit leads,
> From house to house the heavenly fire he spreads;
> Ranges through all the city-lanes and streets,
> And seizes every prodigal he meets.[2]

[1] *Diary*, March 2, 1736.

[2] *Elegy, op cit*, lines 121–9.

Such a youth, engaged thus among persons who had known him since childhood, could not fail to be a centre of attention. Some people treated him with scorn, but many regarded him with an overweening admiration and began to urge that he apply for ordination right away. Some even went so far as to interview the Bishop, Dr Benson, asking that he be placed in Gloucester, that thus he might be near them and be their minister.

But the attention of the Bishop had already been drawn to him by the wealthy Lady Selwyn and, after Whitefield had been in Gloucester about seven months and had just passed his twenty-first birthday, his lordship sent word that he wished to see him. Whitefield obeyed with some reluctance and reported:

He told me he had heard of my character, liked my behaviour in church, and enquired my age. 'Notwithstanding', said he, 'I have declared I would not ordain any under three-and-twenty, yet I shall think it my duty to ordain you whenever you come for Holy Orders.'[1]

Whitefield's admirers found the offer a cause for rejoicing, but in Whitefield himself it occasioned a sense of dread. Some men might look lightly on the ministry, but he felt its spiritual responsibilities so heavily that he said, '. . . that first question of our Ordination Office, "Do you trust that you are inwardly moved by the Holy Ghost to take upon you this office and administration?" used even to make me tremble . . .' To some extent, he was affected, we may be sure, by his native reticence, but far more than this, it was his concept of the ministry as the awesome work of speaking for God to an alien world that overwhelmed him. Even at that early date, as he anticipated the work of a minister, he began to experience the coming upon him of 'the burden of the Lord', and although he felt the solemn attraction of its duties, he also felt it to be a weight that he was not yet ready to bear. Late in life, as he looked back upon these days, he stated:

God alone knows how deep a concern entering the ministry and preaching was to me. I have prayed a thousand times, till the sweat has dropped from my face like rain, that God . . . would not let me enter the Church before he called me and thrust me into his work.

I remember once in Gloucester, I know the room, I look up at the

[1] *Diary*, June 17, 1736.

window when I am there; I know the window, the bedside and the floor upon which I have lain prostrate. I said, Lord, I cannot go; I shall be puffed up with pride and fall into the snare of the devil.[1]

Notwithstanding this dread of the ministry, Whitefield knew he was called of God to its labours and that before long he must enter upon it. Yet as he viewed its responsibilities and remembered his own weakness, he felt he could undertake it only if he received such an assurance from heaven, that he could consider it a Divine commission.

In the face of this need he cried out that God would doubly confirm the call. And his prayer became a very practical one: looking upon graduation as a necessary step towards ordination, he prayed that if God wanted him to be ordained He would reveal it by the miracle of supplying the money for his return to Oxford.

And just such a miracle did he experience. 'When I had given up all hope of money', he confessed, 'it came.' The first gift was from the Rev Sampson Harris, M.A., elder son of the Harrises of Gloucester and vicar in the Cotswold village of Stonehouse. Whitefield had sent him one of his sermons which he asked him to criticize and return, but Harris liked it so well that he preached it and, upon returning it, enclosed a gift of £1. The next day there came the sum of four guineas from Lady Selwyn, and, at that very time, his brother James, a ship's captain, returned from a voyage and gave him five guineas. One of Gloucester's town fathers, Alderman Bell, presented him with £6 and promised to defray the costs of his re-entering the University, Gabriel Harris gave him 'a comfortable coat' and another man gave him a horse to provide his means of transport.[2] Moreover, further evidence that God was opening the way for him came in a letter from Thomas Broughton; Broughton stated that he was needed in Oxford to take over the leadership of the Holy Club, and presented other news which caused Whitefield to say, 'My college wants me in Oxon'.

[1] Sermon, 'The Good Shepherd', in *Sermons on Important Subjects*, *op cit*, *p* 733.

[2] The amount of money Whitefield received would equal the wages paid to a labouring man for thirty or more weeks of work. We cannot be sure whether Alderman Bell's gift for the costs of re-entering the University was included in or was apart from the £6.

Such was Whitefield's joy upon receiving the sudden monetary supply that the day's diary, instead of the usual two pages, required six. He immediately used some of the money to complete his restitution for his boyhood thefts, and it appears that he had felt it wrong for him to leave Gloucester till this was done. He also found another use for some of it, saying, 'It put me in a capacity to help the poor a little'.

*

Whitefield returned to Oxford by horse-back.[1] The journey proved so tiring that during the next two weeks he made such complaints as 'I have been ill most of the day' and 'Body out of order'. He realised that he was still far from well and began taking daily walks for his health, lengthening them from time to time, till in three months he reported, 'The longest walk I have taken yet', and showed considerable improvement.

He found the Holy Club much changed. The Wesleys and Ingham had left during the preceding year in order to become missionaries to Georgia. Gambold, Clayton, Broughton, Kinchin and Chapman had removed to various parts of England and either had already taken or were preparing for Holy Orders. The work was at a low ebb, but under Whitefield's leadership, it showed some improvement and he mentions nineteen men who apparently attended its sessions or were under its influence.[2]

We have an insight into his efforts from the following *Diary* entries:

March 29. Morgan is going out into the world. I hope our friends here will be likewise zealous. Great things are expected of us.

April 30. Hervey writes that Dr Doddridge is praying for us. I believe we have the prayers of all good men in England.

May 1. Evans seems awakened. I gather his mother keeps him back. But I must ply him accordingly. God give me prudence in managing him.

May 3. Turner . . . God give me grace gently to lead that lamb to Christ . . . Turner seems true and sincere. I trust God intends him for great things.

[1] He reached Oxford on March 11 (1736).

[2] Among these are Jones, Webster, Green, Wellington, Smith, Granville, Kent, Jefferys, Turner, Evans and Watson. Some names are not fully legible but may be Sarny, Carill, Rawley, Lauer and Gordsye.

May 5. Had great comfort in Turner. He begins to be greatly ridiculed. I hope he will be a means of strengthening Green, who tomorrow puts on a scholar's gown . . . Good of Almighty God in bringing that young man to us. I hope he will be a worthy member of our despised Society. God will not leave Himself without witness. The prayers for the Church will be heard!

June 12. Granville has begun to be a subscriber to the Castle. I hope his zeal will provoke many.

Whitefield probably conducted the Holy Club meetings after the fashion established by Wesley and continued by Broughton. His *Diary* shows that he made use of the following books at this time: Horneck's *Primitive Christianity*, Archbishop Wake on *The Catechism*, Wright on *Regeneration*, an unnamed work by Bishop Sherlock and another by Bishop Beveridge, and Bishop Burnett's *Pastoral Care* and *History of His Own Times*.[1] These were doubtless his personal reading matter, but it is probable that he used some, if not all, in the Holy Club meetings too. He would endeavour, we may be sure, to inculcate the principles of rigid self-discipline and academic diligence and, above all, would seek in the case of each man, as in that of Turner, 'to lead [him] to Christ'.

The Club's outside activities also came under Whitefield's direction. He conducted a Society which met at the home of a Mr Fox – a former prisoner in whose conversion he had been instrumental earlier – and another which met in the village of Cowley. He held a service in the jail two or three times a week and his *Diary's* frequent use of the abbreviation 'dist.' probably means distributing among the prisoners and the inmates of the poor house the money collected by the Club for this purpose. Beside this, there was the overseeing of the school for the prisoners' children, and Whitefield records that he also started a fund with which to establish a Charity School in Oxford.

At his meetings in the Societies and prisons, although he read the Bible and religious books, Whitefield's chief work was that which he called 'exhorting'. He makes such reports as, 'Full of the Holy Ghost in exhorting friends', 'Continued in exhorting for

[1] Other authors mentioned in the *Diary* are Woodridge, Shepherd, Langhorne, Law, à Kempis, Gill, Watts, Longinus, Reynolds, Ashton, Arndt, Godeau, Hamilton, Foxe, Gouge, Patrick, Francke and Henry.

two hours to-night', 'Was most mercifully assisted in talking almost extempore on the first and second covenants'. Once he writes, 'In regard to exhorting, I never feel the power of the Holy Ghost more than in helping me call to mind everything I have read on a particular subject, though perhaps I scarce ever thought of it again in a long while'. Because he was not yet ordained he would not call this work preaching, but call it what he might, it was excellent preparation for the ministry that lay just before him.

His *Diary* also makes mention of his shyness. In undertaking this leadership he apparently felt his inferiority, for he made such statements as, 'I am of a shy nature', and 'Found I was too bashful. God keep me from a sinful modesty'. Similarly, when he returned to Gloucester, he wrote, 'Mrs Harris says I am grown more shy'.

*

Whitefield's work toward his degree entailed preparations that he terms 'my scheme'. Beginning on May 1, he spent an hour early each morning, one or two more later in the day and, usually, another in the evening working at it. He says:

> I hope I shall now get a little knowledge of the sciences. But there is nothing like knowing Christ and Him crucified!
>
> I am now reading Langhorne, a good ethical book, but deficient in respect of Christianity.
>
> I am now, for some time, obliged to follow different speculative studies. God mercifully enables me to keep up my recollection.
>
> I am obliged to be always learning my scheme. When shall I have time to read the Book of God solely again? No book like that Book of books!
>
> I am to be examined. I hope I have got it pretty perfect. I have spared no pains to get it and therefore I trust God will support me!

These studies led up to a public examination. This was held on May 14, and he writes:

> God mercifully supported me in my examination. Though I had a strict examiner and a school full of Gentlemen, and the Proctor too present (which happens but very seldom) I was not at all surprised. Soon after I got up in the Hall I was enabled to keep my recollection strongly to the true Greek text of Horace and Sallust offhand fluently, and to turn an English book into Latin immediately. It was the more to

be wondered at, because the day before, being put up in the Hall, I could scarce speak a word without trembling, though it was a thing I knew and had been surely used to.

God grant that I may ever come off with as much security and honour; (not that I value these) but had I been plucked it would have brought dishonour to my Tutor, College and Society.[1]

We may be sure that these special circumstances – the presence of the Proctor, a school full of Gentlemen and a strict examiner – did not happen by chance. Whitefield not only bore the general dislike which was shown to all the Holy Club, but suffered a particular disfavour. Dr Panting, the Master of Pembroke, had forbidden him to continue his practice of visiting the prisoners. Whitefield had obeyed at first, but, in the conviction that he was wrong in thus submitting, he had chosen to defy the Master and therewith faced the threat of expulsion. Though this was not fulfilled, it is highly probable that he was forced to face a stricter examination than usual and that the Gentlemen were there in order to embarrass him. When the day was over his *Diary* exulted with 'All praise to God through Christ!'

*

Whitefield's success in the examination largely assured his degree and therefore removed the last obstacle to ordination. Yet still he shrank from entering the ministry; 'I fear I don't think highly enough about Orders', he wrote. 'Oh, it is a dreadful office!'[2] But, at the same time, the certainty that God had commissioned him to His work was becoming weighty within his mind, and he made such *Diary* entries as, 'I am fully persuaded it is His will that I should take Orders', and 'a strong conviction that God immediately calls me'.[3] In his *Journal* he states, 'I began to think that if I held out any longer, I should fight against God. At length I came to a resolution, by God's leave, to offer myself for Holy Orders the next Ember Days.'[4]

For Whitefield, so solemn a step required still more preparation. He records that he 'immediately began self-examination about ordination' and prayed, 'God grant it may be sincere'. He inaugurated the practice of 'setting apart the 16th day of each month as a day of secret fasting for [his] sins', and reports:

[1] *Diary*, May 14. [2] *Ibid*, June 18. [3] *Ibid*, May 29. [4] *Journal*, p 67.

Having made some observations upon the Thirty-Nine Articles and proved them by Scripture, I strictly examined myself by the qualifications required for a minister in St Paul's *Epistle to Timothy*, and also by every question that I knew was to be publicly put to me at the time of my ordination. This latter I drew out in writing at large, and sealed my approbation of it every Sunday at the blessed Sacrament.[1]

*

Whitefield expected to enter upon the active ministry immediately following ordination, for his friend Broughton, who was curate at the Tower of London, had requested him to supply his place there for some weeks. These plans were changed, however, to his great relief, when Broughton wrote urging him instead to return to Oxford and undertake the leadership of the Holy Club on a permanent basis. Letters followed from Hervey and Chapman to the same effect.

They urged [Whitefield wrote], that God had blessed my endeavours *there* as well as at Gloucester; that the University was the fountain-head; that every gownsman's name was Legion, and that if I should be made instrumental in converting one of *them*, it would be as much as converting a whole parish.[2]

To make this arrangement possible, Broughton secured for him an annual allowance of £30 from the pious baronet, Sir John Philips,[3] and Chapman and Broughton stated that they intended to use their influence to have him appointed Chaplain to one of the colleges.

Accordingly, Whitefield set out for Gloucester, there to seek ordination at the hands of Bishop Benson. As he left Oxford he wrote,

I am now about to take Orders and my degree, and go into the world. What will become of me I know not. All I can say is I look for perpetual conflicts and struggles in that life and hope for no other peace, but only a cross, while on this side of eternity.

God make me to reflect how short a time it is since I was a common drawer in a publick-house, and had I not been forcibly drawn out

[1] *Journal*, *p* 68. [2] *Ibid*, *p* 67.

[3] For information on Sir John Philips, see *p* 111. The allowance to Whitefield was £30 if he remained at Oxford and £20 if he did not. The name was also spelled 'Phillips' and 'Philipps'.

from thence by Divine grace, I would have been the most abandoned wretch living.

But now, blessed be free grace, I am appointed as it were, to be the head of the Methodists, have an annuity allowed me of £30 and hopes of being elected Chaplain (but that is as God sees fit).

It is my earnest prayer that I may never have any preferment to hurt me. I am not mine, but His! I give up my body, soul, blood, all, to Him! I am a child! I desire to follow the Lamb whithersoever He goeth.[1]

*

Whitefield journeyed to Gloucester by horseback and again his physical strength did not prove equal to the ordeal. 'Very fatigued by riding', he wrote, 'I could scarce support myself. Alas, what a frail earthen vessel my body is'. He suffered the effects for some days and reproached himself for having been too frugal to travel by coach.

His *Diary* mentions 'the cross God has given me to bear at Gloucester', and there is reason to believe that this is a reference to the separation between his mother and step-father. He probably felt that his own testimony was stained by this open discord in the family and perhaps by some unseemly behaviour on Longden's part. It is possible also that Longden was making trouble and seeking to claim ownership of the Bell, for Richard Whitefield was still experiencing difficulty in obtaining clear possession of it, and George had recently written, 'Again brother Richard has been restrained, but it has not had its desired effect'. At any rate, the family situation was on his mind, for when he first anticipated his return to Gloucester he paid a visit to his friend Gambold and there introduced the subject and asked his advice. The outcome was favourable, for he wrote, 'In many ways he satisfied me as to the lawfulness of my mother's living separate from her husband'.[2]

*

As the day of ordination drew near, Whitefield's dread of the ministry again hindered his efforts. He sought to prepare himself further for any questions the Bishop might ask and to compose a sermon, but as he anticipated the ordeal of the public questioning and the task of preaching, his nervousness became so acute that he lost his powers of concentration.

[1] *Diary*, entry of May 31. [2] *Ibid*, May 27.

I know not what to do [he confessed]; I am asked to preach and I am to be examined, and yet am unable to prepare for either. Strong groanings in prayer. Strong desires after ordination. Reposed in my breast, but shut up as to my head. I think God is preparing me for some great work; the Devil sees it and is permitted to beset me.[1]

His chief work of preparation was the writing out of a self-examination according to 'the qualifications for a minister in St Paul's *Epistle to Timothy*', and on the day of the Bishop's arrival it was still not completed. But, although he was 'greatly obstructed', he forced himself to persevere with it and by one o'clock in the morning had it fairly well finished. Still he reproached himself with 'I fear I have not taken pains enough in my preparation for Holy Orders'.

The following morning he waited on his lordship. Bishop Benson was one of England's better prelates and in that day of the Church's declension realized her need of devout and able men. It is evident that he was delighted in having George Whitefield present himself for ordination. The Bishop had 'heard of his character', and therefore probably knew of his study of the Bible, his prayerfulness, his fasting, his visitation of the prison and was aware of the Society that he had founded during his earlier months in Gloucester. Perhaps he had also heard that, since his recent return from Oxford, he had made certain arrangements whereby several children had begun to attend school, and that he had formed another Society, this one 'for public sinners and holy mourners'. How different was this youth, with his intense earnestness and gracious modesty, from most who came before him for ordination!

He told me [wrote Whitefield], he was glad I offered myself a candidate, and was content with my preparation and delighted that I was to be at Oxon. Said he would ask no questions . . . and was willing to do me all possible service.[2]

With the assurance that there would be no public questioning Whitefield's mind was eased. 'Now my restriction about examination is at an end', he wrote. He had been nervous also about the prospect of becoming a chaplain, but this too was removed. Probably Broughton and Chapman had entertained false hopes in

[1] *Ibid,* June 8. [2] *Ibid,* June 17.

expecting to have a Holy Club man appointed to such an office, but Whitefield noted in his *Diary,* 'Letter from Chapman; no chaplain's place', and his words reveal a sense of relief.

The ordination was appointed for the morning of Sunday, June 20 (1736). As a further preparation Whitefield spent the whole of the Saturday in prayer and fasting and 'in the evening retired to a hill near the town and prayed fervently for about two hours'. On the Sunday he 'arose early and prayed over St Paul's *Epistle to Timothy*, especially that precept, "Let no man despise thy youth" '. At the appointed hour he knelt in the magnificent chancel of Gloucester Cathedral, and later recorded the momentous event in the words:

This day I was solemnly admitted by the Bishop before many witnesses into Holy Orders. Was pure and composed, both before and after, particularly before, when I was melted down as it were and kept from trembling as usual. Read the Gospel pretty boldly. I attempted to behave with unaffected devotion, suitable to the greatness of the office I was to undertake. I hope I answered every question from my heart. I could not help thinking, when I put on the surplice, of poor Samuel who stood before the Lord in a linen ephod. God grant I may be a true, though young, Prophet of the Lord.[1]

*

The conflict of Whitefield's principles with those of other men was immediately manifest. Being invited to dine at the Bishop's palace following the ordination, the abstemious Methodist inwardly criticized the lavishness of the table.

I was mercifully kept [he wrote] from sensuality at the Bishop's . . . Though perhaps I may be too stiff in my spirit, yet I would by all means lead the clergy an example of abstinence and self-denial. I could wish with Bishop Burnett that all high living was taken from Bishop's tables.

By the help of God, I'll never ask for anything, but my friends, great ones, are too forward to do that for me. I hope the good of souls and the glory of God will be my only principle of action. I shall choose a voluntary poverty and give all I have to the poor.[2]

He also began immediately to perform his ministerial duties. That afternoon he ministered to the prisoners and in the evening

[1] *Ibid,* June 20. [2] *Ibid.*

read prayers at a church service. On the Monday he 'christened an infant', on subsequent days read prayers two or three times and on Thursday performed a marriage.

Meanwhile Whitefield's friends clamoured for him to preach. It is evident that they had an exceptional admiration for him, and he wrote:

I find reading prayers pleases the people, but I do not seek to please men, but God. If He was not very merciful I should perish by vain glory, for the people here are too fond of me. They want me to preach, but if I do, I shall tell them the truth and I believe they will not like it . . .

It is true I have a difficult task, but God is all-sufficient, to whose almighty protection I humbly commit myself. I give to Him my soul and body to be disposed and worn out in His labours as He shall think meet. I do hence resolve, by His assistance . . . to lead a stricter life than ever, to give myself to prayer and the study of the Scriptures . . . and to strive as much as possible to be wholly in the ministry.

God give me my health, if it be His blessed will! I give myself wholly to Him.[1]

Although still facing the task with severe apprehension, he consented to preach on the following Sunday. Again his nervousness hindered his preparation, but, after struggling throughout the Monday and Tuesday, on the Wednesday he was 'enabled to compose more freely'.

On Sunday, June 27, in the Church of St Mary de Crypt, he preached his first sermon. We imagine the scene and feel something of its solemn excitement. There, not far in front of the pulpit sits his mother, aged by sorrow before her time; her other sons and her daughter are with her. The town-fathers are represented by former mayor Harris, his wife, their son the Sheriff, Alderman Bell and others. Robert Raikes the publisher is there, as are also the Rev Daniel Bond the schoolmaster, and many of Whitefield's former school-mates. The members of his Religious Society are present in a body, and also the 'public sinners' of his more-recently founded group and the women of the female Society. The ancient church is crowded with some three hundred worshippers, and almost all wait impatiently to hear him.

He enters the pulpit with a solemn and resolute mien. His

[1] *Ibid,* June 20, 21.

countenance is quite boyish, yet marked by a spiritual strength, and radiant in outward reflection of an inner holiness. His nervousness is apparent as he begins to preach, but is soon lost in a realization of authority from on high, and his words flow forth in clarity and power.

His sermon is planned especially for the members of the Societies. It is based on Ecclesiastes 4:9–12, 'Two are better than one . . .'. and bears the title 'The Nature and Necessity of Society in General and Religious Society in Particular'.[1] It expounds the need of mutual assistance in the Christian life, enforces the necessity of regeneration and exhorts to holy living. Most hearts are deeply affected – some tremendously so – but we may best understand the occasion from his own account, written a few days later in a letter:

Glory! glory! glory! be ascribed to an Almighty Triune God. Last Sunday in the afternoon I preached my first sermon, in the church of St Mary de Crypt, where I was baptized and also first received the sacrament of the Lord's Supper. Curiosity, as you may easily guess, drew a large congregation. The sight at first a little awed me, but I was comforted with a heartfelt sense of the Divine presence and soon found the unspeakable advantage of having been accustomed to public speaking when a boy at school, and of exhorting and teaching the prisoners and poor people at their private houses whilst at the University. By these means I was kept from being daunted over-much.

As I proceeded, I perceived the fire kindled, till at last, though so young and amidst a crowd of those who knew me in my infant childish days, I trust I was enabled to speak with some degree of Gospel authority. Some few mocked, but most for the present seemed struck, and I have since heard that a complaint has been made to the Bishop that I drove fifteen mad the first sermon. The worthy Prelate, as I am informed, wished that the madness might not be forgotten before next Sunday.[2]

Such was the effect of Whitefield's first sermon on his hearers. What, however, must have been its effect on the young preacher himself? We may be sure it made him conscious that he possessed marvellous powers of public address, and he would hardly have

[1] This sermon is published in his *Works*, Vol 5, *pp* 107–22.
[2] *Ibid*, Vol 1, *p* 18.

been human had he not realized that these could win him some great place in the world.

But such was not his aim. We have seen his concept of an apostolic ministry, and of a life, not of comfort and peace, but of labour and reproach. He anticipated being regarded 'as a fool for Christ's sake', and spoke of seeing his body 'disposed of and worn out in his service'. He saw his future to be the Pauline one of afflictions and necessities, stripes and tumults, watchings and fastings, but as he considered the effect of his first sermon he must surely have felt pressures which would tend to draw him away from this God-given ministry and turn his thoughts towards earthly success.

He had recently written, 'The people grow too, too fond of me . . . It is time to be going . . . Woe is me if I preach not the Gospel.' Accordingly, on the third day after the triumph of his first sermon,[1] he turned from the adulations of Gloucester and set out for Oxford. Further months of study would prepare him the more for the day when he must undertake the awful burdens of the ministry, and in the meantime, he would labour, he said, to be 'first a saint and then a scholar', at the University.

[1] The preaching of Whitefield's first sermon is commemorated in the Church of St Mary de Crypt. A wooden sounding board, (see Illustration pages) now removed from its position and placed against a near-by pillar, bears the following inscription:

THIS SOUNDING BOARD
(Formerly suspended over the pulpit)
Reverberated the wonderful voice of
The Rev. George Whitefield, A.M.
He preached his first sermon here
On the Sunday following his ordination by
Dr. Benson, Bishop of Gloucester,
27th June, 1736.
GEORGE WHITEFIELD WAS A GLOUCESTER MAN

PART II
The Youthful Ministry

In 1737 Whitefield's appearance, voice and pulpit eloquence drew around him thousands ... in a succession of public services which literally startled the nation. He was a new phenomenon in the Church of England. All eyes were fixed upon him. His popularity in Bristol, London and other places was enormous. His name became a household word. Thousands and tens of thousands were making enquiries concerning him. His position was perilous. Popular favour might have ruined him, but the grace of God preserved him.

LUKE TYERMAN

The Life of George Whitefield

5

Preaching that Startled the Nation

UPON returning to Oxford Whitefield wrote, 'For about a week I continued in my servitor's habit and then took my degree of Bachelor of Arts, after having been at the University three years and three quarters and going on towards the 22nd year of my age'.[1]

There is reason to believe that his degree represented a worthy academic accomplishment. We have seen that, at his earlier appearance, he had a strict examiner and that the Proctor was present, and these circumstances, plus the fact that he suffered Dr Panting's displeasure, suggest that the requirements would be well enforced at this latter time also. This inference is strengthened by his statement that he was obliged to return in six months' time and complete further Determining exercises.[2]

Whitefield settled into his graduate studies, working toward his Master's degree.[3] He led the Holy Club and oversaw its charities, and testifies that these duties, '. . . with the time spent in following my studies, sweetly filled up the whole of my day . . . I began to be more than content in my present state of life and had thoughts of abiding at the University, at least for some years.'[4]

[1] *Journals, p* 75.
[2] *Ibid, p* 82: A. D. Godley, *Oxford in the Eighteenth Century, op cit, p* 173, says, that the Statutes called for 'three public appearances; first, what was called "Disputationes in parviso"; next, an intermediate test, "answering under bachelor"; lastly, the examination for the degree. The subjects were supposed to be grammar, rhetoric, logic, ethics, geometry, Greek Classics and fluency in the Latin tongue.'
[3] 'During the eighteenth century the B.A. degree was not the seal and stamp of a completed education; it was only the preliminary to a course of studies and examinations ultimately qualifying for the Mastership.' Godley, *p* 174.
[4] *Journals, pp* 75, 76.

But this scholastic life was soon interrupted. Broughton, who apparently believed that Whitefield's reticence was holding him back,[1] renewed the request that he supply his place at the Chapel of the Tower of London.[2]

In the face of this invitation Whitefield was again thrust into conflict. Late in life, as he looked back upon these days, he stated, 'I said, Lord, I cannot go! . . . I pleaded to be at Oxford two or three years more and intended to make an hundred and fifty sermons . . . I said, I am undone, I am unfit to preach in thy great name! Send me not, I pray, Lord, send me not yet!'[3]

Nevertheless, after much 'wrestling and striving', convinced that God was indeed sending him, he accepted Broughton's invitation.

With fear and trembling [he writes], I obeyed the summons and went in the stage coach to London. There being no other passenger, I employed myself a good part of the way in earnest supplication to the God of all grace to be my Guide and Comforter.

I could not help praising Him for changing my heart and calling me to preach the Gospel at a place to which, not many years ago, I would have given much money, would my circumstances have permitted, to have gone up and seen a play . . .

As I passed along the streets, many came out of their shops to see so young a person in a gown and cassock, and one cried out, 'There's a boy parson!' This served to mortify my pride and put me upon turning that Apostolic injunction into prayer, 'Let no man despise thy youth'.

No doubt he looked 'a boy parson', but this was forgotten when he stood to preach.

As I went up the stairs almost all seemed to sneer at me on account of my youth. But they soon grew serious and exceedingly attentive, and after I came down showed me great tokens of respect, blessed me

[1] Broughton had urged upon Whitefield the early entry into Holy Orders and into the leadership of the Holy Club, and had previously invited him to supply his place at the Tower. It is highly probable that this was because he saw unusual abilities in Whitefield and wanted him to use them immediately.

[2] Broughton's position brought him into association with persons of importance, and it was for this reason that John Wesley had asked him, in 1735, to use his influence to have him appointed to the Epworth parish following Samuel Wesley's death. Broughton made the request, but it was refused. See Broughton's letter in Tyerman's *Life of Wesley*, Vol 1, *p* 102.

[3] Sermon, 'The Good Shepherd', *Sermons of the Rev George Whitefield, op cit*, *p* 733.

as I passed along and made great enquiry who I was . . . I speedily slipped through the crowd.[1]

*

Doubtless, these reports from Whitefield's *Journals* are a simple narration of fact, but they smack of an egoism which is unbecoming. Nevertheless, the circumstances under which they were written must be noticed.

Each evening Whitefield made his diary entries. Since the diary was meant for no eyes but his own, and as Holy Club practice required utter honesty in such records, he wrote without inhibition. The adulation he received – some of it highly enthusiastic – amazed him, and he made forthright report of it in his diaries.

Two years later, when he was but twenty-four and was experiencing a still greater popularity, he wrote his *Journals*. In doing so he used the diaries as the basis of his reports, and not only transcribed many sections word for word, but also gave some parts a still more highly coloured rendering. By the time a few more years had passed he saw the unwisdom of such glowing accounts and publicly apologized for them. Thus the *Journal* covering the first two years of his ministry contains much of this sort of thing, and though the trait is regrettable, its limited nature and the circumstances surrounding it deserve to be borne in mind.

*

Whitefield's ministry at the Tower lasted for two months and proved a steady attraction. A number of young men, probably from the Religious Societies, were drawn to hear him discourse, he says, 'on the new birth', and some of the titled persons of London, who later were numbered among his followers, first became aware of him at this time.

*

With the return of Broughton to the Tower, Whitefield went back to Oxford. His enjoyment of the University is evident:

Oh what a delightful life did I lead here! What communion did I daily enjoy with God! How sweetly did my hours in private glide away in

[1] *Journals*, *p* 76. This event took place at the Bishopsgate Church.

reading and praying over Matthew Henry's *Comment on the Scriptures*! Nor was I alone happy, for several dear youths were quickened greatly and met daily in my room to build up each other in their most holy faith.[1]

Within six weeks, however, another Holy Club man induced him to undertake ministerial activity. Charles Kinchin, rector at Dummer in Hampshire, expecting to be at Oxford for some time, asked him to officiate in his stead, and he accepted.

Kinchin's parishioners were poor and illiterate, and Whitefield learned a valuable lesson among them. He was becoming too fond of his University associations and admits that, at first, he was ill at ease among the Dummer people and longed for his Oxford friends. But this attitude was soon changed and he wrote, 'The profit I reaped from . . . conversing with the poor country people was unspeakable. I frequently learned as much by an afternoon's visit as in a week's study.'[2] The experience among the Dummer villagers proved effective, for never again was there the least suggestion that he was not equally happy in ministering to the poor and illiterate as to the wealthy and learned.

*

While at Dummer Whitefield made one of the most far-reaching decisions of his whole career. It largely governed the rest of his days on earth. This was his decision to become a missionary to Georgia.

He was confronted first with a very different invitation. People of influence had interceded with the Bishop to have him stationed in London and his lordship offered him 'a profitable curacy' there. He was poor and comparatively unknown, and here was an opportunity which could well lead to competence and prominence. Yet he said, 'I had no inclination to accept it'.

The other call was to hardship in an American Colony. Georgia had but recently been founded and to Englishmen it seemed almost as remote and dangerous as upper Amazonia to-day. In 1734 Dr Burton, a professor at Oxford and a Trustee for Georgia, knowing the Colony needed preachers of heroic mould, had

[1] *Ibid*, *p* 78. [2] *Ibid*, *p* 79.

decided that the zeal of the Holy Club men might well be expended there. In turn, under his influence, John and Charles Wesley, Benjamin Ingham and a Charles Delamotte had made the voyage towards the end of 1735. But by the summer of 1736 Charles Wesley, having suffered trials so severe as nearly to cause his death, set out for home.

John Wesley wrote to the Holy Club for assistance. His first letter had reached Whitefield during his days at the Tower of London, and read, in part, as follows:

In Frederica and all the smaller settlements, there are above five hundred sheep almost without a shepherd. He that is unjust must be unjust still . . . He that is a babe in Christ may be so still . . . Does any err from the right way? here is none to recall him . . . Is any falling? Here is none to lift him up. What a single man can do is neither seen nor felt.

Where are ye who are very zealous for the Lord of hosts? Who will rise up with me against the wicked? . . . Do you ask what you shall have. Why, all you desire: food to eat, raiment to put on, a place where to lay your head (such as your Lord had not), and a crown of life that fadeth not away! . . . I will resign to any of you all or any part of my charge . . . Here are adults from the farthest parts of Europe and Asia, and the inmost kingdoms of Africa; add to these the known and unknown nations of this vast continent and you will indeed have a great multitude which no man can number.[1]

Benjamin Ingham had also been unable to endure the Colony for long. After but slightly more than a year there he too set out for England, and John Wesley, in sore need of helpers wrote a second letter to Whitefield. This reached him while he was at Dummer.

Only Mr Delamotte is with me [said John], till God shall stir up the hearts of some of His servants, who, putting their lives in His hands, shall come over and help us, where the harvest is so great and the labourers so few. What if thou art the man, Mr Whitefield?[2]

Whitefield says of this letter, 'Upon reading it, my heart leaped within me, and, as it were, echoed to the call'.

Despite the alacrity of this response his decision was by no

[1] *The Letters of John Wesley,* Standard ed (Epworth, 1931), Vol 1, *p* 205.

[2] Whitefield's *Journals, p* 79.

means an impulsive one. It was two months since he had received Wesley's first letter and during that time he had considered its request, 'praying again and again that God would not suffer (him) to be deluded'. He had also asked the opinion of several friends and had decided to take no immediate action, but to 'wait and see what Providence might point out'.

Upon receiving the second letter Whitefield carefully weighed the several factors involved. He wrote his reasoning regarding the matter into his *Journals*,[1] and his thoughts may be summarized thus:

1. Kinchin had recently become resident at Oxford and could assume the leadership of the Holy Club.

2. It would be an advantage to work with John Wesley who was his senior by eleven years.

3. He would be happy to share in the future prospects of Georgia – a young Colony with likelihood of much growth.

4. There was great need for Gospel work among the Indians.

5. The ocean voyage, supposedly detrimental to health, might actually assist him in his none-too-robust condition.

6. He would need to come back to England within a year or two to be ordained a priest,[2] and at that time could decide whether or not he wished to return to Georgia.

These were the considerations Whitefield listed, but we may be sure there was also another in his mind. The success that had already attended his ministry was evidence to him that in England he would be constantly faced with the temptations which go with great popularity. If he were to go to Georgia he could escape this trial and avoid the ministerial responsibility for which he still did not feel himself ready. Georgia would provide basic experience in Christian work and would require hardships which would serve to mature him.

It was only after these things were 'thoroughly weighed' that Whitefield made his decision. 'I at length resolved', he writes, 'to embark for Georgia.'

He had not easily made up his mind, but once he had determined upon a course of action he was immovable. In subsequent

[1] *Ibid, p* 80.

[2] Church of England ordination is in two stages: first, that of deacon which Whitefield had already received, and second, that of priest which he was to receive later.

months he faced strong persuasions to alter his plan, but despite their attraction, withstood them all.

*

With this decision Whitefield's outlook was radically altered. He dropped all intention of seeking further study at Oxford or attempting additional ministry in England. He wanted simply to say farewell to his relatives and friends at Gloucester, do the same at Bristol, make final arrangements with the ecclesiastical and Colonial authorities in London, and then set sail.

Despite these intentions, however, he was to find himself detained in England for nearly a year, and in that time was to be thrust out into a ministry which startled the nation.

This ministry began with his farewells. Upon visiting Gloucester he was requested to preach for two Sundays and 'congregations were very large'. At Bristol, after preaching once, he found it necessary to preach every day in the week and twice on Sundays. Churches quickly became crowded, often to overflowing, with many turned away for lack of room. People under spiritual concern sought him continually, and large offers were made with the hope of enticing him to remain in Bristol. But after four weeks of this ministry he brought it to a close and hastened up to London.

There he experienced the forced change in his plans. General Oglethorpe, the Governor of Georgia, was then in London, expecting shortly to sail for the Colony. He stated that Whitefield was to sail on the same vessel as himself and therefore was to remain in England until he should be ready to leave. The date of the Governor's departure, however, depended on several unforeseeable circumstances.

Thus Whitefield was left in a state of uncertainty. His desire, while waiting, was to return to Oxford, but so pressing were some of the requests for his ministry that he gave heed to them.

The first that he accepted was that of the Rev Sampson Harris of the Gloucestershire village of Stonehouse. He was there during April and May – weeks in which the spring in all its glory was coming to the Cotswold countryside – and the heart of Whitefield, alive with a perennial springtime, was moved to spiritual ecstasy. Can we not see him, walking some country lane in April and pausing to commune with God amidst newly blossoming nature, as we read the following account?

Early in the morning, at noonday, evening and midnight, nay, all the day long, did the blessed Jesus visit and refresh my heart. Could the trees of a certain wood near Stonehouse speak, they would tell what sweet communion I and some others enjoyed with the ever-blessed God there. Sometimes, as I was walking, my soul would make such sallies as though it would go out of the body. At other times I would be so overpowered with a sense of God's Infinite Majesty that I would be constrained to throw myself on the ground and offer my soul as a blank in His hands, to write on it what He pleased.

One night it happened to lighten exceedingly . . . In my return to the parsonage, whilst others were rising from their beds, frightened almost to death, I and another, a poor but pious countryman, were in the fields, exulting in our God and longing for the time when Jesus should be revealed from Heaven in a flame of fire.[1]

Such spiritual joy, explains, in part, the extraordinary attraction which people found in his ministry. Other men might talk of the things of God, but in a way which made them appear little more than dry theories; yet as Whitefield expressed them they were full of life and meaning and power. No wonder neither church nor house would hold the throngs that came to hear!

Yet we do well to notice that the youth, so familiar with heaven, was also subject to the little hindrances of earth. 'I know not what to do', he wrote at Stonehouse, 'for the want of a clock in the house' – a severe inconvenience for one who would allow no moment to be lost, but was still too poor to own a watch.

Upon leaving Stonehouse (Oglethorpe was still not ready to sail), Whitefield accepted the invitations which had poured in upon him to return to Bristol. As he approached the city the people heard of his coming and 'multitudes came on foot and many in coaches a mile without the city to meet [him]'. His entrance was something of a triumphal procession and 'almost all saluted and blessed [him] as [he] went along the street'. He was invited to minister in church after church and wrote:

I preached as usual about five times a week; but the congregations grew, if possible, larger and larger. It was wonderful to see how the people hung upon the rails of the organ loft, climbed upon the leads

[1] *Journals, pp* 83–4.

of the church, and made the church itself so hot with their breath that the steam would fall from the pillars like drops of rain. Sometimes almost as many would go away for want of room as came in, and it was with great difficulty that I got into the desk to read prayers or preach. Persons of all denominations flocked to hear. Persons of all ranks not only publicly attended my ministry but gave me private invitations to their houses. A private Society or two were erected. I preached and collected for the poor prisoners in Newgate twice or thrice a week. Many made me large offers if I would not go abroad . . .

But when I came to tell them, it might be that they would 'see my face no more', high and low, young and old, burst into such a flood of tears as I had never seen before. Multitudes, after sermon, followed me home, weeping, and the next day I was employed from seven in the morning till midnight, in giving spiritual advice to awakened souls.[1]

During these days at Bristol Whitefield ministered also at the near-by city of Bath. Bath was the site of mineral springs which drew large numbers of the wealthy of England to seek health by bathing in their waters. The life of the city was marked by pomp and frivolity, yet here, among audiences as fastidious as could be found anywhere on earth, the youthful preacher was received with the same enthusiasm as among the ordinary people of Bristol. He preached four times in the great Abbey Church and once in the Queen's Chapel, and 'received gifts of upwards of £160 for the poor of Georgia'.[2] Moreover, from among these representatives of the élite of England, there came requests that he make his sermons available in print.

*

About this time (June of 1737) Whitefield learned that his benefactor, Sir John Philips, had died.

Sir John was a noteworthy figure in the realm. The fourth Baronet, he had inherited the ancient Picton Castle and its extensive estates. Throughout much of his adult life he had served as a Member of Parliament, and Lady Walpole, wife of the Prime Minister, was his niece.

But it was especially for his religious zeal that Sir John was known. For more than a half century he had championed the

[1] *Ibid, pp* 84–5.
[2] £160 would equal the wages paid to a labouring man for more than 320 weeks of work.

evangelical cause, aiding the Religious Societies and playing a large part in the origin and maintenance of the *Society for Promoting Christian Knowledge*, the *Society for the Reformation of Manners* and the *Society for the Propagation of the Gospel.* During his last years he was infirm and had finally become blind, and his life was saddened by the fact that his own son was utterly a man of the world. In that age of apostasy and sin, Sir John laboured and prayed for a religious awakening, and had he lived to see the dawn of the revival, there would have been no happier soul in the land.[1] But as it was, God took him home.

Whitefield appears not to have been concerned in the least over the loss of the financial assistance which Sir John had been giving him. He was soon granted a stipend of £50 per year as minister of the parish of Frederica in Georgia, but refused to accept it. He chose to look to God for the supply of his needs, feeling that he could regard such Divine provision as a further confirmation of the Divine call.

*

After about a month of marvellous ministry at Bristol Whitefield returned to his studies at Oxford.[2] He allowed himself eight weeks of this pleasant life and then, assuming that Oglethorpe would be ready to sail, went again to London.

Here he made an important new acquaintance: that of James Hutton.

There were two Huttons, father and son. The father, the Rev John Hutton, M.A., had resigned his preferments on a matter of principle and conducted a boarding house for boys attending the Westminster School which was attached to Westminster Abbey. He was a man of learning and his wife was a second cousin of Sir Isaac Newton. Whitefield took up lodgings at the Hutton home.

[1] There is considerable material on Sir John in Mary Clement's *The S.P.C.K. and Wales* (SPCK, London, 1954). The Oxford Diary of his son Erasmus, is published by Macleane, *op cit*, *pp* 323–9.

[2] The time that Whitefield spent at Oxford subsequent to his graduation appears to have amounted to nearly twenty weeks. This was in four short periods of approximately the following dates: in 1736, June 30 to August 4 and October 1 to November 15: in 1737, ten days near the middle of February and from June 26 till past the middle of August.

The son, James, had recently opened his own book business, the *Bible and Sun,* located near Temple Bar. His shop became a gathering place for evangelical Christians and his biographer speaks of it as 'his pulpit from which his customers never retired without some discourse for the good of their souls'. He was a man of outstanding personality; during the ensuing two years he was one of Whitefield's closest associates, and upon the return of the Wesleys from Georgia, held a similar place in their lives.

*

While awaiting Oglethorpe, Whitefield sought to spend his time, he says, 'in my usual practice of reading and praying over the Word of God on my knees'. But his retirement was short, for the fame of his Bristol ministry had preceded him and he was quickly importuned to preach.

Few men would have wanted the task to which he was invited. Some of the Religious Societies held services under their own auspices in certain churches. At these they had a guest clergyman administer the Sacrament and preach, and received an offering for some charitable purpose. However, they were allotted an hour which would not conflict with regular services – usually six o'clock in the morning. As will readily be recognized, at such an hour the hearers were few, the services dull and the offerings small. The sponsors were always looking for a preacher who could put some life into this dreary undertaking and when the eloquent Whitefield appeared on the scene, they immediately sought his help.

> I embraced the invitations [he wrote], and so many came that sometimes we were obliged to consecrate fresh elements two or three times, and stewards found it somewhat difficult to carry the offerings to the communion table.[1]

He was immediately requested to minister also at other services on Sundays and during the week. Here is his amazing story:

> Congregations continually increased and generally, on a Lord's Day, I used to preach four times to very large and affected auditories, besides reading prayers twice or thrice, and walking perhaps twelve miles in going backwards and forwards from one church to the other.

[1] *Journals*, p 87.

But God made my feet like hind's feet, and filled me with joy unspeakable at the end of my day's work. This made me look upon my friends' kind advice to . . . spare myself, as a temptation, for I found by daily experience, the more I did the more I might do for God . . .

Henceforward, for near three months successively, there was no end of the people flocking to hear the Word of God . . . I sometimes had more than a dozen names of different churches, where I had promised to preach, upon my slate-book at once, and when I preached, constables were obliged to be placed at the door, to keep the people in order. The sight of the congregations was awful. One might, as it were, walk upon the people's heads, and thousands went away from the largest churches for want of room. They were all attention, and heard like people hearing for eternity.

I now preached generally nine times a week. The early sacraments were exceeding awful. At Cripplegate, St Ann's and Forster Lane, how often have we seen Jesus Christ, evidently set forth before us, crucified! On Sunday mornings, long before day, you might see streets filled with people going to church, with their lanthorns in their hands, and hear them conversing about the things of God. Other Lecture Churches,[1] near at hand, would be filled with persons who could not come where I was preaching, and those who did come were so deeply affected that they were like persons struck with pointed arrows or mourning for a first-born child.[2]

This ministry lasted four months. It began late in August and did not conclude until he sailed for Georgia at the end of December. We have a further glimpse of it in a letter that he wrote in November:

Last week, save one, I preached ten times in different churches, and the last week seven; and yesterday four times and read prayers twice, though I slept not above an hour the night before, which was spent in religious conversation and interceding . . . I now begin to preach charity sermons twice or thrice a week, besides two or three on Sundays, and sixty or seventy pounds are collected weekly for the poor children. Thousands would come in to hear, but cannot.[3]

It is manifest that much of London – a city then of about five hundred thousand inhabitants – was stirred by Whitefield's

[1] Lecture churches were those in which these meetings sponsored by the Religious Societies were held. Probably, as a means of indicating that these services were not held by the Church, the preaching on such an occasion was referred to, not as a sermon, but as a lecture.

[2] *Journals, pp* 87–9.

[3] *Works,* Vol 1, *pp* 30–1.

The Bell Inn, Gloucester in Whitefield's time.

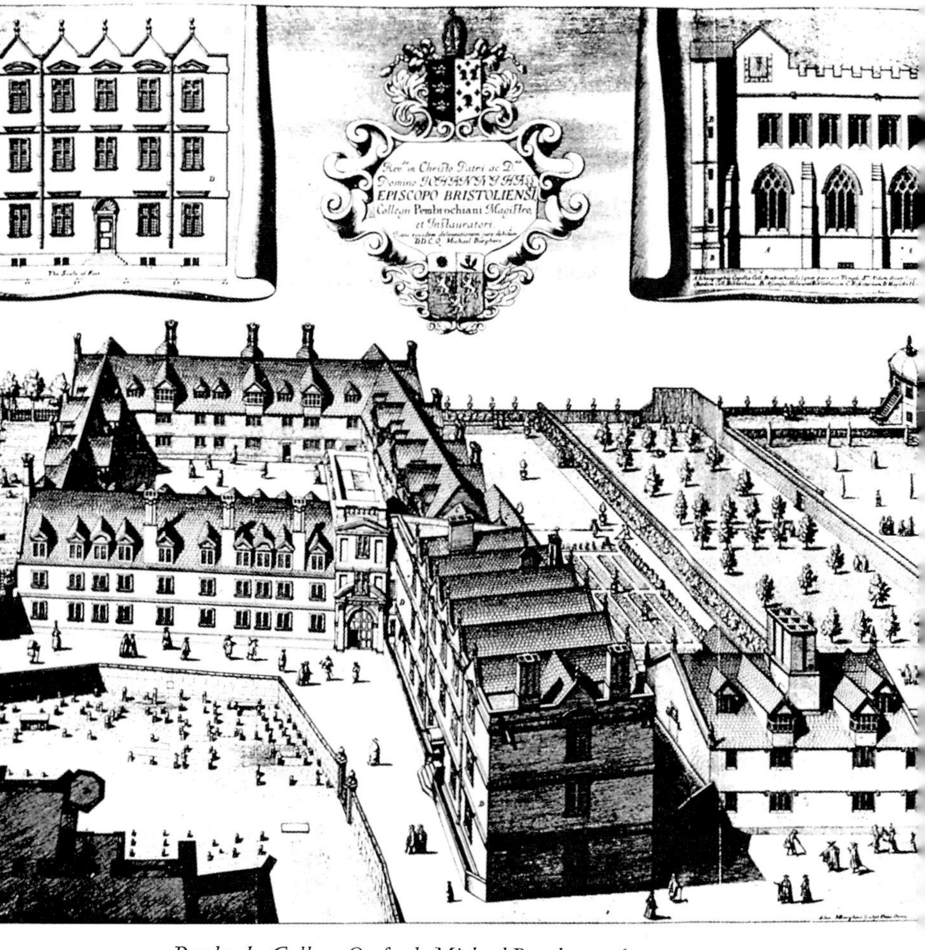

Pembroke College, Oxford. Michael Burghers, 1699.

Insets: (left) Master's Lodgings, (right) St Aldate's Church which stands on the shaded ground shown in bottom left-hand corner of the print. This was used as the College Chapel until 1732.

John Wesley welcoming George Whitefield to the meeting room of the Holy Club, Oxford.

[*By courtesy of Hulton Picture Library*]

The Holy Club in session.
A painting by Marshall Claxton based on originals.
John Wesley, standing, addresses the meeting.
On his right, sitting at the table are James Hervey [nearest Wesley],
William Morgan, Charles Wesley and Benjamin Ingham.
Whitefield is in background between
Hervey and Wesley.

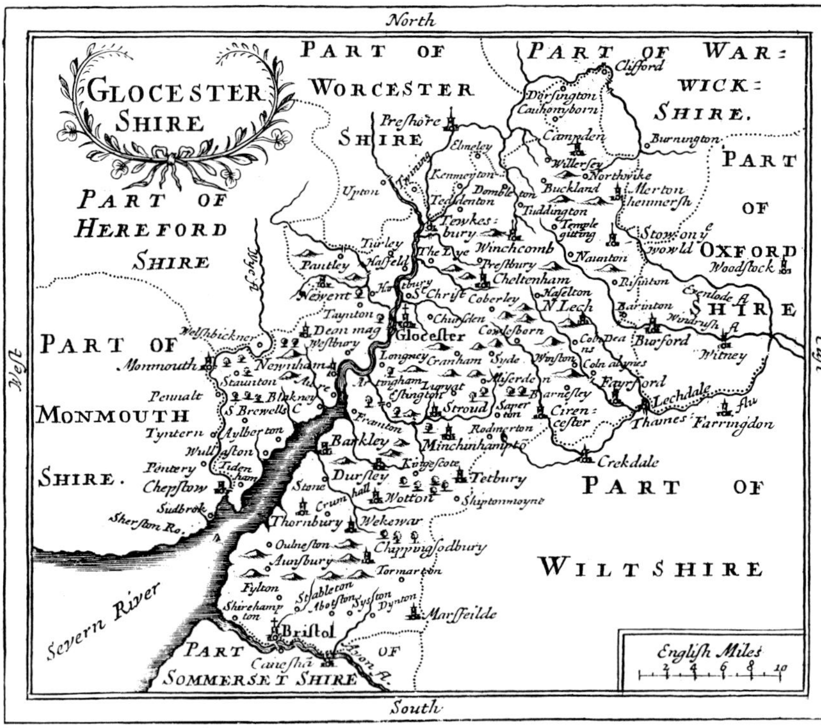

Map of Gloucestershire in 1701 based on Camden's Britannia

Sounding board in St Mary de Crypt Church, bearing the inscription:

This sounding board [formerly suspended over the pulpit] reverberated the wonderful voice of the Rev George Whitefield A.M. He preached his first sermon here on the Sunday following his ordination by Dr Benson, Bishop of Gloucester, 27th June 1736. George Whitefield was a Gloucester man.

Gloucester Cathedral. T. *Bonnor*, 1797.

A hanging at Tyburn by William Hogarth. *See page* 189.
[*By courtesy of Hulton Picture Library*]

The hanging is an occasion of boisterous merriment. Grandstand seats are available, those nearest to the gallows being the most highly priced. At the right foreground a woman seeks customers for a game of throwing a ball into upright cups, and another clutches the face of a boy who is mischievously tipping over a barrow of fruit that she is selling. Behind them a woman in the cart sells gin, and nearby a group of men fight one another with sticks. Toward the centre foreground a man holds a dog by the tail, ready to hurl it at the death cart, and to his right a woman hawks a copy of a death speech recently made by a victim of the gallows. Behind her, a woman has dropped her baby to the ground in order to indulge in a fist-fight with a man.

The carriage near the centre of the picture contains the official chaplain. The executioner reclines atop the gallows, smoking a pipe, and from the top row of the grandstand a homing pigeon is released, to fly back to the prison as evidence that the hanging party has reached Tyburn. A detachment of mounted soldiers accompanies the death cart, and in the cart stands the victim, leaning against his own coffin. In his first draft of this picture, drawn shortly before the beginning of the Revival, Hogarth showed the condemned man alone in the death cart, for 'no man cared for his soul'. But in this second draft, drawn a few years later, he showed a Methodist preacher, Silas Told, in the death cart, and, heedless of the crowd, Told stands with open Bible and upraised hand, declaring to the poor victim the way of life everlasting.

Whitefield preaching at Islington. Gustave Sintzennich. This famous painting, which hung in Whitefield's Chapel, London, was reputedly destroyed when the building was bombed in the Second World War.

Two of the many eighteenth-century cartoons in which, satirically or otherwise, revival scenes were depicted. The first, dated 1739, represents Whitefield's preaching at Moorfields as a performance for women, and the caption, by reference to John Knox, seeks to increase prejudice against his doctrine. In another version of the same picture the caption reads, Enthusiasm Displayed: or, the Moorfields Congregation.

The second cartoon, with scaffolds in foreground [*see page 26*], *gives an idea of the immense crowds which gathered to hear Whitefield.*

[*By courtesy of the British Museum*]

John Wesley, after the painting by J. M. Williams RA, *circa* 1742.

[*By courtesy of Wesley College, Bris*

Charles Wesley, after the painting by Thomas Hudson, circa 1740

[*By courtesy of the Methodist Archives*]

ministry. But why did these people come? What was there in his preaching or his person which attracted such throngs?

Doubtless, the mass of these people were drawn by a deep spiritual hunger. Amidst the conditions that surrounded them – the widespread rejection of moral restraint, blatant denial of the Scriptures, rampant crime and glaring heartlessness – they had long sought in vain for help from the churches. The generality of the parochial clergy were looked upon in bitter contempt, and Bishop Ryle says of these men:

> The vast majority of them were sunk in worldliness and neither knew nor cared anything about their profession . . . They hunted, they shot, they farmed, they swore, they drank, they gambled. They seemed determined to know everything except Jesus Christ and Him crucified. When they assembled it was generally to toast 'Church and King' and to build one another up in earthly-mindedness, prejudice, ignorance and formality. When they retired to their own homes, it was to do as little and preach as seldom as possible. And when they did preach, their sermons were so unspeakably and indescribably bad that it is comforting to reflect they were generally preached to empty benches.[1]

Of course, there were many better men among all denominations, but evangelistic zeal was hardly to be found among them, and strong, unbending convictions regarding Christian truth were rare. The two great figures among the Nonconformists in these days were Isaac Watts and Philip Doddridge, but even these good men were over-fearful of being styled *enthusiasts*, as indeed were the vast majority of ministers, and boldly aggressive Christianity was unknown.

Scores of Londoners, having failed to find food for their souls in the churches, had resorted to the Religious Societies. But so strong seemed the forces of sin and unbelief that, even in these groups there was a sense of defeat, yet at the same time many expressed the longing – perhaps the expectancy – that God would raise up some mighty man to champion His cause.

It was while these conditions prevailed that the voice of George Whitefield began to be heard in the London pulpits. He spoke with the firmest of conviction and his sermons were such that all could understand. He preached nothing but the basic doctrines of

[1] J. C. Ryle, *Five Christian Leaders* (Banner of Truth ed, 1960), *p* 14.

the Church of England; in glowing contrast to the majority of the clergy, his life was marked by personal holiness and everything about him seemed ablaze with zeal. No doubt some people were attracted by curiosity and others by the excitement associated with his going to Georgia; but, above all, it was a spiritual hunger that drew the crowds, and many followed him from church to church, vigorously endeavouring to be present every time he preached.

Moreover, we may be sure that the people found something highly attractive in the young preacher himself. He was always exceptionally neat about his person – an element of his concept of Christian discipline – and his manner was gracious and easy. At this stage of his development, he was still marked by an unassuming youthfulness, but his consciousness of being called of God gave him an extraordinary spiritual authority and courage. To many of his hearers he seemed as a messenger from heaven; his countenance was radiant and he stood as one sent from God, and, like Charles Wesley who spoke of him as 'an angel guest', many were beginning to refer to him as 'The Seraph'.

But this personal attractiveness does not overshadow the fact that Whitefield possessed a most remarkable eloquence. The gift of public utterance which had been evident when he preached his first sermon, had been developed by his months of experience in preaching. Benjamin Franklin, after hearing him frequently during later months, stated:

> . . . every accent, every emphasis, every modulation of voice, was so perfectly well turned and well placed, that, without being interested in the subject, one could not help being pleased with the discourse; a pleasure of much the same kind with that received from an excellent piece of musick.[1]

Yet it would be very misleading to assume that there was anything of a mere performance in Whitefield's preaching. On the contrary, it was the utter lack of anything artificial, and its burning sincerity which were its most noticeable qualities. His delivery was simply the outflow of that spiritual passion which inflamed his whole life.

These are, however, but the human explanations of Whitefield's

[1] *Memoirs of the Life and Writings of Benjamin Franklin,* Vol 1, *p* 87.

success. They reveal the possession of exceptional abilities, but his effectiveness lay not in his eloquence nor his zeal. As we look back from our present standpoint we see that God's chosen time to 'arise and have mercy upon Zion . . . yea, the set time [had] come', and that in raising up Whitefield, He had granted upon him and his ministry 'a mighty effusion of the Holy Ghost'; and it was this, the Divine power, which was the first secret of his success.

On a careful reading, Whitefield's sermons do not seem to be as unworthy of their author as they are reported to be. Though not profound nor wide in range of thought, they are marked by firmness, clarity and sanity in thinking; by force, clearness, fitness, and often beauty of style; by insight, imagination, pathos, breadth of sympathy, and sincere and fervent feeling.

E. C. DARGAN

A History of Preaching

6

The Sermons of a Youth

WHAT did the people hear when they attended Whitefield's services?

Some have supposed that his preaching was of the frothy variety, weak in content but strong on noise, appealing solely to the emotions and seeking to work the congregation into a state of frenzy.

There is no need, however, for supposition in this matter. At this early stage of his ministry Whitefield read his sermons word for word from a manuscript, and, since ten of those that he preached during these months in London were published, we may know precisely what their content was.

These sermons merit our attention first, on the basis of certain negative qualities. If anyone approaches them expecting the marks of present-day sensationalism – such things as spectacular titles, far-fetched interpretations, rhetorical fireworks, eschatological speculations or emotional stories – he will be amazed by their complete absence. Some critics have expressed the view that sermons which proved so remarkably effective ought to exhibit the elements of classical oratory – a finely-ornamented style, soaring flights of fancy and elegance of taste – but these productions make not the slightest attempt at 'excellency of speech . . . or enticing words of man's wisdom'.

Whitefield's preaching is of a very different order. Its chief characteristics are its Biblical content, its doctrinal emphasis and its simplification.

These qualities are to be seen in the following selections, taken from the sermons that Whitefield preached during these opening months of his ministry. As we read them it is necessary to consider not only *what* he said, but also to realize *how* he said it. We must endeavour to visualize him as he stands in one of the London pulpits, his countenance aglow with holy fervour, his voice vibrant and his whole being alive with the consciousness that he is the messenger of God to this people. Thus we view him, as preaching from the text, 'Almost thou persuadest me to be a Christian', he declares:

An almost Christian is one of the most hurtful creatures in the world. He is a wolf in sheep's clothing. He is one of those false prophets of whom our Lord bids us beware, who would persuade men that the way to heaven is broader than it really is, and thereby enter not into the kingdom of God themselves, and those that are entering in they hinder. These, these are the men who turn the world into a luke-warm Laodicean spirit; who hang out false lights, and so shipwreck unthinking benighted souls in their voyage to the haven where they would be. These are they that are greater enemies of the cross of Christ than infidels themselves; for, of an unbeliever everyone will be aware; but an almost Christian, through his subtle hypocrisy, draws away many after him, and therefore must expect to receive the greater damnation.[1]

Man's weakness and need of spiritual aid are Whitefield's theme in his sermon, *The Nature and Necessity of Society in General and Religious Society in Particular*. This was the one he preached following his ordination and he preached it again at Bristol and London. The following passage is representative:

Let us view man a little in his natural estate, since the fall, as having his understanding darkened, his mind alienated from the life of God, as no more able to see the way wherein he should go, than a blind man to describe the sun; that notwithstanding this, he must receive his sight ere he can see God; and that if he never sees Him he never can be happy. Let us view him, I say, in this light (or rather in this darkness) and deny the necessity of society if we can.

A Divine revelation we find is absolutely necessary, we being by nature as unable to *know* as we are to *do* our duty. And how shall we learn except one teach us? But was God to do this immediately of Himself, how should we, with Moses, exceedingly quake and fear!

[1] *The Almost Christian*: 'A Sermon Preached in the Parish Church of St John, Wapping'. This and following selections are taken from the original edition, published in 1738, and not from later editions in which Whitefield made slight alterations. Text, *Acts* 26: 28.

Nor would the ministry of Angels in this affair be without too much terror. It is necessary, therefore (at least God's dealing with us has shewed it to be so) that we should be drawn with the cords of a man; and that a Divine revelation being granted, we should use one another's assistance under God to instruct each other in the *knowledge*, and to exhort one another in the *practice* of those things which belong to our everlasting peace. This is undoubtedly the great end of society intended by God since the fall, and a strong argument it is why we should not forsake the assembling of ourselves together.[1]

About a month after Whitefield's arrival in London the Religious Societies asked him to preach at their Quarterly Meeting which was held in the Bow Church. The event drew an audience that he described as 'a multitude of young professors', and he fittingly used the text: 'Remember now thy Creator in the days of thy youth', and entitled his sermon *The Benefits of an Early Piety*. After shewing 'the unspeakable advantages' of remembering the Creator in the days of youth, he applied his message, asking:

What! Will not a desire of bringing glory to God, honour and comfort to themselves; will not the pleasure of an habitual piety and the comfortable assurance of being sincere; above all, will not the hopes of an honourable old age, a peaceful death and a glorious appearance at the tremendous day of judgment; will not these, I say, prevail with them to leave their husks and return home to eat of the fatted calf?

What! Will they thus requite the Saviour's love? That be far from them! Did He come down and shed His precious blood to deliver them from sin, and will they spend their youthful strength and vigour in the service of it, and then think to serve Christ when they can follow their lusts no longer?

Is it fit that many who are now endowed with excellent gifts and are thereby qualified to be the supports and ornaments of our sinking Church, should notwithstanding forget the God that gave them, and employ them in things that will not profit? O why will they not arise, and like so many Phineas's, be zealous for the Lord of hosts? . . . May we not imagine that young Samuel now rejoices that he waited so soon at the Temple of the Lord? Or young Timothy, that from a

[1] *The Nature and Necessity of Society in General and of Religious Society in Particular:* 'A Sermon Preached in the Parish Church of St Nicholas in Bristol and before the Religious Societies at One of Their General Quarterly Meetings in Bow Church, London.' Text, *Ecclesiastes* 4: 9–12.

child he knew the Holy Scriptures? And if you wish to be partakers of their joy, let me persuade you to be partakers of their piety.[1]

We see something of his vigorous enforcement of Christian principles in the sermon entitled *The Great Duty of Family Religion.* from the text, 'As for me and my house, we will serve the Lord'.

Fifthly and lastly: If neither gratitude to God, love to your children, common justice to your servants, nor even that most prevailing motive, self-interest, will excite, yet let a consideration of the terrors of the Lord persuade you to put in practice the pious resolution of the text. Remember, the time will come, and that perhaps very shortly, when we must all appear before the judgment-seat of Christ; where we must give a solemn and strict account how we have had our conversation in our families, in this world. How will you endure to see your children and servants (who ought to be your joy and crown of rejoicing in the day of Jesus Christ) coming out as swift witnesses against you; cursing the father that begat them, the womb that bare them and the day they ever entered into your houses? Think you not the damnation which men must endure for their own sins will be sufficient that they need load themselves with the additional guilt of being accessory to the damnation of others also? Oh consider this, all ye that forget to serve the Lord in your respective households, lest He pluck you away and there be none to deliver you![2]

Whitefield's denunciation of sin is manifest in the following paragraphs from his sermon against *Cursing and Swearing*:

What shall we say to the unhappy men who think it not only allowable, but fashionable and polite to take the name of God in vain; who imagine that swearing makes them look big among their companions, and really think it an honour to abound in it. Alas! little do they know that such behaviour argues the greatest foolhardiness and degeneracy of mind.

. . . Men dare not revile a general at the head of an army. And is the Almighty God, the great Jehovah, the everlasting King, who can consume them with the breath of His nostrils, and frown them into hell in an instant; is He, I say, the only contemptible being, that may be provoked without fear and offended without punishment?

[1] *The Benefits of an Early Piety*, 'A Sermon Preached at the Bow Church, London, before the Religious Societies, at one of their Quarterly Meetings, on Wednesday, September 28, 1737'. Text, *Ecclesiastes* 12: 1.

[2] *The Great Duty of Family Religion:* 'A sermon Preached at the Parish Church of St Vedast, Foster Lane.' Text, *Joshua* 24: 15.

No! Though God bear long, He will not bear always! The time will come when God will vindicate His injured honour, when He will lay bare His almighty arm, and make those wretched ones feel the eternal smart of His justice, whose power and name they have so often vilified and blasphemed. Alas! What will become of their bravery then? Will they then wantonly sport with the name of their Maker, and call upon the King of all the earth to damn them any more, in jest?

Their note will then be changed. Indeed, they shall call, but it will be for the rocks to fall on them, and the hills to cover them, from the wrath of Him that sitteth upon the throne. Time was when they prayed for damnation for themselves and others, and now they will find their prayers answered.[1]

The personal discipline which Whitefield practised, is sternly enjoined in his sermon on *Self-denial.* He exhorts his hearers,

Thirdly, think often of the pains of hell. Consider whether it is not better to cut off a right hand or foot and pluck out a right eye, if they cause us to sin, rather than to be cast into hell, into the fire that never shall be quenched. Think how many thousands there are now reserved in chains of darkness, unto the judgment of the great day, for not complying with the precept in the text . . . Think you, they now imagine Jesus Christ to be a hard master; or, rather think you not they would give ten thousand times ten thousand worlds, could they but return to life again and take Christ's easy yoke upon them? And can *we* dwell with the everlasting burnings more than *they*? If we cannot bear this precept, how can we bear the irrevocable sentence, 'Depart from me, ye cursed, into everlasting fire, prepared for the devil and his angels'?

Lastly, often meditate on the joys of heaven. Think, think with what unspeakable glory those happy souls are now encircled, who, when on earth were called to deny themselves, and were not disobedient to the call.

Hark! Methinks I hear them chanting their everlasting hallelujahs and spending an eternal day in echoing triumphant songs of joy. And do you not long, my brethren, to join this heavenly choir? Do not your hearts burn within you? As the hart panteth after the water-brooks, do not your souls so long after the blessed company of these sons of God? Behold then a heavenly ladder reached down to you, by which you may climb to this holy hill. If any man will come after them, let him deny himself and follow them. By this we, even we, may

[1] *The Heinous Sin of Profane Cursing:* 'A Sermon Preached at The Parish Church of St Nicholas Cole Abbey.' Text, *Matthew* 5: 34, 'But I say unto you, Swear not at all'.

be lifted into the same blissful regions, there to enjoy an eternal rest with the people of God, and join with them in singing doxologies and songs of praise to the everlasting, blessed, all-glorious, most adorable Trinity, for ever and ever.[1]

These sermons emphasize especially the practical aspects of Christianity, but there were others which were more strongly doctrinal. Whitefield's most widely circulated discourse was the one entitled *The New Birth*. It propounds four arguments as to 'why we must be born again', one of which is as follows:

Now God is described in the Holy Scripture (and I speak to those who profess to know the Scripture) as a Spirit; as a Being of such infinite sanctity as to be of purer eyes than to behold iniquity; as to be so transcendently holy that it is said the very Heavens are not clean in His sight, and the angels themselves he chargeth with folly.

On the other hand, man is described (and every regenerate person will find it true by his own experience) as a creature altogether conceived and born in sin; as having no good thing dwelling in him; as being carnal, sold under sin; nay, as having a mind which is enmity with God.

And since there is such an infinite disparity, can anyone conceive how such a filthy, corrupted, polluted wretch can dwell with an infinitely pure and holy God, before he is changed and rendered, in some measure, like Him. Can He that is of purer eyes than to behold iniquity, dwell with it? Can He in whose sight the heavens are not clean, delight to dwell with uncleanness itself? No! We might as well suppose light to have communion with darkness, or Christ to have concord with Belial.[2]

The most thoroughly theological of these early sermons is the one entitled *Of Justification by Christ*. Taking as his text, 'But ye are washed, but ye are sanctified, but ye are justified, in the name of our Lord Jesus Christ', Whitefield asserts:

These words, beginning with the particle '*But*', have plainly a reference to something that went before; it may not therefore be improper, before I descend to particulars, to consider the words as they stand related to the context.

[1] *The Nature and Necessity of Self-Denial:* 'A Sermon Preached at the Parish Church of St Andrew, Holborn, London.' Text, *Luke* 9: 23.

[2] *The Nature and Necessity of Our New Birth in Jesus Christ in order to Salvation:* 'A Sermon Preached at the Parish Church of St Mary Redcliffe, Bristol.' Text, 2 *Cor.* 5: 17, 'If any man be in Christ he is a new creature'.

This kind of contextual explanation was common with him, as was also the practice of stating his main points at the opening of the sermon, and stating each again as he used it. In this sermon he presents his outline thus:

From these words I shall consider these three things:

First, What is meant by the word *Justified*?

Secondly, I shall endeavour to prove that all mankind in general, and every individual person in particular, stands in need of being justified.

Thirdly and lastly, that there is no possibility of obtaining this justification, which we so much want, but by the precious blood of Jesus Christ.

The sermon proceeds with unity and order. There are no extraneous ideas and the subject is ably argued and Scripturally proved. Under his third heading he declares:

Two things, as was before observed, we wanted, in order to make our peace with God.

1. To be freed from the guilt of original sin; and,

2. From that punishment we had most justly deserved for our actual breaches of God's law. And both these are abundantly secured for us by the death of Jesus Christ. For what says the Scripture?

As to our being freed from the guilt of original sin – it informs us that, 'as in Adam all die, even so in Christ shall all be made alive'. And again, 'As by the disobedience of one man', or by one transgression, namely that of Adam, 'many were made sinners, so by the obedience of one', Jesus Christ, 'many were made righteous'. And again, 'As by the disobedience of one man, judgment came upon all men unto condemnation'; that is, all men were condemned on having Adam's sin imputed to them; 'so by the obedience of one', that is, Jesus Christ, 'the free gift' of pardon and peace 'came upon all men unto justification of life'.

Which clears up (as I promised to do before) that seeming disagreement between God's attributes in imputing Adam's sin to us (namely His justice and His mercy) and wholly takes off that imputation of injustice which wicked men would blasphemously cast upon the righteous Judge of all the earth. Had God imputed Adam's sin to his innocent posterity and left them to perish in it: had He looked upon and punished them all as sinners, without providing them a Saviour, we might have had some pretence to complain of His severity.

But, since 'He has not dealt with us after our deserts, nor rewarded us according to our iniquities': Since the same revelation acquaints us that 'As in Adam all die, even so in Christ shall all be made alive' . . . I say, since these things are so, what reason have such worms as we to quarrel with the most high God? Doubtless, no more than a condemned criminal has to find fault with his judge for condemning him for breaking the law, only that he might give him the pleasure of a reprieve.

No; as for God, His ways are perfect and His dealings with His creatures are holy, just and good. And as in all His dispensations, so more especially in our recovery from our fallen estate by the death of Jesus, we may justly say, 'Mercy and truth have met together, righteousness and peace have kissed each other'.

And after this, can any poor returning sinner despair of mercy? What, can they see their Saviour hanging on a tree with arms stretched out to embrace them, and yet, upon their true repentance, doubt of finding acceptance with Him? No! away with such dishonourable, such desponding thoughts! Look on His hands, bored with pins of iron; look on His side, pierced with a cruel spear, on purpose to unloose the sluices of His blood and 'open a fountain for sin and uncleanness'; and then despair of mercy if you can! No! do but leave those sins he came to die for; . . . do but labour to attain that 'holiness without which no man shall see the Lord', and then, 'though your sins be as scarlet, yet shall they be as wool; though they be red like crimson, yet shall they be whiter than the snow'.[1]

*

One more sermon must be noticed. While at Stonehouse Whitefield preached on Ascension Day from the text, 'Whom He justified, them He also glorified'. He opened by declaring:

This being the day set apart by the Church for the solemn commemoration of our blessed Lord's ascension into heaven, and it being likewise one, if not the chiefest, design of His ascending up thither, to go and prepare a place for us; and as our head and representative, thereby to take possession of that glory which He has purchased for, and will actually confer upon all true believers – I hope it will no way be thought improper or impertinent to the meditations this day's glorious festival ought to suggest, if from the words of the text, I

First endeavour to prove that Christ has purchased for, and in due time will actually confer on all true believers, eternal glory in the world to come.

[1] *Of Justification by Christ:* 'A Sermon Preached in the Parish Church of St Antholin'. Text, 1 *Cor*. 6: 11.

Secondly, I shall endeavour to instance in some particulars, in which that glory and happiness consist.

Thirdly, and lastly, I shall beg leave to conclude with an inference or two naturally arising from what shall have been delivered.

This sermon demonstrates Whitefield's use of the three-point homiletic method, but its chief value lies in its evidence of the measure to which the Calvinistic system was already formed in his thinking.

Although the burden of his message is the assertion that as Christ has ascended, even so must the believer ascend, he bases this truth on certain principles – principles which he continually implies are accepted by both himself and his hearers. These are: 1. That salvation is the work of God, for it is *He* who justifies and *He* who glorifies. 2. The preservation of the believer, for he recognizes an unbreakable link between justification and glorification. 3. The particular nature of redemption, expressed in his statement, 'Christ has purchased for, and in due time will actually confer on all true believers, eternal glory'. These tenets, important elements of Calvinistic theology, are inherent in this sermon, preached when he was twenty-two.[1]

How then are we to appraise these early sermons?

It is true that they contain a few paragraphs in which the thought is immature, and others which reveal that at times he still entertained the idea that human striving necessarily preceded salvation. But it is likewise true that they are far removed from the triviality and emotionalism which has been supposed, also that they are free from the wordiness and tendency toward bombast which mark a short period of his later ministry. Their use of language is correct, the range of subjects is varied, and the presentation, while not always simple, is invariably simplified.

But the chief characteristic of this preaching is its Biblical content. Throughout these sermons there runs one great Scriptural truth – the truth indicated by Whitefield when he summarized his early ministry and its effect, saying, 'The doctrine of the New Birth and Justification by Faith (though I was not so

[1] *A Farewell Sermon*, 'Preached in the Parish Church of Stonehouse, Gloucestershire, on Ascension Day, 1737, by the Rev George Whitefield, B.A.' Text, *Romans* 8: 30. At the request of the hearers, Whitefield left the manuscript of this sermon at Stonehouse. More than a century elapsed before it was published. (Simpkin, Marshall, London, 1842).

clear in it as afterwards) made its way like lightning into the hearers' consciences'. He stood, not as declaring his own message, but that of God as set forth in His Word, 'Ye must be born again'.

In fact, Whitefield in the pulpit was but a reflection of Whitefield in the study. The hours on his knees with the Bible, the Greek New Testament and some rich Puritan volume spread out before him, were his preparation for this pressing and powerful ministry. So fully had he drunk of the wells of Biblical exposition in Matthew Henry that much of his public utterance was little more than the thought of the great commentator – thought that had become assimilated in his own mind and soul, and poured forth spontaneously both as he prepared and as he preached his sermons.

It is foolish to compare,[1] as some have done, the sermons of Whitefield at so early an age with those of other men who wrote in their prime. These sermons must be taken for what they are – the works of a youth – and for what they seek to be: simplified declarations of Scriptural truth. Viewed as such they must be regarded as creditable, and sometimes remarkable, productions.

[1] Whitefield's authentic sermons (excluding seventeen which were published without his knowledge or consent) number sixty-three, forty-six of which he produced before he was twenty-five years of age. Since this circumstance has usually been overlooked by the critics, their complaints are levelled against these youthful productions, equally with those of his later years.

Roused from the sleep of death, a countless crowd,
Whose hearts like trees before the wind are bow'd . . .
Press to the hallow'd courts, with eager strife,
Catch the convincing word, and hear for life,
Parties and sects their endless feuds forget,
And fall and tremble at the Preacher's feet . . .
While yet he speaks the Lord Himself comes down,
Applies and proves the gracious word His own,
The Holy Ghost to thirsty souls imparts,
And writes forgiveness on the broken hearts.

CHARLES WESLEY
An Elegy on Whitefield

7

Lasting Results

AMONG the crowds that thronged to hear Whitefield during these days in London, there were not only the poor and middle classes but several of England's nobility also. The biographer of Lady Huntingdon tells us:

The preaching of Mr Whitefield now excited an unusual degree of attention among persons of all ranks. In many of the city churches he proclaimed the glad tidings of great joy to listening multitudes, who were powerfully affected by the fire which was displayed in the animated addresses of this man of God. Lord and Lady Huntingdon constantly attended wherever he preached and Lady Anne Frankland became one of the first fruits of his ministry among the nobility . . .[1]

Lady Huntingdon became an exceptionally earnest Christian and invited her acquaintances to hear Whitefield. One of these was Sarah, Duchess of Marlborough, the wife of England's famous warrior, the Duke of Marlborough – progenitors of a line that is now noted for its most prominent son, Sir Winston Churchill. The great Sarah was altogether a woman of the world, but she wrote:

My dear Lady Huntingdon is always so very good to me that I must accept your very obliging invitation to accompany you to hear Mr Whitefield . . . God knows we all need mending, and none more than myself. I have lived to see great changes in the world, have acted a conspicuous part myself, and now hope in my old days, to obtain mercy from God, as I never expect any at the hands of my fellow creatures. The Duchess of Ancaster, Lady Townsend and Lady Cobham were exceedingly pleased with many observations in Mr Whitefield's sermon in St Sepulchre's Church, which has made me lament ever since that I did not hear it, as it might have been the means

[1] *The Life and Times of the Countess of Huntingdon* (London, 1840), Vol 1, *p* 20.

of doing me some good; *for good, alas! I do want;* but where, among the corrupt sons and daughters of Adam, am I to find it?[1]

Another of the noble ladies, the proud Duchess of Buckingham replied to Lady Huntingdon's invitation to hear Whitefield thus:

. . . It is monstrous to be told, that you have a heart as sinful as the common wretches that crawl on the earth. This is highly offensive and insulting; and I cannot but wonder that your Ladyship should relish any sentiments so much at variance with high rank and good breeding . . . I shall be most happy to accept your kind offer of accompanying me to hear your favourite preacher, and shall wait your arrival. The Duchess of Queensberry insists on my patronising her on this occasion; consequently she will be an addition to our party.[2]

During his ministry at Bath Whitefield had been a guest at the home of Lady Coxe. From among the nobility who frequented Bath there had come the first gift for the poor of Georgia – a spontaneous act on their part, amounting to £160 – and these people had likewise been the first to urge Whitefield to put his sermons into print. Nor was the interest an empty one, for throughout the years of the revival several from this privileged class were among those converted to Christ in both England and Scotland.

*

The blaze of public attention into which Whitefield was thrust created many difficulties for him. From this early day onward, he could no longer live in the relaxation of the private citizen, but was constantly under the strain of public scrutiny. He was allowed little private life, for awakened souls came crowding into his lodgings at almost any hour, till often he could scarcely find time to eat and his sleep was reduced to a minimum. Isaac Taylor, comparing the extent of his fame with that of other men, asserted there had never been such popularity in the life of so young a

[1] *Ibid*, Vol 1, *p* 25. In another letter the Duchess of Marlborough says, '*When I am alone, my reflections* and recollections *almost* kill me. Now there is Lady Frances Saunderson's great rout to-morrow night – all the world will be there, and I must go. I do hate that woman as much as I do hate a physician, but I must go, if for no other purpose than to mortify and spite her. This is very wicked, I know, but I confess all my little peccadillos to you . . .' *Ibid.*

[2] *Ibid*, *p* 27.

person, either 'in the church or out of it', as that accorded Whitefield 'on his first coming before the world'.[1]

Whitefield reported that, during these days in London,

The tide of popularity began to run very high. In a short time I could no longer walk on foot as usual, but was constrained to go in a coach from place to place, to avoid the hosannas of the multitude. They grew quite extravagant in their applauses, and had it not been for my compassionate High Priest, popularity would have destroyed me. I used to plead with Him to take me by the hand and lead me unhurt through this fiery furnace. He heard my request and gave me to see the vanity of all commendations but His own.[2]

Though Whitefield was fully aware of his extraordinary fame and made frequent mention of it in his *Journals*, he did not allow it to move him from his course. Many a man has been ruined by but a fraction of the adulation that he received, and he did indeed find it 'a fiery furnace'. But God had prepared him for this trial, and shortly after his conversion he had expressed his outlook, praying:

O Heavenly Father, for Thy dear Son's sake, keep me from climbing. Let me hate preferment. For Thine infinite mercies' sake, let me love a low contemptible life, and never think to compound matters between the happiness of this world and the next.[3]

Upon first finding himself subject to the praises of the people at Bristol he had requested in a letter to Gabriel Harris:

O pray, dear Mr Harris, that God would always keep me humble and fully convinced that I am nothing without Him, and that all the good which is done upon earth, God doeth it Himself . . . Sanctify it, Holy Father, to Thine own glory and Thy people's good.[4]

He sought to prevent the displays of attention that the people sometimes attempted. For instance, on the occasion of leaving Bristol he had written:

About three (in the) morning, having thrown myself on the bed for an hour or two, I set out for Gloucester, because I had heard that a great company [of people] intended to see me out of town.[5]

[1] Isaac Taylor, *Wesley and Methodism* (Harper, New York, 1860), *p* 103.
[2] *Journals*, *p* 89. [3] Tyerman, Vol 1, *p* 39. [4] *Works*, Vol 1, *p* 24.
[5] *Journals*, *p* 85.

Such had been Whitefield's attitude already, but amidst the overweening acclaim of London, it grew still stronger. The pressure of popularity was, in fact, used of God in effecting a new and deeper work of grace within his soul, for it caused him to become acutely aware of the coming great day when he would give an account before the judgment seat of Christ. In the light of the all importance of gaining the Saviour's approval on that eternal morning, the acclaims of earth paled into insignificance. Thus we find him making frequent use of such expressions as, 'It is a small thing to be judged of man's judgment – to my Master I stand or fall', and 'In a little while "we must all stand before the judgment seat of Christ", where I shall give a strict account of the doctrine I have preached'. The words, 'He gave me to see the vanity of all commendations but His own', open a window into Whitefield's soul, and this constant awareness of the coming day of accounting became from this time forth one of the underlying principles of his life.

His popularity, however, could have brought him the widest of esteem had that been his aim. With a little compromise here and a little accommodation of his message there, with care not to stand too strongly for anything and not to offend anyone, he could have enjoyed almost unbroken good will and could have avoided entirely the life of conflict. Such would have been to his liking in one sense, for by nature he was a man of peace, and he enjoyed his status of being a very correct and respected young clergyman, and a dutiful son of the Church of England.

Nevertheless, Whitefield had not been in the public eye two or three months before his doctrinal convictions and his ideals regarding the ministry began to bring him into conflict. Aroused by the dearth of Gospel preaching in the churches, he stated in his *Preface* to his published sermon on *The New Birth*:

> I hope it will be permitted me to add my hearty wishes that my Reverend Brethren, the Ministers of the Church of England, would more frequently entertain their people with discourses of this nature, than they commonly do; and that they would not, out of a servile fear of displeasing particular persons, fail to declare the whole will of God.[1]

Of course, such words provoked opposition, and two ministers

[1] *The Nature and Necessity of Our New Birth in Christ Jesus in Order to Salvation*, Preface to 1738 edition, *p* 5.

told him that unless he withdrew them they would never again allow him to use their pulpits.

This was, however, but the first voice of complaint. His popularity and his success in raising money – in four months he 'collected about £1,000 for the Charity Schools and got upwards of £300 for the poor of Georgia, – aroused the jealousy of many a ministerial heart and his zeal disturbed the comforts of the average clerical life.

At first [he writes], many of the clergy were my hearers and admirers; but some soon grew angry, and complaints were made that the churches were so crowded that there was no room for the parishioners and that the pews were spoiled. Some called me a spiritual pick-pocket and others thought I used some kind of charm to get the people's money. A report was spread abroad that, on complaint of the clergy, the Bishop of London intended to *silence* me.[1]

But it was the doctrine of the new birth which proved the especially divisive factor in Whitefield's associations. Without fully realizing what he was doing, he began to carry this teaching through to its logical conclusions. He saw that all who had not experienced regeneration were not truly Christians, and that all who had, even though they might not be members of the Church of England, were his brothers in Christ. Between himself and the former he found a growing sense of separation, while with the latter he could not fail to establish ties of fellowship. Thus he says,

What irritated some of my enemies the more, was my free conversation with many of the serious Dissenters, . . . My practice in . . . associating with them, I thought, was quite agreeable to the Word of God. Their conversation was savoury, and I imagined the best way to bring them over was not by bigotry and railing, but by moderation and love, and by undissembled holiness of life.[2]

Of course, someone used Whitefield's popularity and zeal as a means of expressing the common contempt for the clergy. 'Some ill-minded persons', he states, 'painted me leaning on a cushion, with a bishop looking very enviously over my shoulder. At the bottom were six lines, in one of which the bishops were styled "Mitred Drones". The same person published in the paper that

[1] *Journals*, *p* 89. [2] *Ibid*, *p* 90.

I had sat for it.'[1] At the same time, the Rev Dr Hooker, editor of *The Weekly Miscellany*, the principal Church of England paper, began a series of articles in which, though he did not mention Whitefield by name, he steadily belittled his ministry and sought to give it the appearance of fanaticism.

To such treatment Whitefield constantly turned the other cheek. His followers were quickly aroused by anything said or done against him and when one minister called him 'a pragmatical rascal', it 'stirred up' he says, 'the people's corruptions, and having an overweening fondness for me, whenever they came to church and found that I did not preach, some of them would go out again. This spirit I always endeavoured to quell.'[2] Of another instance he says, 'Hearing that a churchwarden intended to take £8 a year from his parish minister because he refused to let me preach, I composed a sermon on "Love your enemies".'[3] He showed his high regard for the office held by the clergy and his desire to avoid a merely personal strife by exhorting his people, ' "Obey them that have the rule over you", and be always ready to attend on their ministry . . . Think not that I desire to have myself exalted at the expense of another's character.'[4]

Despite this attitude on Whitefield's part, the clerical dislike remained and increased, and more than one man of the cloth looked forward impatiently to the day when this disturber of the peace would be on his way to Georgia.

*

Amidst the commotion aroused by Whitefield's ministry, however, one thing was clear: the fruit it bore was of a solid and abiding nature. Its effect was no mere burst of emotion, here one week and gone the next. Nor did the work in a given location come to a standstill at his departure, but rather, it continued and even grew after he had left. For instance, while at London he frequently received letters that reported 'the springing up and increase of the seed sown in Bristol and Gloucester', though he had not been in these cities within three months.

The solid and lasting effects which accompanied Whitefield's

[1] *Ibid, p* 91. [2] *Ibid, p* 90. [3] *Ibid.*

[4] Sermon, 'Intercession: Every Christian's Duty', *Works*, Vol 6, *p* 342.

ministry must be attributed (in the human sense) to the thoroughness of the methods he used in dealing with souls.

It must be explained that Whitefield made no appeal for people to make a public profession of salvation at his services. His practice (which had also been that of the Puritans) was one of making powerful application of the Gospel as he preached and of therewith leaving the Word to become operative in the heart by the ministry of the Holy Spirit. He looked for the Spirit's work in arousing the sinner to a deep, and even overwhelming, sense of his need, but this work he called, not *conversion*, but *awakening*.[1]

Many of these awakened ones sought him out in private, that they might ask his further counsel and beg a place in his prayers. So large were the numbers of those who came that he found it necessary, both in this early ministry and throughout all his later life, to announce certain hours at which he would be available for this purpose. In these interviews he taught that the illumination of the mind and the implanting of faith in the heart are entirely the work of the Holy Spirit. He urged the seeker to go directly to the Lord, entreating that this saving work might be done within him. He directed the needy soul to the Gospel promises and told him to plead them before God, and, on the basis of them, to seek the assurance that this Divine work was accomplished within his heart.

Yet Whitefield gave no seeker reason to believe that such an interview was essential to, or necessarily productive of, salvation. His emphasis was ever that salvation is a Divine work, a matter between the human soul and the Lord, and many left his presence to continue to seek – some for days and even weeks – and to entreat God to make them the objects of His mercy. But numerous persons came again to Whitefield, and many others wrote to him, telling him, often with abounding joy and deep assurance, that this work had indeed been accomplished within them. Yet, even then, he still refused to count converts. He chose to wait until conversion had been manifested by months of a transformed life, and his attitude is well expressed in his words, 'Only the judgment morning will reveal who the converts really are'.

[1] One of the 1739 editions of Whitefield's sermon on *The New Birth* contained also 'A Prayer for One Desiring to be Awakened to an Experience of the New Birth, and another for One Newly Awakened to a Sense of the Divine Life'.

Whitefield had abundant reason, however, to believe that this work was effected under his ministry in the hearts of many. As we have seen, his reports contain such statements as, 'Several young men came to me under serious impressions', 'The arrows of conviction stuck fast', and 'They were all attention and heard like people hearing for eternity'. At the close of his ministry in Bristol he wrote, 'I was employed from seven in the morning till midnight, in giving spiritual advice to awakened souls'.[1] In the midst of his three months in London he stated, 'Many youths here sincerely love our Lord Jesus Christ, and thousands, I hope, are quickened, strengthened and confirmed by the word preached'.[2] Late in December he reported, 'There was no end of persons coming to me under soul concern. God blessed me more and more and supported me with but very little sleep'.[3] 'There is no end of persons coming and weeping', he says in still another report, 'telling me what God has done for their souls . . . Time would fail me to relate how many have been awakened and how many pray for me. The great day will discover all.'[4]

As the time of his departure for Georgia approached Whitefield made preparations to assist the continued spiritual growth of these people. Together with 'a sweet knot of religious friends', he 'began to set apart an hour each evening to intercede with the Great Head of the Church to carry on the work begun'.[5] Nothing could have been further from his concept of the Christian life than merely to leave these babes in Christ on their own, and since he knew they would find little help from the clergy, he turned to the Religious Societies. The biographer of James Hutton tells us:

> By his [Whitefield's] powerful sermons many were moved and awakened. When they applied to him personally for advice, he, being about to leave England, recommended them to the Society raised by Hutton and his friends, by which it was much increased and made known . . . The elder and new Societies came into a more intimate connection, and the preaching of Whitefield caused a new life to spring up among the members.[6]

In their zeal, their evangelical solidarity and their allegiance

[1] *Journals*, *p* 85. [2] *Works*, Vol 1, *p* 30. [3] *Journals*, *p* 92.
[4] *Works*, Vol 1, *p* 32. [5] *Journals*, *p* 91.
[6] Daniel Benham, *Memoirs of James Hutton* (London, 1856), *p* 14.

to Whitefield, these people constituted the beginnings of a movement. But he had not the least thought of forming a new denomination. On the contrary, he saw his work as within the bounds of the Church of England, as true to her *Articles* and labouring for a renewal of her spiritual life.

*

As 1737 drew to its close, despite the extraordinary success of his ministry, Whitefield decided that he could no longer postpone his sailing for Georgia.

At the beginning of Christmas week [he writes], I took my leave. But, oh, what groans and sighs were to be heard when I said, 'Finally, brethren, farewell!' At Great St Helen's the cry was amazing. I was nearly half an hour going out to the door. All ranks gave vent to their passions. They would run and stop me in the alleys, hug me in their arms, and follow me with wishful looks. Once, in the Christmas before my departure, with many others I spent a night in prayer and praise, and in the morning helped to administer the Sacrament at St Dunstan's . . . But such a Sacrament I never saw before. The tears of the communicants mingled with the cup and had not Jesus comforted our hearts, our parting would have been almost insupportable.[1]

But even then the people would not let it be a final farewell. Whitefield boarded his vessel, the *Whitaker*, at Purfleet (a few miles down the Thames from London) on December 30, and many of his friends followed him there. Since the vessel was not yet ready to sail, Whitefield went ashore and on the New Year's Day (a Sunday) was joined by several more friends who had travelled down the river all night in order to see him once more. It was a day of preaching, prayer and parting.

While awaiting a favourable wind the *Whitaker* put in at the ports of Gravesend and Margate, affording Whitefield the opportunity to go ashore and preach. Finally three weeks were spent at Deal, and during that time his ministry was so used of God that the town and surrounding area experienced blessings similar to those of London. Each evening a crowd surged into the house where he lodged, and so many were they that the poor landlady feared the floor would break. Thus Whitefield had them come in two separate companies, but it was soon necessary to have three and then four, and he expounded from six o'clock

[1] *Journals*, p 92.

till ten. On his last Sunday in England (January 29) he was 'accompanied with a troop of pious friends to Shroulden Church . . . where [he] preached to a weeping and thronged congregation'. Such was the blessing during his three weeks' stay that he exclaimed, 'All Deal seems to be in a holy flame!'

These days marked a further development in Whitefield's ministry. Before leaving London he had begun to pray extempore, and while at these down-river ports he added extempore preaching – a form of ministry without which his later open-air preaching would have been impossible.

We may well wonder if Whitefield did not feel some tinge of regret in leaving so great a work as had been his in England. 'Large offers were made me', he writes, 'if I would stay in London'; yet he was relinquishing all this in order to become a missionary to a sparsely populated colony in a wilderness area of America. The little vessel meant weeks of confinement, poor food and a passage that could hardly fail to entail sickness and danger. But when some of the Gloucester people wrote, urging him to remain, he replied, 'Let not my friends trouble me with temporal offers. I shall accept of no place this side Jordan'.[1]

Accordingly, from aboard the vessel he stated, 'I considered it was the Divine will that placed me here, and therefore I rejoiced. He is unworthy the name of a Christian who is not as willing to hide himself when God commands, as to act in a public capacity.'[2]

Back in Bristol, Gloucester and London, hundreds of people prayed for him, bought his printed sermons and impatiently awaited the reports of his activities abroad that he had promised to send to James Hutton. Charles Wesley, who had returned from Georgia a few months earlier, viewing the marvellous results of Whitefield's preaching wrote: 'The whole nation is in an uproar . . .'[3] Similarly, James Hervey exclaimed, 'All London and the whole nation ring of the great things of God done by his ministry'.[4] And on board the *Whitaker*, Whitefield, apparently thinking of the strange troubles the Wesleys had encountered in Georgia, prayed, 'God give me a deep humility, a well-guided zeal, a burning love and a single eye, and then let men or devils do their worst!'[5]

[1] *Works*, Vol 1, *p* 30. [2] *Journals*, *p* 104. [3] Tyerman, *op cit*, Vol 1, *p* 112.
[4] Tyerman, *The Oxford Methodists op cit*, *p* 215. [5] *Works*, Vol 1, *p* 33.

The remembrance of the happy hours I enjoyed in religious exercises on the deck, is refreshing to my soul. And though nature sometimes relented at being taken from my friends, and little accustomed to the inconvenience of a sea-life, yet a consciousness that I had in view the glory of God and the good of souls, from time to time afforded me unspeakable satisfaction.

WHITEFIELD
Manuscript quoted by Gillies

8

Military Chaplain

WHITEFIELD had made some fairly extensive preparations for his work in Georgia.

He took with him five young men,[1] having selected them with a view to certain requirements of the Colony. Two were teachers, for he planned to establish schools for the settlers' children. Two others were servants and he intended to have them do the housekeeping – a prudent arrangement which would mean a totally male household, and would avoid the necessity of bringing in outside (particularly female) help.

The fifth man, James Habersham, was to be his personal assistant. Whitefield saw goodly qualities in him which he wished to cultivate, and wrote, 'O that I may be made an instrument of breeding him up for God'.[2] While on board ship he gave him lessons in Latin and since he cherished the hope of building an orphan house in the Colony, he already planned to use Habersham as its superintendent.

Whitefield had also taken pains to inform himself of the everyday needs of the colonists, and in the light of this knowledge had purchased a vast array of goods. In keeping with wise public relations he published *An Account of Money Received and Expended for the Poor of Georgia*. Tyerman made an abridgement of this document and in this shortened form the expenditure section reads as follows:

Whitefield's items of disbursement are curious. First there is £50 paid to the Trustees of Georgia 'towards building a church at Frederica'. Then there are divers payments for books, pamphlets and tracts,

[1] The names of four of these have come down to us. They were James Habersham, William Doble, Joseph Husbands and Robert Hows.
[2] *Journals*, p 110.

including Flavel's Husbandry, Jenks' Devotion, Norris On Prudence, Wesley's Forms of Prayer, Law's Call and Perfection, the Bishop of the Isle of Man's Catechism, Reeve's Apology, 100 sermons entitled The Christian Soldier by Thomas Broughton, 150 Common Prayer Books, 25 Copies of Watts' Songs, 130 small Chapmen's Books, 50 Bellamy's Christian Schoolmaster, 50 Spelling Books, 6 Nelson's Festivals, 74 Organist's Pocket Companions, 200 Country Parson's Advice, Arndt's True Christianity, etc., etc.

The clothing, harberdashery, and other kindred items are far too numerous to be detailed, but include the following: stockings for men, women, boys and girls; shoes for ditto; caps for boys; three dozen hats; six dozen women's caps; twenty-four striped flannel waistcoats; twenty-six pairs of canvas breeches; to which must be added Holland tapes, Manchester tapes, beggars' tapes, thread, cotton laces, yard-wide cottons, handkerchiefs, and twelve dozens of shirt buttons.

The hardware list includes the following: a dozen tinder boxes, a dozen tin pots, three dozen ink-horns, two dozen leather ink-pots, four dozen stone seals, six claw hammers, three dozen gunflints, a dozen of six-case knives, a gross of sleeve buttons, thirteen pen-knives for Savannah school, sixteen dozens of corks, fifty pounds of shot, a hundredweight and a quarter of shot, sixty-four pounds of gun-powder, scissors, buckles, corkscrews, ivory combs, horn combs, spoons, pewter porringers, nails, gouges, gimblets, axes, files, chisels, planes, hatchets, saws, shovels, spades, locks, hinges and fishing tackle.

The list of drugs comprises: rhubarb, senna, manna, Jesuit's bark, pearl-barley, ipecacuanha, sago, saffron, snake-root, gentian-root, cochineal, hartshorn powder, isinglass, etc.

Among the household provisions are the following: a firkin of butter, a Cheshire cheese, a Gloucestershire cheese, one hundred lemons, two hogsheads of fine white wine, three barrels of raisins, to which must be added such various items as cinnamon, sugar, brimstone, cloves, mustard, pepper, oatmeal, oranges, potatoes, onions and sage.

The stationery account includes four reams of foolscap writing paper, half a pound of wafers, three thousand second quills, sealing wax, copybooks, lead-pencils, slate pencils and ingredients to make ink.[1]

This is but a partial list of Whitefield's purchases. We may be

[1] Tyerman's *Whitefield*, Vol 1, *pp* 108–10. The form of the quotation from Tyerman is slightly altered; a section in which he listed items in a column, giving the price of each, is changed into a paragraph and the prices are omitted.

tempted to smile as we visualize the youth, shopping around London and gathering this variegated supply of goods, but tinder boxes and stockings, buttons and saffron, cheeses and axes, these and the rest of his items, not only bespeak his benevolence and forethought, but indicate that his boyhood in the inn had given him a goodly understanding of everyday life.

*

While the *Whitaker*, carrying Whitefield *to* America, was waiting to sail out of the port of Deal, the *Samuel*, bringing John Wesley *from* America, sailed in.

Wesley's life at this point stood in marked contrast to that of Whitefield. In later years their careers were to run in parallel channels, with the Divine blessing bountifully bestowed on each, but at this earlier time they were widely different. There lay before Wesley some months of seeking and striving before he was to become a mighty evangelist and we shall notice later the events in which this development took place. But as he returned to England he was heavy with a sense of frustration and failure.

Wesley had gone to Georgia with one supreme purpose: 'My chief motive', he had then declared, 'is the hope of saving my own soul'.[1] He had thought of salvation as coming by way of the Holy Club type of discipline and believed that a continuation of such practices, assisted by the enduring of privations in the Colony, would serve toward that end. He anticipated a pleasant ministry among the Indians and a position of authority among settlers and felt that, with such success, his salvation would largely be achieved.

But he returned to his homeland with these hopes shattered. He was in bitter dejection, for his whole person was shaken by the realization that salvation was not to be gained by any programme of human effort. Now he knew he must be changed inwardly and confessed, 'What have I learned? Why, what I the least of all suspected, that I who went to America to convert others, was never myself converted to God.'[2]

Wesley had been taught this truth by the Moravians. These

[1] John Wesley's *Journal*, Vol 8, *p* 288.

[2] *Ibid*, Vol 1, *p* 422.

were a German people, a small party[1] of whom had been aboard the vessel which carried him out to Georgia. He noticed their willingness to perform menial tasks for the other passengers, but his chief surprise came when the vessel[2] encountered a violent storm. A raging sea broke over the ship and while, as he reports, 'A terrible screaming began among the English', these Germans – men, women and children – calmly sang a hymn of trust and praise.

Wesley was both delighted and startled by their behaviour: delighted to know there was a relationship with God which could provide such peace, and startled to realize that these Christians possessed something to which he was a stranger, for, amidst the storm he admitted, 'I was afraid to die!'[3]

The impression thus made was deepened by further association with these and other Moravians during his months in Georgia. One of their leaders, Augustus Gottlieb Spangenberg, replied to certain of Wesley's questions with the enquiries, 'Does the Spirit of God bear witness with your spirit that you are a child of God?' 'Do you know Jesus Christ?' and 'Do you know He has saved your soul?' To this probing Wesley had no clear answers, but recognized that, scholar and clergyman though he was, he was ignorant of the assurance of which the German spoke. These associations with the Moravians were his first contacts with evangelical Christianity and they left a lasting mark.

Wesley's days in Georgia also taught him that he knew little about human nature. His training had been somewhat unbalanced, for he had left home as a boy of ten to go to the Charterhouse School and from there, at seventeen, directly to the University. Thus, apart from the almost two and a half years in which he had served as curate to his father at Epworth and Wroote, he had known little but the scholastic life.

In later years Wesley proved himself a most astute judge of character but at this earlier time, as Dr Curnock, the editor of his *Journal*, points out, 'He could not discern spirits. He misread

[1] This party consisted of twenty men, besides women and children. An earlier party had sailed in 1735 aboard *The Two Brothers,* and had numbered ten men and some women and children.

[2] 'the Symonds . . . a ship of about 250 tons and 19 sailors.' *Manuscripts of the Earl of Egmont*, Vol 2, *p* 200.

[3] John Wesley's *Journal*, Vol. 1, *p* 138.

the simplest facts . . . for a while he became the sport of fools and hypocrites.'[1] While crossing to Georgia, two unscrupulous women were able to make him the butt of much mischief and, during his stay in the Colony he was kept embroiled in discords with the people in general. It is true that the colonists were a troublesome lot, but a wiser man could have avoided such frictions. A sense of humour would have helped and had he been able to exchange one of his years at school for the experience Whitefield had gained in the inn, he would have understood mankind better.

Charles Wesley had also found little but trouble in Georgia. He had served, not specifically as a missionary but as secretary to General Oglethorpe and this lack of spiritual activity had caused Whitefield, in writing to him, to say:

> My friend will not take it amiss if I inquire why he chooses to be secretary . . . and not rather go where labourers are so much wanted, in the character of a missionary. Did the Bishop ordain us, my dear friend, to write bonds, receipts, etc., or to preach the Gospel?[2]

Charles became involved in a bitter misunderstanding with the General and endured his suspicion and his wrath to such an extent that he grew sick, nigh unto death. In the disputes with the settlers he was sometimes faced with threats of violence, and after less than six months in the Colony, his poetically sensitive soul could stand no more and he returned in despondency to England.

John's stay in the Colony was brought to a close by an innocent but unwise love affair. Sophia Hopkey, the young lady of his affections, finding he would not make up his mind regarding marriage, suddenly married another man. John was deeply wounded, and shortly thereafter debarred her from the communion service. This was a foolish action which crystallized the feelings of the people against him. Sophia's husband sued him for £1,000 for defamation of her character, and a notice was posted for his arrest. John was able, however, to escape under cover of night to Charleston, South Carolina, from whence he

[1] *Ibid, p* 174.
[2] Tyerman's *Whitefield,* Vol 1, *p* 62.

quickly sailed for home. This was the only visit he ever made to America and it had lasted but a year and ten months.

Notwithstanding their difficulties, the Wesleys manifested many ministerial qualities during their Georgia days. Their lives were marked by unceasing industry and self-sacrificing labour. John was exceptionally faithful in his pastoral duties and, though his church services did not draw many (it would appear from his *Journal* that thirty or forty was the usual congregation) those who did attend heard a very earnest preacher. Dr Curnock says that while in the Colony John 'learnt German, Spanish, Italian and conversational French, compiled many grammars and some dictionaries, [and] condensed several books of devotion, biography, theology and ecclesiastical history, . . .'[1] Having become acquainted with German hymns, he translated some of them into English – translations which were almost compositions in themselves and which merit a place among the finest hymns of all time.

One would wonder then, why men of such qualities failed as they did in Georgia. The answer is that they were hindered by certain traits which they had inherited from their father, the Rev Samuel Wesley, M.A., rector of the Lincolnshire parishes of Epworth and Wroote. Samuel was an intense little man, possessing a vigorous mind, quenchless ambition, ripe scholarship and 'courage enough' we are told, 'for a whole troop of British cavalry'. In the labour of the study or the oversight of the flock, few men were more diligent, and anyone seeing only this side of him would regard him as nothing but an earnest and godly clergyman.

But there was also another side to Samuel Wesley. Despite his religious sincerity he was severely domineering, and his daughters and parishioners suffered under his imperious demands. He was sorely impractical in business matters and constantly created antagonisms in his relationships with the public. He was the kind of man who would never admit to being in the wrong, and when his will was thwarted he could be merciless and vindictive. In short, there were two distinct sides to Samuel Wesley, and so contradictory were they that he must be considered as very largely a dual personality.[2]

[1] John Wesley's *Journal*, Vol 1, *p* 425.

[2] Sir Arthur Quiller-Couch, in his *Hetty Wesley* (his story depicting Samuel's heart-

The common practice of overlooking this family background has proved seriously misleading in the study of Charles and John. Along with the magnificent qualities which they had inherited from their mother, these men had manifestly received, in some measure, certain of the characteristics of their father. They too proved impractical, tended to be domineering, and created antagonisms – traits we see in John's own report that while in Georgia Magistrate Horton said to him:

I like nothing you do. All your sermons are satires upon particular persons, therefore I will never hear you more; and all the people are of my mind, for we won't hear ourselves abused.

Besides, they say they are Protestants. But as for you, they cannot tell what religion you are of . . . And then your private behaviour – all the quarrels that have been here since you came have been 'long of you. Indeed, there is neither man nor woman in the town who minds a word you say.[1]

The Earl of Egmont, President of the Trustees for Georgia, likewise saw something of the dual personality in John, saying of him:

He appeared to us to be a very odd mixture of a man, an enthusiast and at the same time a hypocrite, wholly distasteful to the greater part of the inhabitants.[2]

A knowledge of John Wesley's background and of his days in Georgia is essential to our present study. It helps to remove that aura of near perfection which has become attached to him, and lets us see the real man – the man of limitations and faults like other men. It reveals that a struggle lay before him in overcoming his deficiencies and gives us a truer understanding of the man with whom Whitefield was to be associated throughout most of the rest of his life. Above all, it lets us see the troubled situation into which Whitefield was moving as he sailed toward Georgia.

*

less behaviour toward his most gifted daughter) quotes extensively from letters written in the Wesley home as the basis of his narrative. Though Samuel's good side is not sufficiently shown by Sir Arthur, the evidence regarding the other side of his nature is conclusive. This paternal background has never been adequately recognized by John's biographers and the omission is seriously misleading.

[1] John Wesley's *Journal*, Vol 1, *p* 234.

[2] *The Letters of John Wesley*, Vol 1, *p* 365.

The experiences in the Colony proved very hard for Wesley to bear. Though his earlier years had contained little but scholastic success, he was forced to recognize that in his first venture out into the world of practical affairs he was largely a failure. But more grievous still was his sense of spiritual defeat: 'I went to America', he confessed, 'to convert the Indians; but, oh, who shall convert me? who, what is he that will deliver me from this evil heart of unbelief?'[1]

It was in this spirit of depression that Wesley landed at Deal. On the previous evening Whitefield had concluded his three weeks of ministry there. As he had boarded his ship 'the Deal people . . . came running in droves after [him] . . . and with tears and other expressions of kindness praying for [his] success and safe return'.[2] When Wesley arrived Whitefield's vessel was still in the harbour and we may be sure that the town was alive with talk of his preaching.

Strange as it may seem, though Wesley learned of the presence of his young friend, he made no attempt to see him. Instead, he cast a lot – a practice learned from the Moravians – in order to determine whether or not Whitefield should continue his journey. Therewith he despatched a note to him which read, in part, 'When I saw that God, by the wind which was carrying you out, brought me in, I asked counsel of God. His answer you have enclosed.'[3] The answer was the slip of paper he had picked in the lot, and on it were the words, 'Let him return to London'. Having delivered his message and preached in the inn at Deal, he himself set out for London.[4]

Though Whitefield was amazed by Wesley's action, he was in

[1] John Wesley's *Journal*, Vol 1, *p* 418.

[2] Whitefield's *Journals*, *p* 119.

[3] *Ibid*, *p* 572.

[4] The following extenuating circumstances should be noticed: 1. Wesley was probably too depressed to want to see anyone, even an old friend. 2. Since it was at his request that Whitefield was going to Georgia, he felt a personal responsibility in the matter. 3. The only previous association between the two men had been that at Oxford, when Wesley had been a Master of Arts and a Fellow and Whitefield a lowly servitor – a contrast which long remained in Wesley's mind. 4. In view of the conditions under which he had left the Colony, Wesley would probably want to avoid any conversation which might require him to mention them. 5. Wesley believed that the casting of a lot revealed the mind of God and therefore left nothing to be discussed; it needed only to be stated and obeyed. 6 It was probably some time before day dawn when Wesley reached the port of Deal.

no way deterred from his plans. He made an effort to see Wesley, but, finding he had left, wrote to him the following letter:

I received the news of your arrival (blessed be God!) with the utmost composure and sent a servant immediately on shore to wait on you, but found you were gone. Since that, your kind letter has reached me.

I think many reasons may be urged against my coming to London. For first, I cannot be hid if I come there; and the enemies of the Lord will think I am turning back, and so blaspheme that holy name wherewith I am called. Secondly, I cannot leave the flock committed to my care on shipboard, and perhaps while I am in London the ship may sail. Thirdly, I see no cause for my not going forward to Georgia. Your coming rather confirms (as far as I can see) than disannuls my call. It is not fit the colony should be left without a shepherd; and though they are a stiff-necked and rebellious people, yet as God hath given me the affections of all where I have been, why should I despair of finding His presence in a foreign land?[1]

Whitefield's letter speaks for itself. We shall return later to the story of Wesley and his Aldersgate Street experience. In the meantime we notice that Whitefield, after expressing his disappointment at not meeting Wesley at Deal, said, 'I considered God ordered all things for the best', and therewith continued his journey.

*

Whitefield's actions during the passage to America reveal certain important facets of his personality which have usually been overlooked.

On board the *Whitaker*, besides its crew under a Captain Whiting, there were about a hundred soldiers (under a Captain Mackay), twenty or so women and a few children. Two other vessels, the *Amy* and the *Lightfoot*, were travelling with the *Whitaker* and were sailing first for Gibraltar, where more soldiers were to be taken aboard. The military contingent was then to be transported to Georgia, that it might serve in defending the Colony against the Spaniards from Florida.

Whitefield was to act as chaplain to the soldiers, but he looked upon himself as responsible to minister also to all aboard the three vessels. On his first morning aboard the *Whitaker* he held

[1] Tyerman's *Whitefield*, Vol 1, *p* 115.

public prayers and declared his intention 'to know nothing among [them] save Jesus Christ and Him crucified'. His statement met instant scorn and Dr Gillies tells us:

The captains, both of the soldiers and sailors, with the surgeon and a young cadet, gave him soon to understand that they looked on him as an impostor, and for a while treated him as such. The first Lord's Day one of them played on the hautboy and nothing was to be seen but cards, and little heard but cursing and swearing. I could do no more for a season [writes Whitefield], than whilst I was writing, now and then turn my head by way of reproof to a lieutenant who swore as though he was born of a swearing constitution. Now and then he would take the hint, return my nod with a 'Doctor, I ask your pardon', and then to his swearing and cards again.[1]

In the face of this unpromising situation Whitefield began his attempt to reach all on board with the Gospel, and his efforts displayed an admirable blending of tact and zeal. He well revealed his attitude in his expression, 'Oh, that I may catch them with a holy guile!'

'I began to visit the sick,' he writes. The living conditions on such a vessel were undoubtedly wretched, and, because of seasickness and the frequency of other ailments, there were always several persons ill. Among these he went every day, extending encouragement, providing medicines and giving tasty items of food from the supply he had brought. Even while the ship was still in the Thames estuary he stated: 'The sick increased upon my hands, but were very thankful for my furnishing them with sage-tea, sugar, broth, etc. At the sight of so many objects of pity, I was sensibly touched with a fellow-feeling of their miseries. I could not but transverse the prodigal's complaint, "How many of my Father's children are ready to perish with hunger, whilst I have enough and to spare".'[2]

Each morning and evening Whitefield read prayers on the open deck. He did not dare, however, for the time being, add anything to this minimal activity, lest he deter the people from attending. Nevertheless, after four days had passed he began a

[1] Gillies, *op cit, pp* 17, 18. Gillies was here quoting from the earlier editions of Whitefield's Journals. The Journals as known today are the 1756 edition, from which certain passages were deleted.
[2] *Journals, p* 106.

catechism class for the soldiers. Only six or seven were present on this first occasion, but the numbers steadily increased, until in a week's time the class had an attendance of twenty, and the study had been enlarged to include an exposition of the Lord's Prayer. Finding this acceptance he began to preach whenever he read Prayers.

To these public efforts Whitefield added personal associations. These were principally with the officers and his *Journals* contain such reports as: 'Breakfasted with some of the gentlemen in the great cabin, who were very civil and let me put in a word for God.' 'Had an hour's conversation with a gentleman on board, on our fall in Adam and the necessity of our new birth in Christ Jesus, and hope it was not unpleasant to him.' 'Had some religious talk with the surgeon, who seems very well disposed.' 'Had near an hour's conversation with one who, I hope, will become an altogether Christian.' 'Gained an opportunity, by walking at night on the deck, to talk closely to the chief mate and one of the sergeants, and hope my words were not spoken in vain.' Yet he also established friendship with the crew and we find him writing, 'About eleven at night, I went and sat down with the sailors in the steerage, and reasoned with them about righteousness, temperance and a judgment to come.'

Steadily gaining the good will of all aboard, Whitefield quickly began other activities. He held a daily catechism class for the women and soon added a Bible study. He had Habersham give daily instruction in elementary education for the children, and also invited any soldiers and sailors who wished to learn to read and write to attend.

Then the ship's Master, Captain Whiting, began to show favour. Noticing that Whitefield had no place of privacy for study and prayer, he offered him the use of his cabin. Whitefield's practice of discipline and industry made such a place a boon, and in using it he reported, 'I fancied myself in my little cell at Oxford; for I have not spent so many hours in sweet retirement since I left the University'.[1]

While having 'a dish of coffee' with the military captain, Whitefield stated he 'thought it a little odd to pray and preach to the servants, and not to the master, and added withal, that if

[1] *Ibid, p* 108.

he thought it proper he would make use of a short collect now and then to himself and the other gentlemen in the great cabin'.[1] At first the captain demurred, but a few days later came to him to say he had been watching his conduct and 'expressed his appreciation of the good [he] was doing among the soldiers'. Forthwith, Whitefield read prayers in the great cabin each evening, and after a week's time the ship's captain requested that he should not confine himself to prayers, but that he give them a sermon too.

The next step was taken by Captain Whiting. Affected by the work of the Gospel on his own heart, and concerned now for the spiritual welfare of his men, he ordered that chairs be set out on the deck and planks placed across them for the soldiers and passengers to sit on during the services. Thus the deck of the *Whitaker* became a sort of floating chapel and, since Whitefield says that he 'arranged to meet with any soldiers who could sing by note, to join in Divine Psalmody every day', we can but wonder whether he intended to supply it with a male choir.

While passing through the Bay of Biscay the vessel was struck by a terrific storm. Something of its terror may be seen in Whitefield's description:

About twelve at night a gale arose which increased so much by four in the morning that the waves broke in like a great river on many of the poor soldiers who lay near the main hatchway . . . I arose and called upon God for myself and those who sailed with me, for absent friends and for all mankind.

After this I went on deck; but surely a more noble, awful sight my eyes never yet beheld. The waves rose mountains high and sometimes came on the quarter-deck. I endeavoured all the while to magnify God for thus making His power known. Then, creeping on my knees (for I knew not how to go otherwise), I followed my friend Habersham between decks and sang Psalms and comforted the poor wet people.

After this I read prayers in the great cabin, but we were obliged to sit all the while. Though things were tumbling, the ship rocking, persons falling down unable to stand, and sick about me, I never was more cheerful in my life, and was enabled, though in the midst of company, to finish a sermon before I went to bed.[2]

Such a report must not be passed with the mere mention. A winter night at sea, the relentless fury of the storm, the merciless

[1] Gillies, *op cit*, *pp* 18, 19. [2] *Journals*, *p* 124.

pitching of the little vessel – these circumstances were fearful enough, but what must conditions have been below deck? There, amidst darkness relieved only by a flickering lantern or two, with pools of sea water sloshing back and forth, sea-sickness and foul odour, the crying of the children, fear among the women and confusion everywhere, the two young men make their way on hands and knees, singing Psalms and bringing encouragement everywhere. No wonder Whitefield later admitted to being 'a little sick . . . from the heat and smell of the people between decks'.[1]

As the ship neared its first port the change aboard was widely manifest. It was but seven weeks since Whitefield had first met these men – then a scornful, cursing company. But God had so blessed his labours among them that now 'the soldiers stood forth like little children to say their Catechism', many read their Bibles regularly, and almost all attended Divine service morning and evening, seven days a week. Such were the fruits of his labour as the vessel cast anchor in the harbour of Gibraltar.

*

Whitefield found he was already known at the Rock and was treated as something of a celebrity. He was provided with goodly accommodation on shore, the ministers of the Church of England asked him to conduct daily prayers and to preach on Sundays, and the Governor invited him to dine daily at his mansion.

One would suppose that in the eighteenth century a military outpost such as Gibraltar would have been a place of iniquity and irreligion. It proved, however, to be much the opposite. The Governor made it his practice to attend church daily, and several officers followed his example. Whitefield was particularly pleased with the behaviour of the members of a kind of Religious Society called *The New Lights*. In one instance he reported:

> . . . was pleased at my entrance into the church, to see several soldiers kneeling in several parts of the House of God, at their private devotions. O happy Gibraltar, that thou hast such a set of praying men! Some, I hear, often come in by two o'clock in the morning, to pour out their hearts before God.[2]

[1] *Ibid*, *p* 125. [2] *Ibid*, *p* 134.

Whitefield also learned of another Society, *The Dark Lanthorns*. But since they were of the Scotch Church, he was too much an Anglican to visit them, and instead sent them what he called 'some proper books'.

Whitefield's stay at Gibraltar lasted merely fifteen days, but in this short time the winsome personality and fervent zeal which had won the affections of hundreds at London did the same in this military centre. As his visit drew to a close his congregation on two occasions amounted to a thousand. Some of the soldiers who were going to Georgia begged to be allowed to sail on the *Whitaker* so as to be near him. 'Many', he says, 'came to me weeping, telling me what God had done for their souls, desiring my prayers and promising me their's. Others gave me tokens of their love, as cake, figs, wine, eggs, and other necessaries for my voyage, and seemed to want words to express their affection.'[1] The leader of the Jewish synagogue, who had been present when he preached his sermon on *The Heinous Sin of Swearing*, personally thanked him for it.

The Rock had been to Whitefield a place of spiritual happiness, and as he took his leave he depicted his experience by quoting Samson's phrase, 'Out of the strong came forth sweetness'.

*

During the voyage from Gibraltar to Georgia, Whitefield increased his discipline among his floating flock. He says, 'I began to inquire into the faith of those committed to my charge',[2] by which he means that he examined them individually, 'speaking to them one by one to see what account they could give of their faith'.[3]

To this practice he added another. Early in the voyage, upon finding a political paper on the Captain's pillow, he had removed it and left a religious book in its place, and now, on the high seas, he did the same kind of thing among the soldiers and sailors. He writes, 'I exchanged some bad books that were on board (which I immediately threw into the sea) for some good ones. All that I have found with them . . . have been willing to surrender them up.'[4] While visiting the sister ship, the *Lightfoot*, he did the same

[1] *Ibid, p* 137. [2] *Ibid, p* 140. [3] *Ibid, p* 139. [4] *Ibid, p* 144.

with some playing-cards, and his audacious action seems not to have aroused any protest.

We can but regret, however, an incident in Whitefield's dealing with one of the children.

Had a good instance [he wrote], of the benefit of breaking children's wills betimes. Last night, going between decks (as I do every night) to visit the sick and to examine my people, I asked one of the women to bid her little boy say his prayers. She answered his elder sister would, but she could not make him. Upon this I bid the child kneel down before me, but he would not till I took hold of his two feet and forced him down. I then bid him say the Lord's prayer (being informed by his mother he could say it if he would), but he obstinately refused, till at last, after I had given him several blows, he said his prayer as well as could be expected and I gave him some figs for a reward.[1]

This action seems both foolish and cruel by to-day's standards and it is not in any attempt to excuse it that we notice that it was in keeping with the customs of those times. Even so good a woman as Susannah Wesley said that she taught her children, beginning at their first birthday, 'to fear the rod', and that they were allowed only 'to cry softly'. 'The first thing to be done', she wrote, 'is to conquer their will . . . I insist on conquering the will of children betimes.'[2] Nevertheless, we must deplore both the custom and Whitefield's action on the basis of it.

*

During this voyage Whitefield's soul was often moved to awe and praise by the might and majesty of the ocean. His *Journal* contains such phrases as, 'The wind magnified that God at whose word the stormy wind ariseth', 'We praised God to see the floods clap their hands', and 'We rejoiced to see the works of the Lord and the beauty of the great deep.' He records an occasion on which, 'The night was unusually clear and the moon and stars appeared in their greatest lustre;' after viewing the scene he went below but could not stay, for he found himself drawn back to the deck, there to rejoice at length in the glory of the night. He was overawed by the approach of two waterspouts which threatened to engulf the vessel, but when the storm was stilled and the waterspouts had disappeared, he exclaimed, 'Surely the Everlasting I AM said to

[1] *Ibid, p* 146. [2] John Wesley's *Journal*, Vol 3, *pp* 35, 36.

the sea that instant, "Let there be a calm in that place".' Moon and stars, sea and wave, wind and storm spoke to him of their Creator and caused him to cry, 'O that men who occupy their business in great waters would admire God's wonders in the deep!' and 'O Lord, the sea is full of Thy riches! Marvellous are Thy works and that my soul knoweth right well!' There is a poetic beauty in his description, 'The evening was exceedingly calm, the sky clear, and all things conspired to praise that glorious and lofty One Who inhabits eternity, who stretcheth forth the heavens like a curtain and holdeth the waters in the hollow of His hand.'[1]

Whitefield took an interest in the daily affairs of the sailors. He makes mention of such matters as the sighting of a whale, the presence of pilot fish with a shark and the catching of a porpoise. His influence with the people arose in some measure from his familiarity with the common events of their lives and he constantly found ways in which to use such things as illustrations of Divine truth.

*

As the journey continued the effects of the Gospel became increasingly evident.

By this time the Captains made it their practice to stand, one on each side of Whitefield as he preached, and Captain Mackay ordered a drum to beat, calling the soldiers to Divine service every morning. Moreover, there were occasions when the other vessels heard him too, 'for being in the trade winds, the other two ship's companies drew near and joined in the worship of God'.

What a sight this must have been! The calm sea, the three vessels clustered together, the crowded decks ablaze with the red coats of the soldiers, and one deck serving as an open-air chapel, replete with make-shift benches and, possibly, a male choir. Before them stands the young chaplain, a Captain on each side and officers round about. In a voice which can be clearly heard on each of the three vessels, he leads a service which includes the singing of Psalms and the prayers of the Church of England liturgy. Many who recently cursed God now join in the words of petition and praise.

[1] *Journals*, p 99.

The sermon is entitled *The Heinous Sin of Drunkenness.* After showing the Scriptural setting of his text, Whitefield goes on to declare:

Believe me, ye unhappy men of Belial (for such, alas! this sin has made you), it is not without the strongest reasons, as well as utmost concern for your precious and immortal souls, that I now conjure you, in the Apostle's words, 'Not to be drunk with wine, or any other liquor, wherein is excess . . .

But think you, O ye drunkards, that you shall ever be partakers of the inheritance of the saints in light? Do you flatter yourselves, that you, who have made them often the subject of your drunken songs, shall be exalted to sing with them the Heavenly songs of Zion? No, as by drunkenness you have made your hearts cages of unclean birds, with impure and unclean spirits must you dwell . . .

Let not a servile fear of being despised by a man that shall die, hinder thy turning unto the living God. For what is a little contempt? It is but a vapour which vanisheth away. Better be derided by a few companions here than be made ashamed before men and angels hereafter. Better be the song of a few drunkards on earth, than dwell with them, where they shall be eternally reproaching and cursing each other in hell! . . . But turn ye, turn ye from your evil ways. Come to Jesus Christ, with the repenting prodigal saying, 'Father, we have sinned! We beseech Thee, let not this sin of drunkenness have any longer dominion over us!' Lay hold on Christ by faith, and lo! it shall happen to you even as you will! . . .

Behold I have told you before! Remember, you were this day informed what the end of drunkenness would be! And I summon you, in the name of that God Whom I serve, to meet me at the judgment seat of Christ, that you may acquit both my Master and me, and confess with your own mouths that your damnation was of your own selves.[1]

Such was the preaching heard aboard the *Whitaker*, the *Amy* and the *Lightfoot.* At the close of this sermon Captain Mackay arose and 'made a useful speech, exhorting the men to give heed to the things spoken', just as, following Whitefield's earlier sermon against *Swearing*, he had risen to testify that he had been a most notorious swearer, but now had left it off, and urged all to do the same.

*

[1] Sermon, *The Heinous Sin of Drunkenness*; text, *Eph.* 5: 18. *Works*, Vol 6, *pp* 303–16.

Before America was reached an epidemic of fever swept over the ship. Gillies says that, 'For many days and nights Whitefield visited between twenty and thirty sick persons', and, as was to be expected, he contracted the disease himself. The foolish medical practices of the times were used on him; he 'was blistered and vomited once, and blooded thrice', but he became worse and lay at the doors of death for some days. Yet from this extremity he was brought back and later testified:

I earnestly desired to be dissolved and go to Christ; but God was pleased to order it otherwise, and I am resigned, though I can scarce be reconciled to come back again into this vale of misery. I had the Heavenly Canaan in full view and hoped I was going to take possession of it; but God saw I was not yet ripe for glory, and therefore in mercy spared me.[1]

*

The last few days of the passage were marked by pleasant sailing and by much concord aboard. Whitefield made frequent mention of the manifest work of grace in the hearts of the people and we notice such *Journal* entries as, 'Observed still stronger signs of a thorough conversion being wrought in some on board', 'Some more of the sailors are convinced of sin and others send notes to be prayed for', and 'The soldiers come very regularly twice a day to prayer and an oath seems a strange thing among most of them.' A sailor who had been one of the most evil men aboard came to Whitefield, confessing how grievous a sinner he had been and crying to God for repentance. Among those who had first looked upon Whitefield as an impostor, was a cadet – a former university student – who was now so moved upon by the Holy Spirit that he asked Captain Mackay for a release from the military in order that he might devote his life to the service of Christ. 'We live in perfect harmony and peace', said Whitefield, 'loving and beloved by one another.' 'In the great cabin . . . we talk of little else but God and Christ . . . and we shall part with great regret.'

Whitefield's actions during these days under sail reveal an important facet of his personality. Had he been anything of an impetuous individual, or had he been lacking in tact, the opposi-

[1] *Works*, Vol 1, *p* 43.

tion that had faced him as the journey began would have continued till its end. But he had proved himself a man of exceptional patience, his zeal had been exercised with much wisdom, and by the grace of God, his desire, 'Oh, that I may catch them with a holy guile!' had been largely fulfilled.

*

Finally the vessel dropped anchor at the coast of Georgia. 'O what joy appeared in everyone's countenance!' says Whitefield. Four months had elapsed since they had first boarded the *Whitaker* and during that time they had been near to shipwreck, in sickness and through storms together. With the great sea behind them and the new world before them, he gathered all on the deck for a farewell service. His sermon – an example of his apt choice of a text – was on the Scripture, 'So He bringeth them unto the haven where they would be', and was entitled *Thankfulness for Mercies Received, a Necessary Duty*.

After enlarging on the many mercies they had received, Whitefield addressed himself to the soldiers, saying:

> Blessed be God! some marks of a partial reformation, at least, have been visible amongst all you that are soldiers. My weak, though sincere endeavours to build you up in the knowledge and fear of God, have not been altogether vain. Swearing, I hope, is in a great measure abated with you; and God, I trust, has blessed His late visitations by making them the means of awakening your consciences to a more solicitous enquiry about the things which belong to your everlasting peace.

To the women Whitefield said:

> I hope you wives also will suffer the word of exhortation. Your behaviour on shipboard, especially the first part of the voyage, I choose to throw a cloak over . . . However, of late, blessed be God! you have taken more heed to your ways, and some of you have walked all the while as became women professing godliness . . . Beg of God to keep the door of your lips, that you offend not with your tongues; and walk in love, that your prayers be not hindered.

He spoke of his responsibility as a minister, confessing,

> I cannot say I have discharged my duty to you as I ought. No: I am sensible of many faults, for which I have not failed to humble myself in secret before God. . . . I have still stronger obligations to intercede

on your behalf, for God has set His seal to my ministry, in your hearts.

Whitefield concluded by addressing them all thus:

And now brethren, into God's hands I commend your spirits. Excuse my detaining you so long. Perhaps it is the last time I shall speak to you. My heart is full, and out of the abundance of it I could continue my discourse till midnight. But I must away to your new world. May God give you new hearts and enable you to put into practice what you have heard . . . As surely as He hath now brought us to this haven, so surely, after we have passed through the storms and tempests of this troublesome world, will He bring us to the haven of eternal rest . . .[1]

As the sermon finished 'many wept', and from each of the vessels people came, bringing him gifts, expressing their affection and asking for a place in his prayers. And thus they parted, some, no doubt having been truly born again, to go on in the new life in the new world: others never to forget the terrible warnings and loving entreaties they had heard from his lips: and he to enter into a situation made all the more difficult by the fact that, from here, just five months earlier, John Wesley had been maliciously expelled.

[1] Tyerman's *Whitefield*, Vol 1, *pp* 126–7.

. . . thousands of awakened souls who had been gathered by Mr Whitefield . . .

MRS JOHN HUTTON

London, 1738

'Let us consider one another to provoke unto love and good works; not forsaking the assembling of ourselves together' . . . I suppose the assemblies here intended were little private societies . . . Nothing hath of late more alarmed the enemies of the cross of Christ, than the zeal that God hath stirred up in the hearts of many to put in practice this Apostolical injunction.

WHITEFIELD

A Letter to the Religious Societies, 1739

9

Developments in England

WHITEFIELD'S mission to Georgia kept him out of England throughout almost all of 1738. But before we look into his activities in the Colony we must notice certain developments which, in the meantime, were taking place in England.

Several of the London clergy hoped that following his departure his influence would begin to die away and that he would be forgotten. But, with the passing of a few weeks, they were forced to realize that such hopes were false, for they saw that, despite his absence, the effects of his ministry not only remained alive, but even increased.

This continuance was both evidenced and aided by the activities of the publishers. Whitefield had committed the publishing of his sermons to James Hutton. Before he had left England Hutton had produced three of them (one had required a second edition) and after his sailing Hutton produced six others in quick succession, as well as further editions of the former ones. Another publisher went one better: although he had no permission to do so he reprinted the nine sermons and produced them together under one cover. Hutton replied with his own edition of the nine sermons as a single volume, but sought an advantage over his competitor: having formerly used the printer Rivington, he now had the work done by William Bowyer, a member of a coterie of literary élite and a man whom Tyerman describes as 'the most learned and distinguished printer of the age'.[1]

Editions of the nine-sermon volume were produced by other publishers also. One of these men offered a special attraction, for he carried a portrait of Whitefield as his frontispiece, and another

[1] Tyerman's *Whitefield*, Vol 1, *p* 103.

'annexed *A Collection of Forms of Prayer* Recommended by the Same Reverend Author'.

Another publisher reprinted the pamphlet *The Oxford Methodists* which had first been published in 1733. This reprinting was occasioned by the fact that Whitefield's fame would give it wide sale, and the pamphlet now bore as its preface 'A Short Epistle to the Reverend Mr Whitefield, A.B., of Pembroke College, Oxon.' (This could not but have served to strengthen the association of the words 'Methodist' and 'Whitefield' in the mind of the public.) Then a Bristol printer, apparently seeking to outdo his London competitors, went all the way: he produced the nine sermons, appended also *The Oxford Methodists* and prefixed the 'Short Epistle'[1] too.

These various publishers doubtless served themselves well by their multiple editions of Whitefield's sermons, but they also served the cause of the Gospel. The repeated editions and the publishers' competition kept the memory of Whitefield fresh in the minds of the people and thus gave a still more lasting effect to the message he had preached.

The continuing nature of Whitefield's work was especially to be seen in the Religious Societies. The sudden presence of so many people earnestly desiring the spiritual help to be found in these groups gave new life to the meetings of the older ones and brought a similar fervour into the several new ones. Moreover, previous to Whitefield's ministry the Societies had been separate bodies, scarcely conscious of any mutual relationship. But now, in their new zeal and strong allegiance to evangelical doctrine, bonds of fellowship were formed between them, and their London-wide Quarterly Meetings not only revealed a notable spiritual vigour but made it manifest that they were experiencing a new sense of unity also.

Before leaving England Whitefield had taken another step to the end that the souls of those awakened and converted under his ministry might grow, and that God might continue and

[1] Hutton appears merely to have used the title *Sermons on Various Subjects*, by George Whitefield, A.B. Other publishers entitled their editions *Several Discourses Upon Practical Subjects, The Christian's Companion; Or Sermons on Several Subjects* and *Nine Sermons Preached by George Whitefield at Different Parish Churches in London and Bristol*. The Bristol publisher, P. Browne, used the title, *Several Discourses upon Practical Subjects, the Arguments of which May Be Collected from the Contents*.

increase the work of revival that had already commenced. As far back as the days when he was preparing for ordination he had begun observing the 16th day of each month as a time of special prayer and fasting, and during his ministry in London he had sought to institute this practice among his people. He continued to observe it himself while overseas and his *Journals* contain the following entries:

January 16 . . . It being the 16th day of the month, Mr H. and I joined in an hour's intercession and abstinence, with all those who meet together to bewail their own and the sins of the nation.[1]

Feb. 16 . . . Joined with those at night, who set apart this day as a day of fasting and humiliation, to deprecate the judgments our national sins deserve. Lord, hear our prayers and let our cry come unto Thee.[2]

March 16 . . . joined an intercession with those who set apart this day as a day of fasting and prayer for the sins of the nation to which we belong. May they prove as effectual as those which Moses put up for the children of Israel![3]

Whitefield's words imply that the day was observed by many of his followers, and this practice could not but have added to the solidarity of his people and the continuance of the work.

The clergy were well aware that the effects of Whitefield's ministry were not dying away, and as the weeks passed certain of them became aroused by the situation.

It was especially the Societies, in their revived condition, that alarmed them. In these bodies an attitude of independence and even an anti-clerical sentiment was developing. Though each Society was nominally under the direction of a designated clergyman, certain members now made it known that they would submit to no clerical oversight – unless the minister were one of the few thoroughly evangelical men. We may be sure that it was not uncommon for a clergyman to be confronted by some of these people – perhaps his own parishioners – with the question 'Have you been born again?' Doubtless, many a man of the cloth heard his indolence contrasted with Whitefield's zeal, and a contemporary author put the matter plainly when he wrote:

Whitefield has set them an example which they must, in some measure, follow. But for him they could have gone on in their old way as well as ever, and their corn, and their wine, and their pigs, and their eggs

[1] *Journals*, p 110. [2] *Ibid*, p 125. [3] *Ibid*, p 141.

and their apples would have come in as usual. All besides is unnecessary trouble, and they detest the man who has put them upon it.[1]

Furthermore, in the thinking of the clergy, the Societies posed a threat for the future. The spiritual vigour of these groups made them a force to be reckoned with, and were some strong leader to arise in their midst, he might well unify and organize them, and lead them as his own movement. Whether this would be within the Church or out of it, the clergy knew not, and they feared the outcome.

As was but to be expected, some of the clergymen took steps to remove this disturbance of their peace. One prominent minister, in preaching before the University of Oxford, made his message a denunciation of the doctrine of the new birth. He did not mention Whitefield by name, but sought to influence his followers, for, in publishing the sermon, he drew attention to the fact that it was particularly 'Recommended to the Religious Societies'. Others began agitating to have the Societies banned altogether, and asserted that this drastic action alone could provide a solution to the problem.

*

Though the majority of the clergy looked on Whitefield with mounting dislike, there was little they could use against him in his published sermons. However, a weapon in printed form was put into their hands by the surreptitious publication of Whitefield's *Journal*.

During the days when Whitefield was preparing to leave England, his friends had urged him to write to them. As he could not correspond with all, he agreed to send reports of his activities to James Hutton, who, in turn, would read them in his Societies. Thus, Whitefield sent his first report when he reached Gibraltar and his second upon arriving at Savannah. There was nothing new in the sending of such reports, for the Moravians required it of all their missionaries and John Wesley[2] and Benjamin Ingham had each sent a *Journal* from Georgia.

[1] Robert Seagrave, *The Conduct of Mr Whitefield Vindicated from the Aspersions and Malicious Invectives of his Enemies* (London, 1739).

[2] John Wesley sent more than one copy of his *Journal*, and one of these he sent to the printer Rivington, apparently in the hope he would print it.

Charles Wesley wrote, 'My brother's Journal is in everyone's hands . . . I called

Whitefield's situation, however, was different. With such a clamour for anything from his pen, whatever he wrote was sure to be published, and with the hundreds of followers impatiently awaiting news from him, some publisher was certain to get hold of these reports. And thus it happened that an enterprising publisher named Cooper somehow obtained the manuscript and held it long enough to put it into print. It was an underhanded action which Charles Wesley tried to prevent,[1] but Cooper would not be denied so profitable a stroke of business and his edition went forth to the public.

Of course, this account should not have been published. Whitefield wrote with merely his friends in mind – friends among whom he practised little spiritual reserve – and he wrote not only to inform them of his own activities but also to arouse them to zealous efforts for the Lord. But, as seen in the chapter on his journey across the Atlantic, he spoke of his doings in a way which an outsider might look on as egotism, and made mention of people he met in a manner that was far too frank for publication. Had the *Journal* been confined to Hutton's use in the Societies, as Whitefield planned, there could have been little or no objection, but parts were in bad taste when printed for all to read.

Hutton was offended by Cooper's publication and stated that Cooper had acted without Whitefield's knowledge or permission. 'Mr Whitefield', explained Hutton, 'knew himself too well to obtrude his little private concerns upon the world, especially when inter-mixed with such passages relating to others, as none

on Charles Rivington, who gave me letters and a Journal from my brother in Georgia . . . I read it through without either surprise or impatience. His dropping my fatal letter, I hope will convince him of what I never could – his own great carelessness; and the sufferings *that* brought upon him, of his inimitable blindness. His simplicity in telling what and who were meant by the two Greek words, was "outdoing his own outdoings". Surely all this will be sufficient to teach him a little of the wisdom of the serpent, of which he seems utterly void.' (*Journal*, Dec. 5, 7, 1736.)

[1] 'My advice to suppress it being overruled.' Charles Wesley's *Journal*, Aug. 3, 1738. General Oglethorpe appears to have been irked by the complaints made in John Wesley's *Journal* about conditions in Georgia, for Charles says that the General 'talked much about the mischief of private journals, all of which ought to be published or never sent.' *ibid*, Jan. 20, 1737. It is possible that the three publishers who printed Whitefield's *Journal* learned of the General's sentiments through Charles and that they regarded these as partial justification for their action.

but an unthinking person would judge proper to divulge.' Hutton also claimed that Cooper's edition contained certain errors and, therefore, like a good businessman, decided that he should produce an edition of his own. This he did, complaining in his *Preface* of Cooper's inaccurate work. Cooper, in turn, published an advertisement in the *Weekly Miscellany* challenging Hutton to show 'any *passage*, *circumstance* or even *any word*' in his edition which varied from the original. Whereupon, still another publisher put the *Journal* into print,[1] and thus the regrettable fact that it was published at all was complicated by the appearance of three competitive editions.

Hutton said that he published his edition 'at the earnest solicitation of several of Mr Whitefield's friends', and it is evident that, despite the harm done by Cooper's action, the *Journal* was avidly received by Whitefield's followers and helped to maintain and increase his work. Hutton published two more editions in 1738 and another three in 1739, and this work, along with the printing of the sermons, did much to establish Hutton in business.

But the *Journal* quickly became a means of opposition in the hands of Whitefield's enemies. One minister produced a 32-page pamphlet entitled *Remarks on Mr Whitefield's Journal: Wherein His Many Inconsistencies are Pointed out and his Tenets Considered. Addressed to the Religious Societies.* The writer claimed to have been an admirer of Whitefield earlier, but stated, 'I could not help endeavouring to undeceive others, since I had been so deceived in him myself'. Other publications of a similar nature followed, the common attempt of which was to destroy the image formed by his London ministry – that of a widely respected young clergyman – and to replace it with one which carried the stigma of fanaticism. There were many persons, both clerical and lay, ready to believe such charges, and, sad to say, the indiscretions of the *Journal* gave them considerable cause.

It is interesting to notice, however, that the higher clergy did not altogether share the attitude of their lower brethren. Charles Wesley indicates something of the episcopal view in his report:

With my brother I waited on the Archbishop. He showed us great affection and spoke mildly of Mr Whitefield . . . From him we went to

[1] This was the edition of Hunt and Clarke, London, 1738.

the Bishop of London; who denied his having condemned or even heard much of us. G. Whitefield's Journal, he said, was tainted with enthusiasm, though he himself was a pious well-meaning youth.[1]

A few months later Bishop Benson also stated his opinion:

Though mistaken on some points, I think Mr Whitefield a very pious, well-meaning young man, with good abilities and great zeal. I find His Grace of Canterbury thinks highly of him. I pray God grant him great success in all his undertakings for the good of mankind, and the revival of true religion and holiness among us in these degenerate days.[2]

*

Other developments which also had a bearing on Whitefield's work took place while he was in Georgia. Important among these was the increase of Moravianism in England.

The Moravian Brethren were a Protestant people who had long suffered Catholic persecution in their homelands in central Europe. In 1722 a pious nobleman, Count Zinzendorf, came to their aid, and gave them refuge on his estates in Saxony. There they built a communal settlement which they named Herrnhut. In 1727 they experienced a great enduement of spiritual power, as a result of which their past differences were obliterated and an abounding new joy filled their souls. Desiring to maintain so rich a blessing, they instituted a system called *The Hourly Intercession* – a system in which there was always one of their members at prayer, an hour at a time, day and night – and this continuous praying was carried on without a break for over a century.

But the most important result was a new sense of evangelical responsibility. Such was the Moravians' desire to spread the message of Christianity that within twelve years they had established mission bases in the West Indies, Greenland, India, South Africa, Guinea, Ceylon and Turkey, and were also at work among the Jews of the large cities of Holland and Germany. The leading Moravian historian says of their action; 'This was the first time in the history of Protestant Europe that a congregation of orthodox Christians had deliberately resolved to take the Gospel to the heathen.'[3]

[1] Charles Wesley's *Journal,* Feb. 21, 1739. As there is no standard edition of this work, reference is made to it by date rather than by page.

[2] Huntingdon, *op cit,* Vol 1, *p* 196.

[3] J. E. Hutton, *A History of the Moravian Church* (London, 1909), *p* 237.

The settlement at Herrnhut was remarkable for its disciplined order and its spiritual fervour. Life was controlled by a set of strict rules and the Count governed all with a benign but unbending domination. Christianity, as exemplified among the common people, was warm and beautiful and abounded with singing. They practised an unfeigned humility and sought to do good unto all, and the Jews, accustomed to bitter treatment, expressed their amazement at the kindness shown them by the Moravians. These qualities, however, found their highest fulfilment in the lives of the missionaries, for they gladly endured suffering and faced death in order to reach the heathen with the Gospel. History has few records as rich in Christian devotion as those of the Moravians during the first fifteen years after their great blessing in 1727.

Nevertheless, this noble movement was not without its weaknesses. Its historian says that Count Zinzendorf believed in the inspiration of the Augsburg Confession more than in the inspiration of the Bible. The Moravians, he states, 'held that the Bible . . . contained mistakes in detail; that the teaching of St James was in flat contradiction to the teaching of St Paul, and that even the Apostles sometimes made a wrong application of the prophecies. To them, the value of the Bible consisted, not in its supposed infallibility, but in its appeal to their hearts.'[1]

As a result, Moravianism was not a thoroughly Biblical organization. The Bible was not its supreme authority, but authority lay also in personal experience, and, of course, varied according to the sentiments of the individual. Nor was the Bible a book to which they gave diligent study; they regarded it somewhat as a compilation of texts and mottoes, and they had the curious practice of opening it at random and accepting the first verse their eye lighted upon as the immediate guidance of heaven. They employed it also in the casting of lots and we are told that the Count 'carried his lot apparatus in his pocket; he consulted it on all sorts of topics and regarded it as the infallible voice of God'.[2]

The Moravians gave little attention to systematic theology.

[1] *Ibid, p* 264.

[2] *Ibid, p* 274. 'It was a little green book with detachable leaves; each leaf contained some motto or text, and when the Count was in difficulty he pulled out one of the leaves at random.'

Though they taught most earnestly that salvation is by faith alone, they knew little as to the nature of such faith and considered it merely a subjective experience. At first they made much of the substitutionary nature of the atonement of Christ, but this became secondary among them to a kind of moral influence theory, in which help was to be gained from the cross by a mental visualization of Christ's sufferings.

This custom of emphasizing the physical wounds of Christ came about in the following manner. Certain of the Moravian missionaries, in attempting to teach the Lutheran Catechism to the Eskimos, found that such abstract theology failed to interest their unlettered hearers. They discovered, however, that by describing the scourging and crucifixion of the Saviour, they gained their wrapt attention, and so successful was this approach that they made it their regular practice. In turn they reported this new method and its results to Herrnhut, and many of the preachers there, intrigued by the missionaries' success, adopted it also. Thereafter it became the principal element of Moravian preaching, and some of the preachers learned to depict the Saviour's sufferings in vivid detail and with tear-compelling effect. They spoke of the lash, the thorns, the nails and the sword-thrust with ecstatic emphasis and unhallowed familiarity, and this practice they called 'the blood and wounds teaching'.

The influence of the Moravians in London stemmed largely from the short residence there of one of their ablest men, Peter Böhler. Böhler had been a junior lecturer at the University of Jena, but left this position at the bidding of Count Zinzendorf in order to establish a Moravian settlement in Georgia. On his way to America he spent a few months in London learning English, and was soon invited by James Hutton to teach the Society which met at his *Bible and Sun*.[1] Despite his incompetency in the language, Böhler proved a very capable teacher, and attendances so increased that Hutton leased an unused chapel in Fetter Lane and moved the Society there. Many of Hutton's original

[1] This Society is also said to have met at Hutton's home. But as he was then unmarried, he undoubtedly lived in rooms that adjoined his business, and therefore the claims that the Society met 'in his own back parlour' and 'at the *Bible and Sun*' are one and the same.

company and many of these newer members were persons who had been drawn by Whitefield's ministry. Before leaving for America, Böhler instituted a series of Moravian-type rules and, by his personal example and public teaching, left a deep impress of Moravianism's best qualities on the Society.

During 1738 the Fetter Lane Society began to take on a particular importance. The Earl and Countess of Huntingdon frequently attended its services and influenced others of titled rank to do the same. It attracted also several well-to-do business families, and the Delamottes, the Claggetts, William Holland and James Hutton are representatives of this class who come into our narrative. The Wesley brothers made it the chief scene of their activities, and John, although he held no official position, exercised a measure of leadership in its affairs.[1] The Society's gatherings were characterized by an extraordinary fervour, but because of the lack of clear doctrinal teaching, its members proved susceptible to varying religious influences.

Although the Fetter Lane Society was basically one of the many Religious Societies of London, it was steadily becoming more and more a Moravian body. Count Zinzendorf had made an arrangement with the Archbishop of Canterbury, whereby the Moravian Church, wherever it might be planted in Britain or her colonies, was to be considered part of the Church of England. It was, however, to be *a church within a church*; it was to enjoy all the privileges of the state Church yet was to be in no way subject to its control. This plan made possible a dual relationship, and many of the Fetter Lane people, while retaining their status as members of the Church of England, availed themselves also of the warmth of Moravianism. As a result, with the passing of the weeks they found themselves becoming increasingly Moravian at heart, the Society gradually changing into a Moravian body.

*

The religious situation in London was also affected by another people from the continent: a people known as the French Prophets.

[1] It has often been assumed that John Wesley held a position of authority in the Fetter Lane Society. When Thomas Church made that suggestion Wesley replied, 'No, I was but a single, private member of that Society' (*Letters, op cit,* Vol 2, *p* 221). Whatever measure of leadership Wesley exercised was merely the result of his abilities, his training and his innate tendency to dominate others.

The Prophets were the descendants of a large company of Protestants who had suffered severe persecution in France during the previous century. Though the great French Protestant movement in general is worthy of the highest commendation, not only for its zeal and courage, but also for its good sense, the latter cannot be said of the Prophets.

Earlier generations of these people, had been driven to seek refuge in inaccessible areas of the mountains in southern France. There they eked out a pitiable existence amidst constant privation and peril. Since it was both difficult and dangerous for them to possess a copy of the Bible, their knowledge of the Word of God was often limited to a few printed passages or whatever verses they had been able to commit to memory. Under the great strain that they endured, some suffered derangements of the mind and began to experience strange delusions and to undergo convulsive fits, and since they lacked the instruction and comfort of the Scriptures, they sought relief in self-induced trances and attempted to see supernatural visions.

After enduring these conditions for several decades, those who had escaped the sword fled to Protestant lands. Their freedom, however, did not signal a return to the Bible, but they carried their occult practices to their new homes. In England they attracted wide attention by exhibitions which included bodily contortions and unintelligible sounds, all of which they claimed were miraculous. Their most notorious action was the announcement that one of their leaders, a Mr Emms, who had recently died would be raised to life at a given hour. Hundreds gathered around the grave and one can but imagine the disappointment and frustration of the Prophets when the given moment arrived and the dead man failed to come forth.

Nevertheless, following Whitefield's ministry, the Prophets, aware of the new enthusiasm in the Religious Societies, decided that here was a people among whom they might easily make proselytes. This proved especially true of the Fetter Lane Society, and some of its leading men were led to believe that the convulsive fits and unintelligible sounds of the Prophets – since they knew not how to explain them otherwise – must be supernatural.

Both of the Wesleys came into contact with this cult and recorded their experiences.

I lodged at Mr Hollis's [wrote Charles], who entertained me with his French Prophets – equal, in his account, if not superior, to the Old Testament ones. While we were undressing he fell into violent agitations and gobbled like a turkey-cock. I was frightened and began exorcising him with, 'Thou deaf and dumb devil,' &c. He soon recovered out of his fit of inspiration. I prayed and went to bed, not half liking my bed-fellow. I did not sleep very sound with Satan so near me.[1]

The leading figures among the Prophets were women, and John Wesley reported his visit to the home of one of them, as follows:

She seemed to be about four or five and twenty, of an agreeable speech and behaviour. She asked why we came. I said, 'To try the spirits, whether they be of God.' Presently she leaned back in her chair and seemed to have strong workings in her breast, with deep sighings intermixed. Her head and hands, and, by turns, every part of her body, seemed also to be in a kind of convulsive motion. This continued about ten minutes, till she began to speak (though the workings, sighings and contortions of her body were so intermixed with her words that she seldom spoke half a sentence together) with a clear, strong voice, 'Father, Thy will be done . . .'

She spoke much (all as in the person of God, and mostly in Scripture words) of the fulfilling of the prophecies, the coming of Christ now at hand and the spreading of the Gospel over all the earth . . . Two or three of our company were much affected and believed she spoke by the Spirit of God. But this was in no wise clear to me.[2]

Charles Wesley also paid a visit to a Prophetess and wrote of the event:

The Prophet Wise asked, 'Can a man attain perfection here?' I answered, 'No!' The Prophetess began groaning. I turned and said, 'If you have anything to speak, speak it!' She lifted up her voice like the lady on the tripod and cried out vehemently, 'Look for perfection! I say, absolute perfection!' I was minded to rebuke her, but God gave me uncommon command of spirit, so that I sat quiet and replied not. I offered at last to sing, which she allowed, but did not join. Bray pressed me to stay and hear her pray. They knelt; I stood. She prayed most pompously and . . . concluded with an horrible, hellish laugh . . .[3]

[1] Charles Wesley's *Journal,* December 11, 1738.
[2] John Wesley's *Journal,* Vol 2, *pp* 136–7.
[3] Charles Wesley's *Journal,* June 7, 1739.

While it must be stressed that other French Protestant peoples were of a much more Biblical and commendable kind, the Prophets as they existed in London in 1738 are well exemplified in these accounts from the Wesleys.

Such then were the developments that took place in England while Whitefield was overseas. His work continued, the Societies prospered and the clergy opposed. The Moravians brought a spiritual warmth, but, being Biblically weak, introduced superstitious practices. The Prophets interjected the element of fanaticism and posed the threat which pseudo-supernaturalism always constitutes for earnest but unthinking Christian people. The movement at large, in Bristol, Gloucester and London remained and grew, but manifestly needed wise leadership and Scriptural instruction, lest the superstitions and fanaticism spread.

The most significant development, however, was an experience of conversion: the conversion of Charles and John Wesley. That story is of such importance that it merits being told separately.

It is of real importance not to undervalue the human side of great saints. The value of a Francis and a Wesley is not exhausted by their heavenly citizenship . . . Wesley undoubtedly suffered from this semi-idolatry. The spirit which apotheosizes a man destroys the man, *and it is just the man, of like passions with ourselves, as he struggled and conquered, lived and served, who is really a heritage and inspiration.*

J. E. RATTENBURY

Wesley's Legacy to the World

10

The Conversion of the Wesleys

A MINISTRY such as that which Whitefield had exercised in England was something new to Holy Club thinking. While at Oxford, the Wesleys, Clayton, Broughton and the rest had looked forward to a lifetime of enforcing their discipline and practising their High Church ritual, either in a parish in the homeland or in some foreign missionary service. This was their prospect and they had known nothing of the message of conversion that Whitefield had preached, and had possessed no expectation of a ministry which, in a blaze of evangelical zeal, would draw thousands.

Yet when John Wesley, after leaving Deal, arrived at London, it was the fruit of this ministry which greeted him. Merely five weeks had passed since Whitefield had concluded his work there, and the evidence of its results – the thronged Societies, the published sermons, the awakened souls and the reports of Whitefield's immense congregations – undoubtedly filled him with amazement. But no man was more sensitive to the presence of success than Wesley, and the knowledge that so much of it had come to his young friend, could not but have had a powerful effect, helping to relieve his depression and provoking within him a determination that some measure of such success would yet be his.

The acquaintance that Wesley had made in America with evangelical truth also assisted in the brightening of his outlook. Shortly after his return he made an analysis of this alteration in his thinking, stating:

> This, then, have I learned in the ends of the earth– that I 'am fallen short of the glory of God': that my whole heart is 'altogether corrupt and abominable': . . . that, 'alienated' as I am from the life of God,

I am 'a child of wrath', and heir of hell: . . . that, 'having the sentence of death' in my heart, and having nothing in or of myself to plead, I have no hope but that of being justified freely 'through the redemption that is in Jesus'; I have no hope, but that if I seek I shall find Christ, and 'be found in Him, not having my own righteousness, but that which is through the faith of Christ, the righteousness which is of God by faith'.[1]

Such was the new ray of hope that pierced John's gloom. Now he could say, 'if I seek I shall find Christ', and though he knew not how to seek, he was assured that the way to Him was 'by faith'. His confession of failure was an indication that he was stirred to the very depths of his being, but now, in this new understanding, he at least had before him a discernible pathway and it was a pathway that led towards light.

Charles Wesley was also in London and was in much the same condition as John. He seldom preached, and though he was active in pressing the strict religious life on people in personal contacts, his manner was severe and his efforts bore little fruit. He spoke of returning to Georgia and of establishing an Orphan House there, but in reality was too sick in both body and soul to have heart for this or any other labour. Such was his despondency that on his birthday he wrote, 'I began my twenty-seventh year in a murmuring, discontented spirit; reading over and over the third of Job.'[2] After meeting a friend who told him of a report that he had died, Charles remarked, 'Happy for me had the news been true! What a world of misery would it save me!'[3]

Since the Moravians had been the Wesleys' first teachers in evangelical Christianity, John and Charles were drawn to Peter Böhler who was then in England, in the hope that he might instruct them further. Böhler's first attempt was to destroy any remnant of their self-trust, and John recorded, 'I understood him not, and least of all when he said, "My Brother! My Brother! That philosophy of yours must be purged away!" '[4]

Charles had a similar experience with Böhler, saying:

He asked me, 'Do you hope to be saved?' 'Yes!' 'For what reason do

[1] John Wesley's *Journal*, Vol 1, *pp* 423–4.
[2] Charles Wesley's *Journal*, Dec. 18, 1736.
[3] *Ibid*, Jan. 22, 1737.
[4] John Wesley's *Journal*, Vol 1, *p* 440.

you hope it?' 'Because I have used my best endeavours to serve God.' He shook his head and said no more. I thought him very uncharitable, saying in my heart, 'What? Are not my endeavours a sufficient ground of hope? Would he rob me of my endeavours? I have nothing else to trust to.'[1]

John testified further:

I was strongly convinced that the cause of [my] uneasiness was unbelief, and that the gaining a true, living faith was 'the one thing needful' for me. But still I fixed not this faith on its right object: I meant only faith in God, not faith in or through Christ. Again, I knew not that I was wholly void of this faith, but only thought I had not enough of it. So that when Peter Böhler . . . affirmed of true faith in Christ, that it had those two fruits inseparably attending it, 'dominion over sin and constant peace from a sense of forgiveness', I was quite amazed and looked upon it as a new Gospel.[2]

Immediately it struck into my mind, 'Leave off preaching. How can you preach to others, who have not faith yourself?, I asked Böhler whether he thought I should leave it off or not. He answered, 'By no means.' I asked, 'But what can I preach?' He said, 'Preach faith *till* you have it, and then, *because* you have it, you *will* preach faith.'[3]

The views to which the Wesleys were led by these means became of historic importance, for these views influenced the beliefs that they held throughout life. They both spoke of 'seeking Christ', yet as one analyses the pertinent passages in their *Journals* it becomes evident that they were actually seeking *faith* more than they were *Christ*. Faith had become the great *desideratum* in their thinking, insomuch that they began to look upon it as an entity in itself. Under Böhler's instructions they had forsaken their trust in personal endeavours and works, but faith had become a kind of new endeavour which they substituted for their former endeavours and a work which took the place of their former good works. They had still learned nothing about receiving Christ in the fullness of His person and the completeness of His saving work, but were concerned about faith itself and what measure of it might be necessary for salvation. Charles expected that the coming of this faith might be associated with some visible presence of Christ, and John looked for an experience

[1] Charles Wesley's *Journal*, Feb. 24, 1738. [2] John Wesley's *Journal*, Vol. 1, *p* 471.
[3] *Ibid*, *p* 442.

which would be accompanied by an emotional response. 'I well saw', he wrote, 'that no one could, in the nature of things, have such a sense of forgiveness and not *feel* it. But I felt it not.'[1]

*

The Wesleys were not men to do anything by half-way measures, and, spurred on by their fear of being eternally lost, they made their search for faith the passion of their lives.

This became especially evident during the month of May (1738). John described himself as 'sorrowful and very heavy; being neither able to read, nor meditate, nor sing, nor pray'.[2] Charles, grasping for any straw of help, refused the comfortable surroundings of the Reverend John Hutton's home in Westminster, and went to live with a William Bray, of whom he speaks as, 'a poor ignorant mechanic, who knows nothing but Christ; yet by knowing Him, knows and discerns all things'.[3] Bray's living-quarters appear to have been attached to his business – a brazier's workshop in Little Britain, off Aldersgate Street – and Charles was so feeble that he had to be carried there in a chair.

He spent the next few weeks in a bed-ridden condition, but his spiritual search continued. His *Journal* reports:

May 11. We prayed together for faith. I was quite overpowered and melted into tears . . . I was persuaded I should not leave his house before I believed with my heart unto righteousness.

May 12. I waked in the same blessed temper, hungry and thirsty after God . . . This day (and indeed my whole time) I spent in discoursing on faith, either with those that had it, or those that sought it; I joined with Mr Bray in prayer and the Scripture, and was so greatly affected, that I almost thought Christ was coming that moment. I concluded the night with private vehement prayer.

May 13. I waked without Christ; yet still desirous of finding Him . . . At night my brother came, exceeding heavy. I forced him (as he has often forced me) to sing an hymn to Christ, and almost thought He would come while we were singing: . . .

May 14. The beginning of the day I was very heavy, weary, and unable to pray; but the desire soon returned; . . . I longed to find Christ, that I might show Him to all mankind; that I might praise, that I might love Him.

[1] *Ibid*, Vol. 1, *p* 471. [2] *Ibid*, *p* 460.
[3] Charles Wesley's *Journal*, May 11, 1738.

May 16. I waked weary, faint and heartless . . . In the afternoon I seemed deeply sensible of my misery, in being without Christ.

On the following day a new source of spiritual help was introduced into Charles's life. Another earnest seeker, William Holland, a commercial painter 'in rather a large way of business', called on Charles and brought with him a copy of Luther's *Commentary on the Galatians*. The visit and the book proved of the greatest importance to Charles and he wrote:

May 17. To-day I first saw Luther on the Galatians, which Mr Holland had accidentally lit upon. We began, and found him nobly full of faith. My friend, in hearing him, was so affected as to breathe out sighs and groans unutterable. . . . I spent some hours this evening in private with Martin Luther, who was greatly blessed to me, especially his conclusion of the 2nd chapter. I laboured, waited and prayed to feel 'who loved *me*, and gave Himself for *me*.'

But William Holland had a triumphant testimony of this reading of Luther, reporting:

Mr Charles Wesley read the Preface aloud. At the words, 'What, have we then nothing to do? No! nothing! but only accept of Him, "Who of God is made unto us wisdom and righteousness and sanctification and redemption" ', there came such a power over me as I cannot well describe; my great burden fell off in an instant; my heart was so filled with peace and love that I burst into tears. I almost thought I saw our Saviour! My companions, perceiving me so affected, fell on their knees and prayed. When I afterwards went into the street, I could scarcely feel the ground I trod upon.[1]

From this time forth Holland was indeed a new creature in Christ. He spoke of his volume of *Luther on the Galatians* as 'a very precious treasure that I had found', and it would appear that in the days following this reading of it with Charles, he took it to other spiritual seekers and read it with them also.

But Charles knew no relief. 'May 19', he wrote, 'I received the Sacrament, but not Christ . . . I looked for Him all night with prayers and sighs and unceasing desires.' The following morning he began his *Journal* with the words, 'I waked much disappointed,

[1] William Holland, *A Narrative of the Work of the Lord in England*, manuscript in possession of the Moravian Church Library, Muswell Hill, London. This paragraph is cited in John Wesley's *Journal*, Vol 1, *p* 476, fn.

and continued all day in great dejection . . .' But that evening, as Bray read to him the narrative of the healing of the palsied man, with its assurance, 'The Son of Man hath power on earth to forgive sins', Charles said, 'It was a long while before he could read this through for tears of joy; and I saw herein and firmly believed, that his faith would be available for the healing of me.'

The following day, May 21, Pentecost Sunday, became the day of days for Charles. 'I waked in hope and expectation of His coming', he wrote. In his looking for some audible revelation of the Saviour he imagined that the voice of Bray's sister in the house was the voice of the Lord Jesus. He also resorted to the practice of opening the Bible at random and accepting the first verse his eye lighted upon as the message of the Lord to him. At first he spoke of 'violent opposition and reluctance to believe', but later was able to testify, 'The Spirit of God strove with my own and the evil spirit, till by degrees He chased away the darkness of my unbelief. I found myself convinced, I knew not how nor when, and immediately fell to intercession.' That evening he recorded:

I now found myself at peace with God, and rejoiced in hope of loving Christ. My temper for the rest of the day was mistrust of my own great, but before unknown, weakness. I saw that by faith I stood; by the continual support of faith, which kept me from falling, though of myself I am ever sinking into sin. I went to bed, still sensible of my own weakness, yet confident of Christ's protection.

Two days later Charles commemorated the occasion, saying, 'I began an hymn upon my conversion.' Opinions differ as to which hymn it was, but some believe it to have been:

Where shall my wond'ring soul begin?
  How shall I all to heaven aspire?
A slave redeem'd from death and sin,
  A brand pluck'd from eternal fire,
How shall I equal triumphs raise,
Or sing my great Deliverer's praise?

But there is also evidence which points to another hymn – one which several authorities regard as among the foremost hymns of all time:

And can it be that I should gain
  An interest in the Saviour's blood?
Died He for me, who caused His pain?
  For me, who Him to death pursued?
Amazing love! how can it be
That Thou, my God, should'st die for me!

Long my imprisoned spirit lay
  Fast bound in sin and nature's night;
Thine eye diffused a quick'ning ray;
  I woke; the dungeon flamed with light;
My chains fell off, my heart was free,
I rose, went forth, and follow'd Thee.

It matters little which was 'the hymn' of Charles's conversion.[1] Both the above express the transformation he experienced on that memorable day, Sunday, May 21, 1738. That evening John wrote, 'I received the surprising news that my brother had found rest to his soul. His bodily strength returned also from that hour.'

*

John, however, remained despondent and still seeking. 'Monday, Tuesday and Wednesday', he writes, 'I had continual sorrow and heaviness in my heart.' But on the Wednesday morning, chancing to light upon the Scripture, 'Thou art not far from the kingdom', he took it as an omen that his search was soon to end. In the afternoon he attended a service at St Paul's Cathedral and as the choir sang, 'Out of the deep have I called unto Thee, O Lord; Lord, hear my voice. O let Thine ears consider well the voice of my complaint', he found the words an expression of his own deep desires.

That evening he went, as he says, 'very unwillingly to a Society

[1] The writer of an article in the *Proceedings of the Wesley Historical Society*, September, 1966, argues in favour of "Granted is the Saviour's prayer' as the conversion hymn. The evidence in favour of 'And can it be' seems much stronger. The latter is indeed a hymn of conversion; that is its only subject, and it is alive with the joy that Charles experienced on this occasion. Moreover, it bears a relationship with the *Galatians* which was of such influence upon Charles; the emphasis upon the personal pronouns that he makes in his *Journal*, 'I laboured, waited and prayed to feel "Who loved *me* and gave himself for *me*"', is repeated in the lines, 'And can it be that I should gain An interest in the Saviour's blood? Died He for me, who caused His pain? For me, who Him to death pursued? Amazing love! how can it be, That Thou, my God, should'st die for me!'

in Aldersgate Street, where one was reading Luther's preface to the Epistle to the Romans'. There can be little doubt that this 'one' was William Holland, and we may well ask, 'But how did he read?' In the light of the fact that just seven days earlier Luther's message had come to his own soul with such power, flooding his heart with joy and filling his eyes with tears, we can but believe that it was with the same rejoicing and the same glory of spirit that he read now. Surely it was with tears of gladness that he repeated Luther's 'description of the change which God works in the heart through faith in Christ', and as he pronounced the wondrous words, John Wesley, longing with such intensity for that faith, felt in that moment he had received it.

I felt [he says], my heart strangely warmed. I felt I did trust in Christ, Christ alone for salvation; and an assurance was given me that He had taken away *my* sins, even *mine*, and saved *me* from the law of sin and death.[1]

The search which had gone on with so strong a desire since his days in Georgia was suddenly ended. 'I then testified openly to all there', he reports, 'what I now first felt in my heart.'

As soon as the Aldersgate Street meeting was over, John and several companions went to Bray's to break the good news to Charles. 'Towards ten,' writes Charles, 'my brother was brought in triumph by a troop of our friends, and declared, "I believe!" We sang the hymn with great joy and parted with prayer.'[2]

We visualize the scene in Bray's humble home. Charles, yet recuperating from his illness, rises to join with the exulting John, accompanied by Bray, Hutton, Holland and others, as with rejoicing in each heart and gladness ringing through each voice, they sing:

[1] John Wesley's *Journal*, Vol 1, *p* 476. Was it *Romans* or *Galatians* which was being read on this occasion? There is no doubt that it was *Galatians* that Charles and Holland had read seven days earlier, and Holland also read *Galatians* to the Claggett sisters, and Charles states, 'I read Luther as usual to a large company of friends'. Perhaps Holland, having derived such benefit from *Luther on the Galatians* quickly purchased *Luther on the Romans*, but the greater probability is that John Wesley, writing his diary at the close of the day was so overjoyed, that he mistook the one for the other.

[2] Charles Wesley's *Journal*, May 24, 1738.

'Tis mystery all! The Immortal dies!
  Who can explore His strange design!
In vain the first-born seraph tries
  To sound the depths of love divine!
'Tis mercy all: let earth adore,
Let angel minds inquire no more.

What triumph for John, after his months of fear and dejection to be able to cry:

No condemnation now I dread;
  Jesus, and all in Him, is mine!
Alive in Him, my living Head,
  And clothed in righteousness divine.
Bold I approach th' eternal throne,
And claim the crown, through Christ my own.

*

Following conversion, each of the Wesleys looked forward to the transformation that the Moravians had taught them to expect.

The change was noticeable first in Charles. 'I was full of delight', he exclaims, 'and seemed in new heavens and a new earth.'[1]

There were times when he still suffered some heaviness, but amidst such struggles he testified to new victory. The tendency to hasty temper was there yet; of one occasion he says, 'I felt a motion of anger from a trifling disappointment, but it was no sooner felt than conquered.'[2] At another time when his opinion was contradicted, he said, 'I found the old man arise, but I grew calmer and calmer the longer we talked. Glory be to God through Christ!'[3] 'I never knew the energy of sin', he stated, 'till now that I experience the superior strength of Christ.'[4]

Charles began to declare 'salvation by faith' to every soul he could reach. He gave little attention to theological matters, and his particular doctrinal convictions at this time seem to have been little more than the certainty that salvation was received by faith. His *Journal* indicates one or two instances in which he went on to show that this faith was in the work of Christ and that Christ's righteousness was imputed to the believer, but more often it was faith itself that he emphasized. He frequently asserts that

[1] *Ibid,* June 8.
[2] *Ibid,* May 27.
[3] *Ibid,* June 26.
[4] *Ibid,* June 6.

he 'preached faith' and that others 'received faith', and when he was questioned about salvation he triumphantly pointed to his own experience of faith. With great boldness he preached 'salvation by faith' in the few churches to which he found admission, in the Society Rooms, and once in Westminster Abbey. He laboured to lead the family of the wealthy Justice Delamotte to the experience of faith, and after nearly three weeks at their country mansion he wrote, 'I returned to town, rejoicing that God had added to His living church seven more souls through my ministry'.[1]

In a beautiful work of Christian compassion Charles went day after day among the condemned criminals at Newgate prison.

> I visited one of them in his cell [he writes], sick of a fever – a poor black that had robbed his master. I told him of One who came down from heaven to save lost sinners, and him in particular. I described the sufferings of the Son of God, His sorrows, agony and death. He listened with all the signs of eager astonishment; the tears trickled down his cheeks while he cried, 'What? Was it for me? Did God suffer all this for so poor a creature as me?'[2]

Upon visiting the prison again three days later Charles said, 'I . . . rejoiced with my poor happy black; who now *believes* the Son of God loved him and gave Himself for him.' As Charles declared the Gospel's good news to the felons, even in what he called 'the condemned hole', he saw its effect on them, one by one. But he also experienced its effect afresh within his own heart, as dealing with these pitiable individuals in this wretched place, he said, 'I had great help and power in prayer. . . . I found myself overwhelmed with the love of Christ to sinners.'[3]

As the day of execution approached, Charles increased his efforts. At night, he and Bray allowed themselves to be locked in with the condemned men; they 'wrestled in mighty prayer' and saw fear and despair give way to peace and joy on one countenance after another.

On the morning of the hanging, a boisterous crowd, intent on making sport of the victims, gathered as usual at Tyburn. As the death cart drew on to the field, Charles Wesley and a few friends were there to meet it. 'The black had spied me coming

[1] *Ibid,* June 27.
[2] *Ibid,* July 12.
[3] *Ibid,* July 17.

out of the coach', says Charles, 'and saluted me with his looks. As often as his eyes met mine, he smiled with the most composed, delightful countenance I ever saw.'[1] Charles made his way through the crowd and climbed into the cart, but when the official chaplain tried to do the same, 'The prisoners begged he might not come; and the mob kept him down.'[2]

There in the death cart, disdainful of the jeers of the crowd, Charles again spoke words of Scriptural comfort to the poor victims. He and his companions sang for all to hear:

Behold the Saviour of mankind
  Nail'd to the shameful tree!
How vast the love that Him inclined
  To bleed and die for thee!

'Tis done! the precious ransom's paid;
  'Receive My soul', He cries;
See where He bows His sacred head!
  He bows His head, and dies!

A rope from an overhead scaffold was placed around the neck of each prisoner. Charles continued his ministrations, praying with them, giving encouragement and kissing whom he could. As the final moment approached he again broke into song:

To the dear fountain of Thy blood,
  Incarnate God, I fly;
Here let me wash my spotted soul,
  From crimes of deepest dye.

A guilty, weak and helpless worm,
  Into Thy hands I fall;
Be Thou my life, my righteousness,
  My Jesus and my all.

'When the cart drew off,' says Charles, 'not one struggled for life. We left them going to meet their Lord, ready for the Bridegroom ... I spoke a few suitable words to the crowd, and returned full of peace and confidence in our friends' happiness. That hour under the gallows was the most blessed hour of my life.'[3]

[1] *Ibid*, July 19. [2] *Ibid.*

[3] *Ibid.* The gallows at Tyburn was so large that it could accommodate the hanging of twenty victims at once. The famed *Speakers' Corner* in Hyde Park is approximately the spot where the gallows stood.

Despite his University background, Charles remained subject to the mystical influences received from the Moravians. This was seen especially in the practice of opening the Bible at random, which he called 'consulting the oracle',[1] and several *Journal* entries after his conversion show him resorting to it. He used it when he wanted guidance for himself, or when he was seeking to show someone else the way of salvation; and there were also one or two occasions when he employed it in order to ascertain the Bible's teaching on a certain subject. Of course, the practice was fraught with danger, for by it the divine approval might appear to be placed upon an interpretation or application of Scripture which could be utterly false. Moreover, it distorted the Bible from a book whose message was to be gained by rational study, into an instrument of mere chance. In a year or two's time Charles forsook this foolish custom, but during these immediate post-conversion months it played an important part in his relation to the Scriptures.

Charles became a man of rich spiritual emotion and vehement zeal. He prayed continually, prayed anywhere and prayed with strong cryings and tears. He spoke the Gospel with boldness and power wherever he was and to everyone he met. Of a coach ride to Bexley and another to Oxford, he says, 'We prayed and sang and shouted all the way.'[2] In his new liberty he could not be held by forms of prayer and written sermons, but broke forth into free supplication and extempore preaching. His life was filled with spiritual activity and he had time and thought for nothing else.

He was still dogmatic and blunt, and had no scruples about offending anyone if he felt the soul's need required it. He says of one of his meetings in a Religious Society, 'I urged upon each my usual question, "Do you deserve to be damned?" Mrs Platt, with the utmost vehemence cried out, "Yes! I do! I do!" '[3] Of a Sunday service at St Mary's Church, Islington, he reports:

I preached with great boldness. There was a vast audience, and better disposed than usual. None went out, as they had threatened, and frequently done heretofore, especially the well-dressed hearers, 'when-

[1] Charles Wesley's *Journal*, May 28, June 29, 1738.
[2] *Ibid*, June 8, Sept. 27.
[3] *Ibid*, Aug. 31.

e'er I mentioned hell to ears polite', and urged that rude question, 'Do you deserve to be damned?"[1]

One of his poetic compositions contains the lines,

> The unitarian fiend expel,
> And send his doctrines back to hell!

He was probably referring to Mohammed in this instance, but would just as readily have applied his couplet to any clergyman who denied the Trinity or any other Christian doctrine.

However, although Charles's actions indicated that he still possessed something of the inherited abrasiveness, as the weeks passed this aspect of his personality gradually revealed the mellowing that is effected by Divine grace.

Above all, Charles's new relationship with the Lord unlocked the treasury of poetic gifts within him. His soul constantly experienced the soaring emotions of the poet and his mind instinctively invested words with harmony. These talents, long unexpressed, now found boundless exercise in the wonders of the Christian life. Hymns began to flow from his pen in rich abundance, and many of these possess a combination of strength and tenderness which from that day to this has given them a unique place in Christian praise.

Such was Charles Wesley in the months following his conversion: a forceful, courageous, happy man; and his testimony of one day, 'I rejoiced, gave thanks and sang', was virtually a picture of his transformed life.

*

John Wesley also proved to be a new man, but for him the change came much more slowly.

Like Charles, John began to make the newly-received 'faith' his principal theme. His first sermon after his conversion was from the text, 'This is the victory that overcometh the world, even our faith.'[2] He mentions 'faith' in almost every day's entry in his *Journal* and, upon having occasion to preach before the University of Oxford, he chose as his theme, 'Salvation by Faith'. This was a noteworthy event in his career, manifesting his reasoning abilities and declaring his convictions, and the sermon,

[1] *Ibid,* Sept. 24. [2] John Wesley's *Journal*, Vol 1, *p* 480.

when printed some months later, served as a sort of manifesto on the subject.

At this point in Wesley's life, however, we are confronted with some of the assumptions that have been made, and which have falsely aggrandized him. Several authors have assumed that he was suddenly and radically transformed at Aldersgate Street. For instance, one writer asks, 'What was it really happened in that little room . . .?' He supplies the answer, 'Something did happen: something memorable, something enduring. It changed Wesley's life. It lifted him, at a breath, out of doubt into certainty. It transfigured weakness into power.' Then he goes on to speak of '. . . the movement which had its starting-point in that little room on that night . . .'[1] Another author makes the assertion, 'From this hour . . . this ritualistic priest and ecclesiastical martinet was to be transformed into a flaming preacher'.[2]

These statements and others like them which might be cited, are misleading. The truth of the matter is that, instead of being 'lifted out of doubt into certainty' on that night, John Wesley was left struggling with his uncertainty for months; his preaching during that time, rather than becoming flaming, continued to be hindered by his doubts and contained very little that was fiery. In fact, Wesley was so much the same after Aldersgate Street as he had been before that certain writers have been unable to consider that event to be his conversion at all; they state that his conversion apparently took place at an earlier date – probably at the time when he first read William Law while at Oxford.[3]

An understanding of Wesley's post-Aldersgate Street condition is important to this present study. *First*, the above-cited claims that he was suddenly transformed and that 'the movement had its starting-point in that room' are but part of a thesis which almost completely overlooks the great ministry that Whitefield had already exercised – a thesis which makes it appear that there

[1] W. H. Fitchett, *Wesley and His Century* (Toronto, 1906), *p* 126.

[2] J. H. Rigg, *The Living Wesley* (London, 1891), *p* 117.

[3] R. A Knox, *Enthusiasm in the Seventeenth and Eighteenth Centuries* (Oxford, 1950), *p* 437, mentions the following as discountenancing the idea of the Aldersgate experience as Wesley's conversion: Urlin, *A Churchman's Life of Wesley*; Overton, *John Wesley*; Lunn, *John Wesley*; Piette, *John Wesley in the Evolution of Protestantism*, Knox himself also inclines to this view.

was no revival activity until Wesley's conversion, and that the trumpet voice that awakened England was his. *Secondly*, the events of this period of uncertainty had a strong effect on the shaping of the doctrines that Wesley held throughout life, and as it was these doctrines which later caused him to separate from Whitefield, we must give attention to this period of his career.

Within a week of his Aldersgate Street experience Wesley wrote:

> I received a letter from Oxford which threw me into much perplexity. It was asserted therein, 'That no doubting could consist with the least degree of true faith; that whoever at any time felt any doubt or fear was not weak in the faith, but had no faith at all; and that none hath any faith till the law of the Spirit of life has made him wholly free from the law of sin and death.'[1]

Wesley was deeply disturbed by this letter. In his short experience with evangelical doctrine he had not grasped the Biblical teaching of the imputed righteousness of Christ, nor had he seen the great eternal plan of redemption revealed in the Scriptures. Rather, as we have noticed, he had learned to emphasize faith – faith as a subjective experience – and, as a result, his thought turned inward, there to recognize his weaknesses and to concern itself with what measure of faith he might possess. The letter so distressed him that, after making such statements as 'I felt a kind of soreness in my heart, so that I found my wound was not fully healed',[2] and 'My weak mind could not bear to be thus sawn asunder',[3] he decided to seek help by visiting what he deemed to be its most probable source: the Moravian headquarters at Herrnhut in Germany.

Wesley's days at Herrnhut were well spent. He met the good but imperious Count Zinzendorf and rejoiced to see the unquestioned control that he exercised over the communal settlement. He made the acquaintance of several Moravian preachers – men whose souls had been purified in the fires of persecution – listened to their sermons and talked with them personally. He found delight in the spiritual earnestness of the common people, and such was his enjoyment that he stated, 'I would gladly have spent my life here'.[4]

[1] John Wesley's *Journal*, Vol 1, *p* 482.
[2] *Ibid.*
[3] *Ibid, p* 483.
[4] *Ibid*, Vol 2, *p* 28.

But though he derived much stimulation at Herrnhut, Wesley was little helped regarding the matter which had taken him there. He had gone with a specific question, 'What is the full assurance of faith, and how is it received?' The question required an answer from the Scriptures, yet this was the very realm in which the Moravians were weak.

In the preaching and the private conversations of the Moravians, much was said about 'the full assurance', and Wesley made extensive reports of what he heard in his *Journal.*[1] But, since the Moravians formulated their beliefs to a considerable degree on personal experience, their answers to Wesley's enquiry were many and various. One preacher said that 'the full assurance' was a blessing received at the same time as justification, but another asserted that it was a separate experience to be entered into after conversion. Another stated that it was the coming of the Holy Spirit subsequent to conversion, just as He had come to the disciples on the day of Pentecost, and still another claimed that it was no more than a rich Christian maturity and was attained simply by steady Christian growth. In these and other conflicting testimonies the Moravian preachers set forth their views on 'the full assurance of faith', and their statements gave Wesley nothing definite.

None the less, his visit to Herrnhut had certain lasting effects. *First,* it influenced him towards combining Scripture and experience in formulating doctrinal beliefs. *Secondly*, it increased in him the introspective tendency. *Thirdly*, it caused him to believe that the Moravians possessed something which he did not have, and therefore that (as some of them had intimated) a second Christian experience was possible – an experience, he believed, which would accomplish in him that larger victory in which the experience at Aldersgate Street had failed.

By the time he returned to England, Wesley had become something of a Moravian himself. Writing from London to Herrnhut, he mentioned this allegiance and described his activities saying:

> We are endeavouring here also . . . to be followers of you as you are of Christ . . . Though my brother and I are not permitted to preach in

[1] *Ibid*, Vol 2, *pp* 19–49.

most of the churches in London, yet, 'thanks be to God'! there are others left wherein we have liberty to speak the truth as it is in Jesus. Likewise on every evening, and on set evenings in the week at two several places, we publish the word of reconciliation, sometimes to twenty or thirty, sometimes to fifty or sixty, sometimes to three or four hundred persons, met together to hear it.[1]

Any help that Wesley had obtained at Herrnhut, however, proved to be of a temporary nature. The lack of a well-grounded understanding of Biblical teaching was soon apparent, for within four weeks after his return he received another letter concerning 'the state of those who are weak in faith', and he found himself as unable to cope with it as he had been on the earlier occasion. Again he confessed it 'threw me into great perplexity'.[2]

In the face of this problem Wesley's thought turned, not outward to Christ, but inward to himself. With magnificent sincerity he made an examination of his inner being and wrote his findings into his *Journal*.[3] There he defined the various ways in which a person who is truly 'in Christ' is 'a new creation', he stated certain points in which he felt he had reached this standard, but confessed several others in which he knew he had failed. It was a difficult time for him and much of his earlier despondency returned.

Two weeks later John's continuing perplexity caused him to speak of himself as 'doubtful of my own state'.[4] He sought help by opening the Bible at random – as he did in each of these times of trial – but to little avail. After the passing of a few more days, Charles Delamotte, his Georgia companion, with whom he had recently spent a week-end, told him:

You are better than you was at Savannah. You know that you was then quite wrong; but you are not right yet. You know that you was then blind; but you do not see now.

I doubt not but God will bring you to the right foundation; but I have no hope for you while you are on your present foundation; it is as different from the true, as the right hand from the left. You have all to begin anew . . .

You have a present freedom from sin; but it is only a temporary suspension of it, not a deliverance from it. And you have a peace;

[1] *Ibid, p* 92, fn.
[2] *Ibid, p* 89.
[3] *Ibid, pp* 88–91.
[4] *Ibid, p* 97.

but it is not a true peace: if death were to approach, you would find all your fears return.

But I am forbid to say any more. My heart sinks in me like a stone.[1]

Upon hearing these accusations from one who knew him so well, Wesley said, 'I was troubled'. Again he resorted to the practice of opening the Bible at random. Then within another month he made a further examination of his inner self, and, in a considerable measure of dejection, once more wrote his findings into his *Journal*.[2] Finally, eight months after his experience at Aldersgate Street, he made the incredible statement:

My friends affirm that I am mad because I said I was not a Christian a year ago. I affirm I am not a Christian now. Indeed, what I might have been I know not, had I been faithful to the grace then given, when, expecting nothing less, I received such a sense of forgiveness of sins as till then I never knew. But that I am not a Christian at this day I as assuredly know as that Jesus is the Christ.[3]

These amazing confessions raise the question, 'Is Aldersgate Street really to be accepted as the occasion of Wesley's conversion, or are we to believe he had already been converted while at Oxford?' In answer we notice that during his days at Oxford Wesley knew nothing of those truths that are essential to regeneration, and that therefore his several improvements in behaviour while there must be considered as nothing more than personal reformations. In contrast, in the Aldersgate event he fully recognized the worthlessness of his religious efforts and knew that he needed Christ; he spoke of experiencing faith's appropriation of the merits of the Saviour's death, and of the joy and peace which that experience brings. He himself, thereafter, looked upon Aldersgate Street as the occasion of his conversion,[4] and, in an over-all view of his life it does indeed stand out, as far as can humanly be judged, as the point at which the saving change was effected. Nevertheless, the truly noticeable change – the supreme point of alteration in his whole career – came later, as we shall see.

[1] *Ibid, p* 103. [2] *Ibid, pp* 115–16. [3] *Ibid, p* 125.

[4] George Croft Cell in his *The Rediscovery of John Wesley*, (Henry Holt, New York, 1935), *p* 185, says; 'In addition to the common way of timing events *Anno Domini* . . . pursued in his writings, especially the *Journal*, there are scattered throughout the twenty-five volumes of his writings – references, not a *few cases, but numbered by the score*, to his conversion-experience, *anno mea conversionis*.'

How then are we to account for this post-Aldersgate Street confusion in Wesley? It is the common practice, because of his extensive scholarship, to attribute to him a deep learning in all fields and, after recognizing this bewildered condition, simply to pass it by and pay no further attention to it. The truth is, however, that Wesley had entered a realm that was new to him – that of evangelical doctrine – and in which he was as yet quite unlearned. In this, the Reformers and Puritans would have proved valuable teachers, but he had turned, not to them, but to the Moravians, and as a result his approach had become largely an empirical one. Failing to see the Scriptural teaching of his constant *standing* in Christ, he concerned himself with his day-by-day *state* in Christ, and the fluctuations that he experienced caused his uncertainty. In the realm of evangelical truth – the realm in which he was to spend the rest of his life – despite his education, he had as yet little understanding.

It will be recognized that while in this condition Wesley could not be a really effective preacher. Powerful preaching requires clear views and strong convictions, and though he could be dogmatic regarding 'salvation by faith', there was little else of his newly acquired doctrinal position that he could declare with certainty. Undoubtedly, his force of personality gave strength to his pulpit utterance, but his delivery was after the fashion of an Oxford lecture and, as Tyerman says, 'His preaching, as yet, comparatively speaking, had not created much excitement'.[1]

Moreover, during this period Wesley revealed the presence of the inherited severity and disdain of opposition. He seems to have felt it a good thing if he offended his hearers; for instance, at the close of a Sunday in which he had preached three times, he said, 'I believe it pleased God to bless the first sermon most, because it gave the most offence; being indeed an open defiance of that mystery of iniquity the world calls prudence'.[2] He makes several reports of this kind and James Hervey evidently told him that such a manner would hinder his usefulness, for John replied:

> I fear that offspring of hell, worldly or mystic prudence, has drawn you away from the simplicity of the Gospel. How else could you ever conceive that being reviled and 'hated of all men' should make us less fit for our Master's service? How else could you ever think of 'saving

[1] Tyerman's *Whitefield*, Vol 1, *p* 149.

[2] John Wesley's *Journal*, Vol 1, *p* 440.

yourself and them that hear you' without being 'the filth and off-scouring of the world'? To this hour is this scripture true. And I therein rejoice – yea, and will rejoice. Blessed be God, I enjoy the reproach of Christ! O may you also be vile, exceeding vile, for His sake! God forbid that you should ever be other than generally scandalous; I had almost said universally. If any man tell you there is a new way of following Christ, 'he is a liar, and the truth is not in him'.[1]

Of course Wesley's manner as well as the doctrine of salvation by faith did cause opposition among his hearers. Of his first church service after his return from Georgia he wrote, 'I was afterwards informed, many of the best in the parish were so offended, that I was not to preach there any more',[2] and a similar response followed at other churches. There was a vast difference at this point between the ministry that Whitefield had exercised, with its great congregations and lasting spiritual results, and that of Wesley, which caused little stir, other than the offence that it engendered.

This was manifestly a difficult period for Wesley. Within him there dwelt extraordinary powers of mind and heart and an unusual strength of will. Around him he saw the signs of the success that had come to Whitefield, yet he himself was held back from the prominence which his abilities deserved, by reason of his doctrinal uncertainty. Moreover, there can be no doubt that, even at this early date, he felt the challenge presented by the Religious Societies – the challenge to unify and lead them – and to a man possessing such gifts of organization the appeal could not but have been a powerful one.

Two factors were necessary if Wesley was to rise to a position of usefulness commensurate with his talents. *One,* he must arrive at a clear doctrinal position; he must have views which he can declare with deep conviction. *Two,* he must find some great mission in life, some field of labour large enough to call forth all his mighty powers and utilize all his energies.

Given these two conditions John Wesley could rise to the greatness for which he was born. And in the plan of God, and in an unfolding of events which has been but little noticed, this historic experience was soon to be his.

[1] *Ibid,* Vol 2, *p* 218. [2] *Ibid,* Vol 1, *p* 436.

I was really happy in my little foreign cure and could have cheerfully remained among them, had I not been obliged to return to England to receive priest's orders and make a beginning towards laying a foundation to the Orphan House . . . During my stay here the weather was most intensely hot . . . Seeing others do it, I determined to inure myself to hardships, by lying constantly on the ground; which, by use, I found to be so far from being a hardship, that, afterward it became so to lie in a bed.

WHITEFIELD
Manuscript quoted by Gillies

11

Colonial Missionary

At the time of Whitefield's visit to America, Georgia was but five years old. Many of its settlers were released debtors from the prisons of England. General Oglethorpe had conceived the idea of thus bringing them to the new world, believing that, no matter how difficult the colonial life might be, it was better than a jail existence at home. These people were largely of a shiftless sort, in poor health, inexperienced at farming and physically incapable of pioneering a wilderness land.

But others came who were of a better class. Among these were additional Englishmen, a group of pious Germans known as Saltzburgers, a few French-speaking Swiss, a party of Scottish Highlanders and two small companies of Moravians.

The Savannah to which Whitefield came was little more than a clearing in the woods. It probably contained about a hundred houses[1] – many of them but primitive cabins – and had a population of not more than five hundred. The only other sizeable community was Frederica, a military outpost a hundred miles to the south, with about 120 inhabitants. There were four or five small villages, and with the addition of the passengers who had arrived on the *Whitaker* and its two companion vessels, the total population of the Colony was probably less than a thousand. It was in order to minister to this people that Whitefield had left the thronging congregations of Bristol and London.

Immediately upon his arrival Whitefield joined in a prayer meeting with 'a few pious souls' and Charles Delamotte, the one remaining member of Wesley's party. Though still sick from the fever suffered aboard ship, he attempted to begin his duties, and at five the next morning held his first service, with seventeen

[1] In 1740 Secretary Stephens reported '142 houses'.

adults and twenty-five children in attendance. That day, Thomas Causton, the Chief Magistrate, who had been Wesley's persecutor, offered to call on him. But Whitefield reversed the courtesy, visited him and the other Magistrates and so won their favour that they 'promised to build [him] a house and showed [him] much civility'.

Whitefield and his young men lived together at the parsonage. In keeping with his intention to have no female help, the two menservants took over the domestic duties, he set up his system of 'living by rule', and matters worked out so well that he said, 'I find it possible to manage a house without distraction'.[1] He quickly became inured to colonial conditions and when five weeks had passed wrote to his friend Harris at Gloucester, saying:

America is not so horrid a place as it is represented to be. The heat of the weather, lying on the ground, etc., are mere painted lions in the way, and to a soul filled with divine love are not worth mentioning . . .

As to my ministerial office, God (such is His goodness) sets His seal to it here as at other places. We have an excellent Christian school and near a hundred constantly attend at evening prayers . . . I visit from house to house, catechise, read prayers twice and expound the two second lessons every day; read to a houseful of people three times a week; expound the two lessons at five in the morning, read prayers and preach twice, and expound the catechism to servants, etc., at seven in the evening every Sunday.[2]

Whitefield experienced a reception in Georgia similar to that which he had known in England. 'The people receive me gladly', he said, 'into their houses and seem to be most kindly affected towards me.' 'They everywhere receive me with civility and are not angry when I reprove them.' Colonel William Stephens, the Secretary of the Colony, made the following entries in his official *Journal*:

May 21. Mr Whitefield officiated this day at the church,[3] and made a sermon very engaging to the most thronged congregations I had ever seen there.

[1] Whitefield's *Works*, Vol 1, *p* 44. [2] *Ibid.*

[3] There was as yet no church, but, 'The Town Hall at Savannah is furnished with benches, a gallery for bailiffs, a pulpit for the minister, in which Divine service is performed . . . it holds one hundred people.' *Manuscripts of the Earl of Egmont*, Vol 11, *p* 314.

May 28. Mr Whitefield manifests great ability in the ministry.

June 4. Mr Whitefield's auditors increase daily, and the place of worship is far too small to contain the people who seek his doctrine.

June 18. Mr Whitefield went on moving the people with his captivating discourses. A child being brought to church to be baptized, he performed that office by *sprinkling*, which gave great content to many who had taken great distaste at the form of *dipping* so obstinately withstood by some parents that they have suffered their children to go without the benefit of that sacrament, till a convenient opportunity could be found of another minister to do that office.

July 2. Mr Whitefield gains more and more on the affections of the people, by his labour and assiduity in the performance of divine offices; to which an open and easy deportment, without show of austerity, or singularity of behaviour in conversation, contribute not a little.[1]

The Secretary was here manifestly contrasting Whitefield's actions with those of the Wesleys. John and Charles had insisted that baptism be performed by immersion,[2] and the terms 'austerity' and 'singularity of behaviour' refer to those aspects of their personalities which had chiefly caused complaint. No doubt Whitefield was watched for the possible appearance of such traits in him, and it is probable that he had this in mind when he said, 'I have endeavoured to let my gentleness be known among them . . . and have striven to draw them by the cords of love'. He refused to carry tales about the Wesleys or to hear the colonists' criticisms, saying, 'All this I was apprised of, but think it most prudent not to repeat grievances'.[3]

Whitefield did, however, find something commendatory to say. Since defamatory accounts of John Wesley's actions in Georgia were then reaching England, there was need for an on-the-spot report which would counteract them. Despite the opposition that John had met, the integrity of his character could not be denied, and it was impossible but that so able and earnest a

[1] *Collections of the Georgia Historical Society, The Journal of Secretary Stephens*, Supplement to Vol 4, entries of dates indicated, 1738.

[2] On March 14, 1736, Charles Wesley recorded in his *Journal*, 'Mrs Germain retracted her consent for having her child baptized. However, Mrs Colwell's I did baptize by trine [triple] immersion.' John wrote, 'Mary Welch, aged eleven days, was baptized according to the custom of the first Church, and the rule of the Church of England, by immersion (*Journal* 1, *pp* 166–7).

[3] Gillies, *op cit*, *p* 27.

man would make a deep impression on some of the people. The number of such persons was undoubtedly small, but Whitefield, in reporting the effect of Wesley's work, used words which suggested a much larger result. 'The good Mr Wesley has done, under God, in America', he wrote, 'is inexpressible. His name is very precious among the people.'[1] Wesley's own *Journal* makes it evident that his labours were of a very limited nature, and, since the statement was clearly an exaggeration, Whitefield deleted it from the later edition of his *Journals*. But at the time he wrote it, his friend Wesley was in need of such commendation, and Whitefield could not refrain from overstatement in giving it.

In making a comparison, however, of the accomplishments of the two men in Georgia, one must bear in mind that, while Wesley had not been able to bring with him anything other than a few books, Whitefield came with a great array of goods. Wherever he went he had clothing, medicines, books, hardware and foodstuffs to distribute and such gifts could not fail to win him a warm reception.

*

During these weeks Whitefield shared the companionship of Charles Delamotte. When Charles had first considered accompanying the Wesleys to Georgia, his father, who was very well-to-do, sought to deter him by offering to set him up in business in a handsome way. But he refused and went to the Colony, suffering his parents' wrath for doing so. He bore the trials which had been the lot of the Wesleys and, when Charles Wesley and Benjamin Ingham returned to England, he stayed on in the Colony, working with John. Then when John left too, he still remained, faithfully carrying on his work of teaching school and assisting the people in every way possible. He was often in dire need but refused to write to his parents for help.

After his months of loneliness he doubtless found the presence of Whitefield and his party a delight. Moreover, it appears that Whitefield was used of God in his conversion, for when Delamotte returned to England the following November, Charles Wesley said, 'I found . . . he had received forgiveness five months

[1] *Journals*, *p* 157.

ago, and continued in peace and liberty'.[1] Though Charles Delamotte virtually disappears from our narrative at this point, his heroic labours in Georgia merit a lasting remembrance.

*

Whitefield's ministry took him to every settlement in the Colony, and his efforts were directed, not only to the spiritual but also to the temporal affairs of the people. At the villages of Hampstead and Highgate he took notice of their pioneering work and commended it; he gave them a supply of meat for their immediate needs and purchased '8 sows and a pig' in order that they might begin to raise their own supply. He organized a school for the children, placed one of his men, William Doble, there as teacher, undertook the responsibility of his maintenance and had the people begin the construction of a school house. At Savannah he began a school for girls and settled another of his men as the teacher. At Frederica, since there was no building suitable for a church service, he preached out of doors, but rejoiced to see that lumber was being sawn for a church, towards which he had raised £50. He visited the Saltzburgers at Ebenezer, gave them a quantity of goods of various kinds and promised to help their pastor, Martin Boltzius, with money and materials towards the building of a church. The Saltzburgers had a small orphan house that he visited. The results of their labours in clearing and planting the land were remarkable, and he gave them high praise. His accounts covering his purchases in the Colony show that he bought 'a cow and a calf for a poor housekeeper', and that he 'set up a poor baker' with some barrels of flour, and we may be sure that these are typical of several such acts of mercy.

Whitefield entered understandingly into Georgia's economic affairs. Conditions were still very primitive, poverty was widespread, many settlers were defeated in their attempts to make a living, and, both there and in England it was prophesied that the Colony would soon fail completely. In bringing the supply of goods with him, Whitefield had manifested his awareness of this situation and, as he travelled, he familiarized himself with the

[1] Charles Wesley's *Journal*, Nov. 18, 1738. Delamotte was so poor that he was unable to return to England until Whitefield provided the money for his passage. Whitefield was later reimbursed by the Trustees.

state of the economy, recognizing the people's problems and seeking to effect some lasting improvement.

His schools were his first step. Looking, as he did, on ignorance and the wasting of time as among the prime foes of mankind, he expressed a desire to see the whole Colony characterized by discipline and industry of the kind that was practised by the Saltzburgers. He viewed the training of the children as a principal means towards this end. 'I am settling', he wrote, 'little schools in and about Savannah, that the rising generation may be bred up in the nurture and admonition of the Lord.'[1] It was his purpose that the schools should supply, not only basic education, but instruction in the Gospel and a drilling in those principles which he deemed essential to Christianity: hard work and orderliness.

The true need, however, was for something more than these 'little schools'. There were a number of homeless children in the Colony, many of them in a deplorable condition, and they could be permanently helped only by the establishment of an orphan house.

Such a project had been in Whitefield's mind for some time. The Holy Club men had made much of the *Pietas Hallensis,* Professor Francke's account of the great orphan house which God had enabled him to build and maintain at Halle in Germany. In their estimate of the several charitable endeavours, these men had looked on the founding of an orphan house as supreme, and, shortly after his conversion Whitefield had expressed his desire to imitate Francke in this accomplishment.

The primary planning for an orphan house in Georgia had already been done. The large-hearted Oglethorpe had suggested the project to the Trustees, and in 1737 they had asked their Secretary, Charles Wesley, to work out preliminary ideas. By way of preparation Charles re-read the *Pietas Hallensis*, and he identified himself with the undertaking, saying, 'I desired our Orphan House might be begun in the power of faith'.[2] Accordingly, when Whitefield first signified his intention to go to Georgia, Charles informed him of the proposals, and Oglethorpe and the Trustees suggested that he take what action he could toward putting them into effect.

This matter took on critical importance in Whitefield's mind

[1] *Works,* Vol 1, *p* 44. [2] Charles Wesley's *Journal,* Nov. 2 and 7, 1737.

while he was in the Colony. It is evident that he did not give careful consideration to all that might be involved; he merely knew that his heart was moved by the sufferings of the children, and that Christian compassion demanded that he help them, and therewith the matter was largely settled for him. But there were also other factors which influenced his thinking: 1. He had raised large sums of money for the settlers without difficulty and assumed that an appeal for orphaned children would bring a still greater response. 2. He took it for granted that the project would have the lasting support of the Trustees and Oglethorpe, of the Wesley brothers and probably of all the Holy Club men. 3. He was influenced by Francke's example, but gave little heed to the contrast between Francke's location in a populous land and his own in a wilderness. These factors all had a bearing on his thinking, and, in the light of them, he decided that he would return to England as soon as possible and begin to raise money for the construction of an Orphan House.

*

At this time Whitefield also made another very important decision. In this, however, his thinking turned in a tragic direction.

In formulating the laws of Georgia, the philanthropic Oglethorpe had decreed that slavery would not be allowed. The settlers had immediately opposed this legislation, and, during the very months in which Whitefield was in the Colony, agitation against the law was at fever heat and a petition was being circulated to force its repeal.

The argument of the colonists was that they, being Englishmen, and accustomed to a temperate climate, would never be able to endure the heat of the Georgian fields; only those born in a tropical land, they asserted, could labour beneath the summer sun. They claimed that this had already proved true in Carolina and Virginia, and that, because of the importation of the African, these Colonies were flourishing, while Georgia remained in poverty. 'In spite of all endeavours to disguise the point', stated the colonists, 'it is as clear as light itself, that negroes are as essentially necessary to the cultivation of Georgia as axes, hoes, or any other utensil of agriculture'.[1]

[1] *Colonial Records of Georgia,* Vol 2, *p* 93.

At that time such views were widely held. Slavery was practised in every other American colony, in Canada, the West Indies and Central and South America. Very few voices had been raised against it, either in England or the Colonies. Christian leaders condoned the practice, claiming that (as they supposed) the Gospel could not be taken to the African in his native land, but that by bringing him to America it was possible to reach him with its influences.

During his days in Georgia, Whitefield proved susceptible to this propaganda. Let it be understood that in two years' time he published a scathing denunciation of the cruelties practised on the slaves and began the construction of a great institution to provide a refuge for them. Nevertheless, at this earlier date, set down amidst the agitation of the Georgian people, he was influenced towards accepting the principle of slavery.

*

Whitefield's plans to return to England in order to secure a charter and money for an orphan house, caused him to bring his ministry in the Colony to a close. The first farewell service was held at Highgate on August 24, and the occasion was marked also by the opening of the schoolhouse that he had initiated. The final service was held the following Sunday, and Secretary Stephens reported:

> The congregation was so crowded that a great many stood without the doors, and under the windows to hear him, pleased with nothing more than the assurances he gave of his intention to return to them as soon as possible.'[1]

Whitefield took his departure the next day.

'They came to me', he wrote, 'from the morning till the time I left them with tears in their eyes, wishing me a prosperous journey and safe return, and gave me other tokens of their love . . . My heart was full, and I took the first opportunity of venting it by prayers and tears. I think I never parted from a place with more regret . . .'[2]

The passage to England proved to be a long and frightful

[1] *Colonial Records of Georgia,* Vol 4, *Stephens' Journal,* entry of Aug. 27, 1738.
[2] Whitefield's *Journals, pp* 164–5.

ordeal. Contrary winds buffeted the vessel, the *Mary*, from the start, insomuch that, after a week of sailing she was but a few leagues from the American coast. Tempestuous seas were constantly experienced, but then came a furious storm which, says Whitefield,

> . . . put all the sailors to their wits' end. Most of them declared they had never seen the like before. The mainsail was slit in several pieces, and several of the other sails, and much of the tackling all to tatters. Not a dry place was to be found in all the ship. The Captain's hammock, in the great cabin, was half filled with water; and though I lay in the most dry part of the ship, yet the waves broke in upon me twice or thrice. In short, all was terror and confusion, men's hearts failing them for fear, and the wind and sea raging horribly . . . Most of our fresh provisions are washed overboard, and our tackling much out of order . . .[1]

The prospects for the journey before them thus became dark indeed. Because of the loss of the provisions, the daily ration of water was set at a quart per person, and the food was but a small allowance of salt beef and dumplings. Another vessel came by and made contact with them; it was larger and well provisioned, and, learning of Whitefield's presence, invited him to sail with them. But, thinking it not in keeping with a Christian testimony for him to leave others in danger while he alone escaped, he refused the offer.

Day after day the *Mary* struggled on amidst fearful conditions. Here are some of Whitefield's reports:

> Nov. 1 . . . our food is so salt, that I dare eat but little, so that I am now literally in fastings often . . . they have not above three days' water on board.
>
> Nov. 2 . . . Our allowance of water is but a pint a day . . . Our sails are exceedingly thin, some more of them were split last night, and no one knows where we are; but God does, and that is sufficient.
>
> Nov. 6 . . . we were driven some leagues back . . . a little cake or two baked on the coals, and a very little salt beef was all my provision for the day; . . .
>
> Nov. 8. Preached . . . inwardly fainting, and unable to read scarce anything; but, blessed be God, though He slay me, yet will I put my

[1] *Ibid, pp* 167–8.

trust in Him . . . Most in the great cabin begin to be weak and look hollow-eyed . . .

Nov. 11. Still we are floating about, not knowing where we are; . . . The weather now begins to be cold, so that I can say, with the Apostle, I am 'in hunger and thirst, cold and fastings often' . . . My outward man sensibly decayeth, but the spiritual man, I trust, is renewed day by day . . . Our ship is much out of repair, and our food by no means enough to support nature . . . an ounce or two of salt beef, a pint of muddy water, and a cake made of flour and skimmings of the pot.

Whitefield, who had met the temptations incident to great popularity without faltering, proved equally strengthened amidst these trials. 'Most of this week has been spent in searching the Scriptures, and in retirements for direction and assistance in the work before me', he wrote at one time; and at another, 'Last night He lifted up the light of His blessed countenance upon me, and to-day fills me with joy unspeakable and full of glory.'

Although there was little public ministry that he could exercise during this voyage, Whitefield was particularly used of the Lord in a private way. With him there sailed a man named Gladman, a ship's captain, whose vessel had been wrecked on the coast of Florida. He and his crew had existed for thirty days on a sandbank, after which they had drifted for four hundred miles on a raft. They landed on an island near Savannah, and taking refuge in Georgia, Gladman made the acquaintance of Whitefield and received many kindnesses from him. While sailing with him on the return journey to England he was the object of the evangelist's further instructions in the Gospel. We may be sure also that the courage and fortitude which Whitefield demonstrated in the face of the dangers of the voyage were a living witness to Gladman. Before the journey was concluded, the Lord had effected His saving work in the Captain's heart, and in subsequent months he became a stalwart Christian and a personal friend and worthy assistant to Whitefield.

Conditions aboard the *Mary* grew steadily more perilous. Driven day after day at the mercy of wind and wave, with water reduced almost to the last muddy cupful and the food all but gone, it was manifest that death might well be very near. And constantly there was the haunting fear that they were lost – lost upon the trackless immensity of the ocean. 'I am wholly resigned', wrote Whitefield, 'knowing that His grace will be sufficient for me, and that His time is best.'

After nearly nine weeks at sea, the vessel suddenly rang with the cry of 'Land! Land!' All aboard ran on deck to see the sight and Whitefield led them in a prayer and Psalm of thanksgiving. They had reached the west coast of Ireland, and a boat was sent ashore to obtain water and food. On its return it brought the news that a great gentleman, learning of Whitefield's presence, had sent word inviting him to come to his home and 'to stay as long as [he] wished', in order to recuperate from the ordeal through which he had passed.

As the journey thus came to an end Whitefield stated:

> . . . this voyage has been greatly for my good; for I have had a glorious opportunity of searching the Scriptures, composing discourses, writing letters, and communing with my own heart. We have been on board just nine weeks and three days – a long and perilous, but profitable voyage to my soul; for I hope it has taught me, in some measure, to endure hardships as becometh a minister of Christ. My clothes have not been off (except to change me) all the passage. Part of the time I lay on open deck; part on a chest; and the remainder on a bedstead covered with my buffalo's skin. These things, though little in themselves, are great in their consequences; . . .[1]

Whitefield refused, however, to spend any time in recuperation. After accepting the hospitality of the Irish gentleman, Mr MacMahon, overnight, and being furnished by him with three horses, he, with his servant[2] and Captain Gladman, set out for Dublin. As they journeyed, he remarked the poverty of the people and expressed a strong desire to see schools established for their children. Upon arriving at Limerick he found that he was known: the Mayor sent for him and the Bishop had him preach at the Cathedral, showed him much kindness and kissed him when he left. At Dublin the Bishop invited him to dine and the Archbishop courteously received him.

But Whitefield hastened to reach England, and finally, on November 30 (1738), set foot on his native soil at the port of

[1] *Ibid, p* 179.
[2] Joseph Husbands returned with Whitefield.

Parkgate. Eleven months had elapsed since his tearful farewell at London.

*

Herewith there closed a period in Whitefield's ministry. It was also the close of a stage of his personal development. In some senses it was the most attractive period of his whole career, for during this time he had been the winsome youth, the highly respected young clergyman, somewhat naïve and even boyish, but zealous, tactful and strong. Though he was disliked by some persons, he had won the intense admiration of the majority wherever he had been in England and America, and he still had not yet reached the age of twenty-four.

His characteristics during this period had simply been those of his natural self, in the exercise of the traits and faculties that God had placed within him by birth.

Before him, however, there lay circumstances which would require a manner of life for which he was much less fitted by nature. He was soon to become the centre of a violent controversy and to find it necessary to be a warrior for the Lord, and to such conditions he could adjust only with grave difficulty. But, almost as if he foresaw this struggle, as he anticipated taking up his work again he declared:

> With a particular fear and trembling I think of going to London; but He who preserved Daniel in the den of lions, and the Three Children in the fiery furnace, will, I hope, preserve me from the fiery trial of popularity, and from the misguided zeal of those, who, without cause, are my enemies.[1]

[1] *Journals*, p 179.

PART III
The Period of Transition

The clergy, with a few honourable exceptions, refused entirely to countenance this strange preacher. In the true spirit of the dog in the manger, they neither liked to go after the semi-heathen masses of population themselves, nor liked anyone else to do the work for them . . . The plain truth is, that the Church of England of that day was not ready for a man like Whitefield. The Church was too much asleep to understand him, and was vexed at a man who would not keep still and let the devil alone.

BISHOP J. C. RYLE

Christian Leaders, 1868

12

The Offence of the Cross

THE news that Whitefield was again in England startled his foes, but occasioned a burst of joy among his friends.

James Hutton, to whom Whitefield had written from Ireland, could not wait for him to reach London. Along with three others who shared his enthusiasm – Benjamin Ingham, William Holland and William Seward – he set out along the highway and met him about six miles from the city.[1]

Charles Wesley was at Oxford at the time and quickly made his way to London.[2] John, who was in the same area, wrote, 'Hearing Mr Whitefield was arrived from Georgia, I hastened to London . . . God gave us once more to take sweet counsel together.'[3] This was the first time the two men had met since their days in the university three and a half years earlier, and during that period much had taken place of which they would be sure to talk on this occasion. Doubtless, Whitefield would ask about Wesley's visit to Herrnhut; Wesley would enquire as to how Whitefield had fared in Georgia and, we may be sure, would show an intense interest in the ministry he had exercised in Bristol and London. So sweet was the counsel that, according to Wesley's *Diary*, it lasted till 1.30 in the morning and caused him to exclaim, 'Great blessing!'[4]

Whitefield immediately looked for signs of the continuing effects of his former ministry and saw much to rejoice him. On his first evening in London he attended the Fetter Lane Society, and reported, 'I perceived God had greatly watered the seed sown by my ministry when last in London'.[5] Two days later, a Sunday,

[1] The men are identified by Holland in his *A Narrative of the Work of the Lord in England.*

[2] Charles Wesley's *Journal*, Dec. 11, 1738.

[3] John Wesley's *Journal*, Vol 2, *p* 114.

[4] *Ibid.*

[5] Whitefield's *Journals*, *p* 193.

after preaching at St Mary's Church, Islington, where the Wesleys had frequently assisted the minister, he commented, 'Here seems to be a great pouring out of the Spirit, and many who were awakened by my preaching a year ago, are now grown strong men in Christ, by the ministrations of my dear friends and fellow-labourers, John and Charles Wesley'.[1] And when he had been in England long enough to view the situation in some breadth he stated, 'What a great work has been wrought in the hearts of many within this twelvemonth! Now know I that, though thousands might come at first out of curiosity, yet God has prevented and quickened them by His free grace.'[2]

Without delay Whitefield set about making arrangements regarding the proposed Orphan House. He called on the Archbishop of Canterbury and the Bishop of London, reporting that he 'met with a favourable reception'.[3] He attended two meetings of the Trustees for Georgia, and they gave him their written commission to collect money for the project. The Trustees expected that he would be allowed the use of the churches for this purpose, and it is possible that this was tacitly included in the approval given by the Archbishop.

Whitefield hoped to take up his ministry where he had left it off the year before. He anticipated using again the churches that had been previously allowed to him, but this time, together with his Gospel ministry, he would collect, not for the poor of Georgia in general, but specifically for the Orphan House. Such a plan was in keeping with commonly accepted principles of the Church of England: that is, that the use of a church was not necessarily limited to the activity of its incumbent, but was for the service of the Church as a whole. In turn, Whitefield was an ordained man, he preached nothing but the doctrines of the *Articles* of the Church, and was pleading on behalf of orphans in England's poorest colony. Thus he believed that this undertaking ought to have the support of the clergy and the people and that such an activity formed a part of the very purpose for which the churches existed.

This hope, however, quickly proved vain. Though Whitefield knew that opposition had been levelled against his former ministry, he was not aware of the extent to which it had increased

[1] *Ibid.* [2] *Ibid*, p 195. [3] *Ibid*, p 193.

during his absence. The continuation of his influence, the publication of his sermons, the growth of the Societies and the offence caused by the manner of the Wesleys,[1] had combined to create a situation which many of the clergy found very unpleasant, and since it had originated with Whitefield's ministry, they laid the blame at his feet. It had been with a sigh of relief that they had seen him leave for Georgia and with a sense of alarm they learned of his return. In their opinion his presence could but mean further disturbance for them and, in this mind, they determined to have nothing more to do with him. Accordingly, when he came requesting the use of the churches, their reaction was such that, even on the second day after his arrival, he reported, '. . . five churches have already been denied me, and some of the clergy, if possible, would oblige me to depart out of these coasts'.[2] His words suggest more than they actually state; they are doubtless but a polite way of saying they told him to go back to Georgia and that they would do their best to see that he did!

Faced with this refusal Whitefield made no reply and manifested no disappointment. Undergirded by the assurance that God was about to do a mighty work which no man could hinder, he simply went on preaching wherever opportunity afforded, and in so doing entered upon a ministry that busied him literally night and day.

Four churches remained open to him and in these he ministered twice each Sunday and frequently during the week.[3] But to this number others were soon added – no doubt, more by popular demand than by clerical desire – insomuch that, instead of being shut out of the churches, during a period of fifty-six days he preached in seventeen different churches, and a total of fifty-seven times.[4]

[1] Tyerman says, '. . . it is not improbable that his [Whitefield's] expulsion from the churches was partly on their [the Wesley's] account.' Tyerman's *Whitefield*, Vol 1, *p* 150.

[2] *Journals*, *p* 193.

[3] Though two weeks' records (December 11–23) are missing from Whitefield's *Journals*, the events may be largely ascertained by references to Whitefield in the *Journals* of the Wesleys.

[4] These were: St Mary's, Islington; St Helen's; Wapping Chapel; St Katherine Cree; St Antholin's; Christ Church, Spitalfields; Bermondsey; St Michael's, Cornhill; St Mary's, Whitechapel; St Lawrence, Old Jewry; St George's in-the-East;

But it was in the Religious Societies that Whitefield found his largest sphere of labour. Under the excitement engendered by his return these bodies experienced a still greater fervour and his activities among them knew few bounds. Referring, as was his custom, to his ministration in a church as *preaching* and in a Society as *expounding*, he made the following report of the Christmas week:

Sunday, Dec. 24. Preached twice and in the evening went to Crooked Lane Society . . . After I left Crooked Lane I went and expounded to a company at Mr Bray's in Little Britain; then I went to another love-feast at Fetter Lane, and, it being Christmas Eve, continued till near four in the morning in prayer, psalms and thanksgiving.

Monday, Dec. 25. About four this morning went and prayed and expounded to another Society in Redcross Street, consisting of near two or three hundred people, and the room was exceedingly hot. I had been watching unto prayer all night, yet God vouchsafed so to fill me with His blessed Holy Spirit that I spoke with as great power as ever I did in my life . . . At six I went to Crutched Friars' Society, and expounded as well as I could, but perceived myself a little oppressed with drowsiness. How does the corruptible body weigh down the soul!'

'Preached thrice and assisted in administering the Sacrament the same day . . .

Saturday, Dec. 30. Preached nine times this week, and expounded near eighteen times . . . I am every moment employed from morning till midnight. There is no end of people coming and sending to me, and they seem more and more desirous, like new-born babes, to be fed with the sincere milk of the Word.

Sunday, Dec. 31. Preached twice to large congregations, especially in the afternoon, at Spitalfields. I had a great hoarseness upon me, and was deserted before I went up into the pulpit; but God strengthened me to speak so as to be heard by all.

After I left Spitalfields, my cold being very great, I despaired of speaking much more that night; but God enabled me to expound to two companies in Southwark, and I was never more enlarged in prayer in my life.[1]

The Wesleys also were intensely busy during this Christmas season. Charles recorded, 'The whole week was a festival indeed;

St Margaret's, Westminster; Duke's Place; St Peter's, Bexley; St Alban's (Aldate's ?), Oxford; and two unnamed churches at Gravesend.

[1] *Journals*, *pp* 194–5.

a joyful season, holy unto the Lord.'[1] John in particular found his audiences increased by the fervour that followed Whitefield's return; on two occasions he was able to preach to crowded churches and, in the delight of this new experience, was moved to exaggeration; 'I preached', he reported, 'Sunday the 31st, to many thousands in St George's, Spitalfields. And to a yet more crowded congregation at Whitechapel in the afternoon . . .'[2]

Whitefield's return also drew other Holy Club men to London. Kinchin, Hutchings and Hall arrived, to join with the Wesleys, Ingham and himself in a week of prayer and consultation. They entered with intense fervour into the already-ardent meetings of the Fetter Lane Society and we feel something of the enthusiasm they experienced as we read Whitefield's report:

> Sometimes whole nights were spent in prayer. Often have we been filled as with new wine. And often have we seen them overwhelmed with the Divine presence and crying out, 'Will God indeed dwell with men upon earth! How dreadful is this place! This is none other than the house of God and the gate of Heaven!'[3]

But John Wesley had a still more striking account, for, at this time when the wrath of men was rising against them, God granted a rich assurance of his favour. The occasion was New Year's night and as they met at Fetter Lane with 'about sixty brethren' for the Moravian Love Feast:

> About three in the morning [says Wesley], as we were continuing instant in prayer, the power of God came mightily upon us, insomuch that many cried out for exceeding joy, and many fell to the ground. As soon as we were recovered a little from that awe and amazement at the presence of His majesty, we broke out with one voice, 'We praise Thee, O God; we acknowledge Thee to be the Lord!'[4]

How contemptible must human opposition have seemed in contrast with this overwhelming manifestation of the Divine pre-

[1] Charles Wesley's *Journal*, Dec. 26, 1738.

[2] John Wesley's *Journal*, Vol 2, *p* 119. Dr Curnock's footnote reads: 'This is perhaps the first of many instances in which it becomes obviously necessary to discount Wesley's estimate of numbers. His exaggeration of numbers is well known. It was a fault shared with others. Whitefield and Cennick are notable examples . . . "Many thousands" could not have been accommodated in St George's, Spitalfields; and "a yet more crowded congregation at Whitechapel" is unthinkable.'

[3] Gillies, *op cit*, *p* 34, fn.

[4] John Wesley's *Journal*, Vol 2, *pp* 121–2.

sence! The experience proved a predictive beginning of the year 1739 – a year soon to be fraught with the mightiest of labours, with bitter opposition, but also with boundless blessing and the conversion of untold numbers of mankind.

That week the Holy Club men held an important conference. Whitefield described them as 'seven true ministers of Jesus Christ, despised Methodists, whom God has brought together', and said of their conclave:

> What we were in doubt about, after prayer, we determined by lot, and everything else was carried on with great love, meekness and devotion. We continued in fasting and prayer till three o'clock and then parted with a full conviction that God was going to do great things among us. Oh, that He would make us vessels pure and holy, and meet for our Master's use!"[1]

Though Whitefield raised no question at this time about the casting of lots, this is the only instance on record in which he took part in it. But he soon began to view the practice with disfavour and with the passing of a few years, rejected it entirely.[2] At no time did he favour the practice of opening the Bible at random.

*

Early in January Whitefield went to Oxford in order to enter the second stage of the Church of England ministry: that of priest. The rite was performed in the Cathedral by 'good Bishop Benson', the prelate who had previously ordained him deacon. Following the service Whitefield preached at a church that he calls St Alban's,[3] addressing a crowded congregation inside and 'Gownsmen of all degrees outside'. Though these men apparently came out of curiosity or to make mischief, 'they stood attentive at the windows during [the] sermon'.[4]

Bishop Benson had formerly been a tutor to Lord Huntingdon, and, knowing the interest which he and Lady Huntingdon had in Whitefield, the Bishop wrote a letter informing them of the ordination. It was in this that he expressed the

[1] *Journals*, *p* 196.
[2] See this matter considered more fully in Appendix Note 2.
[3] This is probably a slip of the pen. He possibly intended to say 'St Aldate's' which was near Pembroke College.
[4] *Journals*, *p* 199.

opinion of Whitefield that we have already noticed: 'a pious, well-meaning young man, with good abilities and great zeal', and prayed that God would 'grant him great success in all his undertakings for the good of mankind and the revival of true religion in these degenerate days'.

But Dr Benson did not always retain this attitude. In a few years' time, when Whitefield had become the object of wide dislike, he once told Lady Huntingdon he was sorry he had ever ordained him. '"My Lord!" (said the Countess), "mark my words: when you are on your dying bed, that will be one of the few ordinations you will reflect upon with complacence." The Bishop's conduct at that solemn season verified her prediction: for when near his death, he sent ten guineas to Mr Whitefield, as a token of regard and veneration, and begged to be remembered by him in his prayers!'[1]

*

These were days of spiritual growth for Whitefield. 'I find God's grace quickening me more and more', he wrote. 'My understanding is more enlightened, my affections more inflamed and my heart full of love to God and man.'[2] Since the beginning of his voyage to Georgia he had been practising extempore prayer and expounding and, by this time, had probably broken away entirely from his former custom of reading his sermons, and had begun to preach in the manner of using the manuscript as the basis of a free and spontaneous utterance. From the earliest time of his ministry he had preached 'Justification by Faith in Jesus Christ',[3] but during these weeks in London he came to a clearer understanding of this truth.[4] The former slight intermixing of works and grace completely disappeared, and we find him speaking with strong conviction of salvation as altogether the work of God within the soul. This is evident, for instance, in the following passage from a letter that he wrote at this time:

Jesus Christ has begun and He will carry on, He will finish the good work in our souls. – We have nothing to do but to lay hold on Him

[1] Huntingdon, *op cit*, Vol 1, *p* 18. [2] *Journals*, *p* 197. [3] *Ibid*, *p* 81.

[4] Whitefield states (*Ibid*, *pp* 193–4) that upon his return from Georgia he saw 'the old doctrine of Justification by Faith only . . . much revived', and this was probably due to the emphasis placed on it by the Moravians and the Wesley brothers.

by faith, and to depend on Him for wisdom, righteousness, sanctification and redemption. Not but we must be workers together with Him; for a true faith in Jesus Christ will not suffer us to be idle. – No, it is an active, lively, restless principle; it fills the heart, so that it cannot be easy till it is doing something for JESUS CHRIST.[1]

Moreover, another doctrinal emphasis also appeared in him, particularly following his ordination. This related to the Person and work of the Holy Spirit. His *Journals* begin to contain such statements as, 'God has given me a double portion of His Spirit', and 'I was filled with the Holy Ghost. Oh, that all who deny the promise of the Father might thus receive it themselves!'[2] During these weeks he preached and published a sermon entitled, *Marks of Having Received the Holy Ghost*;[3] the burden of its message is that the Holy Spirit abides in every true believer, that salvation is necessarily accompanied by His gradual work of sanctification, and that His presence in the heart is the essential proof of having received the new birth. These views, along with his declaration of salvation as entirely the work of God, were not something new to him; on the contrary, they were but a development along the lines of the earlier movement of his thought – a trend that ever since his reading of Scougal had been in the Calvinistic direction.

*

Though the clergy had debarred Whitefield from certain of their churches, their effect on his usefulness or popularity had been but negligible. His ministerial activity was tremendous, as is evident in such of his reports as, 'Preached six times this week and expounded twice or thrice every night',[4] and 'Near nine times has God enabled me to preach this week and to expound 12 or 14 times'.[5] He was constantly in the midst of crowds: crowded churches, crowded Societies and crowds that flocked around him on the streets. He spoke of as many as four hundred and even seven hundred persons crowded into Society rooms, and mentioned a meeting in a house at which, even after the building was filled to capacity, the crowd in the street still 'pressed mightily to come in'. The wisdom of his attempt to keep on the go day and

[1] *Works*, Vol 1, *p* 47.
[2] *Journals*, *pp* 201, 203.
[3] *Works*, Vol 6, *pp* 161–73.
[4] *Journals*, *p* 197.
[5] *Ibid*, *p* 205.

night is certainly open to question, and we may be tempted to smile at his report that during a night spent in prayer at Fetter Lane he and John Wesley and some others 'went all together, about four in the morning, and broke bread at a poor sick sister's room.'[1]

Whitefield's return to England also sparked a fresh cry for his sermons in print. The printers – Hutton and others – were quick to respond and during the first months of the new year they published first editions of certain new ones and second, third or fourth editions of old ones.

Such was the Divine blessing that Whitefield again found it necessary to set apart definite hours for dealing with the numerous spiritual seekers. The day he chose was Tuesday, and of one of these he says, 'From seven in the morning till three in the afternoon, people came, some telling me what God had done for their souls, and others crying out, "What must I do to be saved?" Being obliged to go out, . . . I deferred several till Thursday.'[2] In reference to a certain 'greatly thronged' congregation, he remarked, 'Surely these are not curious hearers . . . No! Many conversions have been wrought in their hearts. God has set His seal to my ministry.'[3]

Of course, those among the clergy who viewed Whitefield with dislike, were deeply concerned over such activity. The Chaplain to the Prince of Wales sought to warn the people against Whitefield's doctrine by publishing a sermon that strenuously opposed the teaching of the assurance of salvation. He did not mention Whitefield by name, but left no doubt as to his intention, as he spoke of assurance as 'spiritual pride', and 'a grand enthusiasm' which, 'instead of bringing a man nearer heaven, sets him further from it'.[4] About this time there appeared also a second edition of the pamphlet, *Remarks on the Reverend Mr Whitefield's Journals*, 'Wherein his Many Inconsistencies are Pointed Out and his Tenets Considered', which, Tyerman says,

[1] *Ibid, p* 206 (John Wesley's *Journal*, Vol 2, *p* 139, *Diary*).
[2] *Ibid, p* 196. [3] *Ibid, p* 207.
[4] This sermon had been published while Whitefield was returning from Georgia. John Wesley had then visited the author, to state that he did not believe in the kind of assurance against which the sermon was aimed. 'We speak of an assurance', said Wesley, 'of our present pardon; not, as he does, of our final perseverance.' *Journal*, Vol 2, *p* 83.

is 'full of venom'. Moreover, Dr Hooker, the redoubtable editor of *The Weekly Miscellany*, very frequently displayed his powers of ridicule in attacking Whitefield, and constantly sought to make him appear a fanatic.

To these attacks Whitefield still made no reply. He had, as yet, highly exalted views of the ministry of the Church of England and tended to accord to every holder of the office the esteem with which he regarded the office itself. Therefore, with these men he wanted to be at peace – an attitude revealed in the following excerpts from his *Journals*:

Saturday, Jan. 6. Preached six times this week, and should have preached a seventh time, but one minister would not permit me, which caused me to pray for him most earnestly. Blessed be God, I can say, 'I love mine enemies.'

Monday, Jan. 15. Read a pamphlet written against me by a clergyman, I bless God, without any emotion. Prayed most heartily for the author.

Tuesday, Jan. 16. Prayed by name for the author of the pamphlet. Left my auditors in tears, and went home full of love and joy and peace . . .

Sunday, Jan. 21. Went this morning and received the Sacrament at the hands of the minister who wrote against me. Blessed be God, I do not feel the least remonstrance against, but a love for him; . . . Oh that I could do him any good.

Thursday, Jan. 25. Received the Sacrament at Bow, where four of my opposers administered . . . At first a thought darted into my mind that they were of a persecuting spirit, but I soon checked it, and was filled with love towards them. God grant that they may be like-minded towards me.[1]

But despite Whitefield's gracious attitude, he was gradually being forced to see that there was no possible basis for lasting peace between the clergy and himself. He tells us, for instance,

Monday, Jan. 29 . . . sat up till near one in the morning with my honoured brother and fellow-labourer, John Wesley, in conference with two clergymen of the Church of England, and some other strong opposers of the doctrine of the New Birth. God enabled me, with great simplicity, to declare what He had done for my soul, which made them look upon me as a madman . . . I am fully convinced there is a fundamental difference between us and them. They believe only an

[1] *Journals*, *pp* 197, 199, 200, 202.

outward Christ, we further believe that He must be inwardly formed in our hearts also.[1]

The realization that deep doctrinal differences existed between him and the majority of the clergy was of grave significance to Whitefield. These men were the officers of the Church that he respected so highly, yet allegiance to what he knew to be the truth of God separated him from them and required that he stand against them. The role of peace-maker came naturally to him, but it was now necessary for him to become a warrior and for this he was not at all suited by nature. The status of the respected clergyman must go and he must accept a position of being looked upon as a controversialist, subject to bitter misrepresentation and reproach. Moreover, dark storm clouds were gathering and he believed that such was the malice of his enemies that they would do their utmost to make him an outcast, closing if possible all the churches against him and even preventing him from using the Religious Societies. This prospect Whitefield viewed with ready courage – no one could be more willing to bear whatever suffering loyalty to the Lord demanded – yet the thought of being involved in controversy was very distasteful to him.

In meeting this experience Whitefield was aided by the example of the Wesleys. Their self-assertive strength allowed them to face opposition almost with contempt. Charles tells of a conversation with William Chapman, a former Holy Club man, who 'insisted that there is no need of our being persecuted now. I told him', says Charles, 'I was of a different judgment, and believed every doctrine of God must have these two marks: (1) Meeting all the opposition of men and devils: (2) Triumphing over all. I expressed my readiness to part with him and all my friends and relations for the truth's sake.'[2] Bluntly – almost defiantly – Charles asserted his clerical rights in a discussion with the Bishop of London,[3] and said of an interview which he and John had with the Archbishop, 'We told him we expected persecution'.[4]

Influenced by the attitude of the Wesleys, Whitefield began to

[1] *Ibid, pp* 203–4. John Wesley records in his *Diary* (*Journal*, Vol 2, *p* 137) that the men with whom he and Whitefield had this discussion were Mr Venn and Mr Berryman. Dr Curnock suggests that the latter was 'lecturer at St Paul's, and afterwards rector of St Alban's, Wood Street.'

[2] Charles Wesley's *Journal*, July 22, 1738.

[3] *Ibid*, Nov. 14, 1738.

[4] *Ibid*, Feb. 21, 1739.

share their expectancy. Finding it necessary on a certain occasion, in leaving a church, to go out by its back door in order to avoid the acclaim of great companies of his friends, he thought of the growing hostility and said, 'Perhaps, hereafter, I may be let out in the same manner to escape the fury of mine enemies.'[1]

The clergy, frustrated in their attempts to hinder Whitefield's effectiveness, looked for some circumstance which they could use in such a way as to discredit him before the people. They found an event to suit their purpose in what came to be known as the St Margaret's affair. Whitefield reported it thus:

Went to St Margaret's, Westminster; but something breaking belonging to the coach, could not get thither till the middle of prayers. Went through the people to the minister's pew, but, finding it locked, I returned to the vestry till the sexton could be found. Being there informed that another minister intended to preach, I desired several times that I might go home. My friends would by no means consent, telling me I was appointed by the Trustees to preach, and that if I did not, the people would go out of the church. At my request, some went to the Trustees, church-wardens and minister; and whilst I was waiting for an answer, and the last Psalm being sung, a man came to me with a wand in his hand, whom I took for the proper church officer, and told me I was to preach. I, not doubting that the minister was satisfied, followed him to the pulpit, and God enabled me to preach with greater power than I had done all the day before.[2]

Whitefield's innocence in this incident is manifest, but one of London's most notable clergymen, the Rev Richard Venn, D.D., rector of St Antholin's, published the following account:

At St Margaret's, Westminster, there is a *Society* evening Lecture; and when the Reader came, he found in the *churchyard*, at the west door, a number of people singing Psalms. When he got into the *church* he was affronted by some unknown persons as he passed through a great crowd to the vestry. As soon as the clergyman appointed to *preach* came, he was *solicited* (if an *overbearing importunity* may be so called), to resign the pulpit to Mr Whitefield, who (as is supposed by his not appearing at the *prayers*) was waiting at some neighbouring house to know the issue of their application. But the *preacher* continuing as determined to do his duty as Mr Whitefield was to do it for him, they at last effected by *force* that which they could not do by *treaty*. So the

[1] Whitefield's *Journals*, *p* 207.

[2] *Ibid*, *pp* 205–6.

preacher was safely confined in his *pew,* which was locked (the sexton being appointed by the *Society*, and in Mr Whitefield's interest), and guarded by several lusty fellows; while another party conveyed the *unlicensed intruder* triumphantly up into the pulpit, and kept sentry on the stairs for fear he should be taken down in as forcible a manner as he got up.[1]

One of Whitefield's friends published a reply to Venn's charges. He showed precisely what had happened, proving the falsity of the accusations, but the distorted account was spread far and wide and remained fixed in the minds of many as evidence that Whitefield was not to be trusted. But Whitefield himself, though deeply wounded, we may be sure, simply wrote in his *Journal*,

Thou shalt answer for me, my Lord and my God. A little while and we shall appear at the judgment seat of Christ. Then shall my innocence be made clear as the light and my dealings as the noonday.[2]

In the face of the increasing hostility, Whitefield's assurance that God was about to do great things on the earth appears to have become all the stronger. He possessed a conviction that multitudes of people would be brought into the hearing of the Gospel and, moved by the prospect, began to envision a new means of reaching them. This he suggested in his report of a Sunday's ministry:

Preached twice with great power and clearness in my voice to two thronged congregations, especially in the afternoon, when I believe near a thousand people were in the churchyard, and hundreds more returned home that could not come in. This put me first upon thinking of preaching without doors. I mentioned it to some friends who looked upon it as a mad notion. However, we kneeled down and prayed that nothing may be done rashly.[3]

But despite the opinion of his friends, Whitefield continued to entertain the 'mad notion'. He could see the tremendous advantages to be gained from preaching in the open air and, to a man of his temperament and zeal, the prospect was an exciting one. If the day should arrive when the clergy succeeded in depriving him of all the churches, he would be able to gather crowds out of doors far greater than any church could hold. God

[1] Tyerman's *Whitefield*, Vol 1, *p* 172.
[2] *Journals*, *p* 213. [3] *Ibid*, *p* 200.

was about to do great things on the earth – could it be that He was pointing to this as the method to be used? What liberty, what joy, for Whitefield, if forced to admit, 'The churches are closed against me', to be able also to cry, (as soon he did), 'Bless God, the fields are open!'

... in the secret place with his God Harris was in his element. That was his home – his chiefest pleasure. In Carmarthen at this time, when all the town went out to see the arrival of His Majesty's judges, Harris stole away to the secret place to pray. At Llangadog ... he did the same thing instead of joining his companions at dinner. He would retire to the fields – or anywhere – to pray, if he had a moment's leisure ... He prayed for all: for himself, for his peevish mother, who almost cursed him when he was on his knees, for his indifferent brothers, for the ungodly world, and for all classes of religious people.

RICHARD BENNETT
The Early Life of Howell Harris

13

Howell Harris

WHITEFIELD's idea of preaching in the open air did not originate with himself. It had been put into his mind by his exchange of letters with a fearless, tireless, dynamic Welshman, Howell Harris. For three years this man had been exhorting immense throngs of his fellow-countrymen out of doors and had been used of God in the awakening of hundreds. Whitefield, during his earlier ministry, had heard of Harris, and shortly after his return from Georgia, wrote him the following letter:

London, December 20, 1738

MY DEAR BROTHER,

Although I am unknown to you in person, I have long been united to you in spirit, and have been rejoiced to hear how the good pleasure of the Lord prospered in your hand. Go on, my dear brother, go on. Be strong in the Lord, and in the power of His might. There have been, and will be, many adversaries; but be not afraid. He who sent you will assist, comfort and protect you, and make you more than conqueror through His great love. I am a living monument of this, for the Divine strength has often been magnified in my weakness. I have tasted that the Lord is gracious; I have felt His power; and, from experience, can say that, in doing or suffering the will of Jesus Christ, there is great reward.

Blessed be His holy name! There seems to be a great pouring out of the Spirit in London, and we walk in the comfort of the Holy Ghost, and are edified.

You see, my dear Brother, the freedom I have taken in writing to you. If you would favour me with a line or two, by way of answer, you would greatly rejoice both me and many others. Why should we not tell one another what God has done for our souls?

My dear Brother, I love you in the bowels of Jesus Christ, and wish you may be the spiritual father of thousands, and shine, as the sun in the firmament, in the kingdom of your heavenly Father.

Your affectionate, though unworthy brother in Christ,

George Whitefield.[1]

Harris was not ordained and his activities had provoked strong opposition from ministers, magistrates and mobs. A few evangelical clergy had encouraged him, but he was often alone and at one time had written, 'There must be some worthy men in the world of the same mind as myself. Until I meet such I will go on with such support as I have.' Since first hearing of Whitefield he had longed to meet him and upon receiving his letter replied:

Glamorgan, January 8, 1739

DEAR BROTHER,

I was most agreeably surprised last night by a letter from you. Though this is the first time of our correspondence, I am no stranger to you. When I first heard of your labours and success, my soul was united to you, and engaged to send addresses to heaven on your behalf. When I read your Diary, I had uncommon influence of the Divine Presence shining on my poor soul almost continually, but I little thought our good Lord and Master intended I should ever see your handwriting . . .

Oh, how ravishing it is to hear of such demonstrations of the Divine love and favour to London! And to make your joy greater still, I have some good news to send you from Wales. There is a great revival in Cardiganshire, through Mr D. Rowlands, a Church minister, who has been much owned and blessed in Carmarthenshire also. We have also a sweet prospect in Breconshire and part of Monmouthshire. And the revival prospers in this county where I am now. There is here also a very useful young dissenting minister, who is a man of great charity. There is another of the same character in Montgomeryshire . . . There are two or three young curates in Glamorganshire, who are well-wishers to the cause of God; and we have an exceedingly valuable clergyman in Breconshire. But enemies are many and powerful . . .

[1] *Brief Account of the Life of Howell Harris*, (Trevecka,) 1791, *p* 110. This was largely a collection of Harris's own reports of his life, and is best referred to as his *Autobiography*.

I hope the faithful account I have given you will excite you to send again to him that would be sincerely yours in Christ, whilst –

Howell Harris.[1]

This correspondence was the beginning of an association in which Harris became one of Whitefield's closest friends and most valued co-labourers. Therefore we must pause in our narrative and make his acquaintance.

Howell Harris was born in 1714 – the same year as Whitefield. His parents lived at Trevecka in South Wales and were working-class people of sturdy quality and circumspect behaviour. Three boys were born to them, each of whom manifested exceptional force of personality and achieved notable success.

Joseph Harris, the eldest of the brothers, learned the trade of blacksmith in Wales and at the age of twenty set off for London. There he proved to be no ordinary blacksmith, for such was his skill that his work won the attention of Edmund Halley, the *Astronomer Royal.* He invented certain important mechanical devices, published four scientific books and rose to the position of Assay Master at the Royal Mint.[2]

Thomas, the second son, also left Wales for London. Becoming a tailor, he 'acquired a very handsome fortune by his industry and attention to business', and later retired to his native district with an income of £1,000 a year.[3] Joseph and Thomas exhibited outstanding natural abilities, but showed little interest in the things of God.

Howell, the youngest, was notable as a boy for his lively mind and headstrong manner. He says of himself:

When I was at school, although small in stature, I was ever ready to fight, even with friends. I harboured hatred towards those who

[1] H. J. Hughes, *Life of Howell Harris* (Nisbet, London, 1892), *pp* 64–5.

[2] Joseph's principal works are *The Description and Uses of the Celestial Globe and Orrery* and *An Essay upon Money and Coins.* The latter 'was considered the most authoritative statement on trade and commerce previous to *The Wealth of Nations* by Adam Smith'. Because of his position at the Royal Mint Joseph lived at the Tower of London.

[3] Upon retiring to Wales Thomas became Justice of the Peace and Sheriff of Brecknockshire. 'There is an interesting description of him in the *Memoirs of Mary Robinson*, better known to her contemporaries as "Perdita", who had unhappily married his illegitimate son.' Griffith T. Roberts, *Howell Harris* (Epworth, London, 1951), *p* 11.

treated me shabbily, and despised those of my own family when I wore a new suit of clothes. I was skilful at lying to my mother, teacher, or anyone ill-treated by me, and crafty in framing excuses for breaking the Sabbath.[1]

When Howell was thirteen his father took him to visit some relatives. Here he displayed his arrogance; 'I despised all', he says, 'and left with a haughty heart because they were not rich and noble. On our return to Brecon I spurned my father in my heart because he was not sufficiently elegant in manner and speech.' He showed the same contempt towards his mother, but when Joseph came home on a visit from London, Howell gloated over his success, made much of his fine clothes and tried to be seen in his company as often as possible.

Howell received a good general education, with a basic knowledge of Latin and Greek, and sometimes expressed the desire to enter the ministry. At the age of seventeen he became a schoolmaster, but shortly thereafter – lacking parental restraint by reason of the recent death of his father – he 'broke out into the devil's service'. He relinquished his classical studies, 'took no interest in his work and was wholly bent on dice-playing, drinking, gossiping, love-making and improving his personal appearance'.[2] Because of his vivacious spirit and assertive, roistering manner, he was constantly the centre of his social circle and, like his brothers, was a man of the world.

From this life, however, Howell Harris was rescued by sovereign grace and was transformed into a man of God. The Divine work was first manifest in his heart when, at the age of twenty-one, on Palm Sunday, he heard the vicar of the Talgarth Church say, 'If you are not fit to come to the Lord's table, you are not fit to live, and you are not fit to die!' He was alarmed by the words, confessing, 'All my natural faculties were confounded in the shock'.

He immediately began to mend his ways. He asked the forgiveness of any whom he had wronged, and set for himself a vigorous schedule of religious duties. He rigidly kept the Sabbath, studied the Bible, read religious books, gave to the poor and made lengthy fasts, 'hoping', he says, 'thus to subdue my inward depravity'. He struggled mightily against the passions of his

[1] *Autobiography*. [2] Roberts, *op cit*, *p* 13.

vehement nature; but the works of the law brought no peace, and he declared,

The more I searched into the nature of things, the more I saw myself and others to be on the broad road to destruction. I found myself to be void of spiritual life, 'carnal, sold under sin'. I felt that I could no more believe or mourn for my sins than ascend to heaven . . . But as yet I was ignorant of the blood of Christ, as the only 'fountain opened for sin' and a total stranger to the life of faith; and therefore I was all the while in a lost state, and in danger of final destruction.[1]

But the grace which had begun this work of conviction wrought also the work of conversion. As Whitsunday approached, he fasted from Thursday morning till Saturday night and wrote, while on his knees, a list of all his known sins since the age of four. During his weeks of agony he felt a strong urge to give himself to God, but had never heard of any one who had done such a thing. In his darkness he was subjected to atheistic thoughts and, even while he attended the church service on the Whitsunday morning he said, 'Satan roared dreadfully within me, so that I could almost have shouted out'. Yet he went on to testify that, during the sacrament,

The One who is stronger came in . . . At the table Christ bleeding on the cross was kept before my eyes constantly, and strength was given me to believe that I was receiving pardon on account of that blood. I lost my burden; I went home leaping for joy! I knew that my sins were forgiven: Oh blessed day! Would that I might remember it gratefully evermore!

This was Harris's account of his conversion, and it is significant that the other two great leaders of Calvinistic Methodism were also brought to a knowledge of the Saviour at about the same time. For while Harris had been undergoing the deep conviction of sin at Talgarth, Daniel Rowland had been experiencing the same in another part of Wales,[2] and Whitefield the same at

[1] Hughes, *op cit*, *p* 10.

[2] As to the date of Rowland's conversion, our best authority is Harris. He wrote, 'Mr Daniel Rowland was awakened about the same time as myself', M. H. Jones, *The Trevecka Letters* (C. M. Book Agency, Caernarvon, 1932), *p* 209. Jones also asserts, 'It is sufficiently clear from the MSS. of Howell Harris that both, unawares to each other, experienced their spiritual conversion in the same year – 1735', *p* 208.

The spelling of the name Rowland without the final 's' is apparently the more correct.

Oxford. Apparently Whitefield came into the assurance of salvation first, probably in the April of this year (1735), while May 25 was the date of Harris's conversion, and, as far as can be known, this June or July marked the date of the saving experience in the life of Rowland also. Furthermore, John Cennick has left testimony that 'at Easter, 1735, as I was walking hastily in Cheapside, the hand of the Lord touched me', and there began then the profound conviction which led to the conversion which we shall notice later. Thus, almost without a human instrument, four of God's chief servants were raised up by His hand, and it was these who were foremost in proclaiming the truth of His Sovereign Grace during the years of the coming revival.

*

We catch a glimpse of Harris's soul during his post-conversion days as we read the following testimony:

> All thoughts of human applause were quite vanished from my sight; the spiritual world and eternity began to appear; now I began to have other views and motives; I felt some insatiable desires after the salvation of poor sinners; my heart longed for their being convinced of their sin and misery. I also found myself a stranger here; all my heart was drawn from the world and visible things, and was in pursuit of more valuable riches. I now began to be more happy, and could not help telling . . . that I knew my sins were forgiven me, though I had never heard anyone make that confession before, or say it could be obtained; but I was so deeply convinced, that nothing could shake my assurance of it . . . I had never conversed with any that had his face toward Zion, and who could instruct me in the ways of the Lord.[1]

As part of his self-discipline in the Christian life Harris began to keep a *Diary*.[2] At that time he had no thought that it would ever be published; it was merely a confidential document between himself and the Lord, and he wrote into it his thoughts and longings, and expressed his deepest emotions without inhibition. This was to be, he said, 'a daily and weekly catalogue of my

[1] Hughes, *op cit*, *pp* 11–12.

[2] Harris maintained the *Diary* throughout life, and 294 of his Diaries are extant today among the papers he left. He left also nearly 3,000 letters. All these documents are housed at the National Library of Wales at Aberystwyth. M. H. Jones, in *The Trevecka Letters*, *op cit*, has presented a masterly summary of this literature.

sins . . . to be confessed before every Communion', but it became also a transcription of his strivings and his victories, a reiteration of the new life which now surged so powerfully through his soul.

Harris's knowledge of Divine things during these days was small. He simply knew he loved the Lord and wanted to love Him more, and in this pursuit he sought out quiet places where he could be secluded with Him in prayer. One of his favourite retreats was the church at Llangasty – the village in which he then taught school – and on one occasion shortly after his conversion he climbed into its tower to be the more alone with the Lord. There, as he remained in intercession for some hours, he experienced an overwhelming sense of the presence and power of God. That lonely church tower became to him a holy of holies, and he afterwards wrote,

I felt suddenly my heart melting within me, like wax before the fire, with love to God my Saviour; and also felt, not only love and peace, but a longing to be dissolved and be with Christ. There was a cry in my inmost soul which I was totally unacquainted with before, 'Abba Father!' . . . I *knew* that I was His child, and that He loved and heard me. My soul being filled and satiated, cried, 'It is enough! I am satisfied! Give me strength and I will follow Thee through fire and water![1]

This was indeed a hallowed experience to Harris. It proved to be a mighty infilling of the Holy Spirit, empowering him for the ministry of incessant labours, violent opposition and spiritual victories which lay directly before him.

*

Immediately after his conversion Harris began to go to his former companions to testify to them of his experience of grace and warn them of the wages of sin. He visited the sick and aged and gathered the neighbours into his mother's home in order to read religious books to them, and with the passing of a few weeks the house was overflowing with hearers and the whole countryside was talking of the fervent exhorter. His efforts aroused hostility, the clergy opposed him and ruffians attacked him, but he knew no relenting. 'I was carried', he exclaimed, 'as on wings through all my trials . . . I feared nothing, though my

[1] Hughes, *op cit*, *pp* 12, 13.

life was in danger from the threats of such as loved darkness rather than light . . . The fire of God did so burn in my soul that I could not rest day or night without doing something for my God and Saviour.'

With a view to entering the ministry Harris matriculated at St Mary's Hall, Oxford, and his friends expressed the hope that the University life would 'cure him of his enthusiasm'. 'But', he wrote, 'when I saw the irregularities and immoralities which surrounded me there, I became soon weary of the place', and within a short while he returned to his beloved labour in Wales.

Although it was contrary to the laws of the Church of England for an unordained man to go about as a religious teacher, Harris took up this work with increased zeal. He expected to be ordained as soon as he was old enough, but would not sit idle till that time, and we see something of his fervent activity as we read his account:

A strong necessity was laid upon me, that I could not rest, but must go to the utmost of my ability to exhort. I could not meet or travel with anybody, rich or poor, young or old, without speaking to them concerning their souls. I went during the festive season from house to house in our parish, and the parishes of Llangors and Llangasty, until persecution became too hot. I was absolutely dark and ignorant with regard to the reasons of religion; I was drawn onwards by the love I had experienced, as a blind man is led, and therefore I could not take notice of anything in my way.

My food and drink was praising my God. A fire was kindled in my soul and I was clothed with power, and made altogether dead to earthly things. I could have spoken to the King were he within my reach – such power and authority did I feel in my soul over every spirit . . . I lifted up my voice with authority, and fear and terror would be seen on all faces. I went to the Talgarth fairs, denouncing the swearers and cursers without fear or favour.

At first I knew nothing at all, but God opened my mouth (full of ignorance), filling it with terrors and threatenings. I was given a commission to rend and break sinners in the most dreadful manner. I thundered greatly, denouncing the gentry, the carnal clergy and everybody.[1]

Harris was manifestly raised up of God for this extraordinary work. Wales, at that time, was sunk in sin and ignorance, and

[1] *Autobiography.*

Harris was peculiarly gifted to meet the need of the hour. He was utterly unsophisticated, a man of the people, who could speak so as to reach the heart and conscience of the common individual. He had remarkable talent for using simple, yet striking, figures of speech – 'the gift of similitudes' he called it – and he possessed an extraordinary understanding of human nature which enabled him to probe into the inner consciousness and reveal the presence of sin in the hidden parts. He did not call himself a minister, but simply an *exhorter*, and in order to avoid any appearance of usurping the place of the clergy, he began each service by reading from a religious book and he referred to his public work simply as *reading*. But call it what he would, his was a mighty ministry of the condemnation of sin and the preaching of grace.

He made much use of the text, 'I have made Esau bare, I have uncovered his secret places and he shall not be able to hide',[1] and it was representative of his special mission. Remembering the terrible conviction of sin and fear of judgment that he had experienced, he often cried amidst his former companions, 'You who once went with me toward hell . . . flee from the wrath to come!', and one who frequently heard him preach said 'He used to speak of hell as though he had been there himself'. But another hearer reported, 'He could also set forth the riches of salvation in such a way as to cause sinners earnestly to desire an experience of its freedom and power'.

Because he was unordained, Harris refused to practise any kind of formal sermonization, and stood before his congregations without a prepared message. He looked to God for wisdom and power and as he began to speak his soul took fire and his speech became like a mighty torrent and rushed forth with tremendous conviction. It was said, 'The words flowed scorching hot from the preacher's heart', and 'He would go on thus, pouring out old things and new for two, three or even four hours. Indeed, we have instances of his services continuing without a break for six hours'.[2]

This work was mightily used of God. Harris ranged over a

[1] *Jer.* 49: 10.

[2] R. Bennett, *The Early Life of Howell Harris* (Banner of Truth Trust, London, 1962), *p* 42.

wide area of South Wales, and held meetings anywhere and at any time till the whole countryside became conscious of his condemnation of sin. Under the power of the Holy Spirit hearts were broken, and it was not uncommon for people to come under such conviction that they would cry out aloud to God for mercy while he preached. Hundreds were converted – among them, some of the most notorious sinners – and Harris made plans for their upbuilding by organizing them into Societies. He proved to possess exceptional gifts for the organization and oversight of these bodies, and equally valuable talents in his regular examination of the souls of the individuals.[1] He formed his first Society in September of 1736, and the number of Societies so increased that by 1739, according to Whitefield, there were 'nearly thirty'. It deserves to be emphasized that this, the beginning of Welsh Calvinistic Methodism, took place nearly two years before the Wesleys were converted and a year before Whitefield began his regular ministry.

Of course, such activity provoked severe opposition. Harris's mother treated him with bitter scorn and his brother Joseph wrote to him as though he were mentally deranged. Magistrates threatened to throw him in jail and warned that heavy fines would be imposed against all persons who allowed him to minister in their houses. Some of the people, infuriated by his condemnations, became violent against him, seeking to do him bodily harm, and several of the clergy were guilty of arousing the mob in their attempts to have him driven out of their parishes.

> The ministers preached against me as a false prophet [he wrote], the people despised me, pointing at me as I passed by, and young wastrels threatened to murder me, . . . I was persecuted at home, . . . I was threatened with imprisonment many times. In order to keep me humble, the Lord made me a laughing-stock, and a subject of lampoons to all.[2]

Twice Harris applied for ordination, but though his qualifications were superior to those of most Welsh candidates at the time, he was harshly refused. This was because of his unauthorized

[1] Harris said of this talent, 'My being so long in ye country has given me an opportunity to make my observations on man from ye highest to ye lowest, and I have hardly met a man that rightly understands what a soul is, much less its faculties'. *Ibid*, *p* 44.

[2] *Ibid*, *p* 48.

activity and his denunciations of the clergy, and the following paragraph is typical of several of his utterances:

> . . . Many who wear the cloth . . . what good they do I know not. Because I led some hundreds of ignorant people to a knowledge of what it means to be Christians, to live in peace and to exercise morality, I am called a madman by those who claim the office of enlightening the people who are in darkness. They are more contemptible than ordinary business men, who, when they see another doing better business, try to imitate his methods. What have I taken from them or what have I gained? Their churches are fuller and they are revered more than before. I love the religion but I must despise these niggardly professors. Do I fear their rage? What can they set against me, except that I have endeavoured to do good and that God has followed my efforts with His blessing.[1]

Despite these strictures, Harris held the ministry itself, as an institution of the Church, in the highest veneration, and became exceedingly anxious lest his evangelistic labours should constitute a breach of Church law. He feared to reject what he believed was the Divine authority resident in the Church, but he feared still more to disobey what he knew to be the voice of God which had commissioned his special work. The question became a matter of grave concern to him, and brought him into fierce conflict and much calling upon God for a clear indication of His will. And such indication was given, for (using the word 'read' to designate his public ministrations), he wrote:

> Then after I had waited long – O! glad tidings – the Spirit descended with tears and unusual tenderness, an infallible assurance that I was to continue reading. Then I vowed that I would read in spite of swords, fire, or fierce wrath, without fear of being rent to pieces, leaning completely on God for every qualification . . . I am now assured of Thy command, Thy blessing, Thy protection and Thy favour, and without any fear for the future I give myself, body, soul and reputation unto Thee. I cast myself upon Thee; guide me aright. Behold me an instrument in Thy hand. Oh! ye angels, sing His praises louder than ever before, because He hath visited me in the day of my trouble.[2]

Following this reassurance of the Divine call, Harris saw that it was well that he was not ordained. He was not a man who

[1] *Ibid*, *pp* 53–4. [2] *Ibid*, *p* 51.

could ever have confined himself to one parish; he must be free to range at will, wherever man in his need was found, and this unbounded-parish idea became a basic principle of his life. 'If I had it [ordination] in our Church', he wrote, 'it should be so limited within meshes of Parishes, etc., that it is contrary to ye Spirit I am acted by. My desires are general, without any limits.'[1]

Harris often found himself the centre of violent conflicts. Wherever he went he was bitterly hated by many, but loved with equal intensity by many more. He was passionately devoted to the Church of England, yet even among her evangelical clergy some encouraged and others opposed his unordained evangelizing. He made warm friends of a number of the Nonconformist ministers, but these friendships were not without their frictions because of his refusal to leave the Church and join with them. He was not a man of deep Biblical learning, but during these early post-conversion years he gradually grew in knowledge, and has left written testimony regarding the manner in which he came to clear Calvinistic convictions. He gave away his possessions to help the poor and often went without food and without sufficient sleep, until his health began to suffer. His zeal sometimes overran his discretion; for instance, there was an occasion when, as he returned from a very late meeting, trudging in the darkness across the Black Mountains adjacent to his home, he fell exhausted when trying to cross a stile in a farmer's field and was found there asleep at dawn.

But despite his opposers and his excesses, Harris's triumph abounded. When Joseph wrote, reporting complaints which had been made against him, he replied:

> I am no more concerned to hear their threats than to hear a fly. I should tremble to hear a holy man reprimand me, but Drunkards, etc., have not ye keeping of ye door to Christ's vineyard . . . Though I should leave all to follow such a work, I know my enemies shall have no room to insult, for those that honour Him He'll honour.[2]

He estimated that he walked more than 2,500 miles in going to and from his meetings in two years, and said that as he travelled, 'I devoted myself to exhorting everyone I met to flee from the wrath to come'. But there were also secluded places in the Welsh

[1] *Ibid*, p 69. [2] *Ibid*, p 62.

hills where he journeyed alone with God, and 'He speaks again and again of a spiritual feast he enjoyed on Grwyne Fechan mountain, when he seemed to see God so smiling upon him that his heart was near to bursting under the powerful influences of Divine love'.[1]

But there were times when Harris poured out his soul unto God in dejection, as, for example, 'Evil is repaid me for good everywhere. My steps are watched and I am slandered to the utmost . . . Great fears that I have run too quickly. In great straits for guidance . . . Last night I ventured as one about to lose everything and likely to be imprisoned. The clergyman was very cruel . . . I fell down for the fourth time – my knees are painful. Here I am with all that I possess at Thy feet. I will address Thee till my bones tire . . . Sin within frightens me and oppression without'.[2]

Most of his hours before the Lord, however, were of a different nature, and page after page of his *Diary* is filled with his soul's jubilation. The following is representative,

> Oh! Send me where Thou wilt; I obey. I am Thine; manage me as Thou wilt. Here is a hand ready to write, a tongue to speak, legs to carry me – speak but ye word. Oh! this Thine own free gift – as if embracing Him, loving, longing, admiring, praising, melting sick for Love. Oh! Jesus, to hear Thee reproached and say nothing! Let me have ye guidance of Thy Spirit; let me not go till Thou commandest; but when I am called, make me to go; rule me, guide me, assist me. Whatever Thou dost, take not these signs of Thy love away . . . Pity Mother and my Brethren. Oh! let me have this honour of doing something to show my gratefulness. Oh! Let me be setting forth Thy praise continually, Tears in streams, Joys unconceivable, to gain which for one hour it is worth ye labour of one thousand years.[3]

In physical person Harris seems to have been slightly below average height, but of a stocky build. His voice was strong, and rich with the in-born music of the Welsh, although the strain of his preaching caused 'a settled hoarseness upon it'. By birth he was gifted with a certain genius of spirit, which, under the hand of God, remained unspoiled and almost childlike in its simplicity. His nature was intense and his emotions vehement, yet, though he was a powerfully masculine individual, his soul was exceptionally sensitive and full of tender compassion.

[1] *Ibid*, *p* 52. [2] *Ibid*, *pp* 95–7. [3] *Ibid*, *pp* 71–2.

Too long has this Boanerges of the Welsh hills been overlooked. His name should be as well known to-day as the names of Wesley and Whitefield. He was the pioneer of Methodist field-preaching, the originator of its itinerant evangelism and the first to form a number of Societies and link them together in a permanent organization. Wesley's work was patterned after him, and Whitefield was deeply indebted to his stalwart example. Among certain persons of the present day whose knowledge is such as to lend authority to their opinion, Harris is regarded as the greatest Welshman of that day and, indeed, as among the greatest men that Wales has ever produced.

It was a brave day for England when Whitefield began field preaching.

C. H. SPURGEON
Lectures to My Students

At Kingswood Whitefield broke the deadly decorum and spiritual lassitude of his age; there he began a new era in the religious life of England.

G. H. WICKS
Whitefield's Legacy to Bristol and the Cotswolds

14

Into the Open Air

WHITEFIELD was profoundly influenced by Harris's example. Field preaching opened up prospects which moved him to the depths of his being. Here was a means of reaching the vast untouched multitudes and here was a deliverance from all dependency on the availability of the churches or the Society Rooms. Here was a gloriously free and wondrously promising form of evangelism and in all the vigour of his nature he wanted to launch into it right away. 'Howell Harris and I are correspondents, blessed be God', he wrote. 'May I follow him as he does Jesus Christ!'[1]

Nevertheless, Whitefield was not unmindful that along with the advantages there would be disadvantages too.

Open-air preaching is now so commonplace that it is difficult to realize how outlandish it seemed then. There had long been propaganda to the effect that any display of spiritual earnestness might lead to trouble – even to civil disorder – and the generality of Englishmen believed it. Public opinion confined the clergyman to a narrow area of activity, and though this might include such things as drunkenness and gambling, it left no room for evangelistic fervour. Whitefield knew that were he to preach in the fields his enemies would make loud outcry, hurling the word *enthusiast*, ridiculing him personally and using his action as a means of bringing the whole revival movement into disrepute.

But, being soon to return to America, Whitefield could not long delay his decision. Accordingly, shortly after his correspondence with Harris, he made up his mind: he would take the momentous step, making at least one attempt at the open-air preaching.

His decision, however, was not a careless or sudden one. The

[1] *Works*, Vol 1, *p* 47.

previously expressed desire 'that nothing be done rashly' governed his planning, and he determined to make his initial move in a way which would give his opposers the least possible grounds for complaint.

Whitefield's thinking in this matter is evident. The Church of England did not entirely prohibit out-of-doors preaching, but actually allowed it where no church was available, and it was on this principle that missionaries to primitive peoples had always acted. Moreover, a man named Morgan, a clergyman, had recently and on more than one occasion, preached out of doors in England,[1] and his action had apparently been justified by the fact that this had been to an unchurched people – the Kingswood colliers. Kingswood was a coal-mining district near Bristol, and though its inhabitants lived in utter ignorance and degradation, neither church nor school had been built for them and no clergyman had made it his practice to go among them. Because of these conditions, Morgan's preaching, even though it was done out of doors, had probably brought commendation rather than complaint.

Whitefield was quick to see in Morgan's action a precedent which would justify his own. Moreover, such a hope had long been in his mind, for during his early ministry he had been told, 'No need to go to America to find heathens; there are heathens enough at Kingswood!' and ever since, this needy people had been on his heart.

Accordingly, knowing what Morgan had done, he made his plans. He would go to Kingswood and, if at all possible, would preach to the colliers out of doors. If, however, it did not prove feasible for him to do so, he would go on to Wales and there would meet Howell Harris. He would accompany Harris on his rounds, observe him as he conducted some of his meetings in the fields and learn from him how the great task was done. Strengthened by this experience he would return to Kingswood and make

[1] In November of 1737 Whitefield had written, 'Mr Morgan is going amongst the colliers again at Bristol, and a church, I hope, will be built for them'. *Works,* Vol 1, *p* 30. John Cennick says, 'In the year 1738, Mr Morgan, a clergyman of the Church of England, pitying the rude and ignorant conditions of the Kingswood colliers, sometimes preached to them in the fields.' *The Moravian Messenger,* Vol 16. This was probably Richard Morgan, who had been one of the more casual associates of the Holy Club.

the attempt alone, or, if need be, he would ask Harris to come with him and lend his support for the first meeting or two. He also intended to adhere as closely as possible to the precedent set by Morgan, and thus give no unnecessary cause for offence.

It deserves therefore to be pointed out that Whitefield's action in entering upon the open-air ministry was not a reckless plunge – the cast-discretion-to-the-winds affair that some have pictured. It is true that he was driven by a sense of spiritual urgency, but true also that he held himself in check by wise caution. Yet there can be no doubt that he had more in mind than merely preaching to the colliers, for he had a vision of a ministry that would take him to fields and market places far and wide across England.

With these plans in mind Whitefield said his farewells at London and set out for Bristol. The date was February 7, 1739, and less than three months had elapsed since his return from America.

*

At this time a new figure entered Whitefield's life. This was William Seward (1711–40), a young widower who had been born in the home of a country squire and had attained financial success as a stockbroker.[1] During the ten previous years he had been of a strongly religious turn of mind, devoting much time and money to the work of the Charity Schools. Late in 1738 he had experienced a spiritual awakening and, gravitating in search of spiritual help to Fetter Lane, had there met Charles Wesley. Charles described him as 'a zealous soul, knowing only the baptism of John',[2] but a week later said, 'W. Seward testified faith'.[3]

Seward immediately displayed a fervid zeal and upon Whitefield's return from America, became intensely devoted to him. In fact, so strong was his enthusiasm that he offered to place himself and his fortune at Whitefield's disposal and to accompany him wherever he might go.

This was a timely offer. Whitefield needed someone to relieve him of the increasing business detail connected with his under-

[1] Lord Egmont says, 'Seward was originally a broker in stocks in Exchange Alley, and got £8,000 by his trade'. *Colonial Records of Georgia*, Vol 4, *p* 402.

[2] Charles Wesley's *Journal*, Nov. 13, 1738. [3] *Ibid*, Nov. 19, 1738.

takings, especially the Orphan House. Thus, he accepted his offer and took him with him on this trip to Bristol.[1]

During subsequent months Seward proved himself an exceptionally earnest Christian and a most faithful helper. He inscribed himself 'William Seward, Gentleman, Companion in Travel to the Reverend Mr Whitefield'. He readily exchanged what could have been a life of comfort for one of homelessness, backed Whitefield in two costly undertakings in America and served the Lord with a flaming devotion.

*

Whitefield's journey to Bristol led him through Salisbury. Knowing that Mrs Wesley, the aged mother of John and Charles was living there, he paid her a visit, and in writing to her other son, Samuel, she said:

> Mr Whitefield has been making a progress through these parts, to make a collection for a house in Georgia for orphans . . . He came hither to see me, and we talked about your brothers. I told him I did not like their way of living, and wished them in some place of their own, wherein they might regularly preach, etc. He replied, 'I could not conceive the good they did in London; that the greatest part of our clergy were asleep, and that there never was a greater need of itinerant preachers than now.' . . . I then asked Mr Whitefield if my sons were not for making some innovations in the church, which I much feared. He assured me they were so far from it, that they endeavoured all they could to reconcile Dissenters to our communion . . . His stay was short, so I could not talk with him as much as I desired. He seems to be a very good man, and one who truly desires the salvation of mankind. God grant that the wisdom of the serpent may be joined with the innocence of the dove![2]

*

Whitefield hoped that at Bath and Bristol he would be allowed the same use of the churches as during his earlier ministry there. Moreover, he had still greater reason to expect this privilege now, for he came on behalf of orphaned children and carried the written commission from the Trustees for Georgia.

[1] Seward's father had served for some years as private secretary to a nobleman on a great estate near Bristol, and this may have influenced Whitefield in his decision.
[2] George J. Stevenson, *Memorials of the Wesley Family* (London, 1876), *p* 216.

But upon arriving at Bath he discovered that the opposition displayed at London had arisen here also. He had formerly preached twice with high acceptance at the great Bath Abbey, but as he applied for it now he met 'an absolute refusal'. The Trustees' commission meant little, and he was told he must have 'a positive order' from either the Bishop or the King.

Similar conditions confronted him at Bristol. He asked for the use of the Church of St Mary Redcliffe (in size, second only to the Cathedral), but was denied. Refusing to be so easily put off he carried his case to the Chancellor, who virtually forbade him to preach in the diocese. He went next to the Dean, from whom he met a weak evasion. His report of these interviews concludes with the exclamation, 'Why do not the clergy speak the truth – that it is not against the Orphan House, but against me and my doctrine that their enmity is levelled.'[1]

*

While at Bristol on this and subsequent occasions, Whitefield lived at the home of his sister, Mrs Elizabeth Grevil. She was a widow at this time and operated a grocery business, and probably welcomed the added income that we may be sure would result from the presence of the munificent Seward. She and George had doubtless been close in childhood for she was his senior by but eighteen months. Like the other members of the family, she seems to have been amazed at the phenomenal prominence her brother had attained. From this time forth her home became open house for the Methodist preachers, and both John and Charles Wesley made it their Bristol stopping place until the time of the doctrinal separation of 1741. Elizabeth's mother also paid her frequent and lengthy visits.

*

Though rejected at the churches, Whitefield did not immediately resort to the fields. He went instead to the prison and then to the Societies and in these places found an abundant ministry.

The keeper of Bristol's Newgate prison was named Abel Dagge. This man had been converted under Whitefield's ministry in 1737 and, though Newgate had been notorious for its filthiness

[1] *Journals*, p 214.

and cruelty, since his conversion Dagge had laboured to introduce cleanliness and kindness. The poet Richard Savage was his prisoner for some time, and Samuel Johnson, in his biography of Savage, portrays this wholesome change in jailer and jail.[1] Rejoicing in the message which had occasioned so great a transformation in his own life, Dagge was anxious that it be made known also to the unfortunates under his care, and invited Whitefield to come to the prison for an 'exposition and reading [of] prayers' every morning.

In visiting the Societies Whitefield learned that in Bristol, as at London, his former ministry had borne lasting fruit. Old Societies had been revived and new ones had been formed and his return signalled a fresh wave of fervour among them. Having arrived at Bristol on the Wednesday night, he spent the next two evenings in the Societies, and reported,

> Thursday, Feb. 15 . . . At seven, I expounded for an hour with very great power to a young Society, which God has caused to be established since I was here last; . . . Blessed be God! the good seed sown by my ministry, though but as a grain of mustard seed, is now, being watered by the dew of Heaven, beginning to grow into a great tree.
>
> Friday, Feb. 16 . . . expounded from five till near nine to two thronged Societies, one of which chiefly consisted of young men whom God seems to have called to shine as lights in the world . . . Oh, how thankful I ought to be, for seeing these fruits of my poor labours![2]

Despite, however, the opportunities offered by the prison and Societies, Whitefield's thought was fixed on the open air. Before him there stood its challenge – the bursting of the bonds of ministerial confinement, the freedom from dependence on the churches and the possibility of declaring the Gospel to hosts of mankind – and he chafed to enter upon it. Accordingly, he

[1] Dr Johnson says of Savage: 'He was treated by Mr Dagge with great humanity; was supported by him at his own table, without any certainty of recompence; had a room to himself to which he could retire from all disturbance; was allowed to stand at the door of the prison and was sometimes taken out into the fields; so that he suffered fewer hardships in prison than he had been accustomed to undergo in the greatest part of his life. During the whole time of his imprisonment the keeper continued to treat him with the utmost tenderness and civility.' But Johnson fails to recognize that this benevolence sprang from the grace of God in Dagge's life, and that this conversion took place under the ministry of Whitefield, whom Johnson later belittled.

[2] *Journals, pp* 214–15.

wasted no time and on the Saturday afternoon, taking William Seward with him, he made his way out to Kingswood.

Humanly speaking there could hardly have been a more unlikely congregation than the Kingswood colliers. The district contained some thousands of them[1] and the conditions under which they existed were most deplorable. Men, women and children laboured in the dark tunnellings in the earth, working long hours amidst danger and disease, and their lives were never free from the dirt and dust that attended their employment. So notorious was their settlement for viciousness that a stranger seldom ventured into it, and the colliers in turn lived unto themselves, a sad and sullen race who looked out upon the outside world in hatred and fear. Moreover, there had been occasions on which, seized by a wild mob spirit, the colliers had stormed into Bristol, pillaging and terrorizing, till the crazed mood spent itself and they returned to their seclusion and grime.

Such was the district to which Whitefield made his way that Saturday afternoon. He could probably have used the weather as an excuse for not going, for the month was February and the winter was the coldest in then-living memory.[2] But he was moved by a love for these pitiable people: 'My bowels have long since yearned', he wrote at the time, 'toward the poor colliers, who are very numerous and as sheep having no shepherd.'[3] And if he felt any qualms as to his action he dispelled them with the realization of the clear Scriptural precedent: 'I thought that I might be doing a service for my Creator, who had a mountain for his pulpit and the heavens for his sounding board; and who, when his Gospel was refused by the Jews, sent his servants into the highways and hedges.'[4]

Rowland Hill says that, upon arriving at Kingswood, White-

[1] George Eayrs, *Wesley and Kingswood and its Free Churches* (Arrowsmith, Bristol, 1911), *p* 41, says that in 1684 there were more than seventy coal pits, but that 'during the next fifty years the coal works more than doubled, and thousands of colliers were employed in Kingswood'.

[2] John Entick, *A History of London* (London, 1766), Vol II, *p* 467, says of this winter, 'It may be said to have exceeded all others that could be remembered, in its intenseness and its bad effects . . . Many persons were froze to death by land and water. The necessities of the poor were very great, and the excessive cold hindered them in their work; coals were got to such a price that they could not find money to buy firing.'

[3] *Journals, p* 216.

[4] Gillies, *op cit, p* 37, fn.

field called the colliers 'out of their dens and holes in the earth'.[1] How surprised must these 'outcasts of men' have been to see the youthful clergyman accompanied by the well-to-do young gentleman, as they came along their grimy lanes, paused at their hovels, sought them out at their pits and invited them to assemble for the preaching of the Gospel![2]

In keeping with his determination not to leave himself open more than necessary to the charge of innovation, Whitefield took his stand at the place where Mr Morgan had already preached.[3] His report of the historic event is regrettably brief; he merely says, 'I went upon a mount and spake to as many people as came to me. They were upwards of two hundred.'[4] We know, however, that before the service was finished, such was his satisfaction in this first attempt that he announced another meeting: he would be there to preach to them again the following Wednesday.

Upon returning to Bristol Whitefield reflected on what he had done. He expressed nothing but contentment, saying, 'Blessed be God! I have now broken the ice! I believe I was never more acceptable to my Master than when I was standing to teach those hearers in the open fields. Some may censure me, but if I thus pleased men I should not be the servant of Christ.'[5]

Directly following his open-air meeting Whitefield wrote a letter which was of particular significance. This was to the Bishop of Bristol, the famous Dr Joseph Butler. The Chancellor had virtually forbidden him to exercise any ministry in that diocese, and in the letter Whitefield asked the Bishop 'for leave to preach in his Lordship's churches, for the benefit of the Orphan House', thus going over the Chancellor's head and appealing to the higher authority.

This, however, was not the whole import of the letter. White-

[1] William Jones, *The Life of Rowland Hill* (London, 1837), *p* 58.

[2] It has long been stated that Thomas Maxfield, who later became a Methodist lay preacher, was converted on this occasion. It is highly improbable that Maxfield was a resident of Kingswood, but, since Whitefield says that 'another friend' accompanied Seward and himself on this occasion, we may well suppose that this was Maxfield and that he was one of the young men from one of the Societies in Bristol, whose spiritual seeking caused him to go with Whitefield on this occasion.

[3] John Cennick reports this event saying, 'Feb. 17. Mr Whitefield preached for the first time in or near the same spot in Kingswood, called Rose Green or Crates' End, where Mr Morgan had preached last year.' *The Moravian Messenger*, Vol 16.

[4] *Journals*, *p* 216. Whitefield's text was *Matt.* 5: 1–3.

[5] *Ibid.*

field was satisfied that, in preaching in Kingswood where there was no church, he was acting in harmony with Church of England principles, but was he to limit his open-air work to such situations? In answer to this question he had developed the idea that in any instance in which he requested the use of a church for his evangelistic and charitable purposes and it was refused, he might look upon that area as in the same category as Kingswood, and that he would be within his rights in entering it and preaching there out of doors. He would be willing to use the churches if they were allowed to him, but, if not, would take to himself this liberty to enter a parish and preach as opportunity afforded. Accordingly, his immediate course of action – whether he was to minister in the churches or the fields – depended on the Bishop's reply and he eagerly awaited its arrival.

*

In the meantime he went on with his work. His Sunday's labours began at 6 o'clock in the morning, with a meeting for young people at his sister's house. For some reason, three churches were suddenly offered to him, two of which he accepted, preaching in the morning at St Werburgh's and in the afternoon at St Mary Redcliffe. The congregation at the latter service was the largest he had ever addressed. The evening was spent in two of the Societies, and he reports:

> I hastened to a Society in Baldwin Street, where many hundreds were assembled to hear me, so that the stairs and court below, besides the room itself, were crowded. Here I continued expounding for near two hours, and then expounded for as long a time at another Society in Nicholas Street, equally thronged . . . great numbers were quite melted down, and God so caused me to renew my strength, that I was better when I returned home than when I began to exhort my young fellow-soldiers at six in the morning.[1]

The Monday was almost equally busy. There was the service in the prison in the morning and in the afternoon a great meeting in the Church of St Philip and St James. This seems to have been an extraordinary occasion, for 'thousands went away because there was no room for them within', and the sum of £18 was

[1] *Ibid, pp* 216–17.

collected for the Orphan House. The day closed with two more 'greatly thronged' gatherings in the Societies.[1]

Such activity aroused the Chancellor's ire. Despite his prohibition, Whitefield, during his five days in Bristol had preached in three churches, daily at the prison, twice each evening in the Societies and once, in an unheard-of procedure, out of doors. Above all, his popularity was tremendous. Forthwith the Chancellor summoned him to appear before him and the following interview took place:

Chancellor: 'I intend to stop your proceedings! I have sent for the Registrar here, Sir, to take down your answer. By what authority do you preach in the diocese of Bristol without a licence?'

Whitefield: 'I thought that custom had grown obsolete. Pray, Sir, why did you not ask the Irish clergyman this question, who preached for you last Thursday?'

Chancellor: 'That is nothing to you!' Then reading over part of the Ordination Office, and the canons forbidding ministers to preach in private houses, he asked, 'What do you say to these?'

Whitefield: 'I apprehend these canons do not belong to professed ministers of the Church of England.'

Chancellor: 'But they do!'

Whitefield: 'There is a canon forbidding all clergymen to frequent taverns and play at cards! Why is not that put into execution?'

Chancellor: 'Why does not somebody lodge a complaint? In such a case it would.'

Whitefield: 'My principles may be known by all from my printed sermons. Why then am I taken particular notice of?'

Chancellor: 'You preach false doctrine!'

Whitefield: 'I cannot but preach the things I know, and am resolved to proceed as usual!'

Chancellor: 'Observe his answer, Mr Registrar!' (Then turning to Whitefield), 'I am resolved, Sir, if you preach or expound anywhere in this diocese till you have a licence, I will first suspend,

[1] That day Whitefield learned of the death of the Reverend Dr Richard Venn, rector of St Antholin's in London. This was the man who had written the distorted account of the St Margaret's affair. Venn died at the early age of forty-eight. His son, the Reverend Henry Venn became an outstanding evangelical and one of Whitefield's most cherished friends.

and then excommunicate you! What I do is in the name of the clergy and laity of Bristol!'[1]

Following this exchange Whitefield wrote, 'To show how little I regarded such threatenings, after I had joined in prayer for the Chancellor, I immediately went and expounded at Newgate, where God gave me great joy and wondrously pricked many to the heart, as though He would say, "This is the way. Walk ye in it!" '[2] The next day, in fulfilment of his announcement, he went to Kingswood for his second open-air meeting and the congregation this time numbered nearly two thousand.

*

But despite his brave words, Whitefield had his inner uncertainties. In his high esteem for the Church, he wondered if his attitude of setting the leading of the Lord against its accepted customs was wise. He needed someone with whom he could take counsel, and, providentially, the one man most experienced in this kind of conflict was then at Bath. This was an outstanding Welsh preacher, the Reverend Griffith Jones of Llanddowror, and Whitefield paid him a visit.

In many ways, Griffith Jones was the forerunner of Howell Harris and deserves the title he has received, 'The morning star of the Revival'.

Born in 1683, Jones early experienced the work of God in conversion. He was trained for the Church and in 1709 was ordained priest. He became a man of thorough learning, his sermons were rich in Biblical truth, he spoke with spiritual power and was once invited to preach before Queen Anne. We are told:

> When he came into the pulpit it was with reverence and holy fear . . . He had an unassuming solemnity and seriousness in his face, sweetened with all the meekness of charity and love . . . As he advanced, his subject fired him more and more . . . One while he glowed with ardent love to his fellow-creatures; anon, he flamed with a just indignation at the enemies of their souls . . . Every feature, nerve and part of him were intensely animated . . . When he came to the application he seemed to summon up all his remaining force; he gave way to a superior burst of religious vehemence, and, like a flaming meteor, bore down all before him . . . No wonder that his hearers wept. No

[1] *Journals, p* 218. [2] *Ibid, pp* 218–19.

wonder that he was so successful in the conversion of sinners, when it was the Divine Spirit that made the Word effectual. By his preaching drunkards became sober, Sabbath-breakers were reformed, and the prayerless cried for mercy and forgiveness . . . Christ was all to him, and it was his greatest delight to publish his Redeemer's unsearchable riches.[1]

Under such a ministry Jones's church was constantly filled with hearers, and whenever they were too many to be accommodated within the building he transferred the service to the churchyard or an adjacent field. He was frequently invited to preach at other churches and on these occasions often conducted the service out of doors. He also made it his practice to attend the various events which drew the people together – such things as sporting matches, fairs and wakes – and there called the crowd around him to hear the Gospel. His work preceded that of Harris by twenty years, yet it bore an important difference: while Harris preached without clerical approbation, Jones claimed that he never ministered in any parish without first obtaining the permission of the resident clergyman.

Nevertheless, Jones's conduct aroused the wrath of the less-zealous among the clergy and he was frequently called into ecclesiastical courts. In writing to a Bishop in 1715,

He painted a saddening picture of the spiritual starvation suffered by the people, and the inadequacy of the careless clergy to meet their hunger. 'Oh! miserable people, hoodwinked with stupidity and wallowing with greediness in the filth of sin, what a pity is it that so many in the sacred function should be immersed in this inundation of wickedness.' He gently suggested that the Bishop would be better employed 'in stirring up those that preach not, than silencing those that do.'[2]

Though the opposition to Griffith Jones's doctrine and zeal did not succeed in preventing his activity, it was able to place severe hindrances in his way and to keep him involved in ecclesiastical litigation for twenty years.

In the face of these difficulties Jones developed another means of spreading the Gospel – a system of free education called the

[1] David Jones, *The Life and Times of Griffith Jones*. (SPCK, London, 1902) *pp* 224–6.
[2] A. Skevington Wood, *The Inextinguishable Blaze*, *op cit*, *p* 43.

Welsh Circulating Schools. These were not merely of an academic nature, but the Gospel was taught along with reading and writing, and the arrangements which Jones made for the training of his teachers gave a large place to the study of the Bible.

To this work Jones added extensive charitable undertakings. He devoted much labour and money to the provision and circulation of the Scriptures and Christian literature. Since medical help for the poor was almost non-existent, he equipped himself with a considerable knowledge in that field, wrote a hand-book on the treatment of common ailments and freely performed medical services among the common people. So exhaustive were his labours that his health became undermined and it was for this reason that he had resorted to the mineral waters of Bath in 1739.

What advice would Jones have been likely to give Whitefield as they met on this occasion? We may be sure he would encourage him in his evangelistic efforts in general, and would assure him that he was within the bounds of Church practice in preaching in the open air. However, there was doubtless the added caution that before preaching in any parish he ask the permission of the incumbent. The conversation, says Whitefield, 'convinced me that I was but a young soldier, just entering the field. Good God, prepare me to fight manfully whatsoever battles Thou hast appointed for me.'[1]

*

Upon returning to Bristol Whitefield found that the awaited letter from Bishop Butler had arrived.

Providentially, the circumstances under which the Bishop had written were favourable to Whitefield. Dr Butler had just returned from London where he had gone to address the Anniversary Meeting of the *Society for the Propagation of the Gospel*. At that gathering he would have been among many of Whitefield's friends (Lord and Lady Huntingdon were associated with the Society) and could not but have heard much commendatory comment on the evangelist.

In his address the Bishop advocated a rather fervent type of Christianity. Though not of an evangelical mind he was deeply concerned about the evils of the times and recognized the

[1] *Journals*, p 220.

Church's need of zealous men to combat them. He declared that England's colonies abroad were in danger of sinking 'into stupid atheism', and went on to state, 'And there is too apparent danger of the like horrible depravity at home'. He commended the 'several religious associations' and spoke of them as 'societies' which 'contribute more especially towards keeping up the face of Christianity amongst ourselves'. He urged his hearers 'to support Christianity where it must otherwise sink', and warned against those persons who 'discountenance what is good, because it is not better'.[1]

Though the letter to Whitefield has not been preserved, we have reason to believe that in writing it Dr Butler followed his own advice. This we assume from Whitefield's reply to him, in which he said, '. . . your Lordship's letter . . . gave abundant satisfaction to me and many others', and from the fact that he immediately showed it to the Chancellor who was much subdued by its contents. Without doubt, the letter condoned Whitefield's preaching in the open air to the colliers and in any church in the Bristol diocese which might be placed at his disposal by the minister. Moreover, we may be sure the Bishop commended the idea of the Orphan House and very probably gave his tacit approval to Whitefield's programme of evangelization in general.[2]

The reply was a considerable victory for Whitefield. When faced with the letter, the Chancellor made but a few weak complaints and Whitefield closed the interview by telling him he was 'resolved to go on preaching'.

*

[1] *A Sermon Preached Before the Society for the Propagation of the Gospel in Foreign Parts,* at their Anniversary Meeting in the Parish Church of St Mary-le-Bow, on Friday, February 16, 1739. *The Works of Joseph Butler* (Carter, New York, 1842), Section II, *pp* 194–5.

[2] Bishop Butler is remembered for the profound and yet lucid reasoning in his *Analogy of Natural and Revealed Religion.* His belief, however, was more of the head than the heart. 'When he lay dying, he was in distress of soul, and said to his chaplain that, notwithstanding his efforts to live a good life, he was afraid to die. "My lord", said his chaplain, "You have forgotten that Jesus Christ is a Saviour." "True", was his answer, "but how shall I know that He is a Saviour for me?" "My lord, it is written, Him that cometh to me I will in no wise cast out." "True", said the Bishop, "I am surprised that, though I have read that Scripture a thousand times over, I never felt its virtue till this moment, and now I die happy."' J. E. Rattenbury, *Wesley's Legacy to the World* (Epworth, 1928), *p* 89.

Armed with the assurance that Dr Butler had at least countenanced his proceedings, Whitefield pressed into his ministry with renewed vigour.

On the day before his meeting with the Chancellor he had preached at Kingswood to a congregation of 'four or five thousand', but on the day following it (a Sunday) he was there again and faced this time an immense crowd. 'At a moderate computation', he says, 'there were about ten thousand people to hear me. The trees and hedges were full. All was hush when I began; the sun shone bright, and God enabled me to preach for an hour with great power, and so loudly that all, I was told, could hear. Mr B—n spoke right. The fire is kindled in the country; and, I know, all the devils in hell shall not be able to quench it.'[1]

This must have been a tremendous occasion for Whitefield. Though his figures are probably exaggerated (we shall give attention later to the matter of his estimates), still we may be sure that the task of ministering to such a congregation in the fields was very strenuous.

The blessing of God, however, was wondrously manifest on this ministry to the colliers. Although these people were notorious for their brutality, there is not the slightest evidence that Whitefield was ever subjected to a vicious word or gesture among them. On the contrary, they seem to have been immediately moved by his manifest love for them, and not only did the whole community come flocking to hear him preach but it is apparent they held him in deep affection.

In a description which has become classic Whitefield reports his ministry among this pitiable and neglected people. We visualize the scene – the green countryside, the piles of coal, the squalid huts and the deep semi-circle of unwashed faces – as we read his words:

> Having no righteousness of their own to renounce, they were glad to hear of a Jesus who was a friend of publicans, and came not to call the righteous, but sinners to repentance. The first discovery of their being affected was to see the white gutters made by their tears which plentifully fell down their black cheeks, as they came out of their coal pits. Hundreds and hundreds of them were soon brought under deep convictions, which, as the event proved, happily ended in a sound

[1] *Journals*, p 223.

and thorough conversion. The change was visible to all, though numbers chose to impute it to anything, rather than the finger of God.[1]

*

While Whitefield was experiencing this extraordinary ministry in Bristol, John Wesley was also experiencing extraordinary things in London. Some of his hearers had become subject to overpowering emotions, and, regarding these effects as the work of God, he wrote to Whitefield about them. In one letter he reported that 'a woman was seized, as it appeared . . . with little less than the agonies of death . . . Five days she travailed and groaned, . . .'[2] In another, Wesley told of a woman who 'fell into a strange agony, both of body and mind; her teeth gnashed together; her knees smote each other, and her whole body trembled exceedingly.'[3]

Whitefield apparently had no uneasiness over these extremes at the time, but after the passing of a few months Wesley's encouragement of them became one of several points of difference between the two men.

*

After this successful introduction of himself to the open-air preaching, Whitefield set out to make the acquaintance of Howell Harris in Wales. Since his work at Bristol had developed to the place where it could not be dropped, even for a few days, he had John Hutchings come and conduct it in his absence.

Accompanied by Seward, Whitefield met Harris at Cardiff. It was a momentous occasion for each and Whitefield wrote, 'When I first saw him, my heart was knit closely to him. I wanted to catch some of his fire and gave him the right hand of fellowship with my whole heart.'[4] But Harris reported, "The first thing he said to me was "Do you know your sins are forgiven?"'[5]

Whitefield's right hand of fellowship, however, was something more than a friendly greeting. It was his acceptance of Harris on the same basis as if he had been an ordained minister. White-

[1] Gillies, *op cit*, *p* 28.
[2] *The Letters of John Wesley*, Vol 1, *p* 280.
[3] *Ibid*, *p* 282.
[4] *Journals*, *p* 229.
[5] *Bathafarn* (*The Journal of the Historical Society of the Methodist Church in Wales*), Vol 9, 1954, *p* 31.

field wrote, 'Twice he has applied (being every way qualified) for Holy Orders, but was refused, under a false pretence that he was not of age, though he was then twenty-two years and six months. About a month ago he offered himself again, but was put off. Upon this, he was and is still resolved to go on in his work.'[1] In his exalted concept of the ministerial office, Whitefield repudiated the idea of a lay ministry.[2] But he looked on Harris as manifestly ordained of God and, therefore, as fully worthy of human ordination. Since this was denied without valid cause, he regarded Harris's right to it as equivalent to the act itself.

'Indefatigable zeal has he shown in his Master's service', wrote Whitefield. 'For these three years he has discoursed almost twice every day, for three or four hours together . . . Many alehouse people, fiddlers, etc., cry out against him for spoiling their business. He has been made the subject of numbers of sermons, has been threatened with public prosecutions, and had constables sent to apprehend him. But God has blessed him with inflexible courage and instantaneous strength has been communicated to him from above . . . God has greatly blessed his pious endeavours. Many own him as their spiritual father and, I believe, would lay down their lives for his sake . . . He has established nearly thirty Societies in South Wales and still his sphere of action is enlarged daily.'[3]

Harris showed a similar interest in Whitefield's Christian experience. His Diary contains the following note:

> Had soul united to Brother Whitefield. In Cardiff near 4 hearing him preach from John 3: 3. Hearing him again in public, then to about 12 in private. Conversation relating to what God has done for us. Had my soul filled with heaven. To bed there with Brother Whitefield . . . He more mortified than me, sleeping for near a year 3 or 4 hours a night and kneeling on his knees all day long, reading and praying over the Scriptures.[4]

This meeting effected bonds which became of historic importance. 'We took account', says Whitefield, 'of the several Societies, and agreed on such measures as seemed most conducive to promote the common interest of our Lord.'[5] One of the measures was a plan to supply more Christian literature in the

[1] *Journals*, *p* 229. [2] See *p* 304. [3] *Journals*, *p* 229.
[4] *Bathafarn*, *op cit*, Vol 9, 1954, *p* 31. [5] *Journals* *p* 230.

Welsh tongue, and they mentioned specifically translations of some of Whitefield's sermons and 'a new translation of the Welch Bible'.[1] They also arranged that Harris would return with Whitefield to Bristol and that Whitefield would shortly come again to Wales and make a preaching tour with Harris. In listing the Societies Harris would speak for his thirty in Wales, and Whitefield for eight or ten in London, six or seven in Bristol and two or three in Gloucester, and this knowledge would afford them a view of the over-all extent of their work. Although they attempted no formal organization on this occasion, from this time forth Whitefield's work and Harris's work became joined in a broad fellowship, and this provided the foundation on which in four years' time they formed the Welsh Calvinistic Methodist body.

*

Whitefield's Bristol endeavours grew apace. The young people's meeting which met at his sister's home each Sunday morning at 6 o'clock increased so rapidly that within five weeks it had grown from its original fifty to five thousand, and now met as a great open-air congregation on a near-by bowling green. The Societies were so crowded that, in one instance, Whitefield 'was obliged to go up by a ladder through the window', and in another it was necessary for him to 'stand and expound at the window, so that those in the yard, which was full, might hear'. One Society attempted to remedy matters by renting a public auditorium, Weaver's Hall, but of the first meeting there Whitefield said, 'I was almost faint before I could get in through the crowd'.

Whitefield also extended the open-air ministry, holding meetings in several locations. The Bowling Green became his regular Sunday morning appointment with seven or eight thousand always present at 6 o'clock. Being told of a rough section of the city where 'many dwelt who neither feared God nor regarded man', he went into it and, taking his stand in an industrial yard, preached to thousands. Calls came to him constantly from outlying communities, and, saying 'I will, by the Divine assistance,

[1] Two sermons were published in Welsh in 1739 and others later. The plan to obtain a new edition of the Welsh Bible was fulfilled in 1743, by the help of the Society for Promoting Christian Knowledge, of which Whitefield's friend Thomas Broughton had, by that date, become Secretary.

go to as many as I can', he made Bristol a centre from which he daily ranged out into the surrounding area.

But it was in the Kingswood district that he saw the greatest triumphs. He held two services there each Sunday, one at Hanham and the other at Rose Green. No longer were his congregations composed solely of the colliers, but people from Bristol and farmers from the adjacent area – these and many others now came thronging into the formerly forbidden territory and stood shoulder to shoulder with the inhabitants of Kingswood to hear the Gospel.

We sense something of Whitefield's spirit in performing this work as we read the following accounts:

Sunday, March 18. Was taken ill for about two hours, but notwithstanding, was enabled to go and preach at Hanham to many more than were there last Sunday; and in the afternoon, I really believe no less than twenty thousand were present at Rose Green. Blessed are the eyes which see the things which we see. Surely God is with us of a truth. To behold such crowds stand about us in such an awful silence, and to hear the echo of their singing run from one end of them to the other, is very solemn and surprising. My discourse continued for near an hour and a half, and at both places, above £14 were collected for the Orphan House; and it pleased me to see with what cheerfulness the colliers and poor people threw in their mites.[1]

Sunday, March 25. Preached at Hanham to a larger congregation than ever, and again in the afternoon to upwards (as was computed) of 23,000 people. I was afterwards told that those who stood farthest off could hear me very plainly. Oh may God speak to them by His Spirit, at the same time that He enables me to lift up my voice like a trumpet![2]

The tremendous nature of this work must not be overlooked. It required great vocal powers, unusual clarity of enunciation, readiness of mind, and it could not but have cost him the liberal expenditure of physical and nervous energy. The weather must often have been a hindrance and the winter with its record cold was followed by an exceptionally wet spring. There were doubtless many points of technique for Whitefield to learn – standing so as to take advantage of a wind, using a natural eminence as a sounding board and handling disturbers in the crowd – but of

[1] *Journals*, *p* 234. [2] *Ibid*, *p* 238.

these things he says almost nothing. The burning desire to reach the hosts of mankind with the message of saving grace overruled all trials that came in the way, and he testified to the Divine assistance he experienced in learning the task, and the joy that was his as he performed it, saying:

As the scene was new and I had just begun to be an extempore preacher, it often occasioned many inward conflicts. Sometimes, when twenty thousand people were before me, I had not, in my own apprehension, a word to say either to God or them. But I never was totally deserted, and frequently . . . so assisted, that I knew by happy experience what our Lord meant by saying, 'Out of his belly shall flow rivers of living water'. The open firmament above me, the prospect of the adjacent fields, with the sight of thousands and thousands, some in coaches, some on horseback, and some in the trees, and at times all affected and drenched in tears together, to which sometimes was added the solemnity of the approaching evening, was almost too much for, and quite overcame me.[1]

*

It is an amazing fact that this open-air ministry, thus far, was the labour of merely six weeks. It is also amazing that before that time had elapsed, Whitefield made preparations to leave it.

Yet such an action was dictated by his responsibilities to Georgia. He had come to Bristol with the intention of being there but a short while, preaching the Gospel and collecting for the orphans, but now that this great work had developed, he needs must find a man who would come and continue it. After it was in new hands, he would move on, making a wide evangelistic sweep that would take him into Wales, across England and finally into the parks of London. For all of this activity he allowed himself but eight weeks, at the conclusion of which he would sail again for America.

Any doubts about the open-air ministry that Whitefield may have had when he came to Bristol, had now vanished. The unmistakable evidence of the Divine approval, manifest in the conversion of the colliers and others, had overruled the seemingly contradictory commands of the Church, and had given him a mighty boldness in the face of whatever opposition his extra-

[1] Gillies, *op cit*, *p* 38.

ordinary proceedings might provoke. 'My preaching in the fields', he exclaimed, 'may displease some timorous, bigoted men, but I am thoroughly persuaded it pleases God, and why should I fear anything else!'[1]

[1] *Journals*, p 227.

When Wesley and Whitefield met that night . . . any lingering hesitation on the part of Wesley to take up his friend's work must have vanished . . . The last film of the prejudice which dimmed his spiritual sight disappeared. The vision of the English Church on which he had been inclined, previously, to fix his gaze, faded . . . Above it and beyond it he saw Christ and the neglected masses of his fellow countrymen. That revelation made him an evangelist whose sphere was the nation.

J. S. SIMON

The Revival of Religion in England in the Eighteenth Century

15

John Wesley becomes an Open-air Preacher

WHITEFIELD looked for a man who would be able to take over the Bristol work. He was holding nearly thirty meetings a week with audiences which totalled – according to his estimates – forty or fifty thousand. Of course, within so short a time it was yet spontaneous and unconsolidated, but whoever succeeded him would have abundant opportunity to organize it in a permanent form.

The search soon narrowed to one. Whitefield had tried Hutchings, but this quiet man appears not even to have attempted the open air.[1] Seward says he asked Kinchin to come, but he also had few qualifications for such a labour and refused.[2] Harris could have proved equal to the task but he had his own work in Wales.

Accordingly, Whitefield's thought turned to John Wesley. He had reason, however, to wonder if one who was so observant of ecclesiastical propriety would submit to the indignity of field preaching, and, if he did, how successful he might be with the great out-of-doors congregations. Nevertheless, he was well aware of Wesley's invincible spirit and wrote to him, informing him of the crowds in the open air and concluding with, 'You must come and water what I have planted'.

[1] Comment on Hutchings was made by Harris in his *Diary* of March 12, 1739: 'Heard of Brother Hutchings receiving the Holy Ghost, after he had seen his soul (about 12 months ago), as black as hell.' On April 2 of that year John Wesley expressed the opinion, '. . . our Brother Hutchings, who is strong in faith but very weak in body; as most probably he will continue to be, so long as he hides his light under a bushel' (*Letters*, Vol 1, *p* 289). Charles Wesley wrote (*Journal*, Aug. 10, 1739), 'I am tempted to leave off preaching and hide myself like J. Hutchings.'

Hutchings married into one of the wealthy Fetter Lane families, became a Moravian, and was not heard of in the evangelistic circles thereafter. John Byrom spoke of him in 1744 as 'Mr. Hutchins [sic] who was my shorthand scholar, poor Kinchin's curate, and married a fortune' (*Literary Remains*, Vol 2, Part 2, *p* 374).

[2] Tyerman's *Whitefield*, Vol 1, *p* 187.

This letter crossed in the mail with one Wesley had written to him, upbraiding him for accepting Seward's help without having first secured the permission of the Fetter Lane Society.[1] Whitefield had never recognized the Moravian rules, but needed to see to it now that Wesley's submission to them did not prevent his coming to Bristol. Thus, he wrote again, saying:

I thank you most heartily for your kind rebuke. I can only say it was too tender. I beseech you, whenever you see me do wrong, rebuke me sharply. I have still a word or two to offer in defence of my behaviour, but shall defer it till I come to town.

If the brethren, after prayer for direction, think proper, I wish you would be here the latter end of next week. Brother Hutchings sets out to-morrow for Dummer. Mr Chapman brings a horse to London that you may ride. I go away, God willing, next Monday sennight. If you were here before my departure it might be best. Many are ripe for bands. I leave that entirely to you. I am but a novice; you are acquainted with the great things of God.

Come, I beseech you, come quickly! I have promised not to leave this people till you or somebody else come to supply my place . . . P.S. March 23. I beseech you, come next week; it is advertised in this day's journal. I pray for a blessing on your journey, and in our meetings. The people expect you much. Though you come *after*, I heartily wish you may be preferred *before* me. Even so, Lord Jesus, Amen. Our brethren are here together. They advise you should go through Basingstoke, and call at Dummer, and there take the horse that Brother Hutchings rides thither. Whosoever you may appoint shall ride Brother Chapman's. The Lord direct us all in all things![2]

Whitefield was purposely creating circumstances which left Wesley with little choice. The horses would be waiting for him – one at London and one half-way at Dummer – the newspaper had announced his coming and Whitefield was virtually setting a time limit upon his arrival.

For this sudden taking of so momentous a step Wesley was not yet ready. It was but ten months since his Aldersgate Street experience and only eleven weeks had elapsed since his assertion, 'That I am not a Christian I as assuredly know as that Jesus is the Christ'. Physically, he had not been well since his days in Georgia and he tired so easily from his ministrations in the Societies that

[1] Wesley's *Letters*, Vol 1, *p* 287.

[2] Tyerman's *Whitefield*, Vol 1, *p* 193.

he expected soon to die.[1] Whitefield's letter asked him, not only to forsake his churchly proprieties, but to enter upon a labour of preaching to thousands in the fields, and Wesley could but believe that, were he so to do, his death would be hastened.

This fear was curiously confirmed as he sought guidance by the random opening of the Bible. Four times he 'consulted the oracle' and each time the verse he lighted upon referred to death[2] or suffering. Faced with so plain an indication that to accept Whitefield's invitation would mean his demise, Wesley said: 'This I was not at all forward to do; and perhaps a little the less inclined to it (though I trust I do not count my life dear unto myself . . .) because of the remarkable Scriptures that offered as often as we inquired touching the consequence of this removal.'[3]

Upon proposing the matter to the Fetter Lane Society Wesley received the same assurance.

> My brother Charles would scarce bear the mention of it [says John], till, appealing to the oracles of God, he received those words as spoken to himself, and answered not again, 'Son of man, behold, I take from thee the desire of thine eyes with a stroke: yet shalt thou not mourn or weep, neither shall thy tears run down.' Our other brethren, however, continuing the dispute, without any probability of their coming to one conclusion, we at length all agreed to decide it by lot. And by this it was determined I should go.[4]

Charles Wesley added: 'We dissuaded my brother from going to Bristol, from an unaccountable fear that it would prove fatal to him . . . He offered himself willingly to whatsoever the Lord should appoint. The next day he set out, commended by us to the grace of God. He left a blessing behind. I desired to die with him.'[5]

Yet all these forebodings were entirely unnecessary! In going to Bristol, instead of approaching his death, John Wesley was entering into the labour of his life.

[1] This expectancy is commented on by Wesley's friend and biographer, Henry Moore. 'He thought much at this time on death', says Moore, 'and as his constitution seemed to him not likely to support itself long under the great and continual labours he was engaged in, he judged it probable that his course was nearly finished.' Wesley's *Journal*, Vol 2, *p* 157.

[2] *Ibid.*

[3] *Ibid*, *pp* 156–7.

[4] *Ibid*, *pp* 157–8. Dr Curnock says the disputing at Fetter Lane was continued for eleven days. He remarks that this was a time of 'strong emotion' and 'excitement' for Wesley.

[5] Charles Wesley's *Journal*, March 28, 1739.

Wesley reached Bristol on a Saturday evening. He accompanied Whitefield to his regular meeting at Weaver's Hall and reported the attendance as 'about a thousand souls'.

The surprising sights, however, awaited Wesley the next day, Sunday, when Whitefield introduced him to his open-air congregations. Wesley was somewhat overawed and wrote to Hutton, 'Brother Whitefield expounded on Sunday morning to six or seven thousand at the Bowling Green; at noon to much the same number at Hanham Mount, and at five to, I believe, thirty thousand from a little mount on Rose Green.'[1]

In entering the event in his *Journal* John stated:

I could scarce reconcile myself at first to this strange way of preaching in the fields, of which he set me an example on Sunday; having been all my life (till very lately) so tenacious of every point relating to decency and order, that I should have thought the saving of souls almost a sin if it had not been done in a church.[2]

Moreover, the sight of the crowds and Whitefield's ministering to them moved Wesley to pay his friend the greatest compliment he knew. In writing to Hutton he exclaimed, 'O how is God manifested in our brother Whitefield! I have seen none like him – no, not in Herrnhut!'[3]

Whitefield had little time, however, to spend in persuading Wesley to undertake the open-air work. Having shown him how it was done he took steps to thrust him immediately into the doing of it. On the Sunday evening he had John preach in the Nicholas Street Society while he himself went to the one in Baldwin Street, and there he announced that 'Wesley, "whose shoe's latchet I am unworthy to unloose", would preach on the next day "in the Brickyard, at the farther end of St Phillip's Plain." '[4] This was the location where Whitefield had preached

[1] John Wesley's *Letters*, Vol 1, *p* 289.
[2] John Wesley's *Journal*, Vol 2, *p* 167.
[3] Wesley's *Letters*, Vol. 1, *p* 290.
[4] George Eayrs, *Wesley and Kingswood*, *op cit*, *p* 26. In his various references to this event, Wesley speaks of the place at which he preached as 'a brickyard' and 'the Glasshouse'. See his *Diary* at *p* 172 of his *Journal*, Vol 2. Whitefield called the place where he himself had preached the previous Tuesday 'the Glass Houses'. This was the name of a bottle works which adjoined a brickyard, and Eayrs (*p* 125) presents a diagram showing the relation of the two properties. Thus, the place at which Wesley preached his first open air sermon was not a location of his own choosing, but was rather a site chosen earlier by Whitefield and at which he had Wesley minister on this occasion as his substitute.

on the previous Tuesday and he was now stating that Wesley would take his place in conducting the second meeting that he had planned to hold there. Whether or not he had secured Wesley's agreement to this announcement we do not know, but he was manifestly forcing him to overcome his scruples and launch out into the field preaching right away.

Like Whitefield, Wesley was deeply moved by the prospect which such a ministry opened up. The reaching of vast numbers of mankind, the freedom to range at will and preach wherever opportunity afforded – these advantages could not fail to make a powerful appeal to so earnest a man. Moreover, as he looked out on Whitefield's congregation of thirty thousand he could sense that here was a means by which he might escape the limitations of a ministry confined to the Religious Societies, and here was a method of evangelization by which he might use to the full the extraordinary abilities that were his.

Wesley needed no further prompting. 'I submitted to be more vile',[1] he said, and informed Whitefield of his willingness to undertake his Bristol work.

*

Having obtained this assurance from Wesley, Whitefield prepared to take his departure. We see something of the extent of the Divine blessing on his six weeks of labour in Bristol as we read his report:

Spent a good part of the morning in talking with those who came to take their leave; and tongue cannot express what a sorrowful parting we had. Floods of tears flowed plentifully, and my heart was so melted that I prayed for them with strong cryings and many tears. The scene was very affecting. About one, I was obliged to force myself away. Crowds were waiting at the door to give me a last farewell, and near twenty friends accompanied me on horseback.

Blessed be God for the marvellous great kindness He hath shown me in this city! Many sinners, I believe, have been effectually converted; numbers have come to me under convictions, and all the children of God have been exceedingly comforted . . . Several thousands of little books have been dispersed among the people, about £200 collected

[1] Wesley's *Journal*, Vol 2, *p* 172. Whitefield used a similar phrase, saying of his open-air preaching, 'If this is to be vile, Lord, grant that I may be more vile.' *Journals*, *p* 265.

for the Orphan House, and many poor families relieved by the bounty of Mr Seward. What gives me the greater comfort is the consideration that my dear and honoured friend, Mr Wesley, is left behind to confirm those who are awakened.[1]

But before leaving the area Whitefield had an important duty to fulfil at Kingswood. While there four days earlier he had broached the matter of having a school built for the children and had received a considerable sum towards its cost: 'above twenty pounds in money, and . . . above forty pounds in subscriptions'.[2] Besides this 'they all seemed willing to assist, either by their money or their labour, and to offer such things as they had.'[3] And now, after his farewells at Bristol, he came again to Kingswood, 'where', he says, 'the colliers, unknown to me, had prepared a hospitable entertainment, and were very forward for me to lay the first stone of their school. At length I complied, and a man giving me a piece of ground . . . I laid a stone, and then kneeled down and prayed God that the gates of hell might not prevail against our design.'[4]

Whitefield thus had reason to feel that he had made a valuable start toward seeing a school erected at Kingswood. Accordingly, the following day, while on his way to Wales, he wrote to John Wesley, saying, 'I suppose you have heard of my proceedings in Kingswood. Be pleased to go thither and forward the good work as much as possible.'[5]

*

With Whitefield's departure, the responsibility of carrying on the immense work at Bristol fell on Wesley. It is evident that he felt its weight, for, in writing to James Hutton, after reporting Whitefield's ministry, he concluded with,

Pray ye, my dear brethren, that some portion of his spirit may be given to,

Your poor, weak brother,

John Wesley.[6]

[1] *Journals, pp* 242–3. [2] *Ibid, p* 240. [3] *Ibid, p* 241. [4] *Ibid, p* 243.
[5] Shewn in facsimile in John Wesley's *Journal*, Vol 2, *p* 209.
[6] Wesley's *Letters*, Vol 1, *p* 289.

But Wesley proved equal to the challenge. That afternoon he went, as Whitefield had announced, at four o'clock to the Brick-yard. There he found a congregation of about three thousand and, taking his stand on 'a little eminence', 'proclaimed the glad tidings of salvation' to them.

Any misgivings Wesley had in undertaking this work were quickly overcome and he entered upon it with characteristic zeal. For the next few days he felt his way into it slowly, but by the time the Sunday came round he was able very largely to fulfil Whitefield's schedule, holding three services in the open air and one in a Society.

During the following week he increased his activity and so happy was he that, when Charles wrote expecting he would be ready to start back for London, John replied, 'I have so full employment here that I think there can be no doubt whether I should return already or no.'[1] As he became more experienced he added other meetings, until, by the time he had been in Bristol a month and a half, he regularly conducted about fourteen meetings indoors and eight or ten outdoors each week.[2]

In undertaking this work Wesley was labouring under certain disadvantages. In a few months' time he gained his own place among the Bristol and Kingswood people, but during these first weeks he faced their disappointment over the departure of Whitefield. Moreover, while Whitefield was probably as greatly gifted for the open-air preaching as any man in Christian history, Wesley, whose talents fitted him admirably for the Oxford class-room, was not particularly suited to addressing the crowds in the fields. His voice, though apparently a rich tenor, lacked the organ tones of Whitefield's, and his manner of preaching, while intense in its earnestness, had not the popular appeal of White-field's dramatic oratory.

Wesley's records make it evident that he was highly pleased with the size of his congregations. They were, however, much smaller than those of Whitefield. Gone now were the great crowds of ten, twenty and thirty thousand, and in their place Wesley ministered to gatherings of one, three and five thousand.[3]

[1] *Ibid, p* 291.
[2] Wesley outlines his schedule of meetings in his *Journal,* Vol 2, *p* 198.
[3] We are dependent on the estimates given by the two men themselves, and there

At the Sunday morning service on the Bowling Green, however, attendances remained at much their former level and on two fine Sunday afternoons in late spring Wesley estimated his Rose Green congregations at nine and ten thousand.

But Wesley's assumption of this work also conferred upon him strong advantages. He had never been in Bristol before and, in the light of much that has been written, it is necessary to emphasize that, as he began his ministry there, this extensive evangelism was already in operation and was freely placed within his hands.

It was, however, for the meetings in the Societies that Wesley was especially gifted. The rooms were just as crowded as when Whitefield had been there: 'The yard being full, as well as the house, I expounded at the window', he says of one occasion; and of another, 'The room containing but a small part of the company, we opened the doors and windows, by which means all that was spoken was heard clearly by those in the next room, and on the leads, and in the court below, and in the opposite house and the passage under it.'[1] John was completely at home in such gatherings and the closer contact with the people allowed the full force of his personality to be exercised. In implementation of Whitefield's suggestion, 'Many are ripe for bands', he formed groups of four or five persons who 'agreed to meet together regularly to confess their faults and pray for one another', and his abilities were superbly suited to the task of individual examination which the overseeing of the Bands entailed. If his success was less than that of Whitefield outdoors, this was not true indoors, and his *Journal* makes one feel that his personal strength dominated the meetings in the Societies.

*

During these opening weeks in Bristol, Wesley's work bore a twofold relationship. *First,* he regarded himself as Whitefield's appointee. This is evident, for instance, in the matter of the Kingswood School. He did not consider himself free to make the

can be no doubt that they both exaggerated the size of their congregations. However, since there are instances in which they both give the same estimate of a given congregation, we may assume that the measure of exaggeration was much the same in each, and that their figures are comparable.

[1] Wesley's *Letters*, Vol 1, *p* 295.

decision as to where it was to be built, but waited for Whitefield's directions. 'I wish he would write to me, positively and decisively', he said, 'that, "for this reason, he would have the first school there, or as near it as possible".'[1] *Secondly,* Wesley looked on himself as a Moravian missionary. He began to transcribe the Fetter Lane rules for use by the Bristol Societies and, in Moravian fashion, chose the leaders and the members of the Bands by casting lots. The men's and women's Bands met separately and were organized, he says, 'in closest conformity to the Böhler orders.'[2] It was the custom for all Moravian missionaries to make written reports of their activities, and he wrote a series of letters to Hutton (and through him to the Fetter Lane Society) which were a fulfilment of this practice.

These relationships, however, like almost everything else in Wesley's life, soon began to change. In his Bristol ministry he found, for the first time, a labour of sufficient scope to challenge all his immense powers of mind and will. The thronged Societies and the crowds in the fields afforded him a sense of accomplishment superior to any he had ever known. Ministerial success, the phantom his father had sought so long but failed to find, and which had likewise eluded both Charles and himself in Georgia, was now within his grasp. His Moravian letters are alive with a new exhilaration and one needs but to compare the *Journal* entries he had made in London, in their dejection and uncertainty, with these of Bristol, to see the tremendous alteration that he was experiencing.

The belief that he was soon to die gave way before this new elation. During his first week in Bristol he said, 'I believe I have nearly finished my course',[3] but thereafter, his joy in the work drove such thoughts from his mind. At the close of a Sunday on which he had preached seven times – four of them in the open air – he exulted, 'Oh, how has God renewed my strength! who used ten years ago to be so faint and weary with preaching *twice* in one day!'[4]

In all of this fresh vigour of spirits John was richly reinforced by the sight of transformed lives among the Kingswood and Bristol people. He and his brother Samuel had long indulged the

[1] *Ibid, p* 302.
[2] Wesley's *Journal*, Vol 2, *p* 191.
[3] Wesley's *Letters,* Vol 1, *p* 291.
[4] Wesley's *Journal*, Vol 2, *p* 186.

family penchant for debate, exchanging letters in which they exercised their powers of logic with incisive thrust and counter-thrust, and, in replying to a letter in which Samuel had argued against sudden conversions, John stated:

I have seen very many persons changed in a moment from the spirit of fear, horror and despair, to the spirit of love, joy and peace: and from sinful desire, till then reigning over them, to a pure desire of doing the will of God. These are matters of fact, whereof I have been, and almost daily am, an eye or ear witness.

. . . I will shew you him that was a lion till then, and is now a lamb; him that was a drunkard, and now is exemplarily sober; the whoremonger that was, who now abhors the very 'garment spotted by the flesh'. These are my living arguments for what I assert – viz. 'That God does now, as aforetime, give remission of sins, and the gift of the Holy Ghost, . . . If it be not so, I am found a false witness before God. For these things I *do*, and by His grace *will,* testify.[1]

Furthermore, the change in John Wesley was accelerated by the fact that strong emotional effects began to accompany his preaching. He had twice witnessed such things before leaving London, but in Bristol he began to witness them every day. The following are some of his first reports of these occurrences:

We called upon God to confirm His word. Immediately one that stood by . . . cried out aloud, with the utmost vehemence, even as in the agonies of death. But we continued in prayer till 'a new song was put in her mouth' . . . Soon after, two other persons . . . were seized with strong pain, and constrained to 'roar for the disquietness of their heart'. But it was not long before they likewise burst forth into praise to God their Saviour. The last who called upon God, as out of the belly of hell, was John Ellis, a stranger in Bristol. And in a short space he also was overwhelmed with joy and love.[2]

Wesley was deeply affected by this strange phenomenon. He had no doubts as to its source, for he regarded it as entirely the demonstration of the divine power and as a sign that the special approval of heaven had been placed upon him and his ministry.

Several of Wesley's biographers have pointed out the semi-failure of his Aldersgate Street experience, and have been at a loss to discover when and how the real change in his personality

[1] *Ibid,* Vol 2, *p* 202.

[2] *Ibid, p* 180.

came about. But as one studies his first two months in Bristol, it becomes evident that this period marks the point of supreme change in his life. Truly the Aldersgate experience had left him in doubt and dismay, but under the effect of his new success he became a man of confidence and triumph. His native consciousness of superiority, long frustrated by his uncertainties, now burst its restraints, and ambitions commensurate with his talents were stimulated by the fact that the possibility of fulfilment was now before him.

This new man is to be seen, for instance, in the following report, written when he had been in Bristol seven weeks:

> Seeing many of the rich at Clifton Church, my heart was much pained for them, and I was earnestly desirous that some even of them might 'enter into the kingdom of heaven'. But, full as I was, I knew not where to begin in warning them to flee from the wrath to come, till my Testament opened on these words: 'I came not to call the righteous, but sinners to repentance'; in applying which my soul was so enlarged that methought I could have cried out (in another sense than poor vain Archimedes), 'Give me where to stand, and I will shake the earth.'[1]

Gone now was the man of doubts and uncertainties, and here, at last, in a confidence befitting his abilities was the new John Wesley, ready to enter into the great mission of his life.

[1] *Ibid*, *p* 201.

From strength to strength our young Apostle goes,
Pours like a torrent, and the land o'erflows,
Resistless wins his way with rapid zeal,
Turns the world upside down, and shakes the gates of hell!

CHARLES WESLEY
Elegy on Whitefield

16

Into the Open Air in London

AFTER leaving Kingswood, Whitefield gave himself three more weeks of preparation before he made the attempt in the open air at London.

The first week was spent in the experienced company of Howell Harris, on a preaching tour of his section of Wales. Upon entering any parish Whitefield sought out the clergyman and asked for the use of the church. If it was allowed he used it, but if not, he took unto himself the liberty to preach wherever opportunity afforded. He and Harris took their stand on anything that gave them a vantage point – a horse-block before an inn, a table placed in the centre of the street or a stone wall at the edge of a field – these and similar contrivances served as make-shift pulpits from which they addressed the crowds. Harris usually preached first, in Welsh, and Whitefield followed in English.

One incident of this tour – their visit to the town of Abergavenny – was of special significance. A widow lived there, a Mrs Elizabeth James, who was to play an important part in the life of each of these men. Harris had probably met her before and on this occasion mentioned her briefly in his *Diary*. He was soon, however, to become romantically interested in her and to experience an affection characterized by his native vehemence of emotion. Whitefield made no mention of her at this time, but the occasion marked his first meeting with the woman who was later to become the wife, not of Harris, but of himself!

The week in Wales provided Whitefield with valuable experience. He entered into the spirit of Harris's work, rejoiced in the liberty of this itinerant ministry, courageously faced the violence which was sometimes threatened, and treated with disdain an attempt to have the law prohibit their proceedings. Four ministers refused their churches, but four others freely opened theirs. Two of the open-air meetings drew congregations, even in the sparsely-populated Welsh countryside, which Whitefield spoke of as 'many thousands'. He learned that constant preaching and travelling could be very tiring and as they crossed the border back into England (en route to Gloucester) he described himself as 'weak through fatigue'. In anticipation of his work in London, he asked Harris to remain with him and assist him there, and to Harris, who had but once before been out of his native area, the prospect was undoubtedly an exciting one.

Whitefield's arrival at Gloucester provoked a wave of enthusiasm among his friends and an outburst of opposition from his foes. When last in the city (nearly two years earlier) he had been an almost unknown youth on his way to Georgia, but as he returned now he was one of the most famous men in the nation. His rise had truly been meteoric, for it was but seven years since he had been a schoolboy at St Mary de Crypt, and eight since he had served liquor at the Bell.

'When I came to the city', he says, 'I found the devil had painted me in the most horrible colours, for it was currently reported that I was really mad, that I had said I was the Holy Ghost, and that I had walked bareheaded through the streets of Bristol singing Psalms.'[1] Again, he simply went on with his work and let his methods speak for themselves.

Refused the use of the churches (only one was allowed, and that but once) he preached in the fields and in the largest public auditorium, the Booth Hall. He also carried the message to several outlying towns, and from still other communities people came into the city to attend his ministry there. At the end of a week, as he took his departure, he wrote,

> Having dined, prayed with and taken leave of my weeping friends, and dispersed a great many of my sermons among the poor, I took horse. But, oh, what love did the people express for me! How many came to me weeping and telling me what God had done for their souls by my ministry! Oh, how did they pray for my return among them! Lord, I dared not expect such success among my own countrymen.[2]

*

[1] *Journals, p* 252. [2] *Ibid.*

In performing this itinerant evangelism Whitefield was adding a further function of the open-air ministry. In his work at Kingswood he had established the field preaching, but had done so in the sense that it was limited to little more than one location. But in moving from place to place, as he had done in Wales and the Gloucester area, he was creating a free ministry which knew no bounds.

This action raised serious questions of Church of England law. While it is possible that the absence of a church or of clerical attention at Kingswood justified his preaching there, this practice of invading other men's parishes at will, as if the refusal of the church constituted his right to do so, could not be so easily vindicated. In fact, whether or not such a procedure can be accommodated within the rules of the Church of England has long been an undecided question, but Whitefield had convinced himself that it could, and it was on this principle that he was acting. But others rejected the principle and therefore there was conflict in store for him.

Whitefield intended, upon leaving Gloucester, to be in London within a week. He was determined to enter upon the out-of-doors ministry there too, but though he anticipated the immense undertaking with joy, he also looked upon it in weakness and dread. 'Oh dear Mr Harris', he wrote to his bookseller friend, 'My heart is drawn towards London most strangely.'[1]

These feelings did not rise in the least from a fear of suffering. On the contrary, he expected severely increased opposition and went so far as to assume it might mean outright persecution and even imprisonment. These things he freely stated his willingness to bear.

The cause of Whitefield's anxiety was something quite different. The open-air ministry required great zeal, but it also required great wisdom, and as he sought to conduct and extend it, it constantly faced him with the decision as to where the highway of good sense ended and where the by-path of fanaticism began. For instance, when passing through Basingstoke a few weeks later, he mounted the stage where a cudgel game was in progress; he tried to halt it and make the players and the spectators listen while he preached. He finally left the stage with a blow from a

[1] *Works*, Vol 1, *p* 48.

cudgel for his trouble. This was certainly zealous, but no one could say it was wise, and this was the kind of thing that he wished to avoid.

Many of the statements that Whitefield made reveal the difficulty that he faced in seeking to ascertain the median of common sense as he pioneered the open-air ministry. As he approached London he prayed, 'God grant that I may behave so, that when I suffer, it may not be for my own imprudencies, but for righteousness sake.'[1] In a letter that he wrote after beginning his work in London (to run ahead of our narrative) he says,

> O pray, dear, Sir, that my zeal may be always tempered with true Christian prudence. It would grieve me should I bring sufferings causelessly upon myself. A trying time, perhaps, is at hand. O that I may be found faithful![2]

Likewise, certain sermons that he preached during this period contain extensive sections which urge upon his followers the constant exercise of caution and warn against excessive action. 'Do nothing rash – wait on the Lord'; 'We need a proper mixture of the lion and the lamb'; 'The Lord's cause needs not noise and rashness. I desire that no wild fire be mixed with the pure fire of holy zeal upon God's altar' – these were his expressions.

In his sense of loneliness and inadequacy Whitefield looked for help. We have seen how he had taken counsel with Griffith Jones and had opened correspondence with the Erskine brothers that he might be guided by the experience of these older men. In a letter to a prominent Christian (the name is not given, but it was probably William Law) Whitefield spoke of himself as 'a novice in the things of God', and expressed the desire to meet him that he might thereby 'have some spiritual gift imparted'.[3] To an elderly evangelical minister he wrote, 'Your advice would always be seasonable to me, because you have been a long time in the school of Christ', and in a few months' time, when he was in America, he wrote to the great Jonathan Edwards, saying, 'I should rejoice to be instructed by you'.[4]

This youth, insecure in himself and longing for experienced counsel, was as much the true Whitefield as the man who stood

[1] *Ibid.*
[2] *Ibid*, *p* 56.
[3] *Ibid*, *p* 54.
[4] *Ibid*, *p* 121.

before his great audiences with a courage and confidence which seemed virtually boundless.

*

Very shortly after reaching London Whitefield found himself excluded from the church which had formerly been the scene of his warmest welcome. This was St Mary's at Islington, and, though invited to preach by the minister, the Rev George Stonehouse, he was forbidden by the warden. Accordingly, he took his stand in the churchyard and afterwards stated:

God was pleased so to assist me in preaching, and so wonderfully to affect the hearers, that I believe we could have gone singing of hymns to prison. Let not the adversaries say I have thrust myself out. No; they have thrust me out. And since the self-righteous men of this generation count themselves unworthy, I go out into the highways and hedges, and compel harlots, publicans and sinners to come in, that my Master's house may be filled.[1]

Whitefield regarded this rejection as his warrant to enter as fully as possible into the open-air ministry in London. Accordingly he made his plans. Not far from the area where the majority of his people lived (the Fetter Lane–Aldersgate Street area) there was an eighteen-acre park called Moorfields. It was the site of the usual entertainments of the age – bear-baiting, merry-andrew shows, wrestling, cudgel playing and dog fights – and large numbers of people gathered there each evening and on Sundays to wile away their hours in these diversions.

Some of the Fetter Lane brethren, having heard of Whitefield's exploits at Bristol, had already attempted an open-air meeting at Moorfields. They had carried in a table on which to stand, but the mob had quickly broken it to pieces and sent them running in fear for their lives. Whitefield faced the question as to whether or not it was wise for him to try where they had failed, and decided in the affirmative. Gillies says that on the Sunday morning,

Public notice having been given . . . upon coming out of the coach he found an incredible number of people assembled. Many had told him that he should never come again out of that place alive. He went in, however, between two of his friends, who, by the pressure of the

[1] *Journals*, p 259.

crowd were soon parted entirely from him and were obliged to leave him to the mercy of the rabble. But these, instead of hurting him, formed a lane for him, and carried him along to the middle of the Fields (where a table had been placed which was broken in pieces by the crowd) and afterwards back again to the wall that then parted the upper and lower Moorfields; from whence he preached without molestation to an exceedingly great multitude.[1]

Directly following this meeting Whitefield attended the morning service at Christ Church, and there received further evidence of his need to preach in the open air. The preacher, the Rev Dr Joseph Trapp, one of London's ablest clergymen, made Whitefield the subject of his sermon, denouncing his activities, ridiculing his *Journal* and accusing him of lying about the St Margaret's affair. He upbraided the Religious Societies for allowing him to make them into so vigorous a movement and urged their members to follow him no longer.

This attack confirmed Whitefield in his belief that he could expect nothing but opposition from the clergy and that God was thus thrusting him into the fields. He held another open-air meeting that evening. 'Being weakened by my morning's preaching', he wrote, 'in the afternoon I refreshed myself with a little sleep, and at five went and preached at Kennington Common.'

Whitefield manifestly found himself deeply challenged by the conditions of this place. Kennington Common was an area of about twenty acres and lay south of the Thames. It was especially notable as the scene of hangings and its permanent scaffold stood as a constant reminder of the sorrows of sin and the power of the law. If the habitués of Moorfields were rough, those of Kennington were brutal, for here the lowest of London's citizens congregated in teeming numbers. Here were vicious sports and drunken brawlings. Here the harlot and pick-pocket sought the victims of their trades, and here the mob assembled, ready for any act of violence. Here humanity gathered – men, women and children – unwashed and ignorant, wicked and diseased, a vast host of whom it might be said, 'No man cared for their souls'.

Moved with compassion and forgetful of Trapp and all his kind, Whitefield walked out upon Kennington Common and proceeded to take the enemy's citadel by storm. His report reads:

[1] Gillies, *op cit*, *p* 42.

No less than thirty thousand were supposed to be present. The wind being for me, carried my voice to the extremest part of the audience. All stood attentive, and joined in the Psalm and the Lord's Prayer most regularly. I scarce ever preached more quietly in any church. The Word came with power. The people were much affected and expressed their love to me many ways. All agreed it was never seen on this wise before . . . I hope a good inroad has been made into the Devil's kingdom this day.[1]

This Sunday's labours marked the beginning of one of the greatest chapters of Whitefield's entire career. Satisfied with this initial step into the open air in London, he returned to Kennington the following Wednesday and, thereafter, nearly every evening saw him there, and every Sunday morning saw him at Moorfields. We follow his amazing course in the following reports:

Wednesday, May 2. Preached this evening again to above ten thousand at Kennington Common . . .

Thursday, May 3. Was fully employed all day in making preparations for my voyage, and preached at six in the evening (a time I choose that people may not be drawn away from their business) at Kennington, and great power was amongst us. The audience was more numerous and silent than yesterday, the evening calm, and many went affected away.

Saturday, May 5. Preached yesterday and to-day as usual at Kennington Common, to about twenty thousand hearers who were very much affected. The remainder of my time I spent in preparing things for Georgia. I am not usually so much engaged in secular work; but I as readily do this as preach, when it is the will of God. It is a great mistake that some run into, to suppose that religion consists only in saying our prayers. I think . . . he only will adorn the Gospel of our Lord Jesus Christ in all things, who is careful to perform all the civil offices of life . . . with a single eye to God's glory . . . This is the morality I preach.

Sunday, May 6. Preached this morning in Moorfields to about twenty thousand people, who were very quiet and attentive, and much affected. Went to public worship morning and evening, and at six preached at Kennington. Such a sight I never saw before. I believe there were no less than fifty thousand people, and near four score coaches, besides great numbers of horses. God gave me great enlargement of heart. I continued my discourse for an hour and a half, and when I returned home, I was filled with such love, peace and joy that I cannot express it.[2]

[1] *Journal, pp* 260, 261. [2] *Ibid, pp* 261, 262.

So runs the record of Whitefield's first week in the open air in London. It is not to be wondered at that on the Monday he refrained from holding an out-of-doors service and confined his work to preparations for Georgia and expounding in a private house.

But during the following two weeks the same great things continued till the record becomes almost monotonous with meeting after meeting and crowds upon crowds:

Tuesday, May 8. Preached in the evening, as usual, on Kennington Common. Some considerable time before I set out from town it rained very hard, so that once I thought of not going; but several pious friends joined in hearty prayer that God would be pleased to withhold the rain, which was done immediately. To my great surprise, when I came to the Common, I saw above twenty thousand people. All the while, except for a few moments, the sun shone out upon us; and I trust, the Sun of Righteousness arose on some with healing in His wings. The people were melted down very much at the preaching of the Word and put up hearty prayers for my temporal and eternal welfare.

Wednesday, May 9 . . . after God had enabled me to preach to about twenty thousand for above an hour at Kennington, He inclined the hearers' hearts to contribute most cheerfully and liberally toward the Orphan House. I was one of the collectors, and it would have delighted anyone to have seen with what eagerness and cheerfulness the people came up both sides of the eminence on which I stood, and afterwards to the coach doors to throw in their mites. Surely God must have touched their hearts. When we came home we found that we had collected above £46, amongst which were £16 in half pence.

Thursday, May 10. Preached at Kennington, but it rained most of the day. There were not above ten thousand people, and thirty coaches. However, God was pleased so visibly to interpose in causing the weather to clear up, and the sun to shine out just as I began, that I could not avoid taking notice of it to the people in my discourse.

Friday, May 11. Preached at Kennington to a larger audience than last night, and collected £26 15s. 6d. for the Orphan House. The people offered willingly. They could not have taken more pains, or expressed more earnestness, had they all come to receive an alms of me. Being upon the Publican and Pharisee, I was very earnest in endeavouring to convince the self-righteous Pharisees of this generation, and offering Jesus Christ freely to all, who, with the humble publican feelingly and experimentally could cry out, 'God be merciful to me a sinner'.

Saturday, May 12 . . . Many came to me this morning, acquainting me what God had done for their souls by my preaching in the fields. In the evening I preached to about twenty thousand at Kennington, as usual, the weather continuing remarkably fair whilst I was delivering my Master's message. I offered Jesus Christ to all who could apply Him to their hearts by faith. Oh that all would embrace Him! The Lord make them willing in the day of His power!

Sunday, May 13. Preached this morning to a prodigious number of people in Moorfields and collected for the orphans £52 19s. 6d., above £20 of which was in half-pence. Indeed, they almost wearied me in receiving their mites and they were more than one man could carry home. Went to public worship twice and preached in the evening to near sixty thousand people. Many went away because they could not hear, but God enabled me to speak so that the best part of them could understand me well, and it is very remarkable what a deep silence is preserved whilst I am speaking. After sermon I made another collection of £29 17s. 8d., and came home deeply humbled . . .[1]

While conducting this work Whitefield was besieged with invitations to come and minister the Word at other places also. Responding to as many as possible, he preached at Blackheath, Hampstead Heath and Shadwell (municipalities on the outskirts of London) and, viewing these along with Moorfields and Kennington, he exclaimed, 'Blessed be God! we begin to surround this great city!'

He also made a preaching tour into several counties north of London. Leaving Monday morning and returning Saturday night, he ministered at a different town each day, and when the tour was finished he remarked, 'Many sinners have been convicted and many saints comforted. I find there are some thousands of secret ones living amongst us who have not bowed the knee to Baal, and this public way of acting brings them out.'[2]

*

Upon returning from this trip Whitefield began to prosecute his ministry with a still greater urgency. He had already booked passage to America for himself and his party and, since the vessel expected to sail in less than two weeks, the remaining days needed to be filled with final preparations and final preaching. The people flocked to hear him in greater numbers than ever and he reports:

[1] *Ibid, pp* 263–5. [2] *Ibid, p* 275.

Sunday, May 27. Preached this morning at Moorfields, to about twenty thousand, and God manifested Himself still more and more. My discourse was near two hours long. My heart was full of love, and people were so melted down on every side, that the greatest scoffer must have owned that this was the finger of God. Went twice to public worship, received the blessed Sacrament, and preached, as usual, in the evening at Kennington Common to about the same number as last Lord's Day. I was a little hoarse, but God strengthened me to speak, so as not only to be heard, but felt by most who stood near me.

Monday, May 28. Preached, after earnest and frequent invitation, at Hackney, in a field, to about ten thousand people. I insisted much on the reasonableness of the doctrine of the new birth, and the necessity of our receiving the Holy Ghost in His sanctifying gifts and graces, as well now as formerly . . . Great numbers were in tears . . .

Tuesday, May 29. Preached at Kennington to a devout auditory, with much sweetness and power . . .

Wednesday, May 30 . . . At the request of many, I preached in the evening at Newington Common, to about fifteen thousand people. A most commodious place was erected for me to preach from. The Word came with power, and seeing a great multitude, I thought proper to collect for the Orphan House; and £16 9s. 4d. was gathered.

Thursday, May 31. Was taken ill this afternoon, but God was pleased to strengthen me to go to Kennington, where I preached to my usual congregation . . .

Friday, June 1. . . . gave a short exhortation to a few people in a field, and preached in the evening, at a place called Mayfair, near Hyde Park Corner. The congregation, I believe, consisted of near eighty thousand people. It was by far the largest I ever preached to yet. In the time of my prayer there was a little noise, but they kept a deep silence during my whole discourse. A high and very commodious scaffold was erected for me to stand upon, and though I was weak in myself, yet God strengthened me to speak so loud, that most could hear, and so powerfully, that most, I believe, could feel. All love, all glory, be to God through Christ!

Saturday, June 2 . . . Collected by private contributions, nearly £50 for the orphans, and preached in the evening to about ten thousand at Hackney, where £20 12s. 4d. was gathered.

Sunday, June 3. Preached at Moorfields to a larger congregation than ever, and collected £29 17s. 9d. for the Orphan House. Went twice to public worship and received the Sacrament. Preached in the evening at Kennington Common, to the most numerous audience I ever yet saw in that place, and collected £34 5s. When I mentioned my departure from them, they were melted into tears. Thousands of ejaculations and fervent prayers were poured out to God on my behalf . . . Oh what marvellous great kindness has God shown me in this great city! Indeed, I have seen the kingdom of God come with power.[1]

We may well agree with Tyerman, who, after presenting these selections says, '. . . it may be useful to pause and to ponder these marvellous extracts from the young preacher's Journal. Are they not unique? Is there any man, except Whitefield, whose diary for (so many) consecutive days, contains a series of statements like the foregoing?'[2]

*

It would be expected that, following meetings of this kind, Whitefield would be utterly exhausted. When we consider how weary the average minister is after preaching to a few hundred or less, once or twice a Sunday, we should expect that, to stand before these multitudes ten or more times a week, to overcome the opposition of the unruly, command the attention of all, meet the inclemencies of wind and rain and preach for an hour – and sometimes two – would have left him overcome with fatigue. John Foster, in considering the vocal effort alone, remarked:

> With all the advantage of such a power of voice as perhaps no other man possessed, there must still often have been the necessity of forcing it to the last possibility of exertion, in order to his being heard by congregations amounting to many thousands . . .[3]

Yet the amazing fact is that Whitefield makes no suggestion of weariness as the result of these labours. There were times when he was subdued to illness – illness which may have been caused by the strain of his work – but he was able to rise from a sick bed and preach with vigour to the multitude. The sight of the crowds and the task of ministering to them seems to have had an exhilarating effect upon him and, both during and after his great efforts in the fields, he frequently experienced a new strength and a joy which reached the point of ecstasy. We see this in the two following reports:

[1] *Ibid, pp* 275–8. [2] Tyerman's *Whitefield,* Vol 1, *p* 217.
[3] Foster, *op cit, p* 70.

Before I went out to preach, I was very sick and weak; but power was given me from above, so that I continued preaching for an hour and a half. It rained some considerable time, but almost all were unmoved, and I was so enlarged in talking of the love and free grace of Jesus Christ, that I could have continued my discourse till midnight.[1]

When we came home . . . God was pleased to pour into my soul a great spirit of supplication, and a sense of His free, distinguishing mercies so filled me with love, humility, and joy and holy confusion that I could at last only pour out my heart before Him in an awful silence. I was so full that I could not well speak. Oh the happiness of communion with God![2]

*

Amid this tremendous activity Whitefield found time to publish more sermons. In order to appreciate the accomplishment we need to take a closer look at his circumstances. Sermons that are published are usually the work of mature men and are generally produced in surroundings conducive to literary effort. But Whitefield had no true home; he lived at Hutton's bachelor quarters and possibly shared a room with Seward. Beside his preaching, correspondence and travelling, there were his preparations for the Orphan House and the time-consuming work of dealing with numerous spiritual seekers. Yet, despite these labours, he managed to have a sermon a week ready for the printer.

Most of these sermons were prepared by Whitefield before preaching, but as he stood before the congregation, he frequently departed from the written text or even the premeditated line of thought, as the extraordinary circumstances in the fields might require. But some of these sermons he delivered extempore and wrote out later.

Certain of these productions give evidence of fairly careful preparation, but a few look as though the writing was greatly hurried, and one seems to suggest that, though uncompleted, the writing had been suddenly terminated. Whitefield suffered from the fact that he did not need to do careful work in order to achieve wide circulation, and, knowing that hundreds of persons testified to great blessing from his printed discourses, he pub-

[1] *Journals, p* 277. [2] *Ibid, p* 263.

lished them. But some might better have been retained and rewritten.

The public demand is evident in the sale that these discourses attained. During his twenty weeks in London he published twenty-one sermons, and most of these required second and third editions that year. Five were translated into German and two into Welsh. Moreover, eight of those which had been published earlier were reprinted at this time and at least three of these were also published in German, and all, both the old ones and the new, soon went through multiple editions in America.

Whitefield's youthful sermons – those of 1737, along with those of 1739 (the ones we are now considering) plus a few of 1740 – constitute the major portion of all the sermons he ever published. His authentic sermons number sixty-three, and, forty-six of these came from his pen before he was twenty-five years old. Thus, any assessment of Whitefield's printed sermons must take into account the fact that they were the work of so young a man – a fact the critics have usually overlooked.

*

The question arises as to what actually were the attendances at these great open-air meetings? Whitefield's figures during his first four weeks in London range from 10,000 to 20,000 and even to 40,000 and 60,000, and there is one instance in which he suggests 80,000. Adding up his estimates for twenty-four meetings we reach a total of 640,000, or an average of 26,500 per meeting.

There can be no doubt that the Holy Club men were given to exaggeration and that both Whitefield and Wesley, like many lesser preachers, formed far too high an estimate of the size of their congregations. Therefore, in seeking a reliable figure, we must look for other testimony.

The Gentleman's Magazine said of one of Whitefield's meetings at Kingswood, '. . . three mounts and the plains around were crowded with so great a multitude of coaches, foot and horsemen, that they covered three acres and were computed at twenty thousand.'[1] Whitefield also spoke of this congregation as twenty thousand and, since three acres contain 14,520 square yards, this

[1] *The Gentleman's Magazine*, 1739, *p* 162.

number is possible. Another periodical described one of his London congregations as 'a prodigious concourse'; Joseph Humphreys spoke of hearing Whitefield preach to 'a most numerous congregation' and Charles Wesley called Whitefield's hearers 'an innumerable multitude'.

Several further statements of a similar nature, made by Whitefield's friends could be cited, but those of his opposers may be more valuable. Dr Trapp made reference to 'vast multitudes . . . so sottish as to run madding after him', and Thomas Church, after asserting, 'He cannot possibly be supposed to know all . . . those present at his meetings of 30, 50 or 80,000',[1] though he may not have entirely accepted these figures, at least made no attempt to deny them.

The following year, when Whitefield was in America, Benjamin Franklin measured the area reached by his voice and declared, 'I computed that he might well be heard by more than thirty thousand.' Even the collection that contained 'above £20 in half pence' – nearly 10,000 of these coins besides the other money – suggests a large crowd.

Nevertheless, though these congregations were undoubtedly very numerous, there is reason to believe that Whitefield's figures were highly inflated. In the later edition of his *Journals* (revised when he had grown to a more mature judgment) he altered some of them and his estimate of 50,000 for a certain meeting was made to read 'said by some to be above 30 or 40,000'. It is probable that this reduction is still not enough and that a figure which would decrease his estimates by a half would be more correct.

But when this extensive reduction has been made, we are yet faced with the fact that these were indeed 'prodigious congregations'. If we read Whitefield's 60,000 as 30,000 and his 80,000 as 40,000, still the accomplishment looms as colossal. It is highly probable that these crowds, which were the largest of Whitefield's whole career, were also the largest ever reached by the unamplified human voice in the whole history of mankind.[2] And this was the ministry of a youth of twenty-four!

[1] *A Serious and Expository Letter to the Rev George Whitefield*, by the Rev Thomas Church, M.A., Whitfield's *Works*, Vol 4, *p* 114.

[2] The Scriptures record that Moses and Joshua addressed large companies of the children of Israel, and that Samuel, Elijah and Jonah preached out of doors. There are tales of ancient generals addressing whole armies. Many of the friars of the

Such was the beginning of Whitefield's work in the open air in London. He had come to the city overwhelmed with a sense of the greatness of the task and conscious of his own inadequacy. Yet he had attempted it and with this tremendous result. He was somewhat bewildered by it all, but he simply went on with it a day at a time, looking upon the blessing of God that was constantly granted as assurance indeed that, despite human opposition, this was the Divinely-ordered work for him.

Middle Ages were street preachers, and of Peter the Hermit it is said, 'neither churches nor streets nor market places could contain the great concourse that resorted to hear his sermons'. There are, however, no reliable figures regarding these gatherings. Wycliffe's Lollards preached in the open air, as did also some of the Reformers and Puritans, reputedly with large congregations. The same is true of John Bunyan. Spurgeon addressed a counted audience of 23,654 in the Crystal Palace, and it is known that more than 22,000 persons were at one of his open-air meetings. This subject is dealt with by Southey, *Life of Wesley*, Vol 1, *p* 247, and by Spurgeon, *Lectures to My Students*, Second Series, *p* 54.

One rises from a study of Cennick's life, ministry and theological views with a feeling of thanksgiving to God for the great demonstration of His transforming power. His sermons give spiritual light, wisdom and power two hundred years after they were written. His life and ministry establish goals for devotion, labour and zeal that can scarcely be equalled in any day.

VERNON WILLIAMS COULLIARD
The Theology of John Cennick

17

John Cennick

As the time of his departure for America drew near Whitefield made further arrangements for the carrying on of the work in England. He had led John Wesley into taking over the work at Bristol and looked for other men with whom he could do the same at London and at Gloucester. Moreover, having initiated a school for the Kingswood colliers, he looked for a man who would serve as its master. This last position was the first to be filled.

Among his friends in London there was a fervent youth of twenty, named John Cennick. By training he was 'a land surveyor and a writing master' and, since he was also a man of earnest Christian character, Whitefield asked him to undertake the Kingswood task. From this time forth he played a highly important part in Whitefield's life, and therefore must have our attention.

Born in the town of Reading in 1718, John Cennick grew up in a sturdy Church of England home. An outward conformity to piety was thrust upon him, entailing a strict observance of the Sabbath, careful instruction in religious principles and daily attendance at the prayers of the parish church.

A death in the family, which occurred during his tender years, had a lasting influence on his mind. His mother's aunt, as she lay on her death-bed, gave vigorous testimony to the assurance of salvation. 'Who calls me poor?' cried the aged saint, 'I am rich in Christ! I have got Christ! I am rich! . . . This night the Lord stood by me and invited me to drink at the fountain of life freely; and I shall stand before Him, bold as a lion!'[1]

[1] *The Life of Mr John Cennick*, written by himself, *p* viii, hereafter referred to as Cennick's *Autobiography*. Published in his *Village Discourses*, edited by Matthew Wilks (London, 1819). No suitable biography of Cennick has yet appeared.

During years to come, God used this scene of Christian triumph, to bring young Cennick to a realization of his need of Christ. He says of the aunt's dying testimony:

The words she uttered indeed pierced my soul, so that I could not rest day nor night, but was continually wishing, if I thought of sickness or death, O that I may be assured of Heaven before I die! and began to fear greatly. These were the most early convictions I can remember, nor do I know any time between whiles, till my conversion, when I did not meditate on my aunt's last words . . .[1]

As a boy, John was not much different from the other boys around him. He testifies that he 'was fond of play, of fine cloaths, and of praise . . . My natural temper was obstinate, and my lips full of lies'. Just what schooling he had is not known, but we find him at fifteen, reading 'histories and romances . . . singing songs, talking of the heathen gods, of the wars of the Jews and Greeks, of Alexander the Great . . .'[2] He delighted, above all, in reading and seeing plays, and, like Whitefield, appears to have possessed a native affinity for the art of drama. If he differed from others, it was in the high vivacity of his spirits, the extraordinary sensitiveness of his soul and his histrionic talents, and it was these qualities which God used in making him a preacher of great power in days to come.

If we are to understand the tremendous passion with which Cennick later preached, and the zeal which captivated his life, we must first of all realize something of the fears, the sense of guilt, and the intense desire for salvation which he experienced before he knew the Lord. Part of this he records, saying that, at the age of sixteen, during the Easter season in 1735,

As I was walking hastily in Cheapside, London, the hand of the Lord touched me. I felt at once an uncommon fear and dejection, and though all my days had been bitter through the fear of going to hell, yet I knew not any weight before, like this . . . I continued dull and thoughtful, nor would any sights and songs divert my trouble.[3]

His *Autobiography* tells how he continued under the terrible sense of guilt and fear and with an intense longing for salvation and peace, throughout two long years.

He attempted to pray, but could not. He sought to read the

[1] *Ibid*, *p* x. [2] *Ibid.* [3] *Ibid*, *pp* xviii and xix.

Bible, but its passages of condemnation smote upon his stricken soul, and all its promises of mercy seemed not for him. He fought with fears and evil desires, and tried fasting, walking, eating, running, and even medicine to overcome them, but groaned in the realization that he was 'yet carnal, sold under sin!' He says, 'Mine own house behaved as though they knew me not, and all mine acquaintance condemned me and I envied them who were fallen asleep in death'. While working as a surveyor in Wiltshire he became little better than a hermit, wandering day and night in Salisbury Plain, confessing his sins, fighting the devil, 'eating acorns, leaves, crabs and grass', fasting and vowing never to eat again, 'sweating, groaning, and crying aloud for mercy'. Yet amidst all his striving he 'saw no help!' and his fastings, prostrations, tears and travail brought no peace. 'All', he says, 'were vanity and vexation of spirit; the earth seemed full of darkness and cruel habitations, nor could ought bring me comfort. I only wanted to know if I had any part in the Lord Jesus!'[1]

By the summer of 1737 Cennick came to the end of himself. There were no further efforts he could make, and in the awful realization of his failure he was given to see something of the truth that Jesus had accomplished salvation for him upon the cross. This assurance became a ray of light piercing the darkness of his soul. No longer did he plead his works, his innocency or his strivings, but, 'I cried', he says, 'to Jesus to remember His blood and tears and sufferings; and if there was no room for me in His favour, to reveal it to me . . . I pleaded the great oblation and sacrifice of Christ crucified, and I entreated mercy for His sake alone.'[2]

On September 6 he went to church to pray. He confessed that as he walked the street, he was 'like some outcast in a foreign land; my heart was ready to burst; my soul on the brink of hell'. His testimony continues:

When I had entered the church and fallen on my knees, I began murmuring, as I did often, because my cross seemed more heavy than ever was laid on any one beside; and how untroubled all the children of God passed to heaven, and how full of terror I must go down to hell! . . . Near the end of the Psalm these words were read, 'Great are the troubles of the righteous, but the Lord delivereth him out of them all.

[1] *Ibid, p* xxi. [2] *Ibid, p* xx.

He that putteth his trust in God shall not be destitute.' I had just room to think, Who can be more destitute than I? when I was overwhelmed with joy, and I believed there was mercy for me. My heart danced with joy and my dying soul revived. I heard the voice of Jesus saying, I am thy salvation.

I no more groaned under the weight of sin. The fears of hell were taken away, and being sensible that Christ loved me and died for me, I rejoiced in God my Saviour.

. . . I felt great and settled peace from this time. When I laid me down in bed, I laid as in the everlasting arms; and when I rose in the morning the Lord was present, and often my lips have been uttering words of prayer before I well knew whether I was waking or sleeping.[1]

*

Herewith there began for Cennick a life of Christian joy. He daily grew in grace, but he was alone and longed for kindred company. He had never heard of any one who had been through an experience like his own until a copy of Whitefield's *Journal* fell into his hands.

. . . My heart cleaved to him [he asserted as he read the book], believing him not unacquainted with that bitter cup, the dregs of which I had long been drinking. I laid down the book and went straightway into an upper chamber to pray, if by any means God would permit me to come to a knowledge of this man.

When I was on my knees I prayed and said, 'O Lord Jesus, Who knowest well my troubled spirit, Who alone canst give me a companion in my way to Thee, permit me to be intimate with this thy servant now sent forth to preach the Gospel in other lands; incline him to stoop to hear me and to speak humbly to me, and so join us together, that together we may be accounted worthy to rest in the kingdom of God forever'. Before I rose up the Lord answered me; yea, while I was speaking God showed me how I should be conversant with him and be beloved by him. Verily I believed this and rejoiced when I thought the day would soon bring it to pass.[2]

This was written while Whitefield was first in Georgia, but upon his return, Cennick, hearing that he was in London, walked all night to get there, and called on him at Hutton's at 8 the next morning. 'I met my dear brother', he says, 'and fell on his neck

[1] *Ibid, pp* xx, xxi. [2] *Ibid, p* xxiii.

and kissed him. Our communion was sweet and I stayed with him several days'.[1]

*

It was on the basis of this earlier relationship that Whitefield asked him to become master of the Kingswood school. 'The thing seemed to be of God', said Cennick, 'and I was obedient . . . He wrote of the same to Mr Wesley, and I received a pressing letter to come to him.'[2]

But in the providence of God, Cennick's prospect of teaching school was changed to the higher work of preaching the Gospel. When he arrived at Bristol, he found Wesley temporarily out of town, and the school not started. On the next day, as he gathered with the Kingswood people for a service, he learned that the man who was expected to do the preaching had not arrived, and he was asked to do so in his stead.

I had no power to refuse or gainsay [he writes], and though I was naturally fearful of speaking before company, having never done such a thing as this, yet so much was I pressed in the spirit to testify the salvation of Jesus to the people, that I fell on my knees and besought the Lord to be with me in the work, and prevent me if his Majesty was offended . . . Again I prayed; and finding great freedom, I then tarried no longer, but rose up and went to the congregation, the Lord bearing witness with my word, insomuch that many believed in that hour.[3]

The following day he preached again, and 'tears fell from many eyes'. On the next, a Sunday, four thousand gathered to hear him, and 'Here also the power of the Lord was present'. Thereafter, he 'continued preaching to the colliers and to their children, and in the Societies in Bristol . . .', and, with the blessing of God abundantly upon his labour, it was evident that here was a man peculiarly gifted for the work of the ministry.

*

The news that Cennick, instead of teaching school, had begun to preach, came as something of a shock to Whitefield. For one thing, he was surprised to learn that construction of the school

[1] *Ibid*, p xxv.
[2] *Cennick's Diary, op cit,* published in *The Moravian Messenger*, Vol 16.
[3] *Autobiography*, p xxvii.

house had not yet started, as John Wesley had left this work in abeyance while he devoted himself to building a new room for two of the Societies.

Furthermore, Whitefield did not favour lay preaching. In the exalted views that he held of the Christian ministry, he placed strong emphasis on the necessity of the Divine call, on adequate preparation and on ordination. In contrast, at this very time some of the Fetter Lane brethren were casting these principles aside and were asserting their own right to preach and administer the sacraments. Certain entries in Charles Wesley's *Journal* report the attitude of these men, and reveal that he and Whitefield withstood their claims. One written on May 16 (1739) states, 'At Fetter Lane a dispute arose about lay-preaching. Many . . . were very zealous for it. Mr Whitefield and I declared against it.'[1] Several of Whitefield's letters rebuke – some gently and some more severely – various men who tried to enter the ministry without a manifest call or satisfactory training.

When Whitefield heard that Cennick had begun to preach and that another unordained man had done the same, he wrote to John Wesley, saying:

Honoured Sir: I suspend my judgment of Brother Watkins' and Cennick's behaviour till I am better acquainted with the circumstance of their proceeding. I think there is a great difference between them and Howell Harris. He has offered himself thrice for Holy Orders; him therefore and our friends at Cambridge I shall encourage: others I cannot countenance in acting in so public a manner. The consequences of beginning to teach too soon will be exceeding bad. Brother Ingham is of my opinion.[2]

But John Cennick was fully persuaded that God had called him into the ministry. Years later, as he looked back upon that day when he had first stood to declare the Word of the Lord there in Kingswood, he testified:

On the 14th day of June, 1739, the burden of the Lord came upon me, and unto this day, the Lord, according to His word, hath been a mouth to me, and thro' His abundant love, hath kept me from all

[1] When, late in life, John Wesley took to himself the authority to ordain, Charles was highly incensed. He refused to recognize the men on whom his brother laid hands and referred to them disparagingly as 'Melchizedekians'.

[2] Tyerman's *Wesley*, Vol 1, *p* 277.

doubts and murmurings, touching my faith in the blood of the Lamb, and in a settled peace, . . . I now wait till my Master shall call me from His vineyard to sit down in His everlasting Sabbath. And of this I am well persuaded, that when I have done the work for which I am sent, I shall be no more a stranger upon earth, but a fellow-citizen with the saints in the kingdom of my Father, and in the New Jerusalem shall I reign for ever and ever![1]

Truly, John Cennick had heard the call of God to preach and 'the burden of the Lord' had come upon his heart. From that day he preached almost every day, and often twice a day, and preached with great power and blessing till his dying day. The soul that had known the tremendous fears and deep emotions before conversion, now experienced an overwhelming measure of peace and joy, and in this gladness all his hours were filled with a holy passion to win the lost to Christ. But he was poet as well as preacher, and his life is well pictured in his testimonial hymn, 'Jesus my all to Heav'n is gone', especially its last stanza:

> Now will I tell to sinners round,
> What a dear Saviour I have found:
> I'll point to Thy redeeming blood,
> And say, 'Behold the way to God!'[2]

Cennick became not only one of Whitefield's closest friends and, for some time, his chief assistant, but a preacher of such power as to stand, in that day of great preachers, in the rank of the first four or five. For months he teamed up with Howell Harris in the open-air ministry, and day after day the two of them suffered at the hands of the mob. It was, however, one thing for the powerful, masculine Harris to stand such treatment, but quite another for Cennick who was by nature a quiet and inoffensive person and whose every action was peace and love. Cennick later joined the Moravians, under whom he served with great heroism and wondrous success in Ireland. The eighteenth-century Revival produced no more beautiful and holy life than that of John Cennick, and it is a sad loss to the Christian world that his career has been so flagrantly overlooked.

[1] *Autobiography*, p xxix.

[2] Besides this hymn Cennick is remembered for the following: 'Children of the Heav'nly King', 'Thou dear Redeemer, dying Lamb', 'Ere I sleep, for ev'ry favour', and 'Be present at our table, Lord'. 'Lo, He comes, with clouds descending', is largely his, with emendations by Charles Wesley and others.

In dealing with whatever may belong to a process of organization, or of marshalling a host for a single initiatory purpose, Wesley has never been surpassed . . . In that order of mind to which Wesley belonged, it is the irresistible force, or one might say, the galvanic instantaneousness of the intuitions, which forbids and excludes the exercise of the abstractive and analytic power. With him, the grasp of what he thought to be a truth was so sudden and so spasmodically firm as ordinarily to preclude two mental processes . . . namely, first, *a ridding the terms . . . of the ambiguities which infest language; and,* secondly, *the looking through the medium – the verbal proposition, into the very midst of the things so presented.*

ISAAC TAYLOR

Wesley and Methodism, 1860

18

The Beginnings of Wesley's Movement

How well it would be if our story could continue to report nothing but harmony in the relations between Whitefield and John Wesley! But, as is well known, this was not the case. At this point in their lives theological differences began to appear, and before two years had passed a wide separation had occurred.

Strong judgments have often been pronounced regarding this affair, but, strangely enough, little of the evidence has been produced. The view that has entered common opinion is the partial one that was presented by Wesley's first biographers. Therefore, if we are to gain a true understanding of either Wesley or Whitefield, we have no choice but to look into this matter.

The discord first became evident in a sermon which Wesley preached during his early weeks in Bristol. Tyerman says, 'It was . . . in some respects the most important sermon that he ever issued. It led . . . to the division which Whitefield so devoutly deprecates; and . . . the difference between Wesley and Whitefield was really one of the greatest events in the history of Wesley, and even of the religion of the age'.[1] This was his sermon against predestination.

Wesley indicates that, from its start, his work in Bristol was fraught with the danger of dissent. His friends, knowing his penchant for debate and his dislike of the doctrine of predestination, had already warned him to be careful:

Our dear brethren, before I left London [he says], and our brother Whitefield here, and our brother Chapman since, had conjured me to enter into no disputes, least of all concerning Predestination, because this people was so deeply prejudiced for it.[2]

[1] Tyerman's *Wesley*, Vol 1, *p* 317.

[2] John Wesley's *Letters*, Vol 1, *p* 302.

This warning soon proved necessary. Wesley had been in Bristol but three and a half weeks when, having said something which revealed his repudiation of this doctrine, he was faced with opposition. One man wrote and 'handed about' a letter, 'charging me roundly', he says, 'with "resisting and perverting the truth as it is in Jesus" ',[1] while the writer of another letter 'exhorts his friends to avoid me as a false teacher.'[2]

Doubtless, in his better self, Wesley wished to preserve the peace, but to a man of his beliefs, his native gifts and his experience in the arts of disputation, this was a serious challenge. 'I questioned whether I ought not now to declare the whole counsel of God', he said. '. . . However, I thought it best to walk gently, and so said nothing this day.'[3]

It was at this very time, however, that Wesley was witnessing the severe emotional effects among his hearers. He was fully convinced that these convulsive experiences were the sign of the Divine approval upon his ministry, and, therefore, as he considered whether or not to speak out against predestination, he asked that heaven's leading might be made manifest by a recurrence of such effects. This he records in the following account of his preaching at the prison:

> . . . I was led, I know not how, to speak strongly and explicitly of Predestination, and then to pray 'that if I spake not the truth of God, He would stay His hand, and work no more among us. If this was His truth, He would not delay to confirm it by signs following.' Immediately the power of God fell on us: one, and another, and another sunk to the earth; you might see them dropping on all sides as thunder-struck. One cried out aloud. I went and prayed over her, and she received joy in the Holy Ghost. A second falling into the same agony, we turned to her, and received for her also the promise of the Father.[4]

Though deeming himself hereby assured that his stand against predestination was supernaturally approved, Wesley sought for still further proof. 'In the evening I made the same appeal to God', he says, 'and almost before we called He answered. A young woman was seized with such pangs as I never saw before;

[1] Wesley's *Letters*, Vol 1, *p*. 302.
[2] *Ibid.* [3] *Ibid.* [4] *Ibid, p* 303.

and in a quarter of an hour she had a new song in her mouth, a thanksgiving unto our God.'[1]

Before going to bed that night Wesley put the matter to what he believed to be the final test: the casting of a lot. '. . . our brother Purdy pressing me to speak and spare not, we made four lots, and desired our Lord to show what He would have me to do. The answer was, "Preach and print". Let Him see to the event.'[2]

Wesley later made an important point of his claim that he was led by God in the action he thus took. We do well, therefore, to notice that the emotional experiences and the casting of a lot constituted the only authorization by which he took it upon himself to thrust this divisive subject into the revival movement.

But Wesley had already been preparing a sermon in readiness for such directions.[3] Accordingly, having received the directions, he finished it and, despite the warnings he had been given by his friends, on the following Sunday morning he preached it. 'On Sunday morning, being so directed again by lot, I declared openly', he says, 'for the first hour against "the horrible decree" before about four thousand persons at the Bowling Green.'[4] Strange to say, it was but four weeks to the day since Whitefield had trustingly introduced him to his Bristol people on this same spot, having 'conjured' him not to do the very thing he was now doing!

This was the sermon which became Methodism's first rock of division, and we must familiarize ourselves with it.

Wesley entitled his sermon *Free Grace.* Though he used the text 'He that spared not his own Son, but delivered him up for us all, how shall he not with him also freely give us all things?'[5] he made no attempt to expound it or to present its contextual setting. Nor did he deal with the positive aspects of the subject of Grace, and the nature of the sermon is best indicated in his own description of it as 'against predestination'.[6]

[1] *Ibid.* [2] *Ibid.*

[3] See Wesley's *Diary* of Wednesday and Thursday, April 25–26 (*Journal*, Vol 2, *p* 183–4). The Diaries contain several points of information on this whole matter, which have been largely overlooked. Since, however, the Diaries were not deciphered and published till Curnock's work which appeared in 1909, writers of earlier years were without their information.

[4] Wesley's *Letters*, Vol 1, *p* 304. [5] *Romans* 8: 32.

[6] Wesley's *Letters*, Vol 1, *p* 307.

His first assertion was that the doctrine of predestination cannot be held in the varying degrees of opinion that some who believe in it would claim. Addressing himself directly to such persons he declared that despite their various claims to the contrary:

> . . . you still believe, that, in consequence of an unchangeable, irresistible decree of God, the greater part of mankind abide in death, without any possibility of redemption; inasmuch as none can save them but God, and he will not save them. You believe he hath absolutely decreed not to save them; and what is this but decreeing to damn them? It is, in effect, neither more nor less; it comes to the same thing; for if you are dead, and altogether unable to make yourself alive, then, if God has absolutely decreed he will make only others alive, and not you, he hath absolutely decreed your everlasting death. You are absolutely consigned to damnation. So then, though you use softer words than some, you mean the self-same thing; . . .
>
> Call it therefore by whatever name you please, 'election, preterition, predestination, or reprobation', it comes in the end to the same thing. The sense of all is plainly this – by virtue of an eternal, unchangeable, irresistible decree of God, one part of mankind are infallibly saved, and the rest infallibly damned; . . .[1]

This statement provided the primary thrust of the sermon, and it was this interpretation of the doctrine with which Wesley dealt throughout his discourse.

Following this assertion he went on to show the effects of this teaching. He declared that it:

1. Makes all preaching vain. 'It is needless to them that are elected; . . . it is useless to them that are not.'

2. '. . . it wholly takes away those first motives to follow after holiness . . . the hope of future reward and fear of punishment . . .'

3. 'It tends to destroy the comfort of religion.'

4. 'This uncomfortable doctrine directly tends to destroy our zeal for good works.'

5. It has 'a direct and manifest tendency to overthrow the whole Christian revelation . . . In making the Gospel thus unnecessary to all sorts of men, you give up the whole Christian cause.'

[1] *Sermons on Several Occasions* by the Rev John Wesley M.A. (Mason ed, published London, 1847, in three volumes), Vol 3, *p* 359. This sermon will also be found in the various editions of Wesley's *Works*.

6. It 'makes revelation contradict itself.' In support of this assertion Wesley quoted several Bible verses which present the Gospel invitation to all mankind. He declared that these represent 'the whole tenor of the New Testament' and claimed that the passages which the holders of predestination used in support of their position could not mean what they seemed to mean, and therefore must be given a different interpretation.

Much of the spirit of the sermon may be understood from the following paragraphs:

It is a doctrine full of blasphemy; of such blasphemy as I should dread to mention, but that the honour of our gracious God, and the cause of truth, will not suffer me to be silent. In the cause of God, then, and from a sincere concern for the glory of his great name, I will mention a few of the horrible blasphemies contained in this horrible doctrine. But first, I must warn every one of you that hears, as ye will answer it at the great day, not to charge me (as some have done) with blaspheming because I mention the blasphemy of others.

... This doctrine represents our blessed Lord, 'Jesus Christ the righteous', 'the only begotten Son of the Father, full of grace and truth', as an hypocrite, a deceiver of the people, a man void of common sincerity.

... Such blasphemy this, as one would think might make the ears of a Christian to tingle! But there is yet more behind; for just as it honours the Son, so doth this doctrine honour the Father. It destroys all his attributes at once: it overturns both his justice, mercy and truth; yea, it represents the most holy God as worse than the devil; as both more false, more cruel, and more unjust . . .

This is the blasphemy clearly contained in *the horrible decree* of predestination! And here I fix my foot. On this I join issue with every assertor of it. You represent God as worse than the devil; more false, more cruel, more unjust. But you say you will prove it by Scripture! Hold! What will you prove by Scripture? that God is worse than the devil? It cannot be. Whatever that Scripture proves, it cannot prove this; whatever be its true meaning, it cannot mean this. Do you ask, 'What is its true meaning then?' If I say, 'I know not', you have gained nothing; for there are many scriptures the true sense whereof you nor I shall know till death is swallowed up in victory.[1]

Having made these assertions, Wesley adopted for the sake of argument a position in which he supposed the doctrine of pre-

[1] *Ibid*, *pp* 364–5.

destination to be true, and from that position he thus addressed the devil:

'Thou fool, why dost thou roar about any longer? Thy lying in wait for souls is as needless and useless as our preaching. Hearest thou not, that God hath taken thy work out of thy hands; and that He doeth it more effectually? Thou, with all thy principalities and powers, canst only so assault that we may resist thee; but He can irresistibly destroy both body and soul in hell! Thou canst only entice; but his unchangeable decree to leave thousands of souls in death compels them to continue in sin till they drop into everlasting burnings. Thou temptest; He forceth us to be damned, for we cannot resist his will. Thou fool, why goest thou about any longer, seeking whom thou mayest devour? Hearest thou not that God is the devouring lion, the destroyer of souls, the murderer of men? . . .'

O how would the enemy of God and man rejoice to hear these things were so! How would he cry aloud and spare not! How would he lift up his voice and say, 'To your tents, O Israel! Flee from the face of this God, or ye shall utterly perish! But whither will ye flee? Into heaven? He is there. Down to hell? He is there also. Ye cannot flee from an omnipresent almighty tyrant . . . Sing O hell, and rejoice, ye that are under the earth! For God, even the mighty God, hath spoken, and devoted to death thousands of souls, from the rising of the sun to the going down thereof! Here, O death, is thy sting! Here, O grave, is thy victory! . . . Let all the sons of hell shout for joy! For the decree is past, and who shall disannul it?'[1]

Wesley followed this address to the devil with a further declaration of the free offer of the Gospel, and therewith brought his discourse to a close.

This sermon must certainly have had a powerful effect on many who heard it. Students of Wesley's life have accorded a high place to his apostrophe to the devil and Southey terms it 'the most remarkable and powerful passage in all his works'. The force of his language illustrates the elated spirits he was experiencing as a result of his new success and indicates that the powers of the popular orator had, in some goodly measure, been formed within him. We may be sure that a number of his hearers were swept along by his rhetoric and his argument and, accordingly, found themselves in staunch agreement with his views.

However, when we remember that among this audience there

[1] *Sermons on Several Occasions*, pp 366–7.

were many who had recently been described as 'strongly prejudiced in favour of predestination', we must see the Bristol Bowling Green, when Wesley's sermon was finished, as the scene of flaring tempers and bitter debate. Charges and countercharges must surely have been hurled that Sunday morning and Southey says of the aftermath, 'Even temperate Calvinists were shocked and have said that Mr Wesley's "horrid appeal to all the devils in hell gave a sort of infernal tone to the controversy" '.[1]

Julia Wedgwood expresses her opinion of the sermon, saying:

> There is in it something of that provoking glibness with which young or half-cultivated people settle in a few sentences questions that have exercised the deepest minds ever since the dawn of speculation. Wesley was neither young nor uncultivated, but that incapacity for seeing difficulties which is characteristic of an early stage of culture, was a part of his nature.
>
> In this sermon he does not once confront the difficulties which must be accepted by any one who, from his point of view, should reject predestination. He does not see that, if the design of Christ was to save all and the result is that He only saves some, His work was a failure. Indeed, it is evident on reading this sermon, that, of all the deep works which had been written on this subject, Wesley had never read one; he had taken it for granted that the opinion he set himself to confute could be held by none but fools, and his confutation was condemned to that futility by which all such arrogance is punished.
>
> No doubt the sermon produced an effect, for it was preached with all his heart; but that effect, we may confidently assert, was not to shake one mind which had laid hold of the doctrine of election. But if this sermon is futile as an argument, the forcible rhetoric displayed in it goes some way to illustrate his influence as a preacher.[2]

This sermon was of major importance in Wesley's career. It was his first declaration of a distinctive theological position, and, as such, it removed him from standing in a secondary relationship to Whitefield. It won the allegiance of a number of the Bristol hearers, and gave them reason to consider themselves no longer Whitefield's people, but Wesley's. Thus, the sermon 'against predestination' marked the actual beginning of Wesley's own movement, with all the historic results which were to flow therefrom.

*

[1] Southey's *Life of Wesley*, Vol 2, *p* 186.

[2] Julia Wedgwood, *John Wesley* (London, 1870) *p* 226–7.

The following morning Wesley called on a printer,[1] Felix Farley, and less than two weeks later he wrote, 'The lot said "Preach and print" and the sermon on Free Grace was published.'[2] It will readily be seen that this discourse in printed form would be a potent weapon of division, but as Wesley sought to have it circulated in London, he met with hindrance. James Hutton, whose book shop was his outlet there, made it a principle not to handle any literature with which he was not in agreement, and therefore refused the sermon. Thus, in writing to Hutton a second time in the matter, Wesley stated:

Bristol, May, 8, 1739.

Dear Jemmy – You seem to forget what I told you: (1) that, being unwilling to speak against Predestination, we appealed to God, and I was commanded by lot to preach and print against it; (2) that the very first time I preached against it explicitly, the power of God so fell on those that heard, as we have never known before, either in Bristol or London, or elsewhere.[3]

But Hutton was not convinced that God had thus ordered the preaching and printing of this sermon, and for the time being it remained uncirculated at London. It would appear also that Wesley had second thoughts about his action, and therefore kept it at that time from circulation in Bristol also.

Wesley's action in preaching this divisive sermon was something of a breach of the trust that Whitefield had imposed in him. Nevertheless, six weeks later, Wesley paid a visit to London, but did not disclose what he had done. Rather, he reported:

I went with Mr Whitefield to Blackheath, where were, I believe, twelve or fourteen thousand people. He a little surprised me by desiring me to preach in his stead, which I did (though nature recoiled) . . . I was greatly moved with compassion for the rich that were there, to

[1] See Wesley's *Diary* of Monday, May 30, 1739 (*Journal*, Vol 2, *p* 186).

[2] *Ibid, p* 184, fn. It was long assumed that Wesley did not publish this sermon for some months, but the *Diary* and *Letters* make it evident that he had it printed right away.

[3] Wesley's *Letters*, Vol 1, *p* 307. In a letter to Hutton, six days later, Wesley says, 'I give the Homilies and sell the sermons on Free Grace. Is that right?' *Ibid, p* 312. He manifestly intended to circulate the sermon without delay, but undoubtedly did not.

whom I made a particular application. Some of them seemed to attend, while others drove away their coaches from so uncouth a preacher.[1]

Whitefield says of this event:

Had the pleasure of introducing my honoured and reverend friend, Mr John Wesley, to preach at Blackheath. The Lord give him ten thousand times more success than He has given me! . . . I went to bed rejoicing that another fresh inroad had been made into Satan's territories, by Mr Wesley's following me in field-preaching in London as well as in Bristol.[2]

On the following Sunday Whitefield continued to thrust Wesley further into the London work, and had him preach to his regular Moorfields and Kennington congregations. The latter, estimated at 15,000, was the largest Wesley had ever addressed, and the extraordinary advantage he had received by being introduced to Whitefield's crowds at Bristol was more than repeated by this further introduction at London.

During this time, however, Whitefield knew nothing about Wesley's anti-predestination sermon. But a few days later, after Wesley had returned to Bristol, he learned of it, and wrote to him, in part as follows:

I hear, Honoured Sir, that you are about to print a sermon against predestination. It shocks me to think of it! What will be the consequences but controversy? If people ask my opinion, what shall I do? I have a critical part to act. God enable me to behave aright! Silence on both sides will be best. It is noised abroad already that there is a division between you and me, and my heart within me is grieved.[3]

But Wesley's strong words were already in print, and in his declaration, "Here I fix my foot! On this I join issue with every assertor of it!" he had vowed contention. Being assured that he was Divinely commanded to "Preach and print", he would not long be able to refrain from circulating the controversial sermon.

[1] Wesley's *Journal*, Vol 2, *p* 220.

[2] Whitefield's *Journals*, p 288. Tyerman, in his *Life of Wesley*, Vol 1, *p* 228, reports this event, but in later editions of this work Whitefield's words are altered to read 'the Lord giving him ten thousand times more success than He has given me.' This is probably a printer's mistake, but it is typical of errors of this nature which have helped to aggrandize the image of Wesley and detract from that of Whitefield.

[3] *The Methodist Magazine*, 1849, *p* 165.

Nevertheless, Whitefield continued to appeal for peace and to promote Wesley's prominence, but with the prospect of dissension his life began to come under a cloud of sorrow.

*

Wesley's ministry in Bristol soon included a further distinctive teaching – one which gave a still more definite identity to his movement. This was the doctrine of *Christian Perfection.*

This concept had been growing in Wesley's mind for several years. During his days in Oxford he had begun to entertain it, although then in a merely idealistic sense. But following the semi-failure of his Aldersgate Street experience he believed that he needed some further work of grace and, hearing certain Moravian testimonies which could be interpreted as claiming a state of sinlessness, he began to conceive of an attainable perfection.[1] Accordingly, while conducting his ministry at Bristol he began to associate the overpowering emotions that he witnessed with the experience of entire sanctification. Of one man in whom the phenomenon was displayed he said, 'He received a full, clear sense of His pardoning love, and power to sin no more',[2] and these words seem indicative of his general view.

Thereafter Wesley made the teaching of Christian Perfection an important part of his ministry and later presented it in writing in his *A Plain Account of Christian Perfection*. This became a further matter of division, gravely affecting Whitefield's life and the revival in general. Therefore we must seek to understand the doctrine as Wesley taught it, and to ascertain its effect on the movement.

1. By *Perfection* Wesley did not mean merely a high state of Christian development.[3] With such a view the others in the movement were in entire agreement, but the chief point of Wes-

[1] This teaching was held by the French Prophets. Charles Wesley, while visiting them, was asked, 'Can a man attain perfection here?' He replied with a decided 'No!', but was contradicted by the Prophetess who declared, 'Look for perfection; I say, absolute perfection!' Charles Wesley's *Journal*, June 7, 1739.

[2] John Wesley's *Journal*, Vol 2, *p* 185.

[3] Several writers have tried to reduce Wesley's *Perfection* in this way. This avoids the difficulty in the matter and absolves Wesley from the responsibility of the true nature and effect of his doctrine, but it is in direct contradiction of the one plain aspect of his teaching: i.e. entire sanctification.

ley's doctrine was that he was asserting something much more than others believed.

2. Wesley taught an attainable condition in which the sin nature is eradicated and the soul entirely sanctified. This was a state superior to *relative holiness*, and though he refused to term it *absolute holiness*, he continually used the words *all, whole* and *entire* in depicting it. The following description of a person in this special state is representative of many of his passages:

For as he loves God, 'so he keeps His commandments'; not only some, or most of them, but ALL, from the least to the greatest. He is not content to 'keep the whole law, and offend at one point', but has in all points 'a conscience void of offence towards God and towards man'. Whatever God has forbidden, he avoids; whatever God has enjoined, he does . . . all the commandments of God he continually keeps, and that with all his might . . . the talents he has, he constantly employs according to his Master's will; every power and faculty of his soul, every member of his body.[1]

3. Wesley did not clearly define his terms. The whole matter turned on the question 'What is sin?', and therefore required that he define the word *sin* in precise language and that he thereafter use it in that sense and that alone. But he made use of the word in so vague a manner as:

What do you mean by the word sin? Do you mean those numberless weaknesses and follies, sometimes improperly called sins of infirmity? If so, we shall not put off these, but with our bodies. But if you mean it does not promise entire freedom from sin in its proper sense, or from committing sin, this is by no means true, unless the Scripture be false.[2]

The following is probably as clear a definition as any that Wesley made:

Not only sin, properly so called (that is voluntary transgression of a known law), but sin improperly so called (that is involuntary transgression of a divine law, known or unknown), needs atoning blood . . . I believe a person filled with the love of God is still liable to these involuntary transgressions. Such transgressions you may call sins, if you please. I do not.[3]

[1] John Wesley, *A Plain Account of Christian Perfection* (Epworth ed, n.d.) *pp* 15–16.
[2] Wesley's Preface to *An Abstract of the Life and Death of Thomas Halyburton* (London, 1739).
[3] *Christian Perfection, op cit, p* 53.

4. Wesley failed to maintain the distinction between perfection as *entire sanctification* (his particular doctrine) and perfection as *Christian maturity* (the doctrine of other Christians). This distinction was the essence of his teaching, but though he dogmatically stated it from time to time, as he sought to elucidate it, his thought ran back and forth, from one to the other in a contradictory manner. In one passage he may be insisting upon nothing less than 'destruction of the old nature' and 'deliverance from inbred sin', but in another meekly explaining that he means 'nothing higher and nothing lower than this – the love of God and man; the loving God with all our heart and soul and our neighbour as ourselves.'

Though John Wesley could be a master of clarity on most subjects, on *Christian Perfection* he was the very opposite. He propounded a doctrine and propagated it with zeal, yet he left its essential points bewilderingly vague and undefined.

Thrust thus by Wesley into the movement, the *Perfection* teaching became a further cause of dissension.

When Count Zinzendorf learned of it he called Wesley 'a false teacher and a deceiver of souls'. Upon meeting him he asked, 'Why have you changed your religion?' and in the ensuing conversation asserted:

> I acknowledge no inherent perfection in this life. This is the error of errors! I persecute it through all the world with fire and sword! I trample upon it, I destroy it! Christ is our only perfection! All Christian perfection is faith in the blood of Christ. It is imputed, not inherent. We are perfect in Christ: we are never perfect in ourselves.[1]

Howell Harris made such *Diary* entries as, 'Talked over the dreadful errors of the Wesleys', and 'I saw that Perfection is for want of seeing the spirituality of law.'[2] John Cennick says:

> Mr Wesley and I disputed often, and chiefly it was because he said if we have no other righteousness than the righteousness imputed to us, we can't be saved. Also that a soul justified by the blood of Christ, and having the assurance of forgiveness and the witness of God's Spirit bearing witness with his spirit that he is a child of God, can

[1] Original in Latin in Wesley's *Journal*, Vol 2, *p* 488. This translation is taken from Southey's *Wesley*, *op cit*, Vol 1, *p* 218. Southey also cites statements from Böhler and Spangenburg in opposition to Wesley's doctrine of perfection.
[2] *Bathafarn, op cit*, Vol. 9, *p* 34.

finally and eternally perish. Also that a man can become so perfect in this world that he shall not only not commit sin, but he shall be without sin and be inherently as holy as God. All of these I withstood, and at first we reasoned out of the Scriptures mildly for some months, but the number of perfectionists increasing, and Mr Wesley declaring and maintaining such sad things in their vindication, we argued hotly and sometimes were both to blame.[1]

Whitefield saw the Perfection teaching as one of several matters which were beginning to divide the movement. His letter to Wesley – the one cited above regarding the *Free Grace* sermon – goes on to say: 'Honoured Sir, How could you tell that some who came to you "were in a good measure sanctified"? What fruits could be produced in one night's time? "By their fruits", says our Lord, "shall ye know them." '[2]

But Wesley continued to declare the Perfection teaching, and it proved a particularly important factor in the establishing of his cause. In the sermon against Predestination he had made it plain that the position he held differed sharply from that of Whitefield, and in the Perfection teaching he demonstrated a further differentiation from the position of Whitefield and also from that of the Moravians. Wesley was thus bringing into being the distinctive doctrines that he needed if he was to function as a leader in his own right, and it is impossible to conceive of a teaching more suited to his purpose than that of his *Christian Perfection*.

[1] John Cennick, 'An Account of the Most Remarkable Occurrences in the Awakenings at Bristol and Kingswood', *The Moravian Messenger*, Vol 16.
[2] *The Methodist Magazine*, 1849, *p* 165.

A work is not to be judged of by any effects on the bodies of men; such as tears, trembling, groans, loud outcries, agonies of body, or the failing of bodily strength . . .

. . . some have been in a kind of ecstasy, wherein they have been carried beyond themselves, and have had their minds transported into a train of strong and pleasing imaginations, and a kind of visions, as though they were rapt up even to heaven and there saw glorious sights.

. . . Nor are many errors in judgment, and some delusions of Satan intermixed with the work, any argument that the work in general is not of the Spirit of God.

JONATHAN EDWARDS

The Distinguishing Marks of a Work of the Spirit of God, 1741

Perhaps it might be because of the hardness of our hearts, unready to receive anything unless we see it with our own eyes and hear it with our ears, that God, in tender condescension to our weakness, suffered so many outward signs of the very time when He wrought this inward change to be continually seen and heard among us. But although they saw 'signs and wonders' (for so I must term them), yet many would not believe.

JOHN WESLEY

Journal, May 20, 1739

19

Signs and Wonders

WESLEY's Bristol ministry lasted seven months[1] and, day after day during that time the severe emotional effects were experienced among his hearers. This matter must have our attention, not only as part of our study of the eighteenth-century Revival, but as an aid to our understanding of the occurrence of similar phenomena during other revivals in Christian history. Here are some of Wesley's reports:

April 21. A young man was suddenly seized with a violent trembling all over, and in a few minutes . . . sank down to the ground. But we ceased not calling upon God, till He raised him up, full of 'peace and joy in the Holy Ghost'.

April 30 . . . many were offended at the cries of those on whom the power of God came; among whom was a physician, who was much afraid there might be fraud or imposture in the case. To-day one whom he had known many years was the first (while I was preaching) who broke out 'into strong cries and tears'. He could hardly believe his own eyes and ears. He went and stood close to her, and observed every symptom, till great drops of sweat ran down her face and all her bones shook. He then knew not what to think, being clearly convinced it was not fraud nor yet any natural disorder. But when both her body and soul were healed in a moment, he acknowledged the finger of God.

May 1 . . . my voice could scarce be heard amidst the groanings of some and the cries of others . . . A Quaker who stood by . . . was biting his lips and knitting his brows, when he dropped down as thunder-struck. The agony he was in was even terrible to behold. We besought God not to lay folly to his charge. And he soon lifted up

[1] Wesley was in Bristol at later periods of his life also, but at this time his ministry there lasted from March 31 till Nov. 1.

his head, and cried aloud, 'now I know thou art a prophet of the Lord'.

May 2. John Haydon, . . . a man of a regular life and conversation . . . changed colour, fell off his chair, and began screaming terribly, and beating himself against the ground . . . Two or three men were holding him as well as they could. He immediately fixed his eyes upon *me*, and cried 'Aye, this is he who I said was a deceiver of the people; but God has overtaken me. I said it was all a delusion; but this is no delusion.' He then roared out, 'O thou devil! thou cursed devil! yea thou legion of devils! thou canst not stay! . . .' He then beat himself against the ground again, his breast heaving at the same time as in the pangs of death, and great drops of sweat trickling down his face . . . We all betook ourselves to prayer. His pangs ceased, and both body and soul were set at liberty.

May 12. . . . three persons almost at once sunk down as dead. But in a short time they were raised up and knew that 'the Lamb of God who taketh away the sins of the world', had taken away their sins'.

May 21. I was interrupted . . . by the cries of one who . . . strongly groaned for pardon and peace . . . another dropped down . . . a little boy near him was seized in the same manner. A young man who stood up behind, fixed his eyes on him, and sunk down himself as one dead; but soon began to roar out and beat himself against the ground, so that six men could scarcely hold him . . . we continued in prayer, and before ten the greater part found rest to their souls.[1]

*

Our attempt to understand this phenomenon may be assisted by the descriptions made by others who witnessed similar effects.

Something of this nature had occurred in the awakening which took place under the ministry of Jonathan Edwards in New England in 1735. The effects on Edwards' hearers were not so violent as those on Wesley's, and Edwards' attitude differed in that he placed little emphasis on the outward demonstrations themselves, and looked on them as of worth only inasmuch as they clearly resulted from an inward spiritual condition. Edwards wrote an acute analysis of these experiences, and showed that they arose primarily from a deep conviction of sin. He says, for instance:

Persons are sometimes brought to the borders of despair, and it looks as black as midnight to them a little before the day dawns in their

[1] Wesley's *Journal*, entries of dates indicated, 1739.

souls. Some few instances there have been, of persons who have had such a sense of God's wrath for sin, that they have been overborne; and made to *cry out* under an astonishing sense of their guilt, wondering that God suffers such guilty wretches to live upon earth, and that he doth not immediately send them to hell. Sometimes their guilt doth so stare them in the face, that they are in exceeding terror for fear that God will instantly do it; but more commonly their distresses under legal awakenings have not been to such a degree. In some, these terrors do not seem to be so sharp, when near comfort, as before; their convictions have not seemed to work so much that way, but to be led further down into their own hearts, to a further sense of their own universal depravity and deadness in sin.[1]

But Edwards also speaks of strong emotional effects which were occasioned, not by the sense of sin and the fear of its consequences, but by the joy of salvation. Both in direct association with the experience of conversion and subsequent to it, there was frequently a delight which rose to the point of ecstasy, and the following is representative of several of Edwards' descriptions:

. . . some persons have had such longing desires after Christ . . . as to take away their natural strength. Some have been so overcome with a sense of the dying love of Christ to such poor, wretched and unworthy creatures, as to weaken the body. Several persons have had so great a sense of the glory of God, and excellency of Christ, that nature and life seemed almost to *sink* under it; and in all probability, if God had showed them a little more of Himself, it would have dissolved their frame'.[2]

Ralph Erskine had also seen similar things under his preaching in Scotland. Wesley wrote to him, reporting some of the cases he had witnessed and asking his opinion, and Erskine replied, in part, as follows:

As to the outward manner you speak of, wherein most of them were affected who were cut to the heart by the sword of the Spirit, no wonder that this was at first surprising to you, since they are indeed so very rare that have been thus pricked and wounded. Yet some of the instances you give seem to be exemplified in the outward manner wherein Paul and the jailor were at first affected; as also Peter's hearers (Acts ii). The last instance you gave, of some struggling as in

[1] Jonathan Edwards, *A Narrative of Surprising Conversions* (Banner of Truth Trust ed, London, 1965), *p* 25.

[2] *Ibid*, *p* 45.

the agonies of death, and in such a manner as that four or five strong men can hardly restrain a weak woman from hurting herself or others – this is to me somewhat more inexplicable; if it do not resemble the child spoke of in Mark ix. 26, and Luke ix. 42, of whom it is said that 'while he was yet a-coming, the devil threw him down and tare him'. Or what influence sudden and sharp awakenings may have upon the body I pretend not to explain . . . The merciful issue of these conflicts in the conversion of the persons thus affected is the main thing.

When they are brought by the saving arm of God to receive Christ Jesus, to have joy and peace in believing, and then to walk in Him . . . there is great matter of praise.

All the outward appearances of people's being affected among us may be reduced to these two sorts: one is, hearing with a close, silent attention, with gravity and greediness, discovered by fixed looks, weeping eyes, and sorrowful or joyful countenances; another sort is, when they lift up their voice aloud, some more depressedly, and others more highly; and at times the whole multitude in a flood of tears, all as it were crying out at once, till their voice be ready to drown the minister's, that he can scarce be heard for the weeping noise that surrounds him. The influence on some of these, like a landflood, dries up; we hear of no change wrought; but in others it appears in the fruits of righteousness and the tract of a holy conversation.[1]

The above words, 'cut to the heart by the sword of the Spirit', doubtless reveal the basic cause of these extraordinary events. But we may also be sure that a secondary cause applied: that as God began to work upon the hearts of men in this unusual way, the powers of hell also began to oppose with new vigour. Joseph Humphreys, who was one of Wesley's earliest helpers and who later witnessed similar outcryings under his own ministry, made such an explanation, saying:

I think the case was often this; the word of God would come with a convincing light and power into the consciences of sinners, whereby they were *so far* awakened, as to be seized with dreadful terrors. The rebellion of their natures would be raised; the peace of the strong man armed would be disturbed; hell within would begin to roar; the devil, that before, being unmolested, lay quiet in their hearts, would now be stirred up and be most outrageously angry, because of this convincing light and power of the word. Hence, I believe, proceeded some of these agonies of body.[2]

*

[1] Wesley's *Journal*, Vol 2, *pp* 230–1.

[2] Tyerman's *Whitefield*, Vol 1, *p* 226.

It is significant, however, that this phenomenon, in its manifestation in England during 1739, was almost entirely limited to the ministry of John Wesley.

Howell Harris' preaching was accompanied by tremendous conviction of sin and, at times, by outcryings, but not by these extreme effects. Tyerman, after reporting the happenings under Wesley, stated, 'No such results attended Whitefield's ministry, and Whitefield himself regarded them with suspicion and dislike.'[1] Whitefield's audiences were often moved to weeping and there were times when the sobbing became so loud that it almost drowned the sound of his voice, but the effect was not such as to overwhelm the hearers, either in mind or body. Only on certain rare occasions on which Whitefield or Charles Wesley preached where people had learned to induce this kind of thing under the ministry of others did it occur under their own.

The reason for this difference probably lies in the fact that, in the preaching of Harris, Charles Wesley and Whitefield, emotion was freely expressed, while in that of John Wesley it was largely pent up. John was a man of a richly emotional nature; this is evident in his poetry and in much of his writing, but such was his self-control that in preaching he usually remained outwardly placid. His hearers, however, though they found a terrible sense of guilt arising within them, seemed to find themselves forbidden by the preacher's self-command to express their feelings in any way, till these at last burst forth with violence.

*

But though, in its beginnings, the phenomenon undoubtedly resulted from the convicting work of the Spirit of God, it soon suffered the addition of a human element. The original experience began to be imitated, for certain of Wesley's hearers learned to make a practice of effecting a self-induced paroxysm during his services. The responsibility for this addition lay partly with Wesley himself, for, believing the emotional experiences to signify the special approval of God, he desired these demonstrations and encouraged them among the people. John Cennick was Wesley's closest associate during this time and reported:

[1] Tyerman's *Wesley*, Vol 1, *p* 264.

At first no one knew what to say, but it was soon called the pangs of the new birth, the work of the Holy Ghost, casting out the old man, etc., but some were offended and left the Societies entirely when they saw Mr Wesley encourage it. I often doubted it was not of the enemy when I saw it, and disputed with Mr Wesley for calling it the work of God; but he was strengthened in his opinion after he had wrote about it to Mr Erskine in Scotland, and had received a favourable answer. And frequently when none were agitated in the meetings, he prayed, Lord! where are thy tokens and signs, and I don't remember ever to have seen it otherwise than that on his so praying several were seized and screamed out.[1]

Charles Wesley mentions several instances which were clearly of human origin. He says that a girl at Kingswood 'confessed that her fits and cryings out (above thirty of them) were all feigned, that Mr Wesley might take notice of her'.[2] Four years later, when preaching in the north of England Charles wrote:

Some stumbling-blocks, with the help of God, I have removed, particularly the fits. Many, no doubt, were, at our first preaching, struck down, both body and soul, into the depth of distress. Their *outward affections* were easy to be imitated. Many counterfeits I have already detected. To-day, one . . . was pleased to fall into a fit for my entertainment, and beat himself heartily. I thought it a pity to hinder him; so, instead of singing over him, as had been often done, we left him to recover at his leisure. Another girl, as she began her cry, I ordered to be carried out. Her convulsion was so violent, as to take away the use of her limbs, till they laid and left her without the door. Then immediately she found her legs, and walked off. Some very unstill sisters, who always took care to stand near me, and tried which should cry loudest, since I had them removed out of my sight, have been as quiet as lambs . . . Yet the Lord was with us, mightily convincing of sin and righteousness.[3]

There can be little doubt that some of Wesley's people were influenced in these things by the French Prophets, for the self-induced paroxysm was a common practice among them. As we have seen earlier, John Wesley had witnessed an instance in which a Prophetess in London intentionally effected such an experience, till 'Her head and hands and, by turns, every part of her body,

[1] Cennick's 'Account', *op cit.*
[2] Charles Wesley's *Journal*, August 5, 1740.
[3] *Ibid,* June 4, 1743.

seemed to be in a kind of convulsive motion'. On that occasion John had taken with him some of the Fetter Lane people, who were, 'much affected and believed she spoke by the Spirit of God'.[1] Charles Wesley also describes the fanatical doings of the Prophets; he says, 'many of our friends have been . . . carried away with their delusions',[2] and confesses that among these was the companion of his conversion days, Bray the brazier.

The Prophets had established themselves at Bristol too. John reports seeing a Prophetess put herself into a paroxysm, adding, 'her agitations were nothing near so violent as those of'[3] the woman in London. He mentions one of his Bristol men 'who did run well, till he was hindered by those called French Prophets'.[4]

By a process of imitation, the emotional experience was spread from the ministry of John Wesley to that of others. This was true in the case of John Cennick.

> They began to cry out as I was preaching', says Cennick. 'At first I took no notice of it, but its increasing forced me to do all I could to prevent it. One night more than twenty roared and shrieked together whilst I was preaching . . . The chief persons who were affected were Sarah Robins, Betty Somers, Sally Jones and a brother . . . The three former confessed they were demoniacs. Sally Jones could not read and yet would answer if persons talked to her in Latin or Greek.[5] They could tell who was coming into the house, who would be seized next, what was doing in other places, etc . . .
>
> I have seen people so foam and violently agitated that six men could not hold one, but he would spring out of their arms or off the ground, and tear himself, as in hellish agonies. Others I have seen sweat uncommonly, and their necks and tongues swell and twist out of all shape. Some prophesied, and some uttered the worst of blasphemies against our Saviour.

Amidst these fearful scenes Cennick lost his close and happy walk with the Lord. But his report goes on to state:

> Things of this kind were frequent everywhere, and all manner of fancies were preached by such means, and I went far from my first

[1] John Wesley's *Journal*, Vol 2, *p* 137.
[2] Charles Wesley's *Journal*, June 7, 1739.
[3] John Wesley's *Journal*, Vol 2, *p* 214.
[4] *Ibid*, *p* 226.
[5] Though Cennick may have known Latin, it is highly unlikely that he understood Greek, and we must therefore assume that it was Wesley to whom he refers in this instance. If so, was Wesley experimenting to see whether or not this experience paralleled the gift of tongues mentioned in the New Testament?

simplicity. But one day I walked by myself into the wood, and wept before the Saviour, and got again a sensible feeling of His presence, and determined henceforth to preach nothing but Him and His righteousness. And so all fits and crying out ceased wherever I came, and a blessing attended my labours; only this opened the way for Mr Wesley and me to jar and dispute often, . . .[1]

News of the strange things accompanying Wesley's ministry reached Whitefield at London and, in the letter to Wesley already cited regarding the anti-predestination sermon and the perfection doctrine, he stated:

I cannot think it right in you to give so much encouragement to those convulsions which people have been thrown into under your ministry. Were I to do so, how many would cry out every night! I think it is tempting God to require such signs. That there is something of God in it I doubt not; but the devil, I believe, does interpose. I think it will encourage the French Prophets, take people from the written word, and make them depend on visions, convulsions, &c, more than on the promises and precepts of the Gospel.[2]

A few days after writing this letter, Whitefield paid a brief visit to Bristol. He preached, with Wesley present, to one of Wesley's congregations and, during the sermon, violent results occurred, just as they regularly did under Wesley's preaching. Wesley saw the occurrence as a vindication of his own practice, saying, 'From this time, I trust, we shall all suffer God to carry on His own work in the way that pleaseth Him'.[3] But Whitefield was not in the least convinced that these paroxysms were pleasing to the Lord and his dislike of them continued.

*

We shall be able to form an adequate judgment of the phenomenon, however, only if we see it also in the still more violent form in which it finally appeared under Wesley's ministry in Kingswood.

Cennick says, 'In the beginning, when Mr Wesley prayed for them, they recovered', but he goes on to state that, with the passing of some weeks, 'Often-times the same persons were

[1] Cennick's 'Account', *op cit.*

[2] *Methodist Magazine*, 1849, *p* 165

[3] Wesley's *Journal*, Vol 2, *p* 240.

seized again and again and grew intolerable, and though he prayed with them whole nights, they grew worse and worse'.[1] Wesley made statements to the same effect, admitting that matters were getting so far out of hand that he too was becoming afraid. His *Journal* of the latter half of October depicts scenes of hysteria and seemingly-Satanic possession, as in the following entries:

October 23. I was exceedingly pressed to go back to a young woman (Sally Jones) in Kingswood . . . I found her on the bed, two or three persons holding her. It was a terrible sight. Anguish, horror and despair, above all description, appeared in her pale face. The thousand distortions of her whole body showed how the dogs of hell were gnawing her heart. The shrieks intermixed were scarce to be endured. But her stony eyes could not weep. She screamed out . . . 'I am damned, damned; lost for ever. Six days ago you might have helped me. But it is past. I am the devil's now. I have given myself to him. His I am. Him I must serve. With him I will go to hell'. . . . She then began praying to the devil.[2] We interrupted her by calling again upon God; on which she sunk down as before, and another young woman began to roar out as loud as she had done. My brother now came in, it being about nine o'clock. We continued in prayer till past eleven, when God in a moment spoke peace into the soul, first of the first tormented, and then of the other. And they both joined in singing praise to Him who had 'stilled the enemy and the avenger'.

October 25. I was sent for to one (N. Roberts) in Bristol . . . She lay on the ground, furiously gnashing her teeth, and after a while roared aloud. It was not easy for three or four persons to hold her, especially when the name of Jesus was named . . . In the evening . . . she began screaming before I came into the room; then broke out into a horrid laughter, mixed with blasphemy grievous to hear. One who from many circumstances apprehended a preternatural agent, asking, 'How didst thou dare to enter into a Christian?' was answered, 'She is not a Christian. She is mine.'[3] We left her at twelve and called again

[1] Cennick's 'Account', *op cit.*

[2] John Wesley's *Journal*, Vol 2, *p* 298. Sabine Baring-Gould, in his *The Evangelical Revival* (Methuen, London, 1920) *p* 196, quotes this passage from Wesley's *Journal*, adds a few lines from other similar entries by Wesley, and says that the whole is from Whitefield's *Journal*. Baring-Gould wrote with bitterness against both Whitefield and Wesley, and it is probable that, wanting to charge Whitefield with participation in the convulsion experiences, but finding little evidence in Whitefield's own writings, he resorted to the misleading statement that this passage had come from his pen. Other authors have copied and repeated the charge – indicative of the unscrupulous or careless manner in which the commonly-accepted image of Whitefield has been created.

[3] John Wesley's *Journal*, Vol. 2, *pp* 299, 300.

about noon on the 26th. And now it was that God showed He heareth the prayer. All her pangs ceased in a moment; she was filled with peace, and knew that the son of wickedness was departed from her.

Other reports of a similar nature came from Wesley's pen during these weeks. But in the midst of this uncontrollable situation he preached a farewell sermon[1] and set out for London. With his departure the hysteria began to abate and, within a few months had all but ceased in the Bristol and Kingswood area. Such experiences very seldom occurred under his ministry throughout the rest of his career.

Ralph Erskine, in the letter cited earlier, goes on to say:

But I make no question, Satan, so far as he gets power, may exert himself on such occasions, partly to hinder the good work in the persons who are thus touched with the sharp arrows of conviction, and partly to disparage the work of God, as if it tended to lead people to distraction.[2]

Charles Wesley made the following report of one of his services in London:

Thurs. June 12th (1740). The power of the Lord was present in his word, both to wound and heal. The adversary roared in the midst of the congregation; for to him, and not to the God of order, do I impute those horrible outcries which almost drowned my voice, and kept back the glad tidings from sinners.[3]

There can be no doubt that the outcryings proved a severe hindrance to the work. News of the hysterical women at Kingswood spread to London and elsewhere, and people jumped to the conclusion that such things were the chief characteristic of the whole revival movement. For many a year, Methodism was associated in the public mind with emotional frenzy, and Whitefield, despite his opposition to the paroxysms, was portrayed by some persons as the proponent of them.[4]

Nevertheless, during the short time that it lasted, the phenomenon served John Wesley's cause. Many of the people looked upon these experiences as an unmistakable sign of the supernatural – a demonstration of the mighty working of God – and

[1] *Ibid, p* 303, fn. [2] *Ibid, p* 231.

[3] Charles Wesley's *Journal*, June 12, 1740.

[4] See Hogarth's *Credulity, Superstition and Fanaticism*, in illustration pages.

viewing Wesley as the one Divinely used channel of this power, they found him raised to extraordinary heights of esteem in their minds. And when the extreme experience no longer occurred, its place was taken among the people by another experience – often an experience subsequent to conversion, a second experience of grace – which was much milder in nature. This was frequently associated with the profession of having received *Perfection*, or *Holiness* as it was often termed, and this second experience became the chief characteristic of Wesley's movement – the movement-within-a-movement that was steadily forming under his hand.

According to all testimony, the ministry of the national church was, at that time, generally such as to give (with respect, at least, to the excitement of attention) a ten-fold effect to the preaching of Whitefield. It was such a contrast as could not but contribute to magnify him as a stupendous prodigy. He might be called by the ministers of this very church, a fanatic, a madman or a deceiver; he might be proclaimed and proscribed under all terms and forms of opprobrium or execration; but all the while, it was perfectly inevitable, that 'all the world would wonder after the beast.'

JOHN FOSTER
Critical Essays, 1856

20

Whitefield – Right and Wrong

If Wesley's work at Bristol contained certain faults, so also did that of Whitefield at London. Whitefield's mistakes, however, were of a different kind and we have a plain indication of their nature in the following apology that he made later:

> Alas! alas! in how many things have I judged and acted wrong. I have been too rash and hasty in giving characters, both of places and persons. Being fond of Scripture language, I have often used a style too apostolical; . . . I have been too bitter in my zeal. Wild-fire has been mixed with it, and I find that I frequently wrote and spoke in my own spirit, when I thought I was writing and speaking by the assistance of the Spirit of God. I have likewise, too much made inward impressions my rule of acting, and have published too soon and too explicitly what had been better kept in longer or told after my death. By these things I have hurt the blessed cause I would defend . . .[1]

The errors which Whitefield thus confesses marked much of his work in England during 1739 and continued, though in a lesser degree, during his ministry in America throughout the following year. We must looked candidly into this aspect of his career.

Whitefield's errors began to be manifest when he found himself drawn into controversy with the anti-evangelical clergy. Though he had previously adopted the attitude of making no reply to his enemies, as he faced the tremendously increased opposition in London, he began to alter this practice. He still did not answer those who attacked him personally, but he did reply to certain denials of Scriptural truth or rejections of Christian standards of behaviour. His action in these matters was a most commendable fulfilment of the divine injunction, 'Earnestly contend for the

[1] *Works*, Vol. 2, *p* 144.

faith, once delivered to the saints', but the fault lay in his manner – a manner which sometimes displayed the 'style too apostolical' for which he apologized.

We see this fault as we notice the conflict which developed out of the attack made on him (a matter already observed) by Dr Trapp.

Dr Joseph Trapp was an outstanding man. He had been Chaplain to the Lord Chancellor of Ireland, had served for some years as a professor of poetry at Oxford and now held the livings of three important churches and was joint-lecturer at another.[1] His career had been marked by controversy – controversy in which he indulged with manifest relish, with great vigour and much display of his polemic powers.

After preaching against Whitefield at the morning service, Trapp repeated the sermon at his other two services of that day. Then he continued to preach on the same subject in his three London churches for the following three Sundays, and thereafter published 'the substance of [the] four discourses' as a booklet of 69 pages. Thus, Trapp's concentrated attack was conducted throughout Whitefield's first month in the open air in London and, aided as it was by the ridicule that constantly appeared in *The Weekly Miscellany*, Trapp doubtless hoped to do the young evangelist lasting harm.

Here is a little of what Trapp had to say:

For a *clergyman of the Church of England* to *pray* and *preach in the fields* in the country, or in the *streets* in the city, is *perfectly new*, never heard of before; . . . To pray, preach and sing psalms in the streets and fields is worse, if possible, than *intruding into pulpits* by downright *violence* and breach of the peace; and then *denying* the plain fact with the most *infamous prevarication*.[2] I could say much here; but am quite *ashamed* to speak upon a subject which is a *shame* and *reproach*, not only to our *Church* and *country*, but to *human nature* itself. Can it promote the Christian religion to turn it into riot, tumult, and confusion? – to make it ridiculous and contemptible, and expose it to the scorn and scoffs of infidels and atheists? . . . I might here very properly urge the

[1] These were: Christ Church, Newgate Street; St Leonard's, Foster Lane; and Harlington in Middlesex. He was also joint-lecturer at St Martin-in-the-Fields, Westminster. His sermons against Whitefield were preached also in St Lawrence Jewry.

[2] A reference to the St Margaret's affair.

canons of the Church of England, and the *laws* of the civil state. But the thing, though detestable, and of most pernicious tendency, is, in another view, too contemptible to be longer insisted upon. It would likewise be endless, as well as nauseous, to make reflections upon that rhapsody of madness, spiritual pride, and little less than blasphemy, if not quite so, that this *field preacher* calls his *Journal*; and so I say no more of it. Go not after these impostors and seducers; but shun them as you would the plague. Those who run after them are the *enemies* of our *religion* and Church.[1]

Trapp's attack aroused the tongues and pens of other men. London pulpits rang with the *pros* and *cons* of the matter and several pamphlets appeared, some bolstering and others opposing Trapp's efforts. In his favour there came, *A Congratulatory Letter to Dr Trapp Occasioned by his Four Sermons Against Enthusiasm* and *The True Spirit of the Methodists*. But Whitefield was defended by his friends whose productions included, *An Answer to Dr Trapp's Four Sermons Against Whitefield, Dr Trapp Tried and Cast and Allowed to the 10th of May to Recant, The Conduct and Doctrine of the Rev Mr Whitefield Vindicated from the Malicious Invectives of His Enemies,* and *Dr Trapp Vindicated from the Imputation of Being a Christian*. Moreover, William Law, who, because of his writings, was included with Whitefield in certain of Trapp's accusations, decided to reply and wrote *An Earnest Answer to Dr Trapp's Discourses*. Then Trapp entered the lists again; he wrote a sermon, *The Nature, Usefulness and Regulation of Religious Zeal,* preached it before the University of Oxford and published it; and an anonymous article in *The Weekly Miscellany* (which was probably from his pen), gave as the reason for not answering one of Whitefield's friends, that it would be foolish to reply to every 'half-witted murderer of paper'. Thus did the hurricane of controversy roar and Whitefield was at its centre.

This was manifestly an exciting time for Whitefield's followers. During his ministry in the churches they had looked upon him as a mighty hero, but now that he had undertaken the tremendous work in the fields, their admiration knew no bounds. Thus, we may be sure that when they saw him attacked, their feelings were aroused to fever heat, and that many of them (William Seward in

[1] Tyerman's *Whitefield*, Vol 1, *p* 210.

particular) not only demonstrated their own antagonism towards Dr Trapp, but urged Whitefield to get into the fray and give such a 'deceiver' a trouncing.

Though Whitefield was manifestly conscious of these pressures and undoubtedly felt them severely, he found it necessary not to let himself be influenced by them. Nevertheless, such stresses added to his difficulties and there is deep meaning in his statement, 'I dread nothing more than the false zeal of my friends in a suffering hour'.[1]

There were, however, other aspects of Trapp's sermons which proved particularly influential upon Whitefield. Using the text 'Be not righteous over much, neither make thyself over wise: why shouldest thou destroy thyself?' (Ecclesiastes 7: 16) Trapp had warned against Christian zeal, advocated indulgence in the life of worldly pleasure, and charged that Whitefield encouraged foolish austerities by which people were likely to do themselves harm. Because of his long experience and wide learning Trapp carried weight with a certain section of the citizens, and Whitefield, fearing, as he says, 'What advantage might not Satan gain over the elect if the false construction put upon the text by this unseeing teacher, should prevail!' decided to make a reply.

Trapp had entitled his sermons, *The Nature, Folly, Sin and Danger of Being Righteous Over-much*, and Whitefield, using the same text, preached before one of his open-air congregations on *The Folly and Danger of not Being Righteous Enough.*[2] Then, a few days later he used the same text again, preached what he called 'a more particular answer to Dr Trapp'[3] and immediately published both sermons.

In these efforts Whitefield proved himself an able controversialist. He somewhat had his antagonist at his mercy, for Trapp, in appealing to the Scriptures, had chosen a battleground whereon Whitefield moved with familiarity. In each reply Whitefield made a careful exposition of the text and asserted that Trapp had lifted the verse out of the passage and thereby had given it an entirely false interpretation. Thence he proceeded to show what he claimed

[1] *Journals*, *p* 294.

[2] Whitefield's *Works*, Vol 5, *p* 123. *Sermons on Important Subjects, op cit, p* 83.

[3] *A Preservative Against Unsettled Notions, and Want of Principles, in* Regard *to* Righteousness *and Christian Perfection, Works,* Vol 5, *p* 143. *Sermons on Important Subjects, p* 96.

was its true meaning,[1] and to affirm that the believer found the restraints of living a godly life, not a burden but a delight. He closed with a powerful application of the Gospel, and the difference between the two men is graphically illustrated by the negative nature of Trapp's discourses and the fervent declaration of the Gospel with which Whitefield culminated his.

But while much in these sermons of Whitefield's is highly commendable, all is not so. He not only shows his superiority to Dr Trapp, both in the Scriptures and in an understanding of the Christian life, but he rather parades it also. Here are some of his statements:

This earthly-minded minister of a new Gospel has taken a text which seems to favour his naughty purpose of weaning the well-disposed little ones of Christ from that perfect purity of heart and spirit which is necessary to all such as mean to live to our Lord Jesus. O Lord! what shall become of Thy flock when their shepherds betray them into the hands of the ravenous wolf! . . .

But must my angry, over-sighted brother Trapp personate a character so unbecoming his function, merely to overthrow the express injunction of the Lord to us, which obliges us never to give over pursuing and thirsting after the perfect righteousness of Christ till we rest in Him? Father, forgive him, for he knows not what he says! . . . Yet, though he blushes not to assist Satan to bruise our heel, I shall endeavour to bruise the heads of both.

. . . Full well I know that this sermon will not be pleasing to my poor peevish adversary; but correction is not to pleasure but to profit. Few children can be brought willingly to kiss the rod which rebuketh them, though when they become of riper understanding, they will bless the hand that guided it. Thus shall this angry man, I trust, thank me one day for reproving him, when his reason shall be restored to him by the light of the Holy Spirit.

. . . Neither am I insensible how offensive my words will be to worldlings in general, who, loving falsehood better than truth, will prefer the doctor's sin-soothing doctrines to the plain Gospel verities

[1] In this second sermon Whitefield says: 'To come at the true sense of the text it will be necessary to look back to the preceding verse where the wise man, reflecting on the vanities of his youth, puts on, for the moment, his former character. "All things have I seen in the days of my vanity; (and among the rest) there is a just man that perisheth in his righteousness and there is a wicked man who prolongeth his life in his wickedness" . . . Solomon speaks here by way of prosopopeia; not the sense of Solomon, the experienced, the learned, the wise; but of the former Solomon, a vain young fellow, full of self-love and the strong desires of life.'

preached by me. O how my soul pities them! But I have done my duty; I wash my hands and am innocent of the blood of all. I have not sought to please my hearers, but have spoken plain truth, though it should offend.[1]

These paragraphs are here quoted for a definite purpose. Several sections of these sermons against Trapp could be cited which manifest Whitefield's very able use of the Scriptures, his successful argument and his admirable Gospel application, but the above are chosen with the intention of showing, at its strongest, the bravado that had crept into his speech. Here was the kind of behaviour for which he apologized, and his stand for the truth of God, in all its commendable quality, was weakened by the brashness that attended it.

*

Something of the same manner characterized Whitefield's utterances regarding the majority of the clergy during these months.

We have seen descriptions of the carelessness and ignorance which marked the lives of these men. We have also seen the holy awe with which Whitefield viewed the ministerial office and the zeal and purity with which he filled it. It was inevitable that *his* fervour and *their* indolence would come into conflict and, thus, after having met bitter opposition from the clergy during his week in Gloucester, he poured forth his soul in the following declaration:

Cry out who will against this my frowardness, I cannot see my dear countrymen, and fellow Christians everywhere ready to perish through ignorance and unbelief, and not endeavour to convince them of both.

Those who forbid me to preach to these poor baptized heathens, that they may be saved, upon them I call to give a reason for their doing so, a reason which may satisfy not man only, but God. I here cite them to answer it to our common Master . . .

I am and profess myself, a member of the Church of England . . . I keep close to her Articles and Homilies, which, if my opposers did, we should not have so many dissenters from her. But it is most notorious that, for the iniquity of the priests, the land mourns. We have *preached* and *lived* many sincere persons out of our communion . . . they went from the Church because they could not find food for their souls. They stayed among us till they were starved out.

[1] *Works*, Vol 5, *pp* 144–157.

I know this declaration will expose me to the ill-will, not of *all* my brethren, but of all my indolent, earthly-minded, pleasure-taking brethren. But were I not to speak, the very stones would cry out against them. Speak, therefore, I must and will, and will not spare.[1]

Similarly, during his ministry in London he made the following reports:

I could not help exposing the impiety of these letter-learned teachers who say we are not now to receive the Holy Ghost and who count the doctrine of the new birth, enthusiasm. Out of your own mouths will I condemn you. Did you not, at the time of ordination, tell the bishop that you were inwardly moved by the Holy Ghost to take upon you the administration of the Church? Surely, at that time you acted the crime of Ananias and Sapphira over again. You lied, not unto man, but unto God.[2]

I preached at Kennington Common to about thirty thousand . . . God gave me great power and I never opened my mouth so freely against the letter-learned clergymen of the Church of England. Every day do I see the necessity of speaking out more and more. God knows my heart, that I do not speak out of resentment. I heartily wish all the Lord's servants were prophets; I wish the Church of England was the joy of the whole earth. But I cannot see her sinking into papistical ignorance and refined Deism, and not open my mouth against those who, by their sensual, luke-warm lives and unscriptural, superficial doctrines, thus cause her to err. O Lord, send out, we beseech Thee, Thy light and Thy truth.[3]

There can be no doubt that such denunciations were both necessary and beneficial. Had Whitefield attempted to take a vacillating or middle-of-the-road course, his people would have been left in confusion. By his clear-cut stand they were warned of a basic cause of the sorry conditions which then plagued England: the apostasy that characterized so many of the clergy. In taking this action Whitefield was setting forth the divine requirement that a minister be a converted man, and though he may have seemed but a voice crying in the wilderness at the time, his words were not lost. The idea of the necessity of a converted ministry became one of the great underlying principles of the revival among all the denominations it reached, and the entrance of this concept effected changes which continued in force for a century

[1] *Journals, p* 250. [2] *Ibid, p* 276. [3] *Ibid, p* 312.

or more. Furthermore, during his lifetime Whitefield saw many a minister converted and it was the strong stand against the unconverted in the ministry which God used to that end.

Nevertheless, though he was right in his intention, Whitefield was again partly wrong in his manner. His confession, 'I have frequently written and spoken in my own spirit, when I thought I was writing and speaking by the Spirit of God', applies to the declamations against the clergy that he made during these months, and his battle for the Lord would have been still more effective had it been without the sword-brandishing that accompanied it. Strangely enough, many others in more recent days who have found it necessary similarly to 'contend for the faith' have weakened their efforts by the same error.

*

Of course, Whitefield's denunciations of the clergy brought further controversy raging around him. Many a church in which hardly a vigorous word had been spoken in decades began to resound with strong utterances against him, and his enemies battled with his friends over his person and his doctrine in pamphlets which poured forth from the press. Tyerman lists forty-nine publications which were produced during 1739, of which ten were favourable and all the rest opposed. A later writer, in an exhaustive survey, says, 'Of 200 anti-Methodist publications . . . during 1739–40, 154 were aimed at Whitefield'.[1]

The charges were many. They asserted that he was a Dissenter or even a Papist in disguise. They accused him of claiming to be as Divinely inspired as the Apostles. They charged that his preaching in the fields, instead of being an example that they should follow, was sheer fanaticism by which he had 'sunk the house of God below a play-house and turned religion into a farce'. Accusations of pride were frequent; from the pulpit of St Paul's his *Journals* were termed 'a medley of vanity, nonsense and pride, jumbled together', and he was used as the theme of more than one sermon *preached before the University of Oxford*. Many a man made him the object of petty sniping, an instance of which was recorded

[1] Harold King, *God's Dramatist*, Studies in Speech and Drama in Honour of Alexander M. Drummond (Ithica, 1944). Here cited from Albert M. Lyles, *Methodism Mocked* (Epworth, London, 1960), *p* 18.

by a German scholar, Jacobi, who, during a visit to London, wrote:

As for dear Mr Whitefield, there really must be something good in his soul, as so many carnal priests oppose him and want to become famous through him. Last Sunday a young babbler who preached before Dr Trapp in St Martin's, railed abominably against the absent Whitefield and warned his hearers against his doctrine.[1]

Some attacks descended to the indecent. Any publication professing to reveal hidden features of Whitefield's life or ridiculing him in some ribald fashion was sure to gain a wide sale. An anonymous writer produced *The Life of George Whitefield by an Impartial Hand* which presented what it said was his 'most useful and entertaining Catechism for female Methodists', and asserted that, at his meetings he employed 'love confessions' as a 'means whereby the future supply of Methodists is well assured'. Other titles were *The Expounder Expounded*, 'Wherein the Abominable Secret Sin therein mentioned, is Particularly Illustrated and Explained', *Genuine and Secret Memoirs Relating to the Life and Adventures of that Arch-Methodist, Mr G Wh.t.fi.ld*, and *The Amorous Humours of One Whitefield.* Another was *The Methodists: an Humorous Burlesque Poem, Addressed to Mr Whitefield and His Followers.* Tyerman says, 'Parts of this foul production cannot be quoted with decency'.

Many an issue of *The Weekly Miscellany* belittled him in some nasty manner. The editor, Dr Hooker, proved himself a master of sarcasm, but in one instance was guilty of what Tyerman calls 'a foul and filthy falsehood'. Whitefield said of a certain meeting, '. . . being fatigued from my ride, and the sun beating most intensely upon my head, I was obliged to break off [from preaching], being exceedingly sick and weak'. But Hooker reported that Whitefield's trouble on this occasion was that he was drunk – too drunk to continue! And that was from the official Church of England newspaper!

To all of these attacks Whitefield made no answer. Though he felt the sting of such abuse, its effect was continually offset by statements of an opposite nature, as, for example, the following letter that he received from a Quaker:

[1] Byrom, *op cit,* Vol 1, *p* 298.

Basingstoke, July 21, 1739.

My Dear Friend –

When I yesterday went up to thy inn, and found thee gone, I was sorry that I missed an opportunity both of taking my leave of thee, and of expressing the sense I had of the presence and power of God with thee, especially in the latter part of thy sermon, and in thy prayer after it. However, I am truly glad that thou wert preserved out of the hands of cruel men. Thou heardest of the threatenings of many; but the malice of some went further. There were ten or twelve men lying in wait to do thee a private mischief. I know this by the testimony of one of those very men, who boasted to me, 'We should have given him a secret blow, and prevented his making disturbances'.

O thy noble testimony against the profaneness and vanity of the age! It rejoiced me not a little. But when thou camest to the necessity, the nature and the rewards of the new birth, thou wert carried beyond thyself. The fountain of life was opened, and flowed around amongst the living. I, for one, am a monument of free grace and mercy. O God, how boundless is Thy love!

My dear friend, may we finally be received up into the mansions of glory, there to live with all the righteous generations, and to sing with them, hallelujahs, glory and praise, for ever and ever. May the Ancient of Days keep thee in His arms, direct thee by His Spirit, support, comfort and watch over thee, is the fervent prayer of, thine in great sincerity,

J. Portsmouth.[1]

*

One aspect of Whitefield's behaviour, however, caused even certain persons who were sympathetic toward his work to regard him as something of an extremist. This was his practice of speaking about impressions that his mind received, in such a way as to suggest that they were revelations from heaven. For instance, after reaching Ireland, following the stormy passage across the Atlantic, he had written, 'Ever since I have been on board the *Mary,* these words, "Howbeit, we must be cast upon a certain island" . . . have been continually pressed upon my heart . . . Behold, they are now fulfilled.'[2] Upon reaching England he stated, '. . . those parts of the book of Jeremiah which relate to the opposition he met from the false prophets were deeply impressed

[1] Tyerman's *Whitefield,* Vol 1, *p* 267.

[2] *Journals, p* 178.

upon my soul'.[1] Likewise he made such statements regarding the future as, 'But so far as our opposers are permitted to go, shall they go, but no farther'; 'God is going to do great things among us'; and 'There are many promises yet to be fulfilled in me'.

Such expressions were considered very unwise by certain of Whitefield's contemporaries. During his first months in the open-air work Dr Isaac Watts stated:

I wish Mr Whitefield had not risen above any pretences to the ordinary influences of the Holy Spirit, unless he could have given some better evidences of it. He has acknowledged to me in conversation that he knows an impression on his mind to be divine, though he cannot give me any convincing proofs of it. I said many things to warn him of the danger of delusion and to guard him against the irregularities and imprudences which youth and zeal might lead him into; and told him plainly that, though I believe him very sincere, I was not convinced of any extraordinary call he had to some parts of his conduct. He seemed to take this free discourse in a very candid and modest manner.[2]

A Correspondent of Dr Philip Doddridge was of a similar opinion. In a letter dated May 24, 1739, John Barker wrote to Doddridge:

I saw Mr Whitefield preaching on Kennington Common to an attentive multitude and heard much of him at Bath. But, supposing him sincere and in good earnest, I still fancy that he is but a *weak* man – much too positive, says rash things, and is bold and enthusiastic. I think, what he says and does comes but little short of an assumption of inspiration and infallibility.[3]

Bishop Butler also indicated his dislike of Whitefield's impressions. Though he had earlier countenanced Whitefield's work and shortly thereafter made a goodly contribution toward the Orphan House, he soon adopted a different attitude. John Wesley had an interview with Dr Butler in which the Bishop reprimanded him about many things – among them his teaching regarding faith, and 'that many people fall into fits in your societies' – and advised him to get out of his diocese. But, in the course of the discussion, Butler also said, 'I once thought you and Mr Whitefield well-meaning men; but I cannot think so now. For

[1] *Ibid*, *p* 193.

[2] Thomas Milner, *The Life, Times and Correspondence of Dr Isaac Watts* (London, 1834), *p* 638.

[3] *Correspondence and Diary of Dr Doddridge* (London, 1892), Vol 3, *p* 381.

I have heard more of you: matters of fact, sir. And Mr Whitefield says in his Journal: "There are promises still to be fulfilled in me." Sir, the pretending to extraordinary revelations and gifts of the Holy Ghost is a horrid thing – a very horrid thing!'[1]

Doubtless, many people to-day will see little about which to complain in Whitefield's reliance on his impressions. Several writers, however, have pointed to it as a grievous fault and have made it appear that it continued throughout his life. Yet it was but a temporary trait; he soon outgrew it and such men as Watts and Doddridge came to hold him in high esteem.

*

Whitefield also committed another error at this time, one which is regrettable, yet perhaps was hardly avoidable. This was the publishing of additional *Journals*.

One would suppose that, on his return from Georgia, finding that his *Journal* had been printed, he would have done his best to prevent anything further of that kind. But people constantly told him of blessing received through this first *Journal*, and there can be no doubt that James Hutton and other publishers urged him to let them print his later ones too. Moreover, it was evident that, unless he kept this matter in hand by authorizing and controlling the publication, there would be more surreptitious activity – much of it probably so faulty as to harm both himself and the work of the Lord – and in the light of these considerations he decided to continue the publishing.

Accordingly, during 1739 Whitefield published his *Second*, *Third* and *Fourth Journals*.[2] These were the records of his work in Georgia, his return to England, his expulsion from the churches and his ministry in the open air. In these accounts the faults of his *First Journal* – the too frank mention of people and the elated manner of telling about his own doings – were not only repeated, but were aggravated at times by the indulgence of the rather bombastic manner that we have noticed.

[1] Wesley's *Journals*, Vol 2, *p* 257.

[2] *Second Journal*. From his arrival at Savannah to his return to London.

Third Journal. From his arrival at London to his departure from thence on his way to Georgia.

Fourth Journal. During the time he was detained in England by the embargo (the entire period covering May 1738 to August 1739).

These records have been chiefly responsible for posterity's concept of Whitefield. The *Journals* were the production of a man of twenty-three and twenty-four, and portrayed a period of his life that was not normal. The more normal Whitefield was the winsome youth of the first year of his ministry and the matured man whom we shall see in our study of the last twenty-five years of his life. The *Journals* were written at a time when he was in transition between these two stages of development, but since this period fills so large a part of the only account of his life that he ever wrote, it has moulded mankind's thought concerning him.

As he later admitted, he was 'too rash and hasty in giving characters, both of places and persons', and 'published too soon, what had better been told after [his] death'. His error has done his memory harm, and it is necessary that its limited nature be recognized.

*

The controversy which raged around Whitefield was not only personal. Doctrine also was involved and here the conflict centred especially on the doctrine of regeneration.

The one great truth which had been the foundation of Whitefield's ministry from the first was that of the new birth. His most widely circulated sermon, *The Nature and Necessity of Our New Birth in Christ Jesus* could almost be regarded as the manifesto of the movement. There can be no doubt that the man on the street in Bristol, Gloucester and London, had he been asked in 1739, 'What do Whitefield and the Methodists believe?', would have answered 'They claim everybody must be born again'.

Several of the clergy viewed this situation as serious. They looked upon Whitefield's teaching as directly contradictory to that of the Church of England, and in both pulpit and press they declared against it. Aroused to unusual vigour, they produced several pamphlets, of which the following are the more important:

1. *A Letter to Mr Whitefield, Designed to Correct His Mistaken Account of* Regeneration, by Tristram Land, M.A.

2. *An Explanation and Defence of the Doctrine of the Church of England Concerning Regeneration*, by Thomas Church, M.A.

3. *St John's Test of Knowing Christ and Being Born of Him,* 'A Sermon preached in St Paul's Cathedral, London, by Charles Wheatley, M.A.'

4. *The Trial of the Spirits*; 'A sermon preached before the University of Oxford, by John Wilder, M.A.'

5. *The Nature and Proper Evidence of Regeneration*, by Ralph Skerret, D.D.

6. *The Doctrine of Assurance*; 'A sermon by Arthur Bedford, M.A., Chaplain to His Royal Highness, the Prince of Wales'.

7. *A Caution Against Religious Delusion*; 'A sermon on the new birth, occasioned by the pretensions of the Methodists', by Henry Stebbing, D.D.

Such authors as these could not be overlooked. They were men of good scholarship and high position, and the very fact that such high-ranking persons deemed it necessary to counteract Whitefield's influence is an evidence of the success of his ministry. These men had manifestly searched through his printed sermons, there to discover the least contradiction in his statements and to analyse whatever he had said regarding the new birth. In turn, their principal argument was that his teaching was contrary to the accepted practice of the Church, and though they wrote with scholarly ability, sarcasm often coloured their words. The following passage from Wilder's sermon before the University appears largely representative of the matter and manner of all:

> Let us hear what this inspired man saith of the new birth. We find from his writings that the new birth is a conversion and change wrought in the mind of a man by a sensible operation of the Spirit of God; and that those who have not experienced some such sensible change in their hearts are not born again nor in a state of salvation.
>
> If this be true, how few of all the millions of the professors of Christianity are there, that have been or will be saved! Scarce any but the itinerant preacher, a few of his followers and some Quakers. If this doctrine be true, how is the God of all mercy and goodness, the God of love, comfort and joy, turned into a cruel and tyrannical being, that delights not to save, but to destroy mankind!

Whitefield's friends immediately came to his defence. Anonymous writers produced *The Case Between Mr Whitefield and Dr Stebbing* and *A Defence of Mr Whitefield's Doctrine of* Regeneration, *in Answer to Mr Land,* and Jonathan Warne wrote *The Dreadful Degeneracy of a Great Part of the Clergy, the Means to Promote Irreligion, Atheism and Popery*, 'to which is prefixed a letter to the Rev Mr Whitefield'.

Whitefield took no personal part in this conflict, but was, however, lastingly benefited by it. The fact that his enemies scrutinized his statements in order to belittle him and that his friends did the same in order to defend him, made it necessary for him to become exceptionally cautious in his utterance. It required him to think through what he believed about regeneration and to answer within his own mind such questions as the source of salvation, why the saving work was done in some and not in others, and what was its essential nature and its duration. This proved a most valuable experience to Whitefield and became the occasion of a rich maturing of his theological thought – a development which we shall notice shortly.

*

In the midst of Whitefield's immense open-air ministry and the controversies which his activities and teachings were arousing, Dr Benson decided the time had come for the youth to be reprimanded. Recognizing a particular responsibility as the Bishop who had ordained him, Dr Benson wrote to Whitefield,[1] politely but firmly, upbraiding him for 'inveighing against the clergy', and admonishing him to preach only when and where he was 'lawfully appointed thereunto'. As a corrective to Whitefield's teaching the Bishop sent him a copy of Dr Stebbing's sermon.

Whitefield replied at some length, repeating his charges against the clergy, answering Stebbing's arguments and closing with the following declaration:

The doctor and the rest of my reverend brethren are welcome to judge me as they please. Yet a little while and we shall all appear before the great Shepherd of our souls. There, there, my lord, shall it be determined who are His true ministers and who are only wolves in sheep's clothing. Our Lord, I believe, will not be ashamed to *confess us publicly in that day*. I pray God we may all approve ourselves such faithful ministers of the New Testament that we may be able to lift up our heads with boldness.

As for declining the work in which I am engaged, my blood runs chill at the very thought of it. I am as much convinced that it is my duty to act as I do, as I am that the sun shines at noon-day. I can foresee

[1] This letter has been preserved, and is now in the possession of Emory University, Atlanta, Georgia. The handwriting is somewhat quaint, but is firm, round and fully legible.

the consequences very well. They have already, in one sense, thrust us out of the synagogues. By-and-by they will think it is doing God service to kill us. But, my lord, if you and the rest of the Bishops cast us out, our great and common Master will take us up. Though all men should deny us, yet will not He. However you may censure us as evil-doers and disturbers of the peace, yet, if we suffer for our present way of acting, your lordship, at the great day, will find that we suffer only for *righteousness' sake*. In patience, therefore, do I possess my soul.[1]

*

While we candidly recognize the faults which entered Whitefield's activities during these days, we do well to recognize also his wisdom. There is much good sense in the above letter to Dr Benson and the same must be said for a letter which he wrote at this time to the Fetter Lane brethren. The Society had largely become Moravian in belief, but several of its men were strongly influenced by the French Prophets too, and in their lack of Biblical understanding were beginning to copy the Prophets' emotional practices and prophetic speculations. Whitefield saw their danger and wrote, in part, as follows:

June 12, 1739.

My dear Brethren in Christ:

I am jealous over you with a godly jealousy, and therefore write to you this second letter. I find more and more that Satan has desired to have some of you in particular, that he may sift you as wheat, and will strive, if possible, to divide and separate you all.

... Great need have you, my brethren, at this time to take the Apostle's advice and to try the spirits whether they be of God. For the devil is beginning to mimic God's work and, because terrors will not do, he is now transforming himself into an angel of light, in order more effectually to gain his point.

Brother—, as well as brother—, I believe, imagines there will be a power given to work miracles and that now Christ is coming to reign a thousand years on the earth. But, alas! what need is there of miracles, such as healing sick bodies and restoring sight to blind eyes, when we see greater miracles done every day by the power of God's Word? Do not the spiritually blind now see? Are not the spiritually dead now raised and the leprous souls now cleansed, and have not the poor the Gospel preached unto them? And if we have the thing already which

[1] *Journals, pp* 300–2.

such miracles were only intended to introduce, why should we tempt God in requiring further signs? . . . And as for our Lord's coming at this time to reign upon the earth, I answer, it is not for us to know the times and seasons which the Father hath put in His own power. That a great work is begun is evident and that it will be carried on I doubt not; but how it will end, I know not, neither do I desire to know. It is sufficient for me to do the work of the day in its day, and to rest satisfied in this, that all will end in God's glory.

Lately, brother — told me he was shortly, he believed, to be called to some public work. I pray God he may not run before he is called. To teach, I know, is a pleasing thing, but to begin to teach too soon or without a commission, will be destruction to ourselves and of ill consequence to others . . .

Oh, my dear brethren . . . may God give us all a right judgment in all things. Pure unfeigned love causes me to use this freedom. Many of you God has worked upon by my ministry . . . Do not conceive prejudices against each other. Do not dispute, but love . . . Build up each other in your most holy faith. My dear brethren,

I am your common servant in our dear Lord Jesus,

G.W.[1]

Despite the few errors that we have noticed, this kind of common sense approach to the Lord's work characterized Whitefield, even during this period of unusual stress. Charles Wesley spoke of him as 'wise above his years',[2] and a certain group of professional men who frequented London's best coffee shops – John Byrom and his associates – seem to have come to a similar opinion. Byrom had been trained as a medical doctor but became prominent for his invention of a system of shorthand. His circle included a half dozen or so gentlemen of literary and scientific tastes, and Byrom makes mention of their discussing Whitefield as they gathered in Childe's and Lloyd's coffee houses. 'Mr Whitefield is the chief topic of conversation', he wrote on June 14, 1739, 'He had Lords, Dukes to hear him at Blackheath, who gave guineas and half guineas for his Orphan House. He does surprising things, and has a great number of followers, both curious and real'.[3] The attitude of Byrom and his coterie, though

[1] *Works*, Vol 1, *pp* 50–1.

[2] Charles Wesley, *Elegy*, line 337.

[3] Byrom, *op cit*, Vol 2, part 3, *p* 246. Byrom is remembered to-day for his hymn, 'Christians, awake, salute the happy morn'. Byrom's circle included Dr David Hartley, a philosophical writer, and William Bowyer, the man who printed Whitefield's

critical at first, soon grew favourable and later became almost one of admiration.

Yet among such men Whitefield made no compromise of his principles and to a Lombard Street banker who had made profession of the Saviour he wrote:

Cirencester, June 27, 1739.

Dear Mr Blackwell,

Last night, God brought us hither in safety. I have now a few moments' leisure. How can I employ them better than in writing to you? I almost envy you, because, when I left you, you were sick. Glorious lessons, dear sir, you may learn from such a visitation. It may remind you of the much greater sickness and disorder of your soul, and give you an excellent opportunity of retiring in order to prepare yourself for the buffetings of a ridiculing world. Ere I return, I expect to hear you are stigmatized, not only in Lombard Street, but in all the places round about. For Christ's servants have always been the world's fools. And, if you will live godly in Christ Jesus, you, even you, must suffer persecution. But you know in whom you have believed. He is able and willing to deliver you. Go on, therefore, my dear friend, in the strength of Christ. Make mention of His righteousness only. Give Him your heart – your whole heart. Cleave to Him by faith in His blood; and then you may bid men and devils defiance. Oh! Mr Blackwell, I would not have you a Demas for the world. But away with all such thoughts. I cannot bear them. Dearest Mr Blackwell, I am ever yours in our Lord Jesus Christ,

George Whitefield.[1]

Furthermore, though Whitefield may have been wrong in some things and was undoubtedly right in others, all that he did was overshadowed by the magnificence of his ministry. We sense something of the magnitude and the glory of his labours as we seek to see him in the act of conducting one of his great open-air meetings and our thought runs as follows:

It is a Friday evening, and vast numbers of mankind are at

sermons and who is spoken of as 'a learned and excellent printer, the friend of all the distinguished literary ornaments of his age'. Mr Lloyd, in whose coffee shop in Lombard Street the great insurance institution was then developing, was one of Byrom's close acquaintances, as was also William Law.

[1] Tyerman's *Whitefield*, Vol 1, *p* 255.

their usual diversions on Kennington Common. A coach arrives and a shout goes up, 'He's here!' and Whitefield, alighting, walks towards a grassy hillock that rises at one side of the field. People begin to leave their sports and to make their way toward the place where he stands, and soon form a vast semi-circle before him. Some hundreds of his followers take their places near him and remain bowed in prayer. Beyond them are thousands of the common humanity of London, and at the fringe of the crowd there sit many persons on horse-back. Finally several coaches drive on to the field, bearing some of London's wealthy ones, for these persons are as hungry as the more lowly citizens to hear the Gospel.

Whitefield announces a Psalm and his voice becomes the organ that leads this great host in the singing of it. He uses certain of the prayers of the Church of England service and then begins to preach. His sermon, which is entitled *The Pharisee and Publican*,[1] is introduced with a pithy description of the practices of the Pharisees and of the position of the publicans in Biblical times, and these opening sentences provide solid information to gain the ear of the learned and yet are simple enough to be grasped by the poor.

The same is true of the body of the sermon – an explanation of the whole parable – and, in teaching the passage phrase by phrase, Whitefield constantly makes application of its message to his hearers' hearts. Any who have come expecting to make a disturbance are disappointed, for Kennington Common has quickly become a holy place and the multitude stands in hushed solemnity to hear the word of the Lord.

As the sermon advances Whitefield's whole person becomes part of the sublime work of preaching. His countenance takes on an intense energy, as its swiftly changing expressions depict the progressing elements of his message. Even the squint in his eye seems to make his gaze the more penetrating, causing many an individual to feel that the preacher has singled him out and is speaking, as it were, to him alone. The voice – seldom have the

[1] 'Being upon the Publican and Pharisee, I was very earnest in endeavouring to convince the self-righteous Pharisees of this generation, and offering Jesus Christ freely to all who, with the humble Publican, feelingly and experimentally could cry out, "God be merciful to me a sinner!"' *Journals*, 264. The sermon is printed in his *Works*, Vol. 6, *pp* 36–48.

sons of men heard such an instrument[1] – gives expression to every emotion known to the human breast, yet it comes with a direct familiarity, as if its message were uttered into the individual ear.

How real seems the poor repentant Publican as Whitefield declares:

Methinks I see him, standing afar off, pensive, oppressed, and even overwhelmed with sorrow! Sometimes he attempts to look up, but, then, thinks he, the heavens are unclean in God's sight, and the very angels are charged with folly; how then shall such a wretch as I dare to lift up my guilty head! And to show that his heart was full of holy self-resentment, he smote upon his breast; the word in the original implies that he *struck hard* upon his breast . . . his treacherous, ungrateful, desperately wicked breast; a breast now ready to burst: and at length . . . with many tears, he cries out, 'God be merciful to me a sinner!'

Not God be merciful to yonder proud Pharisee! . . . Not God be merciful to me a saint! . . . Not God be merciful to such or such a one; but God be merciful to me, even to me a sinner, a sinner by birth, a sinner as to all my performances; a sinner in whom is no health, in whom dwelleth no good thing; a sinner, poor, miserable, blind and naked, from the crown of the head to the sole of the foot, full of wounds, and bruises and putrifying sores; a self-accused, self-condemned sinner!

The wealthy also, long smug in their self-righteousness, are made to feel their spiritual poverty as he addresses them, saying:

Hear this, all ye self-judiciaries, tremble and behold your doom! A dreadful doom, more dreadful than words can express, or thought conceive! If you refuse to humble yourselves, after hearing this parable, I call heaven and earth to witness against you this day, that God shall . . . pour all the vials of His wrath upon your rebellious heads. You exalted yourselves here, and God shall abase you hereafter; you are as proud as the devil, and with devils shall you dwell to all eternity! Be not deceived! God is not mocked! He sees your hearts!

If you are unjustified, the wrath of God abideth upon you! You are in your blood; all the curses of the law belong to you! Cursed are you when you go out, cursed are you when you come in; cursed are your thoughts, cursed are your words, cursed are your deeds . . . However

[1] There was a report that on a certain occasion Whitefield's preaching at one of these meetings could be heard for a mile and the singing of the congregation for two miles.

highly you may be esteemed in the sight of men, however you may be honoured with the uppermost seats in the synagogues, or in the church militant, you will have no place in the church triumphant! 'Humble yourselves therefore under the mighty hand of God'; pull down every self-righteous thought and every proud imagination . . .; 'for he, (and he alone) that humbleth himself shall be exalted!'

Rich and poor alike sense the eternal truth of his words, and everywhere, men and women are in tears. The sounds of their weeping can be heard far across the Common, as each feels himself standing alone, as it were, before a Holy God, and views in contrast his own unjustified human nature. But still Whitefield continues:

Sinners, I know not how to leave off talking with you! I would fill my mouth with arguments, I would plead with you, 'Come, let us reason together. Though your sins be as scarlet', yet if you humble yourselves, 'they shall be white as snow'! One act of true faith in Christ justifies you for ever and ever; He has not promised you what He cannot perform; He is able to exalt you; for God hath exalted Him and given Him a name above every name – exalted Him to be not only a Prince but a Saviour. O, may He be a Saviour to you! and then shall I have reason to rejoice, in the day of judgment, that I have not preached in vain, nor laboured in vain!

With this powerful entreaty Whitefield brings his sermon to a close. He goes to his knees and begins to pray. Few move and little is heard except the weeping of the wounded of the Lord and the joyous cries of those whose tears of mourning and repentance have now become tears of salvation. Finally he seeks to make his way to a waiting coach, only to be pressed upon by scores who crowd around imploring a place in his prayers and by others who come telling him that God has indeed accomplished His saving work in their hearts.

Without doubt, such, in general, were the features of every service Whitefield held during these months. Day by day Kennington Common became a great sky-domed cathedral, in which the multitude stood in a holy hush and the souls claimed by the Saviour were many. The world might ridicule and the hurricane of controversy might blow, but, when making his later apology for his mistakes, Whitefield also could say, 'I cannot but praise the gracious God, who filled me with so much of His holy fire, and carried me, a poor weak youth, through such a torrent, both of popularity and contempt, and set so many seals to my unworthy ministrations'.[1]

[1] *Works*, Vol 2, *p* 144.

And the Lord God said, It is not good that the man should be alone; I will make him an help meet for him.

Genesis 2: 18

Let nothing interrupt your communion with the Bridegroom of the church.

WHITEFIELD

in a letter to a newly-married friend

21

An Affaire de Coeur at Blendon Hall

ONE of the extraordinary features of Whitefield's life, thus far, was its lack of personal friendships with members of the opposite sex.[1] In a zeal for the Lord that filled his waking hours he had given himself over entirely to his ministry, and the usual pursuits of youth in seeking such company had seemed largely outside his thought. However, during these spring months of 1739 this attitude began to weaken, as an affection for a highly suitable young lady forced its way into his heart. This young lady was Elizabeth Delamotte.

Of course, Whitefield wrote no plain account of so personal a matter. He did, however, make several references to it by which we are able to determine the broad outlines of what took place. But these references imply much more than they actually state. They constantly suggest details, and though our interpretation of these is based on nothing more than strong probability, they cannot be overlooked. In turn, the two together – the known facts amplified by the probable details – allow a fairly clear understanding of this important experience to be obtained.

While in the midst of his open-air ministry in London, Whitefield accepted the invitation of Thomas and Mrs Delamotte to be a guest at their home, Blendon Hall, near Bexley in Kent. This brought him near to the down-river ports from which his vessel might sail at any time. The Delamotte's were well-to-do[2]

[1] The Diary that Whitefield wrote shortly after his conversion mentions two or three times a young lady named Rachel Jones. Since he later told Howell Harris that he had had two acquaintances (that is, one besides Miss Delamotte) we may assume he was referring to this person as the other. This friendship was very brief.

[2] In 1735, when Charles Delamotte stated his intention to go to Georgia, his father sought to deter him by offering to 'settle him in a very handsome way'. This is probably the matter to which the Earl of Egmont refers when, in his *Diary*,

and their home was a fine old country mansion, set in its own park, and possessing a private lake. It adjoined a farm and several other fields and tenements which comprised the Blendon estate.[1] Thomas held the office of *Justice of the Peace* of Bexley County, but his principal occupation was a large sugar-importing business in London. This was located at Fresh Wharf and he maintained a city home near by.

There were five children in the Delamotte family: two sons – Charles, who had been the companion of the Wesleys in Georgia; and William (nicknamed Jacky), a student at Cambridge University; three daughters – Elizabeth (called Betty), Esther (Hetty), and a much younger girl named Molly. Elizabeth and Esther divided their time between Blendon Hall and their London home, and while at the latter attended the services at Fetter Lane.

Whitefield had been acquainted with Elizabeth since the autumn of 1737 – prior to his first trip to Georgia. Their first recorded meeting had come about through Charles Wesley, whose familiarity with the family is revealed in his *Journal*. Charles wrote:

September 10. Calling at Mrs Delamotte's, I found Miss Hetty there. . . . We soon fell into talk about the new birth. She lamented her not being acquainted with me sooner . . .

September 11. (Blendon). I had some serious talk with Miss Betsy.

September 24. I found Miss Hetty . . . We passed two hours in conference and prayer.

October 28. I found Miss Betty at Fresh Wharf and spent an hour or

p 194, he says of Charles, 'He is worth about 3,000£, but was entitled to 20,000£ more'. Early in 1740 Whitefield wrote from America to Mrs Delamotte, saying that he had heard '. . . that you are likely to be cast out of your mother's will, *only* for following Christ' (*Works,* Vol 1, *p* 143). This may have involved a fairly large sum, for one of the younger Delamottes – either Elizabeth or William – had written to Whitefield informing him of the event.

[1] *A Survey of the Manor and Desmenses of Bexley* contains 'A Description of Blendon Hall Estate when Occupied by Sir Edward Brett, 1681.' Mr P. E. Morris, F.L.A., Librarian of the Borough of Bexley Public Libraries, has graciously compiled for the author 'A Chronology of the Occupants of Blendon Hall', covering the period from 1301 till the Hall was demolished in 1934. The majority of the occupants were titled persons. Thomas Delamotte was not an owner, but a tenant, and lived there from 1732 till about 1748. Under the ownership of the Rt Hon Lady Margaret Scott, which began in 1763, the old hall was torn down and replaced by 'a neat mansion', and the park and grounds were much improved. The pictures of Blendon Hall that are available appear to be of this second building, and therefore of little relation to the Delamottes. See Illustration pages.

two with her and Jacky. Next morning I was with her alone and spoke largely of the danger of lukewarmness . . . I never saw her so moved before.[1]

Whitefield was in London at that time. (It was then that he was preaching in the churches and was experiencing his first rise into fame.) Charles Wesley was frequently a member of his congregations, and tells of taking Betty and Jacky Delamotte to one of his early morning services. 'Sunday, Oct. 30,' he writes, 'I waked them at five and attended them to Forster Lane, where we heard Mr Whitefield and communicated together'.[2]

That evening Whitefield and several others gathered at the home of the Rev John Hutton in Westminster. Whitefield usually spent his evenings in an exultation of prayer, praise and the Scriptures, and on these occasions the people who had assembled, drawn by his presence, found their own spirits rising with his to similar heights of Christian joy. This was manifestly such an occasion, and Charles brought Betty and Jacky to it, and reported 'They were much delighted by the singing there, and edified, I hope, by George Whitefield's example. It was near eleven before I left them at their own house'.

In order to understand the significance of this meeting between Whitefield and Elizabeth, we must recall the prominence in which he then stood. These were the days in which Londoners were becoming 'so extravagant in their applauses' that he could no longer walk on foot, but found it necessary to travel by coach in order to 'avoid the hosannas of the multitude'. Scores of people sought access to his presence and some of England's 'Honourable ladies' were even numbered among his admirers.

It was as this exceptionally prominent figure that Whitefield would have appeared in the eyes of Elizabeth on the occasion of their meeting for the first time. Moreover, she heard Whitefield again a few days later, for Charles goes on to report:

November 5. I met and turned back with Betty, to hear Mr Whitefield preach, not with the persuasive words of man's wisdom, but with the demonstration of the Spirit and with power. The churches will not contain the multitudes that throng to hear him.[3]

[1] Charles Wesley's *Journal*, entries of dates indicated, 1737.
[2] *Ibid.* [3] *Ibid.*

Charles Wesley, after his conversion during the following May (Whitefield was on his first trip to America by then) was used of the Lord to lead the Delamotte family to Christ. He reports the conversion of Betty, Hetty, William and Mrs Delamotte, their minister (the Rev Henry Piers of Bexley), two maid-servants and their gardener. Of Elizabeth's experience Charles says (and his words reveal the mystical concepts he held and taught at the time):

June 9, (1738) . . . yesterday Miss Betsy plainly informed me that, after her last receiving the sacrament, she had heard a voice, 'Go thy way, thy sins are forgiven thee', and was thereby filled with joy unspeakable. She said within herself, 'Now I do indeed feed upon Christ in my heart by faith', and continued all day in the spirit of triumph and exultation. All her life, she thought, would be too little to thank God for that day.[1]

In subsequent weeks, according to Charles's accounts, Elizabeth displayed a sincere Christian piety. The same was true of the rest of the family also, and in the joy of their new-found salvation they made Blendon Hall resound with the voice of vigorous prayer and praise. William appears to have been especially fervent, and, attending (like his sisters) the Fetter Lane Society during his frequent visits to London, he began there to make his first attempts at preaching.

*

Whitefield returned to England in December of that year and shortly thereafter paid a visit to the Delamotte home. 'A happier household have I seldom found,' he stated on his first evening there, and the next morning continued:

Rose about five, spent above an hour most agreeably in prayer, singing and reading the Scriptures with the church in Mr Delamotte's house; some of whom . . . passed the whole night in the same delightful employment.[2]

During the following June Whitefield became the guest of the Delamottes (the event at which this chapter opens) and his stay

[1] *Ibid.*

[2] *Journals, p* 203. Blendon Hall possessed its own chapel which was probably used on such occasions as this.

with them lasted almost three weeks. The following are a selection of the *Journal* entries he made while there:

Monday, June 4, 1739 ... Took leave of my weeping friends and went in company with many of them to Blackheath, where there was nearly as large a congregation as at Kennington the last Lord's Day. I think I was never so much enlarged since I have preached in the fields. My discourse lasted nearly two hours, and the people were so melted down, and wept so loud, that they almost drowned my voice. I could not but cry out, 'Come ye Pharisees, come and see the Lord Jesus getting Himself the victory!' Afterwards went to an inn upon the Heath, where many came drowned in tears to take a last farewell.

Tuesday, June 5. Went in the morning to Blendon, five miles from Blackheath, and enjoyed a sweet retreat at the house of Mr Delamotte. Preached with unusual power at Bexley Common, at 11 in the morning, to about three hundred people, and in the evening near Woolwich to several thousands. I returned to Blendon rejoicing and spent the evening most delightfully with many Christian friends who came from London to see me. Oh, how does their sweet company cause me to long for communion among the spirits of just men made perfect! ...

Wednesday, June 6. Breakfasted with many friends and gave a word of exhortation to many more who came from London to bid me adieu. Their hearts were ready to break with sorrow ... hasted to Gravesend, where I read prayers and preached in a church near the town to about six hundred people. I have no objection against, but highly approve of the excellent liturgy of our Church, would ministers lend me their churches to use it in. If not, let them blame themselves, that I pray and preach in the fields.

Thursday, June 7 ... returned in the evening, and preached in Bexley Church ... Here some of Mr Delamotte's family gave us the meeting. After sermon I returned to their house at Blendon, praising and blessing God, that we had once more an opportunity of building up each other in our most holy faith. Oh, how sweet is this retirement to my soul! ... Dearest Lord, sweeten all Thy dispensations with a sense of Thy love, and then deal with me as it seemeth good in Thy sight!

Friday, June 8. Preached at Bexley in the morning and at Charlton in the afternoon, whither I was invited by the Earl and Countess of Egmont. Both before and after sermon they entertained me with the utmost civility.[1] My heart was much comforted by God, and at

[1] The Earl and the Countess were able to sit in their summer house, along with several of their friends, and hear the preaching, as their garden adjoined Charlton Green. Following the sermon the Earl questioned Whitefield closely regarding his

night I returned with my friends to my sweet retreat at Blendon. Oh, the comforts of being all of one mind in a house! It begins our heaven upon earth.

Sunday, June 10. Hastened back to Blendon . . . Preached with more power than ever . . . in Bexley Church. Dined, gave thanks and sang hymns at Mr Delamotte's. Preached with great power, in the evening, on Blackheath, to above twenty thousand people, and collected £16 7s. for the orphans . . .

Monday, June 11 . . . hastened back to Blendon in company with some who love our Lord Jesus in sincerity. Oh how swiftly and delightfully do those hours pass away which are spent in Christian conversation!

Thursday, June 14. Spent the whole day in my pleasant and profitable retreat at Blendon; . . .

Sunday, June 17. Preached in Bexley Church . . . Dined at Blendon and took sweet counsel with many Christian friends.[1]

These reports contain much that is highly significant. Though, while staying at the Delamotte home, Whitefield continued his preaching with unabated zeal, it is evident, nevertheless, that a new joy had entered his life. The urgency that had filled his hours ever since the beginning of his ministry, had now been allowed to slacken slightly and Blendon Hall had become for him 'a sweet retreat' wherein, in 'sweet retirement' he took 'sweet counsel' in 'sweet company' and spoke of finding 'heaven on earth'. These expressions are not accidental, but indicate that he was experiencing something over and above his usual spiritual happiness. Of course, he could not mention Elizabeth by name (he probably says too much, as it is) but when we consider that a friendship sprang up between them in these days which, before ten months had passed, culminated in a proposal of marriage, we may be sure that this new delight was occasioned by his affection for her.

This inference is strengthened by evidence that his views on ministerial celibacy were changing. On June 2, Charles Wesley

doctrines and certain tales that were being circulated, which charged him with truly fanatical actions. The Earl summarized the results of the conversation, saying, 'I believe him perfectly sincere and disinterested, and that he indeed works a considerable reformation among the common people, and that there is nothing in his doctrine that can be laid hold on to his hurt.' *The Diary of the First Earl of Egmont*, *pp* 67–69. [1] *Journals*, *pp* 285–9.

wrote, 'I heard that my friend Stonehouse was actually married. It is a satisfaction to me that I had no hand in it.' But the next day he added, 'G. Whitefield advised me (I thank him for his love) to follow Mr Stonehouse's example.'[1] Whitefield may have been counselling Charles to marry a wealthy Miss Raymond whom he was seeing 'almost every day', or one of the Claggett or Delamotte sisters. But, be that as it may, he was manifestly weakening in his view that the single life was best for the minister and was admitting that marriage might be preferable.

Furthermore, Whitefield was also giving thought to the nature of marriage in general during these days. Being asked to address 'A Society of Young Women' at Fetter Lane on April 28, he chose as his subject *Christ the Best Husband*. From the Scripture, 'Hearken, O daughter, and consider, and incline thine ear; forget also thine own people, and thy father's house; So shall the king greatly desire thy beauty; for he is thy Lord; and worship thou him',[2] he spoke of leaving, if necessary, all things on earth, in order to be joined in salvation unto Jesus Christ. It was a powerful presentation of the great truth of spiritual marriage, but by way of illustration Whitefield constantly drew parallels from natural marriage, and in so doing revealed both an interest in and an understanding of his subject. Later, when we see two letters that he wrote to Elizabeth, we shall find it difficult not to think of him as a heartless individual, quite insensitive to the feelings of a refined young woman. But as we read this sermon we see a man of warm affections, one who had given thought to the paths of wisdom regarding marriage and who even possessed some understanding of that mystery – the workings of the feminine mind in such matters.

Moreover, the circumstances under which Whitefield lived made marriage seem especially desirable to him. Entertained here and there – at Hutton's bachelor quarters in London, at his sister's house in Bristol and the Harris's in Gloucester – his was a homeless life, and while at Blendon he more than once used

[1] Charles Wesley's *Journal*, June 2, 3, 1739.

[2] *Christ the Best Husband: Or an Earnest Invitation to Young Women to Come nd See Christ*. 'Preached to a Society of Young Women in Fetter Lane.' Text, *Psalm* 45: 10, 11. *Works*, Vol 5, *pp* 65–78. It would appear that several of the older ladies found this event particularly attractive, for a number of them were present also.

expressions which suggest a yearning to settle down like other men and have a home of his own. Thus, it is understandable that, under these conditions, Whitefield found himself drawn toward Elizabeth.

Elizabeth appears to have possessed qualities which may well have rendered her both attractive and suitable to Whitefield. She was manifestly a woman of warm spiritual fervour and, though nothing has come down to us describing her person or indicating what her talents or learning may have been, it is evident that her home life could not have failed to impart a goodly measure of culture. A few of her letters are extant and these, we are told, 'are full of sprightly humour as well as devout piety', are written in 'a clear and legible hand-writing', and 'reveal a woman of considerable charm'.[1] A brief autobiographical note which she wrote late in life indicates the presence of firm Christian convictions and personal strength.[2]

Likewise, we have much reason to believe that Whitefield proved attractive in the eyes of Elizabeth. Dr Gillies, on the basis of a long acquaintance, says:

Mr Whitefield's person was graceful and well proportioned: his stature rather above the middle size. His complexion was very fair. His eyes were of a dark blue colour, and small, but sprightly. He had a squint with one of them . . .[3] His features were in general good and regular. His countenance was manly, and his voice exceeding strong; yet both were softened with an uncommon degree of sweetness. He was always

[1] Eluith Griffiths, *Moravians and Methodists. The Journal of the Historical Society of the Presbyterian Church in Wales*, Vol 16, No 3, 1931, *p* 108.

[2] It was the custom of the Moravians for a person of mature years to write out the principal events of his or her life, with emphasis on spiritual experience, and this was to be read at the person's funeral. Having long been a Moravian, Elizabeth wrote such an account sometime after she reached the age of 55. Of her earlier Methodist associations she merely says, 'Mr Ch's Wesley and Mr Whitefield visited us'. The original of Elizabeth's autobiographical sketch was destroyed in the wartime bombing of the Fetter Lane Chapel, but a copy is possessed by the Moravian Church House, Muswell Hill, London. See *Appendix, Note* 5.

[3] There is a note among the papers left by Charles Wesley's son Samuel, to the effect that he had often heard his father speak of the personal attractiveness of Mr Whitefield. Samuel remarks that he could not see how anyone who squinted could be attractive, but his father assured him that in Mr Whitefield's case the defect of his eyes was overruled by the strength and comeliness of his other features. Samuel replied that he still did not see how this could be. One of Whitefield's hearers is reported as stating that a person could not listen to him for five minutes without forgetting that he squinted.

very clean and neat, and often said pleasantly that 'a minister ought to be without spot'. His deportment was decent and easy, without the least stiffness or formality; and his engaging polite manner made his company universally agreeable. In his youth he was very slender and moved his body with great agility . . .[1]

We must surely assume that the young man who bore this description would prove attractive, even apart from his extraordinary fame.

The friendship between Whitefield and Elizabeth was, however, a very unusual one. In his many visits to her home he seldom, if ever, came alone. Almost always, when he came a troop of his followers either arrived with him or, learning that he was there, came flocking after him. His presence created a constant commotion and it would appear that Mrs Delamotte sometimes tried to provide food for these people. Charles Wesley records an instance in which 'Above sixty of the poor people passed the night in Mr Delamotte's barn, singing and rejoicing.' 'I sang and prayed with them before the door,' says Charles. 'George's exhortation left them all in tears.'[2] Whitefield tells of three Saturday nights on which some hundreds of people came down from London, 'singing and praising God'; they remained around the estate all night and urged him – doubtless clamoured for him – first thing in the morning, to come out and preach to them. On the last of these occasions the crowd increased during the Sunday until by three o'clock it amounted to nearly three thousand, and, taking his stand on a stone wall that surrounded the garden, he preached again. Thereafter these people made their way with him to Blackheath to hear him preach once more – this time to an audience of thirty thousand.

It is evident also that the Delamotte family rejoiced to have Whitefield as their guest, and that they entered with fervour into his spiritual labours and gladly bore with this strange upset of their lives. 'When I consider how constantly you attended my ministry', he wrote to Mr and Mrs Delamotte after leaving their home, 'how gladly you received me into your house, and how affectionately you took your last farewell, gratitude obliges me to send you a line.'[3] Mrs Delamotte in particular seems to have

[1] Gillies, *op cit*, *p* 279.
[2] Charles Wesley's *Journal*, June 6, 1739.
[3] *Works*, Vol 1, *p* 88.

shown him favour and in a later letter that he addressed to her personally he thanks her not only for her kindnesses to him but also to his many friends, and prays, 'The Lord reward you ten thousand-fold . . .'[1]

*

But notwithstanding Whitefield's expressions of happiness in the Delamotte home, it is highly probable that his friendship with Elizabeth caused him more sorrow than joy. The fact that, until this point, there had been no feminine attachment in his life, had been a matter of definite and firm intention. He deeply cherished the victory that had long been his over the normal desires of a young man and there can be no doubt that he was speaking by way of personal testimony when, in his sermon on *Early Piety*, he declared:

> . . . we see mere striplings not only practising, but delighting in such religious duties, and in the days of their youth, when, if ever, they have a relish for sensual pleasures, subduing and despising the lust of the flesh, the lust of the eye and the pride of life . . . A young saint does not decline the gratifications of sense because he can no longer 'hear the voice of singing men and singing women', but willingly takes up his cross and follows his blessed Master in his youth . . . He knows not what men mean by talking of mortification, self-denial and retirement as hard and rigorous duties, for he has so accustomed himself to them, that . . . they are now become even natural . . .[2]

Such had been Whitefield's strength, but with the rising in his heart of an affection for Elizabeth, the two competing emotions threw him into conflict. Thus far he had loved the Lord supremely, but how could he continue to do so, were he to allow himself to love a woman too? Ever since his conversion he had given himself to his Master with undivided devotion and in that full consecration he had found his power with God: but was he now to see that strength dissipated and his ministry weakened by an earthly affection? Doubtless, Whitefield's feelings for Elizabeth were strong, but in his determination to love none but the Lord, he sought to trample them under foot, and as a result a fierce battle raged within his soul.

[1] *Ibid, p* 102. [2] *Ibid,* Vol 5, *pp* 159–70.

While at the Delamotte home Whitefield said, 'Were I left to my choice, here would be my rest'. Knowing, however, the requirements of his ministry he immediately repressed the desire, stating, 'But a necessity is laid upon me, and woe unto me if I preach not the Gospel!'[1] Similarly, after bringing his stay there to a close, as he set out at 11 o'clock at night on an all-night and all-day coach ride, he was probably contrasting the homelessness that was before him with the comforts he had left, when he declared, 'Justly may I say, I am a stranger and pilgrim upon earth; for I have here no continuing city. May I always be preparing myself for that which is to come, a city not made with hands, eternal in the Heavens, whose Builder and Maker is God.'[2]

But Whitefield's struggle is particularly manifest in a letter that he wrote a few months later to William Delamotte. It would appear that William had been experiencing the same conflict, and that he and Whitefield had each expressed the conviction that were they to allow anyone to share the place in their lives that belonged solely to the Lord Jesus their deed would be tantamount to idolatry. Thus (to anticipate our story) while crossing the Atlantic Whitefield wrote to William, saying,

> . . . I trust God has enabled you to take the advice you gave me, and that you have been kept from idolatry. Oh my dear brother, let us watch and pray, that we may not be led into temptation. The spirit is willing in both; but the flesh, mine in particular, is exceeding weak . . . At present my heart is quite free . . . I endeavour to resign myself wholly to God. I desire His will may be done in me, by me and upon me.[3]

How, then, are we to think of the relationship between Whitefield and Elizabeth?

There can be little doubt that he was very fond of her. Nevertheless, though there was manifestly some measure of understanding between them, in his determination to allow no one to usurp the place that belonged to the Saviour alone, Whitefield crushed these desires. It is highly probable that he constantly sought to adopt the 'my heart is quite free' attitude and behaved toward her with little more than a special politeness and much spiritual concern.

[1] *Journals, p* 287. [2] *Ibid, p* 294. [3] *Works,* Vol 1, *p* 109.

There can also be little doubt that Elizabeth was deeply attracted to him. When we read Gillies' description of his person and remember how greatly he was admired by hundreds everywhere, we can but believe that she would feel flattered in receiving his attentions. She manifestly joined in the welcome accorded him by her family, and there is evidence which suggests that the friendship was promoted more by her than by him.[1] But in this regard it should be noticed that though he was but twenty-four at this time she had reached the age of twenty-nine.

This association, however, was very probably a source of disappointment to Elizabeth. Despite the wondrous excitement arising from the presence of so famous a young man, there must have been times when she wished he were but an ordinary person – one who could come to her home alone, without all these others coming too, and all this singing and rejoicing going on around the place at all hours of the night. Moreover, the conflict he was experiencing could not but have affected her, and we must assume that she looked on the whole affair with much bewilderment and probably frustration.

But within Whitefield's heart the struggle raged. His *Journals* and letters began to contain a new term: 'inward trials'. It was a term that he reserved for this particular strife and in our study of the subsequent fourteen months of his life we shall see him using it frequently and as an expression of deep sorrow. Truly, his determination not to be disloyal to the Lord whatever the cost to himself deserves our admiration, but his idea that love for Elizabeth would necessarily have constituted such disloyalty must be regretted. Tyerman says he was 'as odd a wooer as ever wooed', and when we see his subsequent proposal of marriage, we shall probably find ourselves in agreement with this statement.

[1] See *pp* 445, 467–8.

May 4, 1740. *London. Was led to hear Bro. Charles Wesley by mere providence. He was begun when I came there. On his showing how dreadful are the sins of a justified person, and on his singing, 'Thy presence calls* Thee *down', I thought my soul was almost drawn out of my body to Christ.*

HOWELL HARRIS

Diary

Peter Böhler, Moravian leader.
[By courtesy of the Moravian Church]

A view of old London from Blackheath, 1776.
Part of the heath is still known as 'Whitefield's Mount'.
[By courtesy of the London Borough of Lewisham]

Credulity, Superstition and Fanaticism by William Hogarth.

This picture graphically and ruthlessly portrays the idea that wild emotionalism was the chief characteristic of early Methodism. It shows Whitefield, as the foremost figure of the movement, vociferating from a high pulpit. His shouting has cracked the sounding board above his head: his wig falls back to reveal the shaven head of a Jesuit and the parting of his gown shows a clown's suit underneath. His suggestion that he wanted his Tabernacle to be 'a soul trap' is changed to read 'St Money Trap'; he dangles Mother Goose in his right hand and the devil in his left, and on the pulpit is his text, 'I speak as a fool'. To his left is a *Scale of Vociferation* (suspended from an open mouth with 'Blood, Blood, Blood' inside it) which ascends from 'Natural Tone' to 'Bull Roar'. Below it there stands a thermometer of the emotions (resting on two books, *Wesley's Sermons* and *Glanvill on Witches*) and nearby is The Poor Box which is actually a mouse trap. Below the pulpit an amorous youth removes the attention of a young lady from her concern about 'Feasting on Jesus' represented in the partly eaten statuette of Christ. The curate in the reading desk is a preacher of scandalous life (he has no connection whatsoever with Whitefield) and his wings are merely duck's wings. Below the reading desk sits a boot-black boy who indicates his repentance by coughing up a stream of stolen hob nails. In the left foreground lies a Mrs Crofts, a woman who won great notoriety for herself and deceived the medical profession of those times by claiming to have given birth on three or four occasions to rabbits. She also was in no way associated with the revival. Behind her, a Jew calmly sacrifices an insect and looks in wonderment on the excitement of the pulpit. Near the left rear of the picture stands John Wesley; he points a frenzied individual to the overhead 'New and Correct Globe of Hell', which marks the locations of the Molten Lead Lake, Pitch and Tar River, the Bottomless Pit, the Horrid Zone, Brimstone Ocean and Eternal Damnation Gulf. Wesley is surrounded by hysterical people, one of whom also puts a figure of Christ to her mouth, attempting to 'Feast on Jesus'. At the window stands a Turk, placidly smoking his pipe and thanking Allah he is not a Christian.

This was Hogarth's second form of this picture. In the earlier one, entitled *Enthusiasm Delineated*, Wesley, who had not yet gained prominence, was not shown. But in place of the basket at the boot-black's left hand, Hogarth placed a rough dog with its mouth widely open, and around its neck was a heavy collar bearing the name 'Whitefield'. Hogarth's concept of Whitefield, as thus revealed, was held also by others of his circle – such men as Sir Joshua Reynolds, Oliver Goldsmith and Samuel Johnson.

Blendon Hall, Kent.
An early nineteenth-century print of a situation familiar to Whitefield through his friendship with the Delamottes; the building shown was not erected, however, until 1763, by which time the family had left Blendon.

Hanham Mount, Kingswood, Bristol, scene of some of Whitefield's most memorable open-air meetings, when colliers listened 'with tears making white channels down their coal-grimed faces'.

John Cennick, one of Whitefield's closest friends and, at one time, his chief assistant.

[By courtesy of the Moravian Church]

Howell Harris. Copy of original print issued by Nathan Hughes.

[By courtesy of the Brecknock Society]

Tennent Church, Freehold, New Jersey.

Old Court-House, Philadelphia. When Whitefield preached to a great throng from the balcony of this building on his first visit to Pennsylvania, Benjamin Franklin walked from the building to as far as his voice could be heard; then, estimating the size of the crowd on the basis of two square feet for each person, he reckoned the number to be so large that he was henceforth reconciled to the newspaper accounts of Whitefield's preaching in England to 25,000 and 30,000.

Plan and Elevation of the Present and Intended Buildings
Georgia ORPHAN HOUSE & Academy

Salt Water Creeke

Landing

The Orphan House, Georgia.

The Whitefield House, Nazareth, Pennsylvania. The building was planned and the foundations laid by Whitefield in 1740; *it was then purchased by the Moravians.*

22

Charles Wesley becomes an Open-air Preacher

As a further preparation for the carrying on of the work during his absence Whitefield took steps to thrust out Charles Wesley also into the open-air ministry, and, in turn, into the leadership of it in London. At the time, Charles was conducting a busy ministry in the Societies and was exerting a strong personal influence among some of the well-to-do Fetter Lane people. In this kind of activity he was happy, but the labour of preaching to the surging crowds in Moorfields and Kennington – this was a responsibility of a totally different nature and one which he was not ready to accept.

Accordingly, Whitefield sought to press him into the task. In order to accustom him to the sight of so many hearers, he had him stand with him, when possible, before his open-air congregations. 'I attended G. Whitefield to Blackheath', says Charles of such an occasion, 'He preached in the rain to many listening sinners.'[1]

A few days later Charles visited a country district and while there made his own first attempt. 'Franklyn, a farmer, invited me', he writes, 'to preach in his field. I did so to about five hundred on "Repent, for the kingdom of heaven is at hand". I returned to the house rejoicing.'[2]

But after returning to London Charles hesitated to take the momentous step there, and was the object of Whitefield's continuing persuasions. Moreover, he saw Whitefield thrust out his brother John, who was paying a short visit to the city, into the field preaching there as he had in Bristol,[3] and this could not but have increased Charles's certainty that he too must soon enter

[1] Charles Wesley's *Journal*, May 16, 1739.
[2] *Ibid*, May 29.
[3] John Wesley's *Journal*, Vol 2, *p* 220.

upon it. Yet he was still reluctant, for it meant a deep self-renunciation and a fearful burden of labour, and, for a person of so sensitive a nature and such strong Church principles, the decision was a harrowing one.

But Whitefield would not brook a long delay and finally informed Charles that he expected him to preach the following Sunday morning to his own regular congregation which would be waiting for him at Moorfields.

My inward conflict continued [says Charles]. I perceived it was the fear of man, and that by preaching in the field next Sunday as George Whitefield urges me, I shall break down the bridge, and become desperate. I retired and prayed . . . for Christ's sake and the Gospel's. I was somewhat less burdened; yet could not be quite easy till I gave up all.[1]

Whitefield understood his man, however, and knew that since he was a Wesley, he could not long remain in fear of any situation. And as he expected, Charles did become desperate and broke down the bridge that Sunday, recording,

I prayed, and went forth in the name of Jesus Christ. I found near ten thousand helpless sinners waiting for the Word, in Moorfields. I invited them in my Master's words, as well as name, 'Come unto me, all ye that travail and are heavy laden, and I will give you rest'. The Lord was with me, even me, His meanest messenger, according to His promise . . . My load was gone, and all my doubts and scruples. God shone upon my path, and I knew this was His will concerning me.[2]

Two weeks later Charles stepped fully into Whitefield's regular Sunday labours, preaching to 'near ten thousand' at Moorfields in the morning, and to 'double that number' at Kennington in the evening. 'The Lord Almighty bowed their hearts before Him', he exclaimed. But the struggle was not over by any means, for, as we have seen in the experience of Whitefield and of John, Charles also found need to adjust himself to this life of extraordinary labour and to the new measure of success and popularity which it brought. He wrote,

I never till now knew the strength of temptation and the energy of sin. Who that conferred with flesh and blood would covet great

[1] Charles Wesley's *Journal* June 23.	[2] *Ibid*, June 24.

success? I live in a continual storm. My soul is always in my hand. The enemy thrusts sore at me, that I may fall, and a worse enemy than the devil is my own heart.[1]

Too well pleased with my success, which brought upon me the buffetings of Satan.[2]

Charles also reported his difficulties in a letter to William Seward, saying,

I preached yesterday to more than ten thousand hearers; am so buffeted, both before and after, that, was I not forcibly detained, I should fly from every human face. If God does make a way for me to escape, I shall not easily be brought back again.[3]

As the time drew near for Whitefield's departure, Charles felt he should inform him, that he was uneasy about the responsibility which he had thrust upon him.

I am continually tempted to leave off preaching, and hide myself like J. Hutchings [he wrote]. I should then be freer from temptation, and at leisure to attend my own improvement. God continues to work *by* me, but not *in* me, that I can perceive. Do not reckon upon me, my brother, in the work God is doing, for I cannot expect He should long employ one who is ever longing and murmuring to be discharged. I rejoice in your success, and pray for its increase a thousandfold.[4]

But Charles's retreat was only in words. He continued the ministry in the fields and daily increased in activity and power. He won the affection of the people: 'I could hardly get from them', he wrote on one occasion. The blessing of God was on his labours too, and he could say, 'Every day we hear of more and more convinced or pardoned'.

Years later, as he looked back upon the days when he had first undertaken the open-air work, he wrote, in lines addressed to Whitefield,

Nor did I linger at my friend's desire,
To tempt the furnace and abide the fire;
When suddenly sent forth, from the highways
I called poor outcasts to the feast of grace;

[1] *Ibid,* July 22.
[2] *Ibid,* August 7.
[3] *Ibid,* August 13.
[4] *Ibid,* August 10.

Urged to pursue the work by thee begun,
Through good and ill report, I still rushed on,
Nor felt the fire of popular applause,
Nor feared the torturing flame in such a glorious cause.[1]

*

Having found no one to assume the Gloucester work, Whitefield had Charles make a preaching tour of the area. He wrote to his friend Harris the bookseller and asked him to 'have Mr Cole and other dear friends appoint places'.[2] One place was a field belonging to Richard Whitefield and Charles's report of his meeting there indicates how tiring the outdoor ministry could be. 'For near an hour and a half', he wrote, 'God gave me voice and strength to exhort about two thousand sinners to repent and believe the Gospel. My voice and strength failed together; neither do I want them when my work is done.'[3]

The new measure of self-renunciation which the open-air ministry had brought to Charles was vividly illustrated at this time. During their Oxford days John and Charles had frequently visited two cultured families who lived near Gloucester, the Granvilles and the Kirkhams. They had been friends particularly with the young ladies in these homes, enjoying with them music, dancing and poetry. But Charles reports that, during this preaching tour:

An old acquaintance (Mrs Kirkham) stood in my way, and challenged me, 'What, Mr Wesley, is it you I see? Is it possible that you who can preach at Christ Church, St Mary's, &c., should come hither after a mob?' I cut her short with, 'The work which my Master giveth me, must I not do it?' and went to my mob, or (to put it in the Pharisees' phrase) this people which is accursed. Thousands heard me gladly, while I told them their privilege of the Holy Ghost, the Comforter, and exhorted them to come for Him to Christ as poor lost sinners. I continued my discourse till night.[4]

Charles went on to Bristol and we notice some of his exploits there:

[1] *The Poetical Works of John and Charles Wesley*, Vol 5, *p* 69.
[2] Whitefield's *Works*, Vol 1, *p* 54.
[3] Charles Wesley's *Journal*, August 25, 1739.
[4] *Ibid.*

September 16th. I preached at the bowling-green, to (by computation) six thousand people. Before I began, and after, the enemy raged exceedingly. A troop of his children, soldiers and polite gentlemen had taken possession of a corner of the green, and roared like their brethren, the two Gergesenes, before the devils were sent into the civiler swine. They provoked the spirit of jealousy to lift up a standard against them. I never felt such a power before, and promised the people that they should feel it too; for I saw God had a great work to do among us by Satan's opposition. I lifted up my voice like a trumpet, and in a few minutes drove him out of the field. For above an hour I preached the Gospel with extraordinary power . . .

Sat., September 22 . . . In the bowling-green I showed the nature and life of faith from Gal. 2. 20, and then justification by faith alone at the Hall.[1] Two clergymen were present. I proved from Scripture and our own Church, that all were Papists, Pharisees, Antichrists and accursed, who brought any other doctrine. Some of my hearers were forced to turn their backs.

Fri., September 28th. Christianity flourishes under the cross. None who follow after Christ want that badge of discipleship. Wives and children are beaten, and turned out of doors; and the persecutors are the complainers. It is always the lamb that troubles the water. Every Sunday damnation is denounced against all that hear us Papists, us Jesuits, us seducers, us bringers in of the Pretender. The clergy murmur aloud at the number of communicants and threaten to repel them; yet will not the world bear that we should talk of persecution. No; for the world is Christian now, and the offence of the cross ceased. Alas! what would they further? Some lose their bread, some their habitations! one suffers stripes, another confinement. Doubtless they will find some other name for it, when they do God service by killing us.

Fri., October 26. I baptized Mr Wiggington in the river by Baptist-Mills; and went on my way rejoicing.[2]

Charles prosecuted the open-air ministry with constant zeal, and suffered frequent and bitter opposition. Yet though the enemy raged Charles met the onslaughts with unflinching courage. John had written a hymn that served as something of a battle song in such emergencies, and Charles' *Journal* entries (quaint, artless and marked by a wry humour) more than once

[1] This was Weaver's Hall, which the Wesleys continued to use.

[2] Charles Wesley's *Journal,* entries of dates indicated, 1739. Four days later Charles wrote to the Bishop of Bristol giving him the names of seven persons who had applied to him for baptism, and stating, 'They choose likewise to be baptized by immersion'. Entry of Oct. 30.

report that when sorely pressed by the foe he 'gave forth with' it:

Shall I, for fear of feeble man,
The Spirit's course in me restrain?
Or, undismayed, in deed and word
Be a true witness for my Lord?

No; let man rage! since Thou wilt spread
Thy shadowing wings around my head:
Since in all pain Thy tender love
Will still my sweet refreshment prove.

The love of Christ does me constrain
To seek the wandering souls of men;
With cries, entreaties, tears, to save,
To snatch them from the gaping grave.

For this let men revile my name,
No cross I shun, I fear no shame;
All hail reproach, and welcome pain,
Only Thy terrors, Lord, restrain.

Give me Thy strength, O God of power,
Then let winds blow or thunders roar,
Thy faithful witness will I be–
'Tis fix'd! I can do all through Thee!

Charles became an open-air preacher of great power. He was more oratorical and dramatic than his brother, and apparently was second only to Whitefield, Rowland and perhaps Cennick in these gifts. A report by one of his hearers has come down to us:

I found him, standing on a table-board in an erect posture, with his hands and eyes lifted up to heaven in prayer; he prayed with uncommon fervency, fluency, and variety of proper expressions. He then preached about an hour in such a manner as I scarce ever heard any man preach. Though I have heard many a finer sermon, according to the common taste ... I never heard any man discover such evident signs of a vehement desire, or labour so earnestly to convince his hearers that they were all by nature in a sinful, lost, undone state ... He showed how great a change a faith in Christ would produce in the whole man ...

With uncommon fervour he acquitted himself as an ambassador of Christ, beseeching them in His name, and praying them in His stead to be reconciled to God. And although he used no notes nor had anything in his hand but a Bible, yet he delivered his thoughts in a rich, copious variety of expression, and with so much propriety, that I could not observe anything incoherent or inanimate through the whole performance.[1]

This was Charles Wesley as an open-air preacher. He had once introduced Whitefield to the Holy Club, but Whitefield had now led him into the free ministry, and, to the work of preaching Christ in the fields Charles devoted himself with heroic courage and tireless zeal throughout much of the remainder of his life. His ministry was marked by spiritual power and rich success, and had immeasurable effect on the whole course of the Wesleyan section of Methodism.

[1] This statement was made by Joseph Williams of Kidderminster; Tyerman's *Wesley*, Vol 1, *pp* 253–4.

Whitefield must be allowed to occupy the luminous centre upon the field of Methodism.

ISAAC TAYLOR
Wesley and Methodism

23

The Methodist Movement in 1739

As Whitefield's days in England drew toward their close it was evident that his ministry had borne very extensive fruits. And he was quick to acknowledge their source, saying, 'This is the Lord's doing! To Him be all the glory!' and 'God has made Himself a willing people in the day of His power!'[1]

Nevertheless, this extraordinary blessing also demonstrated the value of the evangelistic methods that Whitefield had employed.

We have seen his basic practice. He knew nothing of pronouncing a mere outward profession to be conversion, but on the contrary, he looked for a deep and abiding work of the Spirit of God within the heart. This led, in turn, to two further elements of his ministry which we must notice.

The first was an unusual practice which sprang up among his hearers. Many persons among his congregations came under such a deep conviction of sin that, in their yearning for relief, they wrote notes (bills, Whitefield calls them) and passed them to him as he preached. These brought the individual to his attention by name, implored a place in his prayers and often sought an opportunity to talk to him personally. This was a spontaneous act. Whitefield did not ask for it, but he manifestly rejoiced in it, making such reports as, 'The bills that are sent to me plainly prove that God has worked on numbers of souls',[2] and 'I do not know how many have come to me under strong convictions, and what numbers of bills I have received from persons seeking Christ.'[3]

A second of Whitefield's methods was noticeable in his itinerant

[1] *Journals, pp* 295, 325. [2] *Ibid, p* 316. [3] *Ibid, p* 317.

ministry. When he paid a first visit to any community, he looked upon it as a time particularly for the sowing of seed. He expected that it would then be watered by the Spirit of God, and, whenever possible, he returned later to reap the harvest. For instance, four weeks after his first visit to Hertford, he went back there again. 'I was invited', he says, 'by several pressing letters which declared how God had worked by my ministry when I was there last . . . I preached to nearly three thousand people. Many came to me under strong convictions of their fallen estate . . . Many I heard of besides, who had been much worked upon by my preaching; several Christian families, I find, had been comforted and such immediate effects produced that I could not help rejoicing exceedingly.'[1] Though during these months in London he preached regularly at Moorfields, Kennington and Blackheath, he frequently ministered at other places too, and at these his method was this of *preach and return, preach and return*. This also remained the pattern on which he conducted his itinerant ministry (and this was the large proportion of his entire work) throughout the remainder of his life.

The fruits of this ministry, as had those of 1737, proved to be of a thorough and abiding nature. Though Whitefield did not count converts, it is evident that they were numerous and his *Journals* and letters abound with such reports as, 'Was busied all morning in directing those to believe in Jesus Christ, who came asking me what they should do to be saved'.[2] 'Oh, what a sudden alteration does this foolishness of preaching make in the most obstinate hearts! It is but for God to speak the word and the lion is turned into a lamb!'[3] '. . . it would be endless to recount how many come after preaching under strong convictions of their lost estate. God has begun, God will carry on the good work in their souls.'[4] Without doubt, the persons thus influenced amounted to hundreds in Bristol, the same in Gloucester and still more in London, and in the areas surrounding these cities, there were scores or hundreds more.

This work, however, proved to be something more than spiritual results in the hearts of the host of individuals. Here was a work which, beside being lasting, possessed a certain unity – a

[1] *Ibid*, *pp* 289–90. [2] *Ibid*, *p* 316. [3] *Ibid*, *p* 306. [4] *Ibid*, *p* 316.

unity which arose from the common allegiance of its people to evangelical doctrine and their common esteem for Whitefield. Here was a work which, in this wide three-point area of southern England was so definite and abiding as to constitute a religious movement.

As was but to be expected, outsiders soon found names by which to designate this movement and its people. Because of their relationship to Whitefield the people were sometimes called 'Whitefieldites'. But Whitefield himself used another term. Ever since his days at Oxford he had referred to himself as a 'Methodist', having used the word in his *Diary*, his *Journals* and his sermons, and, we may be sure, in private conversation too. Moreover, he applied it not only to himself, but to others also who were of the same beliefs, and by his example it was taken up by the public. As a result his followers were called 'Methodists' and the movement was known as 'Methodism'.

Of this movement Whitefield was the central figure. This is manifest, of course, in the general facts of his career, with which we have been familiarizing ourselves. But it is also manifest in several statements that have come down from those times and which indicate that among his contemporaries he was regarded as both the leader and founder of the movement – the leader and founder of Methodism.

For instance, the Countess of Hertford, writing in 1739 to the Countess of Pomfret who was then on the Continent, said:

> I do not know whether you have heard of our new sect who call themselves Methodists. There is one Whitefield at the head of them – a young man under five and twenty.[1]

In Tindal's *Continuation of Rapin's History, Up to the Present Time* (1763), we read of '. . . one Whitefield, a young clergyman, the founder of a set of fanatics under the name of Methodists', and in his report of the events of 1739 Tindal asserts:

> This year was distinguished by the institution of a set of fanatics under the name of Methodists, of which one Whitefield, a young clergyman, was the founder . . . Striking in with the common fanatical jargon and practices of enthusiasm, he soon found himself at the head of such

[1] Huntingdon, *op cit*, Vol 1, *p* 197.

a number of disciples as might have been dangerous to the public repose, had they attempted to disturb it.[1]

The *St James Evening Post* reported: 'There is at Hamburg a new set of Methodists, much like our Whitefieldites'. A false report of Whitefield's death, published in the *Gentleman's Magazine* in 1748, designated him, 'Whitefield, the founder of the Methodists'.[2] *An Essay on the Character of Methodism,* written in 1781, made mention of '. . . pure METHODISM, as it subsisted under its founder WHITEFIELD, and some of his immediate followers'.[3]

Those who made printed attack on the Revival usually identified Methodism with Whitefield and vice versa. This is seen in the following titles (already noticed) which appeared in 1739: *The Methodists: An Humorous Burlesque Poem Addressed to Mr Whitefield and his Followers, An Expostulatory Letter to Mr Whitefield and the Rest of his Brethren, the Methodists,* and *The Life and Adventures of that Arch-Methodist, Mr G. Wh.t.fi.ld.*

Several writers of later date have pointed out that 'in the contemporary accounts of the Methodists' ('the *Letters of Horace Walpole* and literature of that stamp', says Canon Overton)[4] Whitefield is spoken of as the supreme figure. A present-day Methodist scholar makes the statement:

> A scrutiny of the contemporary records will reveal that in the eighteenth century itself the name of Whitefield figures most prominently of all; . . . it is unquestionable that in the popular view Whitefield was regarded as the primate of the new movement and even as the founder of Methodism.[5]

Moreover, while Whitefield had long used the word 'Methodist', the Wesleys had seldom employed it in reference to themselves. At Oxford John had spoken of the Holy Club men, not as 'Methodists', but as 'our Company', and though the term 'Methodist' came into wide usage with Whitefield's rise to fame in 1737, the Wesleys still did not take up with it. In December of 1738 Charles made the following report:

[1] *Tindal's Continuation of Rapin's History*, Vol 5, *p* 191.
[2] *The Gentleman's Magazine*, May 1748.
[3] *An Essay on the Character of Methodism*, anon. (Cambridge, 1781).
[4] J. H. Overton, *The Evangelical Revival in the Eighteenth Century* (London, 1886), *p* 29.
[5] A. Skevington Wood, *op cit*, *p* 79.

December 21 (1738). At St Antholin's the clerk asked me my name, and said, 'Dr Venn has forbidden any Methodist to preach. Do you call yourself a Methodist?' 'I do not: the world may call me what they please.' 'Well, sir,' said he, 'it is pity the people should go away without preaching. You may preach.'[1]

John's first recorded use of the word in the evangelical sense, as applied to himself, is undoubtedly that of July 31, 1739. Wishing then to enter the controversy which had arisen around Whitefield, he wrote a reply to Dr Stebbing and found it necessary to state in his opening sentence, 'You charge me (for I am called a *Methodist*, and consequently included within your charge) . . .'[2]

*

Whitefield revealed a wide and definite concept of this movement.

He had, of course, not the slightest thought of forming a new denomination. 'Methodism' was simply a term that designated an adherence to evangelical doctrine and a fervent manner of life, and was used then in much the same way as 'evangelical' is used to-day. Although the vast majority of the Methodist people were members of the Church of England, the public applied the term also to those others (Independents, Baptists and Presbyterians) who were noticeably evangelical and showed favour towards the work of the revival.

But Whitefield thought of this movement as particularly within the Church of England. He believed that the doctrines he taught were simply those of her *Articles* and, having convinced himself (whether rightly or wrongly) that his open-air and itinerant proceedings were not contrary to her laws, he sought to induce other members of the clergy to believe the same things and perform the same work. Wherever he had gone he had found some of them who were favourable to his message and who welcomed him to their pulpits and he strove to lead such men forth from what he considered the indolence of preaching merely in the churches and on Sundays, into a ministry which would see them declaring the Gospel in the fields and on every day of the week.

On one occasion Whitefield had three of these men stand with him while he conducted a great open-air meeting, thus identifying

[1] Charles Wesley's *Journal*, Dec. 21, 1738.

[2] John Wesley's *Journal*, Vol 2, *p* 249.

them with his work and accustoming them to the sight of a large crowd out of doors. He frequently wrote into his letters and *Journals* his desire that God would raise up other men who also would undertake the life of fervent evangelism, both in the churches and in the fields. His prayer, 'Lord of the harvest, send forth, we beseech Thee, more labourers into Thy harvest',[1] is typical of many such expressions that appear in his *Journals* and letters. When about to leave England he wrote:

> I cannot but finish this part of my Journal with a word of exhortation to my dear brethren, whoever they are, whom God shall stir up to go forth into the highways and hedges, into the lanes and streets, to compel poor sinners to come in . . . Oh, my brethren, have compassion on our dear Lord's Church which He has purchased with His own blood. Suffer none of them to be as sheep having no shepherd, or with worse than none, those blind leaders of the blind who let them perish for lack of knowledge.[2]

This endeavour to raise up an evangelical ministry in the national Church remained one of Whitefield's principal purposes throughout life. Hand in hand with his denunciations of an unconverted ministry there went his constant encouragement of those who were sound in the evangelical faith, and, as the narrative of his career progresses, we shall see these efforts gradually resulting in the formation of a strong evangelical party within the Church of England.

Whitefield saw this work, however, as extending also to other denominations and other lands. He came into friendly relations with such Independents as Isaac Watts and Philip Doddridge, and by this time, though apparently still refusing to regard Baptist ordination as valid, he had begun to speak highly of certain Baptist pastors and people whom he met. His Presbyterian associations consisted chiefly of his correspondence with the Erskine brothers in Scotland, and though there had long been bitterness between the English Church and the Scottish, of his relation with Ralph Erskine Whitefield said, 'Some may be offended at my corresponding with him, but I dare not but confess my Lord's disciples'.[3] After receiving a letter from Ebenezer Erskine which reported an out-door audience of fourteen thousand, he exclaimed, 'Blessed be God! there are other

[1] *Journals*, *p* 277. [2] *Ibid*, *p* 317. [3] *Ibid*, *p* 312.

field preachers in the world besides myself!'[1] Moreover, in reference to these men in Scotland and to others in Wales and America whom he knew to be fervent in the Gospel, he said, 'Oh, that all who are truly spiritual knew one another!' In this and similar utterances, he manifested his vision of a fellowship which would link together the several evangelical workers in the various lands.

There can be no doubt that Whitefield thought of this inter-denominational and international fellowship as made possible by a basic theological agreement. He and Harris had found that because of the Calvinistic nature of the views that they each held, they could work in full harmony. Such views were also held with great tenacity and understanding by the Scottish men, and it is highly probable that Whitefield had already learned that the vast majority of the American ministers were of the same mind. He envisioned a oneness arising from this common doctrinal position, and letters which came later from himself and Harris reveal that they both, knowing the theological uncertainty that Wesley had manifested even after the Aldersgate Street experience of 1738, hoped that he too would arrive at the same position.

*

We have seen, however, that within the revival movement in England, another movement – that of John Wesley at Bristol – was already forming. Influenced by his able preaching, his distinctive doctrines and the emotional phenomenon, several people of the Societies had become his ardent followers and, in turn, Wesley took steps to link them more closely to one another and to himself. That is, when he had been in Bristol but five and a half weeks, he made preparations to erect a new building which would be a headquarters for his work and a centre for the gathering of his people.

> We took possession [he writes], of a piece of ground near St James's Churchyard in the Horsefair, where it was designed to build a room large enough to contain both the Societies of Nicholas and Baldwin Streets . . .[2]

This action involved Wesley in considerable responsibility. At first he chose eleven feoffees to bear the expense and direction of

[1] *Ibid*, *p* 275. [2] John Wesley's *Journal*, Vol 2, *p* 194.

this work, but, under persuasion, 'from friends in London, Mr Whitefield in particular', he discharged the feoffees and took everything in his own name. 'Money', he states, 'I had not', nor was he yet experienced in the task of receiving large offerings from the congregations. Nevertheless, he 'articled to pay the workmen about 160 pounds as soon as (the work was) finished',[1] and within twenty-four days the construction was sufficiently advanced for him to report, 'We met in the shell of our new society-room'.[2]

But though Wesley had built the New Room with the purpose of uniting the Societies of Nicholas and Baldwin Streets and making the Room the meeting place of the united body, he did not attempt to lead them in this step of unification by himself. Among a people who had recently been described as 'deeply prejudiced' in favour of predestination he doubtless faced considerable opposition, and therefore needed Whitefield's help in order to bring this union about.

Providentially, Whitefield suffered a change of plans which enabled him to be of this assistance to his friend. After he had been ready for some days to set sail, he received word that the British government, fearing an outbreak of war with Spain, had placed an embargo on shipping. With his time in England thus extended he had opportunity to visit the other two centres of the work, Gloucester and Bristol, and while at the latter could help in uniting the two Societies.

His last moments in London, before starting out on this trip, were spent at Hutton's *Bible and Sun.* John Byrom happened to be in the shop at the time and wrote:

> While we were there, there came in the so-much-talked-about Mr Whitefield, and company with him. He stayed about a quarter of an hour, taking leave of his friends, and then the Cirencester coach called and he went to Gloucestershire therein. He has a world of people that like him. I should have liked to satisfy my curiosity a little if he had not been in haste.[3]

Whitefield spent a week of busy ministry in and around Gloucester. The work in this area posed a special problem for him,

[1] John Wesley's *Letters*, Vol 1, *p* 311. [2] John Wesley's *Journal*, Vol 2, *p* 208.
[3] Byrom, *op cit*, Vol 2, *p* 249.

for he needed to find a man who would come and take it over, but no such person seemed available.

While at Gloucester Whitefield received further information about Wesley's sermon against predestination and about other divisive actions he was taking at Bristol. Distressed by the news he wrote to Wesley as follows:

Gloucester, July 2, 1739

HONOURED SIR,

I confess my spirit has been of late sharpened on account of some of your proceedings; my heart has been quite broken within me. I have been grieved from my soul, knowing what a dilemma I am reduced to. How shall I tell the Dissenters I do not approve of their doctrines, without wronging my own soul? How shall I tell them I do, without contradicting my honoured friend, whom I desire to love as my own soul? Lord, for Thine infinite mercy's sake, direct me so to act, as neither to injure myself nor my friend!

Is it true, honoured Sir, that Brother Stock is excluded the Society because he holds predestination? If so, is it right? Would Jesus Christ have done so? . . .

Dear, honoured Sir, if you have any regard for the peace of the church, keep in your sermon on predestination. But you have cast a lot! Oh! my heart, in the midst of my body, is like melted wax. The Lord direct us all!

Indeed, I desire you all the success you can wish for. May you increase, though I decrease! I would willingly wash your feet. God is with us mightily. I have just now written to the bishop.

Oh, wrestle, wrestle, honoured Sir, in prayer, that not the least alienation of affection may be between you and your obedient son and servant in Christ,

George Whitefield.[1]

After another few days Whitefield went on to Bristol. Many of the Bristol people, learning that he was approaching, went out some distance to meet him and the welcoming crowd increased steadily as it drew near to the city. 'The bells were rung, unknown to me', says Whitefield, 'and I was received as an angel of God.'[2] This excitement continued throughout his stay there, and great throngs assembled to hear him whenever he preached. It was like

[1] Tyerman's *Wesley*, Vol 1, *p* 312. [2] *Journals*, *p* 299.

the days of his former ministry over again: six thousand at Baptist Mills, ten thousand on the Bowling Green and twenty thousand at Rose Green – such crowds as had not been seen since his departure. On these occasions Wesley accompanied him, and Whitefield wrote into his *Journals* the evidences of Wesley's accomplishments, and did so with his usual generosity of commendation.

Whitefield also reported, 'I had a useful conference about many things with my honoured friend, Mr John Wesley,'[1] and, in the light of the above letter (and the other like it, noticed earlier)[2] we may be sure that they discussed the matters which were beginning to divide them. Moreover, they manifestly reached an agreement, for Whitefield twice uses the expression, 'We settled some affairs',[3] and on the strength of the conference he took steps to give important advancement to Wesley's work.

The steps he took were these:

The first: the use of his influence in uniting the Nicholas and Baldwin Street Societies. He wrote, 'My brother Wesley and I . . . united the two leading Societies together'.[4] With this action the *New Room* became the meeting place of these United Societies, Wesley's personal headquarters and the recognized centre of his work.

The *second* step related to the raising of money for the Kingswood school. For this project Whitefield had already received from the colliers 'above 20 pounds in money and above 40 pounds in subscriptions', plus the promise of their labour and such materials as they might have. But he agreed to bear further responsibility and, accordingly, all the offerings he received during the rest of his time in England were given to the Kingswood School. Without doubt, these offerings, and the other moneys he raised for this project, were more than enough to defray its total costs.[5]

[1] *Ibid.*
[2] *Pp* 315, 319.
[3] *Journals, pp* 299 and 303.
[4] *Ibid, p* 303.
[5] Howell Harris, writing after the breach between Wesley and Whitefield, says, 'Mr Whitefield sent £200 or £250 toward the Houses & is now turned out of them, when they [the Wesleys] had none toward them too but on his account. O ungratitude!' (*Bathafarn, op cit,* Vol 9 (1954) *p* 35). Wesley implies that the New Room cost £160, and the school house probably cost no more. This matter, with the amounts of Whitefield's offerings, will be presented later.

The *third* step was the introduction of Wesley to Whitefield's congregations in and around Gloucester. Whitefield had found no one to take over this work and, since it was not far from Bristol, he arranged that Wesley should oversee both places. Accordingly, they went together to Gloucester, where, on the following Sunday morning, Whitefield introduced Wesley to his congregation of 'about seven thousand souls'. He left John to minister to this company while he himself went on to preach at adjacent towns and closed the day with a great crowd of 20,000 at Hampton Common. At each place he recommended his honoured friend, instituted him as his successor and, when the day was done, he wrote, 'Their souls were much rejoiced when I told them that Mr John Wesley intended to come after, to feed them. Lord, grant he may be preferred before me wherever he goes.'[1]

These steps were of exceptional importance in the life of Wesley. The uniting of the two societies marked the beginning of his movement as an organized entity. This, however, he did not call *Methodism* but the *United Society*. Before many more months had passed he extended his organization to London and formed his second *United Society* there, and there can be no doubt that he had conceived the idea of extending this activity, uniting other Societies wherever possible.

The introduction of Wesley to the people at Gloucester completed Whitefield's threefold projection of him into his work. With the recommendation at Bristol, London and Gloucester, Whitefield had placed him in prominence before the whole revival movement in England and had given him the advantage of congregations such as few men had ever experienced. He had set Wesley upon his life's work – a work which, as is well known, he prosecuted with tireless zeal and consummate skill for more than half a century.

*

Before Whitefield could sail for America, however, he found himself thrust into another episode of controversy.

Upon returning to London he learned that the embargo was lifted, and while holding farewell services in Moorfields, Kenning-

[1] *Journals, p* 305.

ton and Blackheath was confronted with a highly influential pamphlet against him. This was *A Pastoral Letter by Way of Caution against Lukewarmness on the One Hand and Enthusiasm on the Other,* and the writer was none other than Dr Edmund Gibson, the Bishop of London.

The letter was a work of fifty-five pages, thirty-six of which warned the reader regarding Whitefield's activities. There were nine charges: the first seven accused him of claiming divine inspiration, speaking of himself under the character of the Apostles, professing the spirit of prophecy, and such like. The eighth asserted that, in his doctrine of regeneration, he was propagating a new Gospel; and the ninth stated that, in making his censorious remarks about the clergy, he was 'casting unworthy reflections upon them'.

To these charges Whitefield deemed it necessary to reply. The Bishop was a venerable figure of seventy years, a scholar and a man of manifest earnestness and public esteem. He wrote with authority, his language was restrained and he supported his statements with no less than ninety quotations from Whitefield's *Journals*.

At the time the *Letter* was published, Whitefield had but four or five days before setting sail and, needing a quiet place in which to write a reply, returned to his 'sweet retreat' at the Delamotte home.

But his hope of finding at Blendon Hall the time and solitude for concentrated effort proved largely vain. Arriving on the Saturday morning he devoted himself to the task, only to have to leave it in the afternoon for a great meeting at Blackheath. But the aftermath of the meeting became an event we have noticed: hundreds of his people followed him back to Blendon and stayed on the grounds all night. After preaching to them early in the morning, attending Bexley Church and preaching in Mr Delamotte's yard in the afternoon, he went again to Blackheath and conducted a farewell service of which he says, 'Thousands burst into tears. I continued my discourse till nearly dark.'[1] He spent the night at Lewisham, but spoke of bodily weakness and complained of 'inward trials'. Of the following day (his last in England for nearly two years) he reports: 'Rose early and

[1] *Journals*, p 325.

hastened to Blendon. Finished and sent to the press my answer to his lordship's Pastoral Letter.'[1] Thus, this week-end, with its services, its travel, its crowds and its weariness, represented his attempt to find seclusion in order to perform this important task.

None the less, his *Answer* was an effective one. Point by point he dealt with the Bishop's charges that he made claim to inspiration, etc., respectfully showing that his lordship had read into his statements connotations which he did not intend. He defended his open-air ministry and showed that the doctrine of the new birth was simply that of the Scriptures and of the *Articles* of the Church. But when he came to the accusation that he 'cast unworthy reflections on the clergy', he admitted everything except the word 'unworthy', and, after insisting that many of the ministers were deserving of his terms, 'indolent, earthly-minded and pleasure-taking', he turned the responsibility back upon the Bishop. 'Surely your lordship will not stand up in their defence', he challenged. 'No! I hope your lordship will not fail to rebuke them sharply.'[2]

Tyerman says of the *Answer*:

> It is one of the smartest productions of his pen; its style firm, but quiet and respectful; its language, pure, pointed, forcible and without the diffusiveness which often characterized his writings . . . It is only fair to add that he honestly meets all the charges brought against him, and that, upon the whole, his *Answer* is complete and victorious.[3]

But Whitefield did not stay in England long enough to see his *Answer* in print. When he had finished writing it on the Monday morning, he dined with the Delamotte family, 'took leave', he says, 'of my dear weeping friends',[4] and hastened to Gravesend where his vessel, the *Elizabeth*, was awaiting him and his party.

*

It was but eight months since Whitefield had returned from America and, during the six of them which he had spent in the open air, he had preached (according to his own figures) to nearly two million persons. In his bold step into the fields he had

[1] *Ibid, p* 326.
[2] 'An Answer to the Bishop of London's Pastoral Letter', Whitefield's *Works,* Vol 4, *p* 16.
[3] Tyerman's *Whitefield*, Vol 1, *p* 293.
[4] *Journals, p* 326.

shaken the weak and timid Christianity of the times and had led the way to an aggressive militancy against sin and unbelief. The Wesleys and others were following his example, the battle was being widely pressed and the forces of righteousness were constantly increasing. He had written, 'I was much pleased to think that religion, which had long been skulking in corners and was almost laughed out of the world, should now begin to appear abroad and shew herself openly at noonday',[1] and he followed this up with, 'Go where you will, religion (either for or against it) is the talk'.[2]

But this rejoicing in the past was conjoined with a vision of the future. Whitefield foresaw a glorious advancement of the movement, and declared:

> I believe the Lord will work a great work upon the earth. Whatever instruments He shall make use of in effecting it, I care not. If Christ be preached, if my dear Lord be glorified, I rejoice, yea, and will rejoice.[3]

Sad to say, his words suggest that he already felt that the subject of human primacy in the movement would be made a matter of importance. Nevertheless, in this assurance of future blessings and this resignation to the supremacy of any instrument whatsoever, he sailed for America.

[1] *Ibid, p* 289. [2] *Works,* Vol 1, *p* 63. [3] *Ibid, p* 59.

Once taught to understand the glorious liberty of Christ's Gospel, Whitefield never turned again to asceticism, legalism, mysticism or strange views of Christian perfection . . . The doctrines of free grace . . . took deep root in his heart and became, as it were, bone of his bone and flesh of his flesh. Of all the little band of Oxford methodists, none seems to have got hold so soon of clear views of Christ's Gospel as he did, and none kept them so unwaveringly to the end.

BISHOP J. C. RYLE
Christian Leaders, 1868

24

The Doctrines of Grace

THE tumult of activity which had been Whitefield's life ashore gave way suddenly as he stepped aboard ship. He appears to have been suffering a considerable measure of physical and nervous exhaustion at the time, and made frequent mention of the tranquillity he began to experience while under sail. 'I went to bed almost forgetful that I had ever been out in the world',[1] is a characteristic statement.

He was taking with him a party of 'eight men, four women, one boy and two children',[2] whom he called his 'family'. Out of the many who had begged to go with him he had accepted these persons, having chosen them with a view to their service at the Orphan House. The women were to serve either as its teachers or its domestics, the children (waifs who had come to Whitefield's attention in England) were to be its first guests, and one of the men – a surgeon and apothecary named Hunter – was to oversee its infirmary. Two of the other men were particularly important to Whitefield: one, a youth named John Syms, was to serve as his secretary, and the other, Captain Gladman, the converted ship's Master,[3] had offered to assist in any way possible. Whitefield said of his 'family', 'Most of them have left good places and are willing freely to spend and be spent for the good of the

[1] *Journal, p* 330.

[2] *Journals, p* 329. Another member of the party was Joseph Periam, a young man who, because of the wholesome change which his conversion had made in his behaviour, had been placed in the Bedlam asylum for the insane, from whence he had been released through the influences of Whitefield and Seward (*ibid, pp* 267–70). He proved a faithful helper in Georgia and on Christmas Day, 1740, Whitefield wrote, 'I married Mr Periam to one of the school mistresses whom I brought out from England'. In 1756 Whitefield added, 'After a few years both died; I now have two of their sons in the Orphan House. They are very promising boys.'

[3] For Gladman's conversion, see *p* 210.

Orphan House'. We may well imagine their excitement as they sailed from their native land and looked forward to a new life in this much-talked-of philanthropic project – a life which was soon to lose its glamour amidst the hardships of the remote and primitive Colony.

*

Despite his attempt to find a quiet relaxation while on board, Whitefield maintained his rigid self-discipline. He arose early and filled his days with labour. He read certain theological books for which he had not had time on land, but he busied himself especially by writing. Being removed from active participation in the revival, he seemed to see it in an enlarged – one might say a panoramic – view, and strove to promote it by the one means available: the use of his pen.

He produced two brief works for publication. One was the autobiographical sketch which has been quoted frequently in the narrative of his boyhood and conversion.[1] The other was a pamphlet entitled *A Letter to the Religious Societies of England.*[2]

In this, as in his *Reply to the Bishop of London*, Whitefield proved that when he took time to do so, he could be an effective writer. The style of the *Letter* is simple and its message practical. He states several reasons why the Societies were sorely needed, commends their efforts and argues their legal rights. He gives instruction as to how their meetings might be improved and exhorts the members to holiness of life. He warns them (probably with thought of Wesley's intentions regarding his *United Societies* in mind) not to let themselves be formed into 'a sect or party', and prays that, 'if ever such designs should be set on foot', they may 'fall to the ground'.[3] On the whole the *Letter*, since it arouses to zeal and yet advocates that it be exercised with prudence, is a reflection of his own spirit.

The *Letter* was printed in England as a pamphlet of twenty-eight pages. Within a year it went through three editions and Whitefield designated all the profits from its sale to the building of the Kingswood School – an important contribution that has

[1] 'A Short Account of God's Dealings with George Whitefield from His Infancy to His Ordination.' *Journals*, *pp* 35–72.

[2] *Works*, Vol 4, *pp* 214–34.

[3] *Ibid*, *p* 27.

seldom been noticed. The *Letter* had also other printings: at least one in Scotland, two in America and two in Wales in the Welsh tongue.

*

But the chief labour of Whitefield's pen was his correspondence. Chafing under his enforced idleness, he poured forth his soul in a flow of personal letters, and the following excerpts reveal something of his vision of the revival and of the leadership therein which God had given him.

In a letter addressed to a friend in England he stated:

I wait with impatience to hear how the work goes on in my absence. I trust that by this time, God has sent forth more labourers into His harvest. I verily believe the right hand of the Lord will not only have the pre-eminence, but will also bring mighty things to pass. Oh, how do I long to see bigotry and party zeal taken away and all the Lord's servants more knit together.[1]

To Howell Harris he wrote:

The people of Wales are much upon my heart. I long to hear how the Gospel flourishes among you . . . May you increase with all the increase of God! You will see my letters to Mr Jones, &c. As fast as I can, the rest of our Welch friends shall hear from me . . . Exhort them, my dear brother, to contend earnestly for the faith once delivered to the saints.[2]

The Rev Henry Piers of Bexley had proved timid about declaring the Gospel, and Whitefield entreated him:

Let me exhort you, by the mercies of God, to continue unwearied in well-doing. You have seen the afflictions of God's spiritual Israel. 'Do and live' is the most they hear, and what is this but requiring them to make bricks without straw? Arise, arise then, my dear Mr Piers and proclaim the Lord to be their righteousness . . . Fear not the face of

[1] *Ibid,* Vol 1, *p* 65. There are some sixty letters published in the *Works,* dated 'Philadelphia, Nov. 10', but there can be no doubt that almost all of them were written aboard ship. Gillies appended a footnote saying, 'Many of the letters of this date were written on shipboard during the passage, but were dated when sent off from Philadelphia.' On his second day ashore Whitefield recorded, 'Wrote some letters', but we may be sure that, in the rush of his circumstances, these were few.
[2] *Ibid, p* 87.

man . . . I hope my dear friend ere now hath prevented my exhortations. Methinks I see him, with all boldness, declaring the whole counsel of God and the attentive people joyfully receiving the gracious words which proceed out of his mouth.[1]

He sought to induce others to undertake the open-air ministry, and thus exhorted John Hutchings:

And how does my dear Mr Hutchings? Is he yet commenced a *field preacher*? Ere now I trust God has pointed out his way and he has been upon many a mount, stretching out his hands and inviting all that are weary and heavy-laden to come to Jesus Christ . . . I shall wait with impatience till I hear of my dear brother's progress in the Lord.[2]

Whitefield's appeal to another minister reads:

As the Lord has been pleased to reveal His dear Son in us, O let us stir up the gift of God and with all boldness preach Him to others. Freely we have received: freely let us give. What Christ tells us by His Spirit in our closets, that let us proclaim upon the house top. He who sends will protect us. All the devils in hell shall not hurt us till we have finished our testimony.[3]

The Rev Jacob Rogers of Bedford had already begun to preach in the fields and Whitefield encouraged him:

Press on, my dear Brother, press on and faint not. Speak till you can speak no more. Wait upon the Lord and you shall renew your strength. Though sometimes faint, yet still pursue. Up and be doing and the Lord be with you. See how the fields are white, everywhere ready to harvest. See how our Lord's sheep are scattered abroad, having too, too few true shepherds. I beseech you, go on and point out to them the Redeemer's good pastures . . . Satan no doubt will resist you; he will bid you, out of a false humility, to hold your peace. But let my friend speak out boldly as he ought to speak . . . If prayers may water the good seed, you may depend on mine.[4]

To the few students at Oxford who sought to maintain the Holy Club practices, he wrote:

Oh, that you may be filled with an holy fire and such an ardent zeal for God as may even eat you up! Look round, look round, my brethren, and, in imitation of your Lord, weep over the desolations of the

[1] *Ibid*, *p* 74.
[2] *Ibid.*
[3] *Ibid*, *p* 83.
[4] *Ibid*, *p* 92.

university wherein you live. Alas! how is that once-faithful city become an harlot! Have pity upon her and, whatever treatment you may meet with from an ungrateful world, endeavour at least to rescue some of her sons out of that blindness, ignorance, bigotry and formality into which she is unhappily fallen. Arise, ye sons of the prophets; shine forth, ye who are appointed to be the lights of the world.[1]

In a letter to a wealthy woman he said:

To be made good by the righteousness and spirit of Jesus Christ is a distinguishing blessing. To be made good and yet to be great and rich in this world's goods, is still more extraordinary. Blessed be God who has thus highly favoured you. I trust He hath given you that faith which enables you to overcome the world and emboldens you to confess both our Lord and His servants in the midst of a wicked and adulterous generation . . . May the Lord enable you, more and more, to set your face like a flint and entirely to live above the fear of man.[2]

The above letters, all written to members of the Church of England, are examples of the efforts that Whitefield made toward raising up an evangelical body in the national church.

*

But Whitefield's desire for fellowship which included all who were truly evangelical, whatever their denomination, is also manifest in his letters. In writing to a Presbyterian minister he stated:

Blessed be God that His love is so far shed abroad in our hearts as to cause us to love one another, though we a little differ as to externals. For my part, I hate to mention them. My one sole question is 'Are you a Christian?'[3]

Whitefield wrote in a similar vein to the ministerial students at Dr Doddridge's Academy. Shortly before leaving England he had preached to them and he followed up his admonitions by writing:

I heartily pray God that you may be burning and shining lights in the midst of a crooked and perverse generation. Though you are not of the Church of England, yet, if you are persuaded in your own minds of the truth of the way wherein you now walk, I leave it. However, whether *Conformists* or *Nonconformists*, our main concern should be to be assured that we are called and taught of God . . . Indeed, my dear brethren, it rejoiced me much to see such dawnings of grace in your

[1] *Ibid*, p 80. [2] *Ibid*, p 110. [3] *Ibid*, p 126.

souls. Only I thought that most of you were bowed down too much with a servile fear of man . . . Unless your hearts are free from worldly hopes and worldly fears you will never speak boldly as you ought to speak . . . Study, therefore, brethren, your hearts as well as books. Ask yourselves again and again, whether you would preach for Christ if you were sure to lay down your lives for so doing.[1]

To the Erskine brothers and the ministers associated with them in Scotland Whitefield wrote:

My dear Brethren and worthy fellow-labourers in Christ:

Though I know none of you in person, yet, from the time I heard of your faith and love towards our dear Lord Jesus, I have been acquainted with you in spirit. The good pleasure of the Lord, I find, prospers in your hands . . . Scotland, like England, hath been so much settled upon its lees that I fear our late days may properly be called the mid-night of the church. Blessed be God, who hath sent forth many of His servants with the cry, 'Behold the Bridegroom cometh!' Thousands obey the call and are trimming their spiritual lamps in order to go forth to meet Him.[2]

These several letters provide further evidence of Whitefield's concept of the Revival. They show that he thought of it as a Divine work and as gloriously setting forth evangelical principles; as marked by a oneness which superseded denominational differences and as strongly adverse to any attempts to introduce a party spirit or to form an organization.

Whitefield recognized that God had made his ministry a major factor in this work, and as he looked forward to America and anticipated preaching there, he made such statements as:

I love those that thunder out the Word. The Christian world is in a deep sleep! Nothing but a loud voice can awaken them out of it.[3]

Oh, for a revival of true and undefiled religion in all sects whatsoever! . . . God make me an instrument of promoting it! Methinks I care not what I do or suffer, so that I may see my Lord's kingdom come with power.[4]

The whole world is now my parish. Wheresoever my Master calls me I am ready to go and preach His everlasting Gospel. My only grief is, that I can do no more for Christ.[5]

*

[1] *Works*, Vol 1, *p* 81. [2] *Ibid*, *p* 67. [3] *Ibid*, *p* 73.
[4] *Ibid*, *p* 66. [5] *Ibid*, *p* 105.

The above excerpts, however, reveal but one aspect of the letters that Whitefield wrote while on the Atlantic. Despite the tranquillity that he experienced during his first days aboard, into his correspondence there began to come expressions which indicated severe sorrow and struggle. 'The searcher of hearts alone knows what agonies my poor soul has undergone since my retirement from the world'; 'I groan daily . . . Dearest Redeemer, I come to thee weary and heavy laden'; 'The Lord has been pleased to withdraw from me and to permit Satan to send me a thorn in the flesh'; 'Had I not known that my Redeemer liveth . . . I must have sunk in despair'; 'Sometimes . . . like Elijah, I wish for death' – these were his confessions and, coming from one who had otherwise known little but triumph, they reveal an extraordinary condition indeed.

What caused this strange alteration in Whitefield's spiritual attitude? It is possible that the sudden change from his tremendous activity on land to the quiet life aboard produced a reaction which issued in a sense of depression. Moreover, there can be no doubt that he was constantly concerned over certain of John Wesley's actions, and that he was burdened also in his attempts to subdue his affection for Elizabeth Delamotte (it was at this time that he wrote the letter to her brother about allowing no idols and claiming, 'At present my heart is quite free').[1]

There was, however, another and much weightier cause of Whitefield's distress. Upon entering the vessel he had stated, 'I was very earnest with God to give me grace to improve my present retirement to His glory, the good of His church, and the edification of my own soul'.[2] In fulfilment of this design he made such further reports as, 'I gave myself to reading the Word of God and to prayer the greatest part of this week'[3] and, 'I had a glorious opportunity of spending many hours in close communion with God, to ask pardon for the defects of my public ministry and to pray for strength to prepare me for future work and trials'.[4]

This proved to be no merely casual effort. On the contrary it quickly became a severe self-examination in which, with strong cryings and tears he opened the recesses of his inner being to the searching light of the Word of God. In response to the petition 'Oh, that God may give me to know myself' he was led, first,

[1] See *p* 367. [2] *Journals*, *p* 331. [3] *Ibid*, *p* 334. [4] *Ibid*, *p* 331.

to a new vision of the unapproachable heights of the divine holiness, and then, in contrast, to a new sight of human sin: sin, in something of that blackness in which God sees it: sin, as it exists in fallen human nature, but above all, sin as it dwelt within his own heart. Broken and burdened he found relief in pouring forth his sorrow in his letters to certain close friends, therein making such statements as 'God has been pleased to let me see something of my own vileness',[1] 'I have seen more and more how full of corruption I am',[2] and 'A mystery of iniquity that lay in my heart undiscovered, has been opened to my view'.[3]

It is probable that in these bitter confessions Whitefield was thinking not only of sin in general, but of a certain sin in particular. More than once he accused himself of pride: 'I am blind, I am full of self-pride and self-love',[4] he admitted. He prayed, 'Oh, that these inner conflicts may purify my polluted, proud and treacherous heart!'[5] His most frequent petition was that he might be humbled. There can be little doubt that in asking 'pardon for the defects of [his] public ministry', he was referring to the 'style too apostolical' which had been displayed in his work in London. In his sword-brandishing he had taken unto himself something of the glory that belongs to the Lord Jesus Christ alone, and this, we may be sure, was the sin that especially caused his grief.

While undergoing this bitter contrition Whitefield wrote the *Account* of his early life. No doubt it was in regard to his description of his boyhood and youth that he said, 'The remembrance of my past sins overwhelmed my soul, and caused tears to be my meat, day and night'.[6] Looking upon his great fame as a danger and a stumbling-block, he portrayed himself in such a way as to make the people see that their idol was but a poor, weak sinner. He sought to turn away their attention from himself, saying, for example, to a certain correspondent, 'You have my person too much in admiration. If you look to the instrument less and to God more, it will be better'.[7]

As God thus dealt with him, Whitefield was brought very low. Conscious that the cruel light of public scrutiny played ever upon him, and smitten with the realization that sin was entrenched

[1] *Works*, Vol 1, *p* 82. [2] *Ibid*, *p* 65. [3] *Ibid*, *p* 91.
[4] *Ibid*, *p* 82. [5] *Journals*, *p* 333.
[6] *Works*, Vol 1, *p* 101. [7] *Ibid*, *p* 118.

within his heart, he became greatly burdened. How dangerous was his position! What delight would there be in the camp of his foes, were he ever to be guilty of some conspicuous error! And what shame would such failure bring upon the cause of the Lord! 'I fear not falling finally', he confessed, '. . . but I fear I shall provoke him to let me fall foully and then how will the *Philistines* rejoice!'[1] Twice he made use of the words of Jeremiah, 'My familiars watch for my halting, saying, Peradventure he will be enticed, and we . . . shall take our revenge on him',[2] and the lamentation of the Prophet echoed the cry of his own soul.

Indeed, so severe became his self-reproach that he had thoughts of leaving the ministry. 'A public life is attended with innumerable snares:' he wrote, 'and a sense of my unworthiness and unfitness so weighs me down, that I have often thought it would be best for me to retire.'[3] Recognizing the burden of labour and reproach that his work entailed, he shrank from taking it up again, and there is a plaintive weariness in his words, 'Must I venture myself once more among fire-brands, arrows and death?'[4] He even came to the place where he looked upon himself as unfit to continue his correspondence; 'I feel myself so wretched and miserable, so blind and naked in myself', he confessed, 'that Satan would tempt me to write to no one.'[5]

One of his critics in London had referred to him as 'Crazy, confident Whitefield', yet this weak and fearful youth, bowed in his tears and talking of hiding himself, was as much George Whitefield as the man who stood in matchless zeal and dauntless courage before the great congregations. But he answered his question about venturing forth once more 'among fire-brands, arrows and death' with the assertion, 'Yes, if I come forth in the strength of the Lord God!' and his words reveal the only source of his confidence and his power.

*

But though God gave Whitefield thus to grasp something deeper of the nature of sin, even more did He give him to understand in a new and fuller way the exceeding riches of His grace. Throughout his reports he links these two experiences together, as, while

[1] *Ibid, p* 78. [2] *Jeremiah* 20: 10. [3] *Works,* Vol 1, *p* 77.
[4] *Ibid, p* 106. [5] *Ibid, p* 78.

weighted by his increased sense of guilt, God led him on to an enlarged realization of Divine mercy. Here are two of his statements:

A sense of my actual sins and natural deformity humbled me exceedingly; and then the freeness and riches of God's everlasting love broke in with such light and power upon my soul, that I was often awed into silence and could not speak.'[1]

I underwent inexpressible agonies of soul for two or three days, at the remembrance of my sins and the bitter consequences of them. All the while I was assured that God had forgiven me, but I could not forgive myself for sinning against so much light and love. I felt something of that which . . . Peter [felt] when, with oaths and curses he had thrice denied his Master. At length my Lord looked upon me, and with that look broke my rocky heart, and I wept most bitterly . . . Were I always to see myself such a sinner as I am, and as I did then, without seeing the Saviour of sinners, I should not be able to look up.

This latter part of the week, blessed be the Lord, He has restored me to the light of His countenance, and enabled me to praise Him with joyful lips.[2]

Whitefield's whole outlook, both theological and in relationship to the daily Christian life, was affected by this deeper understanding of Divine grace. In his letters he began to tell forth the truths he had thus experienced and, in so doing, enunciated the basic tenets of a theological system – the system which is known as Calvinism.

These were not new beliefs to him. Earlier pages have shown that shortly after his conversion he had grasped much of the idea of salvation as the work of God within the human heart, and we have seen the confirmation of his soul in these truths as he studied his Bible and read the writings of some of the Reformers and Puritans. These views he had expressed with growing perception in his sermons; for example, the inseparable link between justification and glorification, the indwelling of the Spirit as the seal of redemption, the elect as a particular number whom God will save, and the imputed righteousness of Christ as the gift of God in salvation.

But though Whitefield had held – with an immature grasp – to these views since the beginning of his ministry, he had been

[1] *Journals*, *p* 331. [2] *Ibid*, *p* 334.

greatly strengthened in them by the controversy which had raged around him in London. His opposers had searched his printed sermons in order to find anything they could use against him, and his friends had done the same in order to warn him of any points in which they thought him to be not yet clear. As a result he had been driven to give very careful consideration to his beliefs and thereby had come to an increased understanding and to firm convictions that God is sovereign in the whole plan of redemption.

In this doctrinal development Whitefield had been assisted by his correspondence and his reading. While in England he had exchanged letters two or three times with the Erskine brothers, who were thoroughly learned and deeply convinced Calvinists, and Ralph Erskine's last reply to him was of enormous length, virtually a theological treatise setting forth the Calvinistic tenets with extensive exposition of the Scriptures and profound reasoning.[1] Whitefield mentions also reading Jenks on *The Righteousness of Christ*, Hammond on *Regeneration*, Boston's *Fourfold State of Man* and Ralph Erskine's *Sermons* – works by which his Calvinistic views were confirmed. But the strongest influence came from a book entitled *The Preacher* by John Edwards, a noted seventeenth-century scholar of Cambridge University. After reading an extract from this work Whitefield stated, 'Here are such noble testimonies, given before that University, on justification by faith only, the imputed righteousness of Christ, our having no free will, &c., that they deserve to be written in letters of gold'.[2]

This reading and the deeper insight into the meaning of sin and the fuller knowledge of the nature of grace were all associated together in Whitefield's experience during these days on the ocean. As a result, the awesome truths of the Divine sovereignty filled his thought. He saw them in their relationship to man's

[1] This letter is now in the possession of the Library of Congress, Washington, U.S.A.

[2] *Ibid, p* 335. Tyerman quotes an author who says, 'Whitefield was not a Calvinist till he went to America in 1739. It was there he caught the tone and imbibed the opinions of the great, the searching, but too gloomy Jonathan Edwards. His *Treatise on the Will* was too deep a book for Whitefield and the probability is that the author himself was somewhat out of his depth' (Tyerman's *Whitefield*, Vol 1, *p* 274). Whitefield came to his views in the manner seen above, and it was John Edwards of England, not Jonathan Edwards of America, by whom he was particularly influenced. This error has been copied by many.

redemption and to the daily Christian walk and, with his mind dominated by their greatness and his life enriched by their assurance, he told them forth in letter after letter. From the several passages which might be cited we select the following:

First, two which present a general statement of his views:

This, however, is my comfort, 'Jesus Christ, the same yesterday, today and for ever.' He saw me from all eternity; He gave me being; He called me in time; He has freely justified me through faith in His blood; He has in part sanctified me by His Spirit; He will preserve me underneath His everlasting arms till time shall be no more. Oh the blessedness of these evangelical truths! These are indeed Gospel; they are glad tidings of great joy to all that have ears to hear. These, bring the creature out of himself. These, make him hang upon the promises, and cause his obedience to flow from a principle of love.[1]

Satan will accuse me; my answer shall be, The Lord Jesus is my righteousness; how darest thou to lay anything to the charge of God's elect? I stand here, not in my own, but His robes; and though I deserve nothing as a debt, yet I know He will give me a reward of grace, and recompence me for what He has done in me and by me, as though I had done it by my own power. Oh, how ought this to excite our zeal and love for the holy Jesus![2]

Whitefield declared that he had learned these truths from the Bible. After reaching America he stated, 'My doctrines I had from Jesus Christ and His Apostles: I was taught them of God',[3] and when another two years had gone by he said, 'I embrace the Calvinistic scheme, not because Calvin, but Jesus Christ has taught it to me.'[4] And during the voyage, in writing to his friend Hervey, he asserted:

It is sweet to know and preach that Christ justifies the ungodly, and that all truly good works are not so much as partly the cause, but the *effect* of our justification before God. Till convinced of these truths you must own free will in man, which is directly contrary to the holy Scriptures and the articles of our church. Let me advise dear Mr H., laying aside all prejudice, to read and pray over St Paul's epistles to the Romans and Galatians, and then let him tell me what he thinks of this doctrine.[5]

[1] *Works*, Vol 1, *p* 98. [2] *Ibid*, *p* 97. [3] *Ibid*, *p* 205.
[4] *Ibid*, *p* 442. [5] *Ibid*, *p* 95.

In these truths Whitefield found his defence against Satan and his strength amidst trial:

Nothing could possibly support my soul under the many agonies which oppressed me when on board, but a consideration of the freeness, eternity and unchangeableness of God's love to me.[1]

I need not fear the sight of sin when I have a perfect, everlasting righteousness wrought out for me by . . . Christ Jesus. The riches of His free grace cause me daily to triumph over all the temptations of the wicked one . . .[2]

May he enlighten me more and more to know and feel the mystery of his electing, soul-transforming love. Nothing like that, to support us under present and all the various future trials . . . But the Lord has apprehended us and will not let us go. Men and devils may do their worst; our Jesus will suffer nothing to pluck us out of His Almighty hands.[3]

It was these beliefs which were the source of his zeal.

The doctrines of our election, and free justification in Christ Jesus are daily more and more pressed upon my heart. They fill my soul with a holy fire and afford me great confidence in God my Saviour.[4]

I hope we shall catch fire from each other, and that there will be a holy emulation amongst us, who shall most debase man and exalt the Lord Jesus. Nothing but the doctrines of the Reformation can do this. All others leave freewill in man and make him, in part at least, a Saviour to himself. My soul, come not thou near the secret of those who teach such things . . . I know Christ is all in all. Man is nothing: he hath a free will to go to hell, but none to go to heaven, till God worketh in him to will and to do of His good pleasure.[5]

Oh, the excellency of the doctrine of election and of the saints' final perseverance! I am persuaded, till a man comes to believe and feel these important truths, he cannot come out of himself, but when convinced of these, and assured of their application to his own heart, he then walks by faith indeed! . . . Love, not fear, constrains him to obedience.[6]

To Whitefield the doctrines of grace were not separate tenets, to be accepted or rejected one by one, but a series of truths so joined together as to compose a great system of theology. Thus:

I bless God His Spirit has convinced me of our eternal election by the

[1] *Ibid, p* 65. [2] *Ibid, p* 82. [3] *Ibid, p* 92.
[4] *Ibid, p* 79. [5] *Ibid, pp* 89, 90. [6] *Ibid, p* 101.

Father through the Son, of our free justification through faith in His blood, of our sanctification as the consequence of that, and of our final perseverance and glorification as the result of all. These I am persuaded God has joined together; these, neither men nor devils shall ever be able to put asunder.[1]

Was there any fitness foreseen in us, except a fitness for damnation? I believe not. No, God chose us from eternity, He called us in time, and I am persuaded will keep us from falling finally, till time shall be no more. Consider the Gospel in this view, and it appears a consistent scheme . . .[2]

Finally, Whitefield looked upon these doctrines as the foundation of a most fervent, soul-winning ministry. In writing to Howell Harris he asked to be remembered to his hearers and said:

Put them in mind of the freeness and eternity of God's electing love, and be instant with them to lay hold of the perfect righteousness of Jesus Christ by faith. Talk to them, oh, talk to them, even till midnight, of the riches of His all-sufficient grace. Tell them, oh, tell them, what He has done for their souls and how earnestly He is now interceding for them in Heaven. Shew them, in the map of the Word, the kingdoms of the upper world, and the transcendent glories of them; and assure them all shall be their's if they believe on Jesus Christ with their whole hearts.

Press them to believe on Him immediately! Intersperse prayers with your exhortations, and thereby call down fire from Heaven, even the fire of the Holy Ghost,

To soften, sweeten and refine,
And melt them into love.

Speak every time, my dear brother, as if it was your last. Weep out, if possible, every argument, and as it were, compel them to cry, 'Behold how he loveth us!' Remember me, remember me, in your prayers.[3]

These statements are a direct contradiction of much that had been written regarding Whitefield's theology. The carelessness with which men have dealt with him is nowhere more evident than in this matter. It has been asserted: (1) that he was not a Calvinist until he came under the influence of the New England ministers, and (2) that he had little understanding of what he professed to believe and merely gave assent to this system because

[1] *Ibid, p* 129. [2] *Ibid, p* 90. [3] *Ibid, p* 88.

it agreed with his own experience. Thus, it needs to be emphasized that: (1) Although he became still more confirmed in these views by his later association with the American ministers, it was before he ever met them that he made the above declarations. (2) He had gradually come to these convictions over the period of the four years following his conversion. (3) He possessed a very real understanding of them, not as an abstract system of thought, but as the teachings of the Scriptures and as the basic principles of his daily Christian life.

These doctrines had indeed become 'bone of his bone and flesh of his flesh'. 'I am more and more convinced', he asserted, 'that they are the truths of God; they agree with the written Word, and with the experience of all the saints in all ages.'[1] In a later letter, after again stating these doctrines, he declared, 'The root of the matter is twisted around every faculty of the soul which daily is supported with this assurance that Christ can no more forsake the soul He loves than He can forsake Himself'.[2] Though he sometimes used the word *Calvinism*, he did not give great place to it. He made much more of the fact that the views he held were those he had discovered in the Bible and he more frequently referred to them as the *doctrines of grace*.

*

Such strong and solemn convictions must perforce have their part in Whitefield's public ministry. As long as he had held to these doctrines with lesser understanding of their importance, the policy of 'Silence on both sides', which he had suggested for John Wesley and himself, seemed advisable, but now that he saw them to be so essential to the whole Christian revelation, he had no choice but to preach them. 'Henceforth, I hope I shall speak boldly and plainly,' he wrote, 'and not fail to declare the whole counsel of God.'[3] This might entail conflict with some of his dearest friends, but he was quick to assert that his part therein would be only on the basis of presenting the Scriptures: 'Election, free grace, free justification . . . I intend to exalt and contend for more and more; not with carnal weapons – that be far from me – but with the sword of the Spirit, the Word of God! No sword like that!'[4]

[1] *Ibid, p* 108. [2] *Ibid, p* 162. [3] *Ibid, p* 90. [4] *Ibid, p* 108.

At the thought, however, of discord with John Wesley, Whitefield again became burdened. He was not, as Tyerman suggests, confused about his beliefs, but he was confused at the prospect of strife with his dear friend. He could oppose the enemies of the Lord with vigour, but only with great reluctance could he anticipate facing the opposition of one he loved so well.

Accordingly, after a few assertions about his willingness to be loyal to what he was sure was the truth of God, whatever the cost, he seems to have tried to overlook the whole matter. It may have been that he still expected that Wesley would come to accept the doctrines of grace too, or it may have been that the prospect of strife was simply too much for him, and that he left it, hoping in some vague way that the Lord would work things out. At any rate, the policy on which he conducted his relations with Wesley for months to come was that of refusing to dispute and of seeking harmony on the recognition that they were far apart on these teachings, yet were agreed on the great essentials of Christianity.

Nevertheless, Whitefield was sorely troubled by these things, and longed to reach shore, that he might forget them by plunging himself into vigorous activity again. 'Satan never buffets me more', he wrote, 'than when confined to a ship.' Thus, we may be sure that it was with great joy that, after eleven weeks on the ocean, he had his first glimpse of the American coast.

For the ministry that lay before him in the new world, God had further prepared His servant during the passage. Now, as never before, Whitefield saw the awful nature of sin and had learned, in a deeper way, its remedy in the eternal reaches of God's grace. In this experience something of the brashness that had crept into his work in London had been purged away. 'I would not have lost this voyage for the world,' he declared. 'I am the chief of sinners . . . I desire to make mention only of the Lord's righteousness . . . Like a pure crystal, I would transmit all the light He poureth upon me . . . I would have Jesus all in all.'[1]

[1] *Ibid*, *p* 106.

Was there not a heavenly coincidence in the fact that at the very time when the Holy Club at Oxford was sending out the leaders of the Evangelical Revival which spread over Britain and beyond, the Great Awakening in America was getting under way? And George Whitefield, born again in the Holy Club, was the chosen Apostle of the Lord in linking together these two awakenings that finally merged into the vast movement which changed the religious face of the English-speaking world. He came to America just in time to infuse new energy into the languishing work begun under Edwards, and to thrust it forward like a flaming torch into all the Colonies.

EDWARDS S. NINDE

George Whitefield, Prophet-Preacher, 1924

25

Religious Conditions in America at the Time of Whitefield's Arrival

It was October 30, 1739, when Whitefield set foot on the soil of America. If he had been freshly prepared for a ministry in the Colonies, so also had much of Colonial life been prepared for him.

The religious fervour which had characterized many of the first settlers of the new world had long since died away. In 1706 Dr Cotton Mather asserted:

> It is confessed by all who know anything of the matter . . . that there is a general and an horrible decay of Christianity, among the professors of it . . . The modern Christianity is too generally but a very spectre, scarce a shadow of the ancient. Ah! sinful nation. Ah! children that are corrupters: what have your hands done! . . . So notorious is this decay of Christianity, that whole books are even now and then written to inquire into it.[1]

In the midst of these conditions, however, the winds of heaven had begun to blow upon America. During the years 1720–35 several thorough evangelical revivals were experienced.[2] These took place in several parts of the country and may be summarized under the following heads:

1. *Revivals among the Germans in Pennsylvania.* German people of many denominations – Lutherans, Reformed, Mennonites, Quakers, Moravians, Schwenkfelders, Dunkers (known as Baptists) and others – had settled a rural area north-west of Philadelphia and had formed a community which bore the name *Germantown*. Due to the isolation that many settlers endured in frontier life, organized religious activity was difficult and a

[1] Thomas Prince, *The Christian History*, Boston, Vol of 1743, *p* 104.

[2] This subject is well presented by C. H. Maxson, *The Great Awakening in the Middle Colonies, op cit.*

severe lowering of spiritual and moral values became prevalent. While these conditions prevailed several preachers – some of them unordained – arose to declare the Word of God with great zeal. Among the Mennonites and Baptists especially, powerful awakenings were experienced, many people were converted and the Pietistic influences lingering from the homeland were rekindled.

2. *Revival under the ministry of Theodorus Frelinghuysen in New Jersey.* In 1720 Frelinghuysen (1691–1747) became the minister of four Dutch Reformed Churches in the semi-wilderness country of the Raritan Valley. His people possessed a strong orthodoxy of the head but evinced little or nothing of a regenerate heart, and he began immediately to preach against the emptiness of their religion and to declare the absolute necessity of being born again. He exercised an unrelenting and powerful ministry, covering an extensive area and preaching not only in his meeting houses, but in homes and barns. A man of sound learning, he printed several of his sermons and used them as a declaration of his doctrine. He established schools for the children and also trained several godly young men and used them, though unordained, in the work of evangelism.

Frelinghuysen's message and methods drew bitter opposition. His church members grew so angry that they complained to the denominational authorities in New York, who quickly pronounced him a schismatic and a heretic. Therewith he became a rock of division in the Reformed Church; some ministers stood strongly in his favour, but others were so much against him that they drew up a written *Complaint*, 246 pages long, and sent it to the Church headquarters at Amsterdam. This roused his friends to write and publish in his defence, and a bitter controversy developed and spread till it divided the Reformed Church in America into two hostile camps.

Such, however, was Frelinghuysen's confidence in God that he was unmoved by the storm of opposition. In season and out of season he fulfilled the command, 'Earnestly contend for the faith which was once delivered to the saints', and God abundantly honoured him. With the passing of the months and the years he saw large numbers of people converted; among them were many of the unchurched and several notorious sinners, but among them also were several deacons and elders and church members who earlier had been his severest opposers. Because of his stalwart Christian character, powerful evangelism and militant aggressiveness, Frelinghuysen exercised a strong influence on several other ministers of all denominations, and it is to be regretted that so magnificent a life has been so largely overlooked.

3. *Revivals among the Presbyterians of the Middle Colonies.* During the first three decades of the eighteenth century the Presbyterian Church in America was the victim of a growing spiritual apathy. Not that the faith was actually denied, for verbal assent was everywhere given to the *Westminster Confession*, but the life of the denomination was little more than cold formalism. This condition was noticeable especially in the practice of receiving communicant members; in earlier days all applicants had been obliged to give evidence of having been born again, but this custom had now fallen into disuse and the only remaining requirement was that a person be free from scandalous behaviour. In turn, an unconverted membership brought about an unconverted ministry, for in this sphere also the requirement of regeneration was gradually allowed to atrophy, and intellectual preparation without regard to the new birth became the basis of ordination.

During the years following 1720, however, a voice began to be raised in protest against these conditions. This was the voice of the Rev William Tennent (1673–1745) minister of the Presbyterian Church at Neshaminy in Pennsylvania. Tennent was a man of extensive learning and his ministry was marked by vital evangelism and spiritual power. Both in his pulpit and before the Synod he declared the unchanging necessity of the new birth; he urged that true evidence of regeneration be restored as the requirement for membership, asserted that an unconverted man was unfit for the ministry and pleaded for a return to evangelical fervency of life.

Tennent had four sons, all of whom experienced the call of God to the ministry, and, fearing the baneful influences of the usual places of education, he trained them in his own home. Other young men asked for the same training and in order to accommodate them Tennent built a one-room school house which, in contempt, its detractors termed *The Log College.* His own wide erudition enabled him to provide these men with a thorough theological education; but he did more than that; he nurtured them on evangelical truth and sent them forth, mighty in the faith, fearless for God and aflame with Gospel zeal.

Tennent's actions became a divisive force within the Presbyterian Church. His attempts to arouse the sleeping denomination were greeted with hostility, for the majority wanted no such disturbance. They belittled his efforts, resorted to ecclesiastical machinations in attempts to hinder him, and under the pretence that his school did not possess adequate academic standards, sought to keep its graduates from being ordained. A conflict of opinion arose and spread throughout the denomination; the Tennants and those who agreed with them became a recognized group – later to be known as *New Sides* – and those who opposed them were the body which came to bear the term *Old Sides*. Thus, among the Presbyterians as among the Dutch, two opposing parties came into being.

As William Tennent aged, the leadership of this work passed into the hands of his son Gilbert (1703–64). In 1726 Gilbert was settled at New Brunswick in New Jersey, and eighteen years later, in response to a request for a report of the blessing experienced there, he wrote:

> The labours of the Rev Mr Frelinghuysen, a Dutch Calvinist minister, were much blessed to the people of New Brunswick and places adjacent, especially about the time of his coming among them . . .
>
> When I came there, which was about seven years after, I had the pleasure of seeing much of the fruits of his ministry; divers of his hearers, with whom I had opportunity of conversing, appeared to be converted persons by their soundness in principle, Christian experience and pious practice: and these persons declared that the ministrations of the aforesaid gentleman were the means thereof. This together with a kind letter which he sent me . . . through the divine blessing, excited me to greater earnestness in ministerial labours. I began to be very much distressed about my want of success; for I knew not for half a year or more after I came to New Brunswick that any one was converted by my labours . . .
>
> It pleased God to afflict me about that time with sickness, by which I had very affecting views of eternity. I was then exceedingly grieved that I had done so little for God, and was very desirous to live one half year more, if it was His will, that I might stand upon the stage of the

world as it were, and plead more faithfully for His cause, and take more earnest pains for the salvation of souls. The secure state of the world appeared to me in a very affecting light; and one thing among others pressed me sore; *viz*. that I had spent so much time in conversing about trifles, which might have been spent in examining people's states towards God, and persuading them to turn unto Him. I therefore prayed to God that He would be pleased to give me one half year more, and I was determined to endeavour to promote His kingdom with all my might at all adventures. This petition God was pleased to grant manifold, and to enable me to keep my resolution in some measure.

After I was raised up to health, I examined many about the grounds of their hope of salvation, which I found in most to be nothing but as the sand; with such I was enabled to deal faithfully and earnestly, in warning them of their danger, and urging them to seek converting grace. By this method many were awakened out of their security; and of those, divers were to all appearance effectually converted; but some that I spoke plainly to were prejudiced. And here I would have it observed, that as soon as an effectual door was opened, I found many adversaries, and my character was covered with unjust reproaches, which through Divine goodness did not discourage me in my work.

I did then preach much upon Original sin, repentance, the nature and necessity of conversion, in a close, examinatory and distinguishing way; labouring in the meantime to sound the trumpet of God's judgments, and alarm the secure by the terrors of the Lord, as well as to affect them by other topics of persuasion: which method was sealed by the Holy Spirit in the conviction and conversion of a considerable number of persons, at various times and in different places in that part of the country . . . frequently at Sacramental seasons in New Brunswick there have been signal displays of the Divine power and presence . . . New Brunswick did then look like a field the Lord had blessed; it was like a little Jerusalem to which the scattered tribes with eager haste repaired at Sacramental solemnities; and there they fed on the fatness of God's house and drank of the river of His pleasures.[1]

Gilbert's younger brother William[2] and three other ministers[3] of like faith also settled in New Jersey. These five men were

[1] Prince, *op cit*, Vol of 1743, *pp* 292–4.

[2] William Tennent, jr, succeeded his brother John who died in 1732. He continued in the Freehold pastorate till his death in 1777. The Old Tennent Church, as it is called, is now a memorial to the Tennent family.

[3] These were Jonn Cross, of Basking Ridge; Samuel Blair, a Log College graduate who settled at Shrewsbury; and Eleazer Wales, a Yale man, who was the minister at Kingston.

erected by the Synod into the *Presbytery of New Brunswick* – an act which placed within their hands the right to ordain men to the ministry. This authority the Synod tried to revoke, but the New Brunswick pastors stood their ground, and not only did they exercise this power, but they fiercely denounced the apathy of their opponents. With fiery zeal they evangelized throughout the area under the jurisdiction of their Presbytery and, when occasion required, they crossed the Presbyterial boundary lines into the fields nominally under the responsibility of other pastors. Much of New Jersey and Pennsylvania was aroused to the great truths of the Gospel by the tremendous preaching of the men of the New Brunswick Presbytery.

The ministry of John Rowland, the first man to be ordained by the New Brunswick Presbytery, reveals much regarding the practices of the Tennents and their fellows. Rowland was settled in the New Jersey circuit of Maidenhead, Hopewell and Amwell, but, being denied the use of the meeting houses at the first two places, like Frelinghuysen he resorted to preaching in barns, and we are told that, 'So great were his congregations that the largest barns of his adherents were required'. The nature of his ministry is manifest in the following account:

For six long months Rowland, with terrible earnestness, preached upon the two themes, conviction and conversion. The most arousing texts were selected. Though he divided his ministry among three townships, the interest was not permitted to subside by long intervals between meetings in one neighbourhood. Sunday night meetings were introduced, a marked innovation in the eighteenth century, and week-day meetings, so that the young enthusiast was constantly going from one service to another. Presently the one topic of conversation in these towns was heart religion. Everyone was asking himself whether he was really converted. A deep gloom began to settle over the three New Side congregations. Now one person and now another broke down and owned himself convicted. Yet months passed, and the prophet of woe but increased their anguish by his arraignment of sin and declaration of the Divine displeasure.

Finally, when the number of convicted was very considerable, and the people who looked upon themselves as converted were aroused to earnest effort in their behalf, the preacher changed his method. The most inviting and encouraging subjects were taken. The eye that had flashed the anger of God was now a well of tears. Solemn weeping came over the congregation. From this time on, conversions were numerous. Sometimes it was the aged to whom the joy of pardon came, and sometimes it was children. The negroes were included in the invitation, and Rowland reports that some were very earnest after the word . . . The movement spread beyond the circle of families which originally composed the three New Side congregations . . . many who had been quite indifferent to the claims of religion were reached.[1]

Under Rowland's practice of this lengthy preaching of judgment, not only was there tremendous conviction of sin, but emotional effects occurred which often overwhelmed his hearers. This was true also of the preaching of the other men of the New Brunswick Presbytery, and loud outcryings and faintings were frequently experienced among their congregations.

There were, however, certain Presbyterian ministers who, though pronouncedly evangelical, could not countenance this type of evangelism. The most outstanding of these men was Jonathan Dickinson (1688–1747) of Elizabeth Town, New Jersey. Dickinson was a medical doctor, a Biblical scholar, an able author and a powerful preacher, and, as a theologian he stood second only to Jonathan Edwards. Another was Aaron Burr of Newark (1715–57); he also was a man of high intellectual attainments and his ministry had witnessed the power of God in true revival. A third was Ebenezer Pemberton (1704–77), minister of the Wall Street Church in New York, and the leading ministerial figure of that city. These Presbyterian leaders recognized that there was great need for a stirring of the dry bones of their church and laboured to that end. But they also believed that the men of the New Brunswick Presbytery went too far in their zeal; they disliked the severity of their denunciations and feared the emotional extremes. Though in opposition to those who favoured the prevailing spiritual lethargy, Dickinson, Burr and Pemberton, and a few others of lesser prominence, could not fully co-operate with the Tennent party and, as a result, the Presbyterian Church developed also a third party: that of this more careful and balanced evangelism.

4. *Revival among the Congregationalists of New England.* The chief

[1] Maxson, *op cit, p* 37. A detailed record of this period of America's religious history is to be found in Archibald Alexander's *The Log College* (1851, republished by the Banner of Truth Trust, 1968).

figure in this work was, of course, Jonathan Edwards (1703–58) of Northampton in Massachusetts.

Edwards has long been falsely pictured before mankind. The concept of him as a gloomy individual whose ministry was largely a pronouncement of damnation is utterly erroneous, and the thought of him as an evangelist of the militant type, a son of thunder, is equally untrue. He was gifted with towering intellectual faculties, but to know him only for his mind is to know him incompletely.

To few men could the words, 'The weapons of our warfare are not carnal, but spiritual', be applied so aptly as to Edwards. In reading his writings one feels that here is a man entirely free from such ministerial sins as personal ambition and ecclesiastical politics; that such is his regard for truth that it would be impossible for him to exaggerate or to attempt to deceive in the slightest way.

Edwards' normal exaltedness of mind cast an aura of majesty and spiritual beauty over him in the daily affairs of life. One of his early biographers says, 'His constant, solemn converse with God . . . made his face, as it were, to shine before others. His appearance, his countenance, his words, and whole demeanour, were attended with a seriousness, gravity and solemnity . . .'[1] The records of his ministerial activities reveal him as a warm-hearted pastor; one who, although exercising unbending Scriptural principle in all of his dealings, nevertheless watched over his flock with loving care. The confidence in God which indwelt his soul made him utterly calm amidst the stresses of life, and let him move in unhurried peace.

All of these qualities characterized Edwards as he performed his chief labour: that of the pulpit. There 'his tall slender figure, six foot one in height, stood almost motionless, and his thin face, with its mixture of sweetness and gravity, remained turned towards some distant spot in the building, or more generally towards the manuscript which he held in his left hand . . .'[2] The doctrines of the Gospel, as he preached them, 'were not mere abstract propositions, but living realities, distinctly seen by the

[1] Quoted by Iain Murray, *A Memoir of Jonathan Edwards,* published in *The Select Works of Jonathan Edwards*, (The Banner of Truth, 1958) Vol 1, *pp* 54–5.
[2] *Ibid, p* 54.

author's faith, and painted with so much truth, and life, and warmth of colouring, as could not fail to give his hearers the same strong impression of them, as already existed in his own mind'.[1]

One who knew him, being asked whether Mr Edwards was an eloquent preacher, replied:

> If you mean, by eloquence, what is usually intended by it in our cities; he had no pretensions to it. He had no studied varieties of the voice and made no strong emphasis. He scarcely gestured or even moved; and he made no attempt by the elegance of his style, or the beauty of his pictures, to gratify the taste, and fascinate the imagination. But if you mean by eloquence the power of presenting an important truth before an audience with overwhelming weight of argument, and with such intenseness of feeling that the whole soul of the speaker is thrown into every part of the conception and delivery, so that the solemn attention of the whole audience is riveted from the beginning to the close, and impressions are left that cannot be effaced, Mr Edwards was the most eloquent man I ever heard speak.[2]

This nobility of soul was the direct outcome of the theology that Edwards held. In reading the Scriptures during his boyhood he had grasped the concept of the Divine sovereignty and as he grew to manhood this tremendous idea developed in his mind until it dominated his life. Upon this premise he had seen the necessity of the doctrines that compose the Calvinistic system, all of them inseparably linked and forming a complete whole. Accordingly, these truths constituted the basic teachings of Edwards' ministry, and though they included exceptionally winsome portrayals of the Divine love, they also included the declaration of the Divine justice and wrath.

*

In 1734, fearing the growth of Arminianism, Edwards preached a series of sermons on 'Justification by Faith Alone'. This was followed by another on 'God's absolute sovereignty in the salvation of sinners'. Using such Scriptures as 'I will have mercy on whom I will have mercy', and 'That every mouth may be stopped', he showed 'that God is under no manner of *obligation* to show mercy to any natural man, whose heart is not turned to God: and that a man can challenge nothing either in *absolute*

[1] *Ibid*, p 55. [2] *Ibid*.

justice or by *free promise*, from anything he does before he has believed on *Jesus Christ* or has true repentance begun in him . . . that it would be just with God for ever to reject and cast off mere natural men'.[1]

Edwards states that under this preaching:

> . . . the Spirit of God began extraordinarily to set in and wonderfully to work amongst us . . .
>
> Presently . . . a great and earnest concern about the great things of religion and the eternal world, became *universal* in all parts of the town, and among persons of all degrees and of all ages. The noise amongst the *dry bones* waxed louder and louder; all other talk but about spiritual and eternal things was soon thrown by . . . The only thing in their view was to get the kingdom of heaven, and everyone appeared pressing into it. The engagedness of their hearts in this great concern could not *be hid*, it appeared in their very countenances. It was then a dreadful thing amongst us to lie out of Christ, in danger every day of dropping into hell . . .
>
> And the work of *conversion* was carried on in a most *astonishing* manner, and increased more and more. Souls did, as it were, come by flocks to Jesus Christ.[2]

A knowledge of what Edwards meant by his words, 'the work of conversion', ought to prove highly valuable to our present age. He made it plain that he did not (as so many do to-day) 'take every religious pang and enthusiastic conceit, for saving conversion'.[3] On the contrary, he looked for evidence of a deep and abiding work of the Spirit of God in the heart – a work which, though it varied from one individual to another, necessarily included a weighty conviction of sin, an utter rejection of all trust in things human, and finally, a very definite experience – that which he referred to as 'a saving closure with Christ'.

Edwards regarded this work, both in the individual and in the revival at large, as the operation of the Holy Spirit. His concept is seen in the phrase quoted above, 'The Spirit of God began extraordinarily to set in and wonderfully to work amongst us', and he repeatedly speaks of the revival under such terms as 'the plentiful effusion of God's Spirit', and 'the shower of Divine

[1] Jonathan Edwards, *A Narrative of Surprising Conversions* (1736, reprinted Banner of Truth, London, 1965), *p* 30.

[2] *Ibid, pp* 12–13.

[3] *Ibid, p* 21.

blessing in the converting, renewing, strengthening influences of the Spirit of God'.

The course of this Divine operation in the heart Edwards describes with extraordinary perception. In regard to the conviction of sin as experienced among his hearers, he writes:

When awakenings *first begin*, their consciences are commonly most exercised about their *outward* vicious course, or other acts of sin; but *afterwards* are much more burdened with a sense of heart-sins, the dreadful corruption of their nature, their enmity against God, the pride of their hearts, their unbelief, their rejection of Christ, the stubbornness and obstinacy of their wills: and the like.[1]

Thus awakened by the Spirit of God, many suffered severe anguish of soul. He says:

Persons are sometimes brought to the borders of despair, and it looks as black as midnight to them a little before the day dawns in their souls. Some few instances there have been of persons who have had such a sense of God's wrath for sin, that they have been overborne; and made to *cry out* under an astonishing sense of their guilt, wondering that God suffers such guilty wretches to live upon earth, and that he doth not immediately send them to hell . . .[2]

Together with those fears, and that exercise of mind which is rational, and which they have just ground for, they have often suffered many needless distresses of thought, in which Satan probably has a great hand, to entangle them and block up their way.[3]

A great many people found themselves driven by their distress to seek Edwards' personal counsel. During the winter of 1734–35 so many thus came calling on him that 'it was no longer the tavern, but the minister's house that was thronged, far more than ever the tavern had been wont to be'.[4] Edwards says that in many of these persons, so exalted was the view of Divine holiness and so black the concept of their sinful hearts that they declared 'the glory of God would *shine bright* in their own condemnation'.[5] In this bitter sense of need they cried out to God for mercy, and Edwards describes their varied experiences in receiving it:

. . . in some, the first sight of their just desert of hell, and God's sovereignty with respect to their salvation, and a discovery of all-sufficient grace, are so near that they seem to go as it were together . . .[6]

[1] *Ibid, p* 27. [2] *Ibid, pp* 25–6. [3] *Ibid, p* 24.
[4] *Ibid.* [5] *Ibid, p* 33. [6] *Ibid, p* 34.

More frequently, Christ is distinctly made the object of the mind, in His all-sufficiency and willingness to save sinners . . . Some view the all-sufficiency of the mercy and grace of God; some chiefly the infinite power of God . . . In *some* the truth and certainty of the gospel in general is the first joyful discovery they have; in *others*, the certain truth of some particular promises; in some the grace and sincerity of God in His invitations . . . and it now appears real to them that God does indeed invite them. Some are struck with the glory and wonderfulness of the dying love of Christ; and some with the sufficiency and preciousness of His blood as offered to make an atonement for sin . . .

The way that grace seems sometimes first to appear, after legal humiliation, is in earnest longings of soul after God and Christ; to know God, to love Him, to be humble before Him, to have communion with Christ in His benefits; which longings, as they express them, seem evidently to be of such a nature as can arise from nothing but a sense of the superlative excellency of divine things, with a spiritual taste and relish of them, and an esteem of them as their highest happiness . . .[1]

It will have been noticed that Edwards' description of the experiences of the soul prior to conversion is very different from the common concept to-day. But if the sense of sin and soul distress was deep, so also was the joy that attended conversion, and Edwards goes on to state:

It was very wonderful to see how persons' *affections* were sometimes moved – when God did as it were suddenly open their eyes, and let into their minds a sense of the greatness of His grace, the fullness of *Christ*, and His readiness to save – after having been broken with apprehensions of divine wrath, and sunk into an abyss, under a sense of guilt which they were ready to think was beyond the mercy of God. Their joyful surprise has caused their hearts as it were to leap so that they have been ready to break forth into laughter, tears often at the same time issuing like a flood, and intermingling a loud weeping. Sometimes they have not been able to forbear crying out with a loud voice, expressing their great admiration.[2]

Many have spoken much of their hearts being drawn out in *love* to God and Christ; and of their minds being wrapt up in delightful contemplation of the glory and wonderful grace of God, the excellency and dying love of Jesus Christ . . . Several of our young children have expressed much of this . . . Some persons have been so overcome with a sense of the dying love of Christ to such poor, wretched and unworthy creatures, as to weaken the body.[3]

[1] *Ibid, pp* 34–5. [2] *Ibid, pp* 37–8. [3] *Ibid, pp* 44–5.

Edwards relates at length the spiritual ecstacy experienced by many, and describes such marks of regeneration as humility of mind, gentleness, self-control and prayerfulness which their lives thereafter revealed.

Edwards did not lightly come to the conclusion that a person was converted. There were, however, instances, and many of them, in which, after extensive acquaintance and thorough interrogation, he was convinced that the Holy Spirit had indeed accomplished His saving work, and in such cases he told the person so. But the enemies of the revival complained that in so doing he might be giving a soul a false assurance and Edwards stated:

I have been much blamed and censured by many, that I should make it my practice, when I have been satisfied concerning persons' good estate, to signify it to them . . . But let it be noted that what I have undertaken to judge of, has been *qualifications*, and declared experiences, rather than persons. Not but that I have thought it my duty, as a pastor, to assist and instruct persons in applying scripture-rules and characters to their *own* case . . . and I have, where the case appeared plain, used freedom in signifying my hope of them to others. But I have been far from doing this concerning all that I have had some hopes of; and I believe, have used much more caution than many have supposed. Yet I should account it a great calamity to be deprived of the comfort of rejoicing with those of my flock who have been in great distress, whose circumstances I have been acquainted with, when there seems to be good evidence that those who were dead are alive, and that those who were lost are found.[1]

So clear was Edwards' assurance in these instances that he gave an estimate of the approximate number of conversions. Northampton was a town of about two hundred homes – perhaps twelve to fourteen hundred inhabitants – and after reporting that he received into the communion about a hundred before one sacrament and near sixty before another, he goes on to state:

I am far from pretending to be able to determine how many have lately been the subjects of such mercy; but if I may be allowed to declare anything that appears to me probable in a thing of this nature, I hope that more than three hundred souls were savingly brought home to Christ, in this town, in the space of half a year . . . When God, in so

[1] *Ibid*, *pp* 38–9.

remarkable a manner took the work into His own hands, there was as much done in a day or two, as at ordinary times . . . is done in a year.[1]

The transformation of these hundreds of individuals effected in turn the transformation of the town. Edwards says of Northampton:

. . . it was never so full of love nor of joy, nor yet so full of distress as it was then. It was a time of joy in families on account of salvation being brought unto them; parents rejoicing over their children as new born, and husbands over their wives, and wives over their husbands. The goings of God were then seen in His sanctuary, God's day was a delight and His tabernacles were amiable. Our public assemblies were then beautiful; the congregation was alive in God's service, . . . every hearer eager to drink in the words of the minister, . . . the assembly in general were, from time to time, in tears while the Word was preached; some weeping with sorrow and distress, others with joy and love, others with pity and concern for the souls of their neighbours.[2]

From Northampton the revival spread to other communities, reaching several in Massachusetts and others across the border in Connecticut. This does not mean that Edwards conducted an itinerant ministry and preached in these places, or that ministers of these towns held what would be called *Revival Meetings*. Rather (and in this we see the thoroughness of this work) the people of these places, in coming to Northampton on visits or on business, were so moved by what they saw and heard that 'they had their consciences smitten and awakened, and went home with wounded hearts'.[3] Thereupon they began to seek the Lord. The first community to be thus affected was South Hadley; its people, says Edwards, 'began to be seized with deep concern about the things of religion'.[4] He then goes on to mention twenty-five other places which experienced the work of God in the power of the Holy Spirit, with results like those already experienced at Northampton. He speaks of it as 'This remarkable outpouring of the Spirit of God which extended from one end to the other of this county'.[5]

*

[1] *Ibid, pp* 19, 21.
[2] *Ibid, p* 14.
[3] *Ibid, p* 15.
[4] *Ibid.*
[5] *Ibid, p* 17.

Of course, this work met strong opposition. 'Many scoffed at it and ridiculed it,' says Edwards, 'and some compared what we call conversion to certain distempers.' The severe distress that some experienced brought criticism; reports of it spread far and wide and tales were told which were often highly exaggerated or even totally false. Throughout New England people declared their opinions of the revival, insomuch that two antagonistic bodies began to form, the one favouring it and the other opposing it. These were later to be termed the *New Lights* and the *Old Lights* and the difference corresponded to that between *Old* and *New Sides* in the Presbyterian churches of the Middle Colonies.

*

By the summer of 1735 the revival in the Northampton district began to lose its original force. There remained, however, a rich heritage of spiritual life among the people – a heritage of which, in the autumn of 1736, Edwards stated:

> There is still a great deal of religious conversation continued in the town, amongst young and old; a religious disposition seems to be still maintained amongst our people, by their holding frequent private religious meetings; and all sorts are generally worshipping God at such meetings, on Sabbath nights and in the evening after our public lecture. Many children in the town still keep up such meetings among themselves . . . We still remain a reformed people, and God has evidently made us a new people.[1]

In 1736 Edwards wrote *A Narrative of Surprising Conversions,* an account of the revival as it had taken place in New England. With all the force of his extraordinary mind he analysed the work in general and described instances of conversion in detail, and it will readily be seen with what avidity this book would be seized upon by the great numbers of persons already influenced by the revival. This was true of Edwards' people in New England, and true also of those throughout the extensive area reached by Frelinghuysen and the men of the New Brunswick Presbytery. Thomas Prince, the contemporary historian, records the effect of the *Narrative* in maintaining the fervour that had been experienced in the revival; says Prince:

> The rumour of that surprising work of God resounding through the country, was a special means of exciting great thoughtfulness of heart

[1] *Ibid, p* 72.

in many religious people; and great joy in others, both in view of what the mighty power and grace of God had wrought, and in the hopeful prospect that this blessed work would go on and spread throughout the land.[1]

One of the chief effects of the revival was the burden of supplication that it placed upon the hearts of the people. They who had tasted the heavenly fruit besought God that it might be granted to them in still richer abundance, and Prince goes on to say, 'this hope excited the extraordinary prayers of many'. Edwards describes the burden for the souls of the unsaved, saying:

Persons, after their own conversion, have commonly expressed an exceeding great desire for the conversion of others. Some have thought that they should be willing to *die* for the conversion of any soul, though one of the meanest of their fellow-creatures, or the worst of their enemies; and many, indeed, have been in great distress with desires and longings for it.[2]

Freylinghuysen made it a particular point in his work to organize his people into small companies that met regularly, in homes, or barns or meeting-houses, for Bible study and prayer. Similar groups sprang up from the labours of the New Brunswick men, insomuch that from Maine in the north to the borders of Virginia in the south, there were hundreds of people whose lives were characterized by these spiritual pursuits and whose deepest longing was to see the fires of revival enkindled again and burning throughout the land.

Out of this longing, however, there arose a practice that was foreign to true revival. We have noticed that, in certain instances, extreme emotional experiences had taken place. These had been witnessed under Edwards' ministry and under the preaching of the New Brunswick Presbytery men, though, while the former did not encourage these demonstrations, certain of the latter apparently attached importance to them. Some of the people, however, looked upon such outcryings as an essential feature of revival and developed the idea that the way to reawaken the revival fervour would be to make loud outcryings in the services. This became the practice in some locations in New England and

[1] Prince, *op cit,* Vol 2, *p* 379. [2] Edwards, *op cit*, *p* 47.

in others in the New Brunswick territory – a practice similar to the self-induced paroxysms of the people of Bristol and Kingswood.

Furthermore, the emphasis upon a converted church membership and a converted ministry led to a custom which also was harmful. Certain people began to take it upon themselves to judge as to those who were and those who were not converted, and, in turn, to denounce by name and with severity, those whom they placed in the unregenerate category.

*

It was while these conditions prevailed that the people of the Colonies were aroused by news from England. The newspapers reported the wonderful success of Whitefield's ministry in the churches of Bristol and London during 1737, and then came the reports of his still greater work in the open air in 1739. Such news awakened in the hearts of many a Christian in the Colonies an excitement and fostered a hope that God would send this renowned evangelist to America, and they saw in him the means whereby the revival fires might be rekindled and indeed spread throughout the land. Then word came that Whitefield was on his way to the Colonies and finally that he had arrived in Philadelphia and intended to preach wherever opportunity afforded throughout the Continent.

Such was the situation when Whitefield reached the new world – surely an extraordinary preparation for an extraordinary ministry!

Mr Whitefield arrived some months past at Philadelphia, where, and through the Jerseys and at New York, he preached daily to incredible multitudes with great eloquence and zeal. America is like to do him much honour. He proposes to see Boston in his return to Europe about June next; and our town and country stand ready to receive him as an angel of God. Ministers and people, all but his own Church, speak of him with great esteem and love.

DR BENJAMIN COLMAN
of Boston, in a letter to Dr Isaac Watts, January 16, 1740

26

Making the Acquaintance of America

HAPPY to be released from the confinement of life aboard, Whitefield left the vessel as soon as it reached America. This was at Lewis Town in Delaware, yet even here he found he was known and was requested by the mayor 'to give them a sermon'. After complying he set out to hasten to reach Philadelphia by land while 'the family' continued the journey by water, and such was his delight in being active again that he rode as many as fifty and sixty miles a day.

It was with a definite purpose that Whitefield had sailed for Philadelphia, in preference to going direct to Georgia. Philadelphia was the geographic centre of the Colonies and he intended to use it as a base from which to become acquainted with the rest of America. He needed to learn where he could purchase the materials which would be required for the construction and maintenance of the Orphan House. Moreover, he wished to discover what opportunities there might be for him to exercise his ministry of preaching the Gospel and receiving offerings, for only by this means could he support a charitable institution in an impoverished Colony at the southern extremity of the country.

It is evident that Whitefield felt the challenge of the great new world. Colonial America was but a ribbon of settlement, which, though seldom more than fifty miles in width, stretched for thirteen hundred miles along the Atlantic coast – from Maine in the north to Georgia's Fort Frederica in the south. The total population, exclusive of the Indians, was something under a million, and of these about one hundred and fifty thousand were negro slaves. The largest cities were Boston, New York and Philadelphia, each of which had between twelve and fourteen thousand inhabitants. The next were Charleston with about six thousand and Williamsburg with somewhat less. Although Whitefield could not have been aware of the publicity which the American papers had given to his work in England, there can be little doubt that he foresaw an extensive ministry awaiting him in the Colonies.

*

Whitefield found Philadelphia 'a city of brotherly love' in the reception that it accorded him. After arriving on a Friday night (November 2, 1739) he 'read prayers and assisted at the Church of England on Sunday, made the acquaintance of the Presbyterian and Baptist ministers on Monday, preached in the Church of England on Tuesday and dined with Thomas Penn[1] the Quaker on Wednesday. By that time, however, 'the inhabitants were very solicitous for [him] to preach in another place besides the church', and in response, on the Thursday evening, he held his first open-air service. Though it was late autumn and the days were getting cold, he 'preached from the Court House stairs to about six thousand people'.[2] Therewith Philadelphia's Court House Square became, like London's Kennington, his sky-domed cathedral. On Friday, Saturday and Sunday it was filled with hearers, about eight thousand each time, and of the Friday meeting he reported:

> Before I came all was hushed exceedingly quiet. The night was clear but not cold. Lights were in most of the windows all around us for a considerable distance. The people did not seem weary of standing, nor was I weary of speaking. The Lord endued me with power from on high. My heart was enlarged and warmed with divine love and my soul was so carried out in prayer that I thought I could have continued my discourse all night.[3]

Again people began to press upon him in his private hours. 'As soon as I come home', he writes, 'my house is generally filled with people, desirous to join in Psalms and prayers. They are so eager for the Bread of Life that they scarcely give me time to take bodily refreshment and proper retirement in my closet.'[4]

[1] Thomas Penn, son of William, was the one member of the Penn family then remaining in America. He and his brother Richard 'were possessors of a feudal estate of 25,000,000 acres'. *Encyclopedia Americana*, article PENN, Thomas.

[2] *Journals*, p 343. [3] *Ibid.* [4] *Ibid*, p 345.

It was evident, thus early in his days in America, that the popularity which had been his in England was to be his here too. He had gained the favour of the people and the friendship of the pastors – he says, 'I was visited again by the Presbyterian and Baptist preachers', and 'I was visited in a kind manner by the minister of the parish' (Church of England) – and had he merely desired good will, he could have gone on attracting it as widely as he wished.

He soon manifested, however, his willingness to sacrifice popular acclaim for the sake of Biblical truth. When he had been in Philadelphia but a week, old Mr Tennent paid him a visit, and Whitefield, learning of that venerable disciple's battle against deadness and formality in the churches, immediately took his stand with him. He wrote:

> He and his sons are secretly despised by the generality of the Synod, as Mr Erskine and his brethren are hated by the judicatories of Edinburgh, and as the Methodist preachers are by their brethren in England. Though we are but few and stand alone, as it were like Elijah, yet I doubt not the Lord will appear for us and make us more than conquerors.[1]

Thereupon, Whitefield extended the controversy into his public ministry. Of his Sunday afternoon meeting he said:

> I was much carried out in bearing my testimony against the unchristian principles and practices of our clergy. Three of my reverend brethren were present; I know not whether they were offended. I endeavoured to speak with meekness as well as zeal. Were I to convert Papists, my business would be to show that they were misguided by their priests; and if I want to convince Church of England Protestants, I must prove that the generality of their teachers do not preach or live up to the truth as it is in Jesus. In vain do we hope to set people right till we demonstrate that the way which they have been taught is wrong.[2]

In this action Whitefield aligned himself with the witness which was already dividing the Reformed, Presbyterian, Congregational and Baptist bodies. Through his faithfulness the controversy now entered the Church of England in America and,

[1] *Ibid*, *p* 344. [2] *Ibid*, *p* 345.

as a result, from this point onward he drew upon himself the angry opposition of almost all of its clergy.

*

After nine days in Philadelphia, Whitefield set out for New York. This was part of his plan to gain a first-hand knowledge of as much of America as possible.

At New Brunswick he made the acquaintance of Gilbert Tennent, and suggested that they might travel to New York together. They proved to be kindred spirits; '. . . as we passed along' (says Whitefield) 'we spent our time most agreeably in telling what God had done for our souls'.[1] Upon hearing Gilbert preach at New York he stated:

> I never before heard such a searching sermon. He convinced me more and more that we can preach the Gospel no further than we have experienced the power of it in our own hearts. Being deeply convicted of sin at his first conversion, he has learned experimentally to dissect the heart of a natural man. Hypocrites must either soon be converted or enraged at his preaching . . . He is a son of thunder and does not fear the faces of men.[2]

Whitefield had been invited to New York by two pressing letters from a Thomas Noble of that city. Noble was a man of strong Christian character and extensive financial means, and from later letters it appears that he indicated his intention to assist Whitefield in his undertakings, especially the Orphan House.

After reaching New York Whitefield called on the Rev Mr Vessey, the Commissary of the Church of England, intending to ask for the use of his church. This was in keeping with the practice he had followed in England, of preaching elsewhere only if the church was denied. But before he even had time to ask, Mr Vessey gave him an angry refusal. Thereupon Whitefield preached in a field, and, following that, at the invitation of Dr Pemberton, at the Wall Street Presbyterian Church.

Providentially, we have an eye-witness report of the service in the field, for an anonymous writer who published a letter in the *New England Journal* at the time stated:

> . . . I thought it possible that some *enthusiasm* might have mix'd itself

[1] *Journals, p* 347. [2] *Ibid, pp* 347–8.

with his piety and that his zeal might have exceeded his knowledge. With these prepossessions I went into the fields; when I came there, I saw a great number of people consisting of Christians of all denominations, some *Jews*, and a few, I believe, that had no religion at all.

When Mr Whitefield came to the place before designed, which was a little eminence on the side of a hill, he stood still and beckoned with his hand, and dispos'd the multitude upon the descent, before and on either side of him. He then *prayed most excellently* . . . The assembly soon appeared to be divided into two companies . . . The [one] were collected round the minister, and were very serious and attentive. The other had placed themselves in the skirts of the assembly, and spent most of their time in giggling, scoffing, talking and laughing . . . Towards the last prayer the whole assembly appeared more united, and all became hush'd and still; a solemn awe and reverence appeared in the faces of most, and a mighty energy attended the Word. I heard and felt something astonishing, but I confess, I was not at that time, fully rid of my scruples.

. . . Upon this frame of mind I went to hear him in the evening at the *Presbyterian Church* . . . I never in my life saw so attentive an audience. Mr Whitefield spoke as one having authority: all he said was *Demonstration, Life* and *Power*. The people's eyes and ears hung on his lips. They greedily devoured every word. I came home astonished. Every scruple vanished; I never saw or heard the like; and I said within myself, Surely God is with this man of a truth!

. . . Mr Whitefield is a man of middle stature, of a slender body, a fair complexion and a comely appearance. He is of sprightly cheerful temper and acts and moves with great agility. The endowments of his mind are very uncommon. His wit is quick and piercing, his imagination lively and florid; and, as far as I can discern, both are under the direction of an exact and solid judgment. He has a most ready memory and, I think, speaks entirely without notes. He has a clear and musical voice, and a wonderful command of it. He uses much gesture, but with great propriety. Every *accent* of his voice, and every *motion* of his body, speaks, and both are natural and unaffected. If his delivery be the product of art, 'tis certainly the perfection of it, for it is entirely concealed. He has a great mastery of words, but studies *much plainness of speech*.

. . . He speaks much the language of the New Testament; and has an admirable faculty in explaining the Scriptures. He strikes out of them such lights, and unveils those excellencies which surprise his hearers. He expresses the highest love and concern for the souls of men; and speaks of Christ with the most affectionate appropriation – My *Master*!

My *Lord*! He is no enemy to the innocent freedoms and liberties of the Gospel nor affects singularity in indifferent things. He spends not his zeal in trifles . . . He prays most earnestly, that God would destroy all that *bigotry* and party zeal that has divided Christians. He supposes some of Christ's flock are to be found under every denomination . . . He declares that his whole view in preaching is to bring men to Christ, to deliver them from their false *confidences*, to raise them from their dead formalities, to revive primitive Christianity among them; and if he can obtain this end he will leave them to their liberty, and they may go to what church, and worship God in what form they like best.[1]

The writer of this letter may very probably be identified, and the identity is highly significant. It was believed by many people at that time, and by others since, that the writer was none other than Dr Pemberton himself. Certainly, Pemberton, in seeing Whitefield accompanied by Gilbert Tennent, would be likely to regard him with suspicion, but we know that Pemberton became a warm admirer of Whitefield at this time. If this letter is from his pen, it indicates that this stalwart member of the evangelical moderates satisfied himself as to Whitefield's good sense and became convinced that he conjoined zeal with prudence in the manner described in the letter.

This view is strengthened by the fact that Jonathan Dickinson, the acknowledged leader of the evangelical moderates, invited Whitefield to preach in his church. With this request Whitefield complied, when, after preaching eight times in New York, he called at Elizabeth Town on his journey back toward Philadelphia.

While in New York, however, Whitefield wrote a letter to Jonathan Edwards. He knew he was near to him, yet not near enough to be able to meet him, and therefore introduced himself by correspondence, saying,

REV SIR,

Mr Noble and the report of your sincere love for our dear Lord Jesus, embolden me to write this. I rejoice for the many things God has done for many souls in Northampton. I hope, God willing, to come and see them in a few months. The Journal sent with this will shew you what the Lord is about to do in Europe . . .

[1] Prince, *op cit*, 1743, *pp* 361–3. Maxson, *op cit*, *p* 50. inclines to the view that this letter was written by Pemberton. He says, 'With a deft pen Mr Pemberton, for the article was attributed to him, described Whitefield's preaching . . .'

Our Lord's word begins to be glorified in America. Many hearts gladly receive it. Oh, Rev Sir, it grieves me to see people everywhere ready to perish for lack of knowledge. I care not what I suffer, so that some may be brought home to Christ. I am but a stripling, but the Lord chooses the weak things of this world to confound the strong. I should rejoice to be instructed by you.[1]

During the return journey to Philadelphia, Whitefield's services became rallying occasions for the evangelicals of the area. He mentions meeting 'several ministers whom the Lord has been pleased to honour in making them instruments of bringing many sons to glory'.[2] One of these was Theodorus Frelinghuysen, whom he describes as 'a worthy old soldier of Jesus Christ, . . . the beginner of the great work that I trust the Lord is carrying on in these parts'.[3] Of another, John Cross, one of the original members of the New Brunswick Presbytery, Whitefield says, 'He himself told me of many wonderful and sudden conversions that had been wrought by the Lord under his ministry'. He mentions also a Mr Camel (probably intended for Cambell) who, after a long and able ministry, had realized that he himself had never been converted and had recently experienced the new birth.

But Whitefield's chief joy came when he arrived at Neshaminy, the home of old Mr Tennent and the site of his Log College. Here he preached in the meeting-house yard and reported:

At first the people seemed [to be] unaffected, but in the midst of my discourse the hearers began to be melted down and cried much . . . It is surprising how such bodies of people, so scattered abroad, can be gathered at so short a warning . . . I believe there were nearly a thousand horses. The people, however, did not sit upon them to hear the sermon, as in England, but tied them to the hedges; and thereby much disorder was prevented.

. . . We had sweet communion with each other, and spent the evening in concerting measures for promoting our Lord's kingdom. It happens very providentially, that Mr Tennent and his brethren are appointed to be a Presbytery by the Synod, so that they intend breeding up gracious youths and sending them out into our Lord's vineyard. The place wherein the young men study now is, in contempt, called *the College*. It is a log house, about twenty feet long and nearly as many broad; . . . From this despised place, seven or eight worthy ministers of Jesus have lately been sent forth; . . . Carnal ministers oppose them strongly;

[1] *Works*, Vol 1, *p* 121. [2] *Journals*, *p* 350. [3] *Ibid*, *p* 352.

and because people, when awakened by Mr Tennent or his brethren, see through them and therefore leave their ministry, the poor gentlemen are loaded with contempt, and looked upon as persons who turn the world upside-down.[1]

The ministerial relationships which Whitefield was now experiencing marked another important milestone in his life. While at Oxford, like the rest of the Holy Club he had admitted of no fellowship except with men of the Church of England. But, as we have seen, following his conversion the logical conclusions of the doctrine of the new birth had caused him to embrace the friendship of regenerate men among the Dissenters and at the same time to feel a separation from non-regenerate persons within the Church. And in this direction he had moved still further, until now, in America, the same reasoning had caused him to take his stand against the unconverted among the clergy; this in turn had largely alienated him from his own communion and yet had brought him into this close fellowship with Presbyterians, Dutch Reformed and Baptists. Thus he had come to a position in which not denominational adherence but evangelical soundness was the criterion, and his work had become non-denominational in character.

*

Upon his return to Philadelphia, Whitefield found that the Anglican Church – Christ Church, which he said was 'as large as most of our London churches' – was still available to him, and since the weather was too cold for the out-door ministry, he preached in the church seven times. He also preached at Germantown, a place which contained 'no less than fifteen denominations of Christians'. And then, since Christ Church was proving too small to hold his congregations, despite the weather, he returned to the open air.

These activities caught the attention of Philadelphia's most astute citizen, Benjamin Franklin. This enterprising gentleman, though not interested in Whitefield's message, was attracted to him as a personality and an orator. Franklin also recognized that the publication of his sermons could be a profitable avenue of business. Whitefield merely says, '[A] printer told me he might

[1] *Journals*, pp 354–5.

have sold a thousand *Sermons*, if he had them; I therefore gave [him] two extempore discourses to be published'. Franklin, however, described Whitefield's ministry at some length, saying:

In 1739 there arrived among us the Rev Mr Whitefield. He was at first permitted to preach in some of the churches; but the clergy, taking a dislike to him, soon refus'd him their pulpits and he was oblig'd to preach in the fields. The multitudes of all sects and denominations that attended his sermons were enormous, and it was a matter of speculation with me, who was one of the number, to observe the extraordinary influence of his oratory on his hearers, and how much they admired and respected him, notwithstanding his common abuse of them, by assuring them they were naturally *half beasts and half devils*.[1]

It was wonderful to see the change soon made in the manners of our inhabitants. From being thoughtless or indifferent about religion, it seem'd as if all the world were growing religious, so that one could not walk thro' the town in an evening without hearing psalms sung in different families of every street.

. . . He had a loud and clear voice, and articulated his words and sentences so perfectly, that he might be heard and understood at a great distance, especially as his audiences, however numerous, observ'd the most exact silence. He preached one evening from the top of the Court House steps, which are in the middle of Market-street, and on the west side of Second-street, which crosses it at right angles. Both streets were filled with his hearers to a considerable distance. Being among the hindmost in Market-street, I had the curiosity to learn how far he could be heard, by retiring backwards down the street towards the river; and I found his voice distinct till I came near Front-street, when some noise in that street obscur'd it. Imagining then a semi-circle, of which my distance should be the radius, and that it were filled with auditors, to each of whom I allowed two square feet, I computed that he might well be heard by more than thirty thousand. This reconciled me to the newspaper accounts of his having preached to twenty-five thousand people in the fields . . .[2]

This was the beginning of a long association between the two men. Franklin became Whitefield's principal publisher in America, his personal friend and, at times, his host, and will frequently come into our narrative.

[1] This phrase, to which many writers have objected, was commonly used by the men of the Holy Club and was taken from the works of one of their favourite authors, Bishop Hall.

[2] Franklin's essay, 'George Whitefield,' to be found in the several editions of Franklin's *Works*.

In all of these meetings, Whitefield had, as yet, asked for no offerings. We see something of his tactful approach in this matter as we read his statement: 'Some little presents have been sent for the Orphan House, and a large collection, I believe, might be made for it; but I choose to defer that till my return hither again.'[1] He was planning his *preach and return* procedure; 'It seems necessary', he wrote, 'for the good of the Church in general, and my orphans in particular, that I should visit every place in America whither I have been before.'[2]

*

Having accomplished the purposes which brought him to that part of America, Whitefield prepared to set out for Georgia. Because no proper roads existed throughout much of the eight hundred-mile distance, that journey was usually made aboard a coastal vessel. A friend offered to lend Whitefield a sloop by which to transport *the family* and his large supply of goods for the Orphan House, but William Seward, knowing there would be permanent use for such a ship and that Captain Gladman was available to take command, purchased it, and renamed it the *Savannah*. In this *the family* set sail for Georgia, while Whitefield did a surprising thing: accompanied by Seward and Syms, he began the long and hazardous journey by land.

This decision was not, however, 'a strange freak', as some have suggested. It was part of Whitefield's determination to know America by personal observation and to preach as often as possible. Moreover, while constantly active in travelling he could more easily forget the problems that were on his mind – his affection for Betty Delamotte and John Wesley's sermon against predestination – problems he would find more difficult were he to suffer another period of inactivity aboard ship.

Whitefield's last service in Philadelphia witnessed a great crowd of 'upwards of ten thousand'. On the following morning people began to throng round his door at seven o'clock. 'Oh how bitterly did the poor souls weep!' he wrote. 'As I passed along the street they came running out to the doors . . . Nearly twenty gentlemen accompanied me on horseback out of town. About seven miles off another company was waiting to meet us,

[1] *Journals, p* 357. [2] *Ibid.*

so that at last we were nearly two hundred horse.'[1] And thus, with this procession accompanying him, he left the Philadelphia area and set out on the overland route for Georgia.

During the first hundred miles of travelling the territory was fairly well populated and Whitefield was able to preach to some large crowds. His *Journal* reports:

CHESTER, Thursday, Nov. 29 . . . I preached to about five thousand people from a balcony. It being court-day, the Justices sent word that they would defer their meeting till mine was over.

WILMINGTON, Friday, Nov. 30. Preached at noon and again at three in the afternoon. Received several fresh invitations to preach at various places, but was obliged to refuse them all. Oh, that I had a hundred tongues and lives, they should all be employed for my dear Lord Jesus.

NEWCASTLE, Saturday, Dec. 1. Preached to about two thousand from a balcony, but did not speak with so much freedom and power as usual, God being pleased to humble my soul by inward visitations and a bodily indisposition. Lay on the bed after sermon, which much refreshed me.

WHITECLAY CREEK, Sunday, Dec. 2. The weather was rainy, but upwards of ten thousand people were assembled. It surprised me to see such a number of horses. There were several hundreds of them. I preached from a tent erected for me by Mr William Tennent, . . . I continued my discourse for an hour and a half, after which we went into a log-house near by, took a morsel of bread and warmed ourselves. I preached a second time from the same place. My body was weak . . .[2]

Franklin published an account of these meetings in his newspaper, and his figures, on the average, are higher than those of Whitefield. Moreover, his report of the Sunday gathering says that '3,000 came on horse-back', and one cannot but wonder what commotion must have been caused by the assembling, tethering, feeding and watering of so many animals.

As Whitefield moved on southward he met varied and trying experiences. Not far from North East in Maryland his presence prevented a drinking party at a house where he lodged, and at Annapolis he was 'received with much civility' by the Governor.

[1] *Ibid, p* 361.

[2] *Ibid, pp* 361–4. The William Tennent here mentioned was the son of the elderly William, the founder of the *Log College*.

At Port Tobacco, after he and his party had rowed about a mile in attempting to cross the Potomac, they were driven back by high winds and the approach of night, and he commented that, had they not turned about, 'both we and our horses must have been lost'.[1] In Virginia he found the roads better and the country more settled than in Maryland, but found difficulty in buying food and provender. He sought everywhere to maintain his witness for the Lord and remarked: 'If I talk of the Spirit I am a Quaker! If I say grace at breakfast I am a Presbyterian! Alas! what must I do to be accounted a member of the Church of England?'[2]

By December 14 Whitefield reached Williamsburg, which he termed 'the metropolis of Virginia'. He was happy to find this jewel of civilization amidst the American woods and reported:

> . . . dined with the Governor, who received me most courteously. Paid my respects to the Rev Mr Blair, the Commissary of Virginia, and by far the most worthy clergyman I have yet conversed with in all America . . . He has been chiefly instrumental in raising a beautiful college at Williamsburgh, in which is a foundation for about eight scholars, a president, two masters, and professors in the several sciences. Here the gentlemen of Virginia send their children, and as far as I could learn by enquiry, they are under about the same regulation and discipline as in our Universities at home. The present masters came from Oxford. Two of them, I find, were my contemporaries there.[3]

Between Williamsburg and Charleston there lay three weeks of travel through sparsely settled regions.

On one occasion Whitefield and his companions lost their way in the woods at night. Finding a cabin full of negroes, they supposed them to be a party of run-away slaves who were then being hunted in the area, and, sensing the danger, they hurried on their way.

> Soon after [wrote Whitefield] we saw another great fire near the roadside, and imagining there was another nest of such negroes, we made a circuit into the woods, and one of my friends at a distance observed them dancing round the fire. The moon shining brightly, we soon found our way into the great road again: and after we had gone about a dozen miles (expecting to find negroes in every place), we came to a

[1] *Journals, p* 369. [2] *Ibid, p* 370. [3] *Ibid, p* 371.

great plantation, the master of which gave us lodging and our beasts provender.[1]

Two days later they again reached civilization. This was Charleston in South Carolina and, since the Church of England Commissary was away, Whitefield preached in a Dissenters' meeting-house. He remarked the finery of dress and gaiety of deportment among the people, and, although he saw no effect on the first day, on the following he wrote, 'Many were melted into tears . . . Many of the inhabitants . . . entreated me to give them one more sermon.'[2]

Charleston marked the end of the journey by land, for between it and Savannah there lay not even a trail. Travel was by water along the coast, and they set out in an open canoe rowed by five negroes. On one night they 'lay on the water', and on another they 'made a fire on the shore and slept round it for four hours'. Finally, on January 10, 1740, forty-three days after leaving Philadelphia, they reached their destination, Savannah, Georgia.

The amount of America that Whitefield had now traversed was, to say the least, extraordinary. He had been in the Colonies but two months, yet in that time had travelled the continent from New York to Savannah – a journey which few men, apart from a handful of adventurers, had ever made.

Whitefield's travels, however, had served to increase his prospect of difficulty. Now he could see that the Colony, in which he was about to erect a large charitable institution, was not only impoverished, but also was so isolated as to create many problems in obtaining the necessary supplies. And in this knowledge there was new and deeper significance in his statement that he was not building in a settled land, but 'at the ends of the earth in Georgia'.

[1] *Ibid, p* 383. [2] *Ibid, p* 371.

One of the most blessed results of the spiritual awakening of the eighteenth century, which spread over the whole of the English-speaking world, was the deepening and increasing interest in child welfare. It is exceedingly difficult for us of to-day to appreciate the condition of children, especially of the poor, two centuries ago. We should, therefore, carefully note as we consider Whitefield's love and services for children, that he blazed out new paths which have now become thoroughfares of Christian activity.

EDWIN NOAH HARDY

George Whitefield, the Matchless Soul Winner, 1938

27

A House of Mercy in the Woods of Georgia

WHILE on the journey from New York to Georgia Whitefield undoubtedly told himself that his affection for Betty Delamotte was a thing of the past; that with the broad Atlantic separating them and a great activity before him, he could remove her entirely from his mind. But, alas! when he reached Savannah he found a letter from her awaiting him, and therewith his affection was reawakened and the whole struggle was on him again.

From that point on, his letters reveal a soul torn with conflict. In his determination to allow no lessening of his devotion to the Lord he strove to subdue his desires, and so fierce was the battle that he was more than once reduced to sickness. But after three months of what he calls 'strong cryings and tears and unspeakable troubles with my own heart', he could resist no longer, and in unwilling submission wrote a proposal of marriage.

We shall look into the matter more fully in a later chapter, but in the meantime must bear these circumstances in mind. We must see him mentally burdened, physically weak and suffering a sense of spiritual defeat, and this must be the background against which we view his labours in establishing a home for homeless children.

*

On the day after his arrival in the Colony Whitefield wrote:

Friday, January 11, 1740. Went this morning, with some friends, to view a tract of land, consisting of five hundred acres, which Mr Habersham . . . made choice of for the Orphan House. It is situated in the northern part of the colony, about ten miles from Savannah . . . Some acres, through the diligence of my friend, are cleared. He has also stocked it with cattle and poultry. He has begun the fence and built a hut . . .'[1]

Whitefield expressed his ideal for the institution: 'I called it Bethesda, that is, The House of Mercy; for I hope many acts of mercy will be shown there . . .'[2]

But the 'acts of mercy' could not be left undone till the Orphan House was completed. That would be several months, and in view of the pitiable condition of many children he immediately rented a house – the largest in Savannah[3] – and soon had more than twenty orphans under his care. He also opened an infirmary, supplied it with the medicines he had brought from England, and placed surgeon Hunter in charge.[4] This was expensive work, but its necessity is manifest in Whitefield's statement:

Took in three German orphans, the most pitiable objects, I think, I ever saw. No new negroes could look more despicable, or require more pains to instruct them. They have been used to exceedingly hard labour, and though supplied with provisions from the Trustees, were treated in a manner unbecoming even heathens. Were all the money I have collected to be spent in freeing these three children from slavery, it would be well laid out.[5]

Whitefield also reports: 'I began the cotton manufacture and agreed with a woman to teach the little ones to spin and card. I find annual cotton grows fairly well in Georgia; and to encourage the people, I bought to-day, three hundred pounds weight, and have agreed to take all the cotton, hemp and flax that shall be produced the following year through the whole province.'[6] This was part of his 'design to have each of the children taught to labour, so as to be qualified to get their own living'. The youngsters spent five hours a day at their school work and other hours at this spinning and carding.

[1] *Journals*, *p* 395. [2] *Ibid.*

[3] Colonel Stephens, the Secretary of the Colony wrote: 'Mr Whitefield agreed with David Douglas, to rent his house (much the largest of any private lot in town) at a rent of £20, for half a year only . . . Douglas took advantage of exacting so unreasonable a rent.' *The Colonial Records of Georgia*, Vol 4, *p* 491. Whitefield also rented another house, that of a Mr Bradley, for the women he had brought. He and his men lived at the parsonage house.

[4] Lord Egmont speaks of Hunter as 'an experienced apothecary and surgeon of good substance'. *Diary*, Jan. 16, 1739.

[5] *Journals*, *p* 395. [6] *Ibid*, *p* 396.

With the needs of the children thus met in the temporary location Whitefield launched into construction of the permanent buildings. After suffering two weeks of frustrating delay, due to the pettiness of Colonel Stephens, the Secretary of the Colony, he proceeded with vigour, writing:[1]

> Wednesday, Jan. 30. Went with the carpenter and surveyor and laid out the ground whereon the Orphan House is to be built . . . The house is to be two stories high, with a hip roof; the first ten, the second nine feet high. In all there will be nearly twenty commodious rooms. Behind are to be two small houses, the one for an infirmary, the other for a workhouse. There is also to be a still-house for the apothecary . . . There are nearly thirty working at the plantation already, and I would employ as many more if they were to be had[2].

A project of this nature could not fail to abound with difficulties. The architect's drawings had been prepared in London, and Whitefield, who was totally inexperienced in matters of construction, now found it necessary, with the aid of a carpenter and a surveyor, to make those several decisions which are normally made at the site by the architect. And since artisans in the building trades were few in Georgia we may be sure that, in hiring every available man, he employed several of the former debtors from the prisons of England – men who would be of little use in either arduous toil or precise workmanship.

But the enterprise extended far beyond the construction of the Orphan House buildings. More land had to be cleared, barns built, the fence continued and a dock erected at the river front. Besides this, there was the construction of what Whitefield called 'a great cart road from Savannah, which will be very serviceable to all the plantations thereabout'. This was a distance of ten miles – the largest piece of road construction undertaken in the Colony till that time. Whitefield expected that the Trustees would share the costs of the road, but apart from that, all this work looked to him for decisions as to what to do and for the drive and money to get it done.

*

[1] The property had been deeded the year before to Habersham, who, in taking out the title, had gone over the head of Colonel Stephens and had dealt directly with Governor Oglethorpe. Thus, as Whitefield sought to have the title transferred to himself, Stephens showed his authority by holding up proceedings for two weeks. He finally relented and acted as witness to the transfer.

[2] *Journals*, p 396.

In order, however, to understand the full nature of Whitefield's undertaking and the extent of the problems he faced, we must notice the breadth of his concept.

Of course, Bethesda was to be primarily a home for orphaned children. But Whitefield intended that it should also supply them with a goodly education; not only were the usual subjects to be taught, but he made a list of books of religion, history and literature which he wished the children to read, and in a few months' time he added a Latin Master to the staff. We have noticed the spinning operations, and while the girls learned this employment, for the boys the institution was to be 'a nursery for mechanics and planters'.

Moreover, Bethesda was to be made as self-supporting as possible. From its forests would come the lumber used in its construction and from its plantation (raising chickens, pigs, cattle, fruit and grain) the bulk of its food requirements. The spinning and weaving would supply textiles for clothing and household needs. All surpluses of these products were to be sold, and the sloop was to earn a revenue by carrying freight.[1]

Whitefield also had certain ideals regarding the operating of the institution – ideals which were very important to him. Above everything else, Bethesda was to be a place of Gospel influence, and he deemed it his duty to see that all parentless children, even those in foster homes, were rescued from their usually godless surroundings and brought up in the wholesome atmosphere of the Orphan House. Moreover, we have seen that Whitefield regarded strong discipline as an essential part of the Christian life and that he looked on one's time as a precious gift from heaven which should never be wasted. Thus, the children were to be under steady discipline and were to be taught such virtues as hard work, thrift, promptness, obedience and responsibility. For these reasons it was imperative that the institution be governed with an unbending, though benign, authority.

Finally, Whitefield had a vision that from this institution there would spring another: a university. While crossing the Atlantic he had stated, 'Who knows but that we may have a

[1] We have an example in the following note: 'Charleston . . . where the Captain is to take in freight for the benefit of the Orphan House.' *Ibid, p* 449.

college of pious youths at Savannah?,[1] and after laying the first brick of Bethesda, he said, 'I laid a foundation for a university in Georgia'.[2]

It was with these extensive plans in mind that Whitefield witnessed the beginnings of the House of Mercy. The clearing in the woods rang with the noise of the axe and hammer and the sound of busy men was heard on every side. All of Georgia was full of the excitement of the project, for now work and wages were available for every man and more money was in circulation than the Colony had ever known.

*

As soon as construction had advanced sufficiently to allow him to be absent, Whitefield set out to gather whatever orphans there might be in the other settlements. He wrote:

Monday, Feb. 11. Took in four fresh orphans, and set out with two friends, to Frederica, in order to pay my respects to General Oglethorpe, and to fetch the orphans in the southern parts of the colony.

DARIEN, near Frederica, Friday, Feb. 15. [Lay] on the water two nights, and reached the Scots' settlement to-day at noon. Was kindly received by Mr MacLeod, the minister. Engaged to take four orphans of his flock . . . took boat for Frederica, where we arrived about two in the morning . . .

FREDERICA, Saturday, Feb. 16. Waited upon and was courteously received by the General, with whom I and my friends breakfasted and dined, and spent most part of the day. At night I had a fever which obliged me to go to bed sooner than usual. My mind also was exercised with inward trials.

Sunday, Feb. 17. Found myself better in body, though somewhat weak. Preached in the morning in a room belonging to the storehouse . . . The General, soldiers and people attended very orderly.

Monday, Feb. 18. Rose this morning by one o'clock. Took boat in order to go to St Andrews, but the rudder breaking, we were obliged to return. Went to bed and slept for a few hours. Spent a good part of the day with the General. Received from him a bill of exchange for £150, which he advanced me in order to begin a church at Savannah. About seven o'clock we set off for Darien . . . The wind being contrary, we were obliged to come to a grappling, and did not get to Darien till the next day at noon. Mr MacLeod and his friends received us with joy, and finding me ill, advised me to lie down.[3]

[1] *Works*, Vol 1, *p* 84. [2] *Ibid*, *p* 185. [3] *Journals*, *pp* 397–8.

At Darien Whitefield 'settled a school, both for grown persons and children' – another in the growing list of his accomplishments in this field. At the Saltzburghers' settlement he delivered several items he had brought from England, and with much rejoicing the pastor, the Rev Martin Boltzius, reported the occasion, saying:

He furnished me with many necessaries . . . Besides this, he paid me £52 19s., for raising a public place of worshipping, and bought a large bell for us, and the necessary iron-work for the building of the church.[1]

*

Within two weeks after his return to Savannah, Whitefield left for Charleston, South Carolina. Many of its people had entreated him to come and preach, and, moreover, his brother James, a ship's captain, was arrived there with a packet of letters from England for him.

Upon reaching the city Whitefield applied to the Church of England Commissary, the Rev Alexander Garden, for the use of his church, and met a very angry refusal. But the Independent, Baptist and Presbyterian ministers welcomed him and he preached in their meeting-houses twice a day. His stay lasted only four days, but even in so short a time the city appears to have been deeply stirred. At the request of several people, Whitefield took up a collection for the Orphan House – the first in America. And it augured well, for it amounted to £70 – more than he had ever received at one time in England. He reports that as he took his leave:

Many wept . . . several came to me, telling me how God had been pleased to convince them by the Word preached . . . Many earnestly entreated that I would come among them again . . . and many things concurred to induce me to think that God intended to visit some in Charleston with His salvation.[2]

*

Among the letters brought to Whitefield by his brother there was one from John Wesley. It is to be regretted that this letter has not been preserved, but from Whitefield's reply it is evident that

[1] *Colonial Records of Georgia,* Book 22, Vol 2, *p* 300.
[2] *Journals, pp* 402–3.

Wesley introduced the matters on which they differed and sought to provoke him into dispute. Whitefield answered:

Savannah, March 26, 1740

HONOURED SIR,

Since I returned here, I received your letter and journal – I thank you for both, and shall wait almost with impatience to see a continuance of your account of what God is doing or has done amongst you – He knows my heart, I rejoice in whatever God has done by your hands. *I prae, sequar, etsi non passibus equis.*[1]

I could now send a particular answer to your last; but, my honoured friend and brother, for once hearken to a child, who is willing to wash your feet. I beseech you by the mercies of God in Christ Jesus our Lord, if you would have my love confirmed towards you, write no more to me about misrepresentations wherein we differ. To the best of my knowledge at present, no sin has *dominion* over me, yet I feel the strugglings of indwelling sin day by day; I can therefore by no means come into your interpretation of the passage mentioned in the letter, and as explained in your preface to Mr *Halyburton*. The doctrine of *election*, and the *final perseverance* of those that are truly in Christ, I am ten thousand times more convinced of, if possible, than when I saw you last. You think otherwise: why then should we dispute, when there is no probability of convincing? Will it not in the end destroy brotherly love, and insensibly take from us that cordial union and sweetness of soul, which I pray God may always subsist between us? How glad would the enemies of the Lord be to see us divided? How many would rejoice, should I join and make a party against you? And in one word, how would the cause of our common Master every way suffer by our raising disputes about particular points of doctrines?

Honoured Sir, let us offer salvation freely to all by the blood of Jesus; and whatever light God has communicated to us, let us freely communicate to others. I have lately read the life of Luther, and think it in no wise to his honour, that the last part of his life was so much taken up in disputing with Zuinglius and others; who in all probability equally loved the Lord Jesus, notwithstanding they might differ from him in other points. Let this, dear Sir, be a caution to us, I hope it will to me; for by the blessing of God, provoke me to it as much as you please, I do not think ever to enter the lists of controversy with you on the points wherein we differ. Only I pray to God, that the more

[1] Go before, I follow, though with unequal steps.

you *judge me*, the more I may *love you*, and learn to desire no one's approbation, but that of my Lord and Master, Jesus Christ.

Ere this reaches you, I suppose you will hear of my late excursion to Charles Town. A great work I believe is begun there. Enclosed I have sent you *Mr Garden's letters* – They will serve to convince you more and more, of the necessity you lie under to be instant in season and out of season.

Oh, dear honoured Sir, I wish you as much success as your own heart can wish. Was you here I would weep over you with tears of love, and tell you what great things God has done for my soul, since we parted last. Indeed and indeed, I often and heartily pray for your success in the Gospel: May your inward strength and outward sphere increase day by day! May God use you as a choice and singular instrument of promoting His glory on earth, and may I see you crowned with an eternal and exceeding weight of glory in the world to come! This is the hearty desire of, honoured Sir,

Yours most affectionately in Christ Jesus,

G. W.[1]

This letter requires our attention. We have already noticed two letters which Whitefield wrote to Wesley while yet in England, beseeching him to be at peace, and we shall notice others which he wrote during later weeks of this stay in America. These letters constitute the only part which Whitefield took in the events that led up to the separation which came between Wesley and himself. The above letter certainly breathes a spirit of restraint, respect and a desire for peace, and we shall see a similar spirit in the later letters. Yet, in one of the strangest inversions to be found anywhere in church history, Whitefield's actions in these events have been portrayed as impulsive, abusive and quarrelsome. We do well, therefore, to bear in mind the true nature of this letter, and to pay similar attention to the others that we shall see in due course.

*

After the Orphan House had been under construction for six weeks, Whitefield reported:

[1] *Works*, Vol 1, *pp* 155–7. Gillies, in publishing Whitefield's correspondence, printed each letter as one unbroken paragraph. Many of Whitefield's original letters that are extant to-day, however, are composed of several paragraphs, and for this reason and also in order to facilitate reading, letters that are herein quoted at length are broken into separate paragraphs.

Nearly twenty acres of land are cleared, and almost ready for planting. Two houses are already raised, and one nearly finished. All the timber for the great house is sawn, and most of it brought to the place where it is to be built. A good part of the foundation is dug, and many thousands of bricks ready for use. Nearly forty children are now under my care, and nearly a hundred mouths are daily supplied with food from our store. The expense is great, but our great and good God, I am persuaded, will enable me to defray it.[1]

Whitefield's mention of the greatness of the expense raises some questions. Already the costs of building in this isolated location had proved so high that the fund he had brought from England was all but depleted. Benjamin Franklin stated that, due to the scarcity of workmen and materials in Georgia, the institution might better have been built in Pennsylvania and the children have been transported there. Knowing that it became an immense burden upon Whitefield, weighing him down with debt, impairing his health and shortening his life, we must enquire whether or not the plan was a wise one. Did he rush unthinkingly into so heavy an undertaking without first counting the cost?

These questions have already been answered in part. We have seen that, before his first visit to Georgia, Whitefield had been influenced regarding the need for such an institution by Oglethorpe, the Trustees and Charles Wesley. In turn, upon reaching the Colony he had been so deeply affected by the plight of the orphans that he had virtually found himself left with no choice in the matter: he must build a House of Mercy for them.

Similarly, he had little choice but to build it in Georgia. More than once he stated the desirability of having it in Pennsylvania, but it was on the understanding that it would be erected in Georgia that people had given their money for it. On this understanding also he had made his arrangements with the Trustees, and only under sore provocation and in open defiance of these officials could he have constructed it elsewhere.

Moreover, Whitefield was not proceeding without the prospect of considerable financial and moral support. The Governor, the Trustees, the Archbishop and several Bishops, had shown their favour of the project, and Charles Wesley (indicating, no doubt, a general Holy Club attitude) had spoken of it as 'our Orphan-

[1] *Journals*, p 403.

house.'[1] William Seward took the position of backing the undertaking with his own substance and acted as jointly responsible in its expenses. Whitefield also had reason to believe that assistance, in a goodly measure, would be forthcoming from Thomas Noble and others of similar means, and there was no doubt but that he would be able to receive large collections in both Britain and America. These assurances of monetary aid were in Whitefield's mind and, since the Lord was apparently raising up such support, he could hardly have worked on a lesser scale.

As to errors in judgment, Whitefield could have saved money, no doubt, had he been willing to bargain over the purchase of materials, and he was manifestly a soft touch for anyone in need, either real or professed. Had he been willing to proceed more slowly construction might have cost less. But haggling over prices or refusing anyone who sought his aid – these were not possible with him, and saying 'What is done for the Lord ought to be done with all our might', he drove on with the task and laboured to see it completed.

Nevertheless, Whitefield knew that he was allowing his heart to over-rule his head. He said later that he realized he had not 'proceeded according to the rules of prudence', but added that it was because he 'found their [the orphans'] condition so pitiable, and the inhabitants so poor' that he did not fully consider the cost in coming to their relief. But, as with the passing of the months Bethesda proved a crushing load of debt and care, he resigned himself to it, yet there is poignant meaning to his statement, 'Had I received more, and ventured less, I should have suffered less, and others more'.[2]

After building operations had proceeded for six months, Secretary Stephens rode out to see what progress was being made. Though he had become severely critical of Whitefield he reported:

July 24, 1740 . . . The principal house is a grand edifice. It is in such forwardness as to be ready for the raising of the roof this week. It is well cellared underneath: the foundation walls are of bricks, which rise several feet higher than the surface of the land.

As we approach it there are six good, handsome edifices, three on each side, for the following purposes – viz., a work-house for women and children, opposite is an Infirmary, next a kitchen, opposite to it

[1] Charles Wesley's *Journal*, November 7, 1737.

[2] Gillies, *op cit*, *p* 51.

another of the same size for washing, brewing, &c.; the other two I was not informed what purpose they are designed for.[1]

Thus the House of Mercy arose within woods – a stately and practical structure. Despite whatever might be considered as too ambitious in its concept, as it moved toward completion it constituted a monument to the breadth of heart and strength of purpose of the twenty-five-year-old evangelist who built it.

*

But though Whitefield expected the co-operation of the Trustees, what he actually received was their hindrance. To understand this matter we go back to the story of his earlier relations with them.

On returning to England from his previous mission to Georgia he had informed them of his willingness to undertake the Orphan House, but had been particularly definite regarding the conditions under which he would do so. The Earl of Egmont, President of the Trustees, says that in meeting with them on December 13 (1738) Whitefield stated, '. . . that he would return again, in case certain propositions delivered by him in writing were complied with; otherwise, that he would remain in England'.[2]

Two weeks later Egmont made the further report:

A commission was sealed to the Rev Mr Whitefield to collect money for erecting an Orphan House at Savannah and a church at Ebenezer. At which time (he attending the Board) we acquainted him that we had agreed to his proposals, which were the conditions on which he offered to return . . . We also desired Mr Whitefield to let us know what sum he should have collected by our deputation to him, because we should thereby be judges what might be farther necessary for us to contribute to accomplish the design of erecting the Orphan House.[3]

But shortly after these transactions Whitefield's relations with the Trustees suffered a serious deterioration. He became a field preacher, began to make severe criticisms of the clergy and, in the opinion of many, changed from the respected young clergyman into an ecclesiastical outcast. The Trustees, in turn, were far

[1] Stephens' *Journals, op cit,* entry of July 24, 1740.
[2] *Manuscripts of the Earl of Egmont, Diary of the First Earl of Egmont,* Vol 2, *p* 512.
[3] *Ibid, p* 516.

from happy in being associated with 'a fool for Christ's sake', and they became highly critical when, by reason of the large offerings that he received from his out-of-doors congregations, he told them he did not need their financial help. He returned their commission and Egmont's account of the event is that he told them 'he could not receive a farthing by virtue of it, but that it everywhere met with contempt'.[1]

The Trustees – a body of distinguished Englishmen – were understandably affronted by such a statement. Nevertheless, Whitefield put in writing his request for five hundred acres of land, and stipulated that it be granted,

> with the privilege of leaving it to whom he pleased for the use of the Orphan House, for since that House was to be built with the contributions that he should collect, he thought it but just that he should have the management and disposal thereof. That he desired no salary for himself and friends; wherefore, if the Trustees should not think proper to grant these terms, he thought it best to decline erecting the Orphan House.[2]

After considering this request Egmont wrote,

> We agreed to his terms, that he should have a grant of 500 acres in trust, to be settled in perpetuity for the use of the Orphan House . . .[3]

Likewise, of this meeting Whitefield reported,

> The Honourable Trustees for Georgia . . . agreed to everything I asked, and gave a grant of 500 acres of land, to me and my successors for ever, for the use of the Orphan House.[4]

From these records it is evident that Whitefield's understanding with the Trustees was clear: (1) in return for the grant of land he was to take the responsibility for the orphans of the Colony off their hands; (2) he was to be financially responsible for the whole undertaking, was to have full management of the institution, and was empowered to bequeath it to whomsoever he desired for its continued use as an Orphan House.

Accordingly the Trustees drew up a deed which incorporated these terms, and some weeks after Whitefield reached Georgia they sent him what was supposed to be an exact copy. But when he

[1] *Colonial Records of Georgia,* Vol 5, *p* 166.
[2] *Ibid.* [3] *Ibid.* [4] *Journals, p* 263.

read it he was shocked. The very terms that he had specified and on which alone he was willing to undertake so great a responsibility were deleted. Under the new terms he was not allowed the right to bequeath the institution, but, at his death it was to come under the control of the Trustees; in the meantime (doubtless, as an admission of their superior authority) he was to pay a yearly quit rent of £3, and was to make regular reports to them of all his receipts and expenditures.

The reasons for these changes are manifest. Not only had the Trustees been stung by his statement that their commission 'met everywhere with contempt', but this feeling had been severely aggravated by a letter that he had written to them after arriving in Georgia. Expecting to find certain improvements that had been promised for the Colony completed, but finding, instead, little or nothing done, he wrote to the Trustees, stating, 'If there's no alteration for the better and the Church be not built, I shall think it my duty to inform pious people in a publick manner, how little good has been done with their charitable contributions'.[1] Lord Egmont says that upon reading this letter the Trustees were 'enraged', and in the discussion that followed Whitefield was bitterly denounced. He was called 'a Methodistical madman', his integrity in money matters was impugned, and it was charged that he intended to make the Orphan House 'a school or Seminary for breeding up Methodists'. Egmont came to his defence, speaking of him as 'sincere though mistaken', but the other Trustees, 'in full resentment', claimed that, as a public trust, they could not conscientiously allow Whitefield the authority contained in their original agreement.

But Whitefield also had a public trust to fulfil. The people had given toward the Orphan House, not with the slightest thought of the Trustees, but as putting money into Whitefield's hands for the erecting and operating of an institution conducted on evangelical principles and solely in evangelical control. This trust would be violated if the Trustees were its supreme authority and if, after Whitefield's death, it came into their possession.

Accordingly, Whitefield wrote a stiff letter to the Trustees. He demanded that they return to the terms of their original agreement and categorically refused to pay the quit rent or to give

[1] *Colonial Records of Georgia,* Book 22, Vol 2, *p* 352.

them a report of his financial activities. His report, he stated, would be a printed one, made to the public.

*

This, however, was but the beginning of Whitefield's troubles regarding the Orphan House.

Disagreement soon arose over the failure of the deed to specify whether Whitefield was to have charge of all the orphans or merely the destitute ones.

Whitefield learned that one of the colonists, Bailiff Parker, had two orphan boys named Tondee living with him, and asked that they be brought to the Orphan House. In the case of the younger boy Parker readily agreed, but stated concerning the older one, '. . . being a well-grown lad of 15 or 16 years, it would be a great hardship to have that boy taken from him, now that he is grown capable of doing him some service, after living so long with him when he could do him none'.[1] The boy had been well treated, though Parker had undoubtedly been recompensed by the Trustees[2] for providing a foster home. Nevertheless, Whitefield, believing that all the orphans had been placed under his care, answered 'that the boy would be so much the better for him and his purpose, as he could be employed for the benefit of the other orphans'.

Thereupon Parker grew angry and Whitefield produced his copy of the deed. Even Secretary Stephens (who, by this time, was quite unfriendly toward Whitefield) agreed that the document gave Whitefield control of all the orphans, and on that basis the boy was sent to the Orphan House.

The reports that we have of these matters come almost solely from Stephens, and while they are undoubtedly correct in the main, their language is probably coloured in such a way as to present Whitefield in a disparaging light. Nevertheless, one cannot but feel that Whitefield was unkind to both Parker and the boy, and some of the colonists thought so too. Accordingly, a

[1] Stephens' *Journal*, p 505.

[2] The Trustees had previously employed a man named Edward Jenkins as overseer of the orphans. He had placed the children in foster homes where they were maintained at the Trustees' expense. He had also been empowered to seize any possessions any orphans may have had. When Whitefield arrived there was a formal turning over the accounts from Jenkins to him.

meeting was held between Whitefield, Stephens and the Magistrates in order to define the extent of his authority, and Stephens wrote:

It was the opinion of all present, upon having recourse to the Trust's deed, that there was not any exception made, but that all orphans were included, who either had been or were chargeable to the Trust.[1]

This matter, however, came to a climax in the case of the Mellidge family. The father had been a prominent settler, and, following his death and that of his wife, the two younger children (a boy and a girl) had been brought up by the two older children (also a boy and a girl) who by this time were in their late teens. General Oglethorpe had taken a personal interest in this family.

But Whitefield, believing that there was no Gospel influence in the home, had the two younger children brought to Bethesda. Whereupon the older brother, John, obtained the services of an attorney, Thomas Jones,[2] who carried the matter to Governor Oglethorpe, and after due consideration Oglethorpe made the following statements:

I have inspected the grant relating to the Orphan House . . . The Trustees have granted the *care* of the *helpless* orphans to Mr Whitefield, and have given him five hundred acres of land, and a power of collecting charities, as a consideration for maintaining all the orphans who are in necessity in this province.[3]

. . . as for Mellidge's brother and sister, I think . . . that the taking them away to the Orphan House will break up a family which is in a likely way of living comfortably. Mr Whitefield's design is for ye good of ye people, and the glory of God, and I dare say, when he considers this he will be well satisfied with the boy and girl returning to their brother John.[4]

The Governor's attitude appears both reasonable and kind. But Whitefield, in his conviction that every orphan deserved the privilege of the evangelical environment of Bethesda, and that the discipline of the institution depended on his having the authority

[1] Stephens' *Journal, p* 505.

[2] Egmont, *Journal*, Vol 2, *p* 485, speaks of Jones as having been high Bailiff of Westminster, and says, 'Oglethorpe proposes a great advantage in having him as companion, for he looks on him as a capable man to advise him'.

[3] Stephens, *Journal*, Part 2, *p* 340.

[4] *Collections of the Georgia Historical Society*, 'The Correspondence of General Oglethorpe', letter of April 2, 1740.

to place the children under its care, remained adamant in his interpretation of the deed. Stephens says that when John Mellidge came to him expecting, on the strength of Oglethorpe's letter, to retrieve the children, 'Whitefield gave him for answer, his Brother and Sister were at their proper home, and he knew no other home they had to go to; desiring him to give his services to the Governor, and to tell him so'.[1]

Following this incident Whitefield spent some weeks on an evangelistic tour in the northern Colonies. During his absence, Thomas Jones, acting on behalf of John Mellidge, went to Bethesda and removed the two children. In a few more weeks Whitefield returned, tired and sick and burdened with many cares, and upon learning what had happened became greatly distressed. He complained to Jones and to General Oglethorpe and then carried the matter to the Trustees, writing:

> I know that the produce of all his [John Mellidge's] land will not maintain the children, and therefore they must be supported, either by the Trustees or the General.
>
> But if the children are to be taken by force out of the Orphan House, whenever anyone says he will maintain them, on what a precarious foundation does the house stand? . . . I shall send a copy of this to the General, and let him make what apology he pleases. I honour him as my superior, but whenever he acts inconsistently with his duty, I think it my duty to inform him of it, with the meekness and resolution that becomes a minister of Christ . . .
>
> I must stop my hands, and settle the rest of my friends in Pennsylvania, unless you take care I shall be supported in my undertakings for the good of the Colony.[2]

But Whitefield had no hope of being helped by appealing thus to the Trustees. On the contrary, in their dislike of him they made matters worse, for they placed authority over Bethesda's affairs in the hands of the Magistrates at Savannah. Several of the actions of the Magistrates had shown them to be petty individuals, little men who delighted in exercising authority, but the Trustees

[1] Stephens' *Journal*, Part 2, *p* 324. Since this report came first from the Mellidge youth and then through Stephens' pen, the language attributed to Whitefield is probably coloured. Such sarcasm is out of character for Whitefield – character established by the numerous reliable reports.

[2] Egmont's *Journal*, *p* 374. John Mellidge became the representative of Savannah in the first General Assembly of Georgia.

gave them sole power to place children in and remove children from the Orphan House. They were to make annual visits to the institution, inspecting the buildings and the staff, and to them the Manager was to be responsible, providing them with reports at specified times. The plan to set up looms in the work-house was forbidden, but why so valuable an undertaking should be disallowed it is impossible to say. Whenever a child grew old enough to be of service, the Magistrates might remove him and give his services to whomsoever they pleased. No wonder that, in drawing up this reply to Whitefield, one of the Trustees said, 'He would not but be much disappointed and displeased at the Instructions this day ordered to be sent'.[1]

Other instructions also followed. The Trustees ordered Whitefield to consult with Colonel Stephens before making any expenditure for the Orphan House, and again demanded that he make full financial reports to them. And finally, in what Whitefield must surely have found a crowning indignity, they wrote to the Saltzburghers, stating what amount he had collected for them. Their thought was that otherwise he might retain some portion of what he professed was to be given to these needy people.

As far as he could, Whitefield continued to oppose this interference. Despite the prohibition regarding the weaving, he persevered with his plan and set up the looms. And in writing to the Secretary of the Trustees he asserted:

> . . . I never did and never shall look upon myself as under any obligation to give them a particular account of monies collected or expended by me for the use of the poor, or Orphan House in Georgia. They know full well that I gave up my Commission as insignificant and no way suitable to my design. They know also what has been collected for the Saltzburghers, Orphan house and other poor of Georgia has been owing chiefly to my own particular interest, and therefore I have a right to the sole disposal of it, without consulting Colonel Stephens, or any other person whatsoever. When I come to England the publick will have a specific account of everything . . .[2]

The outcome of the Trustees' actions, however, proved that Whitefield's fears had been well grounded. The Magistrates did not limit themselves to an annual visit but, after a few months had passed, they came almost at will and interfered with the

[1] *Colonial Records of Georgia,* entry of June 5, 1740. [2] *Ibid,* Vol 23, *p* 100.

Orphan House affairs as they wished. Indeed, there was an instance in which they refused to allow some very needy children to be received, with the result that they were put out instead into the semi-slavery that it had been Whitefield's chief purpose to prevent.

And thus, on this sorry basis, Whitefield brought Bethesda towards its completion. During these and immediately subsequent months several trials seemed to combine and roll in upon him at once. Yet amidst these experiences the institution which ought to have been his supreme delight had become such a mixture of joy and sorrow that, recognizing it was likely to be a life-long burden, he declared, 'I am almost tempted to wish I had never undertaken the Orphan House'.[1]

[1] *Works,* Vol 1, *p* 194.

But this I say, brethren, the time is short: it remaineth, that . . . they that have wives be as though they had none;

. . . But I would have you without carefulness. He that is unmarried careth for the things that belong to the Lord, how he may please the Lord;

But he that is married careth for the things that are of the world, how he may please his wife.

THE APOSTLE PAUL

I *Cor.* 7: 29, 32, 33

Ere this reaches you, I suppose you will hear of my intention to marry. I am quite as free as a child: If it be God's will, I beseech him to prevent it. I would not be hindered in my dear Lord's business for the world.

WHITEFIELD

in a letter to John Wesley, May 24, 1740

28

A Proposal of Marriage

WHITEFIELD was in America throughout the whole of 1740.

The activities of the year fell into six different segments, as follow. After getting the construction of the Orphan House under way he made a preaching tour that took him to Philadelphia and New York. This was the area in which he had already preached and in visiting it again he was following his practice of *preach and return*. Upon its conclusion he spent a further period at the Orphan House and then went away on another preaching tour – this time to Charleston. A third period at Bethesda followed, after which he set out on his longest evangelistic tour – one that took him to several places in New England. The journey back to Georgia, however, climaxed the year's work in a great *return* effort that reached from Boston to New York, throughout New Jersey and Pennsylvania to Philadelphia, to certain communities in Virginia and thence to Charleston and, finally, to Savannah.

As a further means of clarification these labours may be seen in outline as follows:

1. Orphan House: January 11 – April 2.
2. *The Spring Tour*: to Philadelphia and New York, April 2 – June 5.
3. Orphan House: June 5 – July 2.
4. *The Summer Tour*: to Charleston: July 2 – July 25.
5. Orphan House: July 25 – August 18.
6. *The Fall Tour*: to New England, returning by way of New York, Philadelphia and Charleston: August 18 – December 14.

This was manifestly a well-planned year. A cursory glance at Whitefield's life has led certain persons to assume that his ministry was without method and that in choosing the scenes of his preaching he simply went hither and yon according to impulse. A little study of the matter, however, reveals the very opposite. He laid his plans with care, worked wherever possible according to his *preach and return* method, and this year with its ministry throughout the Colonies and its final harvesting from north to south is an excellent example of his practice.

We shall look at these tours, one by one, and therefore the reader would do well to keep the outline in mind.

*

Before setting out on his Spring tour Whitefield performed another act of mercy.

There was in Georgia at the time a small company of Moravians. Their leader was none other than Peter Böhler, the man who had been influential in the conversion of the Wesleys. But Böhler and his people were in sore straits, for General Oglethorpe was demanding that, like other inhabitants, they bear arms in defending the Colony from the Spaniards – a duty which, in view of their pacifist principles, they refused to perform. As a result, they planned to move to Pennsylvania, but were without sufficient money to make the journey and, in so impoverished a Colony, could not sell their possessions in order to raise it.

Whitefield learned of their plight and came to their aid. He had entertained a high opinion of the Moravians he had known in London, saying, 'I could not help admiring their great simplicity, and deep experience in the inward life'.[1] Accordingly he offered to use his influence in helping Böhler and his people sell their goods and, if need be, to buy them himself. With his assistance they were able to sell a considerable portion of their possessions, and to find a tenant for their house (one of Whitefield's friends took it, to use as a hospital). They also had a five-hundred-acre property for sale and this they placed in the hands of an agent. Whitefield offered them free passage to Philadelphia aboard his sloop and, until it was ready to sail, provided them with lodging at the two houses he had rented at Savannah.

Whitefield's kindness to the Moravians, while looked upon by them at the time as a heaven-sent deliverance, brought further

[1] *Journals*, p 266.

criticism upon him in Georgia. Faced with the Spaniards' threats the Colony desperately needed to maintain its population, and one of its leading men wrote to the Trustees charging that, despite his profession of wanting to strengthen the Colony, he had weakened it by helping the Moravians to leave.

It was April 2 when the sloop moved out of the Savannah River and set sail for Philadelphia. If Böhler and his people were happy to be aboard, so also was another passenger: James Habersham. This good man had been in Georgia without a break since Whitefield's first arrival there – a period of nearly two years – and in order to provide him a well-earned respite, Whitefield took him on this trip.

*

On the third day out of port Whitefield took one of the most momentous steps of his life: he brought his long-standing conflict regarding Elizabeth Delamotte to a culmination by writing a proposal of marriage. As we look into the matter we see a very human Whitefield, a combination of strength and weakness, a man so driven by his natural, yet altogether proper, desires, that he acts almost against his will. We do well to remember, however, that notwithstanding the foible that he displayed, this was for him a most solemn experience and one which shook him to the very depths of his being.

Despite his endeavours while crossing the Atlantic to put Elizabeth out of his thoughts, the letter from her that he had found waiting at Savannah,[1] manifestly reawakened his affections. Nevertheless, though he answered other letters right away, he let three weeks elapse before he replied to her, and even then his letter was a curious, contradictory thing. He began by adopting the aloof 'my heart is quite free' attitude, and declaring his determination to let nothing share the place in his life that belonged to the Saviour alone; yet before he closed, he reversed himself, and admitted his loneliness for her. Here are the pertinent paragraphs:

[1] Since, in writing to Elizabeth, Whitefield says 'I thank you for your kind letter', and in writing to Howell Harris (*Works,* Vol 1, *p* 150) he speaks of his letter 'which I received on my arrival here', there can be little doubt that the several letters to which he now replied arrived at the same time.

You do well to go about doing good. Your Master did so before you. Dare, dear Miss, to follow his good example . . .

I beseech you by the mercies of God in Christ Jesus our Saviour, to keep up a close walk and communion with God. Nothing else can preserve you from idols; and you know when once the soul is off its watch, the devil makes sad ravages in it. There is nothing I dread more than having my heart drawn away by earthly objects. – When that time comes, it will be over with me indeed; I must then bid adieu to zeal and fervency of spirit, and in effect bid the Lord Jesus to depart from me. For alas, what room can there be for God, when a rival hath taken possession of the heart?

Oh my dear Sister, pray that no such evil may befal me. My blood runs cold at the very thought thereof. I cannot, indeed; I cannot away with it.

In a multiplicity of business, have I wrote you these lines. I thank you for your kind letter, and hope I shall always retain a grateful sense of the many favours I have received from your dear family. My kindest respects attend your sister; I long to hear of her being brought into the glorious liberty of the children of God. How does your father? Oh that he may have a well-grounded interest in Christ! How does my dear brother *Charles*? I pray God to fill him with all joy and peace in believing. And how does your little sister? Dearest Redeemer, keep her unspotted from the world!

My heart is now full. Writing quickens me. I could almost drop a tear, and wish myself, for a moment or two, in *England*. But hush, nature: God here pours down His blessings on

Your sincere friend and servant in Christ,
G. W.[1]

We may best understand the significance of this letter as we view it through the eyes of Elizabeth. She had taken the initiative in writing to him and had waited these months for a reply. But with what result? Only to have it implied that she was a hindrance to him. She knows full well the meaning of his words: she is the 'earthly object' that would draw away his heart from the Lord, and she is the 'rival' whom the devil would use to 'make sad ravages' in his soul. And what is she to think of his assertions, 'My blood runs cold', and 'I cannot away with it', except that he is

[1] *Works,* Vol 1, *p* 148. Gillies, in editing the *Works,* captioned this letter as addressed to 'Mrs Elizabeth D——'. The internal evidence: 'Dare, dear Miss', and the mention of the family, 'your sister', 'your father', 'dear brother Charles' and 'your little sister', plus other references point conclusively to Elizabeth, not her mother, as the recipient.

implying that the relationship between them must be terminated?

But he does not leave the matter there. Despite his attempts to deny his affection, before he concludes he cannot prevent himself from admitting that he longs, almost unto tears, to be with her again, even if but for a moment or two. We may be sure that his words left Elizabeth wounded and confused, yet they also gave her reason to believe he was very fond of her. And we may well assume that the tear that Whitefield mentions did indeed fall as he wrote the letter and that those of Elizabeth flowed in abundance as she read it.

Whitefield's attempt, however, to crush out his feelings with the command, 'But hush, nature', proved to be no more than wishful thinking. During the weeks that followed, nature continued to exert itself, and in his fear that were he to allow himself to have an affection for Elizabeth he would be unfaithful to the Lord and would jeopardize his ministry, his struggle became bitter indeed. In *Journals* and letters he spoke of suffering 'inward trials', and in such phrases as 'very cast down', 'fever . . . and pain of body and mind' and 'unspeakable troubles and anguish of soul', he revealed the presence of mental burdens so severe as to bring him into physical illness.

This conflict forced Whitefield to a decision: he would marry Elizabeth. His plan, however, was not to make a proposal on the basis of affection – such a step would be tantamount to an admission of defeat. Rather, Bethesda was sorely in need of a woman to superintend its affairs, and he decided to offer her the position, and at the same time to suggest marriage as a secondary element of the whole proposition.

This reasoning he set forth in a letter to Benjamin Ingham, saying:

I often have great inward trials. Pray that I may be kept in all changes and seeming chances of this mortal life. I believe it to be God's will that I should marry. One who may be looked upon as a superior, is absolutely necessary for the due management of affairs. However, I pray God that I may not have a wife till I can live as though I had none. – You may communicate this to some of our intimates, for I would call Christ and His disciples to the marriage. If I am deluded, pray that God would reveal it [to me] . . .[1]

[1] *Ibid*, *p* 158.

Sad to say, despite all that was in his heart, it was on this marry-for-the-sake-of-the-Orphan-House basis that Whitefield decided to broach his plans to Elizabeth. He seems to have been so apprehensive that he might be taking the wrong step and yet was so severely driven by his desires that he could not think clearly. He appears not to have realized the nature of his former letter, for he wrote no word of apology; he seems almost to have taken it for granted that she would be willing to marry him, and this without any real attempt on his part to win her affections or to declare his own. One cannot but wonder if she gave him cause for this attitude during their association in London.

Whitefield made his proposal by writing two letters. One was addressed to Mr and Mrs Delamotte, and with it he enclosed the other, to be given, if they saw fit, to Elizabeth.

Had he tried to design his proposal in such a way as to ensure its failure, he could hardly have done better than in these letters. When Charles Delamotte had gone to Georgia, his parents had grieved for him as for a lost son and, like other Englishmen, they had looked on the distant Colony – to them a place of savage Indians and marauding Spaniards – with dread. Yet Whitefield began his letter by telling them that one of the women he had brought from England had died already in Georgia and that another was sick, and that he wanted Elizabeth to exchange the comforts of Blendon Hall for the trials of the Orphan House. But here is his letter to the parents:

April 4, 1740

My dear friends,

Since I wrote last, we have buried our Sister L——. Rachel I left at Philadelphia, and sister T—— seems to be in a declining state; so that sister A—— alone is like to be left of all the women which came over with me from England. I find by experience, that a mistress is absolutely necessary for the due management of my increasing family, and to take off some of that care, which at present lies upon me. Besides, I shall in all probability, at my next return from England, bring more women with me: and I find, unless they are all truly gracious (or indeed if they are) without a superior, matters cannot be carried on as becometh the Gospel of Jesus Christ.

It hath been therefore much impressed upon my heart that I should marry, in order to have a help meet for me in the work whereunto our dear Lord Jesus hath called me. This comes (like Abraham's servant to Rebekah's relations) to know whether you think your daughter, Miss E——, is a proper person to engage in such an undertaking? If so, whether you will be pleased to give me leave to propose marriage unto her? You need not be afraid of sending me a refusal. For, I bless God, if I know anything of my own heart, I am free from that foolish passion which the world calls *Love*. I write only because I believe it is the will of God that I should alter my state; but your denial will fully convince me, that your daughter is not the person appointed by God for me. He knows my heart; I would not marry but for Him, and in Him, for ten thousand worlds. – But I have sometimes thought Miss E—— would be my help-mate; for she has often been impressed upon my heart. I should think myself safer in your family, because so many of you love the Lord Jesus, and consequently would be more watchful over my precious and immortal soul.

After strong cryings and tears at the throne of grace for direction, and after unspeakable troubles with my own heart, I write this. Be pleased to spread the letter before the Lord; and if you think this motion to be of him, be pleased to deliver the inclosed to your daughter – If not, say nothing, only let me know you disapprove of it, and that shall satisfy, dear Sir and Madam,

Your obliged friend and servant in Christ,

G. W.[1]

The letter for Elizabeth reads as follows:

April 4, 1740

Be not surprised at the contents of this: – The letter sent to your honoured father and mother will acquaint you with the reasons.

Do you think you could undergo the fatigues, that must necessarily attend being joined to one, who is every day liable to be called out to suffer for the sake of Jesus Christ? Can you bear to leave your father and kindred's house, and to trust on Him, (who feedeth the young ravens that call upon Him) for your own and children's support, supposing it should please Him to bless you with any? Can you undertake to help a husband in the charge of a family, consisting perhaps of a hundred persons? Can you bear the inclemencies of the air both as to cold and heat in a foreign climate? Can you, when you have a husband, be as though you had none, and willingly part with him, even for a long season, when his Lord and Master shall call him forth to preach the Gospel, and command him to leave you behind?

[1] *Ibid, pp* 159–60.

If after seeking to God for direction, and searching your heart, you can say, 'I can do all those things through Christ strengthening me,' what if you and I were joined together in the Lord, and you came with me at my return from *England*, to be a help meet for me in the management of the orphan-house? I have great reason to believe it is the divine will that I should alter my condition, and have often thought that you was the person appointed for me. I shall still wait on God for direction, and heartily entreat Him, that if this motion be not of Him, it may come to nought.

I write thus plainly, because, I trust, I write not from any other principles but the love of God. – I shall make it my business to call on the Lord Jesus, and would advise you to consult both Him and your friends – For in order to attain a blessing we should call both the Lord Jesus and His disciples to the marriage – I much like the manner of Isaac's marrying with Rebekah, and think no marriage can succeed well unless both parties concerned are like-minded with Tobias and his wife – I think I can call the God of Abraham, Isaac and Jacob, to witness that I desire 'to take you my sister to wife, not for lust, but uprightly;' and therefore I hope He will mercifully ordain, if it be His blessed will we should be joined together, that we may walk as Zachary and Elizabeth did, in all the ordinances of the Lord blameless.

I make no great profession to you, because I believe you think me sincere. The passionate expressions which carnal courtiers use, I think, ought to be avoided by those that would marry in the Lord. I can only promise by the help of God, 'to keep my matrimonial vow, and to do what I can towards helping you forward in the great work of your salvation'. If you think marriage will be in any way prejudicial to your better part, be so kind as to send me a denial. I would not be a snare to you for the world. You need not be afraid of speaking your mind. I trust, I love you only for God, and desire to be joined to you only by His command and for His sake. With fear and much trembling I write, and shall patiently tarry the Lord's leisure, till He is pleased to incline you, dear Miss——, to send an answer to,

Your affectionate brother, friend and servant in Christ,

G. W.[1]

Such was Whitefield's offer of marriage. We may be tempted to smile at his incredible naïveté, but his intense sincerity is manifest in every line. We must admire the noble ideal that would allow nothing to diminish his devotion to Christ, yet at the same time

[1] *Ibid, pp* 160–1.

can but regret the distorted view of marriage which drove him, though he possessed such extraordinary capacities for tenderness and affection, to a proposal so cold and formal as this.

*

Upon reaching Philadelphia Whitefield sent these letters on their way and began therewith the four months' wait necessary in those days for a trans-Atlantic reply. Though burdened in mind and body, he prosecuted, nevertheless, the tremendous course of labours that we shall see in our study of his spring and summer evangelistic tours.

But Whitefield's proposal had less likelihood of success than he realized, for by the time his letters reached England, important changes had taken place in the religious relations of the Delamottes. Along with many others of the Fetter Lane Society they had become fervent devotees of the principles and practices of the Moravians. During the transition John Wesley had attempted to gain control of the Society and, failing, had led several persons out of it and into his own *United Societies* movement. Much bitterness had resulted, insomuch that Charles Wesley, after visiting Blendon Hall in June (very near, no doubt, to the time when Whitefield's letters arrived) wrote:

> I went thence to Blendon: no longer Blendon to me. They could hardly force themselves to be barely civil. I took a hasty leave, and with a heavy heart, weighed down by their ingratitude, returned to Bexley.[1]

This schism was severe and it is possible that Mr and Mrs Delamotte, in their antipathy toward the Wesleys, also cooled in their admiration of Whitefield. At any rate, the change in their adherence could not but have made them look less favourably on him as a suitor for their daughter.

Moreover, we have reason to believe that by this time another man had entered Elizabeth's life. This was William Holland, who, since he became her husband a few months later, was probably keeping company with her at this earlier date. Holland, a successful tradesman, enjoyed a status in life similar to that of the Delamottes, and for some time had been in close fellowship with them

[1] Charles Wesley's *Journal*, June 10, 1740.

in the inner circles of the Fetter Lane Society. And he too had become a devout Moravian.

It would appear then, that Elizabeth, who by now had reached the age of thirty, found herself in a position where she could make choice between two suitors. The one, Holland: a man of the same religious persuasion as herself, one for whom she would not need to leave her native land and who could provide her with comforts like those of her father's house. The other, Whitefield: the famous evangelist, who was not a Moravian and who offered her a life of loneliness and responsibility far away in the woods of Georgia, with marriage as a sort of supplementary factor. This, no doubt, was the choice that Elizabeth pondered.

She wrote a reply and so did her parents, and Whitefield waited nearly four months before these letters reached him. Of their contents we know nothing, except what may be gleaned from Whitefield's few remarks about them. In writing to William Seward he said:

I find from Blendon letters that Miss E—— D—— is in a seeking state only. Surely that will not do. I would have one that is full of faith and the Holy Ghost. Just now I have been weeping and much carried out in prayer before the Lord. My poor family gives me more concern than everything else put together. I want a gracious woman that is dead to everything but Jesus . . . I wait upon the Lord every moment . . . and He assures me He will not permit me to fall by the hands of a woman . . . Looking back upon the workings of my heart in this affair, I am more and more convinced it is of God, and therefore know that He will order things for me as will best promote His own glory. So that my dear Lord's honour does not suffer, I care not what trouble in the flesh I undergo.[1]

Despite these statements, the letters that Whitefield received may not have contained an outright rejection. A few weeks later Captain Gladman, who had been in England and had visited the Delamottes, returned to America, and the news he brought caused Whitefield to say, 'Mr and Mrs Delamotte refuse to give their daughter, but yet I believe she may be my wife'.[2]

[1] *Works*, Vol 1, *p* 194.

[2] Letter from Whitefield to Gilbert Tennent, Nov. 25, 1740, now in possession of the Bridwell Library, Perkins School of Theology, Southern Methodist University, Dallas, Texas.

Thus we have grounds on which to form an opinion as to what took place. There can be no doubt that Mr and Mrs Delamotte registered their strong opposition to having Elizabeth bury herself in the woods of Georgia. But we may assume that Elizabeth did not send a similar reply. The words 'in a seeking state only' may mean that she confessed she was not a mature enough Christian to make all those sacrifices that Whitefield had listed. But his statement, 'yet I believe she may be my wife', suggests that she did not entirely close the door and her answer may very well have been the typically feminine one, 'I'll think it over'.

Nevertheless, following receipt of the letters from Blendon, Whitefield gave evidence of having suffered a very bitter disappointment. He refused to allow his ministry to slacken in the least, yet he was a sorely burdened man.

It was while undergoing this period of disappointment that Whitefield spent a week-end at the home of Jonathan Edwards and there beheld a demonstration of a married life that, instead of hindering, beautifully assisted a ministry. He manifestly saw his own loss and loneliness in contrast to the happiness of Edwards, for he wrote:

> I felt great satisfaction in being in the home of Mr Edwards. A sweeter couple I have not yet seen . . . Mrs Edwards is adorned with a meek and quiet spirit; she talked solidly of the things of God, and seemed to be such a helpmeet for her husband, that she caused me to renew those prayers, which for some months, I have put up to God, that he would be pleased to send me a daughter of Abraham to be my wife.
>
> Lord I desire to have no choice of my own. Thou knowest my circumstances; thou knowest I only desire to marry in and for Thee. Thou didst choose a Rebecca for Isaac; choose one to be a helpmeet for me, in carrying on that great work which is committed to my charge.[1]

It is a pity that Whitefield had not learned earlier that he did not need to look upon marriage as 'falling by the hands of a woman'. It appears that Elizabeth would have made a very suitable wife for him and it cannot be denied that he was fond of her and perhaps in love with her. While it is fruitless to speculate in such matters, we have reason to believe that had he allowed their friendship to have a normal development and made a pro-

[1] *Journals, pp* 476–7.

posal on the basis of affection, she would probably have accepted him.

But after Whitefield received the letters from Elizabeth and her parents, the relation was quickly terminated. Apart from his remark upon hearing from Gladman, he makes no further mention of her whatsoever, though he twice states his satisfaction that he had done the right thing. He returned to England the following March and three weeks after his arrival Elizabeth and Holland were married. (Was the event hurried, we wonder, by Whitefield's return?) Thereafter, however, there is no record that the paths of Whitefield and Elizabeth ever crossed and no reference to Holland ever appears in Whitefield's records. Only once, and that twelve years later, does he so much as mention the family, saying then in a letter to Gladman, 'I suppose Mr Delamotte will acquaint you of my having been at his house; we are kind friends still'.[1]

*

There is, however, a note in Whitefield's correspondence which probably contains a reference to Elizabeth – an evidence, perhaps, that the sorrow of losing her lingered long in his mind. It occurs in a letter that he wrote to a young man who had been prevented by his father from marrying the woman he loved. In an attempt to comfort him Whitefield refers to the Biblical Jacob and Rachel, and then, apparently implying that on the basis of his own experience he is able to enter with full sympathy into the young man's sorrow, he says, 'My affair went as far as yours, but I was called upon to sacrifice my Rachel!'

[1] *Works*, Vol 2, *p* 463.

Field preaching prevails with the vulgar in Philadelphia so much, that industry, honest labour and care for their families, seem to be held by many as sinful, and as a mark that they neglect the salvation of their souls. Mr Whitefield and his adherents have infatuated the multitude with the doctrines of regeneration, free grace, conversion, etc., representing them as essential articles of religion, though in reality they are inconsistent with true religion, and are subversive of all order and decency, and repugnant to common sense.

. . . I have informed you of all this because Mr Whitefield intends to visit Boston in the autumn, where, I understand, he is impatiently waited for. I wish his ministry there may not be attended with the same bad effects as here . . . Mr Whitefield is the more to be guarded against, because, I can assure you, he is qualified to sway and keep the affections of the multitude.

A letter written by a Philadelphian to
The Boston Post Boy, June 23, 1740

29

The Spring Tour—Philadelphia and New York

It was on the morning of Sunday, April 13 (1740) that Whitefield's sloop cast anchor at Newcastle, Delaware. He came ashore, mentally burdened and physically weak, and he arrived both unannounced and unexpected. Yet this was the beginning of his Spring evangelistic tour.

The lack of advance notice, however, proved to be in no way a hindrance. He preached at the morning service of the Church of England, but news of his arrival spread so rapidly that a large crowd assembled for an afternoon meeting. While this service was in progress Charles Tennent and some two hundred of his people came galloping into the churchyard. The report of Whitefield's presence had caused Tennent to cancel his own service at Whiteclay Creek and the post-haste ride brought him and his congregation to Newcastle in time to hear the sermon. The news 'Whitefield is back' rang with joyous excitement throughout the area, and 'People began to invite [him] several ways to come and preach to them'.[1] But he hastened to reach Philadelphia, and the congregation of three thousand that assembled at Wilmington – his one pause to preach on the way – gave evidence that the people were ready to attend.

Upon reaching Philadelphia Whitefield saw, as he had at Bristol and London, that his former ministry was still bearing fruit. 'What gives me greater hope that this work is of God,' he writes, 'is because these convictions have remained on many since I was here last. Blessed be God, there is a most glorious work begun in this province.'[2] William Seward had a further testimony, reporting:

On our arrival many friends came to see us, particularly Mr Jones, the

[1] *Journals, p* 405. [2] *Ibid, p* 408.

Baptist minister, who told us of two other ministers, Mr Treat and Mr Morgan, who were so affected by our brother Whitefield's spirit, that the latter had gone forth preaching towards the sea coast in the Jerseys and in many other places; and the former had told his congregation that he had been hitherto deceiving himself and them, and that he could not preach again at present, but desired them to join in prayer for him.[1]

Whitefield says of this Mr Treat, 'I hope he will be a means of awakening some dead, false-hearted preachers among the Dissenters, who hold the form of sound words, but have never felt the power of them in their own souls.'[2]

Being forbidden the use of the Church of England at Philadelphia Whitefield again resorted to the open air. He preached from a balcony on Society Hill, and of this ministry he recorded:

Wednesday, April 16 . . . Preached upon Society Hill twice; in the morning to about six thousand, and in the evening to near eight thousand people.

Thursday, April 17 . . . preached to upwards of ten thousand people . . . Hundreds were graciously melted; and many, I hope, not only thronged round, but also touched the Lord Jesus Christ by faith . . . The Word of God every day mightily prevails, and Satan loses ground apace.

Saturday, April 19. Was still much engaged in giving answers and praying with divers persons who applied to me under deep convictions. Preached morning and evening to seven or eight thousand people each time; and I was much rejoiced to see with what order and devotion they constantly attend.[3]

On one of these occasions it was reported that the words, 'And he opened His mouth and taught them saying', as pronounced by Whitefield, were distinctly heard at Gloucester point, a distance of two miles by water.

Of course, there was opposition to such activity, and it drew from Whitefield the following rather humorous remark: 'Scoffers seem to be at a stand what to say. They mutter in coffee houses, give a curse, drink a bowl of punch, and then cry out against me for not preaching up more morality.'[4]

[1] William Seward, *A Journal of a Voyage from Savannah to Philadelphia, and from Philadelphia to England* (London, 1740), *p* 4.
[2] *Journals, p* 408. [3] *Ibid, pp* 407–9. [4] *Ibid, p* 409.

On the Sunday Whitefield attended, as a private worshipper, the service of the Church of England, and many people, seeing him go in, followed. The Commissary preached on Justification by Works from James 2: 18, and that evening, using the same text in his sermon on Society Hill, Whitefield refuted the Commissary's doctrine. The occasion was manifestly a great climax to his week of ministry and must have drawn many hearers from the outlying communities, for though the population of Philadelphia was probably not more than twelve thousand, the congregation that night was estimated as fifteen thousand.

This Sunday was of particular importance to Whitefield. The fund he had gathered in England for the Orphan House was now depleted and it was imperative that he raise money immediately. Accordingly, at each of his services this day he received a collection. At the first – 7 o'clock in the morning and with about ten thousand hearers – it amounted to £110 sterling, and at the evening £50.[1] This was but the second time he had collected for the Orphan House since coming to America and, in the weeks that followed, he was careful to ask for a collection only on Sundays or on certain particularly opportune occasions during the week. His tact in this matter deserves attention.

Benjamin Franklin has left striking testimony regarding Whitefield's persuasive powers when pleading for the orphans:

> Mr Whitefield . . . preached up this charity, and made large collections, for his eloquence had a wonderful power over the hearts and purses of his hearers, of which I myself was an instance.
>
> I did not disapprove of the design, but as Georgia was then destitute of materials and workmen, and it was proposed to send them from Philadelphia at a great expense, I thought it would have been better to have built the house here, and brought the children to it. This I advised; but he was resolute in his first project, rejected my counsel, and I therefore refused to contribute.
>
> I happened, soon after, to attend one of his sermons, in the course of which I perceived he intended to finish with a collection, and I silently resolved he should get nothing from me. I had in my pocket a handful of copper money, three or four silver dollars, and five pistoles in gold. As he proceeded I began to soften, and concluded to give the

[1] This latter figure comes from William Seward, who also speaks of the morning collection as but £90. Each Colony had its own currency and in most instances this was well below the value of sterling.

coppers. Another stroke of his oratory made me ashamed of that, and determined me to give the silver; and he finished so admirably that I emptied my pocket wholly into the collector's dish, gold and all.

At this sermon there was also one of our club, who, being of my sentiments respecting the building in Georgia, and suspecting a collection might be intended, had by precaution emptied his pockets before he came from home. Towards the conclusion of the discourse, however, he felt a strong desire to give, and applied to a neighbour who stood near him, to borrow some money for the purpose. The application was unfortunately made, to perhaps the only man in the company who had the firmness not to be affected by the preacher. His answer was, '*At any other time, Friend Hopkinson, I would lend to thee freely; but not now, for thou seems to be out of thy right senses*'.[1]

Of course, the enemies of the revival made loud complaint about such powerful appeals for money. Says Franklin:

Some of Mr Whitefield's enemies affected to suppose that he would apply these collections to his own private emolument; but I, who was intimately acquainted with him (being employed in printing his Sermons and Journals, etc.), never had the least suspicion of his integrity, but am to this day decidedly of the opinion that he was in all his conduct a perfectly *honest man*; and methinks my testimony in his favour ought to have the more weight, as we had no religious connection. He used, indeed, to pray for my conversion, but he never had the satisfaction of believing that his prayers were heard. Ours was a mere civil friendship, sincere on both sides, and lasted to his death.[2]

*

As he entered upon his Spring tour, however, Whitefield faced a new and fierce wave of hostility. While at Charleston he had published two highly controversial *Letters* and now gave them to Franklin that he might publish them also.[3] They were entitled: *To a Friend In London Concerning Archbishop Tillotson,* and *To the Inhabitants of Maryland, Virginia and North and South Carolina Concerning their Negroes*. The latter was a scathing denunciation of

[1] Benjamin Franklin, *Autobiography* (Modern Library, New York ed.) *p* 120.

[2] *Ibid, pp* 120–1.

[3] Whitefield also sent them to a printer in London. Certain of the editions contained a third Letter, entitled '*To a Friend in London Concerning a Book called The Whole Duty of Man.*' This book was a widely-read anonymous work that taught salvation by human works. The Letter to the slave-owners is published in Whitefield's *Works*, Vol 4, *pp* 35–41.

the cruelties practised by the majority of the slave-owners. We shall consider it later, but in the meantime the reader will need to realize the tremendous antagonism such a publication would arouse in that day when slavery was so deeply entrenched in the nation and hardly a voice had been raised against it.

But at the moment we notice the *Letter* regarding Archbishop Tillotson. Though Dr Tillotson (1630–94) had been dead for nearly half a century, his memory was still highly honoured in both Britain and America. He had been a scholar, a popular preacher and a most benign gentleman, and had been particularly effective in presenting Christianity as a sedate ethic and the Christian life as merely cultured, inoffensive behaviour. His printed sermons, by reason of their easy and polished style, gave force to these views and rendered him the idol of the many persons, both within the Church of England and the other denominations too, who held to a belief in salvation by human works.

Since Tillotson's writings were a direct contradiction of the Biblical teaching regarding the new birth, Whitefield had long looked on them as a snare to the souls of men. But having recently heard the testimony of a wealthy South Carolina planter, Hugh Bryan, who stated he had been kept in ignorance of the Gospel for years by reading Tillotson, he deemed it his responsibility to expose such a danger.

Whitefield's *Letter* is calm, reasoned and Scriptural, but it contains one exceptionable phrase. After asserting 'I have observed that all natural men, generally speak well of his works', he goes on to state,

> Any spiritual man who reads them may easily see that the Archbishop knew of no other than a bare historical faith; and as to the method of our acceptance before God, and our justification by faith alone (which is the doctrine of the Scripture and of the Church of England), he certainly was as ignorant thereof as Mahomet himself.[1]

This *Letter* served a valuable purpose. Without doubt, it caused many persons to see the dangers that lay in Tillotson's writings, but above all, it focused the attention of thousands on the great central truth of the revival: the necessity of the new birth.

[1] Cited from Tyerman's *Whitefield*, Vol 1, *pp* 360–1.

But the *Letter* also aroused a storm of protest. Whitefield's words, 'as ignorant thereof as Mahomet', caught the public imagination and were carried as on the wings of the wind. Admirers of the Archbishop were outraged, and in England pamphlets began to come from the press, answering the attack and denouncing its author. In America the *Letter* proved to be the final factor in deciding the ministers of the spiritually lethargic party that he was a dangerous man. Nor was that all, for along with the hostility engendered by the attack on Tillotson there went the still more violent antagonism caused by the accusations against the slave-owners. Accordingly, time after time throughout the rest of this stay in America, and following his return to England, he was to find himself faced with intense and bitter opposition as a result of these *Letters*.

*

Nevertheless, the zeal that caused Whitefield to write the *Letters* also drove him on in an amazing course of evangelistic labour. This we see as we follow him on his Spring tour.

After but nine days in Philadelphia he set out for New York. A seven-hour journey brought him to the home of old Mr Tennent at Neshaminy, where a congregation of five thousand awaited him.

> When I got there [he writes] my body, through heat and labour, was so weak and faint, that my knees smote one against another, my visage changed, and I was ready to drop down as soon as I had finished my prayer. But God was pleased to revive me. Great numbers were melted; . . .

But despite his weakness, he travelled another eight miles that night and another sixteen the following morning. This brought him to the Dutch settlement of Shippack, where he reported:

> Thursday, April 24 . . . It was seemingly a very wilderness part of the country but there were not less, I believe, than two thousand hearers . . . Travelling and preaching in the sun again, weakened me much and made me very sick; but by the Divine assistance, I took horse, rode twelve miles, and preached in the evening to about three thousand people at a Dutchman's plantation . . .[1]

[1] *Journals*, p 412.

The *Journal* continues:

Friday, April 25. Rose before day. Sang and prayed with my own friends and the German Brethren. Set out before sunrising, and reached Amwell, thirty-five miles from Shippack, where I had appointed to preach by six at night. Some thousands of people were gathered together, expecting I would have been there by noon; but Mr Gilbert Tennent, and Mr Rowland, mentioned in my last *Journal,* coming there to meet me, had given the people three sermons. In my way thither, I was brought low by inward trials, and very great weakness of body, occasioned by the heat of the sun, want of sleep, and the length of the journey; but before I had preached six minutes, bodily and spiritual strength was given me, and the Lord set His seal to what He enabled me to deliver. After sermon, a friend took me in his chaise to an old Christian's, who invited me and my company to his house, five miles distant from the place where I preached.[1]

But he was on his way again by eight o'clock the next morning and rode till four in the afternoon, in order to preach for Gilbert Tennent at New Brunswick. He ministered there also to two thousand on the Saturday and 'to near seven or eight thousand' twice on Sunday. On the Monday he reported that he 'underwent great conflicts of soul last night and this morning', but he travelled and preached again that day, and on the following morning went on to New York. 'Surely this frail body cannot hold me long', he wrote. 'When, O Lord, wilt thou set my imprisoned soul at liberty!'[2]

In reference to these experiences Dr Gillies says:

Sometimes he was almost dead with heat and fatigue. Thrice a day he was lifted up upon his horse, unable to mount otherwise; then rode and preached, and came in and laid himself along two or three chairs.[3]

Such extraordinary feats of perseverance caught the attention of the philosophically-minded John Foster, and provoked the following comments:

Whitefield's career permitted him hardly a day of what could be called repose, till he found it in the grave at fifty-six . . . We repeatedly find him, during a state of languor which sometimes sunk him quite down to illness, prosecuting such a course of exertions, as would have been enough to reduce most strong men to that condition; for

[1] *Ibid, pp* 412–3. [2] *Ibid, pp* 414–5. [3] Gillies, *op cit, p* 54.

example, preaching in his ardent and exhausting manner, to vast auditories, several times a day, a number of days successively, when his debility was such that he could not, without much help, mount his horse, to go to his appointed places.

But his mind held such a predominance over his body, and the passion for preaching was so predominant in his mind, that, even when so oppressed with lassitude as to perform with uneasiness the most ordinary actions, if he could but sustain exertion enough to enter on preaching, he quickly became strong and animated . . . The languor returned on him with double oppressiveness after the conclusion, and the man whose powers of voice and action had appeared to evince an extraordinary vigour, would be found half an hour afterwards, extended on two or three chairs, almost helpless and fainting.[1]

Whitefield's work at New York was but a repetition of the ministry and results experienced on the way there. Though unaccepted by his own Church, he was joyfully received by Pemberton the Presbyterian and by the Dutch ministers on Long Island. His congregations and collections were large, but such was his continuing debility that at one time he wrote, '. . . my body was weak and my soul was in an unspeakable agony for near an hour'.[2] And the same circumstances characterized the return journey to Philadelphia.

*

Whitefield spent but five days in Philadelphia on this return visit – Wednesday to Sunday. The congregation at his farewell service was estimated at nearly twenty thousand, and this was undoubtedly the largest gathering in American history to that date.

But during these days a highly important feature developed in connection with his ministry: loud outcryings began to occur while he preached. He reports:

Saturday, May 10 . . . In the evening I went to a Society of young women . . . As soon as I entered the room, and heard them singing, my soul was delighted. When the hymn was over, I desired to pray before I began to converse; but my soul was so carried out that I had not time to talk at all. A wonderful power was in the room, and with one accord they began to cry out and weep most bitterly for the space of half an hour. They seemed to be under the strongest convictions, and

[1] John Foster, *Critical Essays, op cit*, Vol 2, *pp* 68–70. [2] *Journals, p* 415.

did indeed seek Jesus sorrowing. Their cries might be heard a great way off. When I had done I thought it proper to leave them at their devotions. They continued in prayer for above an hour, confessing their most secret faults; and, at length the agonies of some were so strong, that five of them seemed affected as those who are in fits.[1]

Similar strong emotional effects accompanied Whitefield's preaching when, after leaving Philadelphia, he came into the area of Whiteclay Creek and Fagg's Manor. At the latter place the Rev Samuel Blair was the pastor and a few months before Whitefield's visit he had witnessed a marvellous work of the Spirit of God in deep conviction and remarkable conversions. But strong outcryings occurred in connection with this work and, though Blair repeatedly urged his hearers 'to moderate their passions, but not so as to stifle their convictions . . . several would be overcome and fainting; others deeply sobbing, hardly able to contain . . .'[2] Word of these extraordinary events spread to the neighbouring communities and brought people in excited throngs to attend Blair's services, and many of these folk, upon returning to their homes, waited and longed for further experiences of this kind.

Such were the conditions that prevailed when Whitefield came into this area. At Whiteclay Creek he reported, '. . . one cried out most bitterly, as in great agonies of soul.'[3] The following day he was at Nottingham, where he wrote, 'Oh what tears were shed and poured forth after the Lord Jesus. Some fainted; and when they had got a little strength, they would hear and faint again. Others cried out in a manner as if they were in the sharpest agonies of death.'[4] With the passing of another day he was at Fagg's Manor and here his *Journal* entry reads:

The congregation was about as large as that at Nottingham. As great, if not a greater commotion, was in the hearts of the people. Most were drowned in tears. The Word was sharper than a two-edged sword. The bitter cries and groans were enough to pierce the hardest heart. Some of the people were as pale as death; others were wringing their hands; others lying on the ground; others sinking into the arms of friends; and most lifting up their eyes to Heaven and crying to God

[1] *Ibid, p* 421.
[2] Prince, *op cit,* Vol of 1744, *p* 246.
[3] *Journals, p* 424.
[4] *Ibid, p* 425.

for mercy . . . They seemed like persons awakened by the last trump, and coming out of their graves to judgment.[1]

These experiences confronted Whitefield with a difficult question. To what extent were they the work of the Spirit of God, or were they in any measure the result of human attempts to engender emotionalism? This was a question he faced and to which he did not have a complete answer.

Such occurrences, however, were not new in America. Several of the early preachers in New England[2] had witnessed overpowering effects among their hearers and, as we have seen, Jonathan Edwards reported that under his ministry, 'Some few instances there have been, of persons who have had such a sense of God's wrath for sin, that they have been overborne; and made to *cry out* under an astonishing sense of their guilt'.[3] Likewise, under the preaching of certain of the New Brunswick Presbytery men, there had been outcryings and faintings. These had taken place especially under the ministry of John Rowland, and on one occasion,

Rowland, being invited to preach in a Baptist Church, proclaimed the terrors of the Divine law with such energy to those whose souls were already sinking under them, that a few fainted away. His error, however, was publicly corrected by the Rev Gilbert Tennent, who, standing at the foot of the pulpit and seeing the effect produced on the assembly, interrupted the preacher by this address, 'Brother Rowland, is there no balm in Gilead? Is there no physician there?' Mr Rowland, on this, changed immediately the tenor of his address and sought to direct to the Saviour those who were overwhelmed with a sense of their guilt; but before this had taken place, numbers were carried out of the church in a state of insensibility.[4]

Despite Gilbert Tennent's action on this occasion, he tells us that while he himself was preaching, it was not unusual for people to be 'compelled to cry out in the public assembly, both under the impressions of terror and love'.[5] During the short but highly useful ministry of John Tennent at Freehold, 'it was no uncommon thing to see persons sobbing as though their hearts would

[1] *Ibid*, , *pp* 425–6.
[2] See Prince, *Christian History*, Vol of 1743, *pp* 215–7, 220–5, 227, 231.
[3] Edwards' *Narrative*, *p* 25.
[4] Gillies' *Memoirs of Whitefield*, an American ed. published at Hartford, Conn., 1843, *p* 43, fn.
[5] Prince, *op cit*, Vol of 1744, *p* 295.

break . . . and some have been carried out of the assembly (being overcome) as if they had been dead'.[1] And John Cross of Basking Ridge undoubtedly went still further and, valuing emotion for its own sake, virtually encouraged these demonstrations.

It cannot therefore be doubted that in some cases there had been intermixed with the work of the Holy Spirit in conviction, a human work of imitation that was spurious. And where ministers tended to regard the prostrations and outcries as sure signs of the Spirit's working the danger of the counterfeit was all the greater. This fact we noted earlier in connection with Wesley's ministry at Bristol. Explaining the process which led to cases of this type of phenomena Joseph Tracy writes:

> When one happened under some alarming or exciting sermon, other individuals, already predisposed, and strongly moved by the preaching, would be more readily affected in the same way . . . they became a common, though not constant attendant on revivals in New York and Pennsylvania . . . the lenity with which these 'manifestations' were treated, was too great, and the ignorant took occasion to consider them as parts of the revival – of that process by which their souls were to be saved. A more decided discouragement of them would have saved a vast amount of evil.[2]

Whitefield's ministry was of a kind which could easily be affected by the revival conditions described above. He looked for strong conviction by the Holy Spirit within the hearts of his hearers, and we repeatedly find him making such statements as, 'God's Spirit came upon the preacher and the people, so that they were melted down exceedingly', and 'The Word was like both a hammer and a fire, for many were melted'. At the same time he was far from accepting all spiritual emotion as being of divine origin. His attitude in this matter is well expressed in the following letter that he wrote at this time to James Hutton:

> . . . It is very possible the heart may have much joy floating on the top of it, and yet be as hard as the nether millstone. Hence it is that so many, who boast of their flashes of joy, are self-willed, impatient of reproof, despisers of others in a mourning state, and wise in their own conceits. Whereas the believer, who hath been with his Lord in the wilderness, and has a truly broken and contrite heart, though his

[1] *Ibid*, *p* 300.
[2] Joseph Tracy, *The Great Awakening* (Boston, 1842) *p* 225–6.

joy may not be so extravagant, yet it is substantial . . . I shall not be surprised if many, who seemingly began in the Spirit, do end in the flesh . . . How can they possibly stand, who never felt themselves condemned criminals? who were never truly burdened with a sense, not only of their actual, but original sin, especially that damning sin of unbelief? who were never brought to see and heartily confess, . . . that it is only owing to God's sovereign love that they can have any hopes of being delivered from the wrath to come.'

It is for preaching in this manner that I like the Tennents. They wound deep before they heal. They know that there is no promise made, but 'to him that believeth', and therefore they are careful not to comfort overmuch those that are convicted. I fear I have been too incautious in this respect, and have often given comfort too soon.[1]

Yet it was because of this desire to witness so thorough a work of the Spirit of God that Whitefield was confronted by his uncertainty. In his longing to see souls deeply wounded and his determination not to give comfort too soon, he rejoiced to see his hearers weeping and broken, but he was concerned when tears and melting gave way to uncontrolled outcryings and went so far as to cause faintings. Where was the line to be drawn?

This problem, however, was one that others faced too. Jonathan Edwards states the matter thus:

At the beginning of the extraordinary religious commotion . . . neither people nor ministers had learned thoroughly to *distinguish* between solid religion and its delusive counterfeits . . . Even many ministers of long standing and the best reputation, were for a time overpowered with the glaring appearances of the latter.[2]

Nevertheless, as in England, so here also in America, Whitefield was convinced that the extreme emotional outbursts were not of God. On several occasions he made such statements as, 'Satan begins to drive many into fits', and after the first outcries in Philadelphia he plainly expressed himself on the matter, asserting:

Such-like bodily agonies, I believe, are from the devil; and, now the work of God is going on, he will, no doubt, endeavour by *these* to bring an evil report upon it. O Lord, for Thy mercy's sake, rebuke

[1] Whitefield's *Works*, Vol 1, *p* 190.

[2] Edwards' *Life of David Brainerd*, here cited from David Wynbeck, *Beloved Yankee*, (Eerdmans, Grand Rapids, 1961) *p* 29.

him; and though he may be permitted to bite Thy people's heel, fulfil Thy promise, and let the Seed of the Woman bruise his head! Amen, Amen![1]

It must be noticed also that the severe outcryings took place under Whitefield's ministry only where he preached in an area in which people had already experienced them under the ministry of others. This was true in the Fagg's Manor district and, as we shall see, it proved true a few months later when he preached in an area previously aroused under the work of James Davenport. Apart from these instances Whitefield's ministry in America was almost entirely free from the extreme accompaniments, and the abundance of these things that occurred later stemmed not from him but from other men.

*

On the day following his Fagg's Manor meeting Whitefield boarded his sloop to return to Georgia. His Spring tour was ended and though it had lasted but four and a half weeks, its spiritual fruits were everywhere manifest. For instance, during his last days at Philadelphia he had written:

Religion is all the talk; and I think I can say, the Lord Jesus hath gotten Himself the victory in many hearts. I have scarce had time to eat bread from morning to evening; some one or other was generally applying to me under deep soul concern . . .[2]

There is record of four Societies that Whitefield founded at this time, but a resident of the city indicates that many more came into being, for she reports:

The effects produced, in Philadelphia, by the preaching of Mr Whitefield were astonishing. Numbers of almost all religious denominations and many who had no connection with any denomination, were brought to enquire, with the utmost earnestness, what they should do to be saved. Such was the engagedness of multitudes to listen to spiritual instruction that there was public worship, regularly, twice a day, for a year; and on the Lord's-day it was celebrated generally thrice, and frequently four times. The city contained twenty-six societies for social prayer and religious conference.[3]

Shortly after Whitefield left the city the Presbyterian Synod convened there, and a Boston newspaper reported:

[1] *Journals*, *p* 421. [2] *Ibid*, *p* 422.
[3] *The Memoirs of Mrs Hannah Hodge* (Philadelphia, 1806).

Philadelphia, June 12, 1740. During the session of the Presbyterian synod, there were no less than fourteen sermons preached on Society Hill, to large audiences, by the Revs Messrs Tennent, Davenport, Rowland and Blair, besides what were delivered in the Presbyterian and Baptist meetings, and expoundings and exhortations in private houses. The alteration in the face of religion in Philadelphia is surprising. Never did the people show so great a willingness to attend sermons, nor the preachers greater zeal in performing the duties of their function. No books are in request, but those of piety and devotion.[1] Instead of singing idle songs and ballads, the people are everywhere entertaining themselves with psalms and hymns and spiritual songs. All this, under God, is owing to the labours of Mr Whitefield.[2]

*

Whitefield did not sail for Georgia, however, as soon as he had expected. Due to contrary winds the vessel was held up in the Delaware Bay for a week, and though he went ashore on the nearby Reedy Island each day and preached to its few inhabitants, he found himself once more with time to think about his troubles. His proposal to Elizabeth Delamotte was on his mind, as was also the prospect of discord with Wesley and, apparently having received another letter from Wesley, he wrote to him as follows:

May 24, 1740

HONOURED SIR,

I cannot entertain prejudices against your conduct and principles any longer, without informing you. The more I examine the writings of the most experienced men, and the experiences of the most established Christians, the more I differ from your notion about not committing sin, and your denying the doctrines of election, and final perseverance of the saints.

I dread coming to England unless you are resolved to oppose these truths with less warmth than when I was there last. I dread your coming over to America; because the work of God is carried on here (and that in a most glorious manner) by doctrines quite opposite to those you

[1] Benjamin Franklin was quick to profit from this circumstance. 'In 1741 he printed Gilbert Tennent's sermon on "Justification", at the end of which he advertised as lately printed and for sale by himself Erskine's "Gospel Sonnets", Finley's Sermon "Christ Triumphing and Satan Raging", Whitefield's "New England Journal", and "A Protestation of the Presbyterian Synod" which excluded the Tennents and produced "The Great Schism". He also advertised as in press, Gilbert Tennent's "Remarks" on that Protestation, Watts' "Psalms", Alleine's "Alarm".' Tracy, *op cit, p* 53.

[2] *New England Journal*, 24 June 1740.

hold. Here are thousands of God's children, who will not be persuaded out of the privileges purchased for them by the blood of Jesus. Here are many worthy experienced ministers, who would oppose your principles to the utmost. God direct me what to do! Sometimes I think it best to stay here, where we all think and speak the same thing. The work goes on without divisions, and with more success, because all employed in it are of one mind.

I write not this, honoured Sir, from heat of spirit, but out of love. At present I think you are entirely inconsistent with yourself, and therefore do not blame me if I do not approve of all that you say. God himself, I find, teaches my friends the doctrine of election. Sister H—— hath lately been convinced of it; and, if I mistake not, dear and honoured Mr W—— hereafter will be convinced also.

From my soul I wish you abundant success in the name of the Lord. I long to hear of your being made a spiritual father to thousands. Perhaps I may never see you again till we meet in judgment; then, if not before, you will know that sovereign, distinguishing, irresistible grace brought you to heaven. Then will you know that God loved you with an everlasting love, and therefore with loving-kindness did He draw you.

Honoured Sir, farewell. My prayers constantly attend both you and your labours. I neglect no opportunity of writing. My next journal will acquaint you with new and surprising wonders. The Lord fills me both in body and soul. I am supported under the prospect of present and impending trials, with an assurance of God's loving me to the end, yea, even to all eternity . . .

I am now waiting for a fair wind. God blesses the Orphan house. Do not be angry with, but pray for, honoured Sir,

Your unworthy brother and servant in Christ,

George Whitefield.[1]

*

After nine days of sailing Whitefield again reached Savannah. He brought with him two little girls to live at Bethesda, a tailor, a bricklayer and a glazier to help in its construction, and a Latin Master and two maidservants to serve on its staff. He had well accomplished the purposes for which he had taken the tour, for not only had he been mightily used of God in the reviving of the work in the Middle Colonies, but had collected about £500 with which to continue the House of Mercy in Georgia.

[1] *Works*, Vol 1, *pp* 181–2.

Think you, your children are in any way better by nature than the poor negroes? No! In no wise! Blacks are just as much, and no more, conceived and born in sin, as white men are; and both, if born and bred up here, I am persuaded, are naturally capable of the same improvement. And as for the grown negroes, I am apt to think, that whenever the Gospel is preached with power among them, many will be brought effectually home to God.

WHITEFIELD, 1740

A Letter to the Inhabitants of Maryland, Virginia, North and South Carolina, Concerning their Negroes

30

Whitefield and the American Negro

WHEN he had first journeyed overland from Philadelphia to Savannah, making the acquaintance of America, Whitefield had been left with a saddening picture before his mind. His travels through the southern Colonies, with their rich plantations and slave labour, had shown him that the negroes were treated shamefully and often with outright cruelty.

This knowledge presented him with a serious duty. Believing that these conditions were unknown to much of America, he deemed it his responsibility to expose and condemn them. Though aware that a storm of abuse would descend on him in retaliation for such an action, he nevertheless wrote *A Letter to the Inhabitants of Maryland, Virginia, and North and South Carolina Concerning their Negroes* and upon reaching Philadelphia gave it to Franklin to be published. The *Letter* is written in his usual forthright manner,[1] and reads, in part, as follows:

As I lately passed through your provinces, I was touched with a fellow-feeling of the miseries of the poor negroes . . . I have no other way to discharge the concern that lies upon my heart, than by sending you this letter. How you will receive it I know not; but whatever be the event, I must inform you in the meekness and gentleness of Christ, that God has a quarrel with you for your cruelty to the poor negroes. Whether it be lawful for Christians to buy slaves, I shall not take it upon me to determine, but sure I am that it is sinful, when bought, to use them worse than brutes. And I fear the generality of you, who own negroes, are liable to such a charge, for your slaves, I believe, work as hard as the horses whereon you ride.

[1] Charles Maxson, *The Great Awakening in the Middle Colonies*, *op cit*, *pp* 57–7, says, 'He wrote like an Old Testament prophet, stirred by the wrongs of the poor . . . it was the one strong appeal of that time in the interest of the negro, and it turned the newly awakened sympathies of Christian people to the extension of a helping hand to the African in America'.

These, after they have done their work, are fed and taken proper care of; but many negroes, when wearied with labour in your plantations, have been obliged to grind their own corn after they return home.

Your dogs are caressed and fondled at your tables; but your slaves, who are frequently styled dogs or beasts, have not an equal privilege. They are scarce permitted to pick up the crumbs which fall from their masters' tables. Nay, some, as I have been informed by an eye-witness, have been, upon the most trifling provocation, cut with knives, and have had forks thrown into their flesh: not to mention what numbers have been given up to the inhuman usage of cruel task-masters, who by their unrelenting scourges, have ploughed upon their backs, and made long furrows, and at length brought them even to death itself.

I hope there are but few such monsters of barbarity suffered to subsist among you . . . Although I pray God the slaves may never be permitted to get the upper hand, yet should such a thing be permitted by Providence, all good men must acknowledge the judgment would be just.

Is it not the highest ingratitude, as well as cruelty, not to let your poor slaves enjoy some fruits of their labour? Whilst I have viewed your plantations cleared and cultivated, and have seen many spacious houses, and the owners of them faring sumptuously every day, my blood has almost run cold within me, when I have considered how many of your slaves have neither convenient food to eat, nor proper raiment to put on, notwithstanding most of the comforts you enjoy were solely owing to their indefatigable labours . . . 'Go to now, ye rich men, weep and howl, for your miseries that shall come upon you!' Behold the provision of the poor negroes, which have reaped down your fields, which is by you denied them, 'crieth, and the cries of them which have reaped have come into the ears of the Lord of Sabaoth!'[1]

This *Letter* quickly became known to much of America. It was not only published by Franklin (he printed it in pamphlet form along with the *Letter On Tillotson*) but was republished by one newspaper after another throughout the Colonies. Though certain notable figures of earlier years had condemned the practice of slavery,[2] the undeveloped conditions of those times had limited their effectiveness. But Whitefield, besides having arrived in an age of increased population and expanded com-

[1] *Works,* Vol 4, *pp* 35–41.

[2] These were particularly John Cotton, John Eliot and William Penn. The Quakers in general were opposed to slavery.

munications, had attained an unprecedented prominence, and thus his *Letter* focused public attention on the treatment of the slaves as nothing else had done.

Of course, such a publication provoked a vehement response. Slavery was deeply entrenched in the life of the nation and, though Whitefield did not attack the practice itself, he certainly denounced the abuse of it. Slave-owners were furious and sought revenge, and much of the libellous propaganda levelled against Whitefield throughout the rest of his life resulted from the bitterness aroused by this *Letter*.

*

Remembering, however, the suffering he had witnessed, Whitefield did not limit his efforts to merely a printed complaint. He formulated plans to help the negroes in a much more material way, and began immediately to put the plans into effect. His *Journal* entry of April 22 reads:

> Philadelphia . . . This day I bought five thousand acres of land on the forks of the Delaware, and ordered a large house to be built thereon, for the instruction of these poor creatures. The land I hear is exceedingly rich . . . I took up so much because I intend settling some English friends there, when I come next from England. I have called it Nazareth.[1]

In a letter to England Whitefield explained further:

> Pennsylvania seems to be the best Province for such an undertaking. The negroes meet there with the best usage, and I believe many of my acquaintance will either give me, or let me purchase their young slaves at a very easy rate.[2]

The 'English friends' mentioned by Whitefield were persons who had entreated him to help them emigrate to the new world, and he also had in mind others who, he expected, might be driven out of England by anti-Methodist persecution. Thus, he envisioned a fairly extensive development of the five thousand acres, and William Seward says, 'Mr Whitefield's design [is] to have a

[1] *Journals, p* 411.

[2] An unpublished Whitefield letter addressed to Dr Barecroft, Secretary of the Society for Propagating the Gospel in Foreign Parts, now in the possession of the S.P.C.K., London.

town on our land in Pennsylvania, and to call it English Town'.[1]

Seward advanced the money, £2,200, to purchase the property, and shortly thereafter he and Captain Gladman sailed for England. They went at Whitefield's request and had five tasks to perform. (1) They were to call at Blendon Hall, and this, we may be sure, was in order to ascertain what reply Whitefield might expect to his proposal, and to help matters along if possible. (2) They were to make the Nazareth project known and to interest friends in contributing to it. (3) Seward intended to sell certain stocks (*South Sea Company* holdings)[2] in order to cover his outlay of money. (4) They were to enlist the services of others who would be willing to help in America, particularly John Hutchings who, Whitefield hoped, would become his assistant at Bethesda. (5) They intended to purchase an ocean-going vessel, by which to transport both people and supplies from England to the two institutions in America – Nazareth and Bethesda.

*

Besides undertaking this immense project to aid the negroes, Whitefield demonstrated a deep concern for them in both private contacts and public ministrations.

During previous years little had been done to take the Gospel to the black population of America. Slavery with all its enormities was viewed with complacency and it was commonly believed that the negro occupied a place in life somewhere above the animal, but also somewhat below the human. This seemingly removed him beyond the sphere of the Gospel, and only rarely had a voice been raised in protest against this attitude or to proclaim his place in the grace of God.

But as Whitefield came preaching through the Colonies he gave a direct challenge to this state of mind. Eight weeks after arriving in America he recorded,

> . . . I went, as my usual custom is, among the negroes belonging to the house. One man was sick in bed, and two of his children said their prayers after me very well. This more and more convinces me that

[1] William Seward, *Journal of a Voyage from Savannah to Philadelphia and from Philadelphia to England* (London, 1740) *p* 62.

[2] In a letter to Mr Blackwell, the Lombard Street banker, Seward said, 'I desire you, if you can conveniently, to sell for me £1,650 old South Sea annuities, and £585 4s 5d South Sea stock'. Tyerman's *Whitefield*, Vol 1, *p* 378.

negro children, if early brought up in the nurture and admonition of the Lord, would make as great proficiency as any white people's children. I do not despair, if God spares my life, of seeing a school of young negroes singing the praises of Him Who made them . . . Lord, Thou hast put into my heart a good design to educate them.[1]

This sort of attention was in such contrast to the treatment usually accorded the negroes that it was not uncommon, Whitefield says, for them to come to him enquiring, 'Have I a soul?'[2]

William Seward, whose thoughts were often but a reflection of those of Whitefield, expressed particular hopes for the welfare of the black people, saying,

. . . a free Negroe woman came to Mr Whitefield, who was touched by the free grace of God when he expounded in the prison . . . and is a good omen that God intends the salvation of the Negroes, while he passes by their despisers, and worse than Egyptian task-masters. – Oh that many of them may be pricked to the heart, and feelingly enquire after the dear Lord Jesus . . . Praised be the Lord. Methinks one Negroe brought to Jesus Christ is peculiarly sweet to my soul.[3]

Whitefield enlarged upon this remarkable conversion and stated, 'I doubt not, when the poor negroes are to be called, God will highly favour them, to wipe off their reproach, and shew that He is no respecter of persons . . .'[4]

Accordingly, he made it his practice to address himself to the black man as well as to the white in his preaching. 'In my public discourses, I have freely offered the Lord Jesus to them', he says, and we have an example of his practice in his sermon 'The Lord Our Righteousness'. As he drew toward the close of his message he declared:

I must not forget the poor negroes. No, I must not. Jesus Christ has died for them, as well as for others. Nor do I mention you last, because I despise your souls, but because I would have what I shall say make the deeper impression upon your hearts.

Oh that you would seek the Lord to be your righteousness! Who knows but that He may be found of you. For in Jesus Christ there is neither male nor female, bond nor free; even you may be the children of God, if you believe in Jesus. Did you never read of the eunuch belonging to queen Candace? a negro like yourselves. He believed.

[1] *Journals, p* 379.
[2] Gillies, *p* 53.
[3] Seward's *Journal, pp* 6, 7.
[4] *Journals, p* 420.

The Lord was his righteousness. He was baptized. Do you also believe, and you shall be saved. Christ Jesus is the same now as He was yesterday, and will wash you in His own blood. Go home then, turn the words of the text into a prayer, and intreat the Lord to be *your* righteousness. Even so, come Lord Jesus, come quickly into all our souls! *Amen,* Lord Jesus, *Amen* and *Amen*![1]

It is probable that more preachers of that day would have been willing to carry their message to the negroes but failed to do so because of the difficulty inherent in preaching to so primitive a people. But Whitefield's gifts – his ability to simplify Divine truth and to present the narratives of the Scriptures and the message of the Gospel with vivid clarity – rendered him particularly suited to such a ministry. In turn, the negroes found an unusual interest in his preaching, and many of them testified that God used it in bringing His grace to their hearts.

For instance, while at Philadelphia, Whitefield wrote:

Nearly fifty negroes came to my lodgings, to give thanks for what God had done for their souls. How heartily did those poor creatures throw in their mites for my poor orphans. Some of them have been effectually wrought upon, and in an uncommon manner.[2]

At Boston a company of negroes assembled on a certain occasion, and sent word beseeching Whitefield to come and preach to them. This he did, giving them a sermon on 'The Ethiopian's Conversion'. During his stay at Charleston he reported, 'Several of the negroes did their work in less time than usual, that they might come to hear me; and many of the owners, who have been awakened, have resolved to teach them Christianity'.[3] And as he summarized the first fruits of his Spring tour he stated, '. . . the Word hath run and been much glorified, and many *Negroes* also are in a fair way of being brought home to God'.[4]

There is also a report of a negro who was converted under a certain sermon from Whitefield and remained so deeply impressed that he could afterwards repeat it almost word for word. And from the pen of William Seward there came the following note:

Heard of a drinking club, with a negro boy attending them, who used

[1] *Works,* Vol 5, *p* 234.
[2] *Journals, p* 422.
[3] *Ibid, p* 444.
[4] *Works,* Vol 1, *p* 167.

to mimic people for their diversion. The gentlemen bid him mimic our brother Whitefield, which he was very unwilling to do; but they insisting upon it, he stood up and said, 'I speak the truth in Christ; I lie not; except your repent you will all be damned!' This unexpected speech broke up the club, which has not met since.[1]

The relationship between Whitefield and the negroes was a warm and familiar one on both sides. In writing to the overseer of a Society of 'negro women and children' at Philadelphia, he said, '. . . My love to all the Society . . . Shew them, O shew them the necessity of being deeply wounded, before they can be capable of healing by Jesus Christ . . . My love to the Negro Peggy, and all her black sisters. Bid them pray for me'.[2] Of his experience during a period of grave sickness, he reports, 'The poor negroes crowded round the windows, and expressed a great concern for me. Their master had acquainted them, I believe, that I was their friend.'[3] And time after time negro people, as well as whites, came to him expressing their desire to follow him whithersoever he might go.

While the Nazareth institution was under construction Whitefield planned to do something further to meet the needs of the blacks. 'Had I time,' he said, 'and proper schoolmasters I might immediately erect a negro school in South Carolina, as well as in Pennsylvania.'[4] But though he had not the time himself he found others who had: Hugh Bryan, the wealthy planter, and his wife. 'By my advice,' he says, 'they have resolved to begin a negro school. A young stage player who was convinced when I was in New York last . . . is to be their first master.'[5]

*

Besides his efforts on behalf of the negroes Whitefield also gave encouragement to a work that had been begun among the Alleghany Indians. He reports:

Philadelphia, May 8 . . . Was called up early in the morning, as I always am, to speak to poor souls under convictions. The first who came was an Indian trader, whom God was pleased to bring home by my preaching when here last. He has just come from the Indian nation, where he has been praying with and exhorting all he met who were

[1] Seward's *Journal*, *pp* 7–8. [2] *Works*, Vol 1, *p* 176.
[3] *Journals*, *p* 446. [4] *Ibid*, *p* 444. [5] *Ibid*, *p* 450.

willing to hear. He has hopes of some of the Indians, but his fellow-traders endeavoured to prejudice them against him. However, he proposes to visit them again in the autumn, and I humbly hope the Lord will open a door amongst the poor heathen. The conversion of one of their traders will be a great step towards it.[1]

Delighted at this prospect Whitefield wrote to the trader, saying,

I received your letter, and have been reading part of your journal. I think it your bounden duty to go amongst the Indians again, not as a *minister*, but as a private Christian, whose duty it is, when converted himself, to strengthen his brethren . . . it is plain God calls you . . . Be sure you keep a close walk with God . . . Beg of God to give you true notions of our free justification by faith in Jesus Christ. Bring your Indian hearers to believe, before you talk of baptism or the supper of the Lord. Otherwise, they will catch at a shadow and neglect the substance. Improve your leisure time and see that you feel the truths that you speak.[2]

In his desire to further this work Whitefield wrote a letter for the trader to read to the Indians. This was, in reality, a Gospel tract, but in writing it Whitefield did not merely retell and apply a human story or even a Biblical narrative. Rather, in seeking thus to present the Gospel to these primitive people, he presented a summary of Christian doctrine, but set it forth in the simplest manner possible. Beginning with nature's testimony to the existence of God, Whitefield goes on to speak of creation, the fall of man, the meaning of sin, the Bible, the death and resurrection and second coming of Christ, the judgment, the nature of true faith, the transforming power of God in salvation and the glory of the Christian life.

The letter is remarkable for the way in which it sets forth so wide a range of Christian doctrine with utter simplicity. In reading it one is struck with the thought that here is a presentation of Divine truth well suited to reach the mind and heart of the Indian. But the letter leaves also a second impression, for it suggests the plainness with which the Gospel went forth from

[1] *Journals, p* 419.
[2] *Works,* Vol 1, *pp* 170–1. This letter reveals that the trader was a 'Mr. M——', not Samson Occum as suggested in a footnote to the *Journals, p* 419.

Whitefield's lips and therefore found its way likewise to the mind and heart of the negro.[1]

*

In arranging for the construction work at Nazareth, Whitefield again found opportunity to shew kindness to Peter Böhler and his little group of Moravians. While sailing from Georgia aboard Whitefield's sloop, Böhler had looked forward to meeting the Moravian leaders Nitchsmann and Spangenburg in Pennsylvania, having heard they were building a settlement there. But upon arriving he found neither leaders nor settlement, and learned, to his great disappointment, that these men had returned to Germany. He and his people were given temporary lodging in the Germantown area, and there Whitefield, in visiting the district during his Spring tour, renewed fellowship with them. 'When I had done' [preaching], he wrote, 'Peter Böhler, a deacon of the Moravian Church, a dear lover of our Lord Jesus Christ, preached to his countrymen in Dutch.'[2] But Böhler and his people were in need of employment and therefore Whitefield offered to enagage them in building the edifice at Nazareth. This was an act of mercy, rather than of business, on Whitefield's part, for, though some of the men were carpenters by trade, Böhler, who was to oversee the construction, was without experience in this field. But after seeking direction by the casting of a lot, Böhler accepted the offer and within two weeks the woods of Nazareth echoed with the sound of German hymns as the Moravians entered joyfully upon their work.

*

But Whitefield's great plans for Nazareth soon ended in failure. Out of this affair there have come serious charges against Whitefield and therefore it must have our attention.

From the very first there were difficulties inherent in the location. The tract of land was about forty miles from Philadelphia, and its boundaries, which were nothing more than lines on a map, were identified only by a few surveyor's markings in the midst of a wooded wilderness. The only inhabitants were Indians, who bitterly resented the intrusion of the white man, and constantly threatened the Moravians' lives.

[1] *Works*, Vol 1, *pp* 171–4. [2] *Journals*, *p* 412.

The building that Whitefield envisioned was a highly ambitious design. 'The edifice was to be of massive stone, and its plan was so extensive that it would have been a great undertaking even in the populous sections of Pennsylvania; in a wilderness such as constituted its site, difficulties of every kind presented themselves.'[1]

Furthermore, for several reasons, the time-table for the construction proved impossible of fulfilment. The Moravians began their work in June and laboured to have the roof on the great house in time to allow them to occupy it during the winter. But the summer was unusually rainy and Böhler's party was small,[2] and though he hired other workmen, from Germantown, progress was slow. By the first week of September little more than the cellar was finished and £300 had been spent.

This lack of progress necessitated a change in plans for the Moravians. They had already constructed a small log house as their living quarters but, since the large building could not be roofed for many months, they had no choice but to devote their energies to the erecting of another log house, in order to have it ready before winter. Therewith the main construction came to a standstill.

Böhler intended, however, to continue the work as soon as spring arrived, but before that time a change in arrangements between Whitefield and the Moravians halted construction indefinitely.

This arose from a conference that took place between Böhler and Whitefield in November. While Whitefield was moving southward during the final week of his Fall tour, Böhler sought to locate him that he might talk with him about the project. Böhler appears to have caught up with him at Salem – a town near the point where the borders of Pennsylvania, Delaware and Maryland meet.

This was at the time when several trials seemed to be rolling in at once on Whitefield, yet despite them his labours were as manifold as ever. Where he fitted in the conference with Böhler it is

[1] Edmund de Schweinitz, *Some of the Fathers of the American Moravian Church* (The Moravian Historical Society, Bethlehem, Pa., n.d.), *p* 211.

[2] Böhler's party consisted of, besides himself, four men, two women, one child and two indentured lads. Their names are given in the *Transactions of the Moravian Historical Society*, Vol 1, Part 10, 1876, *p* 433.

difficult to say, but it must have been a rather hasty one for he reported the day's activities as follows:

Salem, Thursday, Nov. 20. Preached twice here this day; in the morn- in the Court House; in the afternoon in the open air, before the prison, to about two thousand . . . After service two or three came to me weighed down with the burden of sin, I gave them what advice I thought proper, and about five left Salem.[1]

But besides Whitefield's burdened condition, there were other circumstances which affected this conference. We have seen the gracious letter which Whitefield wrote to the Fetter Lane brethren while in England, warning them regarding certain mystical ideas they were beginning to entertain and urging them to beware of the influences of the French Prophets, but with the passing of the months these tendencies had continued. Moreover, a Moravian teacher, Philip Henry Molther, who had become the leader of the Fetter Lane Society, advocated the neglecting of the Church of England ordinances and taught, in place of spiritual activity, a passive attitude known as 'stillness'. John and Charles Wesley viewed this departure with great seriousness; they fought against it, and John, in his letters to Whitefield, reported it with all the gravity that it held in his thought.

Whitefield's reaction to this news is manifest in several of his letters. We find him writing:

Friends from England write strange things; . . . the Moravians, I think, are sadly erroneous in some points of doctrine.[2]

Some of Fetter Lane society, I fear, are running into sad errors.[3]

I find our friends are got into disputing one with another. – O that the God of peace may put a stop to it![4]

I find I must, if I am faithful, oppose the errors of many who, I believe, fear God. O that I may do it with meekness and wisdom.[5]

Furthermore, these doctrinal differences were not only at Fetter Lane, but had been brought home to Whitefield with painful force at Bethesda. A Moravian named Hagen had been given employment in the building of the orphan house and, during Whitefield's absence, had injected the dispute among the other workmen. When Whitefield returned from his Summer tour he found the

[1] *Journals*, *p* 496.
[2] *Works*, Vol 1, *p* 208.
[3] *Ibid*, *p* 210.
[4] *Ibid*, *p* 213.
[5] *Ibid*, *p* 218.

place in turmoil and, though matters were righted before he left on his Autumn tour, he feared lest it should break out again. Shortly before his conference with Böhler, he declared, 'With fear and trembling, ever since the late disputations, have I opened letters from Savannah'.[1]

Thus it was, in this anxiety regarding 'the Moravian errors', that Whitefield met with Böhler at Salem. As Böhler had as yet learned but little English and Whitefield did not speak German, they conversed in Latin, and the discussion related, of course, to the doctrinal differences.

Nothing is known as to what took place between them, except that Whitefield later wrote:

> I have lately conversed closely with Peter Böhler. Alas! we differ widely in many respects; therefore to avoid disputation and jealousies on both sides, it is best to carry on the work of God apart. The divisions among the brethren sometimes grieve, but do not surprise me. How can it be otherwise, when teachers do not speak and think the same things? God grant we may keep up a cordial undissembled love towards each other, notwithstanding our different opinions.[2]

With this decision 'to carry on the work apart', the construction at Nazareth was again left in abeyance, and the Moravians soon purchased a tract of land of their own, to which they gave the name *Bethlehem*. Nevertheless, Böhler's people remained at Nazareth throughout the winter, and not only they, but others who arrived from Germany – five of Moravianism's élite[3] – spent the winter there too.

It is out of this decision to discontinue the construction that the charges against Whitefield have arisen. One writer states:

> Whitefield returned to Pennysivania in November, 1740, nursing his wrath against Hagen, and finding Böhler to be of the same mind, he peremptorily ordered the Moravians to leave his land. Neighbours interfered, and cried shame on him for turning the little company

[1] *Ibid*, Vol 1, *p* 218.

[2] *Ibid, p* 224. A fortnight later Whitefield wrote to a friend: 'Though he [Böhler] has been washed in the blood of the Lamb, so as to be justified from all his sins, yet like me his feet want washing still, and will till he bows down his head and gives up the ghost.'

[3] These were Bishop David Nitchsmann, an uncle of his, the uncle's daughter, Anna Nitchsmann who later married Count Zinzendorf, Christian Froelich, and Mrs. Molther, wife of the Moravian minister in London.

adrift in the depth of winter, and he finally agreed to let them stay for a while in the log cabin which was sheltering them while they were building the large house.[1]

Another author asserts:

Aroused by a doctrinal dispute with John Hagen, . . . and prejudiced by outside influences against the Moravians, Whitefield, after a futile disputation with Böhler, worthy of the most medieval scholasticism, brusquely ordered the Moravians to leave the tract immediately. The news of this debacle came to the ears of Nathaniel Irish, the miller at Saucon Creek, who, tired of theological polemics and sectarian bigotry, had discarded church connections, but not his Christianity and who now persuaded Whitefield to permit the Moravians to remain on the Nazareth Manor for the winter.[2]

These writers and others who have copied them make not the least attempt to prove their accusations and, certain of their statements, when examined, prove both contradictory and absurd.[3] Nevertheless, the idea that Whitefield drove a company of needy people – men, women and children, it is said – out into the depths of winter, has now become a part of the common concept of him on the American continent.

The kindness which Whitefield had manifested toward the Moravians in rescuing Böhler and his people from their troubles in Georgia and in providing them with employment in Pennsylvania continued to characterize his attitude toward them. Indeed, such was his goodness to them that, some little time later, Gilbert Tennent asserted that he must surely have become one of them, to which Whitefield replied:

Some Philadelphia friends are suspicious that I am joined with the Moravian Brethren, but indeed I am not. My principles are still the same; only as I believe many of them love the Lord Jesus, I would love and be friendly to them, as I would be to all others who I think bear the image of our common Master, notwithstanding some of my principles differ from theirs, and are as far distant as the East is from the West.[4]

[1] Adelaide L. Fries, *The Moravians in Georgia*, 1735–40 (Raleigh, N. C., 1905), p 223.

[2] *Two Centuries of Nazareth, 1740–1940*, by various contributors (Nazareth, Pennsylvania, Bi-Centennial, Inc.), 1940, *pp* 6, 7.

[3] See Appendix: Note 4.

[4] *Works*, Vol 1, *p* 441. In writing to John Wesley, March 11, 1742, Whitefield said, 'I believe Jesus Christ fights for the Moravian Brethren. They will insensibly

Whitefield intended to have others complete the construction of Nazareth, but at this point of time, for reasons that we shall explain later, he lost one of his main financial supports. He was already seriously in debt for Bethesda and it was impossible for him to continue the great schemes he had in mind for a Nazareth settlement.

Thereafter Nazareth was taken over by the Moravians. In 1743 they purchased the property from Whitefield, finished the edifice that he had started, and erected other buildings till, with the passing of years, they had formed a goodly settlement. They did not, however, use it as a refuge for negroes, but as a centre of their communal living, their benevolent enterprises and missionary labours.

*

But though Whitefield failed in this attempt to help the negro, he was successful in others.

More especially was this true of his public ministry. Listening to Whitefield the poor black man heard words that he could understand, and found himself led by them into a rich new realm. As the Bible narratives were told in a vivid, dramatic manner, the negro quickly identified himself with them and seemed to be living their wondrous events over again. Moreover, he heard a message to lighten his burden and ennoble his life, even the life of a slave, and as he returned to his toil he soothed his sorrows in its truths. Amidst the monotony of his labour he repeated over and over some phrase he had heard from the preacher's lips, until the repetition became rhythmic and his natively musical soul spontaneously linked it with melody. The words, the music, the song, remained with him; he sang it again, he added to it, others heard and joined their voices, and the whole was repeated day after day, till it became something permanent with them, a part and parcel of their lives.

Thus was born the *Negro Spiritual*. Though there is no document that actually links this origin with Whitefield's work, such

increase. They get ground dayly. I fear you grieve the Spirit of God, Dear Sir, in speaking against them and us. Oh pray leave it off. I have had free conversation with Mr Spangenburg several times. Indeed I think he is a simple man.' (Letter in the Methodist Archives, London.)

singing came from the acquaintance of the slaves with the truths that he preached and may be traced, in its beginnings, to the time of his first ministry among them.

Whitefield's influence, however, with regard to the position of the negro, was both beneficial and harmful. Harmful, in that within eleven years, he owned slaves at Bethesda, and though they received the same treatment as the whites, they were, none the less, slaves. But the far greater weight of his influence was exerted for the welfare of the black man, for the *Letter* to the slave-owners, the project at Nazareth, the school in Carolina and his public utterances, all combined to declare to America the human dignity and spiritual worth of the negro.

But it is deeply to be regretted that Whitefield did not go all the way and see the necessity of complete abolition. He had the ear of the people as no other man would have it in many years, and how different might have been the lot of the slaves had he fought for their liberation! America was being remoulded in the fires of the revival; new forces of freedom and compassion were being born; how changed might have been the history of the nation had it embarked in that early day on a course of liberty and justice for all, black as well as white!

Nevertheless, Whitefield's contribution to the temporal and spiritual welfare of the slave was rich and lasting, and we may well agree that he was, as a modern author has termed him, 'the first great friend of the American negro'.[1]

[1] Maxson, *op cit, p* 57.

Mr Whitefield goes about his Master's work with diligence and application; and with such cheerfulness as would make one in love with a life of religion, which has so many inward springs of the best comforts, and is not that gloomy, melancholy thing, which prejudice and imagination make it.

He is proof against reproach and invective. When he is reviled he revileth not again, but prays heartily for all his enemies, and that such as oppose the truth may be converted to it. He professes himself to lay down his life for Christ, and to spend and be spent in the service of souls. Such a man has all imaginable claim to our highest love and honour.

JOSEPH SMITH

The Character, Preaching &c. of
The Rev George Whitefield, Charleston, 1740

31

The Summer Tour – Charleston and the Surrounding Area

WHILE Whitefield had been preaching throughout the Middle Colonies – his Spring evangelistic tour – a series of strong attacks had been made on him in South Carolina. These were the work of the Rev Alexander Garden, rector of St Philip's and Commissary of the Church of England at Charleston.

This was not the first time that the Commissary had manifested his enmity. During the previous March Whitefield had called upon him and had found him highly indignant.[1] 'He sneered at me . . .' says Whitefield, 'charged me with breaking the Canons and Ordination vow . . . He told me if I preached in any public church in that province he would suspend me. I replied, I should regard that as much as I would a Pope's bull . . . "Then, Sir," he said in a very great rage, "get you out of my house!" '[2]

Soon after that exchange, however, an action of Whitefield's added fresh fuel to the fire. This was the publication of his two *Letters*, the one concerning Tillotson and the other on the treatment of the slaves. In Charleston, a city strong for the Tillotsonian vogue in religion and the commercial centre for several surrounding plantations, no themes could have been more likely to arouse hostile passions. Thereupon, Garden, acting as spokesmen for the offended churchmen and the angry planters, replied to Whitefield with *Six Letters*[3] of his own.

In his first two *Letters* Garden presents his view of justification – salvation by works. 'In the third . . . Whitefield is accused of "wilful and malicious, arrogant and wicked slander". . . . In reference to Whitefield's saying in his Journal that he has kindled a fire which all the devils in hell will not be able to extinguish,

[1] See *p* 450. [2] *Journals, pp* 400–1.
[3] *Six Letters to the Rev George Whitefield*, by Alexander Garden (Boston, 1740).

Garden remarks: "Alas! the fire you have kindled is that of slander and defamation, – a fire which no devil in hell, nor Jesuit nor Deist on earth, will ever go about to extinguish, but will fagot and foment it with all their might, as too effectually serving their interests." '[1]

Garden's fourth *Letter* makes the charge, '"In your mountebank way you have, David-like, as you fancy, slain your Goliath" [Tillotson] "but his works and memory will long survive after you and your dirty pamphlets are sunk into oblivion".'[2] The sixth *Letter* relates to Whitefield's charges against the slave-owners and, after suggesting that the planters ought to prosecute him for slander, Garden seeks to make a mockery of his accusations, stating, '"I have heard the report of your cruelty to the poor orphans under your care, not only in pinching their bellies, but in giving them up to taskmasters or mistresses, who plow upon their backs, and make long furrows there in a very inhuman manner; . . ."'[3]

Whitefield himself made no reply to Garden's *Letters*, but his cause was taken up by another, the Rev Joseph Smith, minister of Charleston's Independent Church. Smith preached a sermon entitled, *The Character, Preaching, etc., of the Rev Mr Whitefield, Impartially Represented and Supported.*[4] But since he was not widely known, Smith sent the sermon to two of the most noted ministers in New England, the Rev William Cooper and Dr Benjamin Colman of Boston, suggesting that they publish it. This they did, and added a recommendatory preface of their own.

Anything coming from the pens of Cooper and Colman carried weight. Cooper had been offered the Presidency of Harvard, but choosing to remain in the pastorate, had refused to accept it.[5] Colman had been the associate of such men as Howe, Calamy and Burkitt in England, and during his forty-year ministry in America, 'his learning, talents, piety and usefulness [had] secured him universal respect'.[6]

[1] Cited from Tyerman's *Whitefield*, Vol 1, *p* 362.
[2] *Ibid*, *pp* 362–3. [3] *Ibid*, *p* 363.
[4] Published at Boston, June 7, 1740. Republished the same year at Philadelphia and in 1765 at Charleston. It appeared as a Preface in editions of *Whitefield's Sermons* in 1771, 1785, 1792, 1794, 1812, 1825, 1828 and 1838.
[5] Sprague, William B., *Annals of the American Pulpit*, Vol 1, *p* 289.
[6] Tyerman's *Whitefield*, Vol 1, *p* 353, fn.

Smith's effort was well supported by these venerable Boston divines. 'We receive his testimony', they said, 'because we know him to be a gentleman of good sense, and strict veracity, and free from enthusiastic impressions.' And of Whitefield they stated,

. . . he is the wonder of the age; and no man more employs the pens and fills the conversation of people, than he does at this day; none more admired and applauded by some, condemned and reproached by others, – the common lot of the most excellent men the world has ever had to shew.

In the opening paragraphs of his sermon Smith says:

My design is to shew my impartial opinion of that Son of Thunder who has lately graced and warmed this desk, and would have been an ornament to the best pulpit in the province. Happy shall I think myself, if I can but clinch the nails which this great Master of Assemblies has already fastened . . .

After emphasizing that Whitefield's preaching was always doctrinal and listing the doctrines, Smith goes on to speak of the manner of his preaching, saying:

I need not say, nor can my pen describe, his action and gesture, in all their strength and decencies. He is certainly a finished preacher, and a great master of pulpit oratory, though a noble negligence runs through his style. His discourses were very extraordinary, when we consider how little they were premeditated, and how many of them he gave us in the little while he was with us . . .

How did his heart burn within him, while he 'spake of the things touching the king'! How was his tongue as the pen of a ready writer! and touched as with a coal from off the altar! With what a flow of words, – what a ready profusion of language, did he speak to us on the great concerns of our souls! In what flaming light did he set eternity before us! How earnestly did he press Christ upon us! How did he move our passions with the constraining love of the Redeemer! . . .

The awe, the silence, the attention, which sat upon the face of so great an audience, was an argument how he could reign over all their powers. So charmed were the people with his manner of address, that they shut up their shops and forgot their secular business, and the oftener he preached, the keener edge did he put upon their desires of hearing him again . . . Yet he was no flatterer, and did not prophesy smooth things, or sew pillows. He taught the way of God in truth, and regarded not the person of men. The politest of our vices he struck at, regardless of everyone's presence, except His in whose name he spake!

Concerning 'his personal character' Smith asserts:

I challenge his worst enemies to lay anything to the charge of his morals, or to arraign his sincerity, so visible in all his deportment!

He then goes on to make mention of the holiness of his life, his power in prayer, the graciousness of his manner, his selflessness, and diligence.

As for charity [he states], we have few men like-minded . . . Strolling and vagabond orphans, poor and helpless, without father, without mother, without purse, and without friend, he seeks out, picks up, and adopts into his family. He is now building accommodations, and laying the best foundation for their support and religious instruction, without any visible fund. This is a sacrifice well pleasing to God. He hath dispersed abroad and given to the poor. After this, let none call him an uncharitable man, for what brighter evidence of pure religion is there than this, 'to visit the fatherless in their affliction!'[1]

The sermon constituted a worthy defence of Whitefield's cause, but for Garden it administered a measure of defeat. It described a ministry so magnificent that opposition to it seemed contemptible, and the sincerity of Smith's statements made the sarcasm of the *Six Letters* look cheap and petty.

Such was the situation when, during the first week of July, 1740, Whitefield arrived at Charleston. He was still unwell, but he came in response to the pressing invitations of numerous citizens. On the Sunday morning he went as an ordinary worshipper to St Philip's, and Garden made use of the opportunity, first by delivering a virulent tirade against him, and then by refusing him the Sacrament.

But, knowing that Whitefield intended to remain in Charleston for some weeks, Garden laid plans to humiliate him further. In his position as Commissary he possessed an undefined measure of

[1] *The Character, Preaching etc. of the Reverend Mr George Whitefield*, impartially represented and supported in a sermon preach'd in Charles-town, South Carolina, March 26th, Anno Domini, 1740, by Joseph Smith, V.D.M. with a Preface by the Rev Dr Colman and Mr Cooper of Boston, New England. Boston, 1740. Reprinted Philadelphia same year, and Charlestown, 1765. Reprinted also in ***Sermons on Important Subjects*** by the Rev G. Whitefield. Edinburgh, 1825.

authority over Whitefield, and he determined to exercise it to the full. Throughout the history of the Church of England there had never been an ecclesiastical court in any of the British colonies, but Garden decided to hold one. He would force Whitefield to stand trial before him and the outcome shows that he intended to sentence him to the limit of his power.

Accordingly, he issued the following proclamation:

Alexander Garden, lawfully constituted Commissary of the Right Reverend Father in Christ, Edmund, by Divine permission, Lord Bishop of London, supported by the Royal authority underwritten.

ALEXANDER GARDEN

To all and singular Clerks and literate persons whomsoever, in and throughout the whole Province of South Carolina, wheresoever appointed, Greeting; to you conjunctly and severally, we commit, and strictly enjoining, command that you do cite, or cause to be cited, peremptorily, George Whitefield, Clerk and Presbyter of the Church of England, that he lawfully appear before us, in the Parish Church of St Philip's, Charleston, and in the judicial place of the same, on Tuesday, the fifteenth day of this instant July, betwixt the hours of nine and ten in the forenoon, then and there in justice to answer certain articles, heads or interrogatories, which will be objected and ministered unto him concerning the mere health of his soul, and reformation and correction of his manners and excesses, and chiefly for omitting to use the Form of Prayers prescribed in the Communion Book. And further to do and receive what shall be just in that behalf, on pain of law and contempt. And what you shall do in the premises, you shall duly certify us, together with these presents.

Given under our hands, and seals of our office, at Charleston, this seventh day of July, in the year of our Lord, one thousand seven hundred and forty.[1]

The only actual charge against Whitefield in all these high-sounding phrases is that he had omitted 'to use the Form of Prayers prescribed in the Communion Book' when he preached at the Independent and Baptist meeting-houses. It will have been noticed, however, that Garden is careful to declare the unalloyed purity of his motives – he is acting only 'for the health of [Whitefield's] soul'!

During the week that lay between the issuing of the summons and the day of trial, Whitefield continued his offence. He preached

[1] Tyerman's *Whitefield*, Vol 1, *p* 396.

among the Independents and Baptists at several places in and around Charleston, and made such *Journal* entries as:

Monday, July 7. Set out early this morning in company with several whose hearts the Lord hath lately opened, and went to the house of Mr Chandler, a gracious Baptist minister, who lives about fourteen miles from Charleston. After dinner . . . I preached at his meeting-house, to the conviction of some and comfort of others. Sermon being ended . . . I went with some Charleston friends to the home of Mrs P . . . rs, about five miles from the meeting house; but was obliged to lie down (as I now am generally every day) by reason of the violent heat of the weather, and great expense of sweat.

Tuesday, July 8. Left my lodgings at eight in the morning, and hastened to Dorchester, where I preached twice to a large audience in Mr Osgood's meeting-house, a young Independent minister. At four in the afternoon we set out again; . . . and lay at Mr C's at night. Here my bodily strength failed me again; and therefore, being very weak, I retired to bed as soon as possible, but slept very little . . .

Wednesday, July 9. Found myself still weaker; but was strengthened to preach under a tree near Mr C's meeting-house, at ten in the morning, it being now too small to contain the congregation. People seemed to come from all parts, and the Word came with convincing power. Having changed my linen (which I am obliged to do after every sermon, by reason of my prodigious sweating), I hastened to Charleston; but my body was so exceeding weak, and the sun shone so intensely hot, that five miles before I reached town, I called in at a public house, and lay for a considerable time, almost breathless and dead. But God comforted me; and being thereby strengthened in the inner man, I once more set forward . . . reached town about four, and preached at six, with more freedom and power than could have been expected, considering the great weakness of my body.

Saturday, July 12. Went over the water on Thursday, and read prayers and preached at the request of the churchwardens and vestry at Christ's Church. Returned in the evening to Charleston; preached twice there yesterday, and went this morning to John's Island, about twenty miles up the river. We rode to the church, where there was a great congregation. God strengthened me to read prayers and preach twice with much freedom . . . returned to town in the evening, praising and blessing God. Glory be to His most Holy Name, Dagon seems daily to fall before the ark. A lasting impression is made on many hearts; and God, I believe, will yet shew that He hath much people in Charleston . . .[1]

[1] *Journals, pp* 440–2.

After this week of labour and sickness Whitefield again attended the morning service at St Philip's. Garden was well prepared for him. 'Had some infernal spirit been sent to draw my picture,' says Whitefield, 'I think it scarcely possible he could have painted me in more horrid colours.'[1] The Commissary 'seemed to ransack church history' for instances of fanatics to whom he could be likened. He spoke of the Oliverians, Ranters, Quakers and French Prophets, and then, fearing these cases might not be sufficiently known to his hearers, finally produced one which he knew would be both familiar and repulsive to all. This was the case of *The Dutarts*, a family who, fifteen years earlier, had lived in the Charleston area. They had practised weird religious rites, lived as outlaws, and 'were guilty of the most notorious incests and murders;' some of them had finally been arrested and found guilty of murder, and Garden had served as Chaplain at their hangings. The terrible doings of the Dutarts remained strong in the public mind, and it was to these people that Garden likened Whitefield in his Sunday morning sermon.

This, however, was but a preliminary to the indignity that Garden intended to heap upon his victim when he stood before him in trial. The Court assembled on the Tuesday morning, with Garden in the chair, replete with all possible pomp and attended by four clergymen who were to serve as spiritual advisers. 'Spectators were numerous', says Tyerman, for the whole city was stirred by the event.

Garden opened proceedings by handing Whitefield a list of accusations and demanding that he answer them. But Whitefield asserted that he would answer nothing until the Court had proved that it possessed authority to examine him.

The Commissary replied that if he did not answer, the Court would proceed to censure him. This Whitefield countered by 'reminding him of the heathen magistrates who had exceeded their authority in condemning the Apostle Paul, unheard'. With this Garden seems to have lost his aplomb, for he sent for his written Commission from the Bishop of London and then called for another copy which was in Latin. Both of these were met by Whitefield's assertion that they gave him but a 'general commission, and the extent of his jurisdiction was to be determined

[1] *Ibid*, *p* 442.

by particular Acts of Assembly'. He stated also that, since he was a resident of Georgia, he was outside any jurisdiction Garden might possess, and that the Bishop of London, in whose name this action was professedly taken, had never sought to prohibit his preaching in the fields in England. With this he won a begrudged adjournment and therewith went out and held two great meetings that filled the rest of his day.

When the Court reconvened the following morning, Whitefield seized the initiative by presenting a written 'exception' – a *Recusatio judicis* he calls it – claiming that Garden was prejudiced against him and therefore was unqualified to act as his judge. Garden refused to accept this exception, but Whitefield insisted that the matter of the acceptance or rejection of it could not be left to him, but that it be placed in the hands of six arbitrators, three to be appointed by Garden and three by himself. He asserted that until their decision was made he regarded all further proceedings as null and void. Therewith he again walked out of Court and spent the remainder of the day at his Gospel labours.

The following morning Whitefield returned to Court, ready to take his final action. He asked that the Court inform him 'if his exception was to be referred to arbitration or repelled', and being told it was repelled, he made his announcement: 'he would appeal to His Majesty, in the High Court of Chancery, in London'. And once more he left the Court and went about his work.

Garden, however, despite his pedantic observance of technicalities, had overlooked one important point. Accordingly he sent his Apparitor after Whitefield, commanding him to appear in Court again two days later. Whitefield obeyed, and Garden, implying that Whitefield's word was not to be trusted, required him 'to take an oath he would lodge his appeal within a twelvemonth, and caused him to deposit £10, as a guarantee that his oath would be fulfilled'.

By reason of this appeal any further proceedings by Garden were prohibited by law for a period of a year and a day. We may be sure that throughout that time Garden waited eagerly to hear of the outcome in England, hoping the authorities there would pass a strong sentence on Whitefield. But with the passing of the months he learned to his chagrin that they did not even take him and his little Court seriously and had simply dropped the matter unheard.

But – to anticipate our story – Garden would not drop it. As soon as the year and a day were expired he went into action again and reconvened his Court. Whitefield was then in England, but Garden, after once more stating the holiness of his motives – 'having', he wrote, 'first invoked the name of Christ, and setting and having God alone before our eyes' – proceeded to try and sentence his absent victim. His judgment he recorded in another magniloquent document – 'a cloud of high-sounding words' Tyerman calls it – which closed with the following declaration:

> We therefore pronounce, decree and declare that the said George Whitefield, for his excesses and faults, ought duly and canonically, and according to the exigence of the law in that part of the premises, to be corrected and punished, and also to be suspended from his office; and accordingly, by these presents, we do suspend him, the said George Whitefield; and for being so suspended, we also pronounce, decree and declare him to be denounced, declared, and published openly and publicly in the face of the Church.[1]

Such was Garden's verdict. Though no attention was paid to it by any ecclesiastical authorities, it was not without its effect. Whitefield's enemies seized upon it and until his dying day used it as the basis of the charge that he had been defrocked, thus becoming an outcast from the ministry of his own Church.

This trial constitutes Garden's only claim to fame. Nothing else that he did in life has proved worthy of mankind's remembrance. Alexander Garden satisfied his ego with his little game of court and his masquerade as judge, but he himself stands judged before the bar of history, guilty of adding to the burdens of an already sick and weighted man, and of seeking to hinder – to prohibit if he could – a ministry that was being used of God in an unparalleled reviving of Christianity on two continents.

And what of Whitefield's attitude toward his persecutor? Just before leaving Charleston he met Garden and sought to remove at least any misunderstandings in their relationships. Also, in his *Journals* he wrote:

> I did not feel the least resentment against him. No; I pitied, I prayed

[1] Tyerman's *Whitefield*, Vol 1, *p* 400.

for him; and wished from my soul that the Lord would convert him as He once did the persecutor Saul.[1]

The people were very solicitous about my health, when they saw me so weak, and sent me many small presents. I sometimes feared they would be too hot against the Commissary, but I endeavoured to stop their resentment, and recommended peace and moderation to them.[2]

In its final effect, however, Garden's interference helped, rather than hindered, Whitefield's work at Charleston.

The commissary's detaining me here [he says in a letter], has much tended to the furtherance of the Gospel . . . The Lord is bringing mighty things to pass. I am surprisingly strengthened to bear the heat and burden of every day . . . The inhabitants here are wondrous kind. They attend morning and evening most cheerfully on my preaching. We often see the stately steps of our dear Lord in His sanctuary. I am more than happy. I am amazed at the divine goodness. Lord, I abhor myself in dust and ashes! . . . O pray that an humble child-like spirit may be given to,

Ever yours in Christ,

G.W.[3]

Whitefield's stay in Charleston lasted but two and a half weeks. and of his final service his *Journal* states;

Sunday, July 20. Preached in the morning as usual . . . In the evening (though I went off my bed to do it, and was carried in a chaise) the Lord Jesus strengthened me to take my last farewell of the people of Charleston. Many seemed to sympathise with me.

Blessed be God for sending me once more among them. Though the heat of the weather, and frequency of preaching, have perhaps given an irrecoverable stroke to the health of my body; yet, I rejoice, knowing it has been for the conviction, and I believe conversion of many souls. Glory be to God on high, the fields here, as well as elsewhere, are now white, ready to harvest. Numbers are seeking after Jesus . . .

At my first coming, the people of Charleston seemed to be wholly devoted to pleasure. One, well acquainted with their manners and circumstances, told me that they spent more on their polite entertainments than the amount raised by their rates for the poor. But now the jewellers and dancing-masters begin to cry out that their craft is in danger. A vast alteration is discernible in ladies' dresses; and some,

[1] *Journals, p* 442. [2] *Ibid, p* 444. [3] *Works,* Vol 1, *pp* 200–1.

while I have been speaking, have been so convinced of the sin of wearing jewels, that I have seen them, with blushes, put their hands to their ears, and cover them with their fans. But the reformation has gone further than externals. Many moral, good sort of men, who before were settled on their lees, have been awakened to seek after Jesus Christ; and many a Lydia's heart hath the Lord opened to receive the things that were spoken. Indeed, the Word often came like a hammer and a fire.[1]

Moreover, this change of heart produced a true liberality. Mr Smith, the Independent minister, made mention of 'the late very large collection (*six hundred pounds*), for the Orphan House in Georgia. This is an honour to our whole town.'

*

As a result, however, of Garden's opposition, there came a further development in Whitefield's thinking regarding the doctrine of the church. As we have seen, ever since his conversion he had been slowly moving away from the exclusive Church of England position of the Holy Club, and during his days in America this process had been accelerated by his association with the evangelicals among the Presbyterians, Baptists and Independents. Nevertheless, he had continued to attend the Church of England service each Sunday, but after putting up with three consecutive tirades from Garden, he saw reason to amend this practice. Thus, upon returning to Charleston a few weeks later he stated:

Finding when I was here last, that Jesus Christ was not preached in the church, my conscience would not suffer me to attend on those that preached there any more. I therefore went to the Baptist and Independent meeting-houses, where Jesus Christ was preached. I have administered the Sacrament thrice in a private house. Never did I see anything more solemn . . . What was best, Baptists, Church folks, and Presbyterians all joined together, and received according to the Church of England, except two, who desired to have it sitting: I willingly complied, knowing that it was a thing quite indifferent.[2]

Moreover, if the Church was not the best place for him, neither was it for his hearers. 'I advised the people,' he says, 'since the Gospel was not preached in the church, to go and hear it in the meeting-houses.'[3]

[1] *Journals, p* 444. [2] *Ibid, p* 450. [3] *Ibid, p* 444.

This change in Whitefield's ecclesiastical leanings proved a happy event for these other denominations. Later pages will show something of the growth that was made by the Presbyterians and Independents (Congregationalists) from this time onward, but in the southern Colonies it was the Baptists who gained most from his ministry. While in England Whitefield had come but slowly to an acceptance of the Baptists, but his attitude in this regard too had altered rapidly in America. During his days in Pennsylvania he reported, 'I went and heard Mr Jones, the Baptist minister, who preached the truth as it is in Jesus. He is the only preacher I know of in Philadelphia who speaks feelingly and with authority.'[1]

Likewise, at Ashley Ferry, near Charleston, he rejoiced in being in 'the house of a Mr Chandler, a gracious Baptist minister', and of preaching in his meeting-house and, under his auspices, out-of-doors. Of the Charleston area he wrote, 'There are some faithful ministers here among the Baptists', and when he returned to Georgia, one of whom he spoke as 'a serious, lively Baptist minister, named Tilly', came to see the Orphan House, and Whitefield had him stay for some time, and used him as his 'stand in' when he himself was too sick to preach. Tilly's ministry was of such a nature that it won Whitefield's commendation – a high test, indeed – but it also provoked the disapproval of Secretary Stephens, who, in manifest displeasure, reported seeing this 'Baptist teacher' in the Church of England pulpit.

The effect of Whitefield's influence on the Baptists of the southern Colonies is displayed in miniature in the event of his preaching in the Baptist church at Charleston. He wrote:

> I heard afterwards that from the same pulpit, a person had preached not long ago, who denied the doctrine of original sin, the Divinity and Righteousness of our Lord, and the operation of God's blessed Spirit upon the soul. I was led to shew the utter inability of man to save himself, and absolute necessity of his dependence on the free grace of God in Jesus Christ.[2]

From another source we learn that, prior to Whitefield's ministry in Charleston, '. . . this church was nearly extinct, being reduced to five or six communicants, but Whitefield's success

[1] *Journals*, p 419. [2] *Ibid*, p 401.

greatly increased their number, and it thus gained a strength that it has never lost'.[1]

Baptist churches were not numerically strong in America at that time, and were particularly few in the south, and some were threatened, like that of Charleston, with the crippling effects of Deism. But these conditions began to change, and from the time of this early ministry of Whitefield the history of the Baptists of the southern Colonies became one of militant adherence to the evangelical faith, vigorous evangelism and extraordinary growth.

*

This Summer tour concluded with a final week of ministry as Whitefield journeyed from Charleston back to Savannah. His reports of these days are those of a very sick man – yet one who, despite his weakness, frequently forced himself to preach, and sometimes rode as many as forty miles in a day. We notice:

Monday, July 21. Left Charleston very early, accompanied by many of the inhabitants. Read prayers and preached at Ashley Ferry, to a large congregation. The weather continuing extremely hot, sweating and preaching weakened me very much. I went in a carriage to Madam B's, who kindly invited me and my friends to dinner. I ate but little; . . . took horse, and put in for shelter from the rain at Major B's, in the evening, and reached . . . Ponpon, nearly forty miles from town about midnight . . . being quite worn out, I went to rest as soon as possible . . .

Tuesday, July 22. Slept fairly well, but found I was not strong enough to engage in family duty . . . About noon God strengthened me to ride a mile and preach under a great tree . . . I would willingly have preached a second time; but my body was so weak, that, by the advice of my friends, I resolved to continue where I was all night. Surely it cannot be long before this earthly tabernacle will be dissolved.

Wednesday, July 23. Rose some time before day, and about noon got to Hoospanah Chapel, near thirty miles from Mr B's. Here I preached . . . I went on horseback to Good Hope . . . and several followed, hoping I would preach again in the evening. But here my bodily strength so failed me, and I had such longings after God; that I sometimes hoped He was about to set my imprisoned soul at liberty. Surely God then placed me upon Mount Pisgah, and gave me a dis-

[1] Joseph Belcher, *Biography of Whitefield* (American Tract Society, New York, 1857), *p* 146.

tant prospect of the Heavenly Canaan. I stretched for immortality, and longed for blessed angels to come and carry me to Abraham's harbour . . . thoughts of my Saviour's dying love and of the Lord being my Righteousness, melted me into tears. My dear friend and companion was in tears . . . The poor negroes crowded round the windows, and expressed a great concern for me. Their master . . . sat by and wept. But the time of my departure was not yet at hand. In a short time I felt my body grow stronger, and I was enabled to walk about. I joined in family prayer, as well as I could, and asked God, if I was not to die, but live, that it might be to declare the works and lovingkindness of the Lord.

Thursday, July 24. Being too weak to ride on horseback, I went in Mr B's boat to Beaufort. We got thither about ten in the morning, but the heat of the sun almost struck me down, and took away my senses . . . In the cool of the evening I preached . . .

Friday, July 25. Took boat before day, and . . . reached Savannah and saluted my family about five in the evening.[1]

Savannah, however, held but further trials for the weak and weary Whitefield. Sixteen weeks had now elapsed since he had written his proposal of marriage, and the burdened mind and bodily weakness that he had experienced during that time were caused principally by his concern about the outcome. But as he reached Savannah the reply awaited him, the reply which, as we have seen, caused him to say, 'I find from Blendon letters that Miss E—— D—— is in a seeking state only . . . Just now I have been weeping, and much carried out in prayer before the Lord.'[2]

But this disappointment, bitter though it was, was not the only sorrow that Whitefield met at Savannah. He wanted to be able to look upon Bethesda as a source of joy, but to the trouble that arose from the duplicity of the Trustees and the interference of the Magistrates, there had now been added another. It was at this

[1] *Journals, pp* 445–6.

[2] Gillies dates this letter, *Works,* Vol 1, *p* 194, as June 26. This is manifestly an error. Whitefield had written his letters to Blendon on April 4, but could not have placed them on a vessel to England until he reached Newcastle, which was on April 13. It would have been impossible for him to receive a reply by June 26, a period of two months and thirteen days, and at least another month was necessary. Moreover, in the letter to Seward which reports his having had a reply from Blendon, Whitefield says, 'I sent you a packet of letters from Charleston, the middle of this month', and July was the month in which he was in Charleston. Thus, he arrived back in Savannah on Friday, July 25, and there can be no doubt that it was on the following day, July 26, that he wrote to Seward.

time that Hagen, the Moravian, had interjected the doctrinal differences, creating strife among, apparently, both the men employed on the construction and the women engaged in looking after the children.

The discord seems to have been so severe as to create a crisis in Orphan House affairs: 'My family in Georgia was . . . sadly shaken,' Whitefield stated. Thus, notwithstanding the weakness of his body and the fearful preoccupation of his mind, he had no choice but to face the trouble and to take what steps he could towards restoring order. He says nothing about what action he took, but after the passing of three weeks, which he undoubtedly filled with teaching and persuasion, he appears to have been satisfied that conditions had largely returned to normal.

*

It will surely be thought that having conducted such strenuous labours as those of his Spring and Summer tours, and having suffered such a time of sickness and disappointment, Whitefield ought to have made plans to take a vacation – to find a place of peace and quiet, where the body might recuperate and care might be forgotten. But this kind of thing was impossible to George Whitefield and, in less than a month after his return to Savannah, he was on his way north again, launching out upon another and still more extensive evangelistic tour: that of New England.

Lo! by the Merrimac Whitefield stands
In the temple that never was made by hands, –
Curtains of azure, and crystal wall,
And dome of the sunshine over all! –
A homeless pilgrim, with dubious name
Blown about on the winds of fame;
Now as an angel of blessing classed,
And now as a mad enthusiast.
Called in his youth to sound and gauge
The moral lapse of his race and age,
And, sharp as truth, the contrast draw
Of human frailty and perfect law;
Possessed by the one dread thought that lent
Its goad to his fiery temperament,
Up and down the world he went,
A John the Baptist crying – Repent*!*

JOHN GREENLEAF WHITTIER

The Preacher

32

The Fall Tour – New England

NOWHERE in America was Whitefield's coming awaited with such eagerness as in New England. The Boston newspapers had kept their readers informed of his activities in the other Colonies and several of the city's most eminent ministers and laymen had written,[1] earnestly inviting him to come and minister among them. Great numbers of the people fondly remembered the revival at Northampton; they longed to see it renewed, and in the knowledge that extraordinary blessings had accompanied Whitefield's ministry elsewhere, had developed an expectancy that his visit to New England would be the occasion of a revival even mightier than that of former years.

Such was the spirit prevailing in the northern Colonies when, on Sunday, September 14,[2] Whitefield landed at Newport, Rhode Island. Again, as at the beginning of his Spring tour, he came unannounced, and again the news of his arrival caused an immediate excitement and brought the people in throngs to hear him. On the Monday he was begrudgingly allowed the use of the Church of England, and wrote,

At ten in the morning and at three in the afternoon, I read prayers and preached in the church. It is very commodious and will contain three thousand people. It was more than filled in the afternoon, persons of all denominations attending.[3]

[1] Not long after his arrival in America Dr Colman had written a letter of greeting and invitation, and thereafter other ministers had done the same. Mr Josiah Willard, the Secretary of Massachusetts, had exchanged letters with Whitefield two or three times, earnestly entreating him to come. [2] 1740.

[3] *Journals*, p 453. The minister of the Church of England, the Rev James Honeyman, in an unpublished letter now in the possession of the S.P.C.K., London, stated, 'Last Sunday arrived here from South Carolina, the noisie Mr Whitefield . . . he came to my house, attended by an aged Dissenting Teacher and several other

Tuesday, September 16. Although a little low in the morning, I was enabled to read prayers and preach to still greater auditories than yesterday . . . several invitations were given to me to come to other adjacent places. The people were exceedingly attentive; tears trickled down their cheeks; . . .

In the evening I went, privately as I thought, to a friend's house; but the people were so eager to hear the word, that in a short time, more than a thousand were before the door, besides those that were within, and filled every room in the house. I therefore stood upon the threshold, and spake for near an hour . . . It was a very solemn meeting . . .[1]

*

Before Whitefield, however, there lay the fulfilment of the dream of many months: the opportunity to see New England and to minister among the descendants of its Puritan founders. Thus, after but four days in Rhode Island he wrote:

Thursday, September 18. Rose a long while before day, and set out as soon as it was light. Breakfasted at a minister's house on the road. Found the people were apprised of my coming and solicitous for my preaching; but, being resolved, if possible, to reach Boston, we travelled on for near fifty miles and came to Boston about eight in the evening.

When we were within four miles of the city, the Governor's son, with one or two ministers and several other gentlemen, waited at a gentleman's house to give me the meeting. They received me with great gladness, and told me many more would have come, had there not been a large funeral in the city, or if there had been more certain notice of my arriving. I think I can stand anything better than this; it savours too much of human grandeur . . . After stopping a while, we went together to Boston, to the house of Mr Staniford, brother-in-law to the Rev Dr Colman, who long since had sent me an invitation . . .

Friday, September 19. I was visited by several gentlemen and ministers, and went to the Governor's with Esquire Willard, the Secretary of the Province . . . The Governor received me with the utmost respect,

people, and . . . desired leave to preach in my Church . . . He said if I denied him, the Old Teacher had strongly invited him to the Meeting House, and he would accept of it. Whereupon, several of the chief of my people most vehemently pressed upon me to allow him to preach in the Church . . . I at last complied . . . I shall endeavour to correct his mistakes and evince a just distinction betwixt Christianity and enthusiasm.'

[1] *Journals, pp* 454–5.

and desired me to see him as often as I could. At eleven I went to public worship at the Church of England, and afterwards went home with the Commissary. He received me very courteously; and, it being a day whereon the clergy of the Established Church met, I had an opportunity of conversing with five of them together.[1]

At the Commissary's home a discussion occurred which reveals still further the changes that were taking place in Whitefield's thinking regarding the doctrine of the Church. The clergymen questioned him on his associating with persons of other denominations, implying that he ought to have fellowship only with men of the Church of England, and he reports:

. . . one of them began with me for calling 'that Tennent and his brethren *faithful* ministers of Jesus Christ'. I answered, 'I believed they were'. They then questioned me about the validity of the Presbyterian ordination. I replied, 'I believed it was valid'. Then they urged against me a passage in my first *Journal*, where I said, 'That a Baptist minister at Deal did not give a satisfactory answer concerning his mission'. I answered, 'Perhaps my sentiments were altered'. . . .[2]

I then urged 'That a catholic[3] spirit was best, and that a Baptist minister had communicated with me lately at Savannah'. 'I suppose', said another, 'that you would do him as good a turn and would communicate with him.' I answered, 'Yes', and 'urged that it was best to preach the new birth, and the power of godliness, and not to insist so much on the form: for the people would never be brought to one mind as to that; nor did Jesus Christ ever intend it'. 'Yes, but He did', said Dr Cutler. 'How do you prove it?' 'Because Christ prayed "That all might be one, even as Thou Father and I are One".' I replied, 'That was spoken of the inward union of the souls of believers with Jesus Christ, and not of the outward Church'. 'That cannot be,' said Dr Cutler, 'for how then could it be said, "that the world might know that Thou hast sent me"?' He then (taking it for granted that the Church of England was the only true apostolical Church) drew a parallel between the Jewish and our Church, urging how God required

[1] *Ibid, pp* 456–7.

[2] At this point in Whitefield's account there occurs a mention of the views held by 'Mr Wesley . . . when he was at Boston'. This refers to Charles Wesley, who, on his return to England from Georgia, was aboard a vessel that put in at Boston and remained there for four weeks. This was the only place in America, apart from Georgia and Charleston, that either of the Wesleys ever saw.

[3] Whitefield frequently made use of the work 'catholic'. He did so, however, in its basic meaning of 'universal, comprehensive in sympathies and understanding, extending to all mankind'.

all things to be made according to the pattern given in the Mount. I answered, 'Before that parallel could be just, it must be proved that everything enjoined in our Church was as much of a Divine institution as any rite or ceremony under the Jewish dispensation'. I added further 'That I saw regenerate souls among the Baptists, among the Presbyterians, among the Independents, and among the Church folk – all children of God, and yet all born again in a different way of worship . . .' 'What, can you see regeneration with your eyes?' said the Commissary . . .

I also said, 'That if every child was really born again in baptism, then every baptized infant would be saved'. 'And so they are,' said Dr Cutler. 'How do you prove that?' 'Because the Rubric says "that all infants dying after baptism before they have committed actual sin, are undoubtedly saved".' I asked, 'What text of Scripture was there to prove it?' 'Here,' said he (holding a Prayer Book in his hand), 'the Church says so.' . . . Several other things of less consequence passed between us . . .[1]

With this discussion Whitefield's association with the Church of England in America came to an end. During the remainder of this trip to the Colonies he did not again call upon or attend the services of any of its clergy. And of these men in Boston he said, 'Finding how inconsistent they were I took my leave, resolving they should not have an opportunity of denying me the use of their pulpits. However, they treated me with more civility than any of our own clergymen have done for a long while.'[2]

Since the dimensions of these Boston churches are known, we may be sure that Whitefield's estimates, like those he made in England, are highly exaggerated. They need to be reduced – probably by almost a half.

Nevertheless, there can be no doubt that these buildings were overcrowded to the point of grave danger. One or two eyewitnesses have left reports of these gatherings which depict tremendous throngs – humanity pressed into the pews, crowding the aisles, filling the stairways, congesting the doorways and porches, stretching to look in at the windows and covering the pulpit area till they barely left room for the preacher to stand. Doubtless, so packed together was the multitude that (as Whitefield said at London) 'one might, as it were, walk upon the people's heads'.

[1] *Journals, pp* 457–9. [2] *Ibid, p* 459.

Civic officials to-day would not allow such crowding, and in one instance then it proved disastrous. On the Monday afternoon a congregation that filled the New South Church sat waiting for Whitefield to arrive, and amidst the congestion and excitement someone broke a board in order to provide himself with a makeshift seat. The sound of the breaking board caused a sudden alarm and brought a cry that the galleries were falling. Immediately all the place was in a panic. Some people threw themselves out of the windows and others jumped from the galleries to the crowded floor beneath. The multitude pressed to get out at the doors, and in the confusion many were thrown down and trodden upon. 'I happened to come in the midst of the uproar', says Whitefield, 'and saw two or three lying on the ground in a pitiable condition. God was pleased to give me presence of mind; so that I gave notice I would immediately preach on the common. The weather was wet, but many thousands followed in the field, to whom I preached from these words, "Go out into the highways and hedges and compel them to come in". I endeavoured . . . to improve what had befallen us.'[1] Within two days five persons died from the effects of this accident.

Though greatly disturbed by the tragedy, Whitefield did not let it curtail his labours. Each day he preached both morning and afternoon, and each evening ministered to a crowd that thronged into and around the house at which he lodged. On the Wednesday he preached twice to the students at Harvard College, and on the Saturday to a congregation of fifteen thousand on the Boston Common. On the Sunday he took up his first two collections in New England, receiving nearly £200 sterling.[2] Following his second service of the Sunday he 'went and preached to a great number of negroes at their request' and then, upon returning to his lodgings, found a crowd awaiting him, to whom he 'gave a word of exhortation'. 'My spirits were almost exhausted', he writes, 'and my legs ready to sink under me; but the Lord visited

[1] *Journals, p* 461. Certain details of the event as here related are taken from an early *Journal* that Whitefield wrote which is quoted by Belcher, *op cit, p* 159. Students of the life of C. H. Spurgeon will notice the similarity between this tragedy and that experienced by Spurgeon in 1856 while preaching in the Surrey Gardens Music Hall. See Spurgeon's *Autobiography*, Vol 2, *pp* 195 ff. Reprinted 1962, under title *C. H. Spurgeon: The Early Years.* (Banner of Truth Trust), *pp* 429–43.

[2] At that time it required about £5½ in the currency of Massachusetts to equal £1 in sterling.

my soul, and I went to bed greatly refreshed . . . Lord, Thou fillest my soul with marrow and fatness.'[1]

Thus ended Whitefield's first week in New England. During the second week he followed a practice that we have seen him observing in old England – he made a seven-day preaching tour to several outlying towns. This took him to Marble Head, Salem, Ipswich, Newbury, Hampton and Portsmouth, and finally to York in what is now the state of Maine. On the journey back to Boston he preached again at these places – his custom of *preach and return* – and rejoiced to see that tne seed sown the few days earlier was already bearing fruit.

It is evident that the matter of choosing a wife was on his mind, for at Hampton he wrote:

I was pleased to see more plainness in Mr Cotton's house than in any minister's house since my arrival. His wife was as one that serveth. O that all ministers' wives were so! Nothing gives me more offence than to see clergymen's wives dressed out in the pride of life. They generally live up to the utmost of their income; and, being above working, after their husband's decease, they are of all women most miserable. From such a wife, good Lord, of Thy infinite mercy, deliver me![2]

This journey to the north was followed by a final week of ministry at Boston. It proved to be a time of rich harvest, as is manifest in the following selections from his *Journals:*

Tuesday, October 7. Preached both morning and evening in Dr Colman's meeting-house, with much power. People seemed greatly rejoiced at my arrival, it being reported I had died suddenly . . . Gave a word of exhortation to many people, at a house which I trust the Lord will visit with His salvation. Wherever I go people will follow me; and I now, almost hourly, receive letters from persons under convictions, . . .

Wednesday, October 8. Went with the Governor, in his coach, to Mr Webb's meeting-house, where I preached both morning and evening, to very great auditories. Both times, Jesus Christ manifested forth His glory. Many hearts were melted down. I think I never was so drawn out to pray for little children, and invite little children to Jesus Christ, as I was this morning. I had just heard of a child, who after hearing me preach, was immediately taken sick, and said, 'I will go to Mr Whitefield's God'. In a short time he died. This encouraged me to speak to

[1] *Journals, p* 464. [2] *Ibid, pp* 465–6.

little ones; but, oh, how were the old people affected, when I said, 'Little children, if your parents will not come to Christ, do you come, and go to Heaven without them'. There seemed to be but few dry eyes . . .

Thursday, October 9. Every morning, since my return, I have been applied to by many souls under deep distress, and was grieved that I could not have more time with them. Gave, this morning, the public lecture at Dr Sewall's meeting-house, which was very much crowded . . .

Went to a funeral of one belonging to the Council; but do not like the custom at Boston of not speaking at the grave. When can ministers' prayers and exhortations be more suitable, than when the corpse before them silently assists them, as it were; and, with a kind of dumb oratory, bids the spectators consider their latter end? When the funeral was over, I went to the almshouse, and preached on these words, 'The poor received the Gospel', . . . then I went to the work-house, where I prayed with and exhorted a great number of people, who crowded after me, besides those belonging to the house, for near an hour more; and then, hearing there was a considerable number waiting for a word of exhortation at my lodgings, God strengthened me to give them a spiritual morsel. Soon after, I retired to rest. Oh, how comfortable is sleep after working for Jesus! . . .

Friday, October 10. Was still busied, from the very moment I arose until I went out, in answering those that came to me under great distress. About nine, went with Mr Cooper over Charleston ferry, where I preached with much freedom of spirit, and collected £156 for the orphans . . .[1]

Whitefield concluded his twenty-four days in the Boston area (including the one-week tour to the north) with a Sunday which God caused to be a day of jubilee. During its early hours, awakened souls – many more than he had time to deal with – came seeking him at his lodgings, but he had to leave them in order to go and preach at the Old South Church. Upon arriving, however, he found the crowd so great that he could not get in by the doors and was obliged to enter through a window.

He was unwell following the meeting, but went in the afternoon – driven by the Governor in his coach – to the Common for his farewell service. Apparently the vast majority of the inhabitants of Boston were there and many from outlying towns,

[1] *Ibid, pp* 469–71.

for a newspaper reported 'there were, at a moderate computation, twenty-three thousand present.[1] Whitefield wrote:

. . . I preached my farewell sermon to near twenty thousand people, – a sight I have not seen since I left Blackheath – and a sight, perhaps, never seen before in America. It being nearly dusk before I had done, the sight was more solemn. Numbers, great numbers, melted into tears when I talked of leaving them. I was very particular in my application, both to rulers, ministers and people . . . After sermon the Governor went with me to my lodgings. I stood in the passage, and spoke to a great company, both within and without doors; but they were so deeply affected and cried so loud that I was obliged to leave off praying . . .

The remainder of the evening was almost entirely spent in speaking to persons under great distress of soul . . . Blessed be God! for what He has done in Boston. I hope a glorious work is now begun, and that the Lord will stir up some faithful labourers to carry it on.'[2]

The hope expressed by Whitefield was abundantly fulfilled. Thomas Prince wrote an account of the change which, under God, was effected by Whitefield's ministry. He describes the spiritual decline that long had been experienced in Boston and cites, as typical of conditions, the effort put forth at one time by eleven pastors to hold a series of special meetings – 'Lectures', they called them – to deal with the subject of *Family Religion*. 'Yet they had the further sorrow,' says Prince, 'to see these Lectures too thinly attended to expect any benefit from them.[3] Even when the revival at Northampton was spreading to several other towns, Prince could only remark,

. . . the general decay of piety seemed to increase among us in Boston . . . few came to me in concern about their souls. And so I perceive it was in others. And I remember some of the Ministers were wont to express themselves as greatly discouraged with the growing declension, both in principle and practice, especially among the rising generation.[4]

[1] This report was written in Boston and was published in the *South Carolina Gazette*, No 361. As an example of the erroneous fashion with which certain writers have dealt with Whitefield, we notice that, though he reported 'near twenty thousand' and the newspaper said 'twenty-three thousand', Grover C. Loud, *America Evangelized*, *p* 50, misconstrues these figures into the following, 'Whitefield himself thought that about thirty thousand heard his farewell sermon on Boston Common, but the newspapers of the day put the crowd at two thousand three hundred'.

[2] *Journals*, *p* 472.

[3] Prince's *Christian History*, *op cit*, Vol of 1744, *pp* 375–6.

[4] *Ibid*, *p* 379.

Prince then goes on to relate the principal events of Whitefield's visit and continues,

But upon Mr Whitefield's leaving us, great numbers in the town were so happily concerned about their souls, as we had never seen anything like it before . . . our assemblies, both on Lectures and Sabbaths were surprisingly increased, and now the people wanted to hear us oftener. In consideration of which a public Lecture was proposed to be set up at Dr Colman's Church near the midst of the town, on every Tuesday evening . . . When the evening came, the House seemed to be crowded as much as if Mr Whitefield was there. It was the first stated *evening* Lecture in these parts of the world.[1]

At Whitefield's request Gilbert Tennent came to Boston to carry on the work that had been begun. There was not the least thought of starting a new church, for he came to assist, as Whitefield had done, the Boston ministers. But Tennent's ministry, though exceptionally powerful and effective, had little of the sweet entreaties and tender persuadings of Whitefield's.

His preaching [says Prince] was as searching and rousing as ever I heard. He seemed . . . to aim directly at the hearers' hearts and consciences, to lay open their ruinous delusions, shew them their numerous, secret, hypocritical shifts in religion, and drive them out of every deceitful refuge . . .

From the terrible and deep convictions he had passed through in his own soul, he seemed to have such a lively view of the Divine majesty, the spirituality, purity, extensiveness, and strictness of His law, with His glorious holiness, and displeasure at sin, His justice, truth and power, in punishing the damned; . . . The arrows of conviction, by his ministry, seemed so deeply to pierce the hearts, even of some of the most stubborn sinners, as to make them fall down at the feet of Christ, and yield a lowly submission to him.[2]

Tennent remained in Boston for four months, after which he returned to Philadelphia. His work, however, proved to be, in the hand of God, a cultivation of the sowing that had been effected under Whitefield's ministry, and Prince goes on to state:

And now was such a time as we never knew. The Rev Mr Cooper was wont to say, that more came to him in one week in deep concern about their souls, than in the whole *twenty-four years* of his preceding ministry. I can also say the same as to the numbers who repaired to me. Mr

[1] *Ibid, pp* 381–2. [2] *Ibid, pp* 385–6.

Cooper has had about six hundred persons in three months; and Mr Webb has had in the same space above a thousand.

. . . there repaired to us both boys and girls, young men and women, Indians and Negroes, heads of families and aged persons; . . . Persons far advanced in years came, afraid of being left behind, while others were hastening to the blest Redeemer.[1]

Tyerman summarizes these results, saying:

This wondrous movement continued a year and a half after Whitefield's departure from Boston. Thirty Religious Societies were instituted in the city. Ministers, besides attending to their usual work, preached in private houses almost every night. Chapels were always crowded. 'The very face of the town seemed to be strangely altered. Even the negroes and boys in the streets left their usual rudeness, and taverns were found empty of all but lodgers.' 'Our lectures flourish,' wrote Dr Colman in a letter to Dr Isaac Watts, 'our Sabbaths are joyous, our churches increase and our ministers have new life and spirit in their work.'[2]

*

Mention has been made of the attention shown to Whitefield by the Honourable Jonathan Belcher, the Governor of Massachusetts. After graduating from Harvard, Belcher had spent six years – in the manner of the sons of the English nobility – making *the grand tour* of Europe, and in his associations there 'the gracefulness of his person, his talents and property procured him considerable notice'. Appointed in 1730 to the governorship of New England, he continued to live in the aristocratic fashion, delighting in the display of pomp and magnificence. Yet under Whitefield's ministry God humbled him, and on one occasion he said, 'Mr Whitefield, do not spare rulers, any more than ministers, no, not the chief of them'. At another time, 'After sermon the Governor remarked, "I pray God, I may apply what has been said to my own heart. Pray, Mr Whitefield, that I may hunger and thirst after righteousness".'[3] A newspaper report stated, 'Mr Whitefield has not a warmer friend anywhere than in the first man among us. Our Governor can call him nothing less than the Apostle Paul. He has shown him the highest respects and carried him in his coach from place to place; and could not help following

[1] *Ibid*, *pp* 391–2.
[2] Tyerman's *Whitefield*, Vol 1, *p* 425.
[3] *Journals*, *p* 475.

him fifty miles out of town.'[1] Belcher continued to manifest, not only his affection for Whitefield, but a deep concern for the work of the Lord. In 1745 he became Governor of New Jersey, where, in 1746, he played an important part in the establishment of a new Presbyterian school, the College of New Jersey.

*

As Whitefield left Boston there lay before him a privilege he had long anticipated, that of making the acquaintance of Jonathan Edwards at Northampton. Arriving there after four days of travelling and preaching, he recorded:

After a little refreshment, we crossed the ferry to Northampton (Mass.), where no less than three hundred souls were saved about five years ago. Their pastor's name is Edwards, successor and grandson to the great Stoddard, whose memory will always be precious to my soul, and whose books entitled 'A Guide to Christ', and 'Safety of Appearing in Christ's Righteousness', I would recommend to all.

Mr Edwards is a solid, excellent Christian, but at present weak in body. I think I have not seen his fellow in all New England. When I came into his pulpit, I found my heart drawn out to talk of scarce anything besides the consolations and privileges of saints, and the plentiful effusion of the Spirit upon believers. When I came to remind them of their former experiences, and how zealous and lively they were at that time, both minister and people wept much. In the evening I gave a word of exhortation to several who came to Mr Edwards' house.

Saturday, Oct. 18. At Mr Edwards' request, I spoke to his little children, who were much affected. Preached at Hadley, five miles from Northampton, but found myself not much strengthened. Preached at four in the afternoon to Mr Edwards' congregation. I began with fear and trembling, but God assisted me. Few eyes were dry in the assembly. I had an affecting prospect of the glories of the upper world, and was enabled to speak with some degree of pathos. It seemed as if a time of refreshing was come from the presence of the Lord.

Sunday, Oct. 19. Felt great satisfaction in being at the house of Mr Edwards. A sweeter couple I have not yet seen. Their children were not dressed in silks and satins, but plain, as becomes the children of

[1] Postscript to the *South Carolina Gazette*, No 361. This issue contained serial accounts of Whitefield's ministry in Boston, written at the request of Josiah Smith, Whitefield's defender at Charleston. In publishing these accounts Smith doubtless intended they should be news to Whitefield's multitude of friends in the southern Colonies and also that they should serve as an additional rebuttal to Commissary Garden.

those who, in all things, ought to be examples of Christian simplicity. Mrs Edwards is adorned with a meek and quiet spirit; . . .[1]

Preached this morning, and good Mr Edwards wept during the whole time of exercise. The people were equally affected, and in the afternoon the power increased yet more . . . Oh, that my soul may be refreshed with the joyful news, that Northampton people have recovered their first love; that the Lord has revived His work in their souls, and caused them to do their first works![2]

Edwards' report of Whitefield's visit and of the results that followed indicate that Whitefield's prayer was largely answered. Says Edwards:

Mr Whitefield preached four sermons in the meeting-house (besides a private lecture at my house). The congregation was extraordinarily melted by each sermon, almost the whole assembly being in tears for a great part of the time.

Mr Whitefield's sermons were suitable to the circumstances of the town; containing just reproofs of our backslidings, and in a most moving and affectionate manner, making use of our great profession and great mercies, as arguments with us to return to God, from whom we had departed.

Immediately after this, the minds of the people in general appeared more engaged in religion, shewing a greater forwardness to make religion the subject of their conversation, and to embrace all opportunities to hear the Word preached. The revival at first appeared chiefly among professors, to whom Mr Whitefield chiefly addressed himself, but in a very short time among some young persons who looked upon themselves as in a Christless state . . . In about a month there was a great alteration in the town, both as to the revival of professors, and awakening of others . . .[3]

Mrs Edwards also left record of her opinion of Whitefield, for she immediately wrote to her brother, the Rev James Pierpoint of New Haven, as follows:

October 24, 1740

DEAR BROTHER JAMES,

I want to prepare you for a visit from the Rev Mr Whitefield, the famous preacher of England. He has been sojourning with us, and

[1] There follows here the expression of desire 'that God would be pleased to send me a daughter of Abraham to be my wife', which we have seen in the chapter 'A proposal of Marriage', *p* 475.

[2] *Journals*, *pp* 476–7.

[3] Prince's *Christian History*, Vol of 1743, *p* 368.

after visiting a few of the neighbouring towns, is going to New Haven, and from thence to New York.

He is truly a remarkable man, and during his visit, has, I think, verified all we have heard of him. He makes less of the doctrines than our American preachers generally do and aims more at affecting the heart. He is a born orator. You have already heard of his deep-toned yet clear and melodious voice. It is perfect music.

It is wonderful to see what a spell he casts over an audience by proclaiming the simplest truths of the Bible. I have seen upwards of a thousand people hang on his words with breathless silence, broken only by an occasional half-suppressed sob.

He impresses the ignorant, and not less, the educated and refined. It is reported that while the miners of England listened to him, the tears made white furrows down their smutty cheeks. So here, our mechanics shut up their shops, and the day-labourers throw down their tools, to go and hear him preach, and few return unaffected. A prejudiced person, I know, might say that this is all theatrical artifice and display; but not so will anyone think who has seen and known him.

He is a very devout and godly man, and his only aim seems to be to reach and influence men the best way. He speaks from a heart aglow with love, and pours out a torrent of eloquence which is almost irresistible. I wish him success in his apostolic career; and when he reaches New Haven, you will, I know, show him warm hospitality.

Yours in faithful affection,

SARAH.[1]

Despite, however, the mutual happiness occasioned by Whitefield's week-end in the Edwards' home, the two men did not become intimate friends. Upon meeting Edwards, Whitefield immediately recognized his intellectual and spiritual superiority – 'I have not seen his fellow in all New England'. He seems to have felt himself unable and unworthy to seek a close fellowship with so towering a personality, and it may have been for this reason that the natively-reticent young evangelist spoke of 'fear and trembling' when he first stood to preach in the presence of the philosopher-theologian.

[1] Tyerman's *Whitefield*, Vol 1, *pp* 428–9. This letter is, in itself, sufficient answer to the description that has been made of Whitefield, as he came to the Edwards' home, as most 'repulsive', and to the suggestion that, because of the condition of his eyes, womankind would have found him offensive. The supposition that his preaching, during that week-end, was 'whining and sanctimonious', 'shallow' and creating frenzy among his hearers, may be viewed in the light of Mrs Edwards' glowing tributes to its qualities.

This sense of disparity was probably heightened by the fact that Edwards, who was Whitefield's senior by eleven years, sought to warn him regarding the reliance he placed upon his impulses. Edwards says that Whitefield took his advice courteously, but appeared reluctant to converse upon the subject. 'I thought Mr Whitefield liked me not so well for my opposing these things,' he reports, 'and though he treated me with great kindness, yet he never made so much of an intimate with me, as of other men.'[1]

But Whitefield's reserve may well have arisen from an entirely different source. It was during these days that, unknown to Edwards, Whitefield was undergoing the deep disappointment over his proposal of marriage, and his sorrow was manifestly increased during his few days at the Edwards' home. In the comfort and assistance that Mr and Mrs Edwards were to one another, he could not fail to see that he had been wrong in assuming that marriage would prove detrimental to a minister's spiritual life, and while suffering this change of mind and experiencing fresh 'inward trials' he probably found it difficult to be his normal friendly self.

Nevertheless, when Whitefield left Northampton, and resumed his journey, Edwards chose to accompany him. On the second day of travel they arrived at East Windsor, where Edwards' father, the Rev Timothy Edwards, was the minister. After preaching to his people and 'supping at his house', Whitefield said, 'His wife was as aged, I believe, as himself, and I fancied I was sitting in the house of a Zacharias and Elizabeth. I parted from him and his son (who came with me thus far) with regret.'[2]

*

Two days after parting from Jonathan Edwards and his father, Whitefield came to Middletown. His meeting there was not unusual in any way, for he merely says of it, 'Preached to about four thousand people at eleven o'clock.'[3] But one of his hearers penned a description which shows how the mere news that he was to preach created a sudden excitement and brought almost the whole countryside hurrying to hear him. The writer was an unlettered farmer named Nathan Cole, and he wrote:

[1] Tracy, *op cit*, p 100. [2] *Ibid*, p 479. [3] *Ibid*.

Now it pleased God to send mr whitefield into this land & . . . i longed to see & hear him . . . & then one morning all on a Suding there came a messanger & said mr whitefield . . . is to preach at middletown this morning at 10 o'clock i was in my field at work i dropt my tool that i had in my hand & run home and throu my house and bad my wife to get ready quick to go and hear mr whitefield preach at middletown & run to my pastire for my hors with all my might fearing i should be too late to hear him & took up my wife & went forward as fast as i thought ye hors could bear & when my hors began to be out of breth i would get down and put my wife on ye saddel and bid her ride as fast as she could & not Stop or Slack for me except i bad her & so i would run until i was almost out of breth & then mount my hors again . . . fearing we should be too late to hear ye Sarmon for we had twelve miles to ride dubble in little more than an our.

i saw before me a cloud or fog i first thought of from ye great river but as i came nearer ye road i heard a noise something like a low rumbling thunder & i presently found out it was ye rumbling of horses feet coming down ye road & this Cloud was a Cloud of dust made by the running of horses feet it arose some rods into ye air over the tops of ye hills and trees & when i came within about twenty rods of ye road i could see men and horses slipping along – it was like a steady streem of horses and their riders scarecely a hors more than his length behind another – i found a vacance between two horses to slip in my hors & my wife said law our cloaths will be all spoiled see how they look – & when we gat down to ye old meeting hous thare was a great multitude it was said to be 3 or 4000 & when i looked towards ye great river i see ye fery boats running swift forward and backward – when i see mr whitefield come up upon ye scaffold he looked almost angellical a young slim slender youth before thousands of people and with a bold undainted countenance & my hearing how god was with him everywhere as he came along it solemnized my mind and put me in a trembling fear before he began to preach for he looked as if he was Clothed with authority from ye great god and a sweet solemnity sat upon his brow and my hearing him preach gave me a heart wound & by gods blessing my old foundation was broken up & i see my righteousness would not save me.[1]

[1] *The Spiritual Travels of Nathan Cole.* This is Cole's original draft of the narrative, the ms. of which is in the possession of the Connecticut Historical Society. There is also a copyist's version which is edited and corrected as to spelling and grammar, but which lacks the quaintness of the original. Cole's *Spiritual Travels* and particularly this experience are discussed by Leonard W. Larabee in the *William and Mary Quarterly*, 3rd Series, VII, 1950, *pp* 589–90.

Cole describes himself as one who, until this time, was an Arminian and 'intended to be saved by his own works'. After hearing Whitefield, however, he came under a severe sense of sin which continued for two years and then issued in a glorious conversion. He left the *Old Light* church and became an active worker in a *New Light* congregation which was formed at Middletown.

If Cole has given us an insight into the manner in which Whitefield's immense congregations gathered upon such short notice in the sparsely-populated areas of America, another hearer has left us an account which illustrates his ability to use the circumstances of the moment as a means of enforcing the Gospel message. This hearer, describing one of his services in Boston, writes:

There is nothing in the appearance of this remarkable man which would lead you to suppose that a Felix would tremble before him. To have seen him when he first commenced, one would have thought him anything but enthusiastic and glowing. But as he proceeded, his heart warmed with his subject, and his manner became impetuous, till, forgetful of everything around him, he seemed to kneel at the throne of Jehovah, and to beseech in agony for his fellow-beings.

After he had finished his prayer, he knelt for a long time in profound silence; and so powerfully had it affected the most heartless of his audience, that a stillness like that of the tomb pervaded the whole house.

Before he commenced his sermon, long, darkening columns crowded the bright sunny sky of the morning, and swept their dull shadows over the building, in fearful augury of the storm that was approaching.

'See that emblem of human life,' said he, as he pointed to a flitting shadow. 'It passed for a moment, and concealed the brightness of heaven from our view; but it is gone. And where will you be, my hearers, when your lives have passed away like that dark cloud? Oh, my dear friends, I see thousands sitting attentive, with their eyes fixed on the poor unworthy preacher. In a few days we shall all meet at the judgment-seat of Christ. We shall form a part of that vast assembly which will gather before His throne. Every eye will behold the Judge. With a voice whose call you must abide and answer, He will enquire, whether on earth you strove to enter in at the strait gate; whether you were supremely devoted to God; whether your hearts were absorbed in Him. My blood runs cold when I think how many of you will then seek to enter in, and shall not be able. O, what plea can you make before the Judge of the whole earth? Can you say it has been your whole endeavour to mortify the flesh, with its affections and lusts? No! you must answer, I made myself easy in the world, by flattering myself that all would end well; but I have deceived my own soul, and am lost!

'O false and hollow Christians, of what avail will it be that you have done many things? that you have read much in the sacred Word? that you have made long prayers? that you have attended religious duties, and appeared holy in the eyes of men? What will all this be, if, instead of loving God supremely, you have been supposing you should exalt yourself in heaven by acts really polluted and unholy?

'And you, rich men, wherefore do you hoard your silver? Wherefore count the price you have received for Him whom you every day crucify in your love of gain? Why, that, when you are too poor to buy a drop of cold water, your own beloved son may be rolled into hell in his chariot, pillowed and cushioned!

'O sinner! by all your hopes of happiness, I beseech you to repent. Let not the wrath of God be awakened! Let not the fires of eternity be kindled against you! See there!' cried the impassioned preacher, pointing to a flash of lightning, 'It is a glance from the angry eye of Jehovah! Hark!' he continued, raising his finger in a listening attitude, as the thunder broke in a tremendous crash, 'it was the voice of the Almighty as He passed by in His anger!'

As the sound died away, Whitefield covered his face with his hands, and fell on his knees, apparently lost in prayer. The storm passed rapidly by, and the sun, bursting forth, threw across the heavens the magnificent arch of peace. Rising and pointing to it, the young preacher cried, 'Look upon the rainbow, and praise Him who made it. Very beautiful it is in the brightness thereof. It compasseth the heavens about with glory. and the hands of the Most High have bended it.'[1]

Whitefield was as happy in the land of the Puritans as anywhere he went in all his travels. As he concluded his ministry there, he recorded with rejoicing the many commendable features of its life, and stated, 'In short, I like New England exceeding well'.[2] His ministrations had been wonderfully owned of the Lord, in blessings which, a hundred years later, the Quaker poet Whittier described, saying:

[1] J. B. Wakeley, *Anecdotes of the Rev George Whitefield* (Hodder, London, 1900), *pp* 344–7.
[2] *Journals, p* 483.

So the flood of emotion deep and strong
Troubled the land as it swept along,
But left a result of holier lives,
Tenderer mothers and worthier wives.
The husband and father whose children fled
And sad wife wept when his drunken tread
Frightened peace from his roof-tree's shade,
And a rock of offence his hearthstone made,
In a strength that was not his own, began
To rise from the brute's to the plane of man.
Old friends embraced, long held apart,
By evil counsel and pride of heart;
And penitence saw through misty tears,
In the bow of hope on its cloud of fears,
The promise of Heaven's eternal years, –
The peace of God for the world's annoy, –
Beauty for ashes, and oil of joy.[1]

Such, in fulfilment of the design of God, was the trail of blessing Whitefield left behind after his six and a half weeks of ministry in New England.

Indeed, so numerous were the converts throughout the Colonies that many Christians actually began to believe the millennium was coming. Such a prophecy as '. . . the earth shall be full of the knowledge of the Lord, as the waters cover the sea' which had formerly seemed all but impossible of fulfilment, now took on an exciting new reality in the minds of these people; now they could see that the Revival well might spread till it reached every nation and till all mankind were converted, and they believed that to a world made righteous the Saviour would then return to reign. Thus, though Whitefield had virtually been silent on prophetic matters, his ministry effected a strong upsurge in prophetic interest and, strange as it may seem to many to-day, gave vital new meaning and force to the eschatological views generally held in that and the previous two centuries – the views now known as post-millennialism.

[1] John Greenleaf Whittier, *Works* (Houghton, Mifflin ed., Boston, 1882), *p* 254.

I marvel that ye are so soon removed from him that called you into the grace of Christ unto another Gospel; which is not another: but there be some that trouble you and would pervert the Gospel of Christ. But though we, or an angel from heaven, preach any other Gospel unto you than that which we have preached unto you, let him be accursed. As we said before, so say I now again, If any man preach any other Gospel unto you than that ye have received, let him be accursed.

THE APOSTLE PAUL

33

Contending Against an Unconverted Ministry

THUS far we have passed over one of the most significant aspects of Whitefield's work in New England: that is, his protest against the practice of allowing unconverted men to enter the ministry. Therefore, we must pause in our narrative and consider the nature and effect of his action.

This battle had long been fought by others. Since as early as 1720 Theodorus Frelinghuysen had vigorously opposed an unregenerate ministry in the Dutch Church and William Tennent had done the same in the Presbyterian.

In more recent months, however, Gilbert Tennent had brought this matter to the attention of the public with startling force. At the Presbyterian Church in Nottingham (in March of 1740) he delivered a sermon entitled *The Danger of an Unconverted Ministry*. Using the text, 'And Jesus, when He came out, was moved with compassion towards them; because they were as sheep not having a shepherd', he first described conditions in the Saviour's day; there were then, he asserted, plenty of professional ecclesiastics, but most of them were so indolent that the people were left virtually shepherdless. From this he advanced to the statement that the situation in the Presbyterian body of his own times was much the same, and he closed by denouncing the willingness of many persons to put up with an unconverted minister and urged them to leave such men and attend upon those whose lives and doctrines proved them to be regenerate.

Something of the matter and manner of the sermon may be understood from the following selections:

Natural men have no call of God to the ministerial work, under the Gospel dispensation. Remarkable is that saying of our Saviour, 'Follow me, and I will make you fishers of men'. See, our Lord will not make men ministers, till they follow him. Men that do not follow Christ may fish faithfully for a good name, and for worldly pelf; but not for the conversion of sinners to God. Is it reasonable to suppose that they will be earnestly concerned for others' salvation, when they slight their own? – The apostle Paul thanks God for counting him faithful, putting him into the ministry; which plainly supposes that God Almighty does not send Pharisees and natural men into the ministry; for how can these men be faithful, that have no faith? It is true, men may put them into the ministry through unfaithfulness or mistake; or credit and money may draw them; and the devil may drive them into it, knowing, by long experience, of what special service they may be to his kingdom in that office; but God sends not such hypocritical varlets.

Some may say that Judas was sent by Christ. I fear that the abuse of this instance has brought many Judases into the ministry, whose chief desire, like their great-grandfather, is to finger the pence and carry the bag. But let such hireling, murderous hypocrites take care that they do not feel the force of a halter in this world, and aggravated damnation in the next.

. . . such who are contented under a dead ministry, have not in them the temper of the Saviour they profess. It is an awful sign that they are as blind as moles and as dead as stones, without any spiritual taste and relish. And, alas! is not this the same with multitudes? If they can get one that has the name of a minister, with a band and a black coat or gown to carry on Sabbath days among them, although never so coldly and unsuccessfully; if he is free from gross crimes in practice, and takes good care to keep at a good distance from their consciences, and is never troubled about his unsuccessfulness; O! think the poor fools, that is a fine man indeed; our minister is a prudent and charitable man; he is not always harping upon terror and sounding damnation in our ears, like some rash-headed preachers, who, by their uncharitable methods, are ready to put poor people out of their wits, or run them into despair.[1]

This sermon was published by Benjamin Franklin and, of course, immediately became the subject of wide discussion and bitter attack. One reply after another – as vehement in tone as was the sermon itself – appeared in print, and from pulpits throughout the Middle Colonies, the debate was carried on, some ministers vigorously commending Tennent's statements and others with

[1] Tracy, *The Great Awakening, op cit, pp* 66–8.

equal fervour condemning them. 'Neither friends nor enemies', says Joseph Tracy, 'would let the sermon rest.'

*

As we have seen, even before the appearance of Tennent's sermon, Whitefield had taken his stand on this question. We notice again that within a week after his first arrival at Philadelphia he had allied himself with old Mr Tennent in his contention within the Presbyterian body, and had also projected the dispute into the Church of England, saying:

> I was much carried out in bearing my testimony against the unchristian principles and practices of our clergy. Three of my reverend brethren were present . . . I endeavoured to speak with meekness as well as zeal. Were I to convert Papists, my business would be to shew that they were misguided by their priests; and if I want to convince Church of England Protestants, I must prove that the generality of their teachers do not preach or live up to the truth as it is in Jesus.[1]

Similarly, two weeks later, after attending the service of the Church of England in New York he wrote:

> . . . felt my heart almost bleed within me, to consider what blind guides were sent forth into her. If I have any regard for the honour of Christ and the good of souls, I must lift up my voice like a trumpet, and shew how sadly our Church ministers are fallen away from the doctrines of the Reformation.[2]

But since Whitefield's relations in America soon proved to be, not with his own Church, but with the Dissenters, he was careful to declare the seriousness of this matter among them also. For example, of a service that he held at the Presbyterian Church in Elizabeth Town (April, 1740), he wrote:

> Ten Dissenting ministers were present, and two Church ministers; but they did not tarry very long . . . I dealt very plainly with the Presbyterian clergy, many of whom I am persuaded, preach the doctrines of grace to others, without being converted themselves. No doubt some were offended: but I care not for any sect or party of men. As I love all who love the Lord Jesus, of what communion soever, so I reprove all, . . . who take His Word into their mouths, but never felt Him dwelling in their hearts.[3]

[1] *Journals, pp* 345–6. [2] *Ibid, p* 350. [3] *Ibid, p* 414.

Whitefield took similar action when he stood amidst the Reformed Church – a people among whom Frelinghuysen's declaration of the necessity of the new birth had met bitter antagonism. After preaching at Flatbush (Long Island) Whitefield reported:

. . . the Dutch ministers received me with all civility, . . . There were also seven or eight Dissenting ministers present. I continued discoursing on the knowledge of Jesus Christ, near an hour and a half. Many people, and some of the ministers wept. My own soul was wonderfully carried out; and, at last I applied myself to the ministers themselves. Oh, that we all were a flame of fire![1]

But the practice of allowing the unconverted to enter the ministry had taken on special importance in New England. Though the churches in the Middle Colonies had merely drifted into the custom, the Church in Massachusetts had made it its stated policy, and not only condoned but defended it. The great Solomon Stoddard (the grandfather of Jonathan Edwards) had been a leader in introducing this change and, in the apathy of the times, the principle 'A converted minister is best, but an unconverted one cannot fail to do *some* good' had become almost everywhere accepted.

Before going to New England Whitefield had been informed by the Tennents of the situation that existed there. After arriving at Boston he further acquainted himself with it and then began to declare against it. Of this, in reporting a service at Dr Sewall's Church, he says:

When I got into the pulpit I saw a great number of ministers sitting around and before me. Coming to these words, 'Art thou a master in Israel, and knowest not these things?', the Lord enabled me to open my mouth boldly against unconverted ministers . . . The reason why congregations have been so dead is, because they have dead men preaching to them . . . How can dead men beget living children? It is true, indeed, that God may convert people by the devil, if He chooses; and so He may by unconverted ministers; but I believe He seldom makes use of either of them for this purpose. No: He chooses vessels made meet by the operations of His Blessed Spirit. For my own part, I would not lay hands on an unconverted man for ten thousand worlds.[2]

[1] *Ibid*, *p* 416. [2] *Ibid*, *p* 470.

This matter took on particular importance for Whitefield when he visited Harvard College. He says:

Wednesday, September 24. Went this morning to see and preach at Cambridge, the chief college for training the sons of the prophets in New England. It has one president, four tutors, and about a hundred students. The college is scarce as big as one of our least colleges at Oxford; and, as far as I could gather from some who knew the state of it, not far superior to our Universities in piety. Discipline is at a low ebb. Bad books are become fashionable among the tutors and students. Tillotson and Clarke are read, instead of Shepard, Stoddard, and such-like evangelical writers; and therefore I chose to preach from these words, 'We are not as many, who corrupt the Word of God'. A great number of neighbouring ministers attended.[1]

Before leaving Boston Whitefield paid a second visit to Harvard. 'I discoursed', he says, 'on these words, "Noah, the eighth person, a preacher of righteousness", and endeavoured to show the qualifications for a true evangelical preacher of Christ's righteousness.[2]

While at Northampton Whitefield could not but reflect on the strange inconsistency of Solomon Stoddard. Stoddard had been the pastor there for the extraordinary span of sixty years, and though he had preached the Gospel and had witnessed what he called 'five harvests' – five periods of remarkable blessing – he had advocated admitting the unregenerate into both the membership and the ministry. Thus, Whitefield, after leaving Northampton, preached at Suffield and wrote:

Meeting with a minister who said 'it was not absolutely necessary for a Gospel minister, that he should be converted', I insisted much in my discourse upon the doctrine of the new birth, and also the necessity of a minister being converted before he could preach Christ aright . . . Many ministers were present. I did not spare them. Most of them thanked me for my plain dealing. One of them, however, was offended; and so would more of his stamp if I were to continue longer in New England. Unconverted ministers are the bane of the Christian Church. I honour the memory of that great and good man, Mr Stoddard; but I think he is much to be blamed for endeavouring to prove that unconverted men may be admitted to the ministry.[3]

Following this event (and following his preaching at Middle-

[1] *Ibid*, *p* 462. [2] *Ibid*, *p* 471. [3] *Ibid*, *p* 478.

town) Whitefield moved on to New Haven. This was the site of Yale College which, like Harvard, had been established principally for educating men for the ministry. He dined with the President, the Rev Thomas Clap, and afterwards preached twice at the College. Standing before this body of young men – men who would later fill the pulpits of Connecticut – he again felt the gravity of his task and sought to make the fullest use of his opportunity. 'I spoke very closely to the students', he says, 'and shewed the dreadful ill consequences of an unconverted ministry. Oh, that God may quicken ministers! Oh, that the Lord may make them a flaming fire!'[1]

*

Such was the action that Whitefield took in New England. The question arises, however, as to whether or not he was wise in doing so, and, in reply it must be noticed that when he revised his *Journals* sixteen years later he said:

> In my former Journal, taking things by hearsay too much, I spoke and wrote rashly of the colleges and ministers of New England, for which, as I have already done it when at Boston last from the pulpit, I take this opportunity of asking public pardon from the press. It was rash and uncharitable and though well-meant, I fear did hurt.[2]

It cannot be doubted that Harvard and Yale were more sound in both faith and practice than Whitefield had been given to believe. He manifestly placed too much confidence in the opinions of the New Brunswick men – opinions that were often coloured by the extreme nature of their zeal and the excessive fervour with which they opposed apostasy – and it was for this exaggerated judgment, not for his stand in general, that he apologized.

And Gilbert Tennent's sermon is also open to criticism. He preached with an urgency that befitted the occasion – the souls of men were placed in eternal jeopardy by the unregenerated condition of their ministers – yet despite his earnestness, one cannot but feel that the sermon reveals something of the sword-brandishing and the display of heroics that we have seen in Whitefield's controversies in London.

Nevertheless, Tennent's sermon proved highly effective. Tracy

[1] *Journals*, *p* 480. [2] *Ibid*, *p* 462, fn.

says of Tennent, 'Though he spoke with an anger that debased his style and wrought evil, yet he spoke truth, mainly from good motives. The sermon . . turned the tide of popular opinion against unconverted ministers; and to no other agency, probably, so much as to this sermon, is it owing that Presbyterian ministers at the present day [1842] are generally pious men.'[1]

The warnings which Whitefield gave also proved to have a beneficial and lasting effect. This was especially true at Harvard, and a few weeks after he had left New England Dr Colman stated, 'The College is entirely changed. The students are full of God. Many of them appear truly born again. The voice of prayer and praise fills their chambers; and joy, with seriousness of heart, sits visibly on their faces. I was told yesterday that not seven, out of the one hundred in attendance, remain unaffected.[2] And the Honourable Josiah Willard wrote to Whitefield, saying, 'Divers young men in this town, who are candidates for the ministry, have been brought under deep convictions by your preaching'.[3,4]

In like manner, three months after Whitefield's visit to Yale, that College also experienced a spiritual revival. Jonathan Edwards reports:

> This awakening was . . . for a time very great and general at New Haven; and the college had no small share in it. That society was greatly reformed, the students in general became serious, many of them remarkably so, and much engaged in the concerns of their eternal welfare . . . there have been manifestly happy and abiding effects of the impressions then made on the minds of many of the members of that college.[5]

David Brainerd was a student at Yale at this time and, under the

[1] *Tracy, op cit, p* 70.
[2] Tyerman's *Whitefield*, Vol 1, *p* 418, fn.
[3] Belcher, *op cit, p* 213.
[4] Edward Holyoke, the President of Harvard, after stating, in reference to the charges Whitefield had made, '. . . the college hath not deserved the aspersions which have of late been made upon it', went on to pay warm tribute to the results of the labours of Whitefield and Tennent. '. . . these two pious and valuable men', he said, '. . . have been greatly instrumental in the hands of God, to revive this blessed work . . .' Likewise Colonel Brattle, one of Boston's most notable citizens, '. . . vindicated the college at Cambridge against Whitefield's strictures', but he also stated, '. . . by the preaching of Whitefield and Tennent, the students *in general* have been deeply affected, and their enquiry now was, What shall we do to be saved?' Tyerman, *p* 423, fn.
[5] Jonathan Edwards, *Memoirs of David Brainerd* (edition of J. M. Sherwood, Funk and Wagnalls, 1884), *p* 16.

awakening that followed Whitefield's visit, reported, 'I was much quickened and more abundantly engaged in religion'.[1] His fellow student, Samuel Hopkins, also left a similar testimony. Due, however, to the attendant practice of categorizing certain men as unconverted, Brainerd said of one of his tutors, 'He has no more grace than this chair', and it was this remark which, reaching the ears of the Faculty, caused his expulsion. There can be little doubt that Brainerd's diary contained a valuable record of this revival at Yale, but posterity has been denied it. Regrettably, while on his death bed, Brainerd ordered the destruction of the diaries that covered two or three years of his life, and these happened to include this period of awakening.

Moreover, it was not only at the Colleges but throughout the Colonies that Whitefield witnessed the results of his warnings regarding the unconverted clergy. He had reason to believe that God was honouring his stand, for he saw it as the agency used in the conversion of many a minister and ministerial student. The following incident that took place at New York reveals a case in point:

> At dinner I spoke with such vigour against sending unconverted ministers into the ministry, that two ministers with tears in their eyes, publicly confessed that they had laid hands on two young men without so much as asking them, 'whether they were born again of God, or not'. After dinner I prayed, and one old minister was so deeply convicted, that calling Mr Noble and me out, with great difficulty (because of this weeping), he desired our prayers, 'for', said he, 'I have been a scholar, and have preached the doctrines of grace a long time, but I believe I have never felt the power of them in my own soul'. Oh, that all unconverted ministers were brought to make the same confession![2]

This latter prayer was answered in many an instance – so many, indeed, that when Whitefield came back to America in 1744, 'there were no less than twenty ministers in the vicinity of Boston who considered him as the means of their conversion'.[3] And this proved to be the case so widely during this later trip that in city after city and town after town he was greeted by pastors who came to tell him that their conversion, under God, had resulted from the ministry he had exercised during 1740.

*

[1] *Ibid*, *p* 16. [2] *Journals*, *p* 482. [3] Tracy, *op cit*, *p* 393.

Moreover, not only was Whitefield's protest used of God in the conversion of many ministers, but it bore fruit also in leading many others to the same conviction regarding the necessity of regeneration.

The response among the ministers of Boston provides a case in point. With the exception of Dr Chauncy, in no city on earth at that time could there have been found a company of men who so eminently combined a firm belief in the foundational truths of Christianity with deep learning and extensive Christian experience. Mention has already been made of the high qualifications of Dr Colman and William Cooper. Thomas Prince was a scholar of such attainments that even Chauncy pronounced him 'the most learned man in New England, except Cotton Mather'. Joseph Sewall's ministry gave evidence that he possessed many of the abilities of Samuel, his father, New England's noted diarist and judge. And similar qualities characterized also the other men: Foxcroft, Checkley, Webb, Gee, Walter, Byles and Welstead. On the whole these Boston ministers, marked as they were by their strength of character, thoroughness of erudition and spiritual earnestness, stood as worthy sons indeed of their mighty Puritan forefathers.

Yet among these men, as they themselves testified, Whitefield 'was received, almost as an angel from heaven'. Nor was this a blind admiration, for they made mention of the faults (minor though they were)[1] that they saw in him. But in his holiness of life, his unfailing zeal and unparalleled preaching, they recognized very much the fulfilment of their own ministerial ideals – ideals which they, like other ministers, in varying measure had failed to attain.

And from this association these Boston pastors received lasting benefit. 'I can truly say', wrote one of them, 'that his preaching has quickened me, and I believe it has many other ministers besides',[2] and several made similar statements attesting that, from this point on, their lives were transformed. But this was not

[1] Thomas Prince wrote: 'Though Mr Whitefield now and then dropped expressions that were not so accurate and guarded as we should expect from aged and long-studied ministers, yet I had the satisfaction to observe his readiness to receive correction as soon as offered.' 'Although I can by no means go his length in censuring,' said another, 'yet I can make allowance for such things when I see the fervour of his soul.' Postscript to the *South Carolina Gazette*, No 361.

[2] *Ibid.*

all. Influenced by Whitefield's clear-cut stand against an unconverted ministry, any among them that had drifted into the idea that 'an unconverted minister cannot fail to do *some* good', began to abandon it. And in turn, the whole body of them were strengthened in the Scriptural practice of making a distinction between those who have received life from on high and those who were strangers to its presence and power.

This fellowship, however, proved mutually beneficial. In associating with such stalwart men and finding them to hold with the strongest convictions to the Calvinistic system, Whitefield became the more confirmed in his own adherence to these doctrines. And it was at this very time that John Wesley, by his frequent letters, was forcing Whitefield to see that discord on this subject could not long be avoided; yet, how weak must have seemed Wesley's position – his immaturity in things evangelical and his undefined Perfectionism – in contrast with the wide learning and deep evangelical experience of these Boston pastors.

Furthermore, Whitefield's actions among the ministers, not only in Boston but wherever he went throughout the Colonies, were but a fulfilment of a great over-all purpose. His stand against an unconverted ministry had its counterpart in his labours to strengthen the hands of every pastor who gave evidence of being regenerate. Among such men Whitefield was ever the *Mr Great Heart*, encouraging the downcast, helping the poor and befriending the lonely, and, though he sometimes administered a well-deserved word of rebuke, his aim was to see every ministerial life consumed with a burning zeal for God. He constantly decried that easy ministry which is content to preach merely on Sundays, and urged men to get out into the highways and hedges seven days a week. 'Oh, that all ministers were a flame of fire!' – this was both his exclamation and his aim.

The ministers among whom Whitefield thus associated were the more drawn to him by the humility of his manner. Despite his great fame, there was no suggestion of superiority, but rather the opposite; he was not only one with the others, but he sought to be their servant. '"Less than the least of all" shall be my motto still'[1] – in this and several similar expressions he revealed his inner self.

[1] *Works*, Vol 1, *p* 175.

Moreover, he even asked his friends to reprove him when they saw him to be in the wrong in any way. For instance, in a letter to a minister in England he says:

> . . . why did you not write me a letter of reproof, and smite me friendly for what you thought amiss in the discourse between me and a friend at Bristol? I should have taken it kindly at your hands. When I am unwilling to be told of my faults, dear Sir, correspond with me no more. If I know anything of this treacherous heart of mine, I love those most who are most faithful to me in this respect.[1]

Several statements like this could be cited from Whitefield's pen and, though perverse human nature may find this difficult to believe, the whole context of his life demonstrates that in such statements he was entirely sincere.

One further evidence of Whitefield's humility in his relations with evangelical ministers must be noticed. He would frequently write a letter to some man he had met but once or twice, or even to one he had never met at all, in order to respond to some need of which he had learned in the man's life. It might be a spiritual disappointment or some trial in church or family affairs, but Whitefield, having learned of it, would write to show kindness, but he wrote just as though he and the man had been familiar friends for many years. In reading this correspondence one can but imagine what some poor, backwoods pastor must have felt upon receiving such a letter, a letter from the famous evangelist, knowing that he had not only taken time to write to him, but was concerned about his affairs and acted towards him as a long-standing personal friend.

But Whitefield's association with Gospel pastors was particularly beautiful in his esteem for those of advanced age. 'I love to be acquainted with the true and old servants of Jesus Christ', he wrote, 'because I delight to sit at their feet and receive instruction from them.'[2] Such an one he met at Newport, and reported:

> Several gentlemen of the town soon came to pay their respects, amongst whom was Mr Clap, an aged Dissenting minister, and the most venerable man I ever saw in my life. He looked like a good old Puritan, and gave me an idea of what stamp those men were who first settled in

[1] *Ibid, p* 82. [2] *Ibid, p* 120.

New England. His countenance was very heavenly . . . He is full of days; a bachelor, and has been minister of a congregation in Rhode Island upwards of forty years. People of all denominations respect him. He abounds in good works, gives all away and is wonderfully tender of little children . . . Whenever he dies, I am persuaded he will be able to say with old Simeon, 'Lord, now lettest Thou Thy servant depart in peace'. . . . Although very old, yet he followed me from one end of the town to another; so that people said I had made old Mr Clap young again. Oh what a crown of glory is a hoary head, when found in the way of righteousness![1]

Such was Whitefield in his behaviour towards the evangelical pastors. In turn, as was but to be expected, he became the object of their warmest admiration and undying affection – feelings they expressed in such terms as 'Ye wonder of ye age' and 'The man greatly beloved'.[2]

*

But Whitefield's statements regarding the unconverted soon brought a fresh wave of opposition upon him.

After leaving New England he set out on the final stage of his Fall tour – the return journey that was to take him, preaching *en route*, back to Georgia. Upon reaching New York he experienced the first overt antagonism to his protests, particularly to his assertion that several of the Presbyterians, though they preached the doctrines of grace, had never felt the power of them in their hearts. 'I met with a bitter pamphlet written against me', he wrote,[3] 'by some of the Presbyterian persuasion. I long since expected opposition from that quarter.'[4]

The pamphlet was a clever yet subtle piece of work. The authors did not reveal their identity and therefore both they and the pamphlet became known as *The Querists*. They sought to convey the idea that they were lay people but undoubtedly the work was that of two or three ministers from the Whiteclay

[1] *Journals, pp* 452–5.

[2] Postscript to the *South Carolina Gazette*, No 361.

[3] *An Extract of Sundry Passages Taken out of Mr Whitefield's Printed Sermons, Journals and Letters: Together with Some Scruples Proposed in Proper Queries Raised on Each Remark, by some Church-Members of the Presbyterian Persuasion.* This was published at the time by Benjamin Franklin in Philadelphia, and shortly after at Boston, New York, Charleston and London. At Philadelphia it went through three editions, and probably saw more than one edition in the other cities.

[4] *Journals, p* 484.

Creek Presbytery who had attempted, but without success, to draw Whitefield into theological debate during his visit to that area.[1] They declared that they wrote only with a view to the welfare of Whitefield's hearers: unwary souls might well be led astray by certain imprecise statements he had made and they deemed themselves responsible to issue a warning. Their efforts revealed, however, that the supposed danger was not at all apparent, for, though they had searched through everything he had ever put into print, they had been able to come up with nothing more than a few inconsequential expressions.

Failing thus to find any basis for outright accusation against Whitefield's orthodoxy, the writers resorted to innuendo and used it to strong advantage. Their method was that of citing a phrase from him that either contained some doctrinal inexactitude or on which they could place such a construction, and of then posing several queries about it. These queries they left unanswered, but by their very questioning they left the impression that this man who so openly cast doubts on the orthodoxy of others was at least an untrustworthy guide in spiritual matters, and might actually, if the truth were fully known, be unsound in the faith himself!

A single example of *The Querists'* manner of attack will suffice. In one of his earliest sermons Whitefield had spoken of 'the righteousness of Christ' as being 'imputed to and inherent in' the true believer.[2] By 'inherent' he simply meant that the presence of such righteousness would be manifest in the daily walk of life, but *The Querists* seized upon the word and insinuated that it might represent a rank heresy. Would not, they asked, an 'inherent' righteousness rule out all need for an 'imputed' righteousness? Certainly, Whitefield had failed to observe the punctilio of theological terminology in this statement, and this error is typical of the several expressions that they cited as constituting stumbling-blocks to the common man.

The Querists also found fault with Whitefield in a number of more personal matters. His willingness to have fellowship without

[1] One of these was a Presbyterian minister named Anderson who later met Whitefield at Whiteclay Creek and sought 'a conference'. Whitefield says, 'I told him, "Since he had begun by sending the queries in public, I was resolved to decline all private conversation." This, I found out afterwards, highly offended him.' *Ibid, pp* 496–7.

[2] *The Querists, p* 23.

regard to denominational adherence drew their fire, and they suggested that, since he showed friendship to Lutherans, Arminians and Quakers, he might be expected to turn Papist were he ever to set foot in Rome. They decried his expressions of admiration for John Wesley, and made mention of the 'antinomian absurdities' that Wesley 'has sent abroad to poison the world'.[1] They sought to link Whitefield with responsibility for the 'strange fits and convulsions' that had taken place, questioned the truth of his reports about the good works done by the Holy Club, and closed by charging that the people who favoured the revival were often irreligious and full of 'hatred and rage against their former pious ministers'.

Ought Whitefield to answer such a pamphlet? Its authors challenged him to do so, assuring their readers that if he failed to reply they would recognize that it was because he could not. Moreover, the charges undoubtedly carried weight with a certain section of the people, for the writers were associated with certain friends of the Tennents and posed as defenders of the faith. Accordingly, fearing that the pamphlet might harm the work, Whitefield decided to answer it.

His *Letter*[2] of reply is marked by a frankness that stands out in sharp contrast to the subtlety of his opponents. He thanks them 'for the opportunity they had furnished him of publicly correcting some errors in his printed sermons', and goes on to state:

> I think it no dishonour to retract some expressions that formerly dropped from my pen, before God was pleased to give me a more clear knowledge of the doctrines of grace. St Augustine, I think, did so before me.[3]

Whitefield then proceeds to deal with the complaints one by one. He admits that in most of them he is wrong and *The Querists* are right. But more than that, he says, 'to convince you that I am not ashamed to own my faults, I can inform you of other passages as justly exceptionable',[4] and he points out several errors in his writings that they had overlooked. He states that he intends to correct these matters in the next edition of his sermons and concludes by saying:

[1] *The Querists, p* 25.
[2] 'A Letter to Some Church-Members of the Presbyterian Persuasion, Whitefield's *Works*, Vol 4, *pp* 43–9.
[3] *Ibid, p* 45.
[4] *Ibid, p* 47.

God . . . knows my heart, My one design is to bring poor souls to Jesus Christ. I desire to avoid extremes, so as not to be a bigot on one hand, or confound order and decency on the other . . . Surely your insinuations are contrary to that charity that hopeth and believeth all things for the best. And I appeal to your own hearts, whether it was right, especially since you heard the constant tenor of my preaching in America has been Calvinistical, to censure me as a Papist or Arminian, because a few unguarded expressions dropped from my pen, just as I came from the University of Oxford.[1]

Whitefield says of this reply, 'God enabled me to write it with the spirit of meekness', and a Boston minister expressed the opinion, 'The excellent meekness of Mr Whitefield's answer to *The Querists* will honour him . . .'[2] *The Querists* had succeeded in proving nothing more than their own pedantry but, sensing their failure, they quickly issued another pamphlet in which the *Letter* of reply was subjected to the same petty criticism they had given the sermons and *Journals.*[3]

*

The work of *The Querists*, however, was but a single episode in a long and fierce paper warfare. Whitefield's protest against an unconverted ministry took its place alongside his charges against Tillotson and his *Letter* to the slave-owners as targets of bitter attack. His enemies began to produce tracts and pamphlets in abundance, belittling his person and disparaging his work, and though he made no further reply himself, his friends published in his defence. Several wrote in confirmation of his stand for a converted ministry, and one, the Rev Andrew Croswell, produced a tract which went to the very crux of the matter, even in its title: *What is Christ to Me – If He is not Mine?*

*

But what was the final outcome of this struggle? As a result of

[1] *Ibid, p* 49.

[2] Postscript to the *South Carolina Gazette*, No 361.

[3] *A Short Reply to Mr Whitefield's Letter*, which he wrote in answer to The Querists wherein said Querists testify their satisfaction with some of the amendments Mr Whitefield proposes to make of some of the exceptionable expressions in his writings, together with some other remarks upon what seems exceptionable in the present letter; which seem to occur to the Querists . . . Philadelphia: printed for the Querists (and sold by B. Franklin), 1741.

the stand that Whitefield took against an unconverted ministry, aided by the similar action on the part of Gilbert Tennent, the tide of public opinion began to turn. Opposers might ridicule these two men at will, but little by little their assertion gained acceptance, until with the passing of a decade the majority of the people throughout the Colonies were convinced that a minister must be a regenerate man. Among Congregationalists, Presbyterians and Baptists there came a widespread return to the practice of requiring a candidate for ordination to give clear evidence of his conversion, and this basic alteration was the outcome of the protests first made by Frelinghuysen and William Tennent and then continued by Gilbert Tennent and Whitefield.

Joseph Tracy, taking a view of the movement as a whole, asserts:

> There can be no doubt that a considerable number of ministers were converted during the revival . . . Of nearly equal importance was the conversion of a considerable number of students, preparing for the ministry . . . The value of such an infusion of life into the ministry was incalculable. Every such conversion relieved the church of a 'bane' and gave her a blessing . . .
>
> But this was not all the revival did for the ministry. It fully and finally killed the doctrine that an unconverted ministry might be tolerated.[1]

In the light of such results we do well in our own day to press Croswell's enquiry: *What is Christ to Me – If He is not Mine?*

[1] Tracy, *op cit*, *pp* 393–4.

Whitefield was the greatest single factor in the Awakening of 1740. *He zealously carried the work up and down the colonies from New England to Georgia. Among the revivalists, his influence alone touched every section of the country and every denomination. Everywhere he supplemented and augmented the work with his wonderful eloquence. He literally preached to thousands as he passed from place to place. He was the one preacher to whom people everywhere listened – the great undying agency in the Awakening, the great moulding force among the denominations.*

W. M. GEWEHR

The Great Awakening in Virginia

34

Joy and Sorrow Amid the Harvest

WHITEFIELD's journey from New England to Georgia proved to be a time of constant spiritual harvest. In his earlier visits – this was his sixth to many places in New York, New Jersey and Pennsylvania, and his eighth to Charleston – he had abundantly sown the seed, and now, after months of nurture by the Spirit of God, it was everywhere springing up and bringing forth fruit.

But the joy of the harvest was counterbalanced by a multiplicity of trials. As his days in America drew towards their close, troubles seemed to surround him and press in upon him from every side and, though he did not altogether realize it, he was speedily approaching the supreme crisis of his life.

*

One of these troubles lay in the danger that fanaticism might creep into the work. While at New York Whitefield received a visit from a prominent Long Island minister, the Rev James Davenport, and more than from any other source, the danger arose from this man.

James Davenport came of one of the foremost of Colonial families. His great-grandfather, the Rev John Davenport (1597–1670) had been famous as the founder and principal figure of the New Haven settlement, and has long been recognized as 'one of the great men of early New England, who united learning with piety, and knowledge of men with kindness of heart'.[1]

[1] *The Schaff-Herzog Encyclopedia of Religious Knowledge*, art., DAVENPORT, John. John Davenport was born in England and graduated from Oxford in 1616. While in the ministry he adopted Puritan principles which brought him under the suspicion of Bishop Laud, and, as a result, in 1637 he emigrated to America. In the following year he founded New Haven, where he remained as pastor and a chief civic leader

But James did not possess the stability of his renowned forebear. While a student at Yale College he proved to be brilliant of mind, but applied himself with such extreme diligence that he suffered a nervous breakdown. He went on, however, to graduate and after entering the ministry in 1732 distinguished himself by the unusual measure of learning, zeal and piety with which he filled the pastoral office. So elevated seemed his manner of life that he gained the highest esteem of his fellow pastors – an esteem recorded by several of them,[1] and expressed, for instance, by the Rev Jonathan Parsons in the statement 'that not one minister whom he had seen was to be compared with Mr Davenport, for living near to God, and having his conversation always in heaven'.[2]

Stimulated by the excitement that accompanied the revival, Davenport became still more vigorous in his labours. He undertook an itinerant ministry over a wide area, but the effects of his breakdown remained upon him to such an extent that, after the passing of some months (in 1742, some time after Whitefield had returned to Britain), he developed a condition very near to insanity. His behaviour became utterly fanatical (he preached on one occasion for twenty-four hours) and, as we shall see, brought lasting discredit on the whole revival movement.

Upon first meeting Davenport some months earlier Whitefield had stated, 'He is looked upon as an enthusiast and a madman by many of his reverend pharisaical brethren'.[3] But he had also learned of the high esteem in which he was held by the evangelical pastors and, accordingly, as he met him again at this later date, knowing his repute, he accepted him for just what he appeared to be: an exceptionally zealous and heavenly-minded minister.

Nevertheless, though Davenport conducted himself in general with good sense, there had frequently been loud outcryings under his preaching and he had not discouraged them. In turn, these happenings had stimulated the practice that already existed among some of the people – the practice of seeking to engender the

for thirty years, after which he moved to Boston. During the controversy surrounding the *Half-Way Covenant* he stood strongly against this new measure and drew upon himself severe opposition. John Davenport was the peer, both intellectually and spiritually, of such great ones among his contemporaries as Richard Mather, John Cotton and Thomas Hooker.

[1] Tracy, *op cit*, *pp* 230–1. [2] *Ibid*, *p* 230. [3] *Journals*, *p* 416.

excessive emotions during the services. And this was the situation in New York and northern New Jersey (the area to which Davenport's influence had reached) at the time when Whitefield made this return visit.

Although nothing whatsoever of this emotionalism had attended Whitefield's ministry in New England, it began to occur as soon as he came where Davenport had been. Of his first service at New York he says, 'Two or three cried out',[1] and of his second, 'Crying, weeping and wailing were to be heard in every corner; men's hearts failing them for fear, and many were to be seen falling into the arms of their friends'.[2]

Similar things took place when Whitefield moved on southward and came to Baskinridge. There the Rev John Cross had looked on the emotional outbursts with favour, and they occurred again when Whitefield preached to his people. Whitefield reports:

> When I came to Baskinridge, I found Mr Davenport had been preaching to the congregation . . . It consisted of about three thousand people. I had not discoursed long, when, in every part of the congregation, someone or other began to cry out, and almost all were melted into tears.[3]

The same was the case when, after preaching for a week at Philadelphia, he came into the Fagg's Manor and Nottingham area. Here also the people had learned to seek the outcryings and faintings, and, accordingly, Whitefield said of one service (at Cohansie), 'two cried out in the bitterness of their souls',[4] and of another (at Whiteclay Creek), 'Several cried out, and others were to be seen weeping bitterly'.[5]

In witnessing these outbursts Whitefield was again confronted with the question as to where the work of the Spirit of God ended and where the human imitation began. As has already been observed, he desired to see hearts broken under the hammer blows of the Word of God, and it was to his liking to report, as he did at New York, 'There was a great and gracious melting among the people both times, but no crying out'.[6] But he sought to prevent the displays of mere emotionalism, as, for example,

[1] *Ibid, p* 484. [2] *Ibid, p* 485. [3] *Ibid, p* 487.
[4] *Ibid, p* 496. [5] *Ibid, p* 497. [6] *Ibid, p* 485.

at Baskinridge; there he stopped preaching on account of the outcrying, prayed over the affected persons, sang a hymn and therewith closed the service.[1] And likewise at Philadelphia 'there was such a universal commotion in the congregation' that he 'broke off prayer after sermon sooner than otherwise [he] would have done'.[2]

*

The spiritual harvest that was everywhere apparent is epitomized, for instance, in the report that Whitefield made following his visit to Philadelphia. He was there but eight days and wrote:

> It would be almost endless to recount all the particular instances of God's grace, which I have seen this week past. Many who before were only convicted, now plainly proved that they were converted. My chief business was now to build up and to exhort them to continue in the grace of God . . . Several Societies are now in the town, not only of men and women, but of little boys and little girls. Being so engaged, I could not visit them as I would, but I hope the Lord will raise me up some fellow-labourers, and that elders will be ordained in every place; then shall we see a glorious church settled and established in Philadelphia.[3]

This desire that there might be some permanent establishing of the work in this city came to a notable fulfilment. When Whitefield had first been denied the use of Christ Church (Church of England) several of his followers, incensed by the refusal, had determined to build a large auditorium which would serve primarily as a place for his ministrations. But he viewed the idea unfavourably, fearing that it might indicate an attempt on the part of the people to begin a new church formed around their allegiance to him.

Nevertheless, they carried out their plans, and when he returned to the city on this occasion the structure had advanced to the point where the walls were completed and ready for the roof. Accordingly, he preached in it twice a day, and also laid down a policy for its use. Benjamin Franklin, who was one of the Trustees, wanted to see the New Building, as they called it, made available to everyone. '. . . even if the Mufti of Constantinople were to send a missionary to preach Mohammedanism to us', said Frank-

[1] *Ibid, p* 487. [2] *Ibid, p* 492. [3] *Ibid, p* 493.

lin, 'he would find a pulpit at his service'.[1] But Whitefield, whose word was the more weighty in the matter, stated that it was to be limited to converted men: 'None but orthodox ministers are to use it, and such are to have free liberty, of whatever denomination.'[2]

But the plans called for the New Building to serve also as 'a Charity School' and 'an House of Public Worship'. Thus, on weekdays it accommodated a number of children at school and on Sundays it was the meeting-place of a large company of Christians. These people were followers of Whitefield and they included several of the most prominent of Philadelphia's families.[3] Most had been converted under his preaching, and since they found little food for their souls in the average church, they came together in this way, seeking to preserve the effects of the revival and to take steps to provide for a truly evangelical ministry. Thus, in 1743 they called Gilbert Tennent to be their pastor, and after some years of meeting in the New Building, Tennent led them forth in the construction of a magnificent new church home, the Second Presbyterian Church.

And the Charity School also was but the beginning of great things. After three or four years the school developed into an Academy, and this institution steadily increased till it became a College, and the College in turn grew into a University. This became the *University of Pennsylvania* of the present day.

*

While at Philadelphia Whitefield made specific mention of two striking instances of conversion which came to his attention there.

The first was that of a man in the civic employ and 'eminent in his profession', who had long been a Deist and virtually an atheist. He was, however, upright in his manner of life, and laboured to bring others, especially those of a similar type of behaviour, to accept his beliefs. But shortly after Whitefield had

[1] Franklin's *Autobiography*, *op cit*, *p* 119.

[2] *The Pennsylvania Gazette*, Dec. 4, 1740. Here cited from Maxson, *op cit*, *p* 68.

[3] Maxson, *p* 85, in reference to the Second Church, says, 'The names of its Hodges, Bayards, Boudinots, Hazards, Eastburns, Redmonts, Bourns, Shippens and Grants were widely known in the eighteenth century, and many of them in the nineteenth as well'.

first arrived at Philadelphia, this man had heard him as he preached from the Court House stairs, and thereupon the Lord laid hold of his heart. During months of conviction he 'followed on to know the Lord', and so evident were the fruits of the new life that Whitefield, becoming acquainted with him on this later occasion, stated, '. . . he is now, I believe, born of God'.[1]

Of the second he wrote:

The other is Captain H——, formerly as great a reprobate as ever I heard of; almost a scandal and reproach to human nature. He used to swear to ease his stomach, and was so fond of new oaths that he used to go on board the transport ships, and offer a guinea for a new oath, that he might have the honour of coining it. By God's grace, he is now, I believe, a Christian. Not only reformed, but renewed. The effectual stroke, he told me, was given when I preached last spring at Pennytack, though he had been under good impressions before. Ever since, he has been zealous for the truth; stood firm when he was beaten and in danger of being murdered some time ago by many of my opposers; and, in short, shews forth his faith by his works.[2]

Whitefield mentioned these instances of conversion because he saw them to be 'remarkable proofs of God's eternal election . . .' Such men as these could never have been saved by anything which began with a human power; only that which both began with and was carried on by power from on high could have effected such miracles as these. Thus, in the light of these instances, Whitefield went on to declare:

Whatever men's reasoning may suggest, if the children of God fairly examine their own experiences – if they do God justice, they must acknowledge that they did not choose God, but that God chose them. And if He chose them at all, it must be from eternity, and that too without anything foreseen in them. Unless they acknowledge this, man's salvation must be in part owing to the free-will of man; and if so, . . . Christ Jesus might have died, and never have seen the travail of His soul in the salvation of one of His creatures. But I would be tender on this point, and leave persons to be taught it of God. I am of the martyr Bradford's mind. Let a man go to the grammar school of faith and repentance, before he goes to the university of election and predestination.[3]

*

[1] *Journals, p* 490. [2] *Ibid, p* 490–1. [3] *Ibid, p* 491.

Whitefield's thought was particularly drawn at this time to the doctrine of election and to these two outstanding instances of its truth by the fact that he had recently received further letters from John Wesley opposing it. Moreover, other friends in England had also written, informing him that Wesley had continued to project the points of difference, insomuch that there were now bitter disputings and sad divisions in the work over there.

But Wesley had written to Whitefield on these things with significant frequency during the year that the latter had been in America, and each time Whitefield had replied. We have already noticed two of these replies and must now notice others. Furthermore, we have observed that, though Whitefield stood his ground regarding the doctrines under discussion, he wrote in a most gracious manner and constantly sought to persuade Wesley to desist from his divisive activities. The same spirit characterizes these later letters too – a spirit manifest in the following petition that he wrote upon learning of the strife in England: 'Lord, do Thou cause even this to work for good, and give me grace to oppose such errors, without respect of persons, but with meekness, humility and love.'[1]

We begin our further look into this correspondence by retracing in the narrative to the point of Whitefield's return to Georgia at the close of his Spring tour. There he found several letters awaiting him and, in replying to one from James Hutton, he said, 'My dear brother, . . . for Christ's sake desire brother Wesley to avoid disputing with me. I think I had rather die than see a division between us; and yet, how can we walk together, if we oppose each other?'[2]

There was a letter there also from John Wesley, and Whitefield's reply to it reads as follows:

Savannah, June 25, 1740

MY HONOURED FRIEND AND BROTHER:

I thank you for, and heartily say *Amen* to all the petitions you have put up on my behalf. I want to be as my Master would have me; I mean, meek and lowly in heart. Dear Sir, bear with me a little longer; pray

[1] *Ibid*, *p* 459. [2] *Works*, Vol 1, *p* 185.

for me with great earnestness; and who knows but my God may give me to abhor myself in dust and ashes! He that hath given us His Son, will He not with Him freely give us all things?

. . . If possible, dear Sir, never speak against election in your sermons: no one can say that I ever mentioned it in public discourses, whatever my private sentiments may be. For Christ's sake, let us not be divided amongst ourselves: nothing will so much prevent a division as your being silent on this head.

I should have rejoiced at the sight of your Journal. I long to sing a hymn of praise for what God has done for your soul. I am glad to hear that you speak up for an attendance upon the means of grace, and do not encourage persons who run (I am persuaded) before they are called. The work of God will suffer much by such imprudence.

I trust you will still persist in field preaching. Others are strangers to our call. I know infinite good hath been done by it already . . . May God bless you more and more every day, and cause you to triumph in every place . . .[1]

Whitefield's mention in this letter of 'attendance upon the means of grace' and 'persons who run before they are called' is a reference to the practices that were springing up among the Fetter Lane people. Some of them were refusing to observe the sacraments of the Church of England and seeking instead what they called 'stillness', and in the matter of opposition to these things Whitefield and Wesley were in entire agreement. Moreover, certain of the men had taken it upon themselves to serve as preachers in the Society, and to the foremost of these, John Bray, Whitefield wrote, saying:

. . . My dear Bray, I write in love. For Christ's sake, try your spirit. I fear you were never yet truly humbled . . . O that you had been in the wilderness a little longer! Then you might have been an experienced teacher; but I fear you are now only a novice. May the Lord keep you from falling into the condemnation of the devil. I write this not to damp, but to regulate your spirit; if you are humble, you will take it kind. God knows, I wish all the Lord's servants were prophets; but I would not have my Master's work suffer by too heady a way of proceeding. Why should you dishonour Him by acting above your sphere, whereas you might honour Him by acting in it? Every one is not fit to be a public expounder. To build up awakened sinners in private is what is more wanted at present than young unexperienced preachers . . .[2]

[1] *Ibid*, *pp* 189–90.

[2] *Ibid*, *pp* 196–7.

While in Charleston on his Summer tour Whitefield received another letter from Wesley and with it a section of Wesley's *Journal* that had recently been published. Whitefield had been unwise in publishing his *Journals*, but the same was true of Wesley, for Wesley's account told the story of his days in Georgia and therefore revealed the imprudencies and failure which had marked that period of his life. This *Journal* also carried his confession that he did not possess the witness of the Spirit – a confession that he also made repeatedly following his Aldersgate Street experience. Such an admission gravely weakened his statements against the Calvinistic doctrines, especially since it was by these doctrines that Whitefield and Harris and others whom Wesley was opposing had come to a triumphant assurance. Moreover, the lack of the Spirit's witness and of personal assurance surely robbed his Perfection teaching of its validity. The vulnerability of his position was manifest, but Whitefield was gentle in pointing this out to him, saying:

Charles-Town, Aug. 25, 1740

Dear and Honoured Sir,

Last night I had the pleasure of receiving an extract of your journal. – This morning I took a walk and read it. I pray God to give it his blessing. Many things I trust will prove beneficial, especially the account of yourself.

Only give me leave, with all humility to exhort you not to be strenuous in opposing the doctrines of *election* and *final perseverance*, when, by your own confession, 'you have not the witness of the Spirit within yourself', and consequently are not a proper judge. I remember dear Brother E—— told me one day, that 'he was convinced of the perseverance of the saints'. I told him you was not. He replied, but he will be convinced when he hath got the Spirit himself. I am assured, God has now for some years given me this living witness in my soul . . . When I have been nearest to death, my evidences have been the clearest. I can say, I have been on the borders of Canaan, and do every day, nay, almost every moment, long for the appearing of our Lord Jesus Christ; not to evade sufferings, but with a single desire to see His blessed face. I feel His blessed Spirit daily filling my soul and body, as plain as I feel the air which I breathe, or the food I eat.

Perhaps the doctrines of election and of final perseverance hath been abused (and what doctrine has not,) but notwithstanding, it is children's bread, and ought not, in my opinion, to be with-held from them, supposing it is always mentioned with proper cautions against the abuse.

Dear and Honoured Sir, I write not this to enter into disputation. I hope, at this time, I feel something of the meekness and gentleness of Christ. I cannot bear the thoughts of opposing you: but how can I avoid it, if you go about (as your brother Charles once said) to drive John Calvin out of Bristol. Alas, I never read anything that Calvin wrote; my doctrines I had from Christ and His apostles; I was taught them of God; and as God was pleased to send me out first, and to enlighten me first, so I think He still continues to do it. My business seems to be chiefly in planting; if God send you to water, I praise His name. – I wish you a thousandfold increase.

I find by young W——'s letter, there is disputing among you about *election* and *perfection*. – I pray God to put a stop to it, for what good end will it answer? . . .

Adieu, Honoured Sir, Adieu! My health is better since I last left Charles Town, and am now freed from domestic cares. With almost tears of love to you, and the brethren, do I subscribe myself, honoured Sir,

Your most affectionate brother and servant in Christ,

G. W.[1]

During his New England tour Whitefield also received a letter from Howell Harris. Harris, who more than once expressed his opinion that Wesley would yet come to understand and accept the doctrines of grace, had recently discussed the matter with him. In replying to Harris Whitefield stated:

I hope your conversation was blessed to dear Mr Wesley. O that the Lord may batter down his free-will, and compel him to own His sovereignty and everlasting love . . . My coming to England will try my fidelity to my Master. Nothing but His strength can enable me to hear all contradictions with meekness, and to preach with love His everlasting truths. O that all would study the covenant of grace! The more I look into it the more is my soul delighted . . .[2]

Similarly, in writing to Benjamin Ingham Whitefield said:

My dear brother, my heart's desire and prayer to God is that we may all think and speak the same things. – For, if we are divided among ourselves, what an advantage will Satan get over us! Let us love one

[1] *Ibid, pp* 204–5. [2] *Ibid, p* 210.

another, excite all to come to Christ without exception, and our Lord will shew us who are His.[1]

While in New England Whitefield also received a number of letters at once – a packet of them that had been more than six months in reaching him. Among them was another from Wesley, and his reply reads, in part:

To the Rev. Mr. J. W.

Boston, Sept. 25, 1740

HONOURED SIR,

This is sent in answer to your letter dated March 25. – I think, I have for some time known what it is to have righteousness, peace and joy in the Holy Ghost. These, I believe, are the privileges of the sons of God: But I cannot say I am free from indwelling sin; . . . I am sorry, honoured Sir, to hear by many letters, that you seem to own a *sinless perfection* in this life attainable . . . I do not expect to say indwelling sin is finished and destroyed in me, till I bow down my head and give up the ghost . . . I know many abuse this doctrine, and perhaps wilfully indulge sin, or do not aspire after holiness, because no man is perfect in this life. But what of that? must I therefore assert doctrines contrary to the Gospel? God forbid . . .

Besides, dear Sir, what a fond conceit is it to cry up *perfection*, and yet cry down the doctrine of *final perseverance!* But this and many other absurdities you will run into, because you will not own *Election*. And you will not own election because you cannot own it without believing the doctrine of *Reprobation*. What then is there in reprobation so horrid? I see no blasphemy in holding that doctrine, if rightly explained. If God might have passed by all, He may pass by some. Judge whether it is not a greater blasphemy to say, 'Christ died for souls now in hell'. Surely, dear Sir, you do not believe there will be a general *gaol delivery* of damned souls hereafter.

O that you would study the covenant of grace! O that you were truly convinced of sin, and brought to the foot of sovereign grace! *Elisha Coles* on *God's Sovereignty*, and *Veritas Redux*, written by Doctor *Edwards* are well worth your reading.

But I have done. If you think so meanly of Bunyan, and the Puritan writers, I do not wonder that you think me wrong. I find your sermon has had its expected success; it has set the nation a-disputing; you will have enough to do now to answer pamphlets. Two I have already seen. O that you would be more cautious in casting lots! O that you would

[1] *Ibid, p* 214.

not be too rash and precipitant! If you go on thus, honoured Sir, how can I concur with you? It is impossible; I must speak what I know.

Thus I write out of the fulness of my heart; I feel myself to be a vile sinner. – I look to Christ; I mourn because I have pierced Him. Honoured Sir, pray for me. The Lord be with your dear soul. About Spring you may expect to see,

Ever, ever yours in Christ,

G. W.[1]

This letter, while abridged, is given at considerable length, not with the suggestion that it contributes anything new regarding Whitefield's views, but because it is the strongest of all his replies to Wesley. Let it be repeated: Whitefield at his most emphatic in the breach with Wesley is found in this letter, and the reader will judge for himself as to the spirit therein displayed.

Whitefield's graciousness, however, in dealing with Wesley, brought criticism upon him from the Calvinists in England. Certain of them believed that, because of his deep love for Wesley, he was unwilling to stand up to him, and that this, coupled with his dread of discord, was causing him to compromise the great truths that he professed to hold. Consequently, some of them wrote to him, making charges to this effect. To one of them, a 'Mr A——', Whitefield wrote a reply which began by saying, 'I thank you for your letter: May the Lord enable me to send you an answer of peace', and then proceeded to declare in no uncertain terms his adherence to the doctrines of grace.[2]

And to another such correspondent, a woman who appears to have been aggressive in propagating her Calvinistic convictions, Whitefield wrote:

To Mrs J—— L——, in Bristol.

Charles-Town, Aug. 26, 1740

DEAR J——,

I hope you and your little society go on and prosper. I hear there are divisions among you. Avoid them, if possible. The doctrines of election, and of final perseverence, I hold as well as you. – But then, they are not to be contended for with heat and passion. Such a pro-

[1] *Ibid, pp* 210–12.

[2] *Ibid, p* 209. The name of the man addressed in this letter was undoubtedly 'Acourt'.

ceeding will only prejudice the cause you would defend. Pray shew this to your other friends. – Exhort them to avoid all clamour, and evil speaking, and with meekness receive the ingrafted word . . .[1]

Certain of the Arminians in England also wrote to Whitefield, seeking to dispute the doctrinal differences with him. One of these men wrote several times and apparently in an arrogant fashion, and since Whitefield terms him 'a babe in Christ', he was probably a young upstart. At any rate, Whitefield finally replied and, in doing so, gave him something of the verbal spanking that he manifestly deserved. Here is the letter:

To Mr W——, at Bristol.

Boston, Sept. 28, 1740

DEAR BROTHER W——,

What mean you by disputing in all your letters? May God give you to know yourself, and then you will not plead for ***absolute perfection***; or call the doctrine of election a 'doctrine of devils.' My dear brother, take heed; see you are in Christ a new creature. Beware of a false peace; strive to enter in at the strait gate; and give all diligence to make your calling and election sure. Remember you are but a babe in Christ, if so much. Be humble, talk little, think and pray much. Let God teach you, and He will lead you into all truth. I love you heartily; I pray you may be kept from error, both in principle and practice. Salute all the brethren. If you must dispute, stay till you are master of your subject; otherwise you will hurt the cause you would defend. Study to adorn the Gospel of our Lord in all things; and forget not to pray for,

Your affectionate friend and servant,

G.W.[2]

The person to whom Whitefield wrote in this manner was probably one of the young men whom he mentions as having been drawn to Bristol's Religious Societies under his ministry, and was possibly the 'young W——' who had written a month earlier about the trouble in Bristol.[3]

But though this note was of little significance in itself, eighty years after it was written it suddenly became extraordinarily important. Robert Southey, noticing that the recipient's name began with a 'W' and that he lived at Bristol, jumped to the conclusion

[1] *Ibid*, *p* 206. [2] *Ibid*, *pp* 216–7. [3] See *p* 571.

that the 'W' meant 'Wesley'. Southey seems not to have realized that many factors rendered this assumption highly improbable[1] and without giving his readers the slightest hint that the letter, as published in Whitefield's *Works,* was addressed merely to an unidentified 'Dear Brother W——', altered the heading and printed it as 'Dear Brother Wesley'.[2]

On the basis of this assumption Southey charged Whitefield with adopting 'a tone of superiority, which Wesley . . . was little likely to brook',[3] and since this letter was so different from his others, he not only accused him of being inconsistent but suggested that he appeared somewhat hypocritical too.

This error on Southey's part has proved lastingly misleading. Almost every writer since his time who has dealt at all with the Wesley–Whitefield controversy has copied him in this mistake. Moreover, because of the assumption that Whitefield acted arrogantly towards Wesley, the true nature of his actions (that which is revealed in the letters cited above, for instance) is virtually overlooked. In turn, the whole conflict is viewed in the light of this misconception and the view that has resulted is well stated in a certain reference work which describes it as, 'a personal estrangement in which Wesley displayed much kindness and forbearance, and Whitefield the very opposites, together with a singular narrowness of spirit'.[4]

[1] Whitefield addresses this man as 'at Bristol', but Wesley was in London during these months. It was from London that his letters to Whitefield would have been written and therefore to London that Whitefield would have addressed his replies. Regrettably, Dr Gillies, in printing Whitefield's *Works,* failed to indicate any destination regarding these letters to Wesley. (Wesley spent the major part of October, 1740, in the west of England, including a week in the Bristol area, but this brief change of location would undoubtedly have been unknown to Whitefield.)

Among the letters that Whitefield wrote to Wesley at this time, one is headed 'To Mr J—— W——', but all the others are marked 'To the Rev Mr J—— W——'. Throughout this correspondence Whitefield addresses Wesley as 'Honoured and dear Sir', or 'My dear and Honoured Friend', and even when most strenuously differing from him in doctrine, treats him with the utmost respect. Moreover, it is most improbable that, having written a letter of considerable length to Wesley on September 25, he would write another a mere three days later, especially as both letters would likely be sent to England by the same means of carriage. And there cannot be the slightest possibility that Whitefield would say to Wesley, 'Remember you are but a babe in Christ', or tell him to 'talk little and pray much'. These words are undoubtedly written to a much younger man, one to whom, as to John Bray, Whitefield deemed it necessary to administer a rebuke.

[2] Southey's *Life of Wesley,* Vol 1, *p* 231.

[3] *Ibid, p* 228.

[4] *The Cyclopedia of American Biography,* Art. WHITEFIELD, George.

But Whitefield's letters to Wesley require no defence. They need simply to be made available, and in their restraint, their respect and their desire for peace they speak for themselves.

*

Whitefield's hope, however, of avoiding discord proved fruitless. Wesley gave his sermon on *Free Grace* wide circulation in England and also sent several copies to America. He even sent a copy to Alexander Garden, and it was from this adversary that Whitefield, upon reaching Charleston, first learned that it was being circulated in the Colonies.[1] Since Wesley had long been aware of the Commissary's bitter treatment of Whitefield[2] this action can hardly be viewed as anything but an outright breach of friendship. Finally, Wesley went all the way and had it published at Philadelphia, and shortly thereafter at Boston.[3] It will readily be seen that in its printed form this sermon was a powerful weapon in Wesley's battle. J. P. Gledstone, an author who writes from a pro-Wesley standpoint, states:

> . . . its thrilling denunciations of Calvinistic doctrines almost produce the persuasion that they are as horrible and blasphemous as Wesley believed them to be. The headlong zeal of the preacher allows no time, permits no disposition, to reason. You must go with him; you must check your questions, and listen to him. At the end it seems as if the hated doctrines were for ever consumed in a flame of argument and indignation.[4]

Of course, controversy followed hand in hand with the circulating of this sermon. In the declaration, 'Here I fix my foot. On this I join issue with every asserter of it', Wesley had vowed contention. In his false presentation of the views of his opponents, his several accusations of blasphemy and his address to the

[1] In a letter to Charles Wesley, written after he had returned to England, Whitefield says, 'How can you say you will not dispute with me about election, and yet print such hymns, and your brother send his sermon against election to Mr Garden and others in America?' Tyerman's *Whitefield,* Vol 1, *p* 465. Tyerman, *Ibid, p* 463, quotes Wesley's friend, Dr Whitehead, who says Wesley sent a copy of his sermon 'to Commissary Garden, at Charleston, where Mr Whitefield met with it'.

[2] Writing to Wesley during the previous March Whitefield said, 'Enclosed I have sent you Mr *Garden's Letters*'. *Works,* Vol. 1, *p* 156.

[3] *Free Grace*: A sermon preached at Bristol, by John Wesley M.A., Fellow of Lincoln College, Oxford, Reprinted at Philadelphia by Andrew Bradford and sold by Edward Pleadwell in Front Street. 1740–1, 32 pp, 8vo. Reprinted and sold by B. Franklin in Philadelphia, 1741. Reprinted and sold by T. Fleet in Boston, 1741.

[4] Gledstone, *op cit, p* 240.

devil, Wesley's words were sure to inflame men's passions and set them in heated debate one against another, and such was the sermon's effect as it spread abroad in England and America. Well did Whitefield say, '. . . your sermon has had its expected success; it has set the nation adisputing'.

Wesley's action placed Whitefield in a very difficult situation. It was not a matter of feeling a personal affront, but rather of standing against the denial of what he believed with all his heart to be the truth of God. 'I hope nothing will cause a division between me and the Messrs Wesley', he said again, 'but I must speak what I know and confute error wheresoever I find it.'[1] Yet it was with heaviness that he faced the struggle and phrases such as 'My heart was low' and 'I found myself weighted down'[2] began to reappear in his records. He felt his need of special wisdom: 'I want to have a proper mixture of the lion and the lamb', he wrote, 'of the serpent and the dove.'[3]

Here was the very situation he had foreseen and had striven so earnestly to prevent, but now that it was forced upon him, bewildered though he was by it all, he determined to take action. For one thing, even though, as he stated, he would have been far happier to remain in America, he decided that he had no choice but to return to England and do what he could to restore order in the work there. Furthermore, despite his affection for the Wesleys, he could no longer be silent on the great doctrines in question; John's sermon was in print and was achieving its divisive effect, and he deemed himself responsible to counteract its influence by writing a reply.

Accordingly, some time during his journey from New England to Georgia (the return journey of his Fall tour) Whitefield wrote a *Letter to the Rev Mr John Wesley in Answer to His Sermon Entitled Free Grace*. He did not, however, immediately put it into print. Instead, he carried it with him during the rest of his stay in America, showed it to some of the most experienced ministers and asked their advice. He still hoped that Wesley would cease his aggressive actions and thus obviate the need for him to print the *Answer* or to introduce the conflict into his preaching. Thus, in replying to two more of Wesley's letters, he said:

[1] *Works*, Vol 1, *p* 213. [2] *Journals*, *p* 495. [3] *Works*, Vol 1, *p* 195.

. . . Perhaps in the Spring, we may see each other face to face . . . The king of the church shall yet over-rule all things for good. My dear brother . . . do not oblige me to preach against you; I had rather die. Be gentle towards the —— ——. They will get great advantage over you, if they discover any irregular warmth in your temper. I cannot for my soul unite with the Moravian brethren. Honoured Sir, Adieu!

Yours eternally in Christ Jesus,

G. W.[1]

Whitefield was not the only one who thus felt it necessary to put Wesley on his guard concerning his temper. Similar references were made by Hutton and Harris in these early days of Wesley's ministry and by several of his preachers during the later years of his life. This tendency had been particularly evident in his father and was to be seen in Charles too, and the concept of the Wesleys needs to be remoulded to include this characteristic if there is to be a true understanding of so important a period of history as the eighteenth-century Revival.

But there, for the time being, the matter of the controversy rested. While Wesley laboured his distinctive doctrines at London and Bristol and circulated his sermon, Whitefield let his answer remain unpublished, intending to wait till he reached England before taking any action and hoping against hope that all such action might still be avoided. The dread that he faced in the prospect is manifest in his repeated statements to Wesley to the effect: 'I would rather die than oppose you.'

*

This, however, was not Whitefield's only burden. Other troubles in quick succession came crowding in upon him during his last months in America.

He was again thrust into the struggle regarding his affection for Elizabeth Delamotte. It was at this time that, as we have seen, Captain Gladman returned from England and brought news which caused Whitefield to say, 'Yet I believe she may be my wife', and therewith emotions that he undoubtedly thought had been crushed for the last time were reawakened to plague him.

[1] *Ibid, p* 225. It is probable that the words deleted from the letter by Dr Gillies and indicated with the two blanks were 'French Prophets'.

By the middle of December, 1740, the long Autumn tour ended with his arrival at Georgia. He found that the orphans had been moved out of the rented house at Savannah and were living at Bethesda in the four auxiliary buildings that had been erected as part of the institution. But the Great House was almost finished and in a few more weeks would be ready for occupation.

Yet all was not well. The magistrates had begun the interfering with the management of the place that has already been noticed, disturbing the staff and causing problems among the children. Moreover, the Spaniards had recently captured 'a schooner loaded with bricks and other provisions to a considerable value'.[1] This was a serious financial loss, and one which Whitefield could ill afford. Along with the costs of constructing and maintaining the institution, which had proved utterly exorbitant, it had placed him heavily in debt and he found that he owed the large sum of about £500 sterling.[2]

Moreover, in the matter of this debt Whitefield was in for a terrible shock: he learned that William Seward who had acted as jointly responsible in the financing of Bethesda would no longer be able to share the burden with him.

Seward's activities in England had proved unfortunate in more ways than one. John Wesley had been labouring to make as much of the work exclusively his own as he could. This was true of the New Room at Bristol, the costs of which, in a considerable measure, had come out of Seward's pocket.[3] It was true also of the Kingswood School, for which Whitefield had raised the bulk of the money.[4] But Wesley was endeavouring to remove Whitefield's influence from these places, and Seward, at first amazed and then angered at his proceedings, had attempted to fight for Whitefield's

[1] *Works,* Vol 1, *p* 230.

[2] This would equal the total amount that an English labourer would have been paid at that time for twenty years of work.

[3] Seward remarks on 'God's marvellous ways of working . . . to order it so that I should be refused at ye Society which ye Lord had made me instrumental in great measure to its being and its well being'. William Seward's *Third Journal,* unpublished and in the possession of Chetham's Library, Manchester, England, entry of Sept. 23, 1740. Whitefield's sister and others of his friends wanted Seward, since he had contributed so largely to the New Room, to claim it. Dr Curnock (John Wesley's *Journal,* Vol 2, *p* 395, fn.) says, 'He had probably contributed generously for the building of the New Room in the Horse Fair'.

[4] See *p* 276. A full statement of this matter will be given in Vol 2.

rights. But Seward proved rather unwise in his actions and there can be no doubt that he did Whitefield's cause more harm than good and unnecessarily aggravated the situation between the two opposing camps.

Seward also tried to preach, but his efforts demonstrated more zeal and courage than ability. Charles Wesley, reporting a meeting among the colliers, said, 'Mr. Seward spoke a few works to them which did not convince me of his call to preach'.[1] But Seward went with Howell Harris on his open-air work in Wales, standing with him as he addressed the unruly mobs, and of a meeting at Caerleon (the date was September 9, 1740) Seward wrote:

We had been singing and praying and discoursing for half an hour, when the mobb began to be outrageous, and to pelt us . . . The Lord gave us courage to withstand it for an hour and a half – sometimes singing the hymn in a tumult. The noise often drowned our voices, till at length I was struck with a stone upon my right eye, which caused me so much anguish that I was forced to go away to the Inn. It was given me to pray all the way for the poor people, and especially for the person who struck me.

Bro. Harris continued to discourse for some time afterward . . . I got my eye dressed and went to bed as soon as possible.

Wed. Sept. 10. This morning Bro. Harris was much excited to discourse again at ye same place, and the Lord having abated my pain, I was led by the hand . . . and we had freedom to discourse as long as we pleased.[2]

The blow to the right eye caused a sympathetic blindness in the left. Nevertheless, the following morning the all-but-sightless Seward went with Harris to preach at a horse race and climbed with him to the roof of a booth that was to serve as a pulpit. A drunk tried to pull them down, but they held their ground and continued to declare the word of life. Later that day they stood on a table in the market-place:

We had continual showers of stones, walnuts, dirt, a cat and also a dead dog thrown at us. I was much afraid of the hurt on my eye, but the voice to me was 'Better endure this than hell!' I was struck on my forehead and under my right eye again, and also on my side with a stone.

A drum was ordered to be beat, which drowned the voices, but then

[1] Charles Wesley's *Journal*, Sept. 23, 1740. [2] William Seward's *Third Journal*.

we sung the hymn in ye tumult till the Book was all covered with dirt. After Bro. Harris had done, I spoke a few words, but I found my call was more to suffer than to preach.[1]

Seward's words proved prophetically true. Harris, Whitefield, the Wesleys and Cennick possessed rare powers of public utterance with which to command a hearing before the unruly mobs, but Seward, lacking these gifts seemed to be made the target of their violence. In the month of October he and Harris were viciously assaulted as they stood ministering on the Green in the town of Hay, and Seward was struck by a heavy stone from close range. The blow felled him to the ground and he was carried from the scene unconscious. For a few days he hovered between life and death, but sank steadily lower till, on October 22 (1740), his spirit passed away. He was but thirty-eight years of age. The earth of the churchyard in the nearby village of Cusop received his remains, and there to-day the inscription 'To die is gain' marks the grave and interprets the death of 'the first Methodist martyr'.

Seward's career was commendable indeed in its Christian earnestness. Shortly before his death he had given testimony before a Society at Cardiff: 'I declared', he writes, 'that I had found the Pearl of Great Price, even Jesus Christ, and that I had sold what I had to buy it. I told them I might have kept my Footman and my brace of geldings, and might have gone to Bath and Tunbridge like any other Gentleman.' He then went on to speak of the delight he had experienced in giving more than £10,000 to the Lord's work and to express his gratitude for the privilege of being associated so closely with Whitefield.

Nevertheless, an appraisal of William Seward cannot be limited to commendation. There was a marked element of imprudence in him and a fervour so intense that it tended to overstep the bounds of common sense. He was at his best while under Whitefield's restraining hand, but admitted that, even then, 'Satan . . . made me think Brother Whitefield's zeal was not so great as my own, and therefore kept me on the reserve to him – whereas, in Truth, he only feared I should do hurt by my impetuosity'.[2]

[1] *Ibid.*

[2] William Seward, *Journal of a Voyage from Savannah to Philadelphia and from Philadelphia to England* (London, 1740), *p* 27.

After he sailed from America Whitefield found it necessary to write to him,[1] pointing out mistakes he had made, and mentioning certain results thereof which he himself was being required to correct.

Though Whitefield sought to control Seward's extremism there can be no doubt that, to some extent, it influenced his own behaviour. The fourteen months during which Seward was with him comprised one of the most important periods of his life – a period in which he was blazing a trail in the open-air preaching and taking up battle positions in the fight against apostasy. In regulating these new activities and formulating these new concepts he faced decisions which called for the calmest of consideration, yet during such critical times the inner counsels of his life were shared by this too fervent an associate. The several errors for which Whitefield later apologized – his 'manner too apostolical' and his attack on Tillotson, for instance – occurred during this period, and although the blame for such actions must be placed at his own door, there must also be a recognition of the pressures which Seward's presence placed upon him.

Seward's death left Whitefield in sore straits. Though he himself was entirely responsible for having undertaken the Orphan House, he would probably not have proceeded in so extensive a manner had it not been for Seward's urging and on the understanding that Seward was bearing its burdens with him. The same was largely the case with the Nazareth institution too. But Seward appears not to have made a will,[2] and Whitefield, reflecting on the event some months later, stated, '. . . I was embarrassed with Mr Seward's death. He died without making any provision for me, and I was at the same time much indebted for the Orphan House.'[3]

Whitefield's heart was already heavy with his other trials, and this – the loss of a personal friend, the knowledge of the brutality under which he had died, and the financial load which now came upon his shoulders alone – could not but have added sorely to his burdens.

[1] *Works,* Vol 1, *pp* 169–70, and *pp* 180–1.

[2] Seward was a widower and had a young daughter whom he had placed under a governess in England. John Byrom says that, before going to America, he 'settled £1,000 upon his daughter', and Byrom seems to suggest that if he had not done so she would have been left without substance.

[3] *Works,* Vol 1, *p* 362.

This proved a focal point in Whitefield's life. From this point onward the debt for the Orphanage was ever upon him – a constant burden that weighted his spirits, affected his health and shortened his life, and which he bore, amidst a strange unconcern on the part of his multitude of friends, till within two years of his death.

*

Before sailing for England, however, Whitefield met still another trial.

He had recently corrected a letter which Hugh Bryan was preparing for the press, and since the letter contained the suggestion, 'the clergy break their canons', both Whitefield and Bryan were hailed into court, charged with libel. Whitefield posted bond, guaranteeing that he would appear by an attorney 'at the next quarter sessions, under penalty of £100 proclamation money'. The case was obviously a contrivance, a fresh act of persecution and one for which Alexander Garden was undoubtedly responsible. Under the circumstances, Whitefield had every reason to believe that the court would be biased against him, and the whole affair became but a further burden added to those he already bore.

*

Whitefield's last activity in America was a work of kindness in response to an appeal from John Wesley. A citizen of Georgia named Captain Williams had recently been in England, where he had sworn out a lengthy affidavit which charged Wesley with breaking certain laws and jumping bail while in the Colony. This document exaggerated the unwise actions of which Wesley had been guilty and contained further statements which were both false and slanderous and which brought Wesley under suspicion in England. Wesley needed an authoritative denial of the charges and therefore 'wrote to Mr Whitefield, then in America, to contradict the falsehoods it contained by making inquiries in the place where the misdemeanours were said to have occurred'.[1]

Whitefield's response was two-fold. He informed one of Georgia's magistrates, a man named Brownfield, of Wesley's need, and Brownfield wrote a letter which provided the basic

[1] John Wesley's *Journal*, Vol 8, *p* 256.

facts regarding the bail and cleared Wesley of wrong-doing in the matter. Whitefield also wrote a vindication himself, declaring that his inquiries had entirely satisfied him concerning Wesley's actions. '. . . the Rev Mr Wesley has been much injured', he stated, 'both in respect to anything criminal in his character and as to his going from his bail . . . the whole prosecution, I verily believe, was groundless'.[1] Dr Curnock says of this letter, 'Whitefield . . . fully rebuts the charges.'[2]

*

After spending Christmas at Bethesda, Whitefield set out for Charleston, where he was to board a vessel for England. While at Charleston, knowing that Wesley's sermon was being circulated in America, he concluded that he could no longer postpone the publishing of his answer to it. Thus, he gave a copy to a printer at Charleston, and sent another copy to Boston. A third he carried with him in order to publish it in London should he find that circumstances there required him so to do. And on January 24, the *Minerva* which was carrying him homeward, 'sailed over Charleston bar'.

*

Merely fourteen and a half months had elapsed since his arrival in the New World, yet in that brief time, how tremendous had been his labours and, under the Divine blessing, how great his accomplishments!

This was true of the extent of his travels. His first journey, 'making the acquaintance of America', had taken him from Philadelphia to New York and then overland all the way to Georgia, and this had been followed by the Spring tour to the Middle Colonies, the Summer tour to Charleston and the Fall tour to New England and back to Georgia. So extensive a coverage of the land gave evidence of very careful planning, and it is difficult to conceive of an itinerary which could have reached America more widely or more effectively.

Moreover, there can be little doubt that far more than half of the total population of the Colonies had heard him preach. Nathan Cole's report of the flocking of the whole countryside to

[1] *Ibid, p* 257. [2] *Ibid.*

his service at Middletown is indicative of the excitement that was aroused wherever the announcement 'Mr Whitefield is to preach' was made.

The results were lasting and of many kinds. Not only was Bethesda in operation but the very existence of 'America's first charity' had awakened the Christian conscience to a new concern for orphans and for the needy of mankind in general. Whitefield's efforts on behalf of the slave (while regrettably insufficient) had done much to elevate the black man in the mind of the public and had set in motion vigorous forces that laboured for his welfare.[1] The cleavage between the people who favoured the Revival and those who opposed it had been deepened, and while the opposers closed their ranks in denouncing this work, the others, though of several denominations, experienced an unprecedented unity on the basis of their oneness in the evangelical faith. The people of the Revival had begun to accept a new responsibility to take the Gospel to the Indian – a work undertaken in strong devotion by several men, but in which David Brainerd was soon to become the most prominent. Bibles were in greater demand than ever before and a large market for religious books had now come into being.

Above all, there were the numerous persons who had been converted under Whitefield's ministry. Of course, he made no estimate as to their number and, judging always by the fruit of the Spirit in a lastingly transformed life, he said, 'When I return from England it will be evident who the converts really are'. But hosts of people who had come to the full assurance of salvation now thronged the evangelical churches and gathered in groups in homes and barns to study the Scriptures and pray. The figure was given of thirty Societies that had been established in Boston and there were also several – Societies for children,

[1] Whenever he was in Philadelphia, Whitefield was the welcome guest at the home of a prominent Quaker, Anthony Benezet. Though but twenty-five years old, Benezet had already achieved considerable financial success. Since he was deeply concerned about the welfare of the negroes he took a strong interest in the Nazareth project and undoubtedly was the one in whose hands Whitefield placed its affairs in his absence. With the passing of a few years Benezet retired from business in order to devote his time and his possessions to bettering the lot of mankind, and in this endeavour became America's supreme champion of the negro cause and a powerful advocate of abolition. Benezet testified to the impetus which had come to his life as a result of Whitefield's ministry at the time of this association in 1740.

Societies for young people, Societies for women, Societies for black people and Societies for black and white together – in Philadelphia, and much the same was true of New York. It needs to be emphasized that all of these were related to the local churches, and that Whitefield not only made no attempt to organize them as his own work, but that he was strongly averse to any suggestion of a new denomination or a personal party of any kind. He was the friend of the evangelical pastors, and had no thought in labouring among them but that of strengthening their hands.

Such were some of the results that Whitefield was leaving behind in the Colonies, and we do well to observe that the man whose ministry had already been used in so amazing a manner in both England and America had but recently reached his twenty-sixth birthday.

*

While crossing the ocean Whitefield wrote, 'I never had such a variety of trials and changes of life lying before me as at this time'.[1] He expected soon to appear in court concerning the excommunication he had received at Alexander Garden's hands and, whatever the outcome, the affair would undoubtedly prove very expensive. He faced a tremendous debt for the orphan house and would need to be able immediately to draw huge congregations and receive large offerings, but what would he do were he to find the people separated from him by the doctrinal disputations? He thought of the possibility of meeting Elizabeth Delamotte again, and after earnest prayer about it, the next morning wrote, 'Last night, I think I received as full satisfaction as I could desire, in respect to my marriage. I believe what I have done is of God.'[2]

But Whitefield also faced the prospect of open discord with the Wesleys. He still entertained the hope that it might be avoided. 'I feel a great union of soul with Mr W——;' he wrote, 'we differ in principles, but I hope the Lord will make us of one mind.' But knowing that he must stand for what he believed to be truth he followed up this statement with the words, 'You must not be surprised, if I publish an answer to Mr John W——'s sermon, entitled, *Free Grace*. It is wrote in much love and meekness.'[3] As

[1] *Journals, p* 506. [2] *Works,* Vol II, *p* 245. [3] *Ibid p.* 248.

one reads his letters it becomes evident that he expected that he and John and Charles would sit down in conference and fully discuss their differing views. If a suitable agreement could be reached, well and good; if not, they would agree to work apart, but he expected that their relationships would always be characterized by mutual affection and good will.

Despite these hopes, however, Whitefield seems to have suffered during the voyage and to have anticipated his arrival in England with anxiety. In his letters he made such confessions as, 'I am now entering on a scene of trials',[1] 'Since I have been on board, the Lord hath heard the voice of my weeping',[2] and 'I have sought the Lord by prayer and fasting, and He assures me He will be with me.'[3] In preparation for the difficulties before him he pleaded for a deeper work of Divine grace within his heart, saying to one correspondent, 'I am panting after the compleat holiness of Jesus my Lord',[3] and to another, 'Be always crying out, "Lord, let me know more of myself and of Thee; O let me receive grace for grace of thy dear Son." This, at present, is the full desire of my soul.'[5]

And in this mind Whitefield moved toward England, anxious but hopeful, yet still unaware that before him lay disappointment and disillusion, and experiences which would constitute the supreme trial of his life.

[1] *Ibid, p* 246.
[2] *Ibid.*
[3] *Ibid, p* 250.
[4] *Ibid, p* 237.
[5] *Ibid, pp* 245–6.

APPENDIX

Note 1

On Samuel Wesley, Sr.

IN 1725, while John Wesley was at Oxford, his older sister Emilia wrote to him regarding conditions in the home at Epworth. She complained of her father's costly attendance at Convocation in London, saying,

Then came on London journeys, convocations of blessed memory, that for seven winters my father was at London, and we at home in intolerable want and affliction; then I learnt what it was to seek money for bread, seldom having any without such hardships in getting it that much abated the pleasure of it. Thus we went on, growing worse and worse; all of us children in scandalous want of necessaries for years together; vast income, but no comfort or credit with it . . .

Emilia goes on to relate the events of three years that she spent in London and other years in which she served as housekeeper to her parents at Wroote, and continues:

. . . this winter, when my own necessaries began to decay and my money was most of it spent (I having maintained myself since I came home, but now could do it no longer), I found what a condition I was in – every trifling want was either not supplied, or I had more trouble to procure it than it was worth. I know not when we have had so good a year, both at Wroote and at Epworth, as this year; but instead of saving anything to clothe my sister or myself, we are just where we were. A noble crop has almost all gone, beside Epworth living, to pay some part of those infinite debts my father has run into . . . While my mother lives I am inclined to stay with her; she is so very good to me, and has so little comfort in the world beside, that I think it barbarous to abandon her . . . – Stevenson, *Memorials of The Wesley Family, op cit, pp* 263–4.

John Wesley left an account illustrative of his father's arrogance, as follows:

The year King William died, my father observed my mother did not say Amen to the prayer for the King. She said she could not, for she did not believe the Prince of Orange was King. He vowed he would never cohabit with her until she did. He then took his horse and rode away, nor did she hear anything of him for a twelvemonth. He then came back and lived with her as before, but I fear that his vow was not forgotten before God. – *The Arminian Magazine*, 1784, *p* 606.

The income from Epworth was unusually high. While the average church living was about £40 per year, Epworth yielded between £150 and £200. To this Samuel added the income of the Wroote parish, where, besides being rector, he managed a farm. Trevelyan uses the Epworth living as an example of how high a clerical income might be in those years.

Note 2

Whitefield's Attitude toward the Casting of Lots

In his report of the conference held by 'seven true ministers of Jesus Christ, despised Methodists', at Islington on January 5, 1739, Whitefield says: 'What we were in doubt about, after prayer, we determined by lot . . .' The seven men present on that occasion were John Wesley, Charles Wesley, Westley Hall, Benjamin Ingham, Charles Kinchin, John Hutchings and Whitefield. With regard to Whitefield's attitude we notice:

1. This is the only instance on record in which he took part in the practice of casting lots.

2. There is an earlier instance in which he sought to have one of his servants in Georgia, Joseph Husbands, submit to a lot as to whether or not he should return to England. – Tyerman's *Whitefield*, Vol 1, *p* 193.

3. He had already shown by his rejection of Wesley's 'Let him return to London', received in a lot, that he did not accept such a result as necessarily revealing the mind of God.

4. In his answer to *The Querists* (1740) he stated: 'I am no friend to casting lots; but, I believe, on extraordinary occasions, when things can be determined no other way, God, if appealed to and waited on by prayer and fasting, will answer by lot now as well as formerly.' – *Works*, Vol 4, *p* 48.

5. A few months after making this statement he showed still less favour toward the practice, saying to Wesley, 'Oh that you

would be more cautious in casting lots'. – *Works,* Vol 1, *p* 212.

6. In 1748 Whitefield asserted: 'Casting lots I do not now approve of, nor have I for several years; neither do I think it a safe way (though practised, I doubt not, by many good men) to make a lottery of the Scriptures, by dipping into them upon every occasion.' – *Works,* Vol 4, *p* 245. This latter reference is to the custom of opening the Bible at random – a practice in which Whitefield had never indulged.

Thus, though while he was twenty-three and twenty-four he was associated with men (the Moravians and the Wesleys) who placed credence in these things, Whitefield was influenced toward the casting of lots for but a brief while, after which he gradually came to reject the practice.

Note 3

William Law's Attitude towards Whitefield

The impression has often been given that William Law thought poorly of Whitefield. This has probably arisen from a passage in Charles Wesley's *Journal*, where, in his entry of August 10, 1739, he says: 'He [Law] blamed Mr Whitefield's Journals and way of proceeding. . . . Among other things, he said, "Was I so talked of as Mr Whitefield is, I should run away and hide myself entirely".'

But Dr John Byrom, who was a close acquaintance of Law, writes: 'Mrs Hutton told William Law that she asked a certain young man how Mr Law did, and he said he was so strangely altered, grown sour, and that he had been railing against Mr Whitefield like anything, which greatly surprised Mr Law, as well it might.' – *Life and Literary Remains,* Vol 1, part 1, *p* 278.

It is probable that the 'young man' mentioned by Mrs Hutton was Charles Wesley. Moreover, Charles's words may mean no more than that Law, like Watts, Doddridge and others, saw many ill-advised statements in Whitefield's *Journals,* and that he felt the severe blaze of publicity in which Whitefield was forced to live was something that he himself could not bear. Throughout Byrom's *Remains* there are further references to both his and Law's high regard for Whitefield.

Note 4

Whitefield and the Moravians at Nazareth

The chronology of events related to this matter is basic to an understanding of it.

Böhler's conference with Whitefield, at which it was decided 'to carry on the work of God apart', took place on or shortly after November 20, at Salem or in that area at the head of the Bay of Delaware. Following the conference Böhler would have travelled back to Nazareth, a trip of about one hundred and twenty miles, part of it through wilderness country, and which would likely have taken a week at least. If upon his arrival at Nazareth he and his little party – five men, two women, one small boy and two indentured lads – began preparations to leave, it would undoubtedly have been in the early part of December before they could have started out on their journey. By this time Whitefield was on his way to Georgia, where he remained till late in December, after which he returned to Charleston, and on January 24 set sail for England.

What actually happened regarding Böhler and his little company is not altogether known. If they set out from Nazareth their plan would have been to return to the Germantown and Skippack area, thirty or forty miles to the south, where they had friends or relatives, and with whom they had been lodging at the time when Whitefield arranged for them to construct the Nazareth school. Since the home of Nathaniel Irish, the miller of Saucon Creek, was about ten miles south of Nazareth, and since Böhler was well acquainted with him (having walked to his mill for supplies on several occasions), the Moravians would undoubtedly plan a stop-over at his place, and by this time it would have been the first or second or even the third week of December.

Whitefield never did see the Nazareth property and, indeed, was not even within twenty-five or thirty miles of it.[1] He placed the management of its affairs in the hands of a few friends in Philadelphia, and one of these was undoubtedly Anthony

[1] That is, at this time. There is an entry in the Moravian records at Nazareth to the effect that nearly thirty years later Whitefield paid a visit to the institution the Moravians operated there and expressed his pleasure in seeing that they had largely fulfilled his own early ideals.

Benezet. At that time Benezet was a prosperous young tradesman, but within a few years he relinquished his commercial pursuits in order to devote himself to Christian labours. He championed the negro, proved a warm friend to the Moravian cause (possibly becoming a Moravian himself), and was known throughout the Colonies for his philanthropy. From Benezet, as Whitefield's chief agent, Böhler and his party would have met with nothing but kindness.

We have seen the charges, however, that Whitefield turned the little company of Moravians 'adrift in the depths of winter', that 'neighbours cried shame' and that Nathaniel Irish, 'who, tired of theological polemics and sectarian bigotry, had discarded church connections but not his Christianity, . . . persuaded Whitefield to permit the Moravians to remain on the Nazareth Manor for the winter'. Regarding these charges we notice:

1. The only neighbours were the Indians. Under the leadership of a fierce chieftain, Captain John, they refused to accept the white man's claims to their land and constantly threatened the lives of the intruders. Henckwelder, the Moravian historian nearest to these events, says that it was the hostility of the Indians, together with the financial difficulties Whitefield experienced as a result of the death of William Seward, that necessitated the removal of the Moravians from Nazareth. (J. Henckwelder, *A Narrative of the Mission of the United Brethren Among the Delaware and Mohegan Indians,* 1740–1808.) Other Moravian writers make similar statements.

2. It was impossible for Nathaniel Irish to have seen Whitefield to accomplish the supposed 'persuading'. The assumption is based on the idea that Whitefield was somewhere near at hand. Of course, in so short a time Irish could not have gone to Georgia and back; in fact his claim to have seen and persuaded Whitefield is absurd.

3. What probably happened was that the little band of Moravians reached Irish's place amidst wintry weather and dreaded the remaining thirty or so miles of the journey that were yet before them. Irish then may well have urged them to return to Nazareth, bitterly denouncing the theological differences between Whitefield and these people, and assuring them that, since he was a man

of some influence in the Colony, he would see Whitefield's agents and secure their approval.

4. One version of the tale about Whitefield's expulsion of the Moravians states that it was certain Irish settlers in the area of the community of Bath (some miles south and west of Nazareth) who did the persuading, and there is as much truth, no doubt, in the one 'Irish' story as the other.

5. The fact that four prominent Moravians from Germany spent the winter at Nazareth speaks for itself. It is difficult to believe that if Whitefield had 'peremptorily ordered the Moravians off the land', such outstanding persons as Bishop David Nitchsmann, an uncle of his, a cousin named Anna who later became the second wife of Count Zinzendorf, and Mrs Molther, wife of the Moravian minister at London, would have made Nazareth their home for three or four months. Their action requires the conclusion that they looked on their relationship with Whitefield, despite the theological differences, as one of warm friendship and that they would not have taken up residence there unless they knew they were welcome to do so.

The authors who have told the tale about Whitefield driving the little band of Moravians off his property undoubtedly obtained their information from *A History of Bethlehem, Pennsylvania*, written by Bishop Joseph Mortimer Levering in 1903. The Bishop, however, fails to cite any authority whatsoever for his statements.

John Henckwelder, the Moravian historian who was nearest to these events wrote *A Narrative of the Mission of the United Brethren to the Delaware and Mohegan Indians*. He makes not the least suggestion that it was due to theological differences that Whitefield asked the Moravians to leave Nazareth; rather, he says that it was on account of his financial embarrassments that he could not go on with the building. He places most of the cause for the Moravian withdrawal on the Indians, 'who had indeed manifested hostile intentions, in case these should not withdraw from the land.' (*p* 18.)

Note 5

The Delamotte Family

Charles Delamotte, after returning from Georgia, became active in his father's sugar business. On one occasion, John Wesley, disappointed that Charles did not show strong interest in Christian labours, said, '. . . his sugar has quite eaten him up'. On two other occasions Wesley spoke of meeting him and having warm fellowship with him. Charles attended the Moravian meetings at Hull, where he lived, but did not join the Moravian movement, and in his last years probably attended a Methodist Society. He died in 1790.

William Delamotte attended Cambridge University. He joined the Moravians and did some preaching along with Benjamin Ingham in Yorkshire. He did not marry, and died in 1743.

Esther Delamotte married Charles Kinchin late in 1741. Early in 1742 Kinchin died of smallpox, and before the year closed Esther was married a second time, this time to Ernst Schlit, the Moravian minister at London.

The father, Thomas Delamotte, proved a devoted Moravian. In 1742 he and Captain Gladman, who had also become a Moravian, advised the Brethren regarding the purchase of an ocean-going vessel which was to serve their foreign missionary works. Thomas appears to have contributed freely towards the purchase. He died in 1749.

Elizabeth Delamotte's written testimony, read at her funeral, is as follows:

I was born in London, April 17, 1710. My father was a merchant in good repute, who lived at Greenwich. When 12 years old we moved into Derbyshire, where I lived 11 years and then moved again into Kent. In this time, till I was twenty-eight years of age, I pursued the pleasures of this world. In 1738 Mr Ingham came from Georgia; he visited my Father and preached in the Parish Church; this was the first time any word made any impression on my poor heart. Some time after, Mr Ch's Westley & Mr Whitfield visited us.

I then became acquainted with the Brethren, whom I first saw at Br West's. They soon became to me like my flesh & bone. March 31, 1741, I was married to Wm Holland, a painter who lived in the City in great business. We had 6 children, 5 of them are gone happily to our Saviour & 1 daughter is now in the Cong'n.

The September following, my husband being called out of his business into the Labour we moved into a room in Wild St. Nov'r 1743 we were sent to Yorkshire, where my troubles began through my husband getting confused. In Sept'r 1745 we were called to Germany, where we were greeted with greatest tenderness, but all would no do. In Aug't, 1746 we returned & my Husband was advised to go again to business, which he did Dec'r 1747. He then left the Cong'n, the pain & tears this cost me our dear Saviour only knows. Feb. 26, 1761 my husband departed very suddenly. I was left with 2 children, one of these departed Feb. 26th, 1765.

A note appended by some contemporary hand reads:

Oct'r 20, 1771 she succeeded Sr. Stehman as Widdows Labouress & faithfully laboured among them till her departure, which took place after painful and lingering illness about 10 at night Oct. 26, 1780. Her remains were interred on Wednesday, Nov'r 1st, by Br. Clemens after a discourse on Isaiah 35 v. 10.

Elizabeth was buried at Chelsea. Her husband's confusion arose from the gradual breaking down of the idea that a person might be both a Moravian and loyal member of the Church of England. With the growth of Moravianism in England into the status of a denomination in its own right, Holland began to feel he must make choice between one or the other. The Moravians, however, seem to have believed he was becoming a Methodist, for one of them wrote, 'That miserable man, Holland, . . . is on the point of going over to the Wesleyans'.[1]

Note 6

Whitefield's Sloop

In Whitefield's *Journals* (Banner of Truth edition), *p* 27, the statement is made that Whitefield's sloop was wrecked off the American coast. This was an error on the part of the present writer, who gave this information to the publishers. An entry in the *Colonial Records of Georgia* states that shortly before setting out for England in January, 1741, Whitefield sold the sloop to a Captain Mackay at Charleston.

[1] *Provincial Pilgrim House Diary,* Dec. 16, 1747.

An Index will appear at the end of volume 2.